COUNTY
STREET ATLAS

EAST SUSSEX

Ordnance Survey

COUNTY
STREET ATLAS

EAST SUSSEX

3½ INCHES TO 1 MILE

3rd edition

COUNTY STREET ATLAS
EAST SUSSEX

First Edition published 1988
Second Edition published 1990
Third Edition published 1992 by

Ordnance Survey   and   George Philip Ltd
Romsey Road   59 Grosvenor Street
Maybush   London W1X 9DA
Southampton SO9 4DH

ISBN 0 540 05663 4 [George Philip]
ISBN 0 319 00304 3 [Ordnance Survey]

Printed in Great Britain by
Butler & Tanner Ltd, Frome and London

CONTENTS

Key to map pages   vi-vii

Administrative boundaries   viii

Street maps   1-190

Index explanation and abbreviations   192

Index of towns, villages and rural localities   193

Index of street names   194-212

KEY TO MAP SYMBOLS

British Rail Station	Motorway and Dual Carriageway
London Transport Station	Main or through road
Private Railway Station	A27(T) Road numbers (Dept of Transport)
Bus or Coach Station	Gate and obstruction to traffic (restrictions may not apply at all times and to all vehicles)
(H) Heliport	
Police Station (may not be open 24hrs)	Footpath } The representation in this atlas of a road, track or path is no evidence of the existence Bridleway } of a right of way.
Hospital with Casualty Facilities (may not be open 24hrs)	120 Adjoining Page Indicator
Post Office	
Place of Worship	
Important Building	
P Parking	

Amb Sta	Ambulance Station	Liby	Library
Coll	College	Mus	Museum
FB	Foot Bridge	Sch	School
F Sta	Fire Station	TH	Town Hall
LC	Level Crossing		

The large letters and numbers around the edge of the maps form the referencing system. An explanation of how to use the system for locating the position of street names appears on page **192**.

The small numbers identify the 1 kilometre National Grid lines.

Scale of Maps is 3½ inches to 1 mile (1 : 18103)

0   ¼   ½   ¾   1 Mile

0   250m   500m   750m   1 Kilometre

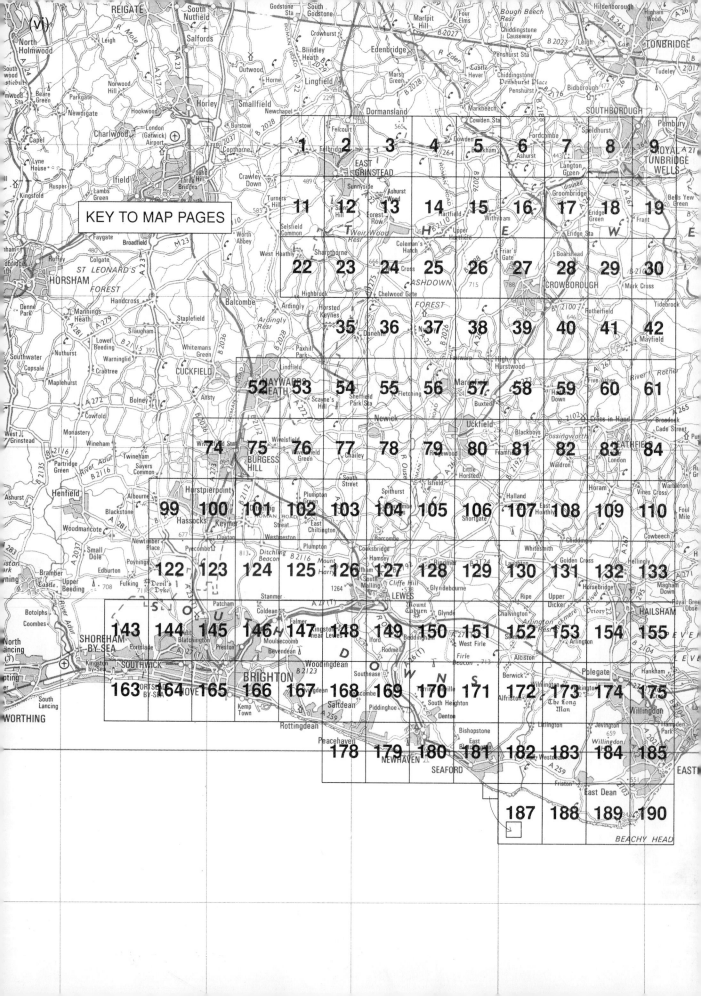

KEY TO MAP PAGES

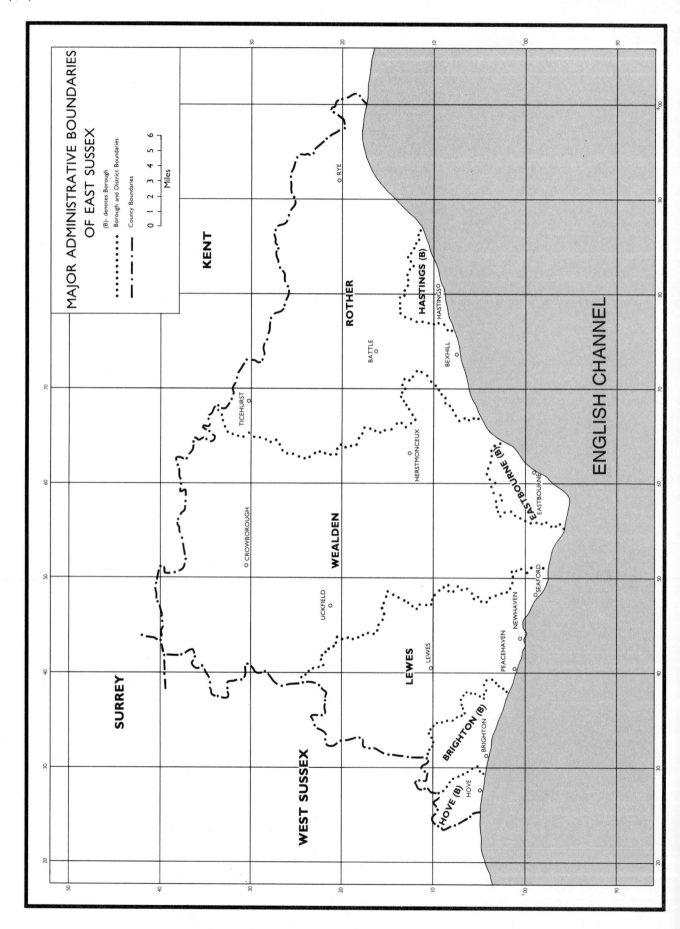

MAJOR ADMINISTRATIVE BOUNDARIES
OF EAST SUSSEX

(B)- denotes Borough

•••••••• Borough and District Boundaries

—·—·— County Boundaries

0 1 2 3 4 5 6

Miles

KENT

ROTHER

RYE

HASTINGS (B)

HASTINGS

BATTLE

BEXHILL

TICEHURST

HERSTMONCEUX

EASTBOURNE (B)

EASTBOURNE

CROWBOROUGH

WEALDEN

UCKFIELD

SEAFORD

LEWES

LEWES

NEWHAVEN

PEACEHAVEN

SURREY

WEST SUSSEX

BRIGHTON (B)

BRIGHTON

HOVE (B)

HOVE

ENGLISH CHANNEL

1

A B C

Quarry Farm
EAST PARK LA
B 2028
WEST PARK RD
Eastpark Farm
Churchill Stud
HOBBS INDUSTRIAL ESTATE
Laylands Farm
A 22
EASTBOURNE RD
WIRE MILL LA
Nurseries Hotel
Wire Mill Lake
Felcourt Farm
High Wood
4
Woodcock Bridge
Wire Mill Wood
Stockriding Wood
Sewage Works
HEATHERWAY
Cooper's Moors
41
MILLHURST LA
Hedgecourt
Moat
WOODCOCK HILL
Domewood
Hedgecourt Lake
MILL LA
Green Meadow
Park Farm
3
Park Wood
EASTBOURNE RD
Chartham Wood
A 264
TANGLE OAK
COPTHORNE RD
ROMAN ROAD (course of)
THE LIMES
40
LAKE VIEW RD
Yewtree Farm
ROWPLATT LA
TWITTEN LA
TITHE ORCH
Sch
THE GLEBE
Whittington College
Felbridge
FELLCOT RD
CHESTERFIELD CL
Fellcot Farm
Miles's Farm
WARREN WHEELERS WAY
Pixiewood Farms
Crawley Down RD
A 264
FELBRIDGE RD
Felbridge Hotel
FURZE LA
PINE GR
LOWDELL'S LA
North End
2
Furnace Wood
Gibbshaven Farm
FURNACE RD
Nurseries
FELBRIDGE RD
Felbridge Water
STANDEN CL
THE PARADE
STREAM PK
LONDON RD
YEW LA
BUTTER FIELD
BACKVILLE CL
A 22
The Felbridge Centre
BIRCHES
INDUSTRIAL ESTATE
Works
HALSFORD GREEN
IMBERHORNE LA
Furnace Wood
HOPHURST HILL
CUTTINGLYE RD
Nurseries
The Birches
School
HALSFORD LA
39
Park Fields Farm
HOPHURST LA
Hophurst Farm
Imberhorne Farm
IMBERHORNE LA
HEATHCOTE DR
FAIRLAWN DR
FAIRLAWN CRES
GREEN RD
HURST ROOM GDNS
1
GAGE CL
TILTWOOD DR
AVIARY WAY
THE MARTINS
Dismantled Railway
Railway Shaw
CHAPMAN'S LA
CAMPBELL CRES
GARDEN ROOM
THE BUTTONS

35 36 37 38

A B C

2

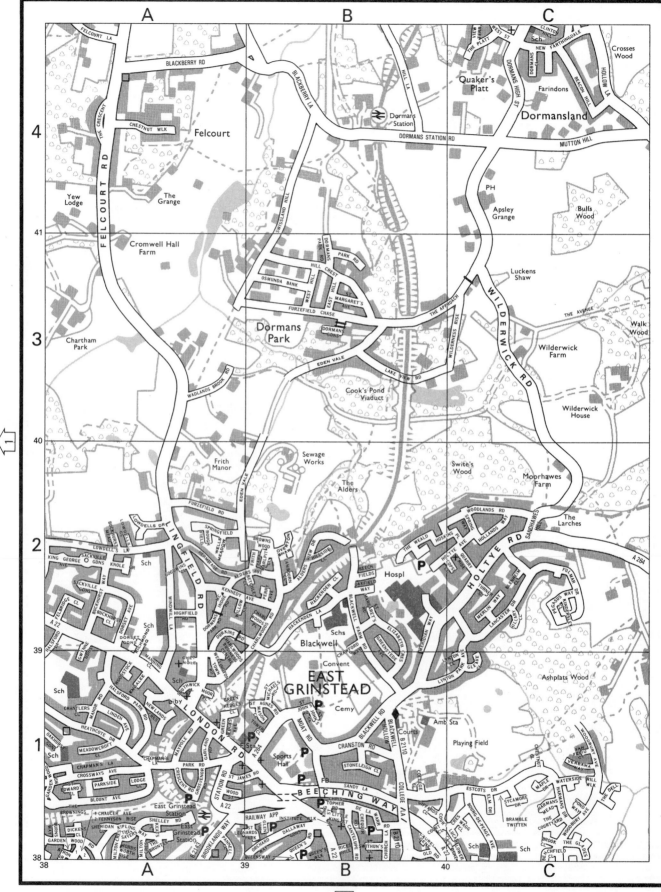

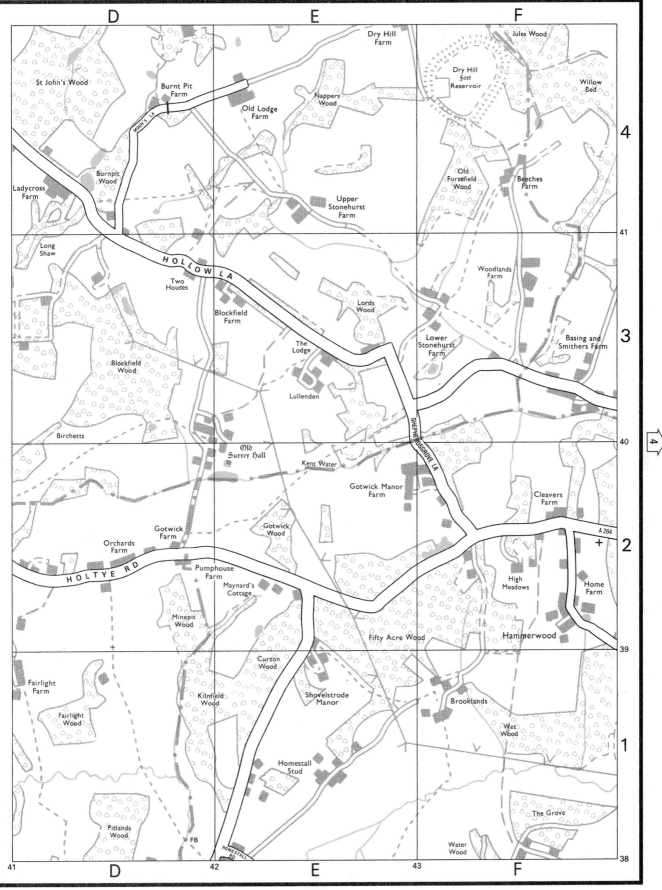

D   E   F

4

St John's Wood

Burnt Pit Farm

Old Lodge Farm

Dry Hill Farm

Nappers Wood

Jules Wood

Dry Hill Fort Reservoir

Willow Bed

Ladycross Farm

Burnpit Wood

Long Shaw

Old Furzefield Wood

Beeches Farm

41

HOLLOW LA

Two Houses

Blockfield Farm

Lords Wood

Woodlands Farm

Basing and Smithers Farm

3

Blockfield Wood

The Lodge

Lower Stonehurst Farm

Upper Stonehurst Farm

Lullenden

Birchetts

Old Surrey Hall

Kent Water

SHEPHERDSGROVE LA

40

Gotwick Manor Farm

Cleavers Farm

Gotwick Farm

Gotwick Wood

Orchards Farm

Pumphouse Farm

A 264

2

HOLTYE RD

Maynard's Cottage

High Meadows

Home Farm

Minepit Wood

Fifty Acre Wood

Hammerwood

39

Fairlight Farm

Curzon Wood

Fairlight Wood

Kilnfield Wood

Shovelstrode Manor

Brooklands

Wet Wood

1

Homestall Stud

The Grove

Pitlands Wood

FB

HOMESTALL RD

Water Wood

38

41   D   42   E   43   F   38

not continued, see key diagram

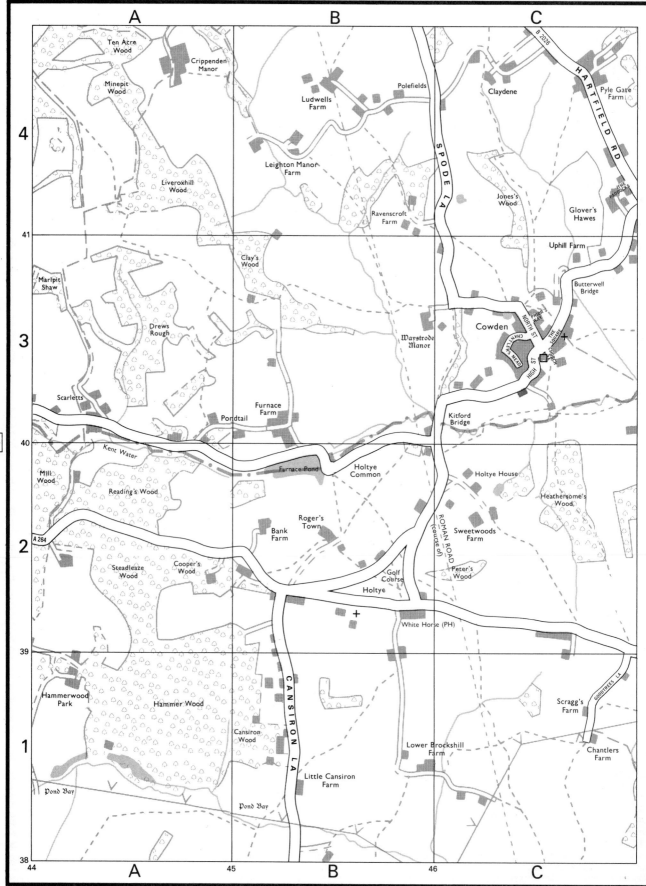

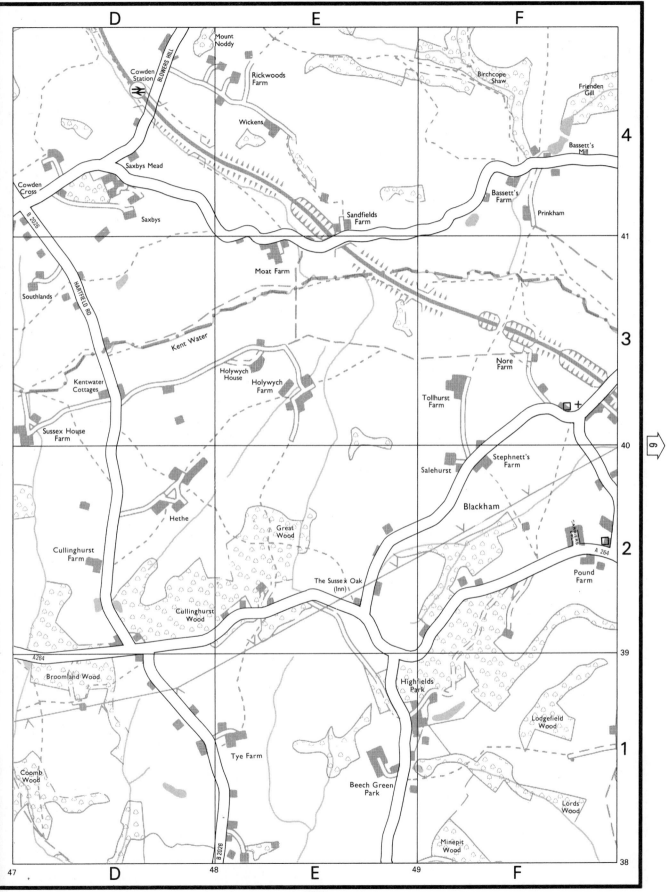

D   E   F

Mount
Noddy

Cowden
Station

Rickwoods
Farm

BLOWERS HILL

Birchcope
Shaw

Frienden
Gill

Wickens

4

Bassett's
Mill

Saxbys Mead

Cowden
Cross

Bassett's
Farm

Prinkham

B 2026

Saxbys

Sandfields
Farm

41

Moat Farm

HARTFIELD RD

Southlands

Nore
Farm

3

Kent Water

Holywych
House

Holywych
Farm

Tollhurst
Farm

Kentwater
Cottages

Sussex House
Farm

Stephnett's
Farm

40

Salehurst

Hethe

Great
Wood

Blackham

CARRIERS RD

Cullinghurst
Farm

2

A 264

Pound
Farm

The Sussex Oak
(Inn)

Cullinghurst
Wood

A 264

39

Broomland Wood

Highfields
Park

Lodgefield
Wood

Tye Farm

1

Coomb
Wood

Beech Green
Park

Lords
Wood

B 2026

Minepit
Wood

38

47   D   48   E   49   F

6

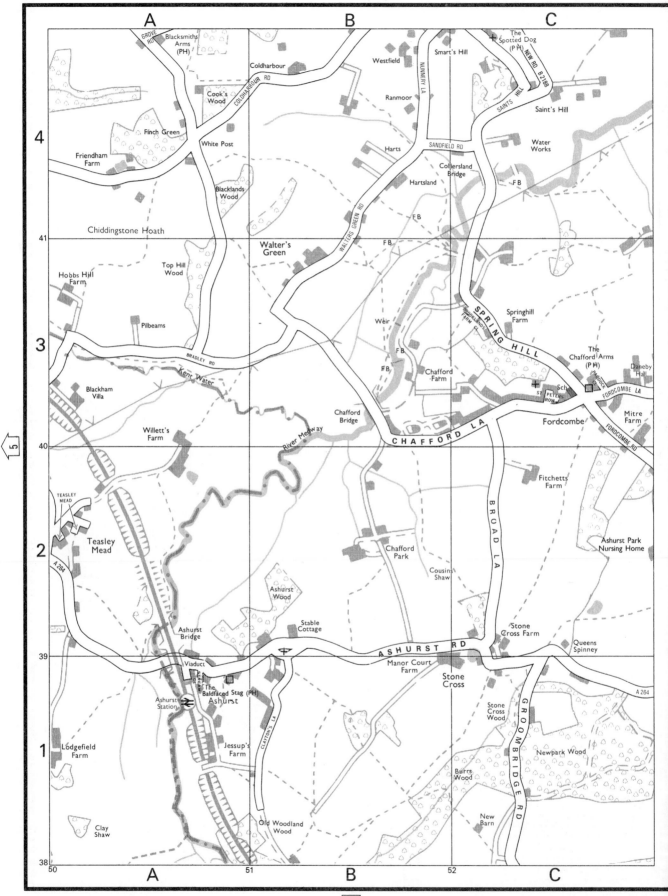

A   B   C

GROVE ROT
Blacksmiths Arms (PH)
The Spotted Dog (PH)
Smart's Hill
Westfield
NUNNERY LA
SAINTS HILL
NEW RD B 2188
Coldharbour
COLDHARBOUR RD
Cook's Wood
Ranmoor
Saint's Hill
4
Finch Green
White Post
SANDFIELD RD
Harts
Water Works
Friendham Farm
Collersland Bridge
Hartsland
FB
Blacklands Wood
WALTERS GREEN RD
FB
41
Chiddingstone Hoath
Walter's Green
FB
Top Hill Wood
Hobbs Hill Farm
SPRING HILL
Springhill Farm
BROOKLANDS FARM CL
Pilbeams
Weir
The Chafford Arms (PH)
Daneby Hall
3
BRADLEY RD
FB
Kent Water
FB
Chafford Farm
St PETERS ROW
Sch
FORDCOMBE LA
Blackham Villa
Chafford Bridge
Mitre Farm
Willett's Farm
River Medway
CHAFFORD LA
Fordcombe
FORDCOMBE RD
40
Fitchetts Farm
5
TEASLEY MEAD
BROAD LA
Ashurst Park Nursing Home
Teasley Mead
Chafford Park
Cousins Shaw
2
A 264
Ashurst Wood
Stone Cross Farm
Ashurst Bridge
Stable Cottage
Queens Spinney
39
Viaduct
ASHURST RD
Manor Court Farm
Stone Cross
A 264
The Baldfaced Stag (PH)
Ashurst Station
Ashurst
CLAYTON'S LA
Stone Cross Wood
GROOMBRIDGE RD
Lodgefield Farm
Jessup's Farm
Newpark Wood
1
Burrs Wood
Clay Shaw
Old Woodland Wood
New Barn
38
50   A   51   B   52   C

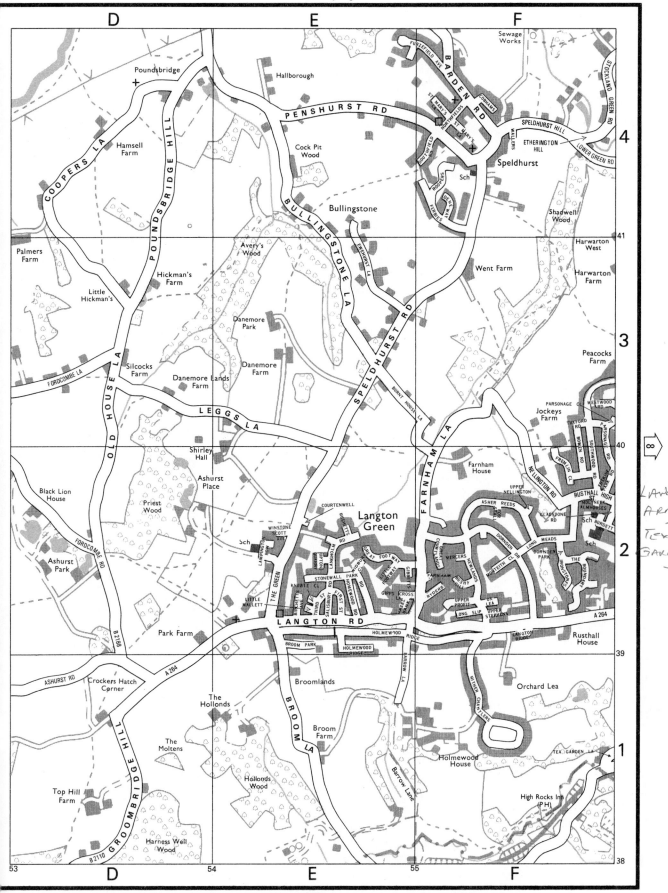

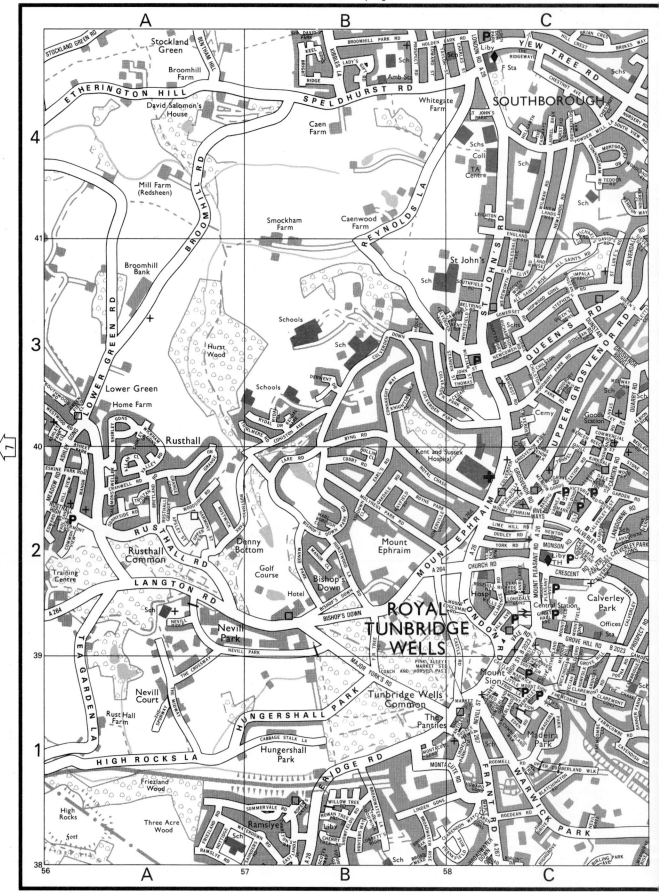

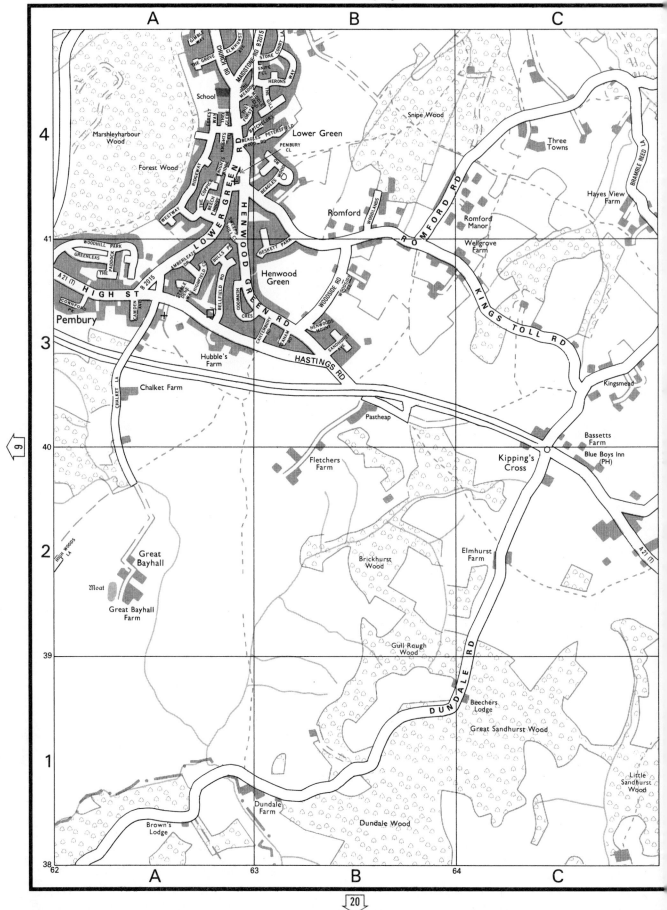

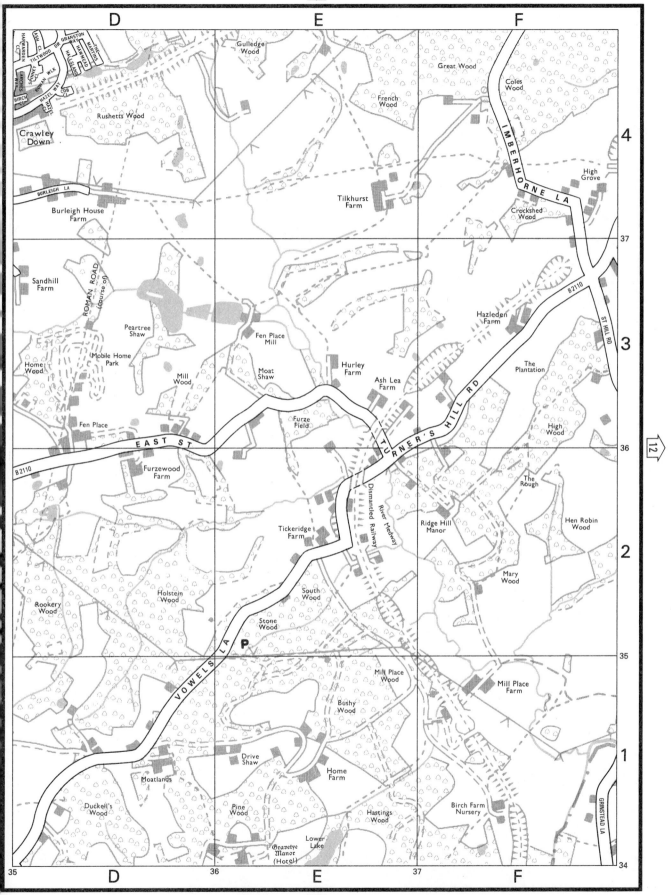

D   E   F

4

3

2

1

37

36

35

34

12

Crawley Down

ASH CL
TILTWOOD DR
GRANSTON WAY
THE MARTINS
HAWARDEN
HAZEL END
STANNEY CLOSE
ROMAN WLK
HAZEL WAY
COB CL
BIRCH
ARCHES WAY
HAWARDEN

Rushetts Wood

BURLEIGH LA

Burleigh House Farm

Gulledge Wood

Great Wood

Coles Wood

French Wood

IMBERHORNE LA

High Grove

Tilkhurst Farm

Crockshed Wood

Sandhill Farm

ROMAN ROAD (course of)

B 2110

ST HILL RD

Peartree Shaw

Fen Place Mill

Hurley Farm

Hazleden Farm

The Plantation

Home Wood

Mobile Home Park

Mill Wood

Moat Shaw

Ash Lea Farm

TURNER'S HILL RD

High Wood

Fen Place

Furze Field

EAST ST

B 2110

Furzewood Farm

The Rough

Dismantled Railway

River Medway

Ridge Hill Manor

Hen Robin Wood

Tickeridge Farm

Rookery Wood

Holstein Wood

South Wood

Mary Wood

VOWELS LA

Stone Wood

P

Mill Place Wood

Mill Place Farm

Bushy Wood

Moatlands

Drive Shaw

Home Farm

Duckell's Wood

Pine Wood

Hastings Wood

Birch Farm Nursery

GRINSTEAD LA

Gravetye Manor (Hotel)

Lower Lake

35   D   36   E   37   F

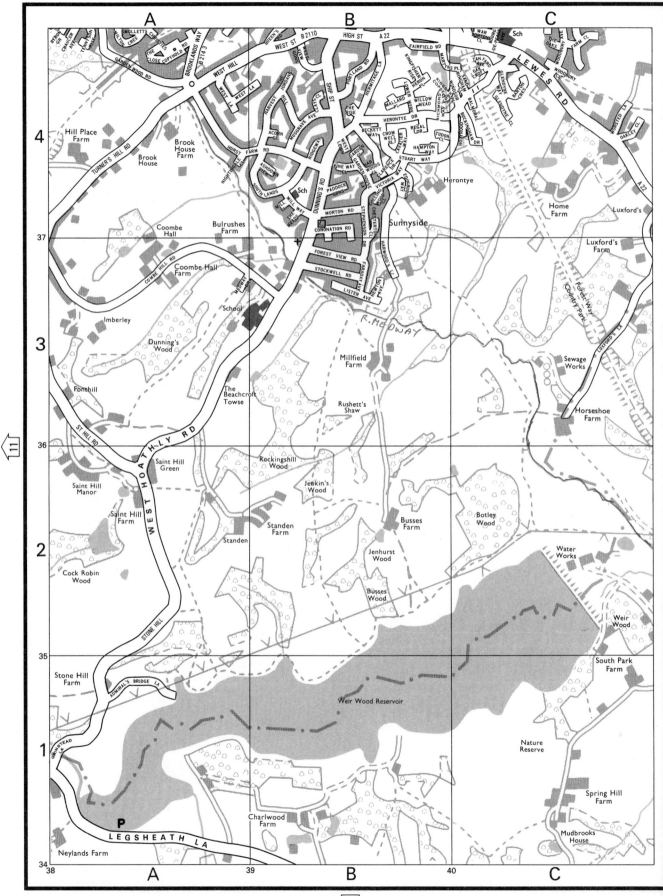

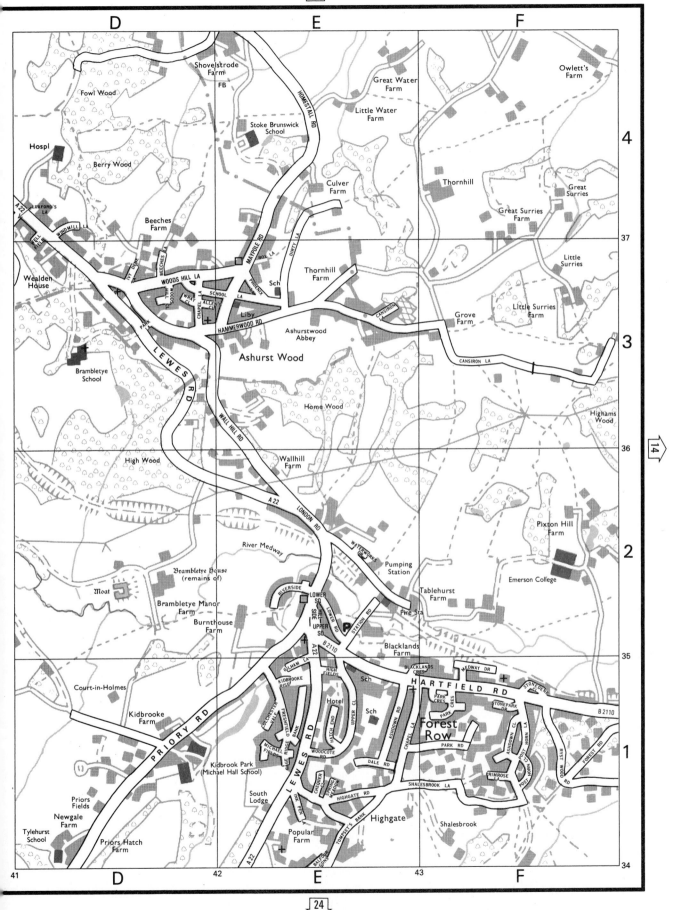

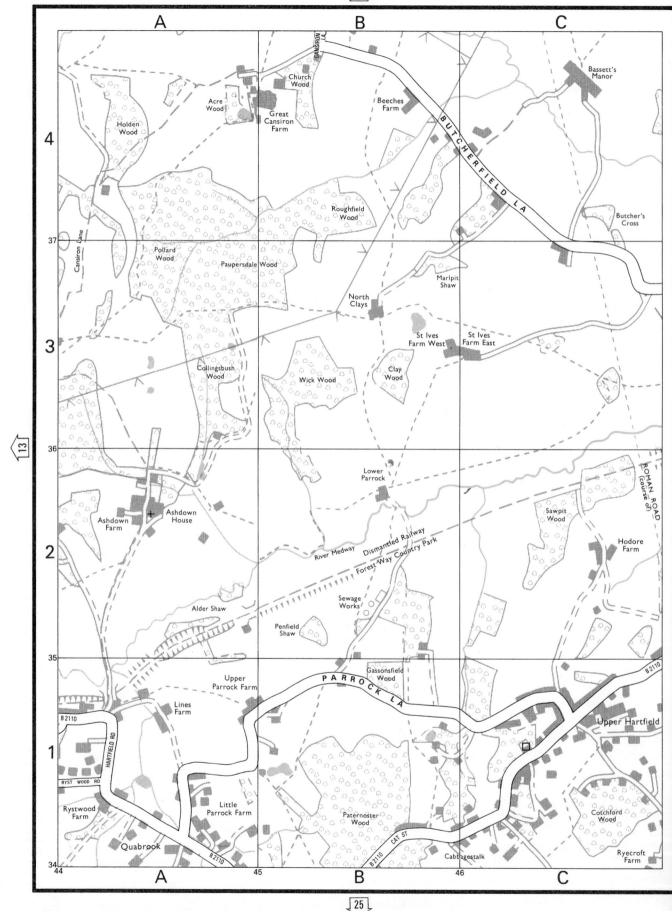

A B C

4

Holden
Wood

Acre
Wood

Church
Wood

Great
Cansiron
Farm

CANSIRON LA

Beeches
Farm

BUTCHERFIELD LA

Bassett's
Manor

Butcher's
Cross

Roughfield
Wood

Marlpit
Shaw

37

Cansiron Lane

Pollard
Wood

Paupersdale Wood

North
Clays

St Ives
Farm West

St Ives
Farm East

3

Collingsbush
Wood

Wick Wood

Clay
Wood

13

36

Lower
Parrock

Sawpit
Wood

ROMAN ROAD (course of)

Ashdown
Farm

Ashdown
House

Hodore
Farm

2

Alder Shaw

River Medway

Dismantled Railway

Forest Way Country Park

Penfield
Shaw

Sewage
Works

35

Gassonsfield
Wood

PARROCK LA

Upper
Parrock Farm

Lines
Farm

B 2110

Upper Hartfield

B 2110

HARTFIELD RD

1

RYST WOOD RD

Rystwood
Farm

Little
Parrock Farm

Paternoster
Wood

CAT ST

Cotchford
Wood

Quabrook

B 2110

B 2110

Cabbagestalk

Ryecroft
Farm

34
44

A

45

B

46

C

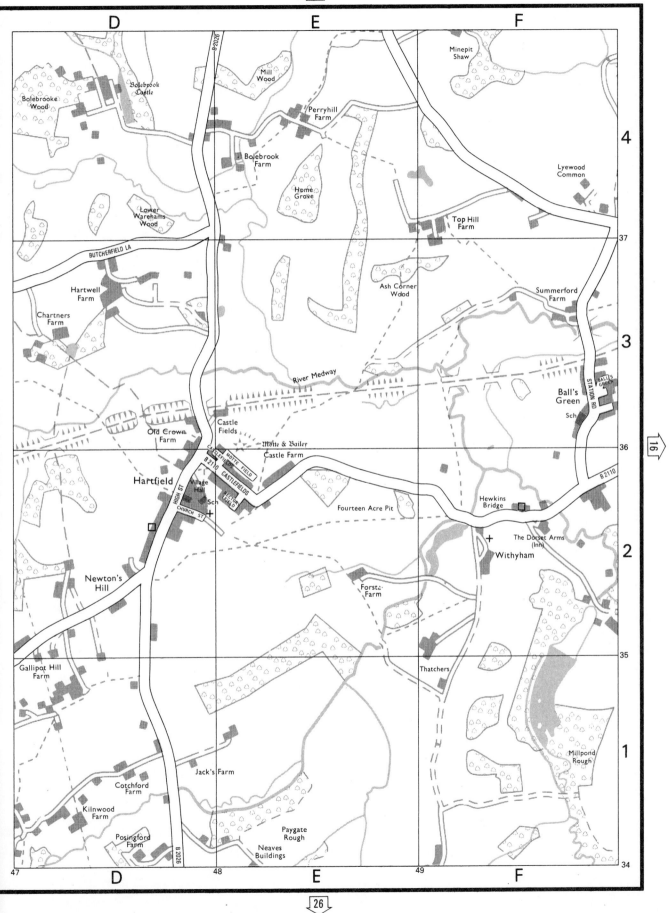

D   E   F

4

Minepit
Shaw

Bolebrooke
Wood

Bolebrook
Castle

Mill
Wood

Perryhill
Farm

Lyewood
Common

Bolebrook
Farm

Home
Grove

Lower
Warehams
Wood

Top Hill
Farm

37

BUTCHERFIELD LA

Hartwell
Farm

Ash Corner
Wood

Summerford
Farm

3

Chartners
Farm

River Medway

Ball's
Green

STATION RD

BALL'S
GREEN

Sch

Old Crown
Farm

Castle
Fields

Motte & Bailey

Castle Farm

36

CASTLEFIELDS

B 2110

B 2110

Hartfield

Village
Hall

Fourteen Acre Pit

Hewkins
Bridge

RECTOR FIELD

HIGH ST

Sch

The Dorset Arms
(Inn)

2

CHURCH ST

Withyham

Newton's
Hill

Forsta
Farm

35

Gallipot Hill
Farm

Thatchers

Millpond
Rough

1

Jack's Farm

Cotchford
Farm

Kilnwood
Farm

Paygate
Rough

Posingford
Farm

B 2026

Neaves
Buildings

34

16

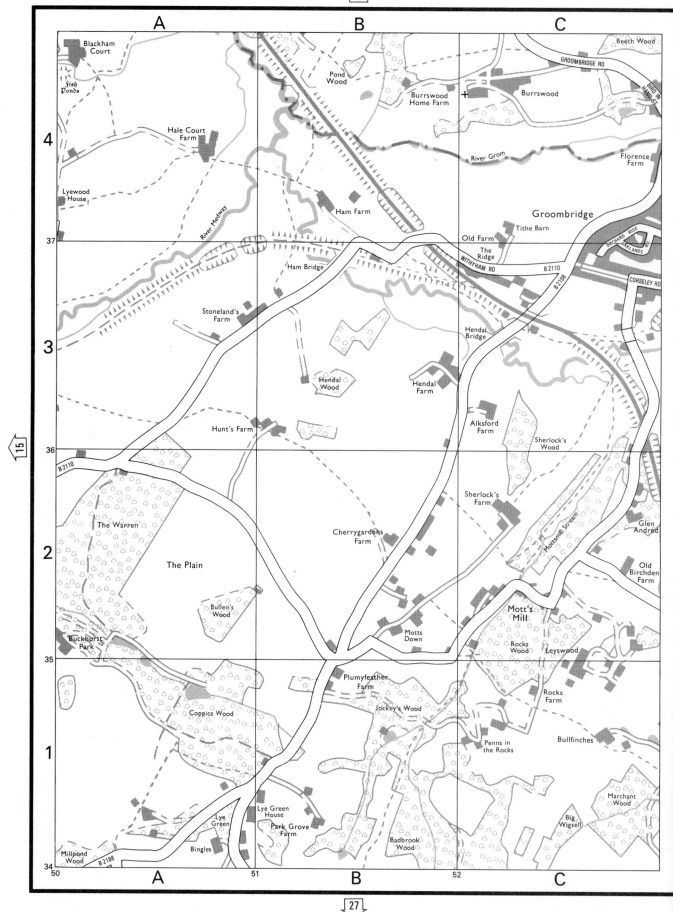

Blackham Court

Fish Ponds

Hale Court Farm

Lyewood House

River Medway

Pond Wood

Burrswood Home Farm

Burrswood

River Grom

Beech Wood

GROOMBRIDGE RD

BIRD IN HAND ST

Florence Farm

Groombridge

Tithe Barn

Old Farm

The Ridge

WITHYHAM RD

B 2110

B 2188

ORCHARD RISE

OAKLANDS RD

CORSELEY RD

Ham Farm

Ham Bridge

Stoneland's Farm

Hendal Bridge

Hendal Wood

Hendal Farm

Alksford Farm

Sherlock's Wood

Hunt's Farm

B 2110

The Warren

The Plain

Bullen's Wood

Buckhurst Park

Coppice Wood

Cherrygardens Farm

Sherlock's Farm

Mottsmill Stream

Glen Andred

Old Birchden Farm

Mott's Mill

Rocks Wood

Leyswood

Motts Down

Plumyfeather Farm

Jockey's Wood

Rocks Farm

Penns in the Rocks

Bullfinches

Lye Green House

Park Grove Farm

Lye Green

Bingles

Millpond Wood

B 2188

Badbrook Wood

Marchant Wood

Big Wigsell

50   51   52

A   B   C

34 35 36 37

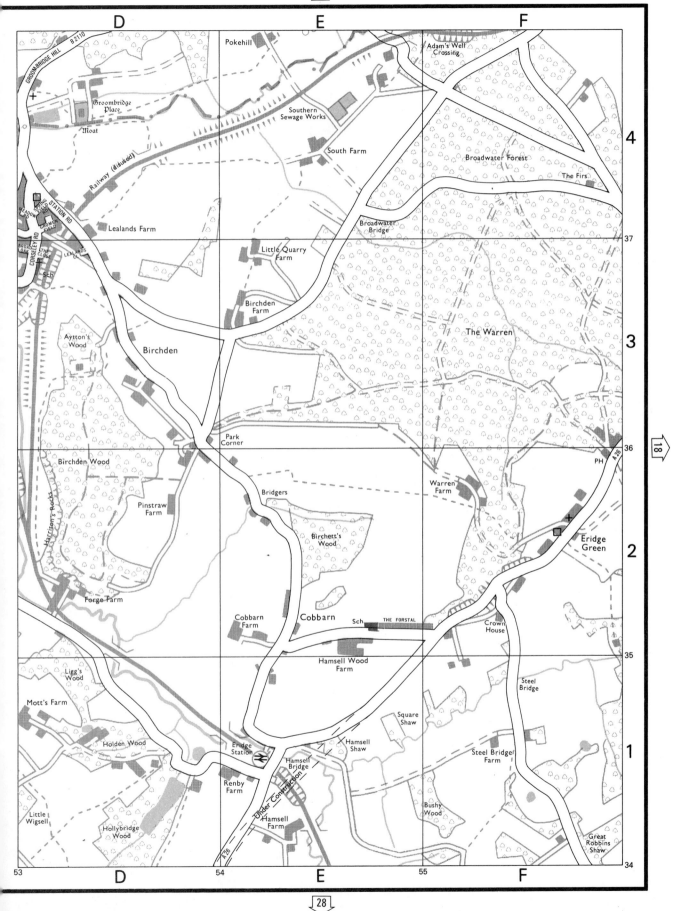

D   E   F

GROOMBRIDGE HILL

B 2110

Pokehill

Adam's Well Crossing

Groombridge Place

Southern Sewage Works

Moat

South Farm

4

Broadwater Forest

Railway (disused)

The Firs

SPRING MEADOW RD
FIELD
GROMB FIELD
STATION RD

Lealands Farm

Broadwater Bridge

BROAD RD
CORSELEY RD
THE CLOSE
LEALANDS CL.

37

Little Quarry Farm

Sch

Birchden Farm

The Warren

3

Aytton's Wood

Birchden

Harrison's Rocks

Birchden Wood

Park Corner

36

PH

A 26

18

Bridgers

Warren Farm

Pinstraw Farm

Birchett's Wood

Eridge Green

2

Forge Farm

Cobbarn

Cobbarn Farm

Sch   THE FORSTAL

Crown House

35

Hamsell Wood Farm

Ligg's Wood

Steel Bridge

Mott's Farm

Square Shaw

Holden Wood

Eridge Station

Hamsell Shaw

Steel Bridge Farm

1

Hamsell Bridge

Renby Farm

Under Construction

Bushy Wood

Little Wigsell

Hollybridge Wood

Hamsell Farm

A 26

Great Robbins Shaw

34

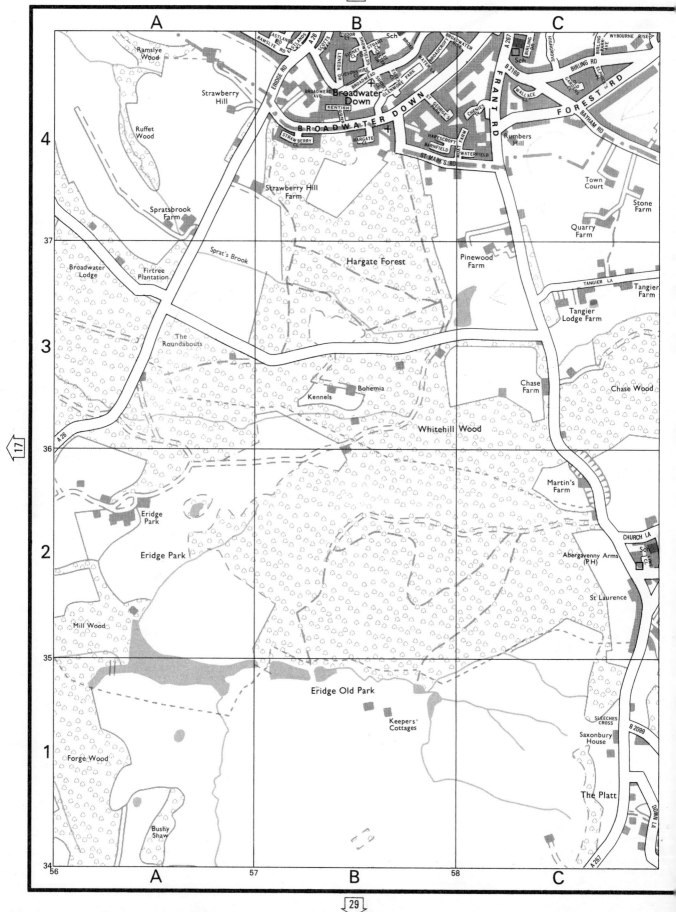

A   B   C

Ramslye Wood

Strawberry Hill

Ruffet Wood

EASTLANDS
RAMSLYE RD EASTLANDS
A 26
SCOTTS
TUDOR CT
SIDNEY CL
SHOEFIELDS
STUART CL
BROADWATER
Sch
BROADWATER
HIGHGROVE
WYBOURNE RISE
A 267
BIRLING RD
BIRLING RD
Sch
B 2169
ELPHIC'S
BIRLING
BRANWOOD
AVE

ERIDGE RD
DEVONSHIRE CL
BROADMEAD
SURREY CL
GLENMORE PARK
WALLACE
OLD
GLADYS
GDNS
FOREST RD

Broadwater Down

BROADMEAD AVE
KENTISH GDNS
Broadwater Down

FRANT RD
BAYHAM RD
FOREST RD

B R O A D W A T E R   D O W N

STRAWBERRY
HARGATE
ST GEORGE'S PARK
HARESCROFT
BARNFIELD
MUST FARM
WATERFIELD
CHEYNE CL
Rumbers Hill

4

ST MARK'S RD

Town Court

Strawberry Hill Farm

Stone Farm

Spratsbrook Farm

Quarry Farm

37

Sprat's Brook

Hargate Forest

Pinewood Farm

Broadwater Lodge

Firtree Plantation

TANGIER LA

Tangier Farm

Tangier Lodge Farm

3

The Roundabouts

Kennels

Bohemia

Chase Farm

Chase Wood

A 26

Whitehill Wood

36

Martin's Farm

Eridge Park

CHURCH LA

Sch

2

Eridge Park

Abergavenny Arms (P H)

SCH CL

St Laurence

Mill Wood

35

Eridge Old Park

SLEECHES CROSS

B 2099

Keepers' Cottages

Saxonbury House

1

Forge Wood

The Platt

DOWN LA

Bushy Shaw

A 267

34

56   A   57   B   58   C

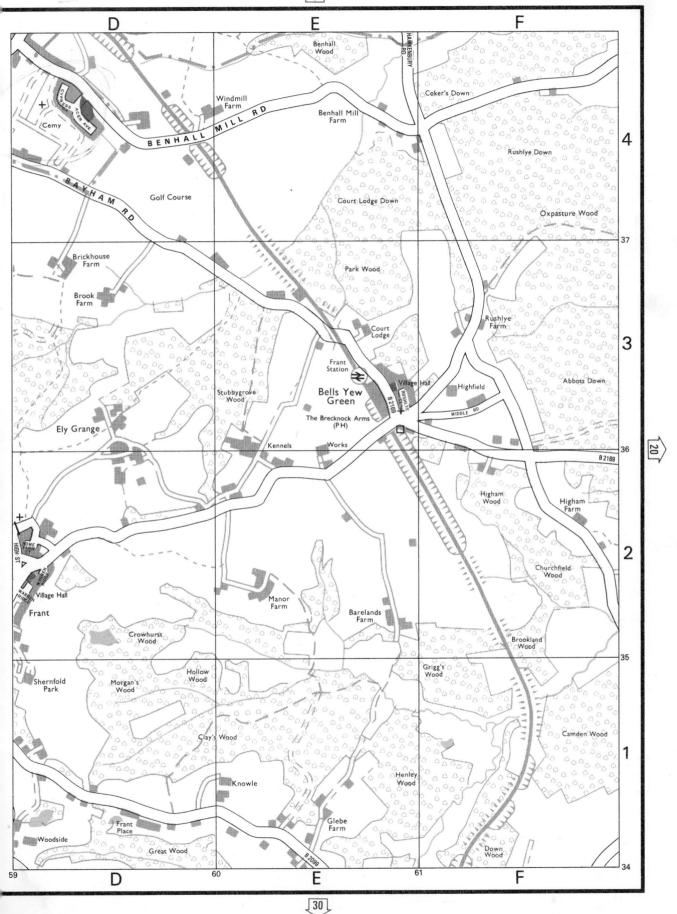

D
E
F

Benhall
Wood

HAWKENBURY RD

Windmill
Farm

Coker's Down

BENHALL MILL RD

Benhall Mill
Farm

4

Cemy

+

CYPRESS
ACER AVE

Rushlye Down

BAYHAM RD

Golf Course

Court Lodge Down

Oxpasture Wood

37

Brickhouse
Farm

Park Wood

Brook
Farm

Rushlye
Farm

3

Court
Lodge

Frant
Station

Stubbygrove
Wood

Bells Yew
Green

Village Hall

Highfield

Abbots Down

B 2169

RUSHLYE

The Brecknock Arms
(PH)

MIDDLE RD

Ely Grange

Kennels

Works

36

B 2169

Higham
Wood

Higham
Farm

HOME
FARM
ST

HIGH ST

WARREN RIDGE

Village Hall

Churchfield
Wood

2

Frant

+

Manor
Farm

Barelands
Farm

Crowhurst
Wood

Brookland
Wood

35

Hollow
Wood

Grigg's
Wood

Shernfold
Park

Morgan's
Wood

Camden Wood

Clay's Wood

1

Knowle

Henley
Wood

Frant
Place

Glebe
Farm

Woodside

Great Wood

B 2099

Down
Wood

34

59
D
60
E
61
F

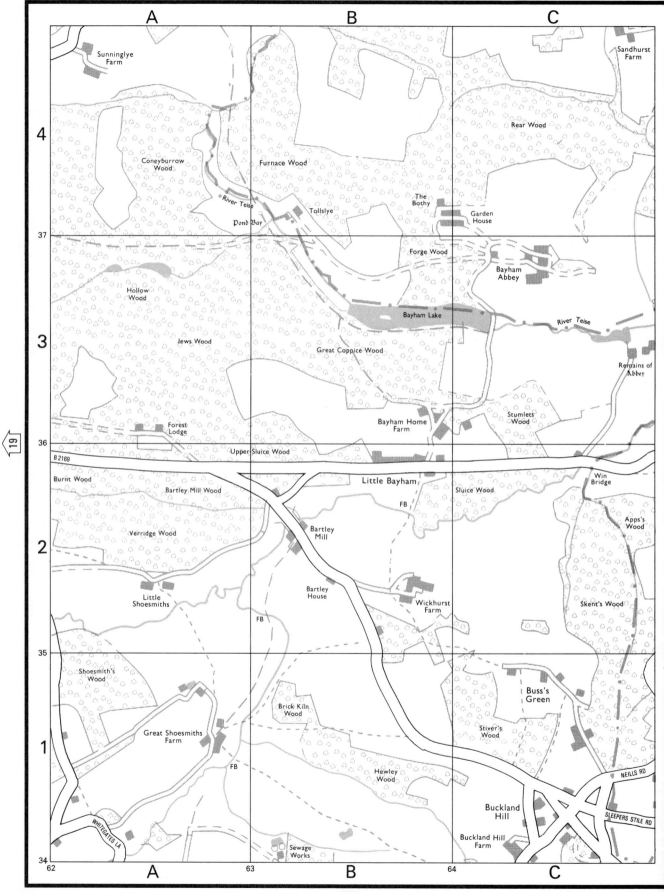

A B C

4

Sunninglye Farm

Coneyburrow Wood

Furnace Wood

Rear Wood

Sandhurst Farm

River Teise

Tollslye

The Bothy

Garden House

Pond Bay

37

Forge Wood

Bayham Abbey

Hollow Wood

Jews Wood

Great Coppice Wood

Bayham Lake

River Teise

3

Remains of Abbey

Forest Lodge

Bayham Home Farm

Stumlets Wood

36

Upper Sluice Wood

B 2169

Burnt Wood

Bartley Mill Wood

Little Bayham

FB

Sluice Wood

Win Bridge

Verridge Wood

Bartley Mill

Apps's Wood

2

Little Shoesmiths

Bartley House

Wickhurst Farm

Skent's Wood

FB

35

Shoesmith's Wood

Brick Kiln Wood

Buss's Green

Great Shoesmiths Farm

FB

Stiver's Wood

1

Hewley Wood

Buckland Hill

NEILLS RD

WHITEGATES LA

Sewage Works

Buckland Hill Farm

SLEEPERS STILE RD

34

62

A

63

B

64

C

19

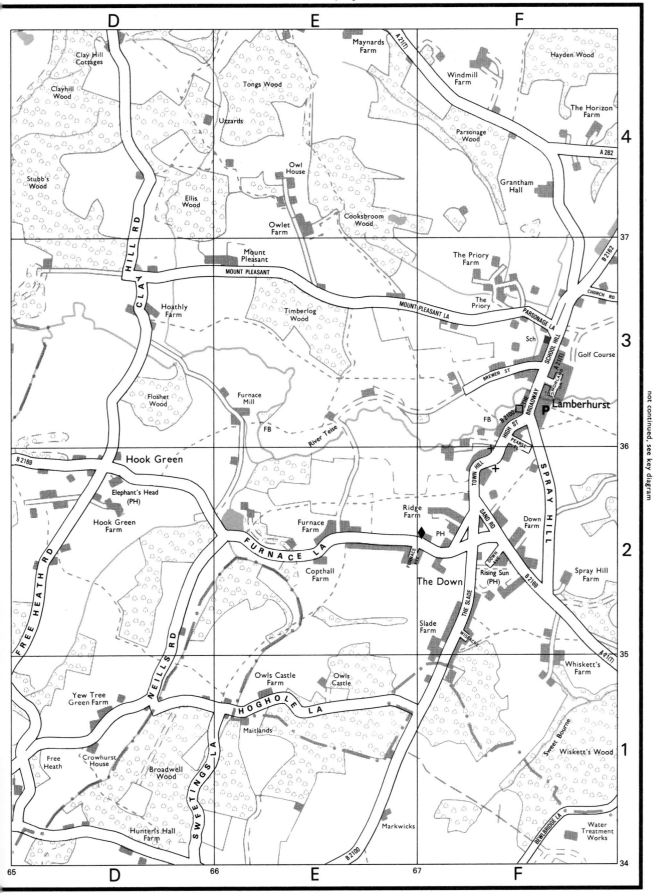

Maynards Farm
Clay Hill Cottages
Clayhill Wood
Tongs Wood
Uzzards
Stubb's Wood
Ellis Wood
Owl House
Owlet Farm
Cooksbroom Wood
Windmill Farm
Hayden Wood
The Horizon Farm
Parsonage Wood
Grantham Hall
A 262

CLAY HILL RD
MOUNT PLEASANT
MOUNT PLEASANT LA
Mount Pleasant
Hoathly Farm
Timberlog Wood
The Priory Farm
The Priory
PARSONAGE LA
SCHOOL HILL
CHURCH RD
B 2162
Sch
Golf Course
BROADWAY
A 21(T)
BREWER ST
Lamberhurst
P
37
3

Floshet Wood
Furnace Mill
FB
River Teise
FB
HIGH ST
B 2100
Town Hill
PEARSE
X
36

B 2169
Hook Green
Elephant's Head (PH)
Hook Green Farm
FURNACE LA
Furnace Farm
Copthall Farm
Ridge Farm
PH
The Down
FURNACE AVE
SAND RD
DOWN AVE
Rising Sun (PH)
B 2169
Down Farm
SPRAY HILL
Spray Hill Farm
A 21(T)
2

FREE HEATH RD
NEILLS RD
SWEETINGS LA
HOGHOLE LA
Owls Castle Farm
Owls Castle
Yew Tree Green Farm
Maitlands
THE SLADE
Slade Farm
WISEACRE
Whiskett's Farm
35

Free Heath
Crowhurst House
Broadwell Wood
Hunter's Hall Farm
Markwicks
B 2100
BEWLBRIDGE LA
Sweet Bourne
Wiskett's Wood
Water Treatment Works
1
34

D   65   E   66   E   67   F

32

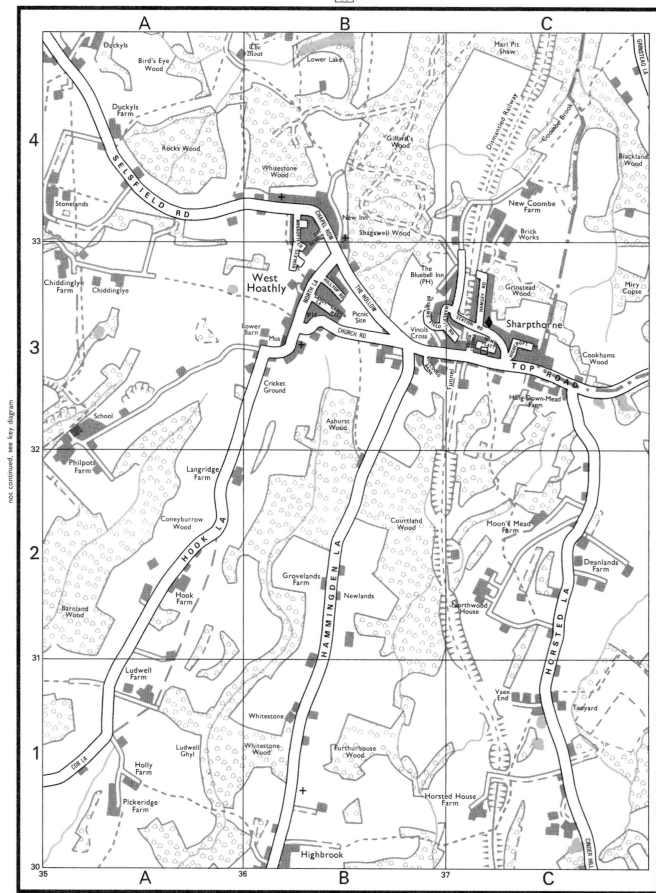

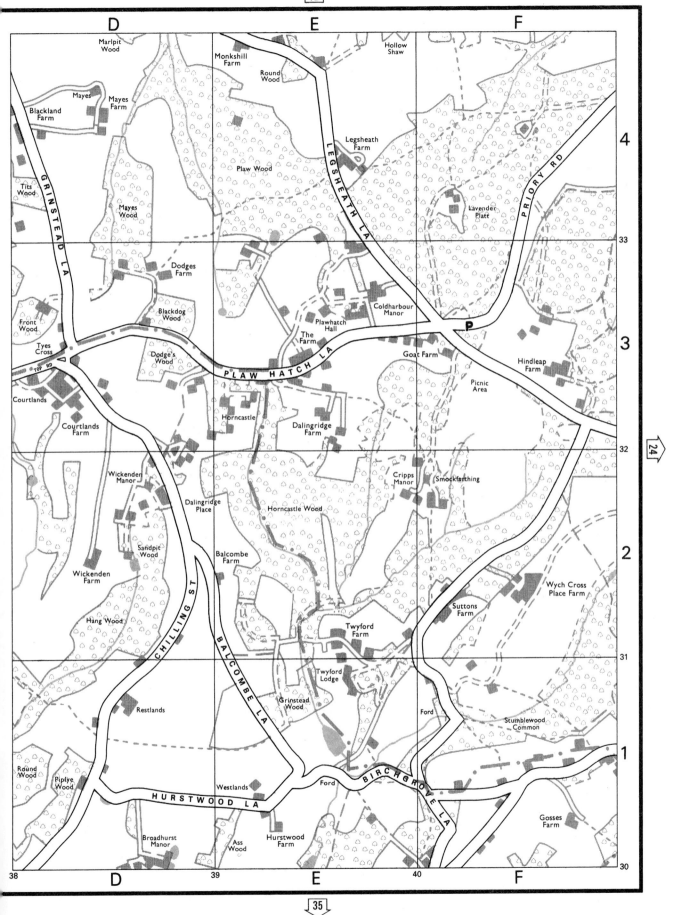

D   E   F

Marlpit Wood
Monkshill Farm
Round Wood
Hollow Shaw
Mayes
Blackland Farm
Mayes Farm
Legsheath Farm
PRIORY RD
4
Tits Wood
Plaw Wood
Lavender Platt
Mayes Wood
33
Dodges Farm
GRINSTEAD LA
Coldharbour Manor
Front Wood
Blackdog Wood
Plawhatch Hall
P
3
Tyes Cross
The Farm
Goat Farm
Hindleap Farm
TOP RD
Dodge's Wood
PLAW HATCH LA
Courtlands
Horncastle
Picnic Area
Dalingridge Farm
Courtlands Farm
32
Wickenden Manor
Cripps Manor
Smockfarthing
Dalingridge Place
Horncastle Wood
Sandpit Wood
Wych Cross Place Farm
2
Balcombe Farm
Wickenden Farm
CHILLING ST
Suttons Farm
Hang Wood
BALCOMBE LA
Twyford Farm
31
Twyford Lodge
Restlands
Grinstead Wood
Ford
Stumblewood Common
1
Round Wood
Piplye Wood
Westlands
Ford
BIRCHGROVE LA
HURSTWOOD LA
Gosses Farm
Broadhurst Manor
Ass Wood
Hurstwood Farm
30

38   D   39   E   40   F

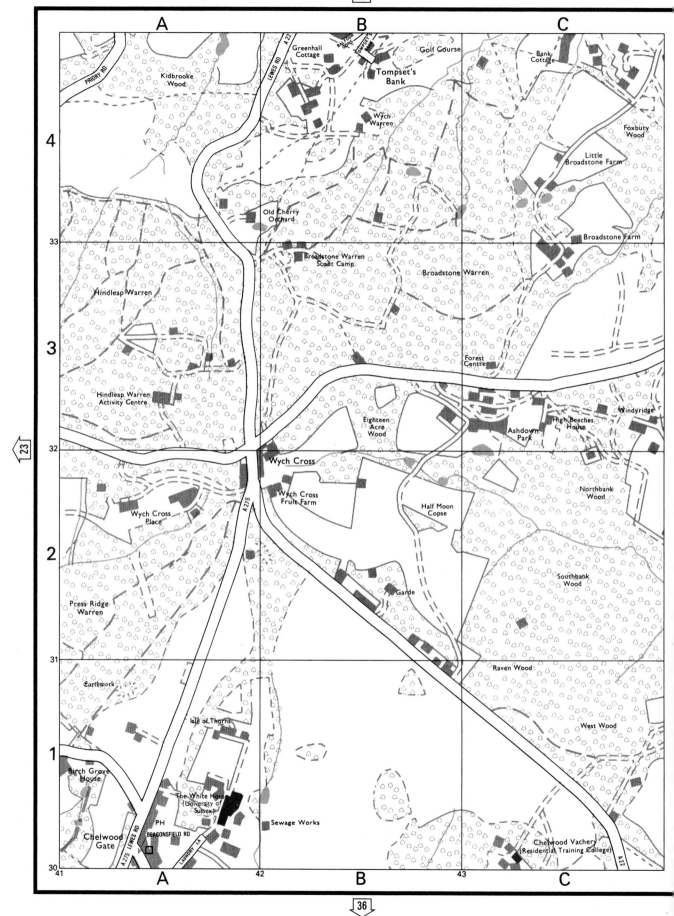

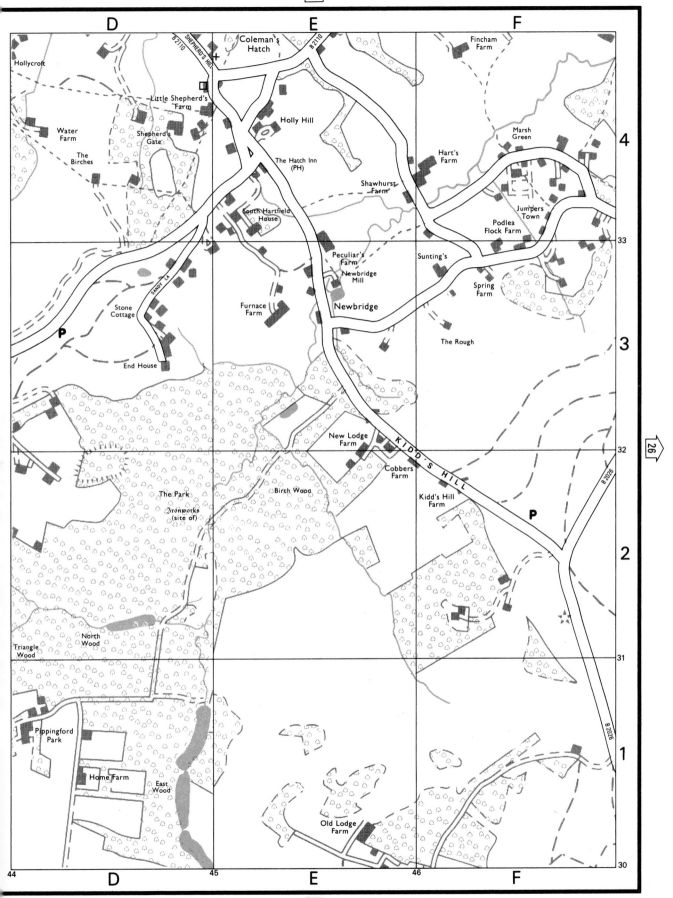

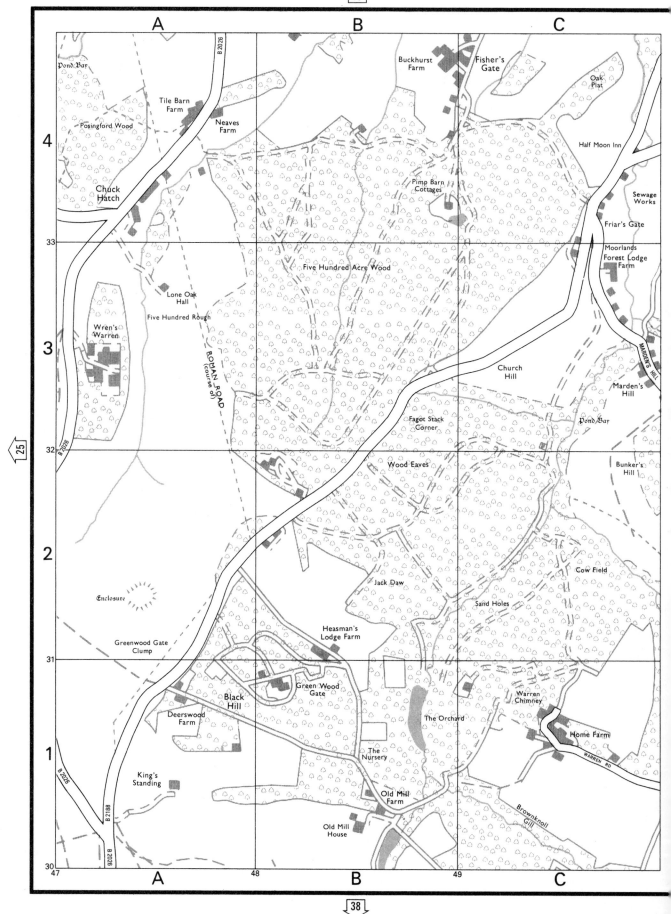

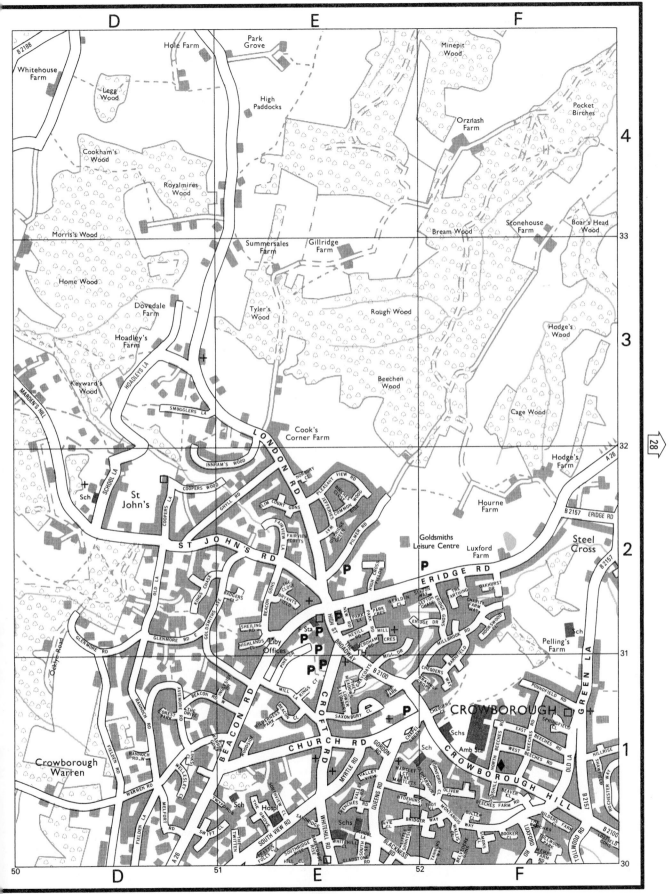

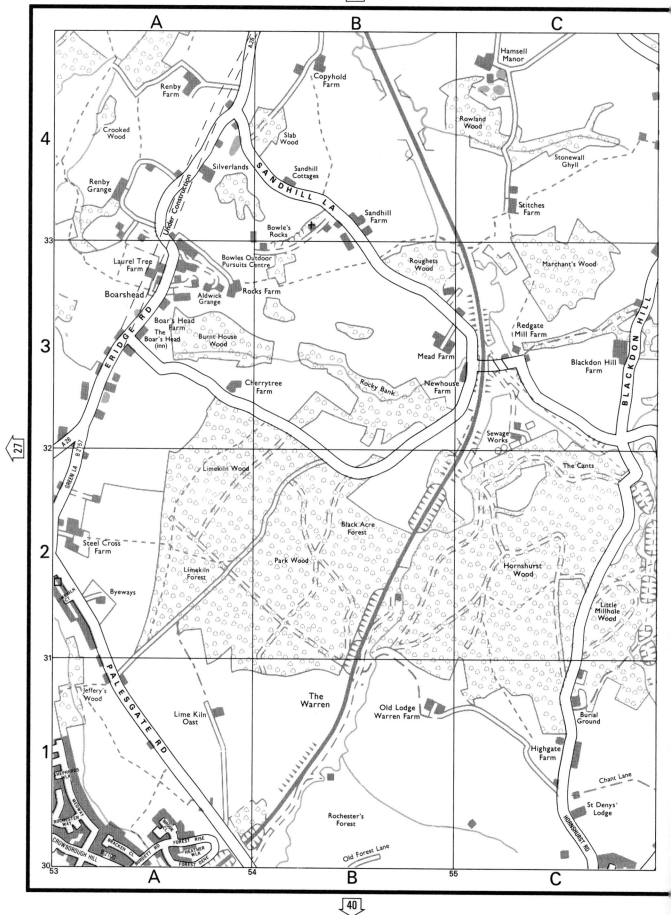

A   B   C

Hamsell Manor

Renby Farm

Copyhold Farm

Rowland Wood

Crooked Wood

4

Slab Wood

Stonewall Ghyll

Silverlands

SANDHILL LA

Sandhill Cottages

Renby Grange

Under Construction

Sandhill Farm

Stitches Farm

Bowle's Rocks

Marchant's Wood

33

Laurel Tree Farm

Bowles Outdoor Pursuits Centre

Roughets Wood

Boarshead

ERIDGE RD

Aldwick Grange

Rocks Farm

Redgate Mill Farm

BLACKDON HILL

Boar's Head Farm

Blackdon Hill Farm

3

The Boar's Head (inn)

Burnt House Wood

Mead Farm

Cherrytree Farm

Rocky Bank

Newhouse Farm

32

A 26 B 2157

Sewage Works

GREEN LA

Limekiln Wood

The Cants

Black Acre Forest

Steel Cross Farm

Hornshurst Wood

2

Park Wood

Limekiln Forest

Byeways

Little Millhole Wood

31

PALESGATE RD

Jeffery's Wood

The Warren

Old Lodge Warren Farm

Burial Ground

Lime Kiln Oast

Highgate Farm

1

SHEPHERDS WLK

Chant Lane

MEDWAY

ROCHESTER WAY

St Denys' Lodge

HORNSHURST RD

CROWBOROUGH HILL

BRACKEN CL

BURDETT RD

FOREST RISE

HEATHER WLK

FOREST DENE

B 2100

Rochester's Forest

Old Forest Lane

30
53   54   55

A   B   C

27

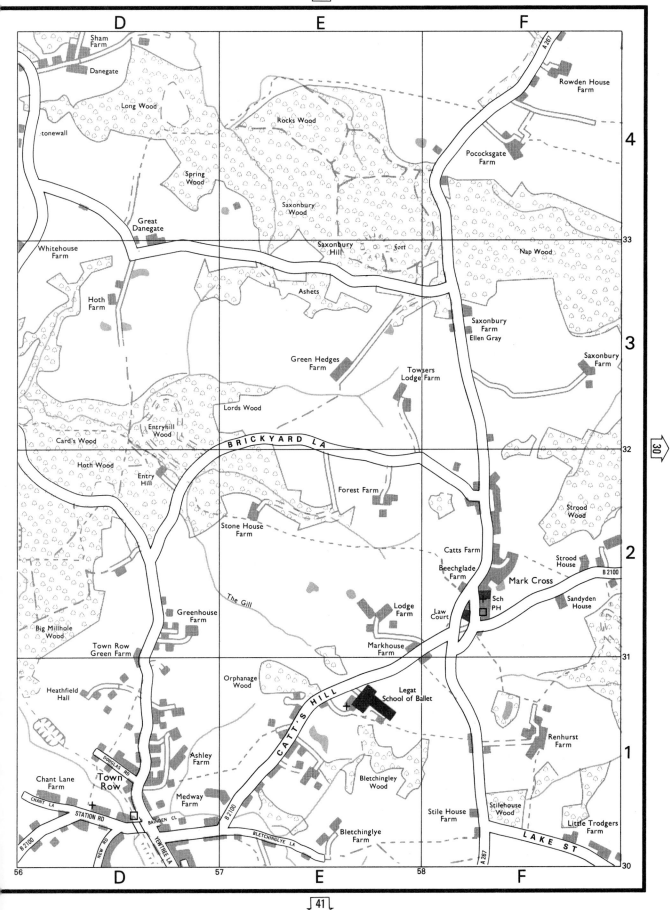

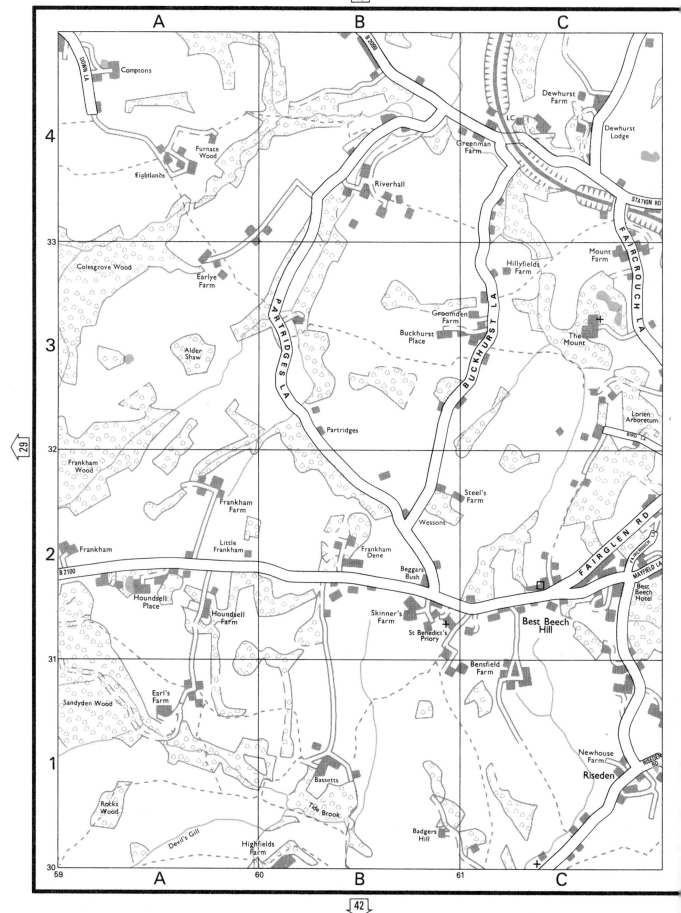

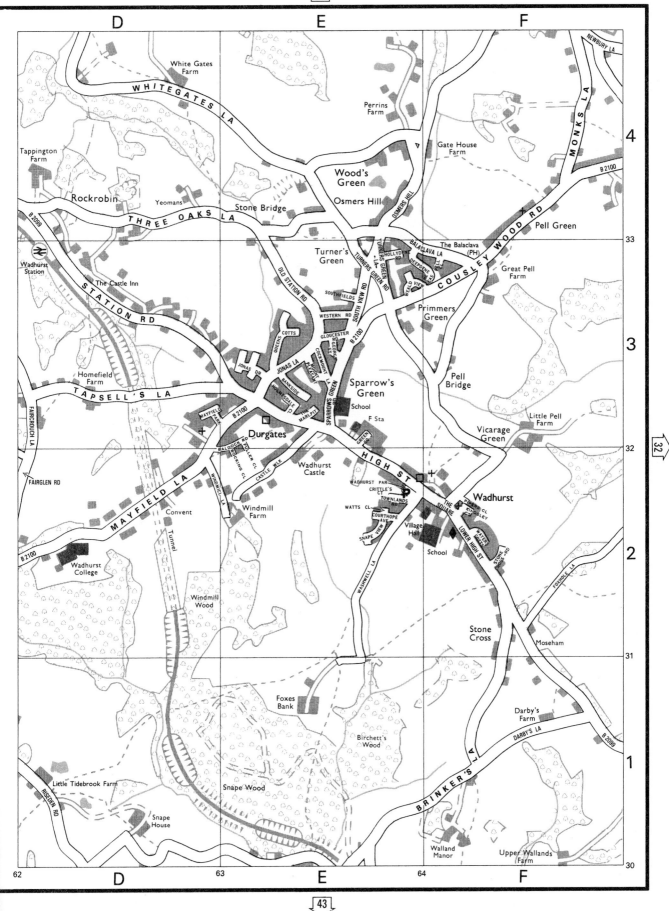

D   E   F

NEWBURY LA

White Gates Farm

WHITEGATES LA

Perrins Farm

Tappington Farm

MONKS LA

Gate House Farm

4

B 2100

Wood's Green

Rockrobin

Yeomans

Osmers Hill

Stone Bridge

THREE OAKS LA

OSMERS HILL

Pell Green

COUSLEY WOOD RD

B 2089

33

Turner's Green

The Balaclava (PH)

BALACLAVA LA

Wadhurst Station

The Castle Inn

STATION RD

OLD STATION RD

TURNERS GREEN RD

HOLLYDENE RD

DEEPDENE

WEALD VIEW

Great Pell Farm

SOUTHFIELDS

SOUTH VIEW RD

Primmers Green

WESTERN RD

GLOUCESTER RD

COCKMOUNT LA

B 2100

3

Homefield Farm

QUEENS COTTS

JONAS DR

JONAS LA

PARK PLEASANT

Pell Bridge

TAPSELL'S LA

BANKSIDE

HOLMESDALE

SPARROWS GREEN

Sparrow's Green

Little Pell Farm

FAIRCROUGH LA

MARLPIT

School

PINE

MAYFIELD PARK

B 2100

Vicarage Green

F Sta

32

Durgates

GREEN

32

FAIRGLEN RD

BALDOCK RD

FULLER CL

BECKING CL

CASTLE WLK

Wadhurst Castle

HIGH ST

WADHURST PAR

CRITTLE'S CL

TOWNLANDS RD

KINGSLEY CL

Wadhurst

WINDMILL LA

WATTS CL

Windmill Farm

Convent

MAYFIELD LA

COURTHOPE AVE

SNAPE VIEW

THE SQUARE

WATERS

LOWER HIGH ST

STONE CROSS RD

Tunnel

Village Hall

School

2

B 2100

Wadhurst College

WASHWELL LA

FOXHOLE LA

Windmill Wood

Stone Cross

Moseham

31

Foxes Bank

Darby's Farm

B 2089

Little Tidebrook Farm

Birchett's Wood

DARBY'S LA

1

RISDEN RD

BRINKERS LA

Snape House

Snape Wood

Walland Manor

Upper Wallands Farm

30

62   D   63   E   64   F

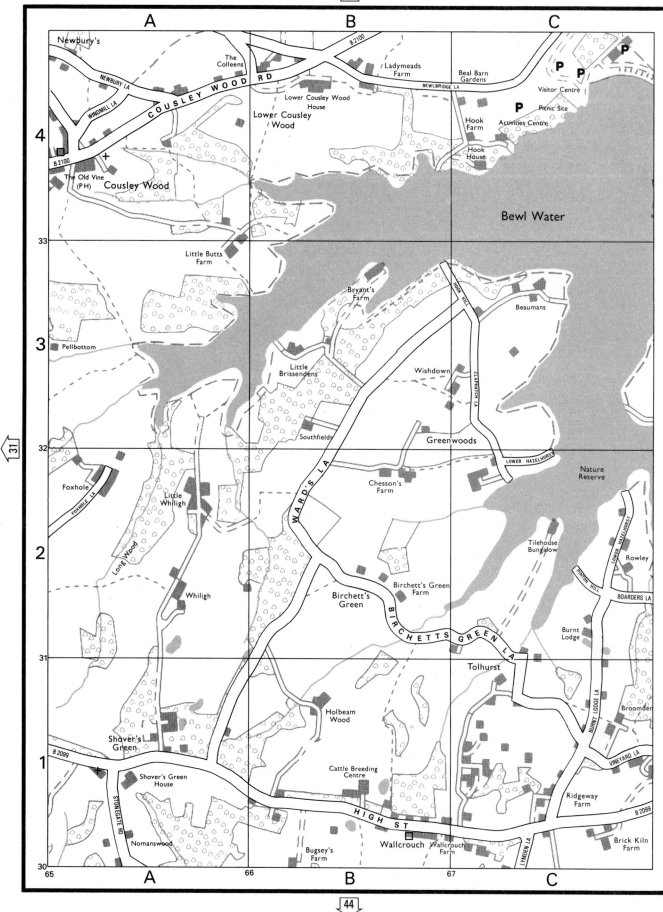

A   B   C

Newbury's

The Colleens

NEWBURY LA

Ladymeads Farm

COUSLEY WOOD RD

B 2100

Beal Barn Gardens

BEWLBRIDGE LA

Lower Cousley Wood House

Visitor Centre

P P P

P

WINDMILL LA

Lower Cousley Wood

Hook Farm

Picnic Site

Activities Centre

4

B 2100

Hook House

The Old Vine (PH)

Cousley Wood

Bewl Water

33

Little Butts Farm

Bryant's Farm

Beaumans

3

Pellbottom

Little Brissendens

Wishdown

HOOK HILL

CLAPIATCH LA

Greenwoods

Southfields

LOWER HAZELHURST

32

Nature Reserve

Foxhole

Little Whiligh

Chesson's Farm

FOXHOLE LA

Tilehouse Bungalow

Rowley

LOWER HAZELHURST

2

Long Wood

PIXTON HILL

BOARDERS LA

WARD'S LA

Whiligh

Birchett's Green Farm

Birchett's Green

Burnt Lodge

BIRCHETTS GREEN LA

31

Tolhurst

Broomden

Holbeam Wood

BURNT LODGE LA

Shover's Green

VINEYARD LA

1

B 2099

Cattle Breeding Centre

Ridgeway Farm

B 2099

Shover's Green House

STONEGATE RD

HIGH ST

Brick Kiln Farm

Nomanswood

Bugsey's Farm

Wallcrouch

Wallcrouch Farm

LYMDEN LA

30

65   A   66   B   67   C

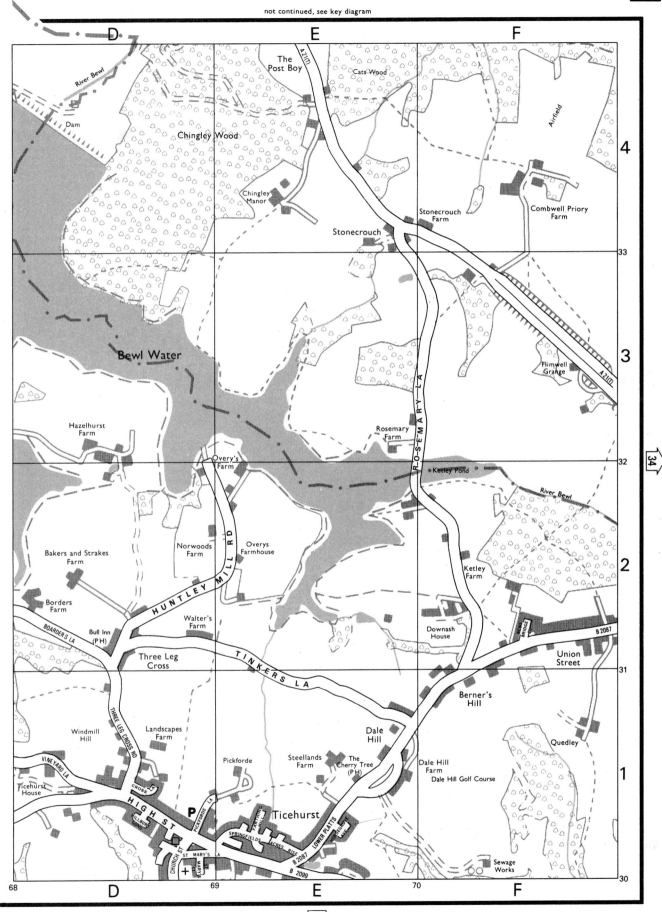

D   E   F

The Post Boy

Cats Wood

A 21(T)

Airfield

River Bewl

Dam

Chingley Wood

4

Chingley Manor

Stonecrouch Farm

Combwell Priory Farm

Stonecrouch

33

A 21(T)

Bewl Water

3

Flimwell Grange

R-O-S-E-M-A-R-Y LA

A 21(T)

34

Hazelhurst Farm

Rosemary Farm

Overy's Farm

Ketley Pond

River Bewl

32

Bakers and Strakes Farm

Norwoods Farm

HUNTLEY MILL RD

Overys Farmhouse

Ketley Farm

2

Borders Farm

Walter's Farm

Downash House

BEWL BRIDGE

B 2087

BOARDER S LA

Bull Inn (P H)

Union Street

Three Leg Cross

TINKERS LA

31

Berner's Hill

THREE LEG CROSS RD

Windmill Hill

Landscapes Farm

Dale Hill

Quedley

VINEYARD LA

Pickforde

Steellands Farm

The Cherry Tree (P H)

Dale Hill Farm

Dale Hill Golf Course

1

Ticehurst House

CROSS ST

HIGH ST

P

PICKFORDE LA

Ticehurst

TILLBURY GDNS

SPRINGFIELDS

ACRES RISE

LOWER PLATTS

CHURCH ST

ST MARY'S LA

B 2087

B 2099

Sewage Works

30

68   D   69   E   70   F

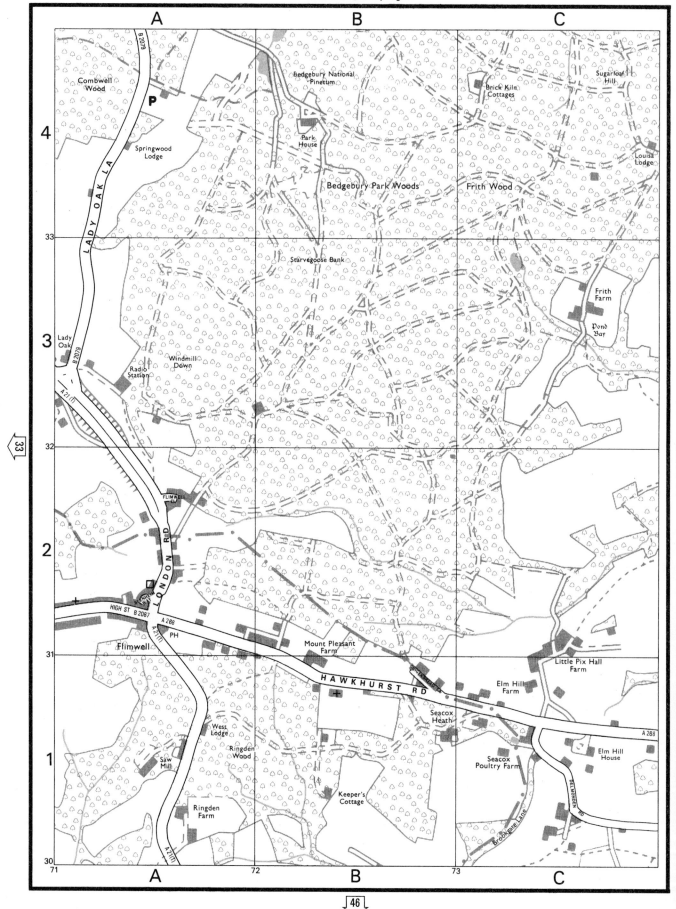

A   B   C

4

Combwell
Wood

Bedgebury National
Pinetum

Brick Kiln
Cottages

Sugarloaf
Hill

Springwood
Lodge

Park
House

Louisa
Lodge

Bedgebury Park Woods

Frith Wood

33

Starvegoose Bank

Frith
Farm

3

Lady
Oak

Pond
Bay

Radio
Station

Windmill
Down

32

FLIMWELL

2

LONDON RD

BLENHEIM PARK

HIGH ST B 2087

A 268

Mount Pleasant
Farm

Little Pix Hall
Farm

31

Flimwell

PH

HAWKHURST RD

Elm Hill
Farm

A 268

West
Lodge

Seacox
Heath

1

Saw
Mill

Ringden
Wood

Seacox
Poultry Farm

Elm Hill
House

BELMONDEN RD

Keeper's
Cottage

Ringden
Farm

Brookgate Lane

30

71   72   73

A   B   C

33

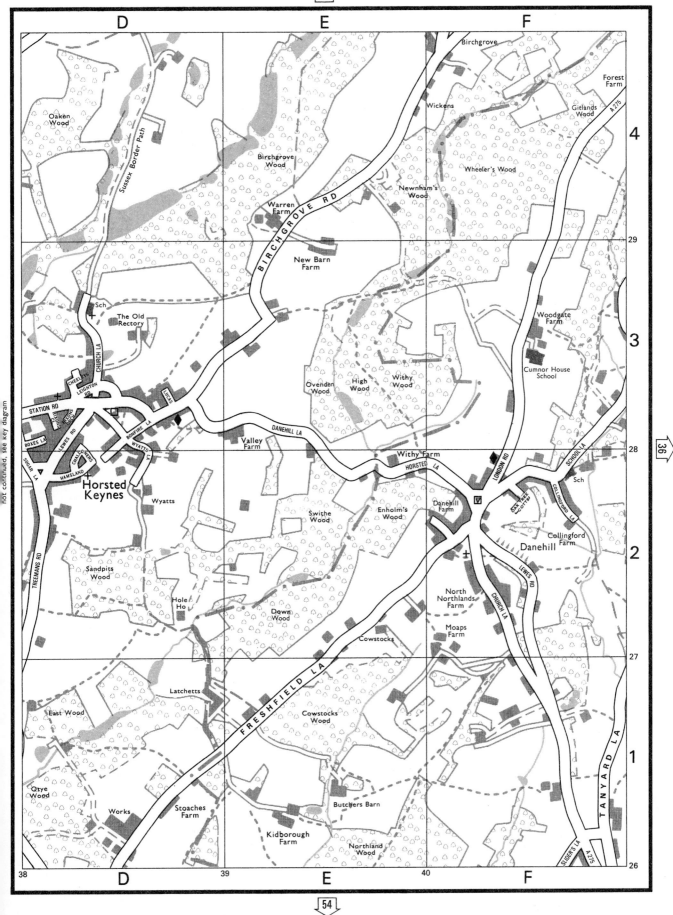

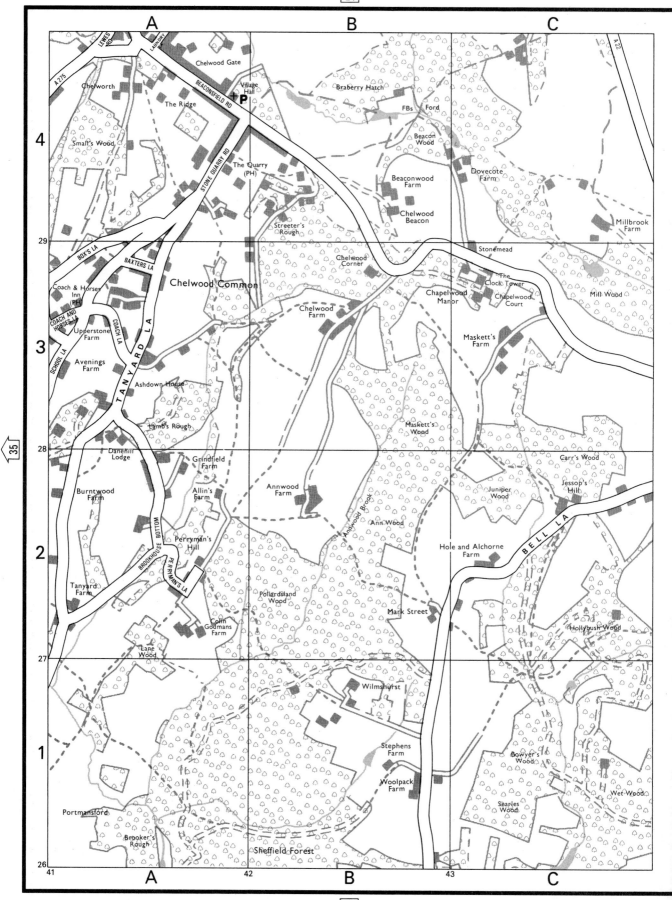

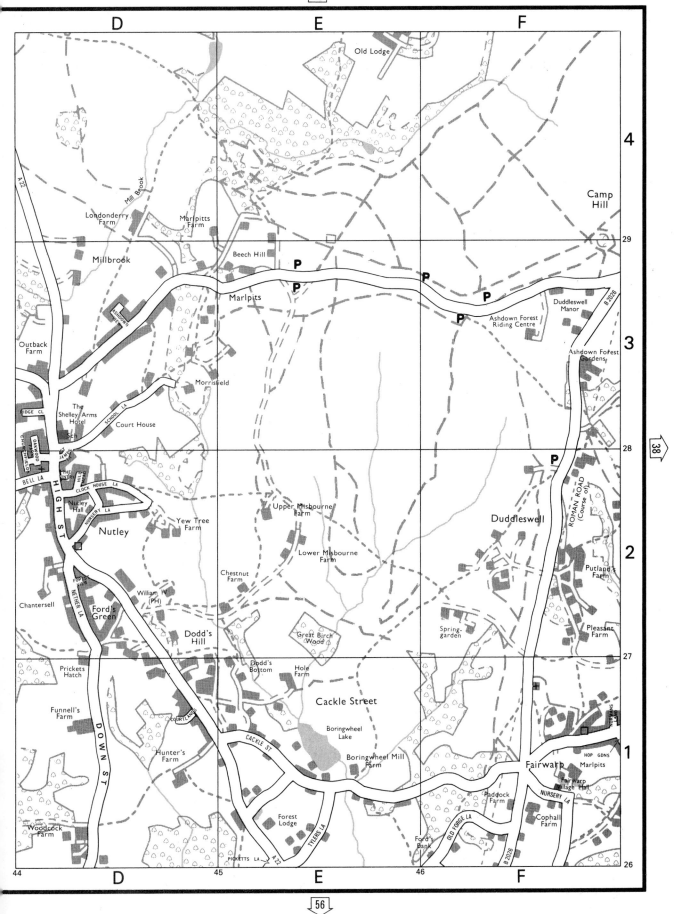

D

E

F

4

Camp Hill

29

A22

Mill Brook

Old Lodge

Londonderry Farm

Marlpitts Farm

Millbrook

Beech Hill

P

Marlpits

P

P

P

P

Duddleswell Manor

B 2026

Outback Farm

Ashdown Forest Riding Centre

3

Ashdown Forest Gardens

Morrisfield

The Shelley Arms Hotel

SCHOOL LA

Court House

RIDGE CL

OAKWOOD FARM

CHURCHFIELD

ST JAMES

CLOCK HOUSE LA

THE CHANTRY

BELL LA

HIGH ST

Nutley Hall

NURSERY LA

Yew Tree Farm

Upper Misbourne Farm

Duddleswell

P

28

ROMAN ROAD (Course of)

38

Nutley

Lower Misbourne Farm

2

Putland's Farm

Chantersell

FORGE VIEW

NETHER LA

Ford's Green

William IV (PH)

Chestnut Farm

Pleasant Farm

Dodd's Hill

Great Birch Wood

Spring-garden

27

Prickets Hatch

Dodd's Bottom

Hole Farm

Cackle Street

+

Funnell's Farm

DOWN ST

COURTLANDS

Boringwheel Lake

HOP GDNS

Marlpits

NORMANS LA

1

Hunter's Farm

CACKLE ST

Boringwheel Mill Farm

Fairwarp

Fairwarp Village Hall

NURSERY LA

Woodcock Farm

TYLERS LA

Paddock Farm

Cophall Farm

Ford's Bank

OLD FORGE LA

Forest Lodge

PICKETTS LA

A22

B 2026

26

44

D

45

E

46

F

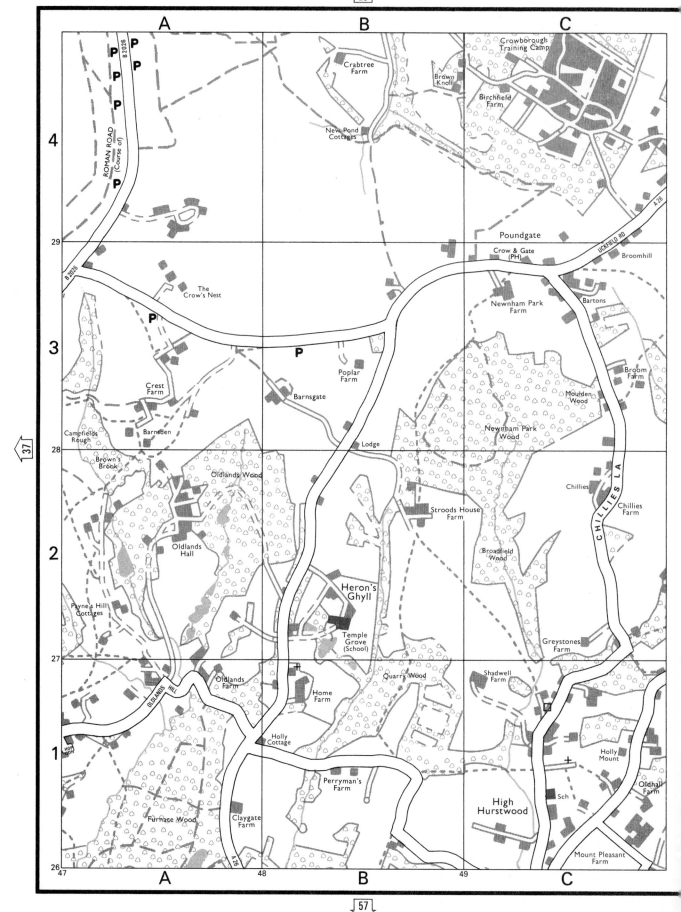

A   B   C

4

P P P
P P
P

ROMAN ROAD (Course of)

B 2026

Crabtree Farm

Brown Knoll

Crowborough Training Camp

Birchfield Farm

New Pond Cottages

P

A 26

29

Poundgate

B 2026

Crow & Gate (PH)

UCKFIELD RD

Broomhill

The Crow's Nest

Newnham Park Farm

Bartons

3

P

P

Poplar Farm

Broom Farm

Crest Farm

Barnsgate

Moulden Wood

Campfields Rough

Barnsden

Newnham Park Wood

Brown's Brook

Lodge

28

Oldlands Wood

Chillies

Stroods House Farm

Chillies Farm

CHILLIES LA

2

Oldlands Hall

Broadfield Wood

Payne's Hill Cottages

Heron's Ghyll

Temple Grove (School)

Greystones Farm

27

Shadwell Farm

Oldlands Farm

Quarry Wood

OLDLANDS HILL

Home Farm

Holly Cottage

Holly Mount

1

HDH DN

Perryman's Farm

High Hurstwood

Sch

Oldhall Farm

Furnace Wood

Claygate Farm

A 26

Mount Pleasant Farm

26

47   A   48   B   49   C

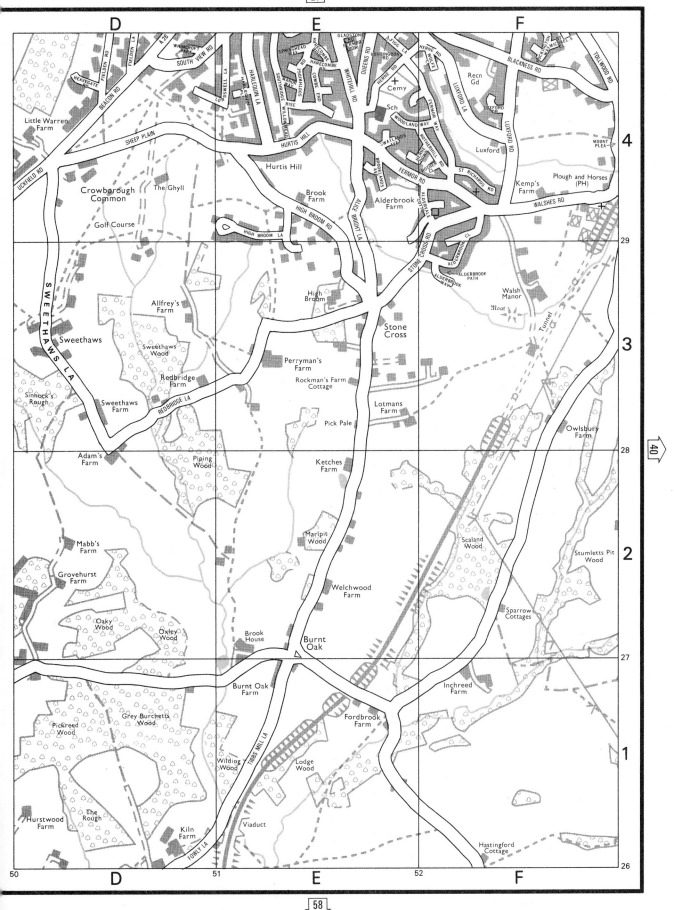

28

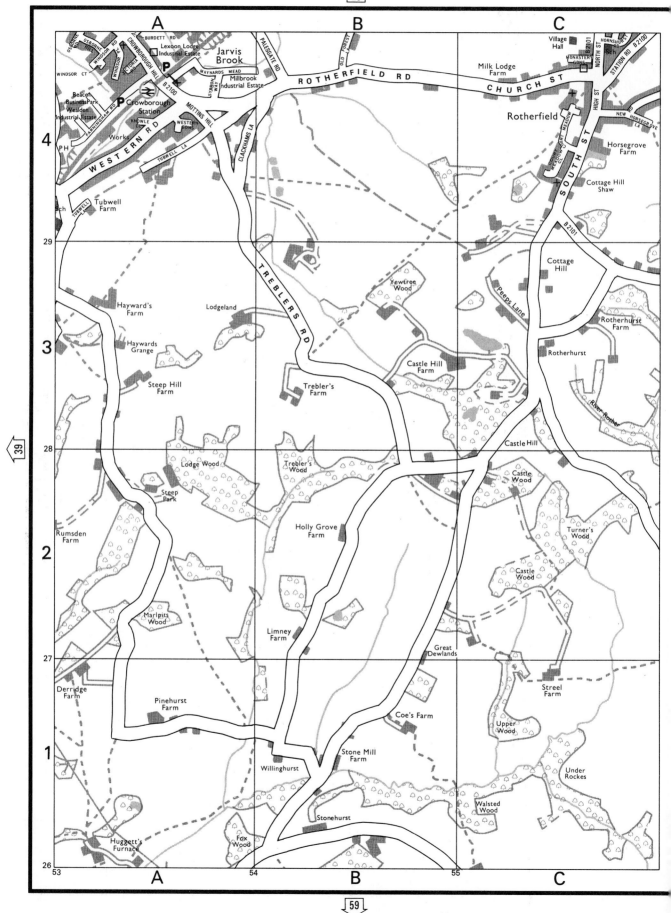

39

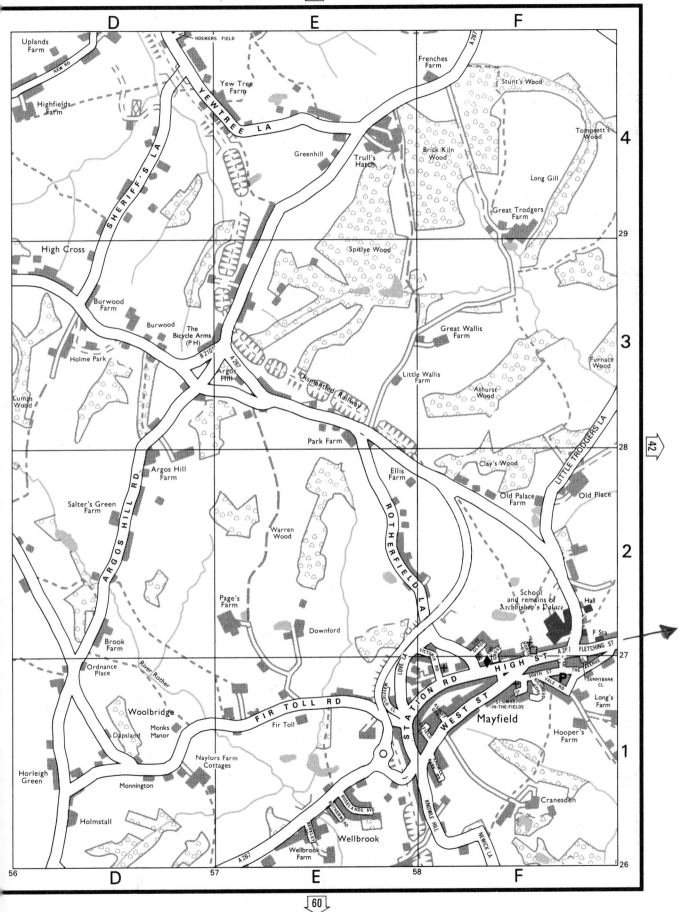

D   E   F

HOSMERS FIELD

Uplands Farm

NEW RD

Highfields Farm

Frenches Farm

A 267

Stunt's Wood

Yew Tree Farm

YEW TREE LA

Tompsett's Wood

4

Greenhill

Trull's Hatch

Brick Kiln Wood

Long Gill

SHERIFF'S LA

Great Trodgers Farm

29

High Cross

Spitlye Wood

Burwood Farm

Great Wallis Farm

3

Burwood

The Bicycle Arms (P H)

B 2101

A 267

Holme Park

Argos Hill

Dismantled Railway

Little Wallis Farm

Furnace Wood

Lumps Wood

Ashurst Wood

Park Farm

28

LITTLE TRODGERS LA

42

Argos Hill Farm

Ellis Farm

Clay's Wood

Old Place

Salter's Green Farm

ARGOS HILL RD

Warren Wood

Old Palace Farm

2

ROTHERFIELD LA

Page's Farm

School and remains of Archbishop's Palace

Hall

F Sta

Brook Farm

Downford

FLETCHING ST

A 2F1

27

Ordnance Place

River Rother

Love La

VICTORIA RD

THE GLEBE

GROVE

NORTH

HIGH ST

THE AVENUE

SUNNYBANK CL

Long's Farm

Woolbridge

FIR TOLL RD

STATION RD

SOUTH ST

VALE RD

WEST ST

P

Dapsland

Monks Manor

Fir Toll

ST. MARY-IN-THE-FIELDS

Mayfield

Hooper's Farm

1

Horleigh Green

Naylors Farm Cottages

KNOWLE HILL

Cranesden

Monnington

ROSELANDS AVE

ROTHERHEAD

BERKLEY RD

A 267

NEWICK LA

Holmstall

Wellbrook Farm

Wellbrook

26

56   D   57   E   58   F

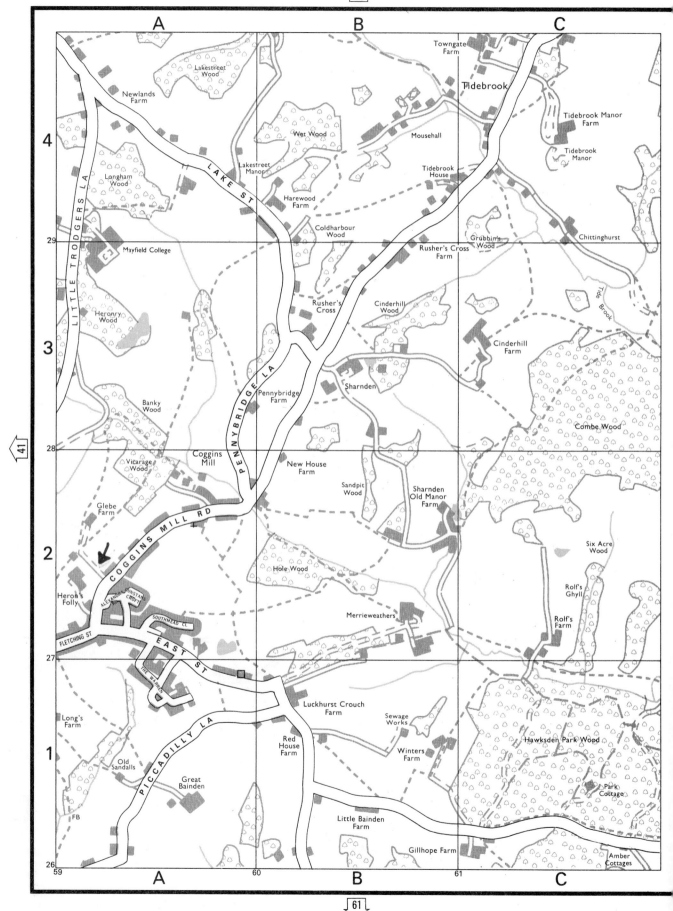

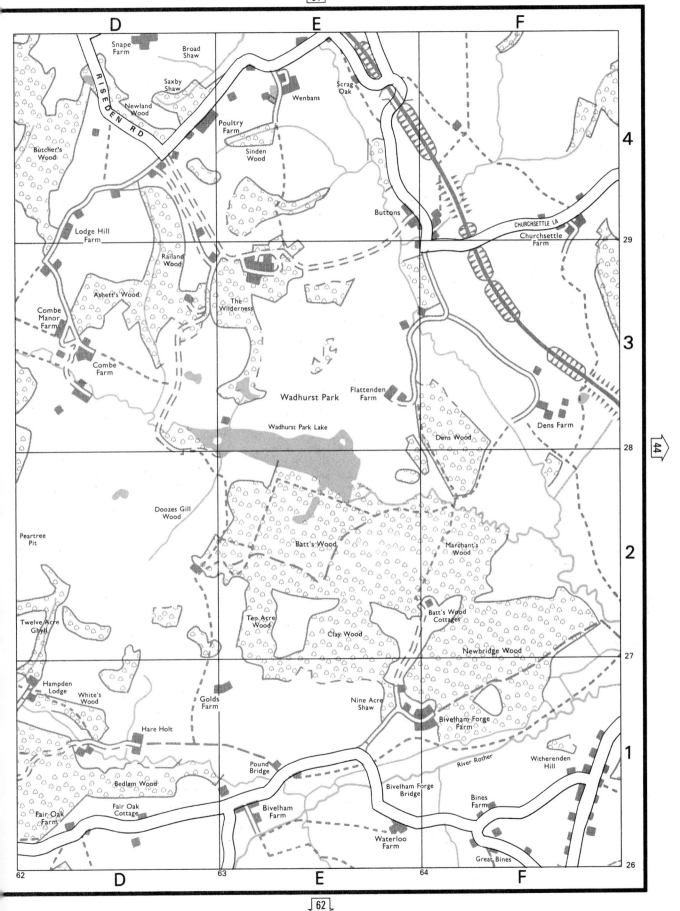

D

E

F

Snape
Farm

Broad
Shaw

Saxby
Shaw

Wenbans

Scrag
Oak

RISEDEN RD

Newland
Wood

Poultry
Farm

4

Butcher's
Wood

Sinden
Wood

Buttons

CHURCHSETTLE LA

Churchsettle
Farm

29

Lodge Hill
Farm

Railand
Wood

Ashett's Wood

The
Wilderness

Combe
Manor
Farm

3

Combe
Farm

Wadhurst Park

Flattenden
Farm

Dens Farm

Wadhurst Park Lake

Dens Wood

28

Doozes Gill
Wood

Peartree
Pit

Batt's Wood

Marchant's
Wood

2

Twelve Acre
Ghyll

Ten Acre
Wood

Clay Wood

Batt's Wood
Cottages

Newbridge Wood

27

Hampden
Lodge

White's
Wood

Golds
Farm

Nine Acre
Shaw

Bivelham Forge
Farm

1

Hare Holt

River Rother

Witherenden
Hill

Pound
Bridge

Bivelham Forge
Bridge

Bines
Farm

Bedlam Wood

Fair Oak
Cottage

Bivelham
Farm

Fair Oak
Farm

Waterloo
Farm

Great Bines

26

D

E

F

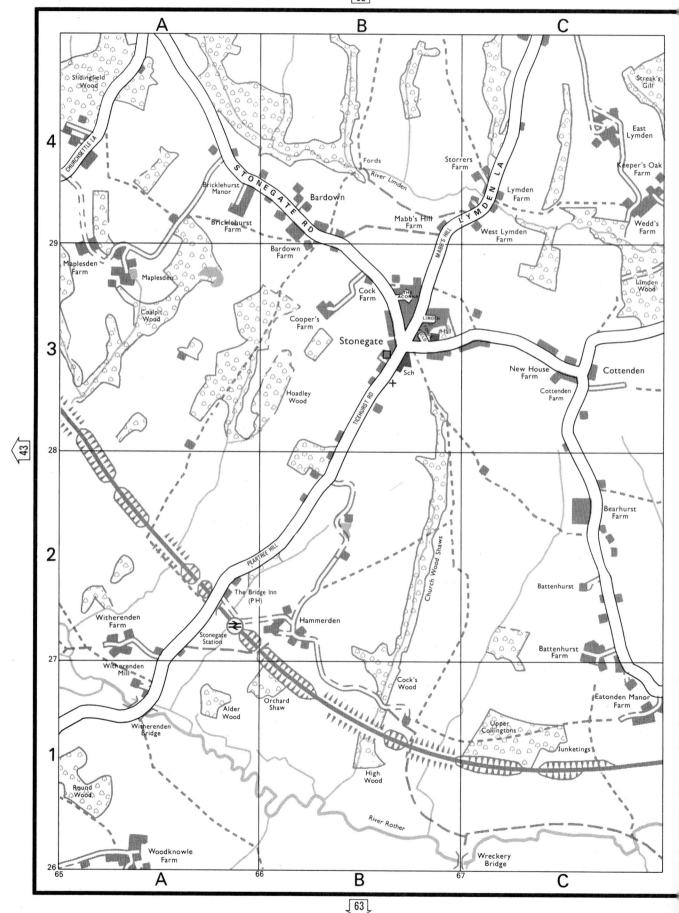

A   B   C

Slidingfield Wood

Streak's Gill

CHURCHSETTLE LA

East Lymden

4

STONEGATE RD

Fords

Storrers Farm

Keeper's Oak Farm

River Limden

LYMDEN LA

Bricklehurst Manor

Bardown

Mabb's Hill Farm

Lymden Farm

Wedd's Farm

Bricklehurst Farm

West Lymden Farm

29

Bardown Farm

Maplesden Farm

Cock Farm

THE ACORNS

Limden Wood

Maplesden

Cooper's Farm

Stonegate

LIMDEN

Hall

Coalpit Wood

New House Farm

Cottenden

3

Sch

Cottenden Farm

TICEHURST RD

Hoadley Wood

+

28

Bearhurst Farm

Church Wood Shaws

2

Battenhurst

PEARTREE HILL

The Bridge Inn (P H)

Hammerden

Battenhurst Farm

Witherenden Farm

Stonegate Station

Cock's Wood

Eatonden Manor Farm

27

Witherenden Mill

Alder Wood

Orchard Shaw

Upper Collingtons

Junketings

1

Witherenden Bridge

High Wood

Round Wood

River Rother

Wreckery Bridge

Woodknowle Farm

26

65   66   67

A   B   C

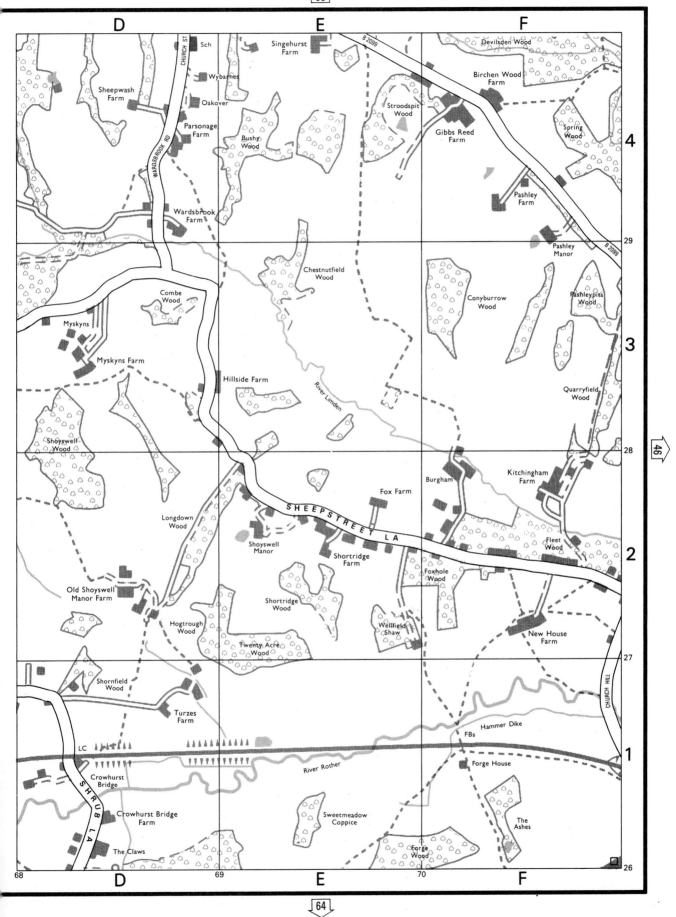

D   E   F

CHURCH ST

Sch

Singehurst Farm

B 2098

Devilsden Wood

Wybarnes

Sheepwash Farm

Oakover

Birchen Wood Farm

Parsonage Farm

Bushy Wood

Stroodspit Wood

Gibbs Reed Farm

Spring Wood

4

WARDSBROOK RD

Wardsbrook Farm

Pashley Farm

29

Pashley Manor

B 2099

Combe Wood

Chestnutfield Wood

Conyburrow Wood

Pashleypits Wood

Myskyns

Myskyns Farm

River Limden

Quarryfield Wood

3

Hillside Farm

28

46

Shoyswell Wood

Burgham

Kitchingham Farm

Longdown Wood

SHEEPSTREET LA

Fox Farm

Old Shoyswell Manor Farm

Shoyswell Manor

Shortridge Farm

Foxhole Wood

Fleet Wood

2

Hogtrough Wood

Shortridge Wood

Twenty Acre Wood

Wellfield Shaw

New House Farm

27

Shornfield Wood

CHURCH HILL

Turzes Farm

Hammer Dike

FBs

LC

River Rother

Forge House

1

SHRUB LA

Crowhurst Bridge

Crowhurst Bridge Farm

Sweetmeadow Coppice

The Ashes

The Claws

Forge Wood

26

68   D   69   E   70   F

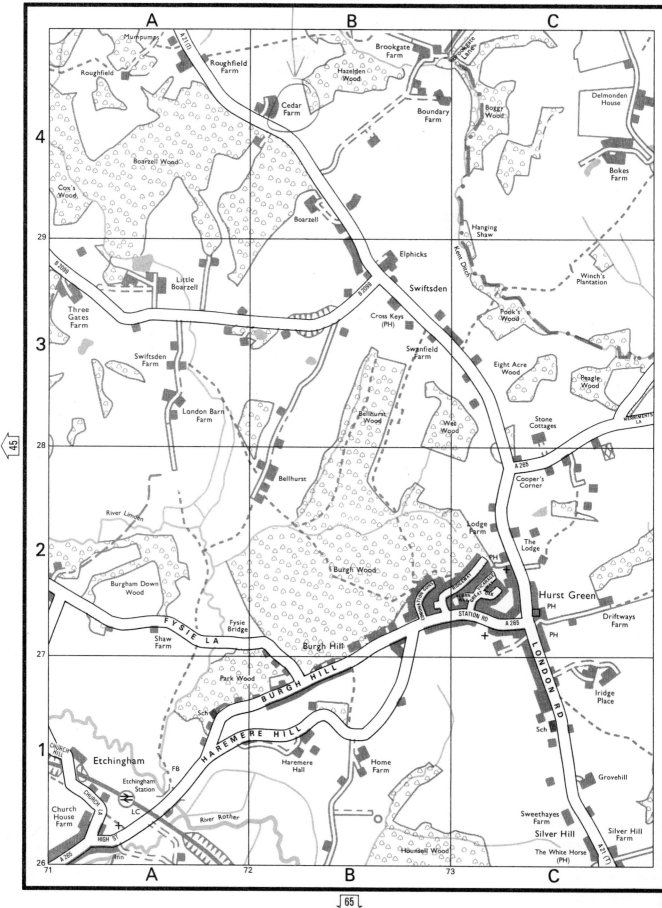

ACAN 34

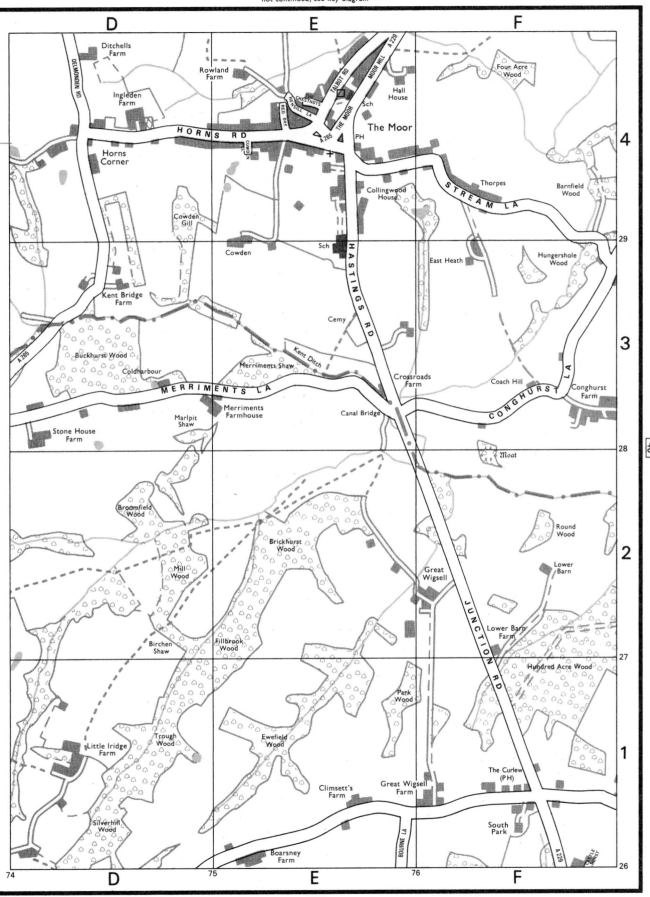

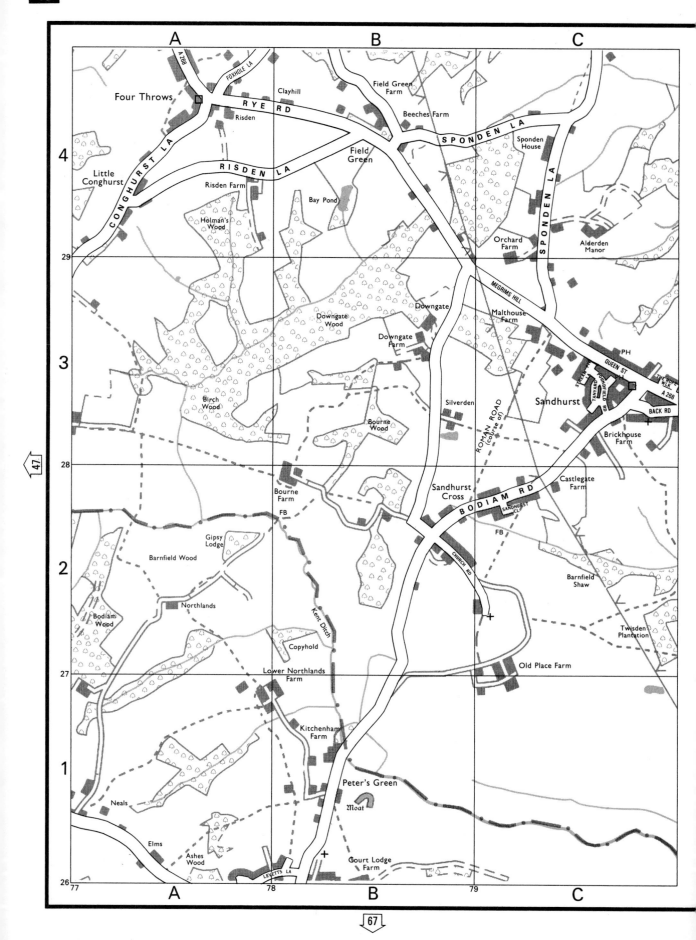

A   B   C

FOXHOLE LA

A 268

Four Throws

Clayhill

Field Green Farm

RYE RD

Risden

Beeches Farm

SPONDEN LA

Sponden House

4

Field Green

RISDEN LA

Little Conghurst

Risden Farm

Bay Pond

CONGHURST LA

Holman's Wood

Orchard Farm

Sponden La

Alderden Manor

29

Downgate Wood

Downgate

MEGRIMS HILL

Malthouse Farm

Downgate Farm

47

3

Birch Wood

Bourne Wood

Silverden

ROMAN ROAD (course of)

Sandhurst

QUEEN ST

PH

TANYARD

POUNDFIELD RD

STREET LA

THE ROPE WLK

A 268

BACK RD

Brickhouse Farm

28

Bourne Farm

FB

Sandhurst Cross

BODIAM RD

Castlegate Farm

SANDHURST CL

FB

Gipsy Lodge

Barnfield Wood

2

Northlands

Kent Ditch

Copyhold

CHURCH RD

Barnfield Shaw

Bodiam Wood

Twisden Plantation

27

Lower Northlands Farm

Old Place Farm

Kitchenham Farm

1

Peter's Green

Neals

Moat

Elms

Ashes Wood

Court Lodge Farm

LEVETTS LA

26

77   A   78   B   79   C

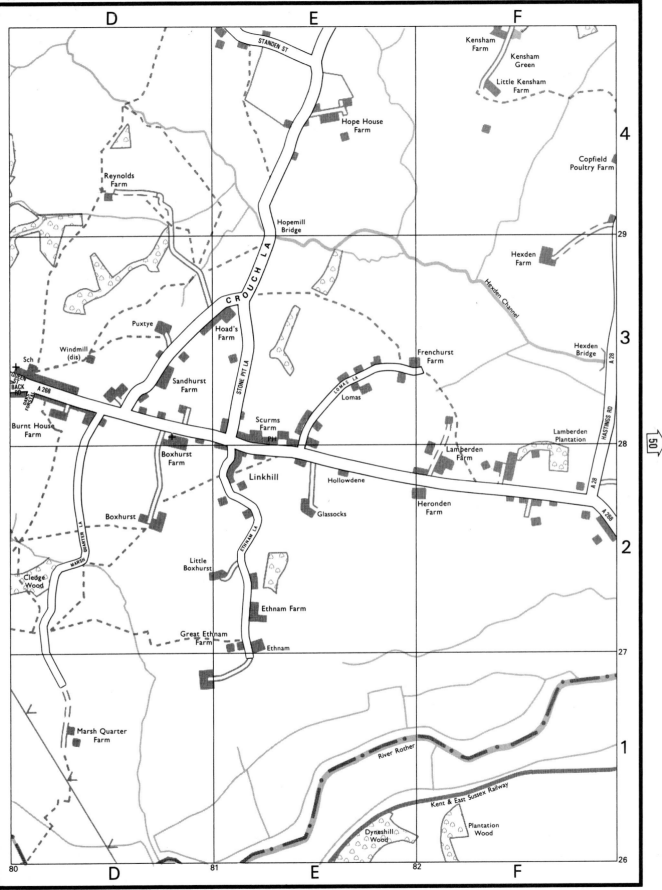

D E F

STANDEN ST

Kensham
Farm

Kensham
Green

Little Kensham
Farm

Hope House
Farm

4

Copfield
Poultry Farm

Reynolds
Farm

Hopemill
Bridge

29

Hexden
Farm

Hexden Channel

C
R
O
U
C
H

L
A

Puxtye

Hoad's
Farm

Hexden
Bridge

3

Windmill
(dis)

Sch

Sandhurst
Farm

Frenchurst
Farm

A 28

QUEEN
ST
BACK
RD

A 268

S
T
O
N
E

P
I
T

L
A

LOMAS LA

Lomas

HASTINGS RD

Burnt House
Farm

Scurms
Farm
PH

Lamberden
Plantation

50

Boxhurst
Farm

Lamberden
Farm

28

Linkhill

Hollowdene

A 28

M
A
R
S
H

Q
U
A
R
T
E
R

L
A

Boxhurst

Glassocks

Heronden
Farm

A 268

2

E
T
H
N
A
M

L
A

Little
Boxhurst

Cledge
Wood

Ethnam Farm

Great Ethnam
Farm

Ethnam

27

Marsh Quarter
Farm

River Rother

1

Kent & East Sussex Railway

Dyneshill
Wood

Plantation
Wood

26

80 D 81 E 82 F

not continued, see key diagram

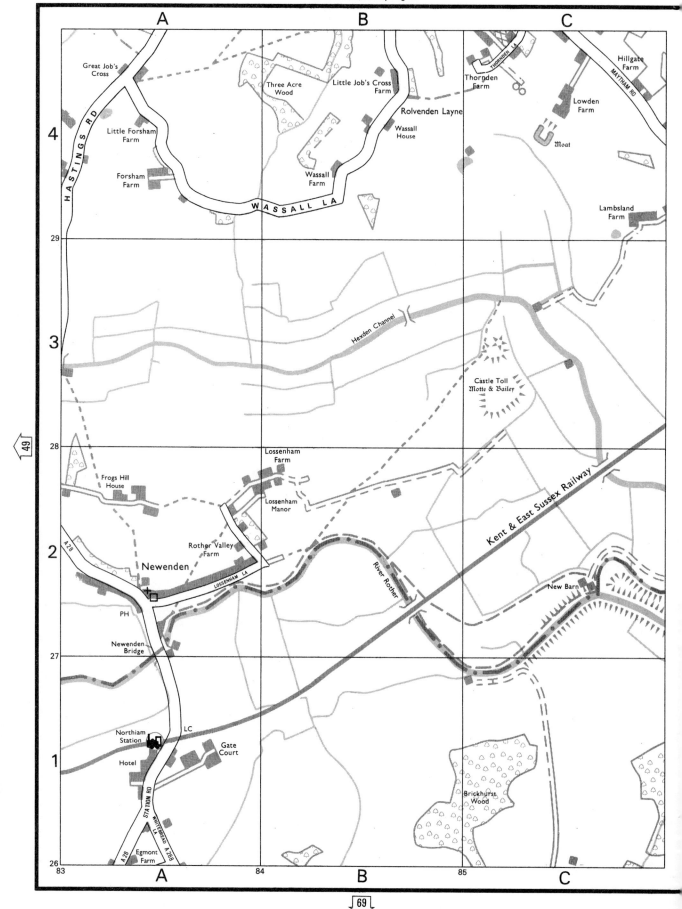

A   B   C

Great Job's Cross
Three Acre Wood
Little Job's Cross Farm
Rolvenden Layne
Thornden Farm
Hillgate Farm
THORNDEN LA
MAYTHAM RD
Lowden Farm
4
HASTINGS RD
Little Forsham Farm
Wassall House
Moat
Forsham Farm
Wassall Farm
WASSALL LA
Lambsland Farm
29
Hexden Channel
3
Castle Toll Motte & Bailey
28
49
Frogs Hill House
Lossenham Farm
Kent & East Sussex Railway
Lossenham Manor
2
A28
Rother Valley Farm
Newenden
LOSSENHAM LA
River Rother
New Barn
PH
Newenden Bridge
27
LC
Northiam Station
1
Hotel
Gate Court
Brickhurst Wood
STATION RD
WHITEBREAD LA
A28
A268
26
Egmont Farm
83
84
85
A   B   C

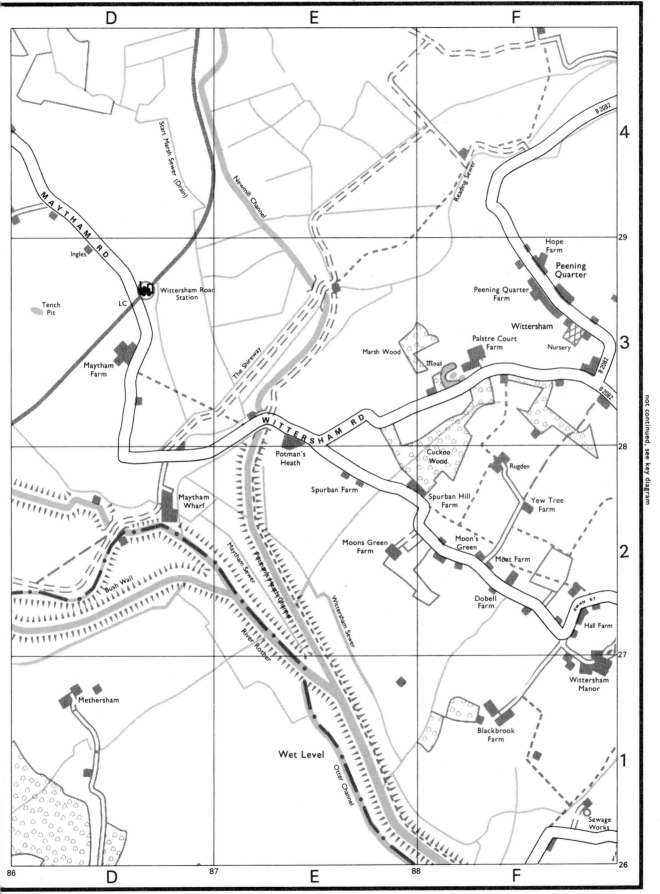

not continued, see key diagram

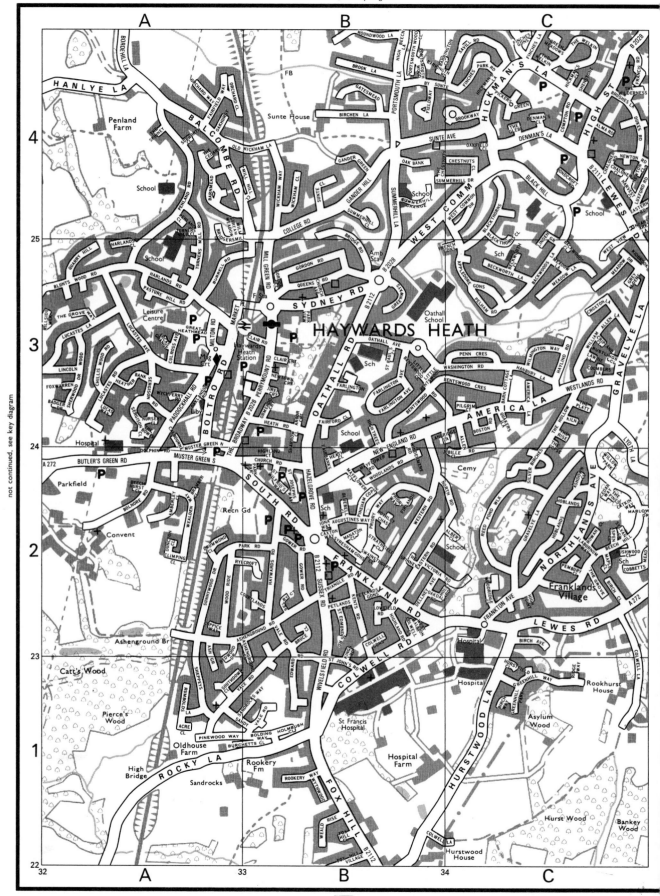

HAYWARDS HEATH

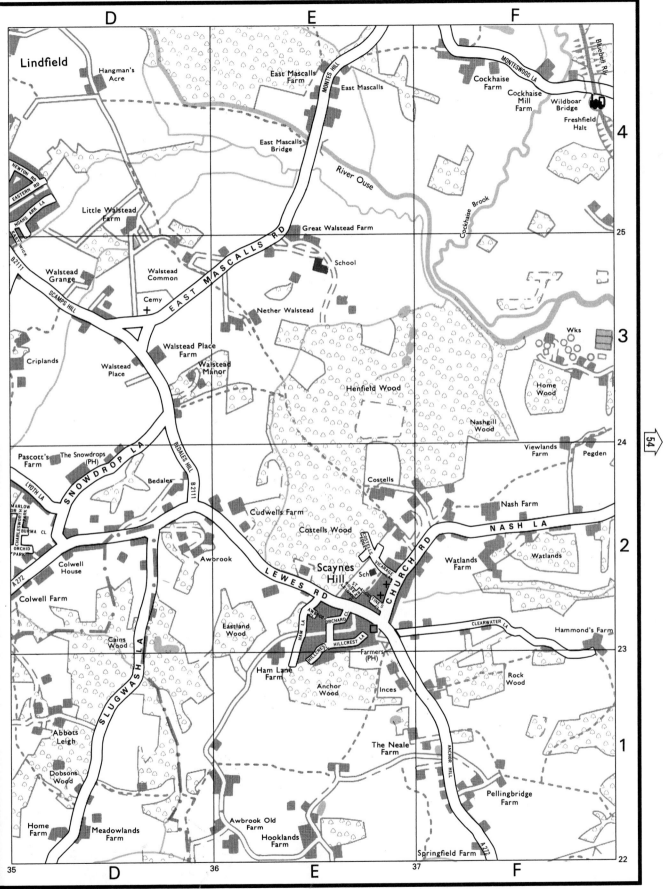

D　　　　　　　E　　　　　　　F

Lindfield

Hangman's Acre

East Mascalls Farm

East Mascalls

MONTESWOOD LA

Bluebell Rly

Cockhaise Farm

Cockhaise Mill Farm

Wildboar Bridge

Freshfield Halt

4

East Mascalls Bridge

MONTES HILL

River Ouse

NEWTON RD

EASTERN RD

NOAHS ARK LA

EAST WICK

Little Walstead Farm

Great Walstead Farm

School

Cockhaise Brook

25

B2111

Walstead Grange

SCAMPS HILL

Walstead Common

Cemy

EAST MASCALLS RD

Nether Walstead

Wks

3

Criplands

Walstead Place Farm

Walstead Place

Walstead Manor

Henfield Wood

Nashgill Wood

Home Wood

SNOWDROP LA

Pascott's Farm

The Snowdrops (PH)

BEDALES HILL

Bedales

B2111

Costells

Viewlands Farm

Pegden

24

54

LYOTH LA

MARLOW DR

BURMA CL

CHARLESWORTH

ORCHID PARK

Cudwells Farm

Costells Wood

Nash Farm

NASH LA

2

A272

Colwell House

Awbrook

LEWES RD

Scaynes Hill

Sch

VICARAGE

ST AUGUSTINE'S

LEYLANDS

CHURCH RD

Watlands Farm

Watlands

Colwell Farm

Cains Wood

Eastland Wood

HAM LA

AWBROOK

ORCHARD CL

HILLCREST

HILLCREST LA

Farmers (PH)

CLEARWATER LA

Hammond's Farm

23

SLUGWASH LA

Ham Lane Farm

Anchor Wood

Inces

Rock Wood

Abbots Leigh

The Neale Farm

ANCHOR HILL

1

Dobsons Wood

Pellingbridge Farm

Home Farm

Meadowlands Farm

Awbrook Old Farm

Hooklands Farm

Springfield Farm

A272

22

35　　　　D　　　　36　　　　E　　　　37　　　　F

35

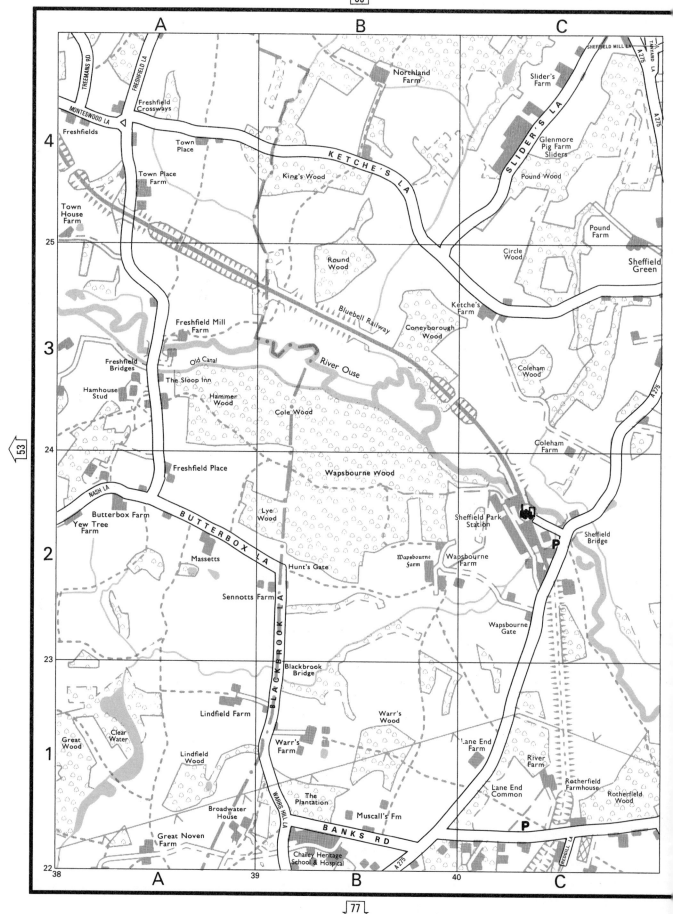

53

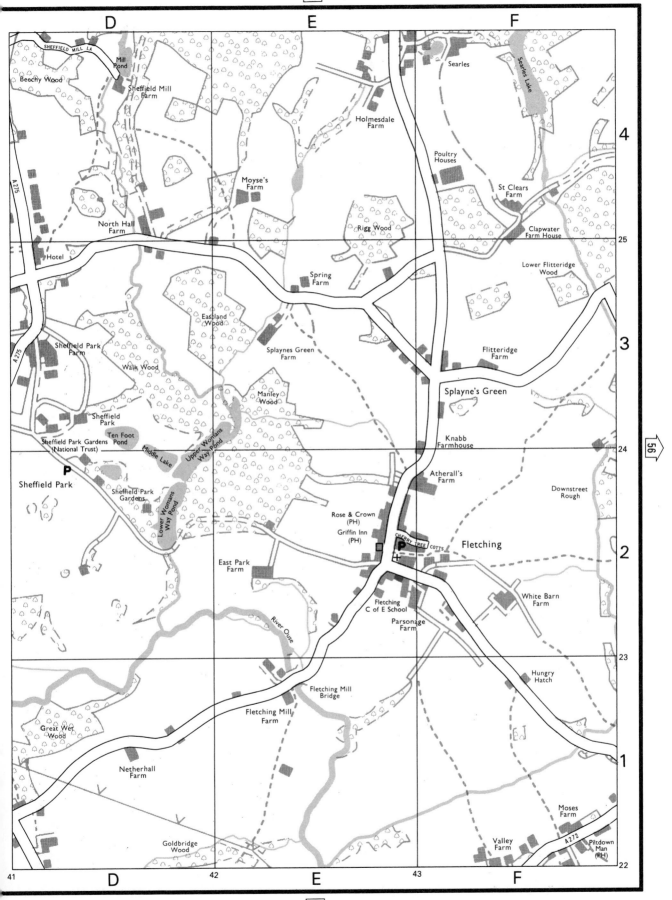

D E F

SHEFFIELD MILL LA

Mill Pond

Beechy Wood

Sheffield Mill Farm

Searles

Searles Lake

Holmesdale Farm

4

Moyse's Farm

Poultry Houses

St Clears Farm

A 275

North Hall Farm

Rigg Wood

Clapwater Farm House

25

Hotel

Spring Farm

Lower Flitteridge Wood

Eastland Wood

A 275

Sheffield Park Farm

Walk Wood

Splaynes Green Farm

Flitteridge Farm

3

Manley Wood

Splayne's Green

Sheffield Park

Knabb Farmhouse

24

Sheffield Park Gardens (National Trust)

Ten Foot Pond

Middle Lake

Upper Womans Way Pond

Atherall's Farm

Downstreet Rough

P

Sheffield Park

Sheffield Park Gardens

Lower Womans Way Pond

Rose & Crown (PH)

Griffin Inn (PH)

CHERRY TREE COTTS

P

Fletching

2

East Park Farm

White Barn Farm

River Ouse

Fletching C of E School

Parsonage Farm

23

Hungry Hatch

Fletching Mill Bridge

Fletching Mill Farm

Great Wet Wood

1

Netherhall Farm

Moses Farm

Goldbridge Wood

Valley Farm

A 272

Piltdown Man (PH)

22

41 D 42 E 43 F

56

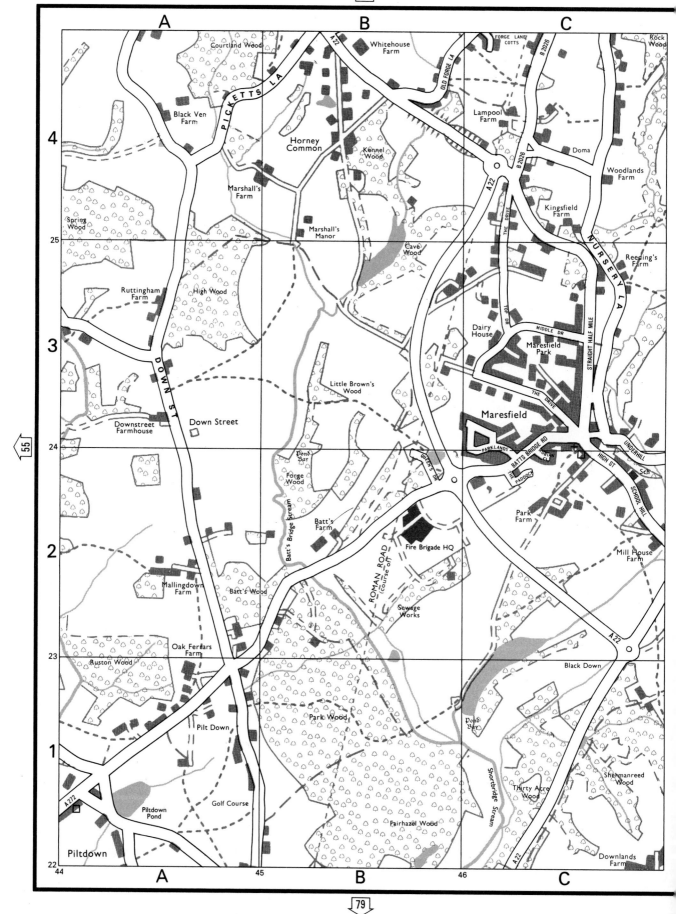

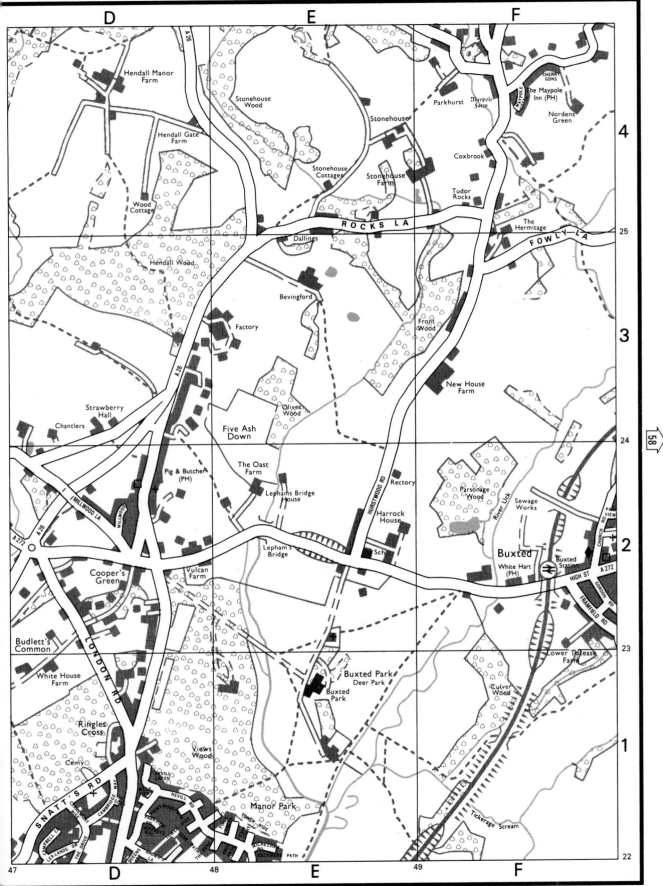

D | E | F

4

Hendall Manor Farm

Stonehouse Wood

Stonehouse

Parkhurst

Maypole Farm

CHERRY GDNS

The Maypole Inn (PH)

Nordens Green

MAYPOLE GDNS

Hendall Gate Farm

Stonehouse Cottages

Stonehouse Farm

Coxbrook

Tudor Rocks

Wood Cottage

25

ROCKS LA

The Hermitage

FOWLY LA

Dallings

Hendall Wood

Bevingford

Front Wood

3

Factory

New House Farm

A 26

Strawberry Hall

Olives Wood

Chantlers

Five Ash Down

24

58

Pig & Butcher (PH)

The Oast Farm

Rectory

Parsonage Wood

River Uck

Sewage Works

PARK VIEW

MILLWOOD LA

MILLWOOD

Lephams Bridge House

Harrock House

CHURCH RD

A 272

A 26

A 272

Vulcan Farm

Lepham's Bridge

Sch

Buxted

2

Cooper's Green

White Hart (PH)

Buxted Station

HIGH ST

GORDON RD

FRAMFIELD RD

Budlett's Common

LONDON RD

23

Lower Totease Farm

White House Farm

Buxted Park Deer Park

Culver Wood

Ringles Cross

Buxted Park

Views Wood

SNATTS RD

Cemy

NEVILL GREEN

1

Manor Park

NEVILL RD

Tickerage Stream

CAMPBELL CT

LEA LANDS DRIVE

THE DRIVE

CAMBRIDGE WAY

QUEENS

BROWNS LA

TOWER RIDE

MICHELHAM RD

CUCKMERE

PATH

22

D | E | F

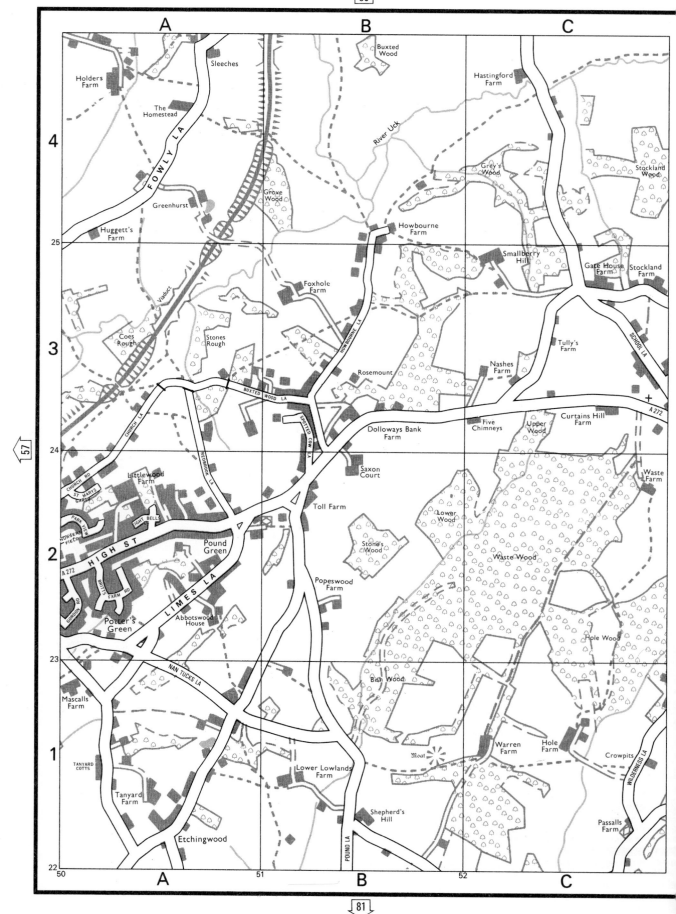

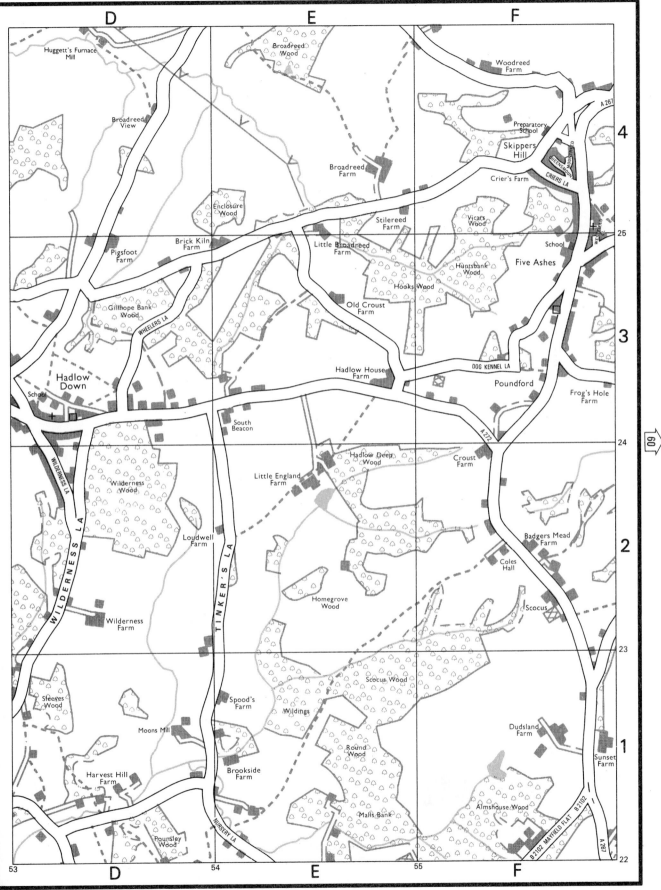

D

E

F

Huggett's Furnace Mill

Broadreed Wood

Woodreed Farm

A 267

Broadreed View

Preparatory School

4

Skippers Hill

Broadreed Farm

Crier's Farm

CRIERS LA

Enclosure Wood

Stilereed Farm

Vicars Wood

School

25

Brick Kiln Farm

Little Broadreed Farm

Huntsbank Wood

Five Ashes

Pigsfoot Farm

Hooks Wood

Gillhope Bank Wood

Old Croust Farm

WHEELERS LA

3

DOG KENNEL LA

Hadlow House Farm

Poundford

Frog's Hole Farm

Hadlow Down

School

South Beacon

A 272

24

Hadlow Deep Wood

Croust Farm

60

Little England Farm

Wilderness Wood

WILDERNESS LA

Badgers Mead Farm

2

Loudwell Farm

TINKER'S LA

Coles Hall

Homegrove Wood

Scocus

Wilderness Farm

23

Steeves Wood

Scocus Wood

Spood's Farm

Dudsland Farm

Moons Mill

Wildings

1

Sunset Farm

Round Wood

Brookside Farm

Harvest Hill Farm

Almshouse Wood

B 2102 MAYFIELD FLAT

A 267

B 2102

Malis Bank

NURSERY LA

Pounsley Wood

22

53

D

54

E

55

F

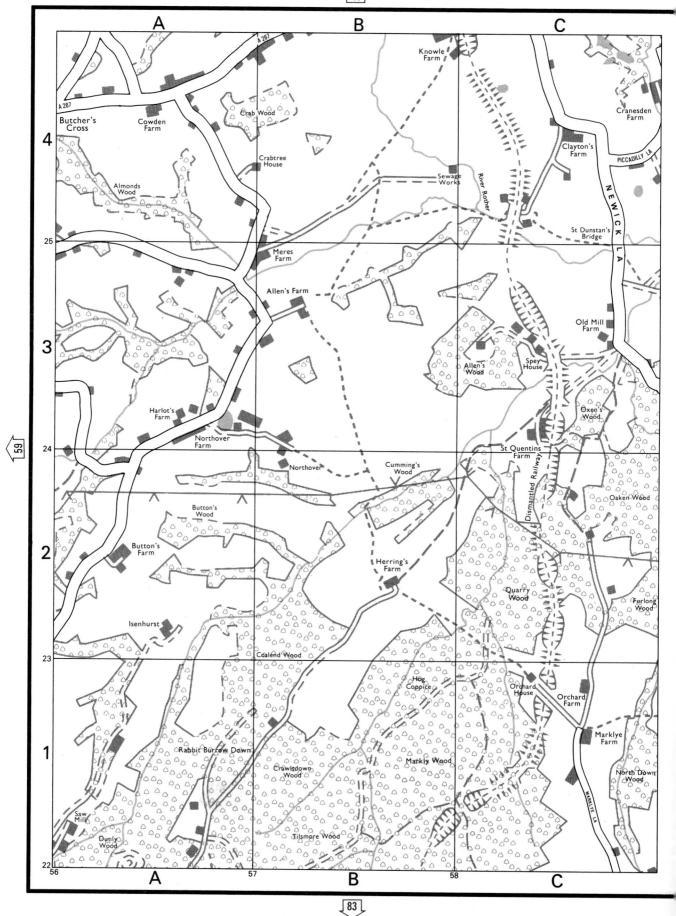

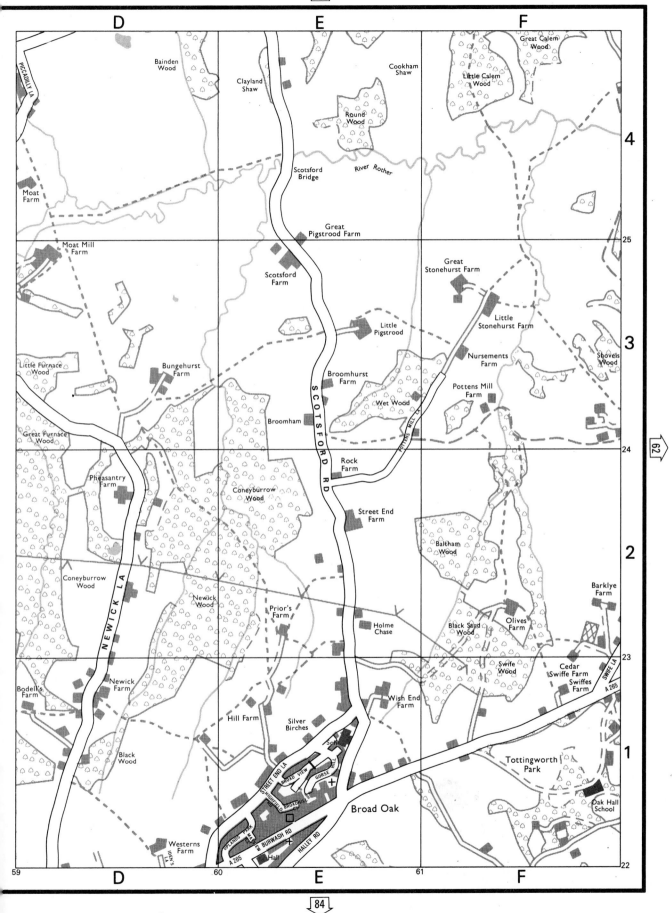

D E F

Piccadilly La

Bainden
Wood

Clayland
Shaw

Cookham
Shaw

Great Calem
Wood

Little Calem
Wood

Round
Wood

4

River Rother

Scotsford
Bridge

Moat
Farm

Great
Pigstrood Farm

25

Moat Mill
Farm

Scotsford
Farm

Great
Stonehurst Farm

Little
Pigstrood

Little
Stonehurst Farm

3

Little Furnace
Wood

Bungehurst
Farm

Broomhurst
Farm

Nursements
Farm

Shovels
Wood

Scotsford Rd

Wet Wood

Pottens Mill
Farm

Great Furnace
Wood

Broomham

Pottens Mill La

24

Rock
Farm

Pheasantry
Farm

Coneyburrow
Wood

Street End
Farm

Newick La

Baltham
Wood

2

Coneyburrow
Wood

Newick
Wood

Prior's
Farm

Holme
Chase

Black Sand
Wood

Olives
Farm

Barklye
Farm

Bodell's
Farm

Newick
Farm

Swife
Wood

Cedar
Swiffe Farm
Swiffes
Farm

23

Swiffe La

A 265

Hill Farm

Silver
Birches

Wish End
Farm

Black
Wood

Street End La

Broad View

Gorse Hill

Broadhill

Highfield

Tottingworth
Park

1

Broad Oak

Oak Hall
School

Westerns
Farm

Iden's La

Uplands Park

Main Rd

Burwash Rd

Halley Rd

A 265

Hall

22

59 D 60 E 61 F

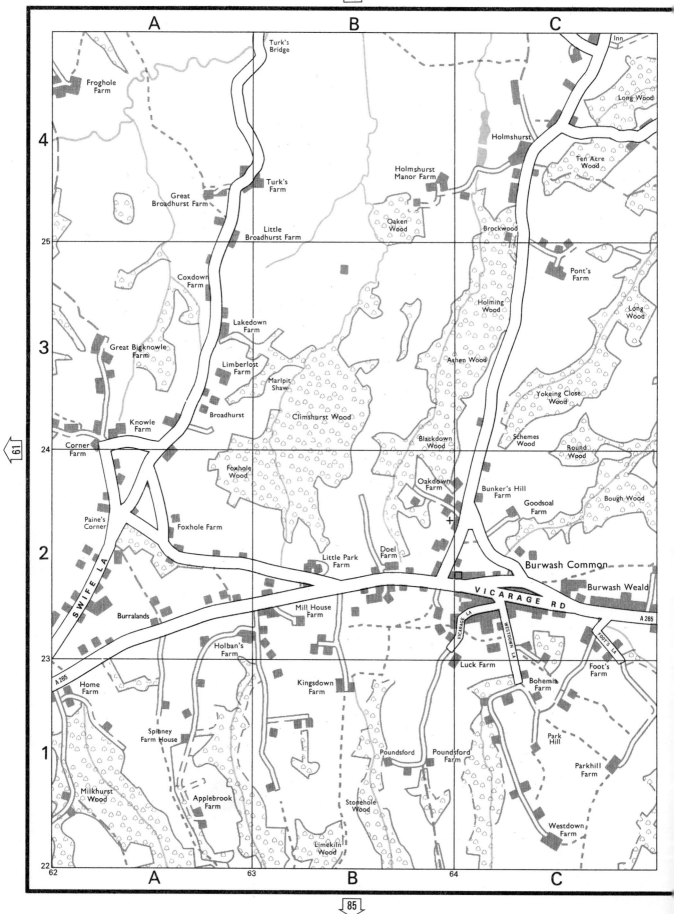

A B C

Turk's Bridge

Froghole Farm

Long Wood

4

Holmshurst

Holmshurst Manor Farm

Ten Acre Wood

Great Broadhurst Farm

Turk's Farm

Brockwood

Oaken Wood

Little Broadhurst Farm

25

Coxdown Farm

Pont's Farm

Holming Wood

Long Wood

Lakedown Farm

3

Great Bigknowle Farm

Limberlost Farm

Ashen Wood

Marlpit Shaw

Yokeing Close Wood

Broadhurst

Climshurst Wood

Schemes Wood

Knowle Farm

Blackdown Wood

Round Wood

24

Corner Farm

Foxhole Wood

Oakdown Farm

Bunker's Hill Farm

Bough Wood

Goodsoal Farm

Paine's Corner

2

Foxhole Farm

Doel Farm

Burwash Common

Little Park Farm

Burwash Weald

SWIFE LA

VICARAGE RD

A 265

Burralands

Mill House Farm

VICARAGE LA

WESTDOWN LA

FOOT'S LA

Holban's Farm

23

Luck Farm

Foot's Farm

A 265

Home Farm

Kingsdown Farm

Bohemia Farm

Park Hill

Spioney Farm House

1

Parkhill Farm

Poundsford

Poundsford Farm

Milkhurst Wood

Applebrook Farm

Stonehole Wood

Westdown Farm

Limekiln Wood

22

62 63 64

A B C

Inn

61

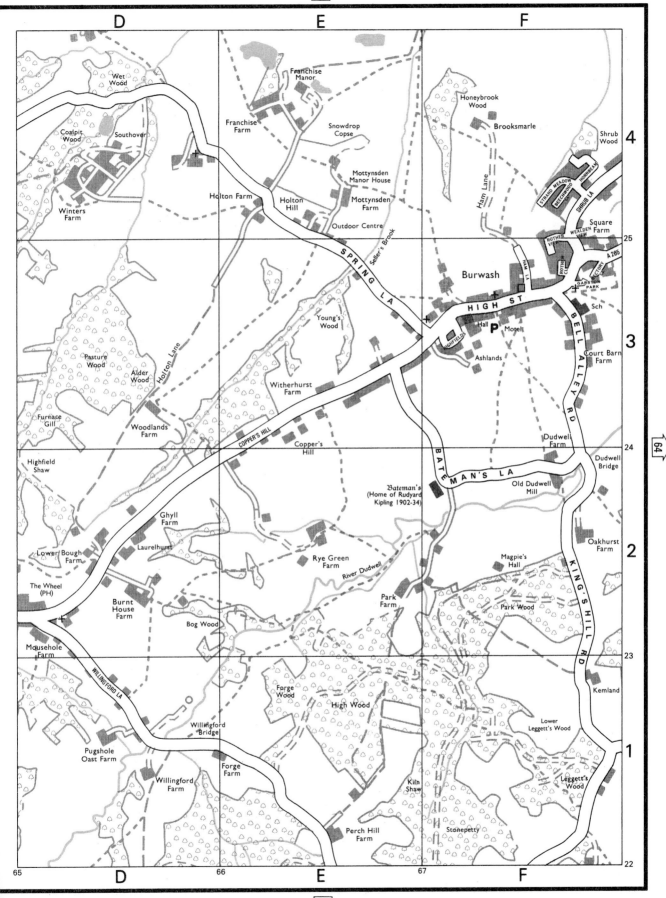

D   E   F

Wet Wood

Coalpit Wood

Southover

Franchise Manor

Franchise Farm

Snowdrop Copse

Honeybrook Wood

Brooksmarle

Shrub Wood

4

Winters Farm

Holton Farm

Holton Hill

Holton Farm

Mottynsden Manor House

Mottynsden Farm

Outdoor Centre

Ham Lane

STRAND MEADOW
BEECHWOOD
HORNBEAM

SHRUB LA

Square Farm

ROTHER VIEW
WEALDEN VIEW

A 265

25

SPRING LA

Seller's Brook

Burwash

HAM LA

ROTHER CL

GARSTON PARK

RECTORY CL

Holton Lane

Young's Wood

HIGH ST

Sch

3

Pasture Wood

Alder Wood

Witherhurst Farm

Hall

Highfield

P

Motel

Ashlands

BELL ALLEY RD

Court Barn Farm

Furnace Gill

Woodlands Farm

COPPER'S HILL

Copper's Hill

Dudwell Farm

24

64

Highfield Shaw

BATE

MAN'S LA

Old Dudwell Mill

Dudwell Bridge

Ghyll Farm

Laurelhurst

Bateman's (Home of Rudyard Kipling 1902-34)

Oakhurst Farm

Lower Bough Farm

Rye Green Farm

River Dudwell

Magpie's Hall

KING'S HILL RD

2

The Wheel (PH)

Burnt House Farm

Bog Wood

Park Farm

Park Wood

Mousehole Farm

WILLINGFORD LA

Forge Wood

High Wood

Kemland

23

Pugshole Oast Farm

Willingford Bridge

Forge Farm

Lower Leggett's Wood

1

Willingford Farm

Kiln Shaw

Leggett's Wood

Perch Hill Farm

Stonepetty

22

65   D   66   E   67   F

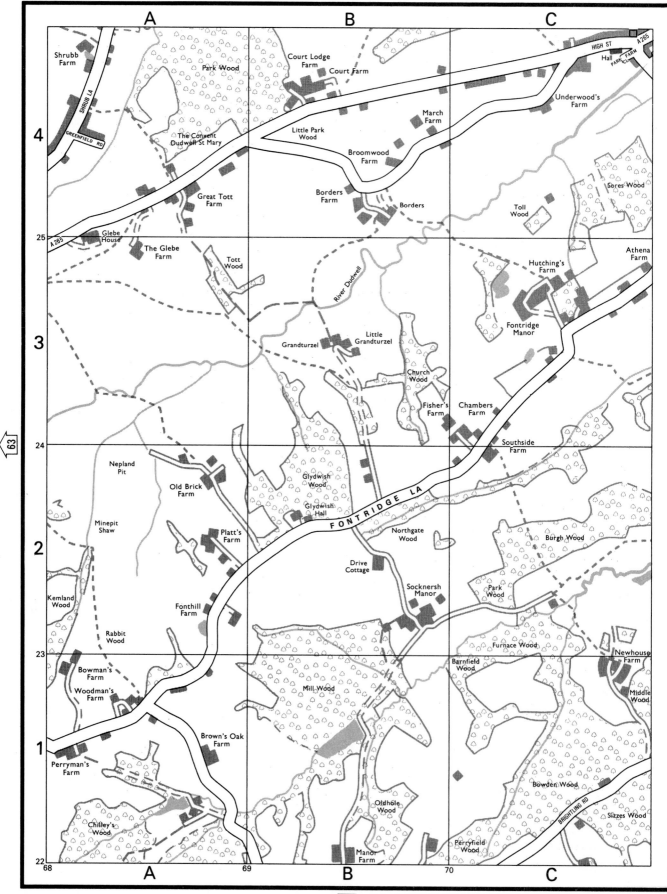

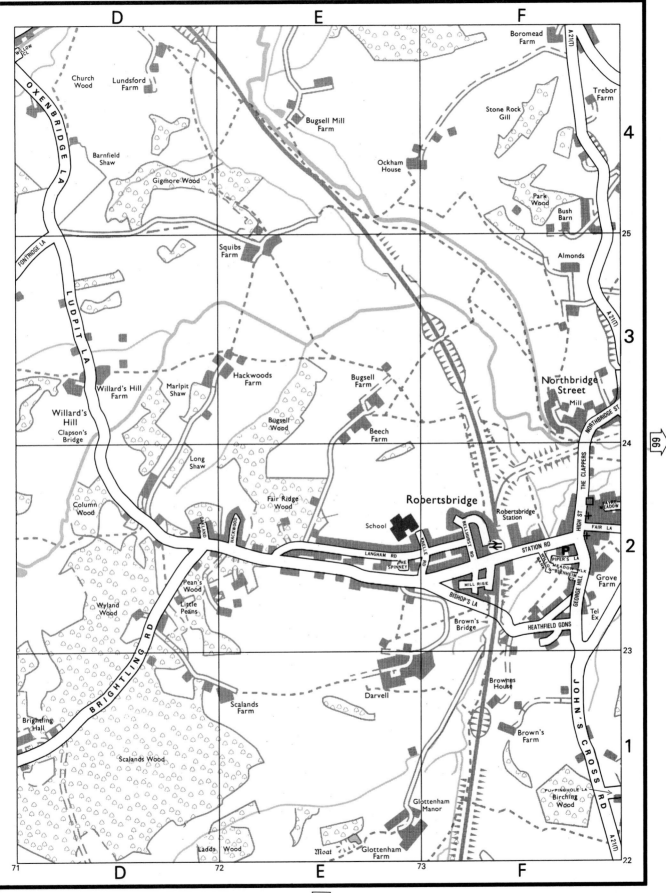

D | E | F

WILLOW CL

Church Wood

Lundsford Farm

OXENBRIDGE LA

Barnfield Shaw

Gigmore Wood

Bugsell Mill Farm

Boromead Farm

Trebor Farm

Stone Rock Gill

A21(T)

Ockham House

Park Wood

Bush Barn

4

25

FONTRIDGE LA

LUDPIT LA

Squibs Farm

Almonds

3

Hackwoods Farm

Bugsell Farm

Willard's Hill Farm

Marlpit Shaw

Bugsell Wood

Beech Farm

Northbridge Street

Mill

NORTHBRIDGE ST

Willard's Hill

Clapson's Bridge

Long Shaw

24

Column Wood

Fair Ridge Wood

School

Robertsbridge

Robertsbridge Station

THE CLAPPERS

FAYRE MEADOW

HIGH ST

FAIR LA

2

OAKLAND

HACKWOOD

BELLHURST RD

KNELLE RD

LANGHAM RD

THE SPINNEY

STATION RD

P

WILLO MEADOW WLK BLENHEIM WLK PEAN'S

GEORGE HILL

Grove Farm

Pean's Wood

Little Peans

MILL RISE

Tel Ex

Wyland Wood

BISHOP'S LA

Brown's Bridge

HEATHFIELD GDNS

BRIGHTLING RD

23

Brightling Hall

Scalands Farm

Darvell

Brownes House

JOHN'S CROSS RD

Brown's Farm

1

Scalands Wood

PUPPINGHOLE LA

Birching Wood

A21(T)

Ladds Wood

Moat

Glottenham Farm

Glottenham Manor

22

71 | D | 72 | E | 73 | F

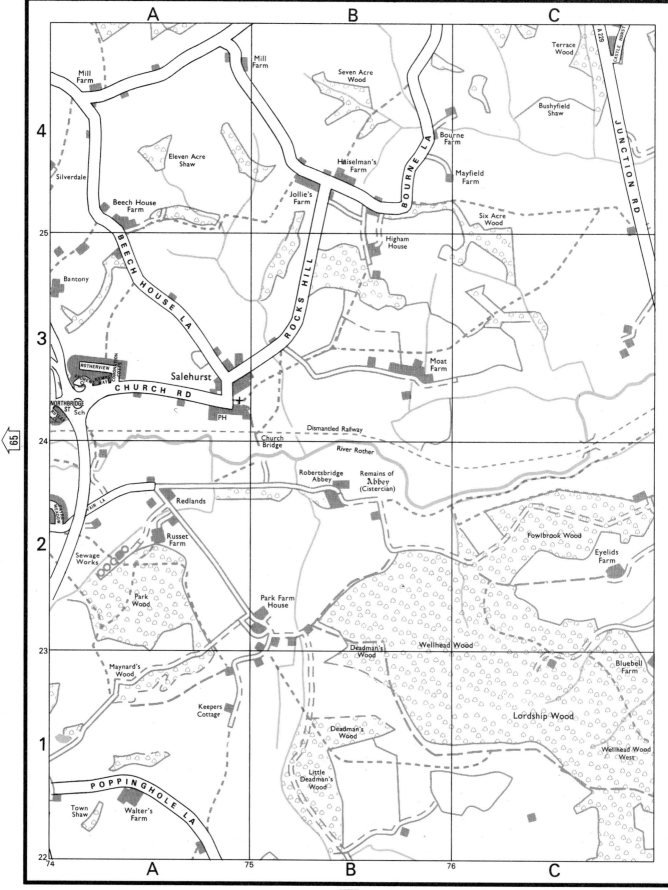

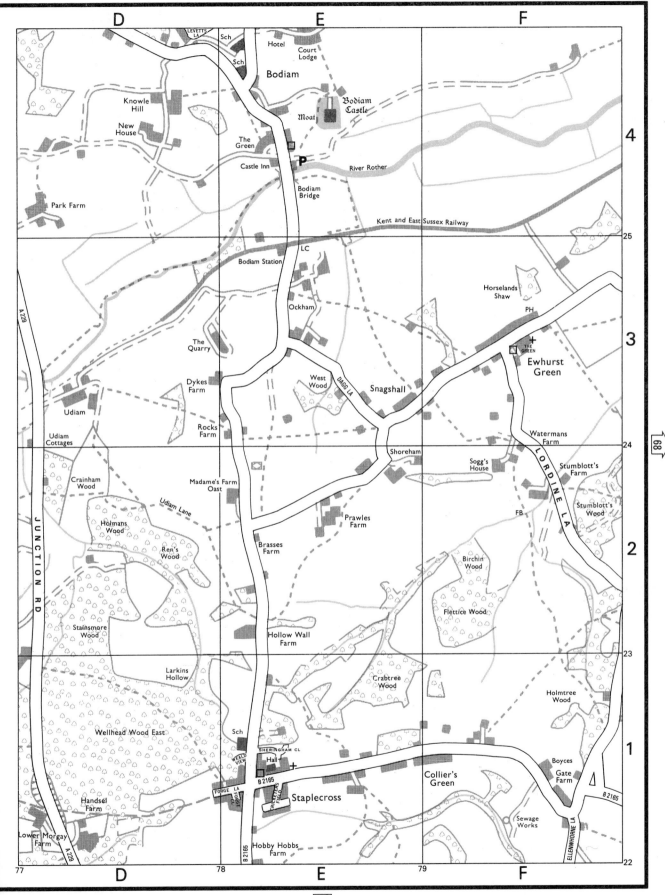

D   E   F

LEVETTS LA

Sch

Sch

Hotel

Court Lodge

Bodiam

Knowle Hill

Bodiam Castle

New House

Moat

The Green

Castle Inn

P

River Rother

4

Bodiam Bridge

Park Farm

Kent and East Sussex Railway

25

LC

Bodiam Station

Ockham

Horselands Shaw

PH

THE GREEN

The Quarry

Ewhurst Green

3

Dykes Farm

West Wood

DAGGS LA

Snagshall

Udiam

Watermans Farm

Rocks Farm

Udiam Cottages

Shoreham

24

Crainham Wood

Madame's Farm Oast

Sogg's House

Stumblott's Farm

Udiam Lane

FB

Stumblott's Wood

Holmans Wood

Prawles Farm

Ren's Wood

Brasses Farm

Birchin Wood

2

JUNCTION RD

A 229

Stainsmore Wood

Flettice Wood

Hollow Wall Farm

23

Larkins Hollow

Crabtree Wood

Holmtree Wood

Wellhead Wood East

Sch

WEALD VIEW

SHERINGHAM CL

Hall

Collier's Green

Boyces Gate Farm

1

B 2165

FORGE LA

CRICKETERS FIELD

Staplecross

Sewage Works

B 2165

Handsel Farm

Lower Morgay Farm

A 229

B 2165

Hobby Hobbs Farm

ELLENWHORNE LA

22

77   D   78   E   79   F

68

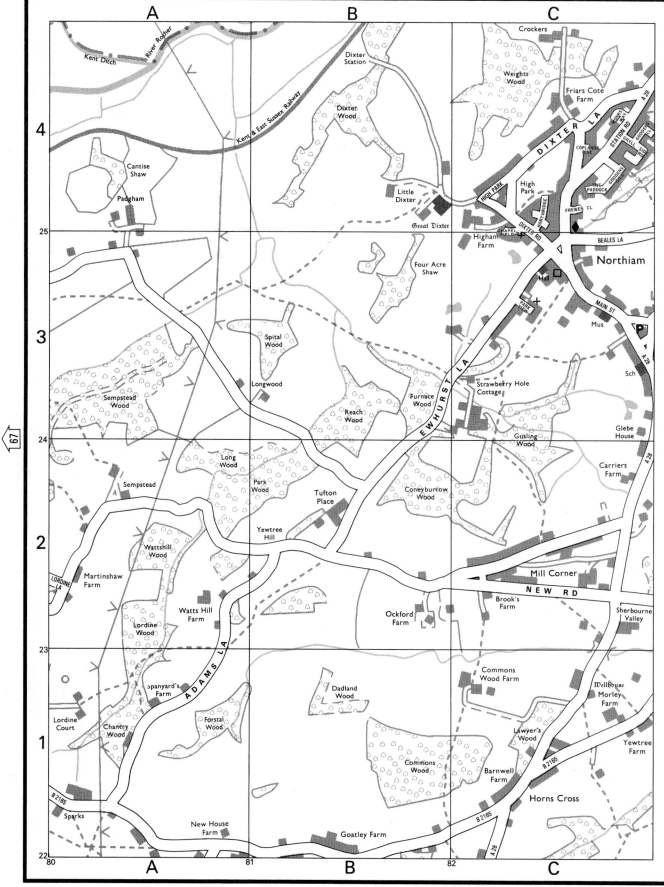

A   B   C

4

Kent Ditch

River Rother

Kent & East Sussex Railway

Cantise
Shaw

Padgham

Dixter
Station

Dixter
Wood

Little
Dixter

Great Dixter

Crockers

Weights
Wood

Friars Cote
Farm

DIXTER LA

A 28

STATION RD

GOODE CL

COPLANDS
RISE

HIGH PARK

High Park

NORTHBRIDGE

THE
PADDOCK

GODDENS
GILL

FREWEN CL

25

Higham
Farm

CHAPEL
FIELD

DIXTER RD

BEALES LA

Northiam

3

Four Acre
Shaw

Spital
Wood

Longwood

Sempstead
Wood

Reach
Wood

Furnace
Wood

NEWHURST LA

Strawberry Hole
Cottage

Hall

PARK
VIEW

Mus

Sch

A 28

Gusling
Wood

Glebe
House

24

Sempstead

Long
Wood

Park
Wood

Tufton
Place

Yewtree
Hill

Coneyburrow
Wood

Carriers
Farm

A 28

2

Wattshill
Wood

Martinshaw
Farm

LORDINE
LA

Watts Hill
Farm

Lordine
Wood

Ockford
Farm

Brook's
Farm

Mill Corner

NEW RD

Sherbourne
Valley

23

ADAMS LA

Spanyard's
Farm

Lordine
Court

Chantry
Wood

Forstal
Wood

Dadland
Wood

Commons
Wood Farm

Wellhouse
Morley
Farm

Lawyer's
Wood

Yewtree
Farm

1

Commons
Wood

Barnwell
Farm

B 2165

Horns Cross

B 2165

Sparks

New House
Farm

Goatley Farm

B 2165

A 28

22

80   A   81   B   82   C

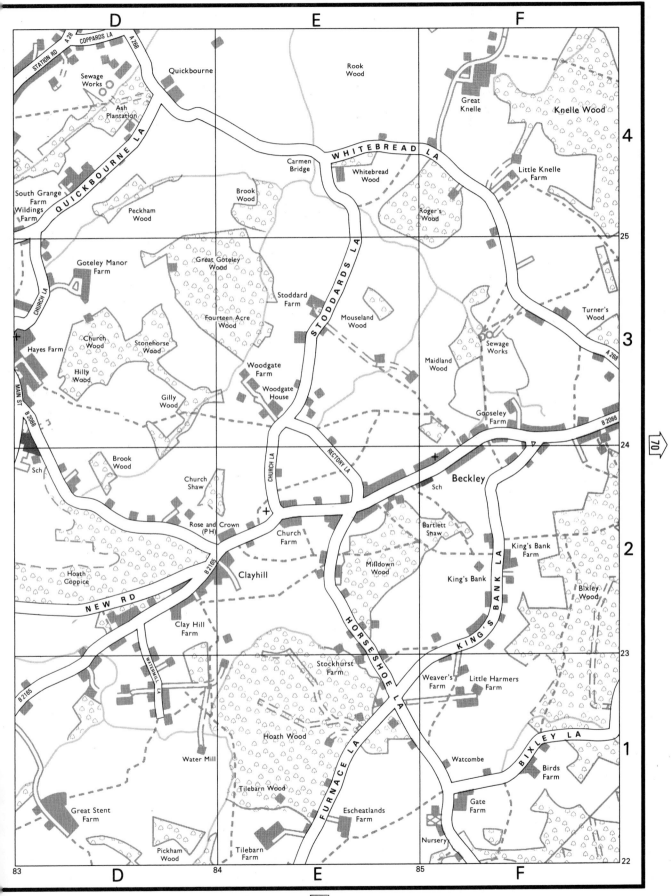

D   E   F

COPPARDS LA

STATION RD

A 28

A 268

Quickbourne

Rook Wood

Great Knelle

Knelle Wood

4

Sewage Works

Ash Plantation

QUICKBOURNE LA

WHITEBREAD LA

Carmen Bridge

Whitebread Wood

Little Knelle Farm

South Grange Farm

Wildings Farm

Brook Wood

Peckham Wood

Roger's Wood

25

CHURCH LA

Goteley Manor Farm

Great Goteley Wood

Stoddard Farm

STODDARDS LA

Mouseland Wood

Turner's Wood

A 268

3

Church Wood

Stonehorse Wood

Fourteen Acre Wood

Maidland Wood

Sewage Works

Hayes Farm

Hilly Wood

Woodgate Farm

Gilly Wood

Woodgate House

MAIN ST

B 2088

Gooseley Farm

B 2088

Brook Wood

Church Shaw

CHURCH LA

RECTORY LA

24

70

Sch

Beckley

Sch

2

Rose and Crown (P H)

Church Farm

Bartlett Shaw

King's Bank Farm

Milldown Wood

King's Bank

KING'S BANK LA

Bixley Wood

Hoath Coppice

Clayhill

B 2165

NEW RD

Clay Hill Farm

HORSESHOE LA

23

WATERMILL LA

Stockhurst Farm

Weaver's Farm

Little Harmers Farm

B 2165

Water Mill

Hoath Wood

FURNACE LA

Watcombe

BIXLEY LA

Birds Farm

1

Great Stent Farm

Tilebarn Wood

Escheatlands Farm

Gate Farm

Nursery

Pickham Wood

Tilebarn Farm

83   D   84   E   85   F   22

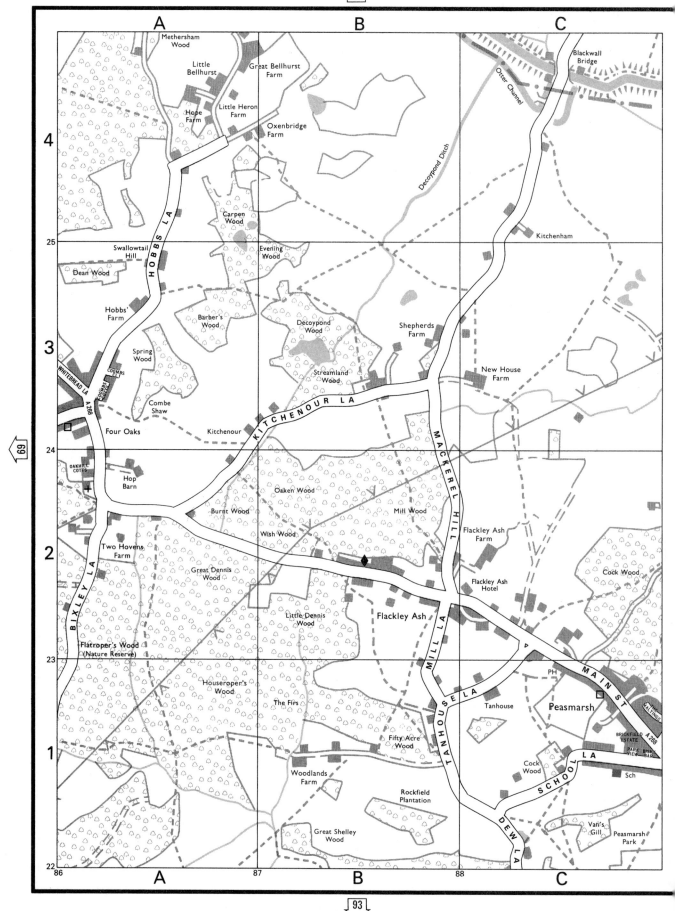

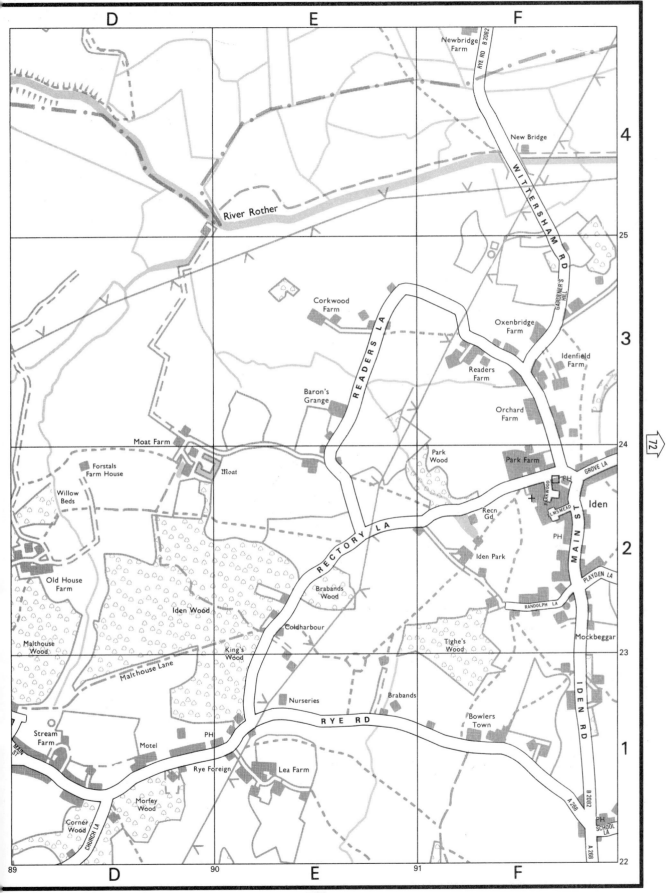

D E F

4

River Rother

Newbridge Farm

RYE RD B 2082

New Bridge

WITTERSHAM RD

25

GARDENER'S HILL

Corkwood Farm

READERS LA

Oxenbridge Farm

Idenfield Farm

3

Readers Farm

Baron's Grange

Orchard Farm

24

72

Moat Farm

Moat

Park Wood

Park Farm

PH

GROVE LA

Forstals Farm House

Willow Beds

RECTORY LA

Recn Gd

PARKWOOD

ELMSMEAD

+

Iden

MAIN ST

2

Old House Farm

Iden Wood

Brabands Wood

Iden Park

PH

PLAYDEN LA

RANDOLPH LA

Malthouse Wood

King's Wood

Coldharbour

Tighe's Wood

Mockbeggar

23

Malthouse Lane

IDEN RD

Nurseries

Brabands

Bowlers Town

Stream Farm

PH

Motel

RYE RD

1

Rye Foreign

Lea Farm

A 268

B 2082

Morfey Wood

PH SCHOOL LA

Corner Wood

CHURCH LA

A 268

89 D 90 E 91 F 22

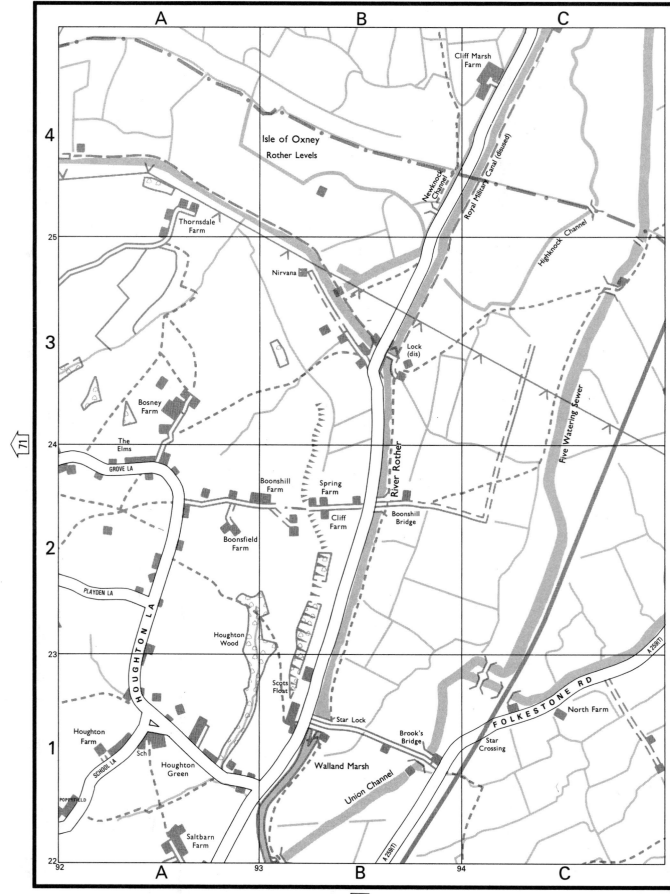

A   B   C

Cliff Marsh Farm

Isle of Oxney

Rother Levels

Newknock Channel

Royal Military Canal (disused)

Highknock Channel

25

Thornsdale Farm

Nirvana

4

3

Lock (dis)

Five Watering Sewer

Bosney Farm

The Elms

24

GROVE LA

Boonshill Farm

Spring Farm

River Rother

Boonshill Bridge

Boonsfield Farm

Cliff Farm

2

PLAYDEN LA

HOUGHTON LA

Houghton Wood

23

A 259(T)

FOLKESTONE RD

North Farm

Scots Float

Star Lock

Brook's Bridge

Star Crossing

Houghton Farm

Sch

Houghton Green

1

SCHOOL LA

Walland Marsh

Union Channel

POPPYFIELD

Saltbarn Farm

A 259(T)

22

92   A   93   B   94   C

71

95

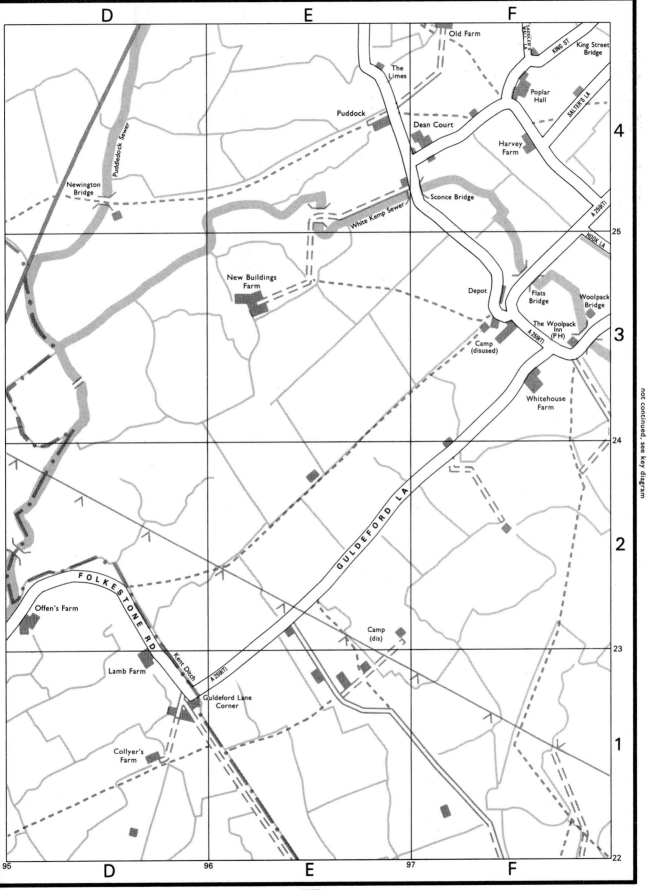

D   E   F

Old Farm

The Limes

Puddock

Dean Court

Poplar Hall

SADDLER'S WALL LA

KING ST

King Street Bridge

SALTER'S LA

Harvey Farm

4

Newington Bridge

Puddledock Sewer

Sconce Bridge

White Kemp Sewer

A 259(T)

HOOK LA

25

New Buildings Farm

Depot

Flats Bridge

Woolpack Bridge

The Woolpack Inn (PH)

A 259(T)

3

Camp (disused)

Whitehouse Farm

24

GULDEFORD LA

2

FOLKESTONE RD

Offen's Farm

Kent Ditch

Camp (dis)

23

Lamb Farm

A 259(T)

Guldeford Lane Corner

1

Collyer's Farm

22

95   96   97

D   E   F

not continued, see key diagram

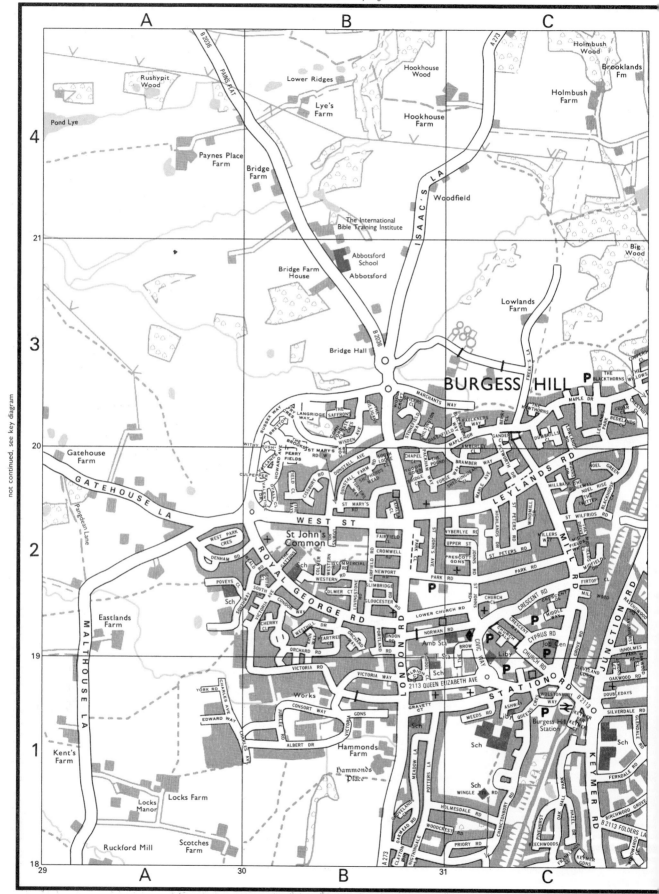

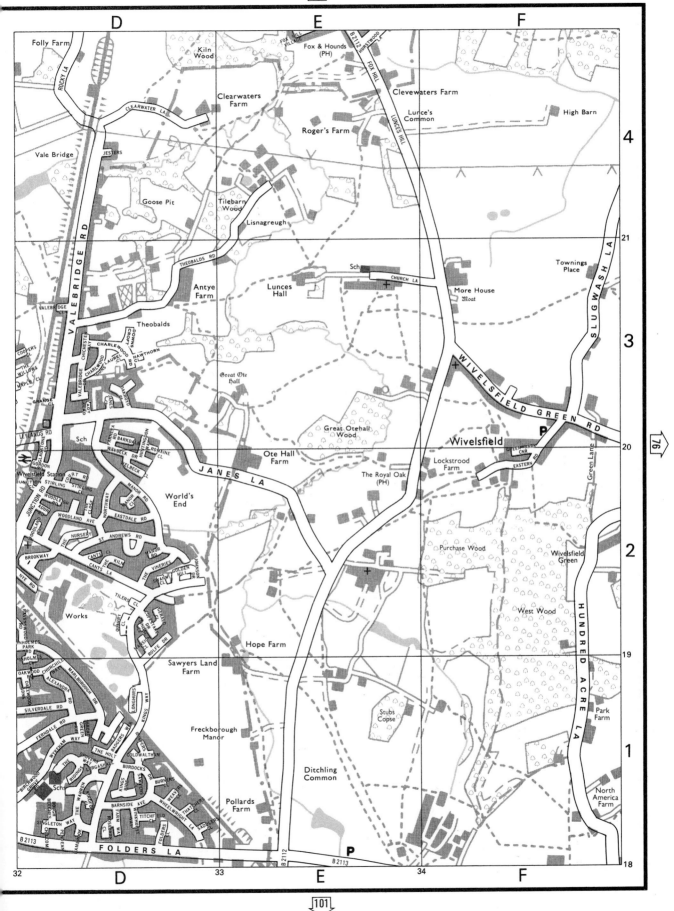

52

D E F

Folly Farm

Kiln Wood

Fox & Hounds (PH)

Clearwaters Farm

Clevewaters Farm

Lurce's Common

High Barn

Roger's Farm

4

Vale Bridge

JESTERS

ROCKY LA

CLEARWATER LA

Goose Pit

Tilebarn Wood

Lisnagreugh

21

VALEBRIDGE RD

THEOBALDS RD

Antye Farm

Lunces Hall

Sch

CHURCH LA

More House Moat

Townings Place

SLUGWASH LA

VALEBRIDGE DRIVE

COOPERS

THE WILLOWS

MAPLE CL

GRANGE CL

Theobalds

CHICHESTER WAY

CHARLEWOOD

DOWNS CROFT

LAUREL

HAWTHORN

CHARLWOOD RD

ADV

Great Ote Hall

WIVELSFIELD GREEN RD

3

LEYLANDS RD

Sch

PRINCE

BARKDALE

HUNTINGDON

ROMAINE CL

WEBECK DR

WELBECK CL

Great Otehall Wood

Wivelsfield

P

20

Wivelsfield Station

JUNCTION RD

GORDON RD

COURT RD

STIRLING

STIRLING CL

MANOR RD

JANES LA

Ote Hall Farm

The Royal Oak (PH)

Lockstrood Farm

GREEN FARM CNR

EASTERN RD

Green Lane

World's End

WOODLEIGH

ADUR

WOODLAND

WOODLAND AVE

NORTHWAY

EASTDALE RD

MANOR CL

MANOR RD

Purchase Wood

Wivelsfield Green

2

THE NURSERY

St ANDREWS RD

BROOKWAY

CANTS CL

THE KILN

CANTS LA

THE VINERIES

GOLDEN HILL

JOHNSON DR

HUNDRED ACRE LA

NYE RD

Works

TILERS CL

West Wood

GILBERT CL

GEERA CL

ROLFE DR

Hope Farm

19

HOLMES PARK RD

WHOLM RD

OAKWOOD

CHURCHILL

MARLBOROUGH DR

LONGHURST

KINGS WAY

Sawyers Land Farm

Stubs Copse

Park Farm

SILVERDALE RD

ALEXANDRA

DRIVE

Freckborough Manor

1

FERNDALE RD

WYCKHAM WAY

BRAMBLE

THE HOLT

COLDWALTHAM

BURDOCKS

BADGERS WLK

Ditchling Common

North America Farm

BIRCHWOOD

BEECHES

Sch

THE RIDINGS

THE WARREN

KINGS

BURNERS

WEAVERS

Pollards Farm

BARNSIDE AVE

WHEELWRIGHT LA

THATCHERS

SADDLERS

SINGLETON WAY

FOLDERS LA

18

B 2113

101

32 D 33 E 34 F

53

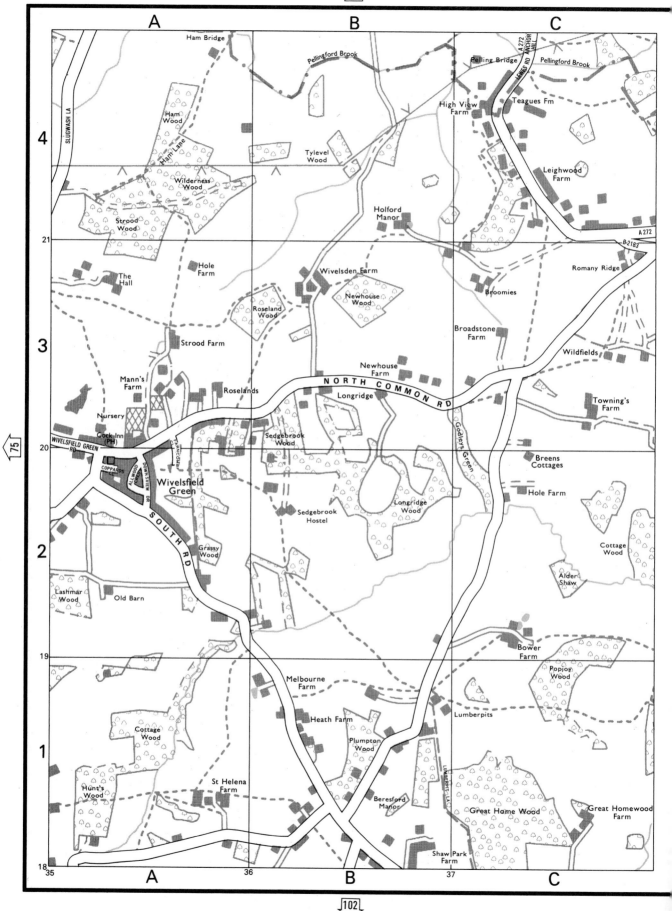

A   B   C

4

Ham Bridge

Pellingford Brook

Pelling Bridge

Pellingford Brook

SLUGWASH LA

Ham
Wood

Ham Lane

Tylevel
Wood

High View
Farm

Teagues Fm

A 272

LEWES RD

ANCHOR HILL

Wilderness
Wood

Leighwood
Farm

Strood
Wood

Holford
Manor

21

A 272

B-2183

3

Hole
Farm

The
Hall

Wivelsden Farm

Broomies

Romany Ridge

Roseland
Wood

Newhouse
Wood

Strood Farm

Broadstone
Farm

Wildfields

Mann's
Farm

Roselands

NORTH COMMON RD

Newhouse
Farm

Towning's
Farm

Longridge

Nursery

Cock Inn
(PH)

Godley's Green

75

20   WIVELSFIELD GREEN RD

Sedgebrook
Wood

Breens
Cottages

COPPARDS CL

DOWNS VIEW DR

ALL WOOD

PARK GMER

Wivelsfield
Green

Longridge
Wood

Hole Farm

Sedgebrook
Hostel

2

SOUTH RD

Grassy
Wood

Cottage
Wood

Lashmar
Wood

Old Barn

Alder
Shaw

19

Bower
Farm

Popjoy
Wood

Melbourne
Farm

1

Cottage
Wood

Heath Farm

Lumberpits

Plumpton
Wood

LUMBERPITS LA

Hunt's
Wood

St Helena
Farm

Beresford
Manor

Great Home Wood

Great Homewood
Farm

Shaw Park
Farm

18
35   A   36   B   37   C

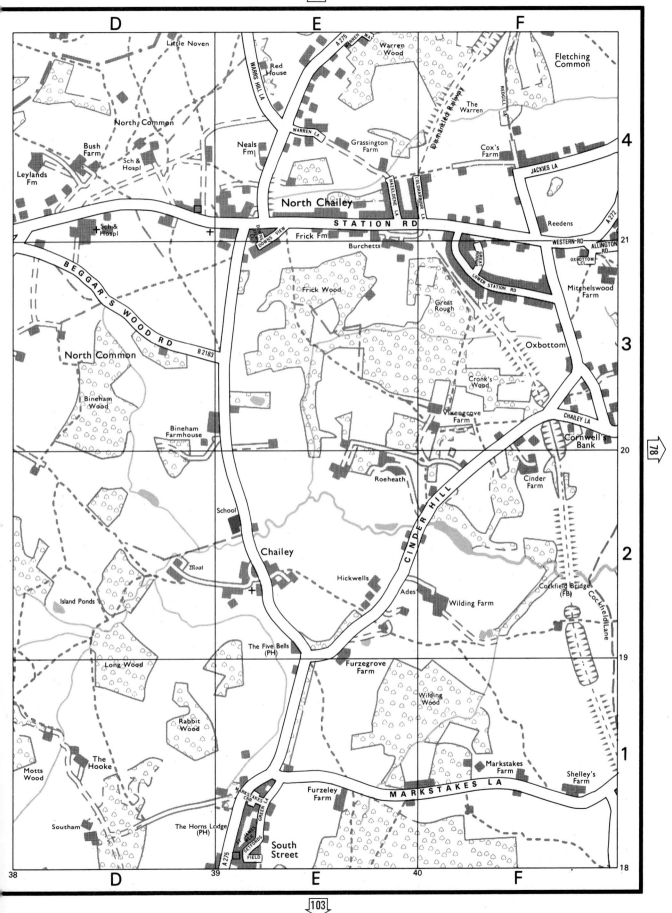

Little Noven

North Common

Bush Farm

Leylands Fm

Sch & Hospl

Sch & Hospl

BEGGAR'S WOOD RD

B 2183

North Common

Bineham Wood

Bineham Farmhouse

Island Ponds

Long Wood

Moat

Rabbit Wood

The Hooke

Motts Wood

Southam

WARRS HILL LA

Red House

Neals Fm

WARREN LA

Grassington Farm

North Chailey

HAZELDENE LA

OLDHARBOUR LA

STATION RD

Frick Fm

DOWNS VIEW

Burchetts

Frick Wood

School

Chailey

Hickwells

Ades

The Five Bells (PH)

Furzegrove Farm

The Horns Lodge (PH)

MARKSTAKES CNR

GREEN LA

HAMES MEAD

SEFFORDS

FIELD

A 275

South Street

Furzeley Farm

MARKSTAKES LA

WARREN WAY

A 275

Warren Wood

Dismantled Railway

The Warren

REDGILL LA

Fletching Common

Cox's Farm

JACKIES LA

A 272

Reedens

WESTERN RD

ALLINGTON RD

OXBOTTOM CL

Mitchelswood Farm

GREAT ROUGH

LOWER STATION RD

Great Rough

Oxbottom

Cronk's Wood

Vixengrove Farm

CHAILEY LA

Cornwell's Bank

Roeheath

CINDER HILL

Cinder Farm

Wilding Farm

Cockfield Bridge (FB)

Cockfield Lane

Furzegrove Farm

Wilding Wood

Markstakes Farm

Shelley's Farm

78

4

21

3

20

2

19

1

18

38

39

40

D

E

F

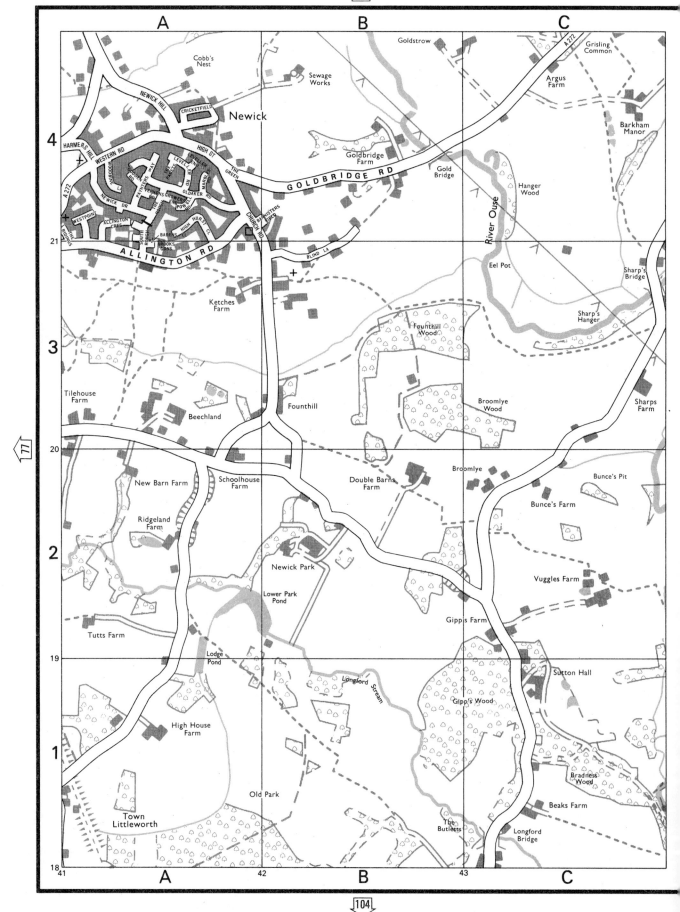

56

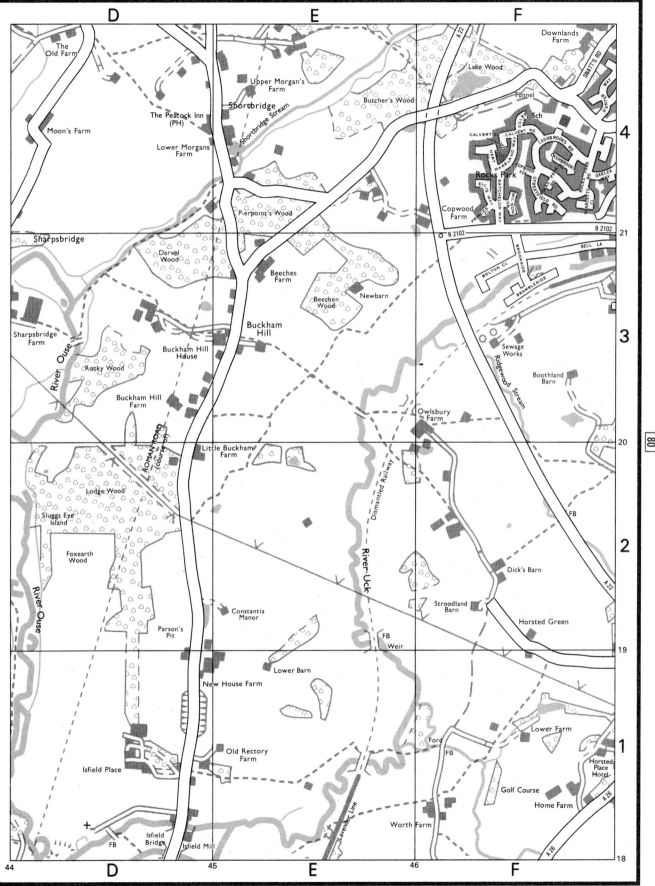

80

57

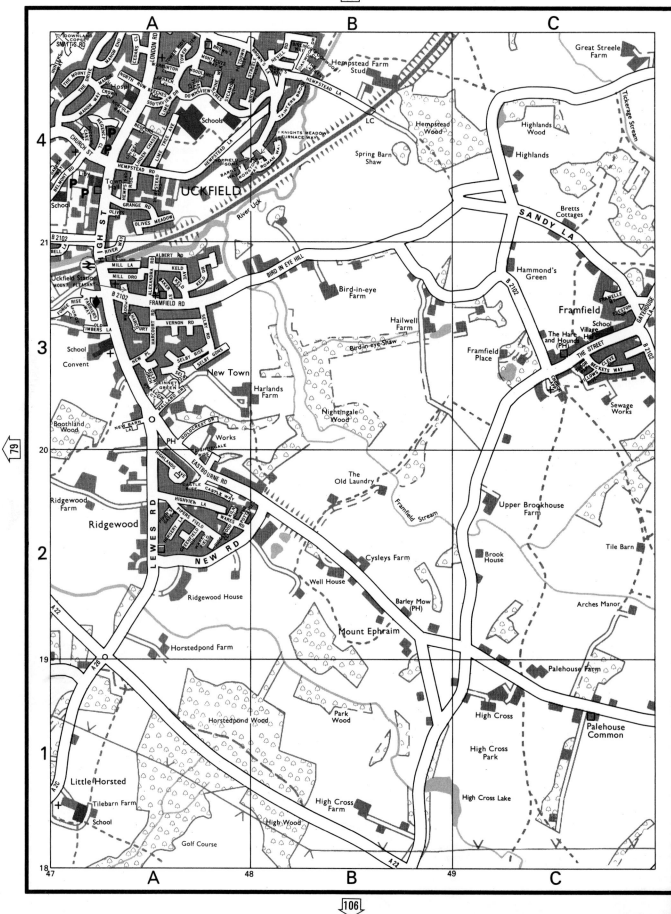

79

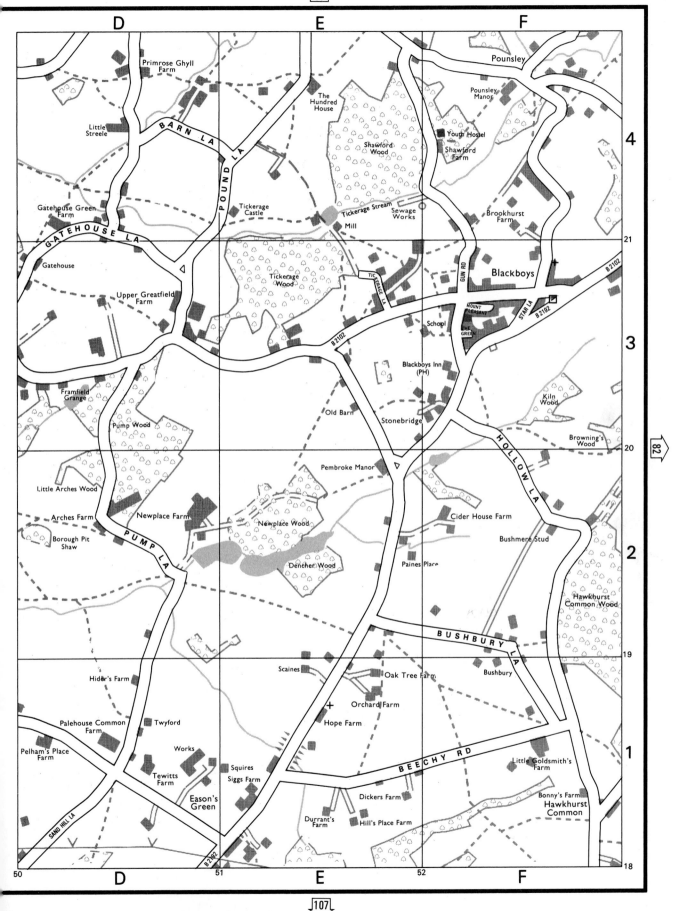

D

E

F

Pounsley

Primrose Ghyll Farm

The Hundred House

Pounsley Manor

Little Streele

BARN LA

Youth Hostel

Shawford Wood

Shawford Farm

4

Gatehouse Green Farm

POUND LA

Tickerage Castle

Tickerage Stream

Sewage Works

Brookhurst Farm

GATEHOUSE LA

Mill

21

Gatehouse

Tickerage Wood

TICKERAGE LA

GUN RD

Blackboys

B 2102

Upper Greatfield Farm

B 2102

MOUNT PLEASANT

STAR LA

B 2192

3

School

THE GREEN

Blackboys Inn (PH)

Framfield Grange

Kiln Wood

Old Barn

Pump Wood

Stonebridge

HOLLOW LA

Browning's Wood

20

Little Arches Wood

Pembroke Manor

Arches Farm

Newplace Farm

Newplace Wood

Cider House Farm

Borough Pit Shaw

PUMP LA

Bushmere Stud

2

Dencher Wood

Paines Place

Hawkhurst Common Wood

BUSHBURY LA

19

Scaines

Oak Tree Farm

Bushbury

Hider's Farm

Orchard Farm

Palehouse Common Farm

Twyford

Hope Farm

BEECHY RD

1

Pelham's Place Farm

Works

Little Goldsmith's Farm

SAND HILL LA

Tewitts Farm

Squires Siggs Farm

Dickers Farm

Bonny's Farm

Eason's Green

Durrant's Farm

Hill's Place Farm

Hawkhurst Common

B 2192

18

50

D

51

E

52

F

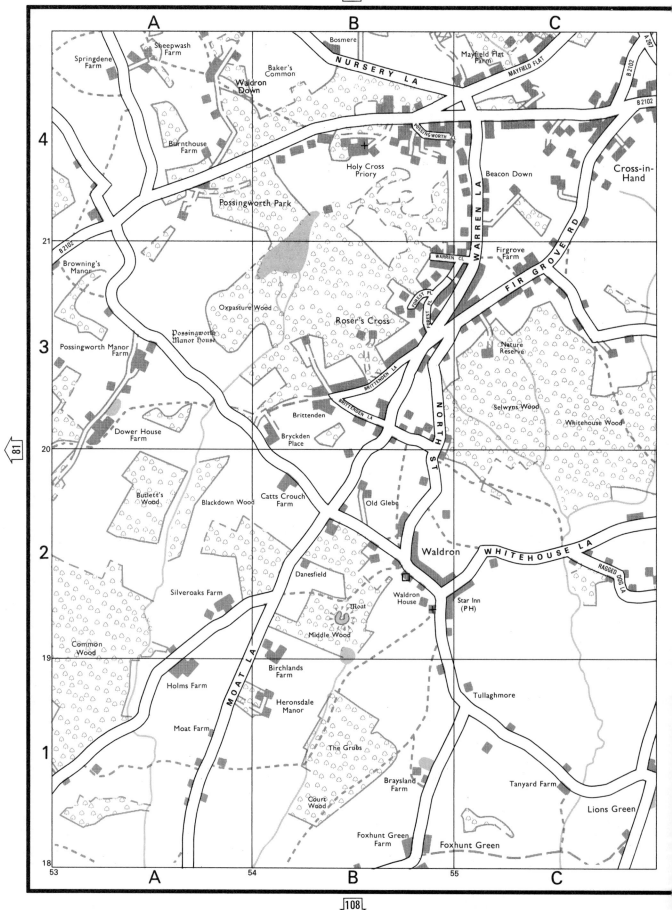

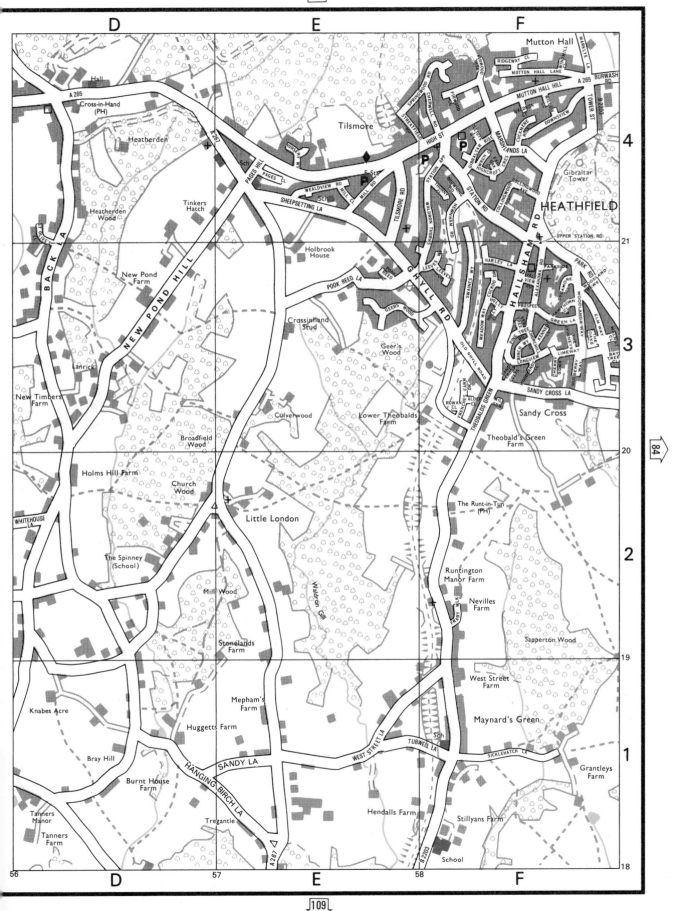

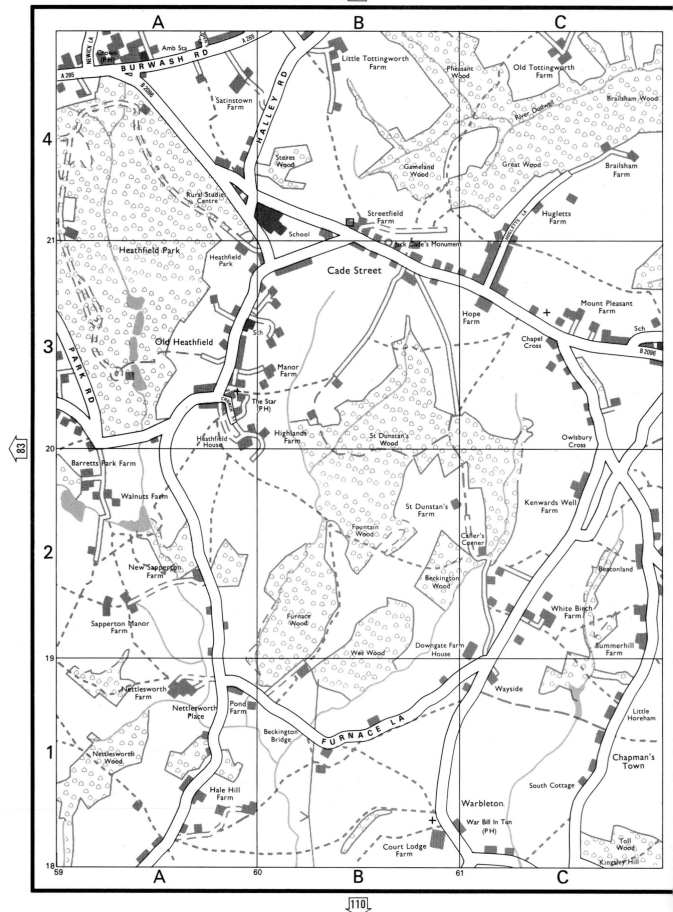

62
86

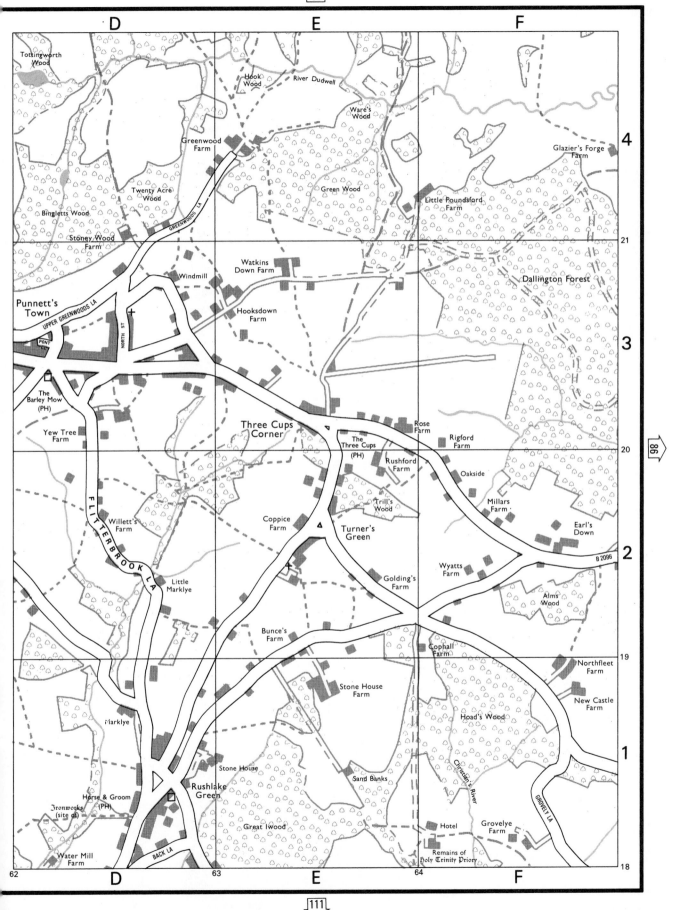

D   E   F

Tottingworth Wood

Hook Wood
River Dudwell
Ware's Wood

Greenwood Farm
Green Wood

Glazier's Forge Farm

4

Twenty Acre Wood

Little Poundsford Farm

Bingletts Wood

GREENWOODS LA

Stoney Wood Farm

21

Watkins Down Farm
Windmill

Dallington Forest

Punnett's Town

UPPER GREENWOODS LA

NORTH ST

Hooksdown Farm

3

PONT

The Barley Mow (PH)

Yew Tree Farm

Rose Farm

Three Cups Corner

The Three Cups (PH)

Rigford Farm

20

Rushford Farm

Oakside

FLITTERBROOK LA

Willett's Farm

Coppice Farm

Trill's Wood

Turner's Green

Millars Farm

Earl's Down

Little Marklye

Golding's Farm

Wyatts Farm

B 2096

2

Alms Wood

Bunce's Farm

Cophall Farm

Northfleet Farm

19

Stone House Farm

New Castle Farm

Marklye

Hoad's Wood

Christian's River

1

Stone House

Sand Banks

Horse & Groom (PH)

Rushlake Green

GROVELY LA

Ironworks (site of)

Great Iwood

Hotel

Grovelye Farm

Water Mill Farm

BACK LA

Remains of Holy Trinity Priory

18

D   E   F

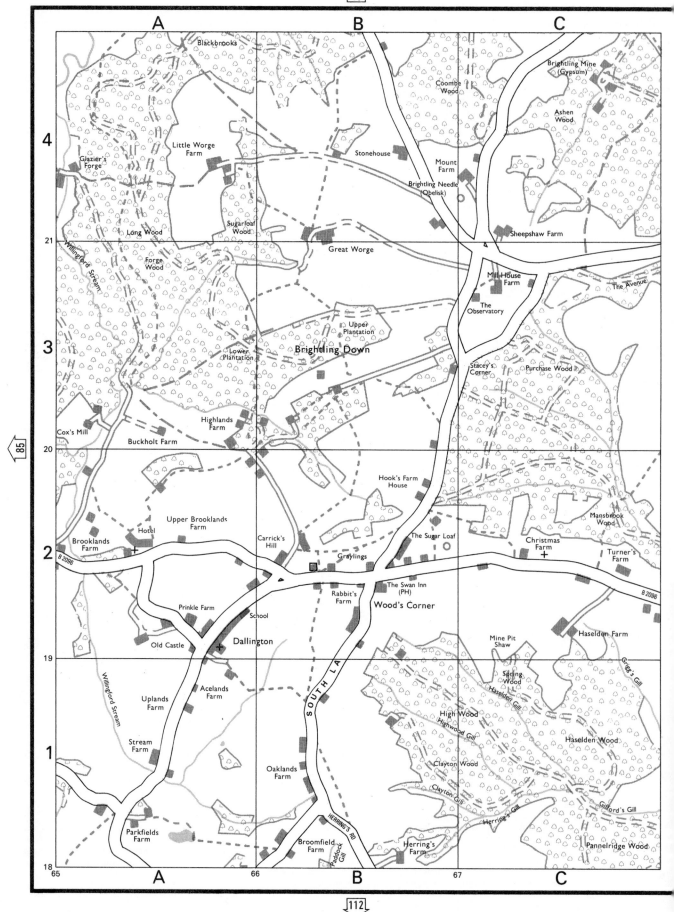

A · B · C

Blackbrooks

Coombe Wood

Brightling Mine (Gypsum)

Ashen Wood

4

Glazier's Forge

Little Worge Farm

Stonehouse

Mount Farm

Brightling Needle (Obelisk)

Long Wood

Sugarloaf Wood

Great Worge

Sheepshaw Farm

21

Willingford Stream

Forge Wood

Mill House Farm

The Avenue

Upper Plantation

The Observatory

3

Lower Plantation

Brightling Down

Stacey's Corner

Purchase Wood

Cox's Mill

Highlands Farm

Buckholt Farm

20

Hook's Farm House

Mansbrook Wood

Upper Brooklands Farm

Carrick's Hill

The Sugar Loaf

Christmas Farm

Turner's Farm

Brooklands Farm

Hotel

Graylings

2

B 2096

The Swan Inn (PH)

B 2096

Prinkle Farm

Rabbit's Farm

Wood's Corner

Mine Pit Shaw

Haselden Farm

School

Old Castle

Dallington

SOUTH LA

19

Spring Wood

Haselden Gill

Gregg's Gill

Willingford Stream

Uplands Farm

Acelands Farm

High Wood

Highwood Gill

Haselden Wood

1

Stream Farm

Oaklands Farm

Clayton Wood

Clayton Gill

Gilford's Gill

Herring's Gill

Parkfields Farm

Broomfield Farm

Paddock Gill

HERRING'S RD

Herring's Farm

Pannelridge Wood

18

65 · A · 66 · B · 67 · C

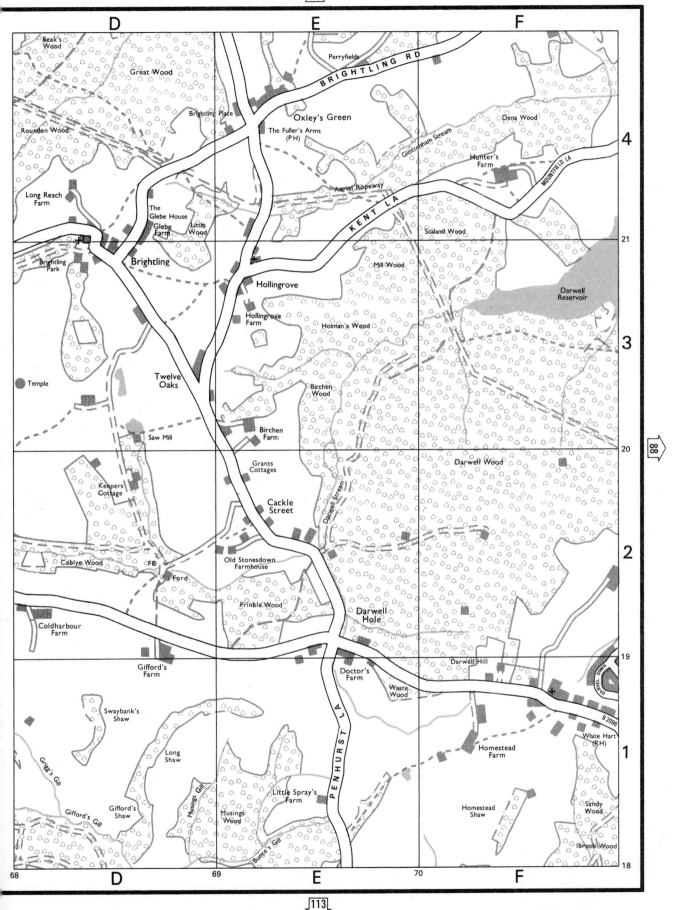

D   E   F

Beak's Wood

Great Wood

Perryfields

BRIGHTLING RD

Rounden Wood

Brightling Place

Oxley's Green

Dens Wood

The Fuller's Arms (P H)

Glottenham Stream

4

Hunter's Farm

MOUNTFIELD LA

Long Reach Farm

The Glebe House

Glebe Farm

Little Wood

Aerial Ropeway

KENT LA

Scaland Wood

21

Brightling Park

Brightling

Hollingrove

Mill Wood

Darwell Reservoir

Hollingrove Farm

Holman's Wood

88

Temple

Twelve Oaks

Birchen Wood

3

Saw Mill

Birchen Farm

Keepers Cottage

Grants Cottages

Darwell Wood

20

Coblye Wood

FB

Ford

Cackle Street

Old Stonesdown Farmhouse

Darwell Stream

2

Coldharbour Farm

Prinkle Wood

Darwell Hole

Gifford's Farm

Darwell Hill

DARWELL TOWN

19

Doctor's Farm

Waste Wood

B 2096

White Hart (P H)

Swaybank's Shaw

PENHURST LA

Homestead Farm

1

Grigg's Gill

Long Shaw

Musings Gill

Little Spray's Farm

Homestead Shaw

Sandy Wood

Gifford's Gill

Gifford's Shaw

Musings Wood

Ibrook Wood

Bunce's Gill

18

68   D   69   E   70   F

65

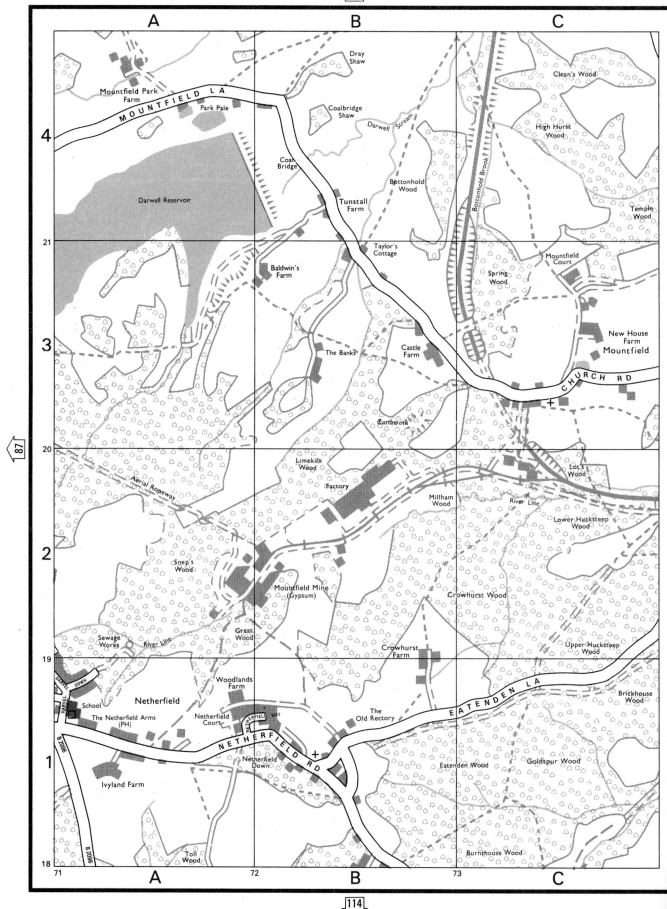

87

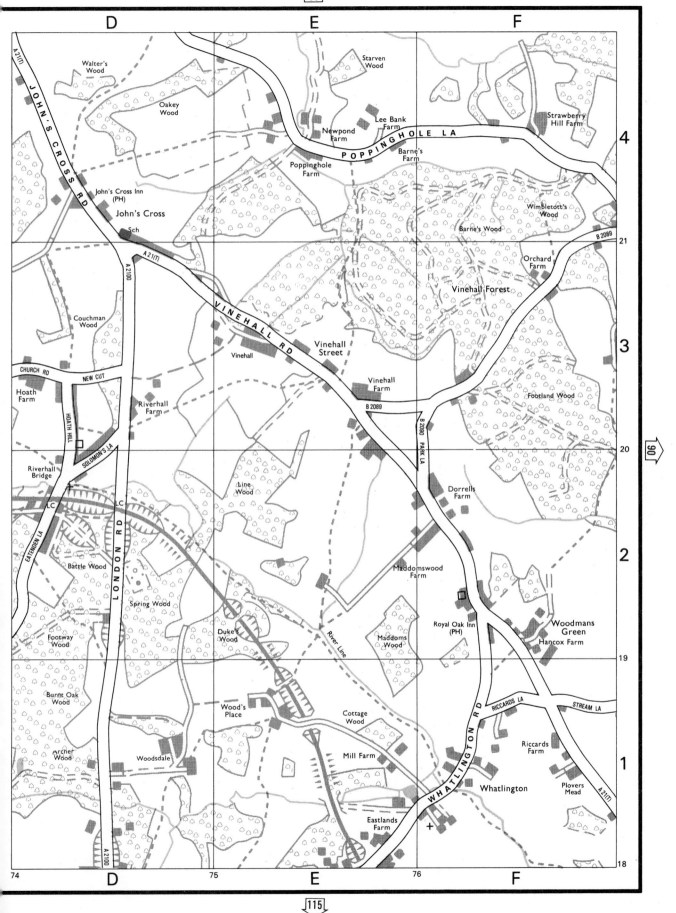

D E F

A 21(T)

JOHN'S CROSS RD

Walter's Wood

Oakey Wood

Starven Wood

Lee Bank Farm

Newpond Farm

POPPINGHOLE LA

Strawberry Hill Farm

Barne's Farm

John's Cross Inn (PH)

John's Cross

Poppinghole Farm

Wimbletott's Wood

Sch

Barne's Wood

B 2089

21

A 21(T)

A 2100

Orchard Farm

VINEHALL RD

Vinehall Forest

Couchman Wood

Vinehall Street

Vinehall

CHURCH RD

NEW CUT

Vinehall Farm

Hoath Farm

Riverhall Farm

B 2089

Footland Wood

HOATH HILL

SOLOMON'S LA

B 2090

PARK LA

20

Riverhall Bridge

LC

LC

Line Wood

Dorrells Farm

EATENDEN LA

LONDON RD

Battle Wood

Maddomswood Farm

2

Spring Wood

Royal Oak Inn (PH)

Woodmans Green

Footway Wood

Duke's Wood

River Line

Maddoms Wood

Hancox Farm

19

Burnt Oak Wood

Wood's Place

Cottage Wood

WHATLINGTON RD

RICCARDS LA

STREAM LA

Archer Wood

Woodsdale

Mill Farm

Whatlington

Riccards Farm

Plovers Mead

A 21(T)

1

A 2100

Eastlands Farm

74 D 75 E 76 F

18

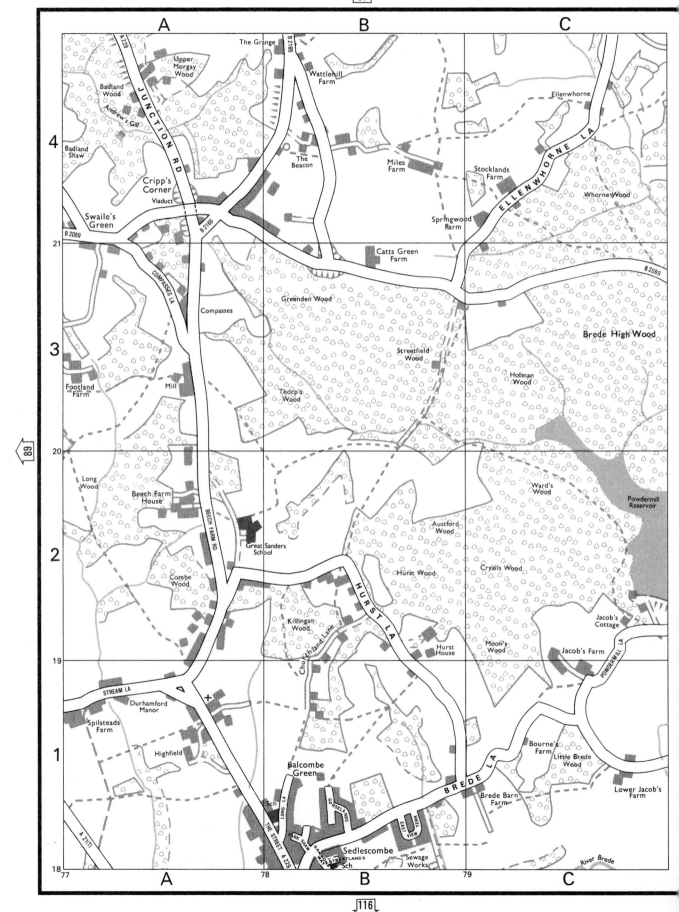

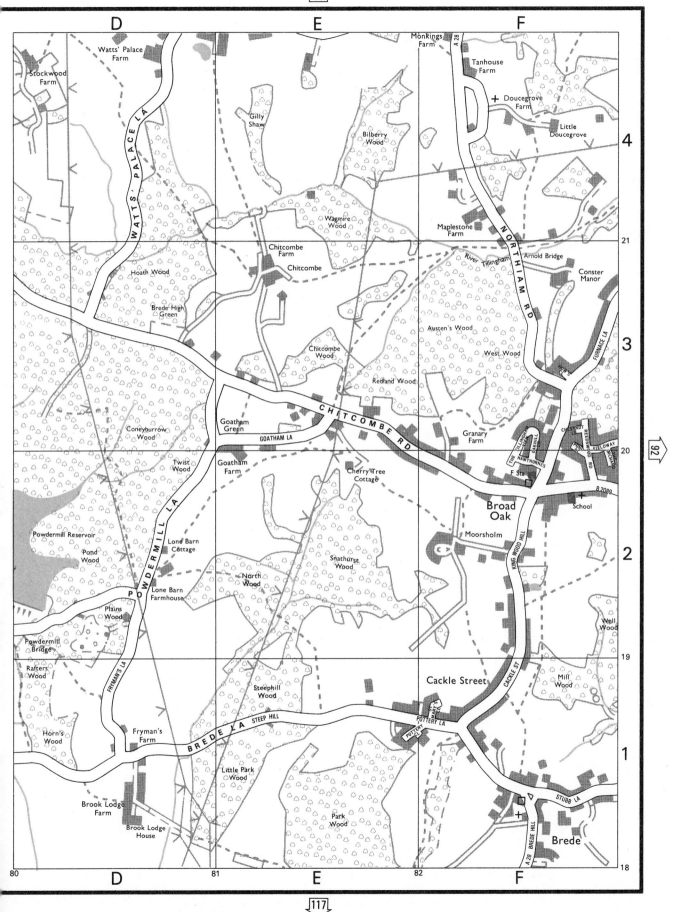

D

E

F

4

21

3

20

2

19

1

18

Stockwood Farm

Watts' Palace Farm

WATTS' PALACE LA

Gilly Shaw

Bilberry Wood

Monkings Farm

A 28

Tanhouse Farm

Doucegrove Farm

Little Doucegrove

Wagmire Wood

Maplestone Farm

NORTHIAM RD

Hoath Wood

Chitcombe Farm

Chitcombe

River Tillingham

Arnold Bridge

Conster Manor

Brede High Green

Austen's Wood

West Wood

FURNACE LA

Chitcombe Wood

Redland Wood

Coneyburrow Wood

Goatham Green

CHITCOMBE RD

GOATHAM LA

Granary Farm

CHESTNUT

THE HAWTHORNES

OAKHILL

PONDWOOD RD

REEDSWOOD RD

FIELDWAY

ORCHARD

F Sta

Twist Wood

Goatham Farm

Cherry Tree Cottage

Broad Oak

School

B 2089

Powdermill Reservoir

Pond Wood

Lone Barn Cottage

Snathurst Wood

Moorsholm

KING WOOD HILL

POWDERMILL LA

North Wood

Well Wood

Plains Wood

Lone Barn Farmhouse

Powdermill Bridge

Rafters Wood

FRYMAN'S LA

Steephill Wood

Cackle Street

CACKLE ST

Mill Wood

Horn's Wood

Fryman's Farm

BREDE LA

STEEP HILL

ST MARY'S

POTTERY LA

POTTERY

Little Park Wood

Brook Lodge Farm

Brook Lodge House

Park Wood

STUBB LA

BREDE HILL

A 28

Brede

80

81

82

D

E

F

69

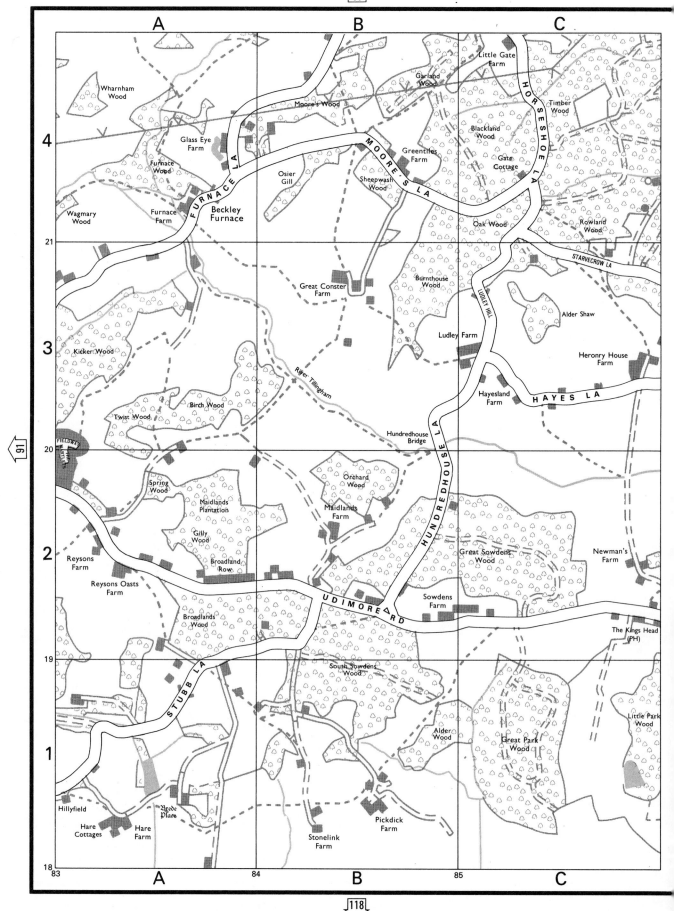

91

A   B   C

Wharnham
Wood

Moore's Wood

Little Gate
Farm

Garland
Wood

HORSESHOE LA

Timber
Wood

4

Glass Eye
Farm

Osier
Gill

Sheepwash
Wood

Greentiles
Farm

Blackland
Wood

Gate
Cottage

Furnace
Wood

MOORE'S LA

Furnace
Farm

Wagmary
Wood

Furnace
Farm

FURNACE LA

Beckley
Furnace

Oak Wood

Rowland
Wood

21

STARVECROW LA

Great Conster
Farm

Burnthouse
Wood

LUDLEY HILL

Alder Shaw

3

Kicker Wood

River Tillingham

Ludley Farm

Heronry House
Farm

Birch Wood

Twist Wood

Hayesland
Farm

HAYES LA

20

FIELDWAY

HILL
MARTLE'S

Hundredhouse
Bridge

Spring
Wood

Orchard
Wood

Maidlands
Plantation

Maidlands
Farm

HUNDREDHOUSE LA

Gilly Wood

Great Sowdens
Wood

Newman's
Farm

2

Reysons
Farm

Broadland
Row

Reysons Oasts
Farm

Sowdens
Farm

The Kings Head
(PH)

Broadlands
Wood

UDIMORE RD

19

STUBB LA

South Sowdens
Wood

1

Hillyfield

Brede
Place

Alder
Wood

Great Park
Wood

Little Park
Wood

Hare
Cottages

Hare
Farm

Stonelink
Farm

Pickdick
Farm

18

83   84   85

A   B   C

118

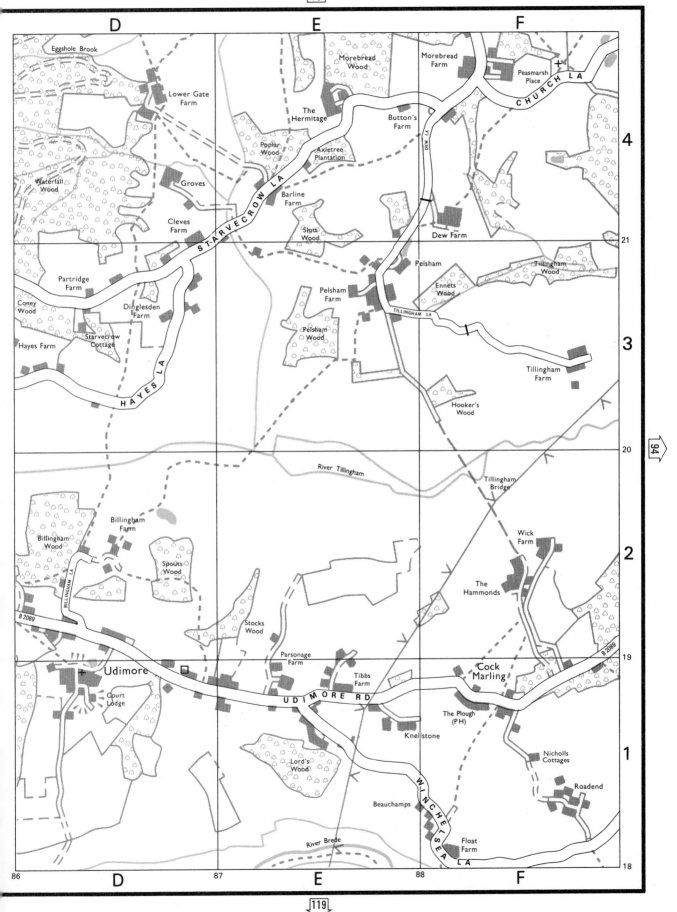

D

E

F

Eggshole Brook

Morebread
Wood

Morebread
Farm

Peasmarsh
Place

CHURCH LA

Lower Gate
Farm

The
Hermitage

Button's
Farm

DEW LA

4

Poplar
Wood

Axletree
Plantation

Waterfall
Wood

Groves

Barline
Farm

Cleves
Farm

Sluts
Wood

Dew Farm

21

STARVECROW LA

Pelsham

Tillingham
Wood

Partridge
Farm

Pelsham
Farm

Ennets
Wood

Coney
Wood

Dinglesden
Farm

TILLINGHAM LA

Hayes Farm

Starvecrow
Cottage

Pelsham
Wood

Tillingham
Farm

3

HAYES LA

Hooker's
Wood

River Tillingham

Tillingham
Bridge

20

94

Billingham
Farm

Wick
Farm

Billingham
Wood

Spouts
Wood

The
Hammonds

2

BILLINGHAM LA

B 2089

Stocks
Wood

B 2089

Parsonage
Farm

19

Udimore

Tibbs
Farm

Cock
Marling

Court
Lodge

UDIMORE RD

Knellstone

The Plough
(P H)

Nicholls
Cottages

1

Lord's
Wood

Roadend

WINCHELSEA LA

Beauchamps

Float
Farm

River Brede

18

86

D

87

E

88

F

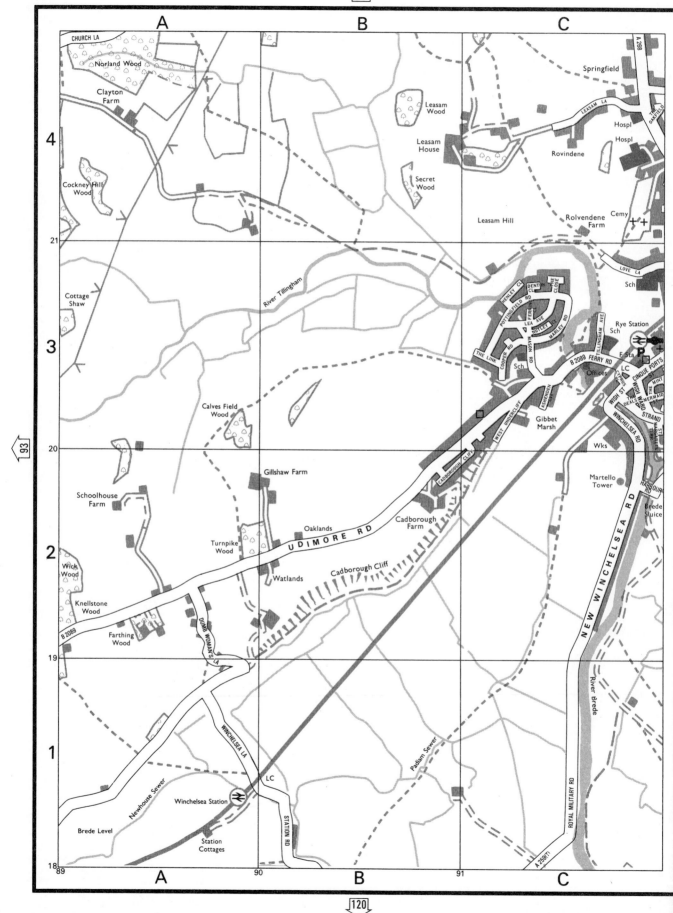

A B C

CHURCH LA
Norland Wood
Clayton Farm
Cockney Hill Wood

Leasam Wood
Leasam House
Secret Wood
Leasam Hill

A 268
Springfield
LEASAM LA
Hospl
Hospl
Rovindene
Rolvendene Farm
Cemy

4

Cottage Shaw

River Tillingham

LOVE LA
Sch

DENTON CL
HENLEY CT
POTTINGFIELD RD
FERRING
THE CLOSE
LEA AVE
MASONS
NUTLEY RD
MARLEY RD
TILLINGHAM AVE
Rye Station
Sch
F Sta
P

3

Calves Field Wood

THE LINK
COOPER RD
Sch
B 2089 FERRY RD
Offices
ASHENDEN
WEST UNDERCLIFF
CADBOROUGH CLIFF
Gibbet Marsh
CINQUE PORTS
WISH ST
WISH WARD
THE STRAND
THE MINT
LC
WINCHELSEA RD
MERMAID ST
DEALS
ST MARGARET'S TERR
Wks

20

Schoolhouse Farm

Gillshaw Farm

Oaklands
UDIMORE RD
Cadborough Farm
Martello Tower
HARBOUR RD
Brede Sluice

2

Wick Wood

Turnpike Wood
Watlands
Cadborough Cliff

Knellstone Wood
B 2089
Farthing Wood
DUMB WOMAN'S LA

NEW WINCHELSEA RD

19

1

WINCHELSEA LA
LC
STATION RD
Padiam Sewer

River Brede
ROYAL MILITARY RD

Newhouse Sewer
Winchelsea Station
Brede Level
Station Cottages

18
89

A 90 B 91 C

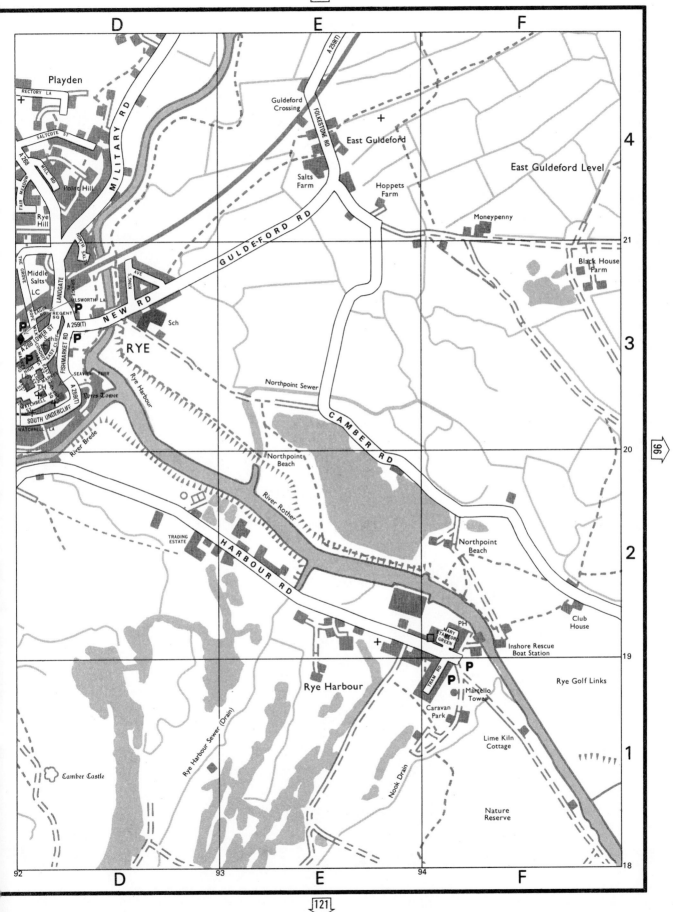

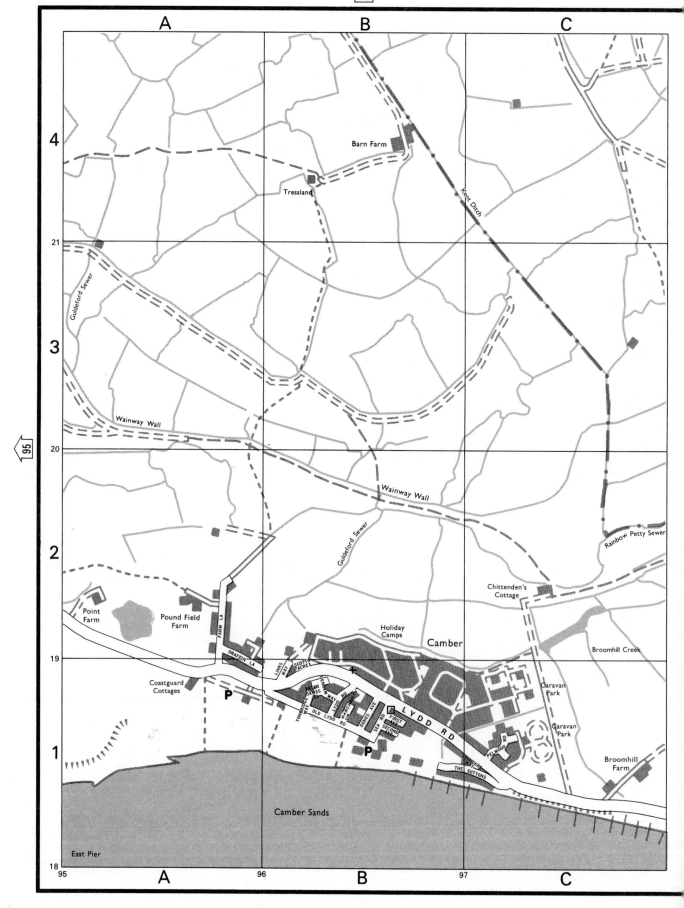

95

A   B   C

4

21

3

20

2

19

1

18

95   96   97

A   B   C

Barn Farm

Tressland

Kent Ditch

Guldeford Sewer

Wainway Wall

Wainway Wall

Guldeford Sewer

Rainbow Petty Sewer

Chittenden's Cottage

Broomhill Creek

Point Farm

Pound Field Farm

FARM LA

DRAFFIN LA

Coastguard Cottages

Holiday Camps

Camber

Caravan Park

Caravan Park

Broomhill Farm

LINKS WAY

SCOTTS ACRES

TONBRIDGE WAY

OLD LYDD RD

BROADWAY

MARCHMONT

DUNES AVE

SEA RD

FIRST AVE

SECOND AVE

LYDD RD

PELWOOD RD

TUNBRIDGE WAY

THE SUTTONS

P

P

Camber Sands

East Pier

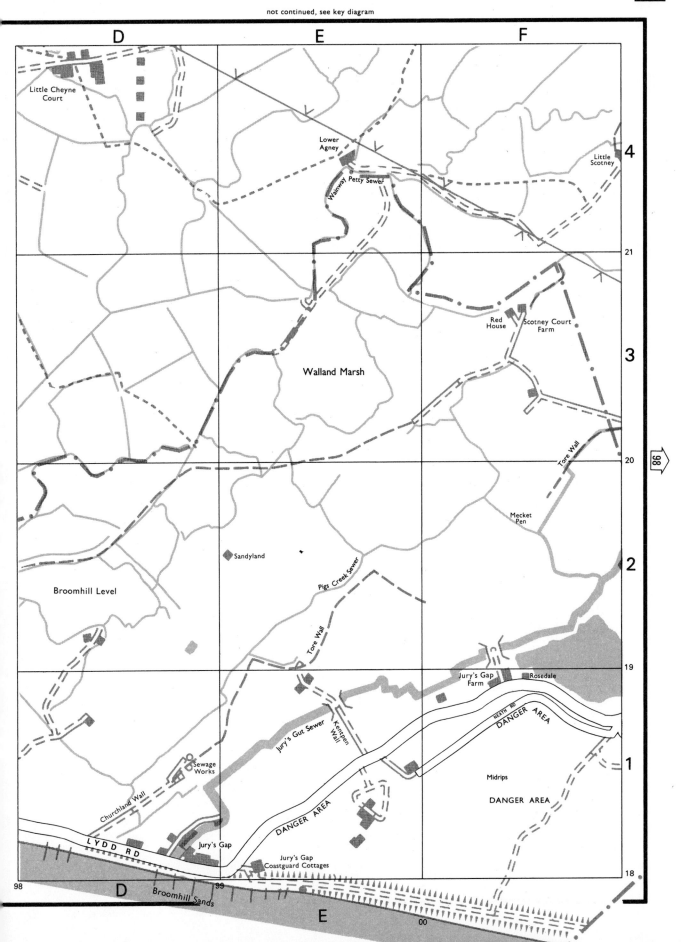

D   E   F

Little Cheyne
Court

Lower
Agney

Wainway Petty Sewer

Little
Scotney

4

21

Red
House

Scotney Court
Farm

Walland Marsh

3

Tore Wall

20

86

Mecket
Pen

Sandyland

2

Broomhill Level

Pigs Creek Sewer

Tore Wall

19

Jury's Gap
Farm

Rosedale

NEATH RD

DANGER AREA

Jury's Gut Sewer

Kentpen
Wall

Midrips

1

Sewage
Works

DANGER AREA

Churchland Wall

DANGER AREA

LYDD RD

Jury's Gap

Jury's Gap
Coastguard Cottages

18

98

D

Broomhill Sands

99

E

00

F

not continued, see key diagram

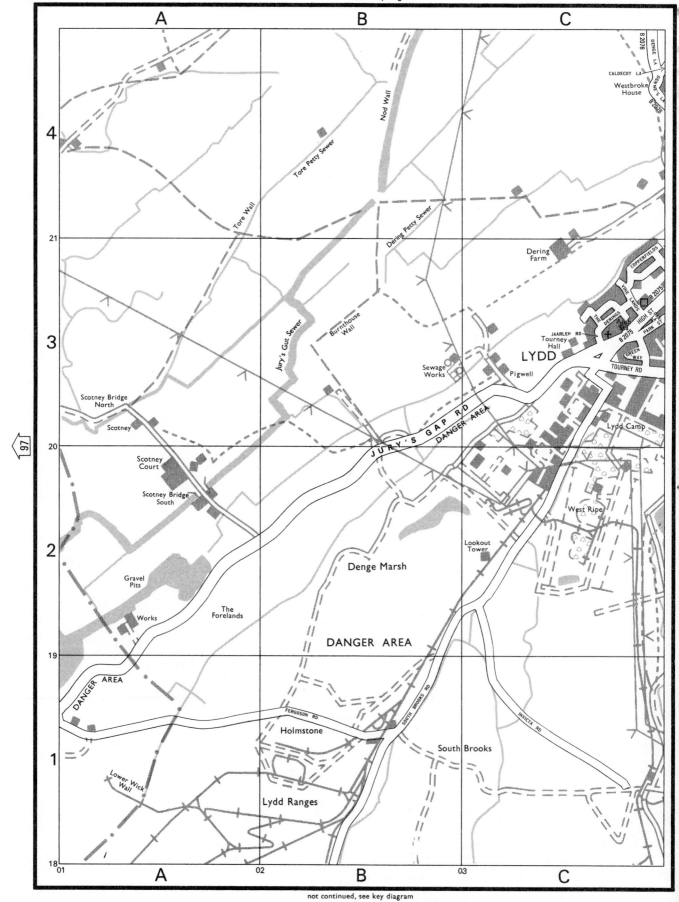

A B C

Westbroke House

B 2076
DENGE LA.
CALDECOT LA.
DENGE'S LA.
B 2076

4

Nod Wall

Tore Petty Sewer

Dering Petty Sewer

Tore Wall

21

Dering Farm

COPPERFIELDS
VINE LANDS
THE DERINGS
HIGH ST
B 2075

Jury's Gut Sewer

Burnthouse Wall

JAARLEN RD.
Tourney Hall

3

Sewage Works

Pigwell

LYDD

GREEN WAY
B 2075
PARK ST
TOURNEY RD.

Scotney Bridge North

Scotney

JURY'S GAP RD
DANGER AREA

Lydd Camp

20

Scotney Court

Scotney Bridge South

West Ripe

Denge Marsh

Lookout Tower

2

Gravel Pits

Works

The Forelands

DANGER AREA

19

DANGER AREA

FERGUSON RD.

SOUTH BROOKS RD

INVICTA RD

Holmstone

South Brooks

1

Lower Wick Wall

Lydd Ranges

18
01 02 03

A B C

97

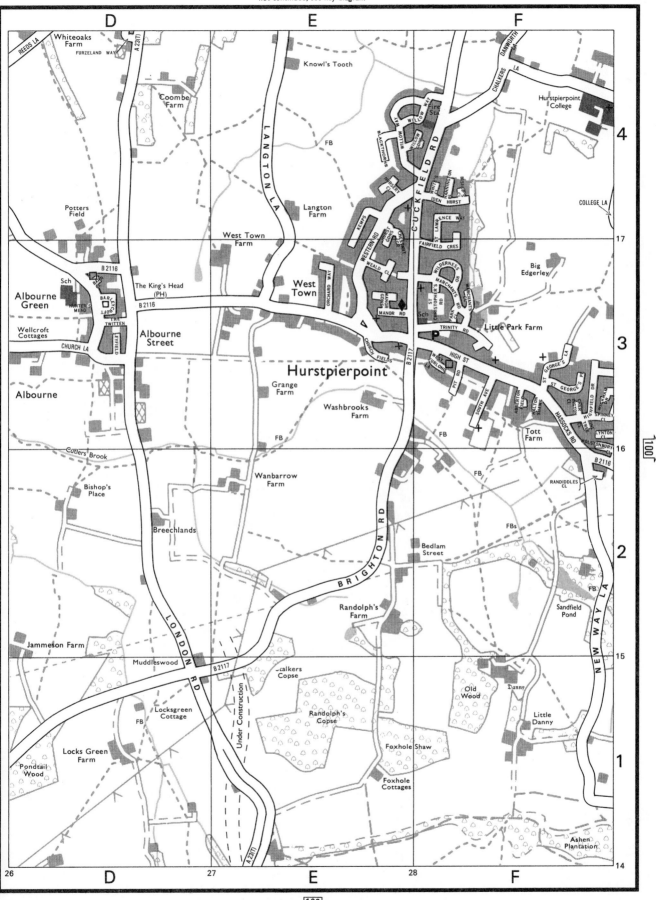

Hurstpierpoint

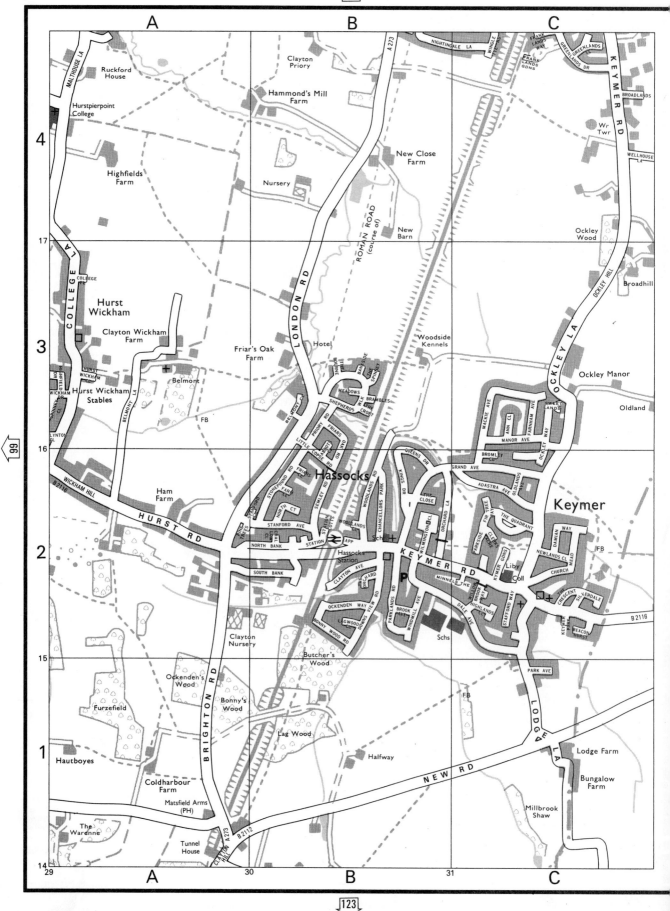

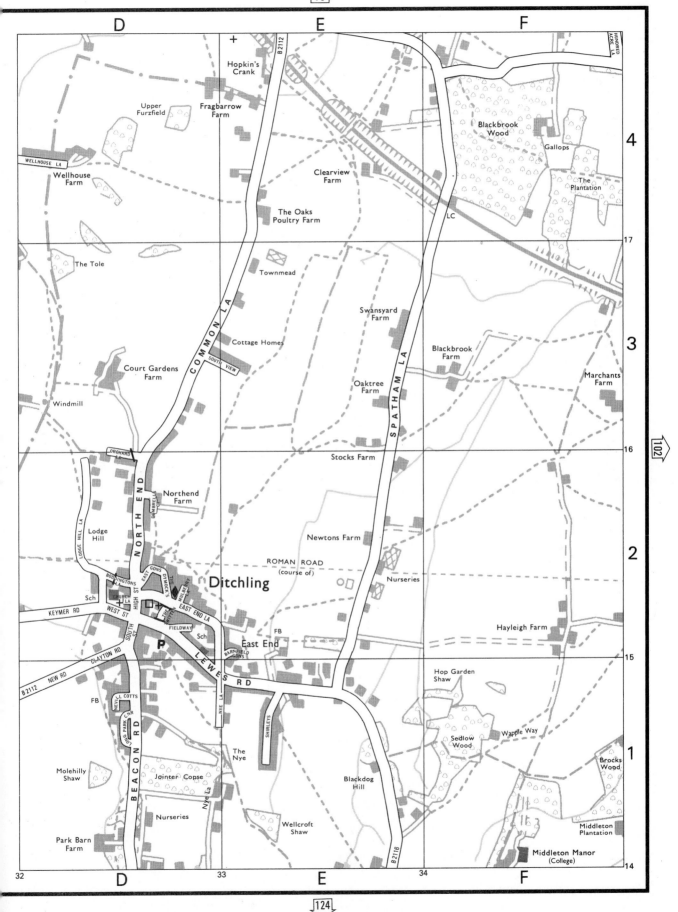

D E F

HUNDRED ACRE LA

Hopkin's Crank

B 2112

Upper Furzfield

Fragbarrow Farm

Blackbrook Wood

Gallops

4

Wellhouse Farm

WELLHOUSE LA

Clearview Farm

The Plantation

The Oaks Poultry Farm

LC

17

The Tole

Townmead

Swansyard Farm

Blackbrook Farm

3

Court Gardens Farm

Cottage Homes

SOUTH VIEW

COMMON LA

Oaktree Farm

SPATHAM LA

Marchants Farm

Windmill

ORCHARD LA

Stocks Farm

16

NORTHEND

Northend Farm

DAMBRELLS RD

Newtons Farm

Lodge Hill

LODGE HILL LA

ROMAN ROAD (course of)

2

Nurseries

BODDINGTONS

GDNS

HIGH ST

THE DYMOCKS

MULBERRY

Ditchling

EAST END LA

Sch

CHURCH LA

Hayleigh Farm

KEYMER RD

WEST ST

SOUTH ST

THE TWITTEN

FIELDWAY

Sch

East End

FB

BARNFIELD GDNS

15

CLAYTON RD

P

LEWES RD

Hop Garden Shaw

NEW RD

B 2112

FB

NEVILL COTTS

DOG PARK CNR

BEACON RD

NYE LA

SHIRLEYS

Sedlow Wood

Wapple Way

Brocks Wood

1

Molehilly Shaw

Jointer Copse

The Nye

Nye La

Blackdog Hill

Middleton Plantation

Nurseries

Park Barn Farm

Wellcroft Shaw

B 2116

Middleton Manor (College)

14

32 D 33 E 34 F

102

76

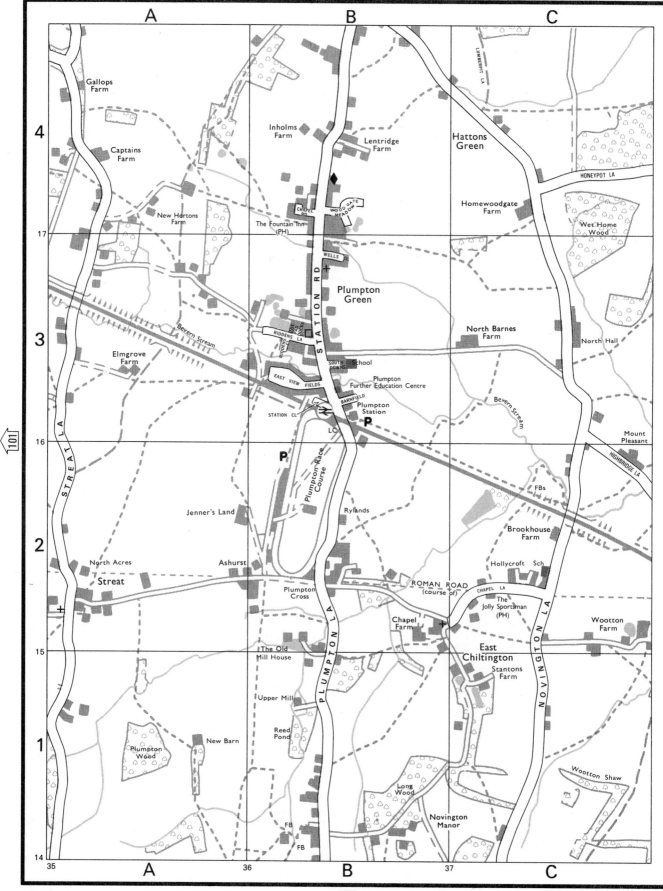

A   B   C

Gallops Farm

Captains Farm

Inholms Farm

Lentridge Farm

Hattons Green

LUMBERPIT LA

HONEYPOT LA

New Hortons Farm

CHAPEL RD

WOODGATE MEADOW

Homewoodgate Farm

Wet Home Wood

The Fountain Inn (PH)

17

WELLS CL

Plumpton Green

STATION RD

North Barnes Farm

North Hall

Elmgrove Farm

Bevern Stream

RIDDENS LA

EDGE END ROAD

SOUTH DOWNS

School

Plumpton Further Education Centre

Bevern Stream

3

EAST VIEW FIELDS

BARNFIELD

Plumpton Station

STATION CL

P

16

LC

Mount Pleasant

HIGHBRIDGE LA

P

Plumpton Race Course

FBs

Jenner's Land

Rylands

Brookhouse Farm

2

North Acres

Ashurst

Hollycroft Sch

Wootton Farm

Streat

Plumpton Cross

ROMAN ROAD (course of)

CHAPEL LA

The Jolly Sportsman (PH)

NOVINGTON LA

STREAT LA

101

Chapel Farm

East Chiltington

15

The Old Mill House

Stantons Farm

Upper Mill

PLUMPTON LA

1

Plumpton Wood

New Barn

Reed Pond

Long Wood

Novington Manor

Wootton Shaw

FB

FB

14

35   A   36   B   37   C

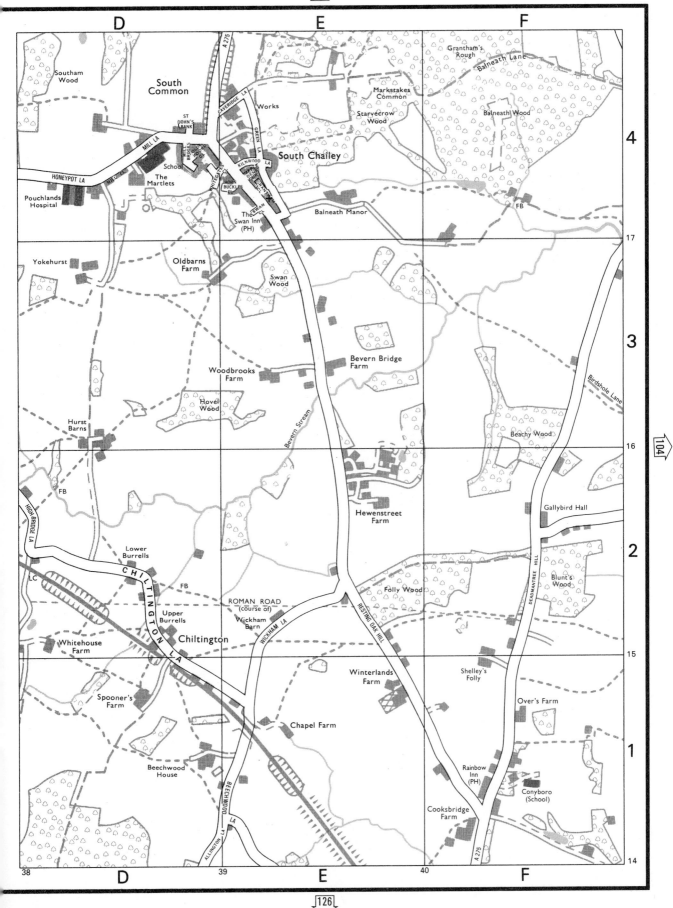

78
103

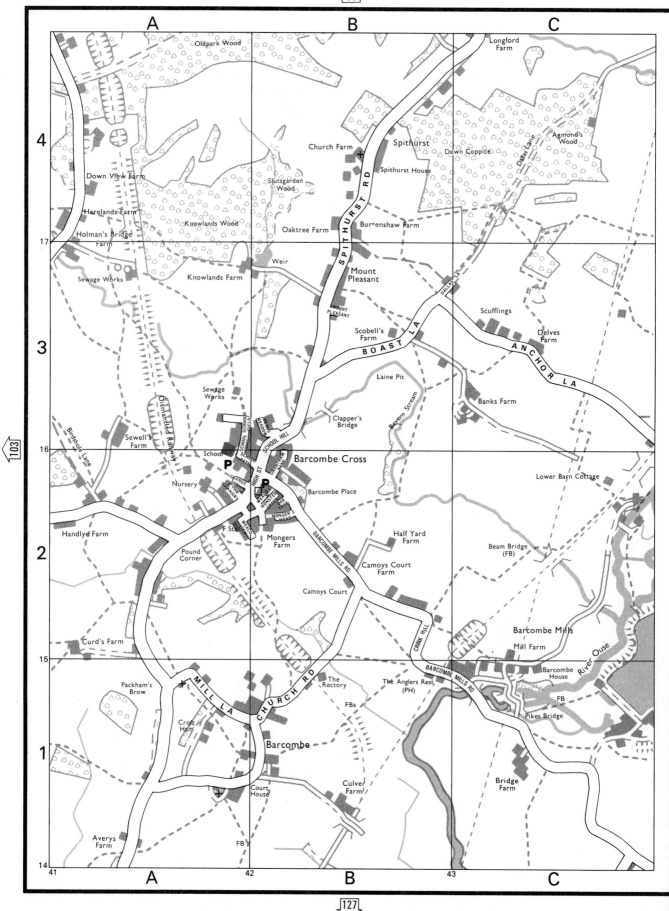

A B C

Oldpark Wood

Longford Farm

Church Farm
Spithurst

Down Coppice

Agmond's Wood

Dallas Lane

4

Down View Farm

Slutsgarden Wood

Spithurst House

Harelands Farm

Knowlands Wood

Oaktree Farm

Burtenshaw Farm

SPITHURST RD

Holman's Bridge Farm

17

Weir

Mount Pleasant

Sewage Works

Knowlands Farm

MOUNT PLEASANT

Scobell's Farm

Scufflings

Delves Farm

Dallas La

BOAST LA

ANCHOR LA

3

Laine Pit

Bevern Stream

Banks Farm

Birdhole Lane

Dismantled Railway

Sewage Works

Clapper's Bridge

Sewell's Farm

SCHOOL SCHOOLS

SCHOOL HILL

16

School

SCHOOL FIELD

Barcombe Cross

Lower Barn Cottage

Nursery

HIGH ST

GRANGE

Barcombe Place

Handlye Farm

GRANGE

WELD LA

MINSTER

MONGER'S MEAD

Half Yard Farm

Beam Bridge (FB)

2

Pound Corner

F Sta

WEALD

Mongers Farm

BARCOMBE MILLS RD

Camoys Court Farm

Curd's Farm

Camoys Court

Barcombe Mills

Mill Farm

CRINK HILL

15

Packham's Brow

MILL LA

The Rectory

The Anglers Rest (PH)

BARCOMBE MILLS RD

Barcombe House

River Ouse

CHURCH RD

FBs

FB

Croft Ham

Pikes Bridge

1

Barcombe

Bridge Farm

Court House

Culver Farm

Averys Farm

FB

14

41 A 42 B 43 C

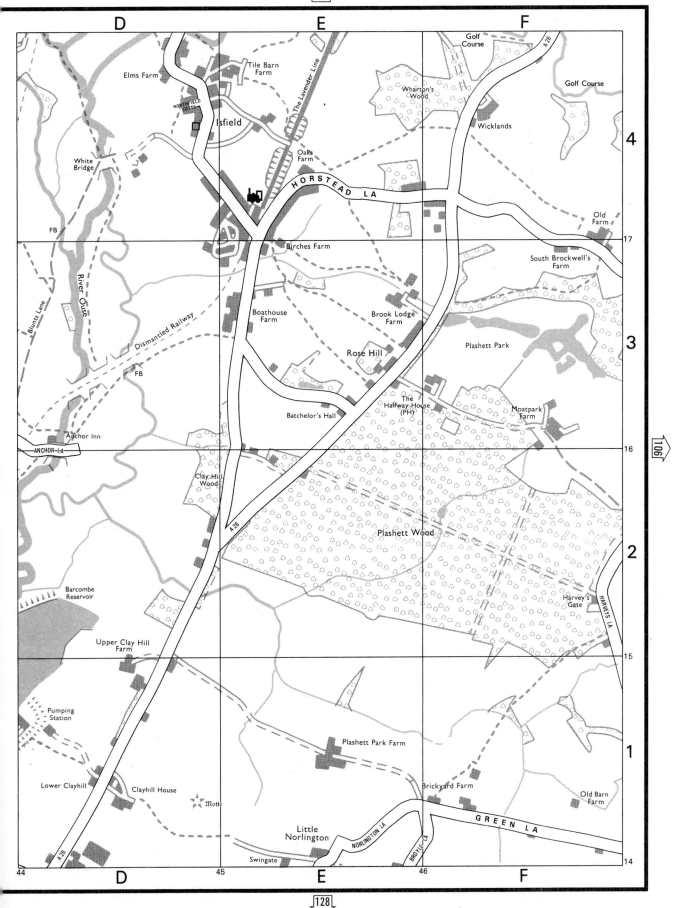

106

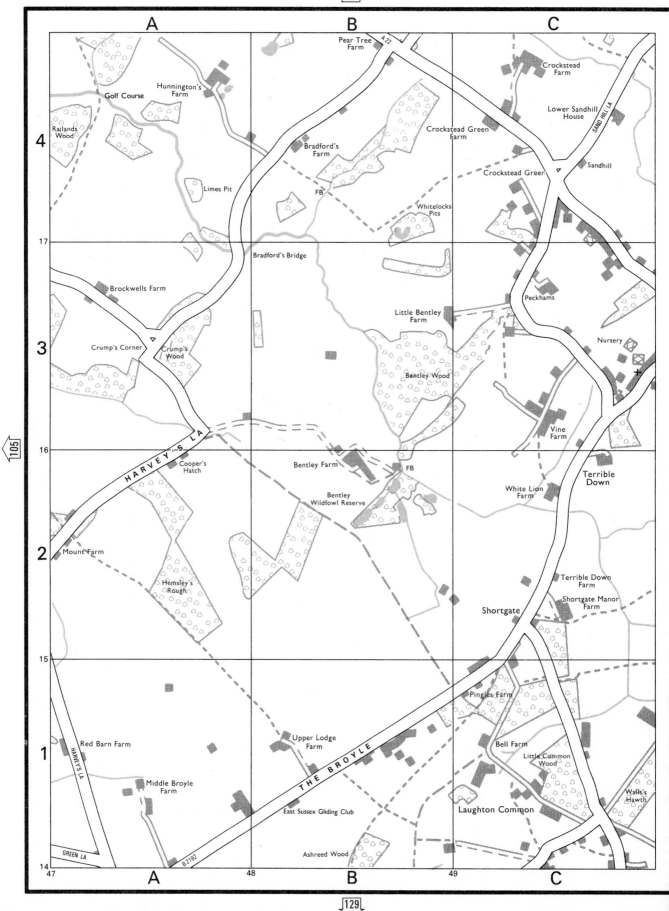

A   B   C

Pear Tree Farm

A 22

Crockstead Farm

Hunnington's Farm

Lower Sandhill House

Golf Course

SAND HILL LA

Railands Wood

Crockstead Green Farm

4

Bradford's Farm

Limes Pit

Crockstead Green

Sandhill

FB

Whitelocks Pits

17

Bradford's Bridge

Brockwells Farm

Peckhams

Little Bentley Farm

Crump's Corner

Crump's Wood

Nursery

3

Bentley Wood

+

HARVEY'S LA

Vine Farm

16

Cooper's Hatch

Bentley Farm

FB

Terrible Down

Bentley Wildfowl Reserve

White Lion Farm

2

Mount Farm

Hemsley's Rough

Terrible Down Farm

Shortgate Manor Farm

Shortgate

15

Pingles Farm

Red Barn Farm

HARVEY'S LA

Upper Lodge Farm

Bell Farm

Little Common Wood

1

THE BROYLE

Middle Broyle Farm

Walls's Hawth

East Sussex Gliding Club

Laughton Common

GREEN LA

B 2192

Ashreed Wood

47   A   48   B   49   C

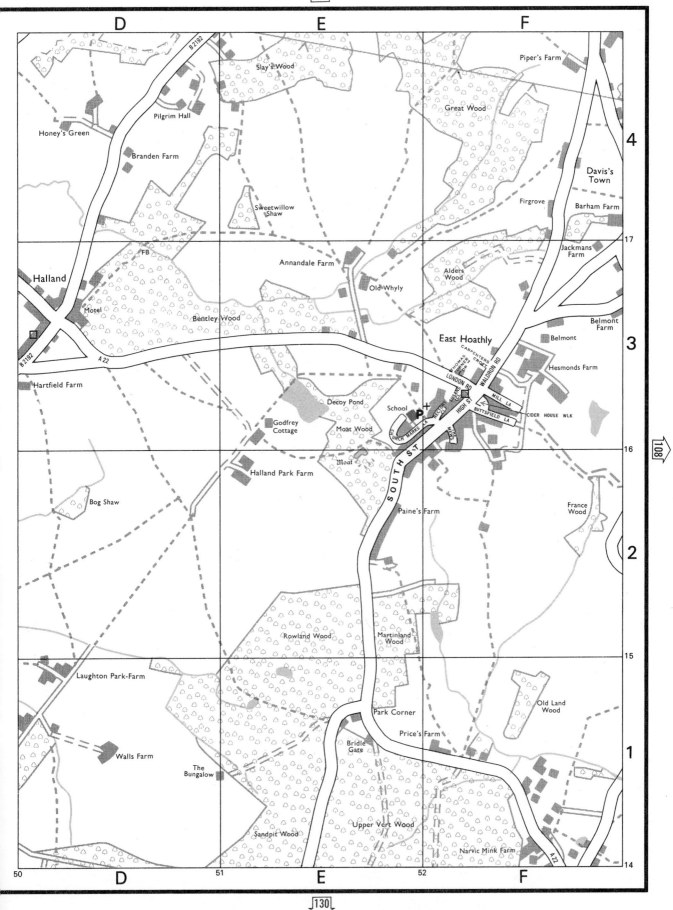

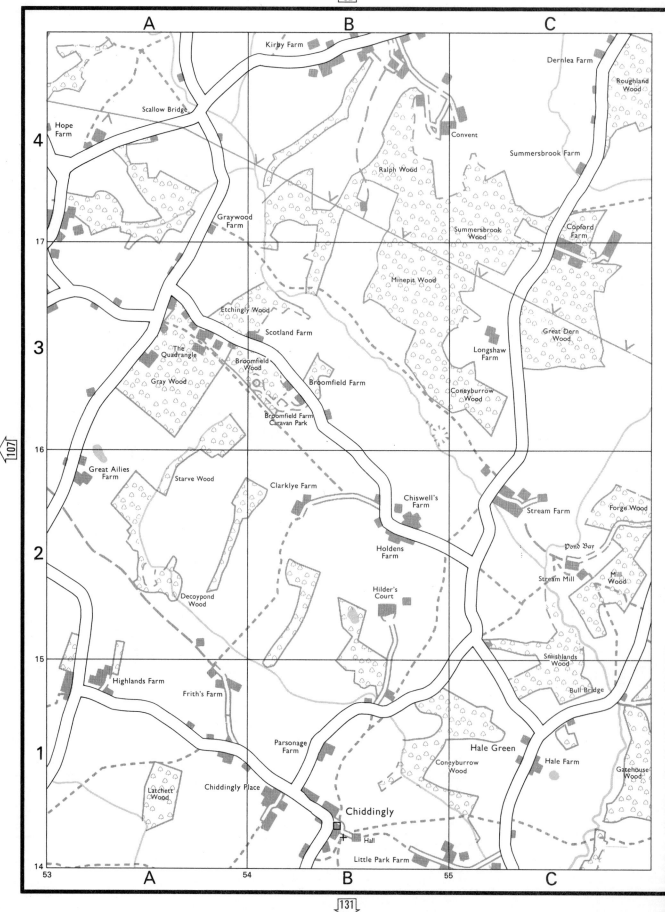

A B C

Kirby Farm

Dernlea Farm

Roughland Wood

Scallow Bridge

Convent

Hope Farm

4

Summersbrook Farm

Ralph Wood

Graywood Farm

Summersbrook Wood

Copford Farm

17

Minepit Wood

Etchingly Wood

Scotland Farm

Great Dern Wood

3

The Quadrangle

Broomfield Wood

Longshaw Farm

Gray Wood

Broomfield Farm

Coneyburrow Wood

Broomfield Farm Caravan Park

16

Great Ailies Farm

Starve Wood

Clarklye Farm

Chiswell's Farm

Stream Farm

Forge Wood

Pond Bay

Holdens Farm

Mill Wood

2

Stream Mill

Decoypond Wood

Hilder's Court

15

Smithlands Wood

Highlands Farm

Bull Bridge

Frith's Farm

Parsonage Farm

Hale Green

Hale Farm

1

Coneyburrow Wood

Gatehouse Wood

Latchett Wood

Chiddingly Place

Chiddingly

Hall

Little Park Farm

14

53 A 54 B 55 C

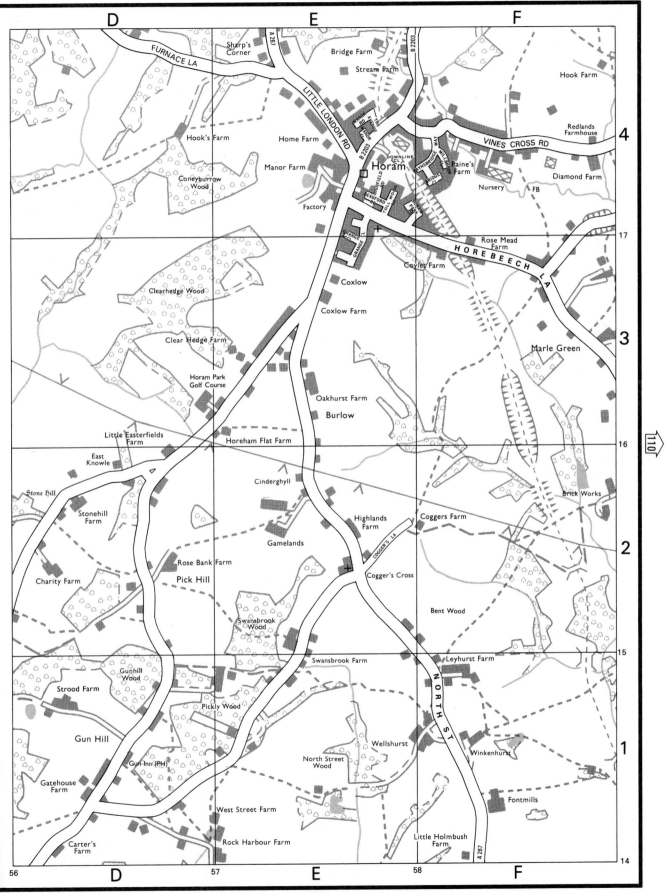

D E F

FURNACE LA
Sharp's Corner
Bridge Farm
Stream Farm
Hook Farm
A 267
B 2203
Hook's Farm
Home Farm
Redlands Farmhouse
VINES CROSS RD
4
LITTLE LONDON RD
MANOR RD
FRAME
MANOR
Manor Farm
Coneyburrow Wood
DOWNLINE CL
Horam
AYNSBRIDGE RD
KYM MILLBROOK
Paine's Farm
Diamond Farm
HIGHFIELD RD
Nursery
FB
Factory
BEAUFORD
BRIDGE CL
TOLL WOOD
HORAM PARK
GRANGE CL
Rose Mead Farm
17
GRANGE CL
HOREBEECH LA
Coylet Farm
Coxlow
Clearhedge Wood
Coxlow Farm
Clear Hedge Farm
Marle Green
3
Horam Park Golf Course
Oakhurst Farm
Burlow
Little Easterfields Farm
Horeham Flat Farm
16
East Knowle
Brick Works
Stone Hill
Cinderghyll
Coggers Farm
Stonehill Farm
Highlands Farm
COGGER'S LA
2
Gamelands
Charity Farm
Rose Bank Farm
Pick Hill
Cogger's Cross
Bent Wood
Swansbrook Wood
Swansbrook Farm
Leyhurst Farm
15
Gunhill Wood
NORTH ST
Strood Farm
Pickly Wood
Gun Hill
Wellshurst
Winkenhurst
1
Gun Inn (PH)
North Street Wood
Fontmills
Gatehouse Farm
West Street Farm
Little Holmbush Farm
Carter's Farm
Rock Harbour Farm
A 267
14

56 D 57 E 58 F

110

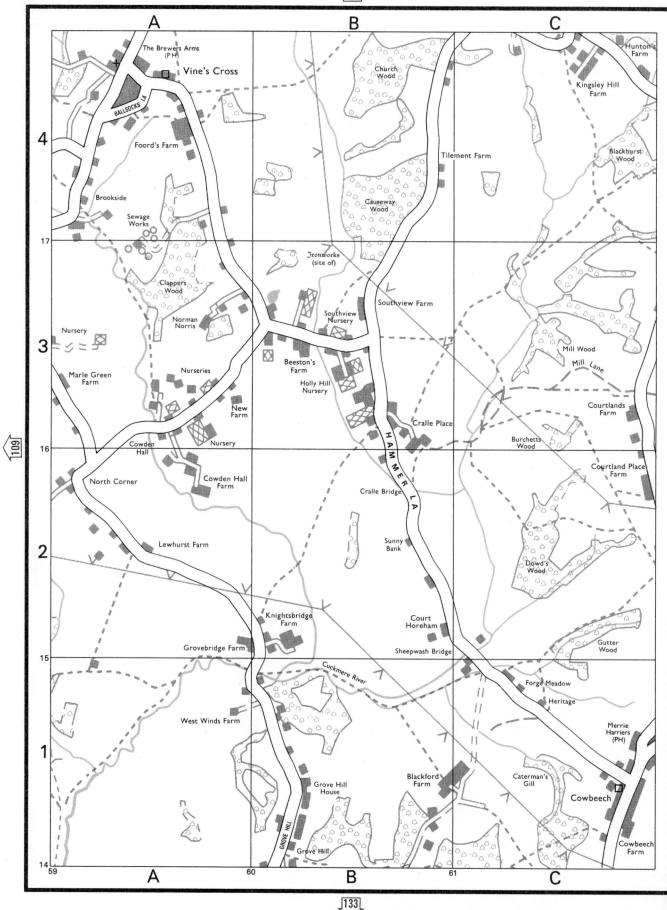

A B C

The Brewers Arms (P H)
Vine's Cross
BALLSOCKS LA
+

Church Wood

Hunton's Farm

Kingsley Hill Farm

Foord's Farm

Tilement Farm

Blackhurst Wood

4

Brookside

Causeway Wood

Sewage Works

17

Ironworks (site of)

Clappers Wood

Southview Farm

Norman Norris

Southview Nursery

Mill Wood

Mill Lane

Nursery

Nurseries

Beeston's Farm

Holly Hill Nursery

Courtlands Farm

3

Marle Green Farm

New Farm

Cralle Place

Burchetts Wood

H A M M E R   L A

Cowden Hall

Nursery

Courtland Place Farm

16

North Corner

Cowden Hall Farm

Cralle Bridge

Lewhurst Farm

Sunny Bank

Dowd's Wood

2

Knightsbridge Farm

Court Horeham

Gutter Wood

Grovebridge Farm

Sheepwash Bridge

15

Cuckmere River

Forge Meadow

Heritage

West Winds Farm

Merrie Harriers (PH)

1

Grove Hill House

Blackford Farm

Caterman's Gill

Cowbeech

GROVE HILL

Grove Hill

Cowbeech Farm

14

59   A   60   B   61   C

109

133

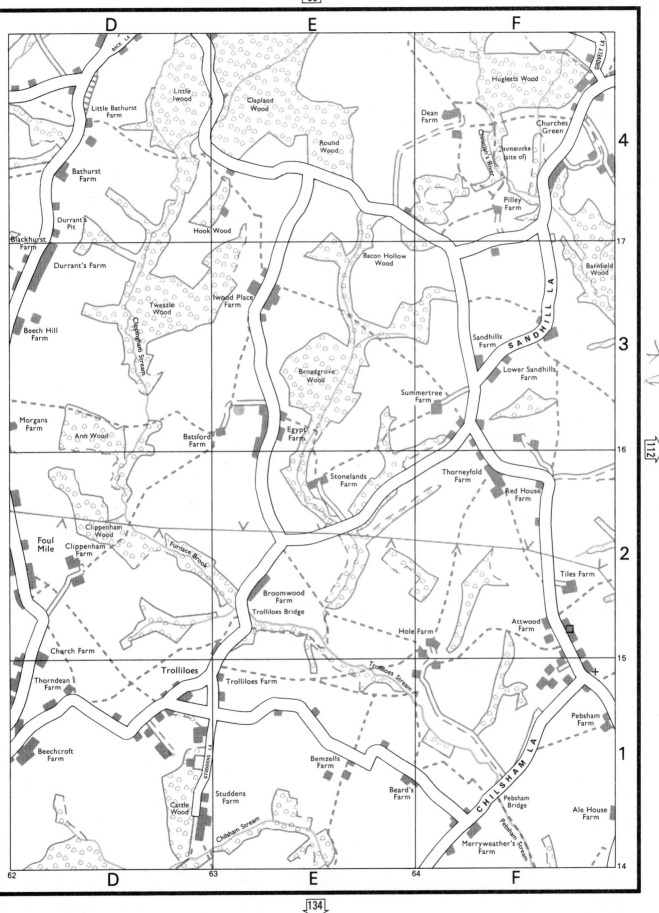

D   E   F

BACK LA

GROVELY LA

Little Iwood

Little Bathurst Farm

Clapland Wood

Hugletts Wood

Dean Farm

Churches Green

4

Round Wood

Christian's River

Ironworks (site of)

Bathurst Farm

Durrant's Pit

Pilley Farm

Blackhurst Farm

Hook Wood

17

Durrant's Farm

Bacon Hollow Wood

Barnfield Wood

Beech Hill Farm

Tweazle Wood

Iwood Place Farm

Clippingham Stream

Sandhills Farm

SANDHILL LA

3

Broadgrove Wood

Lower Sandhills Farm

Morgans Farm

Ann Wood

Batsford Farm

Egypt Farm

Summertree Farm

16

Stonelands Farm

Thorneyfold Farm

Red House Farm

Clippenham Wood

Foul Mile

Clippenham Farm

Furnace Brook

2

Tiles Farm

Broomwood Farm

Trolliloes Bridge

Hole Farm

Attwood Farm

Church Farm

15

Trolliloes

Trolliloes Farm

Trolliloes Stream

Pebsham Farm

Thorndean Farm

STUDDENS LA

1

Beechcroft Farm

Bemzells Farm

Beard's Farm

CHILSHAM LA

Pebsham Bridge

Ale House Farm

Studdens Farm

Cattle Wood

Chilsham Stream

Merryweather's Farm

Pebsham Stream

14

62   D   63   E   64   F

112

86

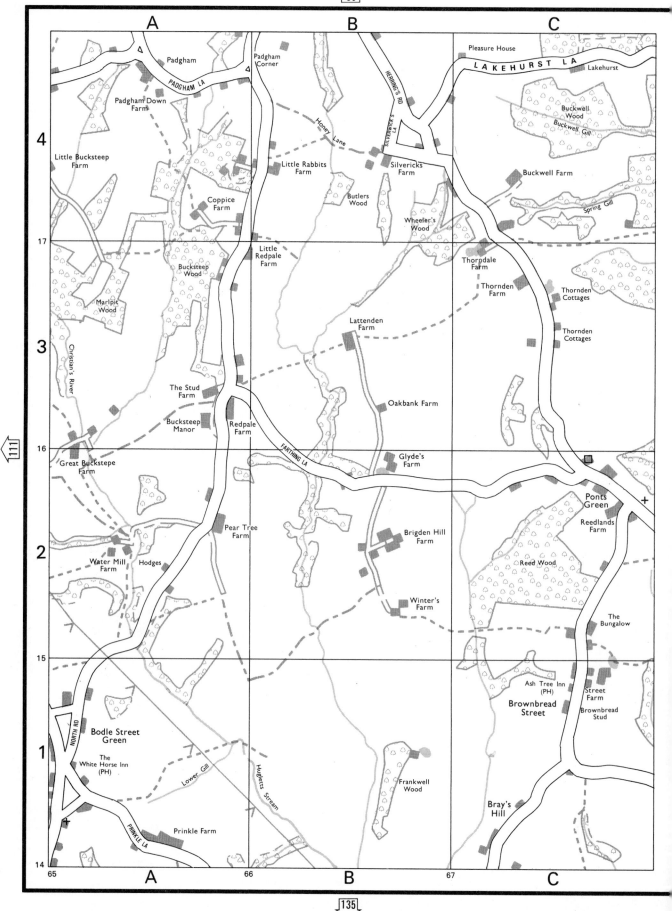

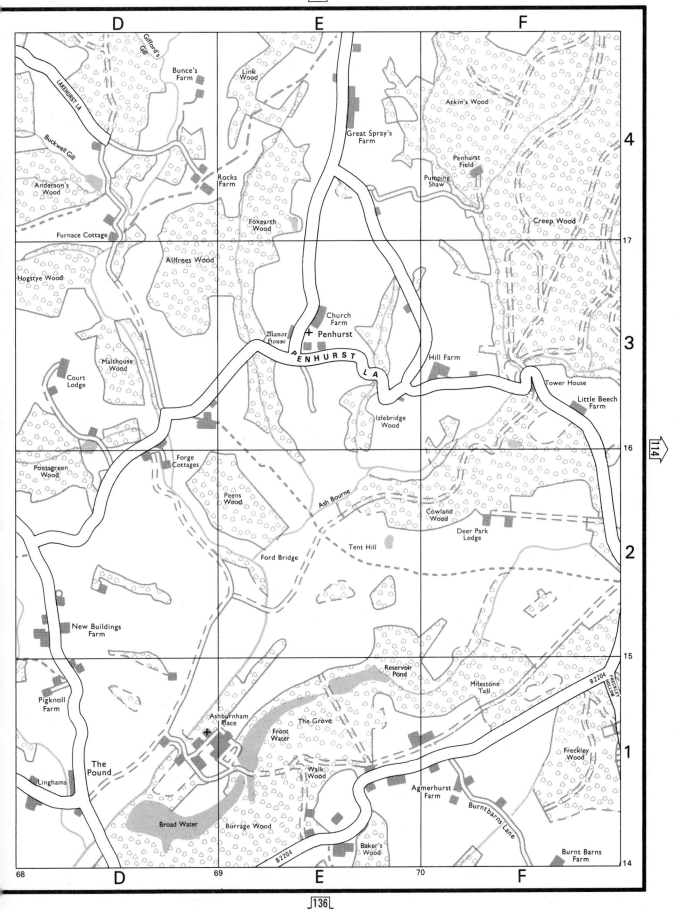

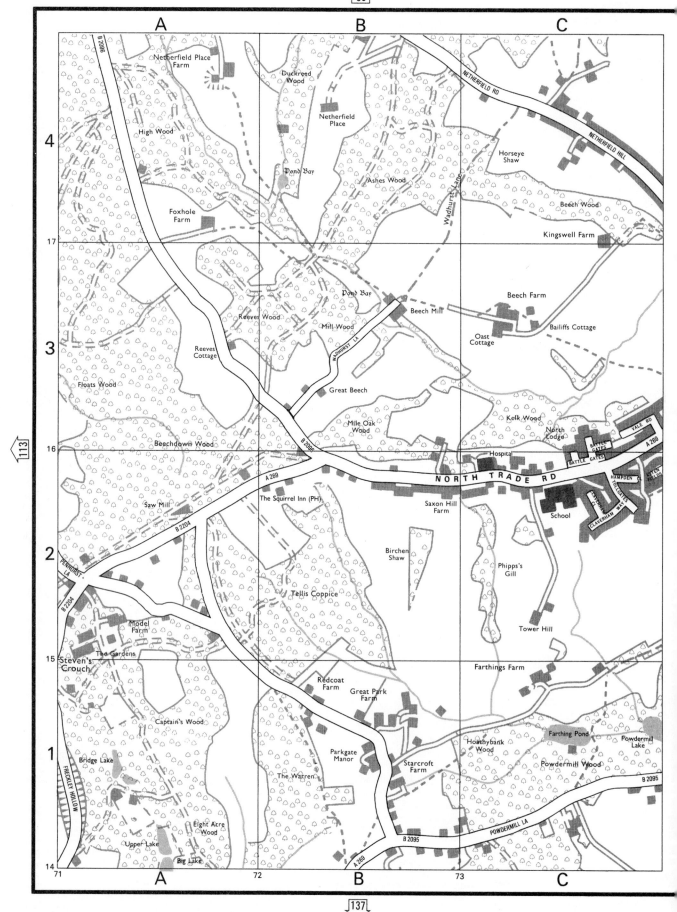

A B C

4

17

3

16

2

15

1

14

71 72 73

A B C

B 2096
Netherfield Place Farm
High Wood
Foxhole Farm
Duckreed Wood
Netherfield Place
Pond Bay
Ashes Wood
NETHERFIELD RD
NETHERFIELD HILL
Horseye Shaw
Beech Wood
Kingswell Farm
Wadhurst Lane
Reeves Wood
Mill Wood
Pond Bay
Beech Mill
WADHURST LA
Reeves Cottage
Floats Wood
Great Beech
Mile Oak Wood
Beech Farm
Oast Cottage
Bailiffs Cottage
Kelk Wood
North Lodge
VALE RD
A 269
B 2096
Beechdown Wood
Hospital
BATTLE GATES
BATTLE GATES
A 269
Saw Mill
The Squirrel Inn (PH)
NORTH TRADE RD
Saxon Hill Farm
HAMPDEN
TOLLGATES
CLAVERHAM WAY
School
B 2204
PENHURST LA
B 2204
Birchen Shaw
Phipps's Gill
Tellis Coppice
Tower Hill
Model Farm
The Gardens
Steven's Crouch
Farthings Farm
Redcoat Farm
Great Park Farm
Captain's Wood
Hoathybank Wood
Farthing Pond
Powdermill Lake
Powdermill Wood
FRECKLEY HOLLOW
Bridge Lake
Parkgate Manor
The Warren
Starcroft Farm
B 2095
POWDERMILL LA
B 2095
Eight Acre Wood
Upper Lake
Big Lake
A 269
B 2095

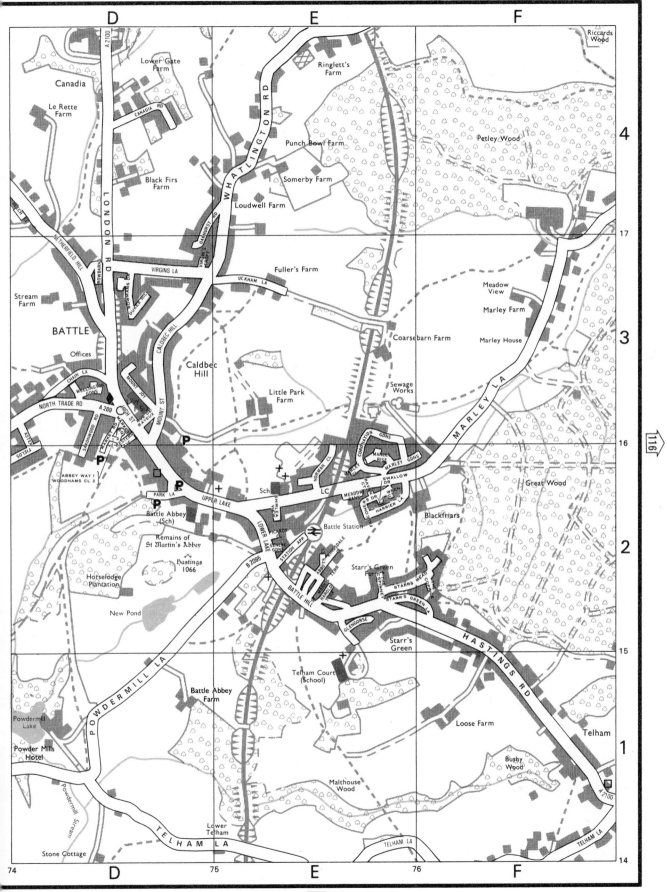

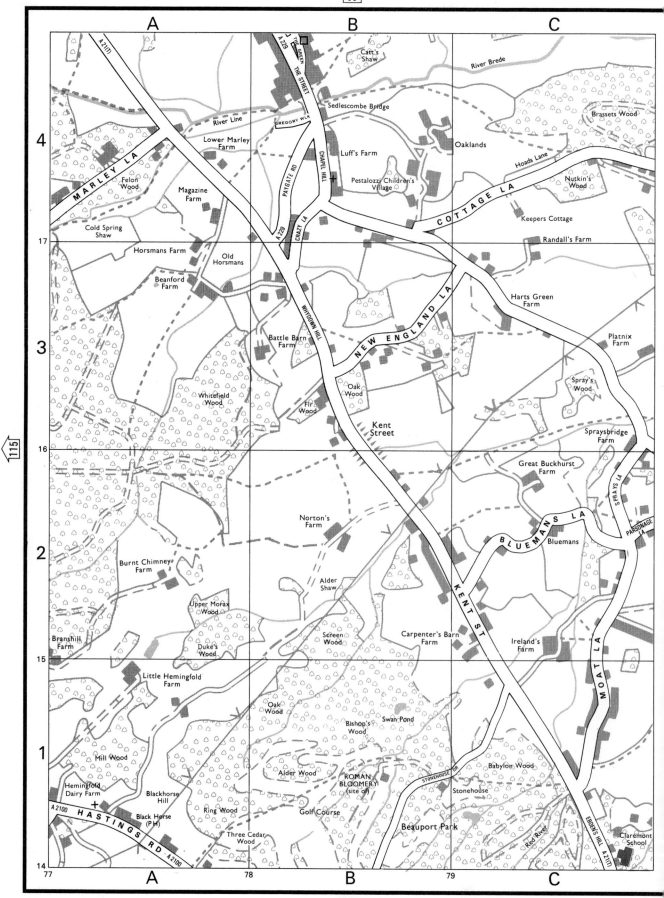

A   B   C

4

17

3

16

2

15

1

14

77   78   79

A21(T)
MARLEY LA
River Line
Lower Marley Farm
Felon Wood
Magazine Farm
Cold Spring Shaw
Horsmans Farm
Old Horsmans
Beanford Farm
Whitefield Wood
Burnt Chimney Farm
Upper Morax Wood
Duke's Wood
Branshill Farm
Little Hemingfold Farm
Mill Wood
Hemingfold Dairy Farm
Blackhorse Hill
Black Horse (PH)
A 2100
HASTINGS RD
A 2100
Three Cedar Wood
Ring Wood

THE GREEN
A 229
THE STREET
GREGORY WLK
Sedlescombe Bridge
Luff's Farm
PAYGATE RD
CHAPEL HILL
Pestalozzi Children's Village
A 229
CRAZY LA
WHYDOWN HILL
Battle Barn Farm
Fir Wood
Oak Wood
Kent Street
Norton's Farm
Alder Shaw
Screen Wood
Oak Wood
Bishop's Wood
Alder Wood
ROMAN BLOOMERY (site of)
Golf Course
Swan Pond

Catt's Shaw
River Brede
Brassets Wood
Oaklands
Hoads Lane
Nutkin's Wood
COTTAGE LA
Keepers Cottage
Randall's Farm
Harts Green Farm
NEW ENGLAND LA
Platnix Farm
Spray's Wood
Spraysbridge Farm
Great Buckhurst Farm
SPRAYS LA
PARSONAGE LA
BLUEMANS LA
Bluemans
KENT ST
Carpenter's Barn Farm
Ireland's Farm
MOAT LA
Babylon Wood
STONEHOUSE DR
Stonehouse
Beauport Park
Red River
EBDENS HILL
A21(T)
Claremont School

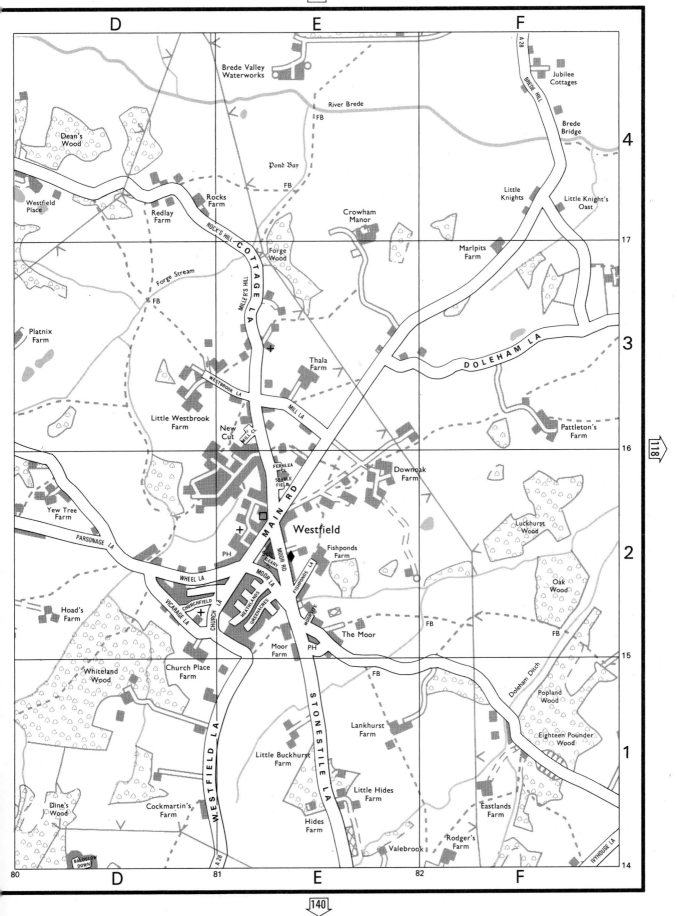

D — E — F

Brede Valley Waterworks

River Brede

FB

Pond Bay

FB

Dean's Wood

Westfield Place

Rocks Farm

Redlay Farm

ROCK'S HILL COTTAGE LA

MILLER'S HILL

Forge Wood

Crowham Manor

Forge Stream

FB

Platnix Farm

WESTBROOK LA

MILL LA

Thala Farm

Little Westbrook Farm

New Cut

MILL CL

FERNLEA CL

SEABLE FIELD

Downoak Farm

A 28

BREDE HILL

Jubilee Cottages

Brede Bridge

Little Knights

Little Knight's Oast

Marlpits Farm

DOLEHAM LA

Pattleton's Farm

Luckhurst Wood

Oak Wood

Yew Tree Farm

PARSONAGE LA

WHEEL LA

VICARAGE LA

CHURCHFIELD

CHURCH LA

MAIN RD

Westfield

PH

Sch

GEARY RD

MOOR RD

MOOR LA

HEATHLANDS

GRESN AC CRES

FISHPONDS LA

Fishponds Farm

MOOR SIDE

The Moor

PH

FB

FB

Hoad's Farm

Whiteland Wood

Church Place Farm

Moor Farm

WESTFIELD LA

STONESTILE LA

FB

Doleham Ditch

Popland Wood

Eighteen Pounder Wood

Lankhurst Farm

Little Buckhurst Farm

Little Hides Farm

Hides Farm

Eastlands Farm

Rodger's Farm

Valebrook

Dine's Wood

Cockmartin's Farm

BARDSLOW DOWN

A 28

IVYHOUSE LA

4

17

3

16

2

15

1

14

80 — D — 81 — E — 82 — F

92

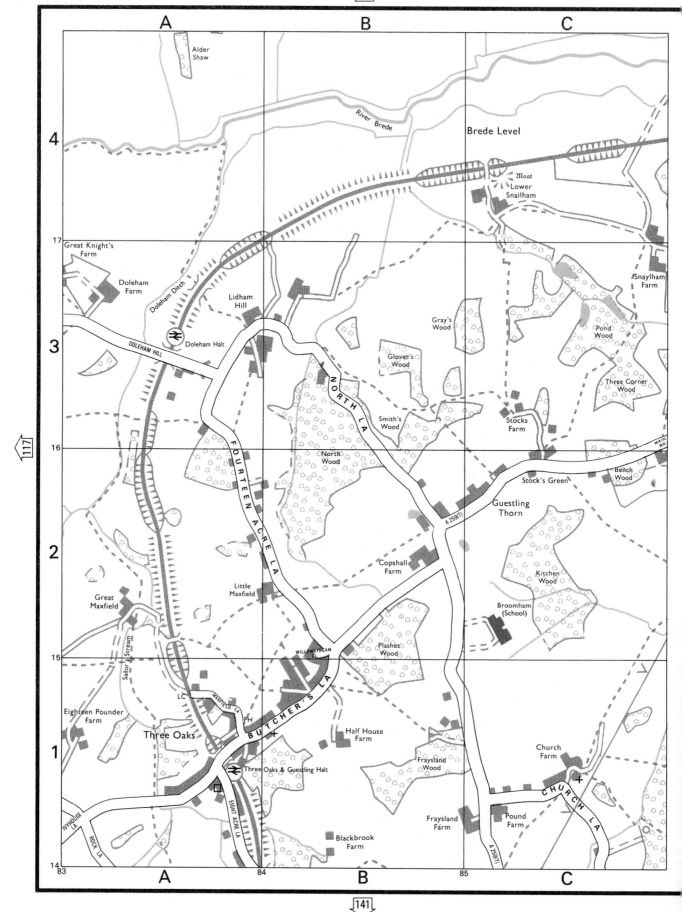

117

141

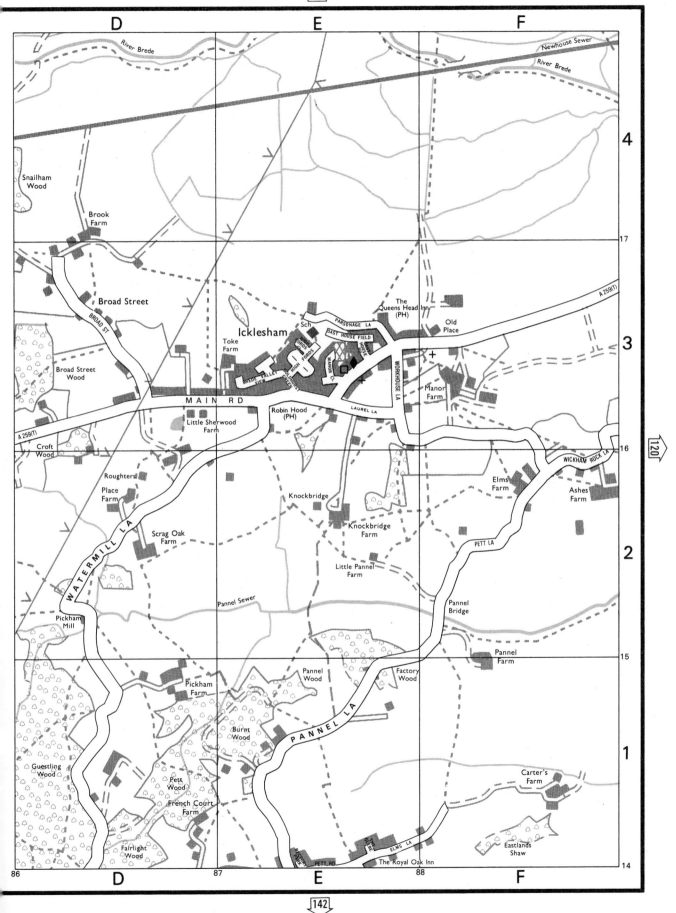

D   E   F

River Brede

Newhouse Sewer

River Brede

4

Snailham
Wood

Brook
Farm

17

Broad Street

A 259(T)

BROAD ST

The Queens Head Inn
(PH)

Old
Place

120

Icklesham

Sch

PARSONAGE LA

OAST HOUSE FIELD

3

Toke
Farm

BREDE VALLEY VIEW

RICHARDS & HIGH FOODS

ROBERTS GREEN

MANOR CL

OAST HOUSE

WORKHOUSE LA

Manor
Farm

Broad Street
Wood

MAIN RD

LAUREL LA

A 259(T)

Robin Hood
(PH)

Little Sherwood
Farm

Croft
Wood

16

WICKHAM ROCK LA

Roughters

Elms
Farm

Ashes
Farm

Place
Farm

Knockbridge

WATERMILL LA

Scrag Oak
Farm

Knockbridge
Farm

PETT LA

2

Little Pannel
Farm

Pannel Sewer

Pannel
Bridge

Pickham
Mill

15

Pannel
Farm

Pickham
Farm

Pannel
Wood

Factory
Wood

PANNEL LA

Burnt
Wood

1

Guestling
Wood

Carter's
Farm

Pett
Wood

French Court
Farm

Fairlight
Wood

PETT RD

THE STREET

ELMS LA

The Royal Oak Inn

Eastlands
Shaw

14

86   D   87   E   88   F

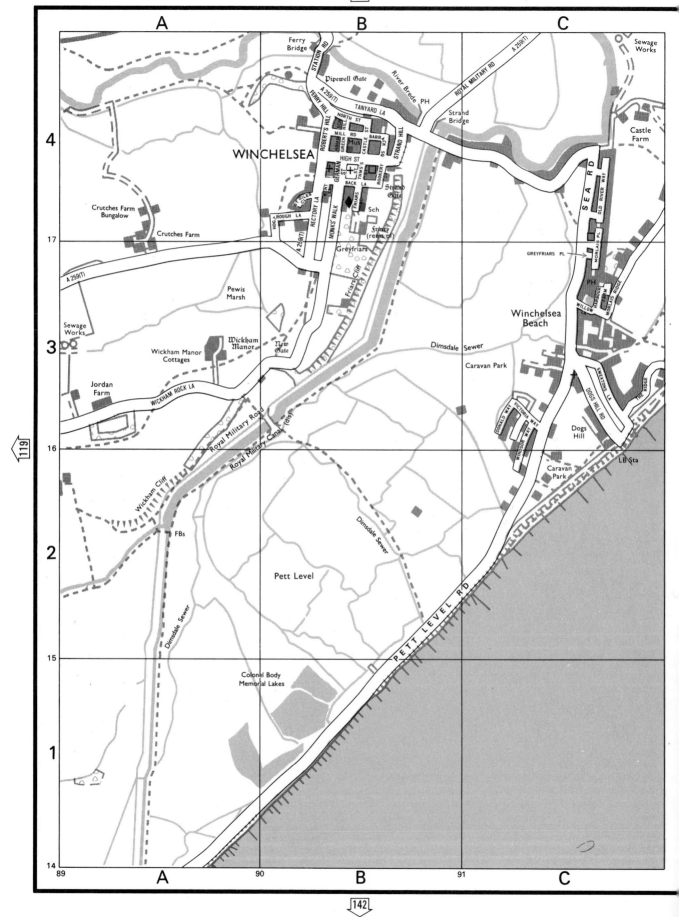

119

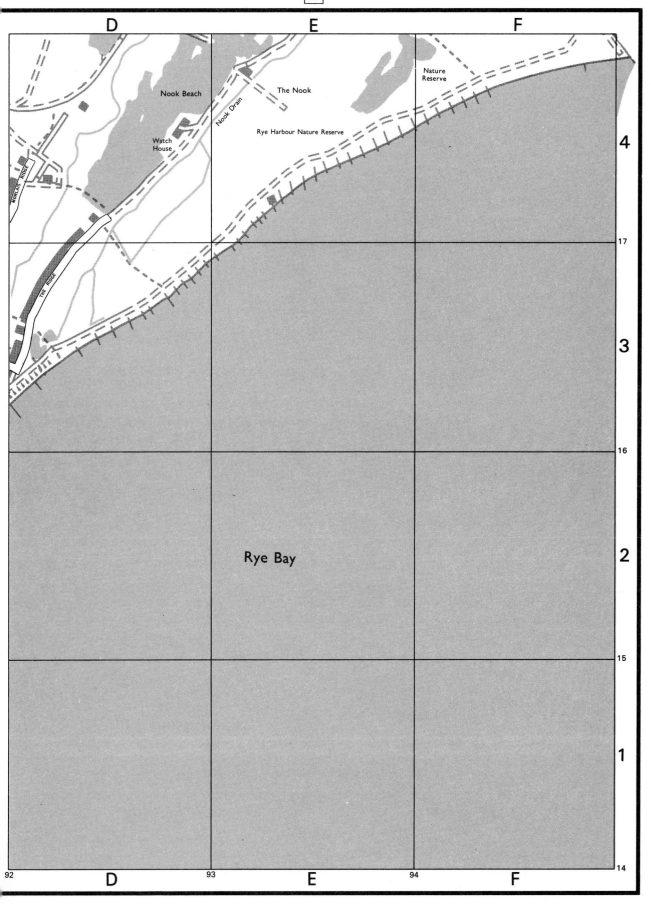

D   E   F

Nook Beach

The Nook

Nature
Reserve

Nook Drain

Watch
House

Rye Harbour Nature Reserve

MORLAIS RIDGE

THE RIDGE

Rye Bay

4

17

3

16

2

15

1

14

D   93   E   94   F

99

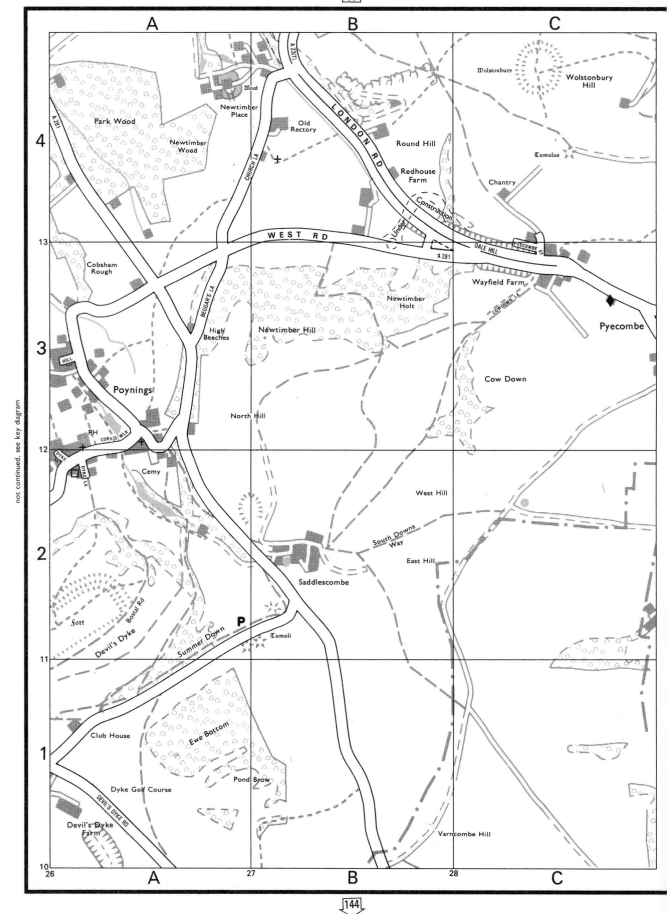

A B C

A 23(T)

Park Wood

Newtimber
Place

Moat

Newtimber
Wood

Old
Rectory

LONDON RD

Round Hill

Redhouse
Farm

Construction

Under

Wolstonbury

Wolstonbury
Hill

Tumulus

Chantry

4

A 281

CHURCH LA

13

Cobsham
Rough

WEST RD

A 281

DALE HILL

PYECOMBE

Pyecombe

BEGGAR'S LA

High
Beeches

Newtimber Hill

Newtimber
Holt

Wayfield Farm

COWDOWN LA

3

HILL

Poynings

North Hill

Cow Down

CORAI'S WLK

RH

West Hill

12

DYKE LA

DYKE LA

Cemy

South Downs
Way

Saddlescombe

East Hill

2

Fort

Bostal Rd

Devil's Dyke

Summer Down

P

Tumuli

11

Club House

Ewe Bottom

Varncombe Hill

1

DEVIL'S DYKE RD

Dyke Golf Course

Pond Brow

Devil's Dyke
Farm

10

26 27 28

A B C

not continued, see key diagram

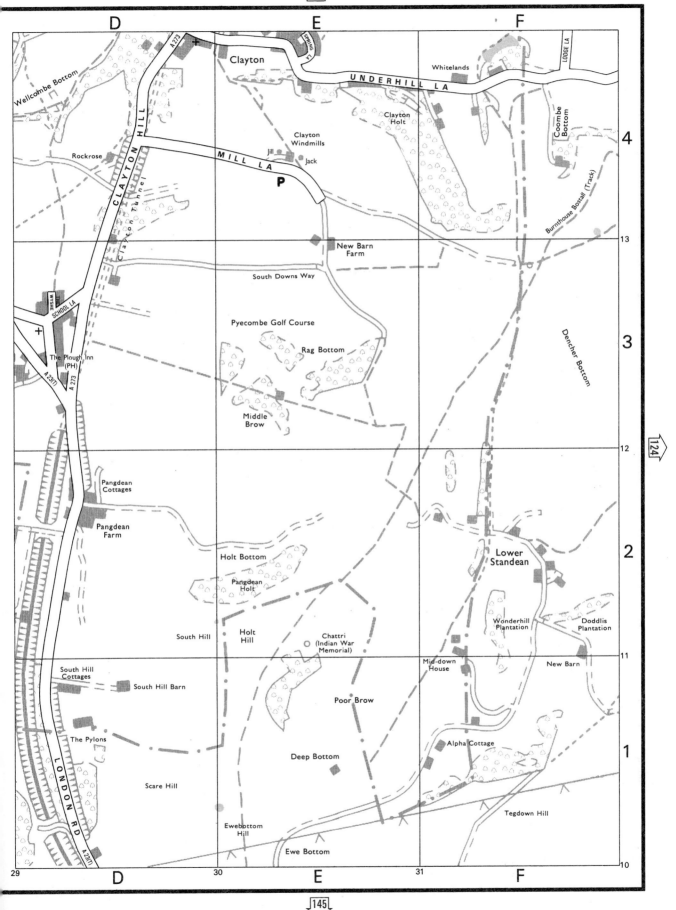

D   E   F

Wellcombe Bottom

CLAYTON HILL

A 273

Clayton

SPRING LA

UNDERHILL LA

Whitelands

LODGE LA

Clayton Holt

Coombe Bottom

Rockrose

Clayton Tunnel

MILL LA

Clayton Windmills

Jill

Jack

P

4

Burnthouse Boxall (Track)

13

New Barn Farm

South Downs Way

Dencher Bottom

THE WYSHE

SCHOOL LA

Pyecombe Golf Course

Rag Bottom

The Plough Inn (PH)

A 23(T)

A 273

Middle Brow

3

12

Pangdean Cottages

Pangdean Farm

Holt Bottom

Lower Standean

2

Pangdean Holt

Wonderhill Plantation

Doddlis Plantation

South Hill

Holt Hill

Chattri (Indian War Memorial)

Mid-down House

New Barn

11

South Hill Cottages

South Hill Barn

Poor Brow

The Pylons

Alpha Cottage

1

Scare Hill

Deep Bottom

LONDON RD

A 23(T)

Ewebottom Hill

Ewe Bottom

Tegdown Hill

29   D   30   E   31   F   10

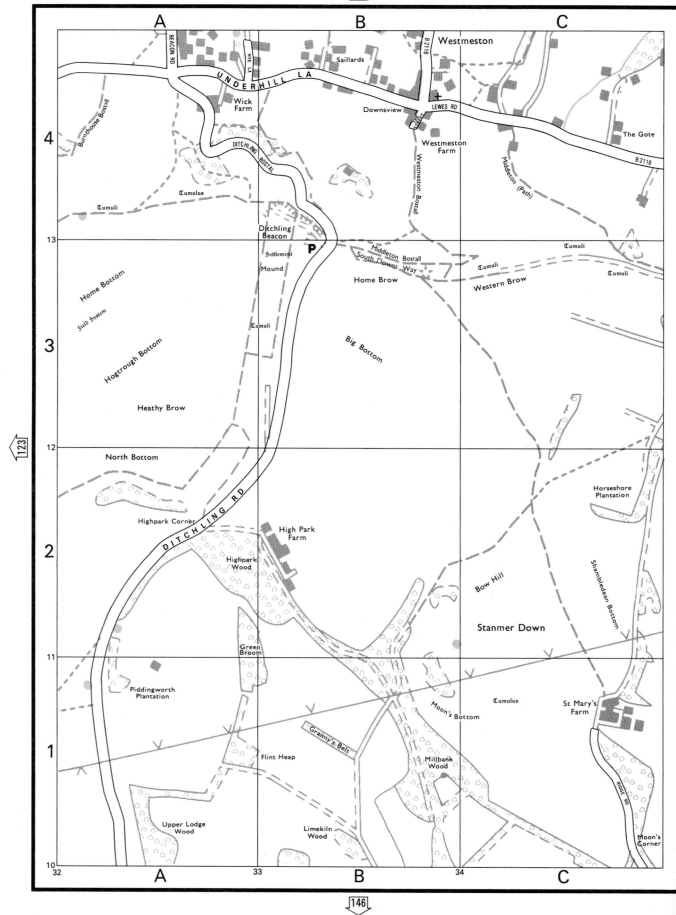

A B C

Westmeston

BEACON RD

NYE LA

B 2116

Saillards

UNDERHILL LA

Wick
Farm

Downsview

LEWES RD

The Gote

4

Burnthouse Bostall

DITCHLING BOSTALL

Westmeston Bostall

Westmeston
Farm

Middleton (Path)

B 2116

Tumuli

Tumulus

Ditchling
Beacon

Settlement

Mound

P

Middleton Bostall
South Downs Way

Tumuli

Tumuli

13

Tumuli

Home Bottom

Home Brow

Western Brow

Tumuli

Field System

Tumuli

Big Bottom

3

Hogtrough Bottom

Heathy Brow

North Bottom

12

Horseshore
Plantation

Highpark Corner

DITCHLING RD

High Park
Farm

Shambledean Bottom

2

Highpark
Wood

Bow Hill

Stanmer Down

Green
Broom

11

Piddingworth
Plantation

Moon's Bottom

Tumulus

St Mary's
Farm

Granny's Belt

1

Flint Heap

Millbank
Wood

RIDGE RD

Upper Lodge
Wood

Limekiln
Wood

Moon's
Corner

10

32

A

33

B

34

C

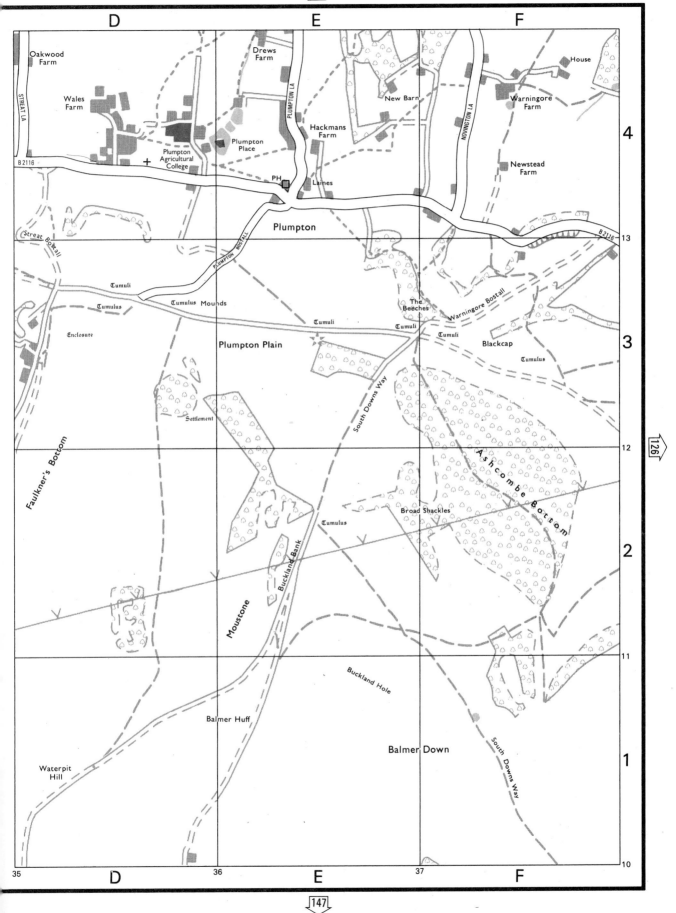

D · E · F

126

Oakwood Farm

STREAT LA

Wales Farm

B 2116

Drews Farm

PLUMPTON LA

Hackmans Farm

Plumpton Place

Plumpton Agricultural College

PH

Laines

New Barn

NOVINGTON LA

House

Warningore Farm

Newstead Farm

4

Plumpton · B 2116 · 13

Streat Bostall

PLUMPTON BOSTALL

Tumuli

Tumulus Mounds

Enclosure

Tumulus

Plumpton Plain

Tumuli

Tumuli

The Beeches

Warningore Bostall

Tumuli

Blackcap

Tumulus

3

Faulkner's Bottom

Settlement

South Downs Way

Ashcombe Bottom

12

Broad Shackles

Tumulus

Buckland Bank

Moustone

2

11

Buckland Hole

Balmer Huff

Balmer Down

South Downs Way

1

Waterpit Hill

35 · D · 36 · E · 37 · F · 10

103

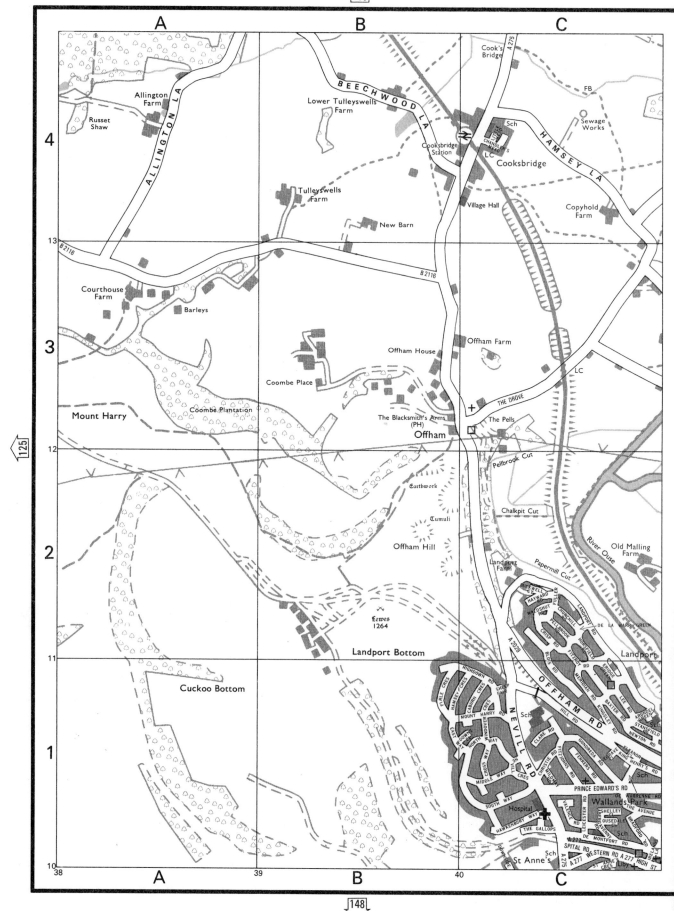

125

148

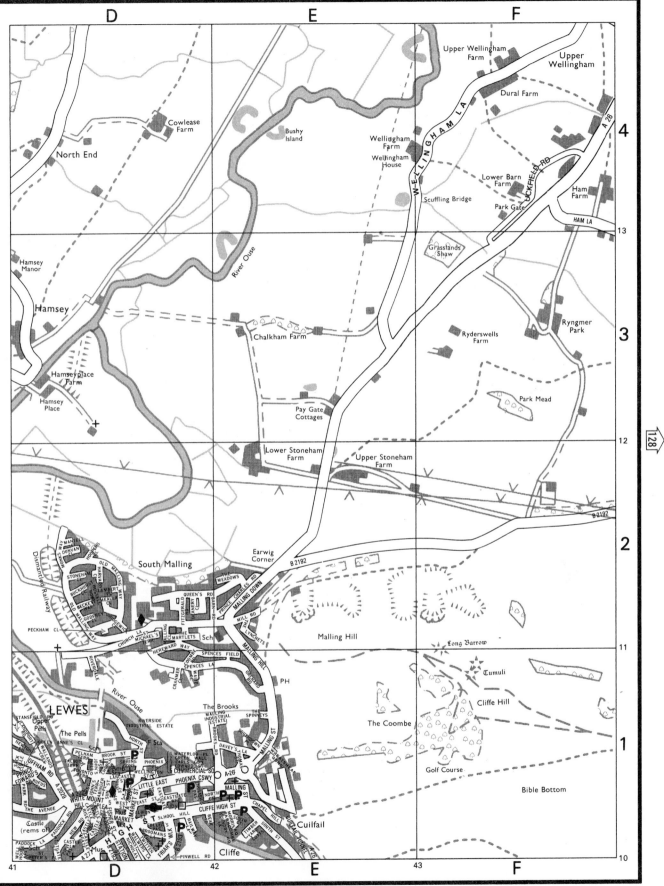

D   E   F

Upper Wellingham Farm

Upper Wellingham

Dural Farm

Cowlease Farm

North End

Bushy Island

Wellingham Farm

Wellingham House

Scuffling Bridge

Lower Barn Farm

Park Gate

Ham Farm

HAM LA

4

13

Hamsey Manor

River Ouse

Grasslands Shaw

Ryderswells Farm

Ryngmer Park

Hamsey

Chalkham Farm

3

Hamseyplace Farm

Hamsey Place

Pay Gate Cottages

Park Mead

12

Lower Stoneham Farm

Upper Stoneham Farm

B 2192

Dismantled Railway

South Malling

Earwig Corner

B 2192

2

MANTELL
WAY
DUNVAN
SNOW
HILL
HOOGERS
OLD MALLING WAY
STONEHAM
BUCKHAM
BECKET
WESTDEAN
GODFREY
PECKHAM CL
OLD MALLING WAY

THE MEADOWS
FITZGERALD
DEANERY
QUEEN'S RD
PRINCE CHARLES RD
BARN RD
MALLING DOWN
MILL RD
LYNCHETS

Malling Hill

Long Barrow

11

CHURCH LA
ST MICHAEL'S
HEREWARD WAY
CRANMER
SPENCES FIELD
SPENCES LA
ORCHARD RD
MALLING HILL

THE MARTLETS Sch

PH

Tumuli

Cliffe Hill

RIVERDALE

River Ouse

The Brooks
MALLING INDUSTRIAL ESTATE
THE SPINNEYS
SOUTH VIEW
MALLING ST

The Coombe

LEWES

STANSFIELD RD
Upper Pells
The Pells

RIVERSIDE INDUSTRIAL ESTATE

DAVEY'S LA
ST THOMAS LA

1

Golf Course

Bible Bottom

P

Phoenix
WELLINGTON
LANCASTER
COMMERCIAL SQ
PHOENIX CSWY
MALLING
CHAPEL HILL

Cuilfail

Castle (rems of)

CLIFFE HIGH ST

Cliffe

A 277

10

41   D   42   E   43   F

128

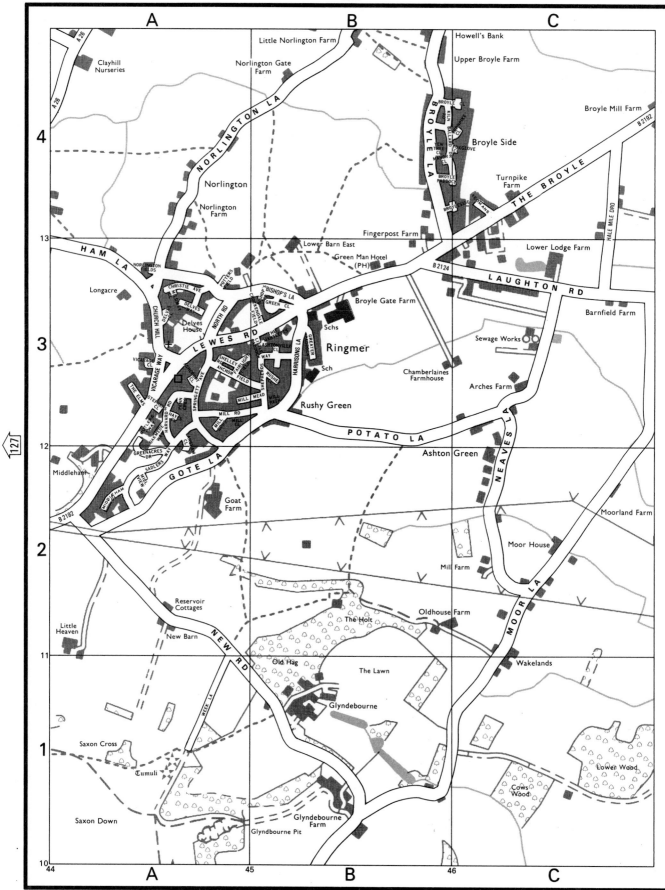

A   B   C

Clayhill Nurseries

A 26

Little Norlington Farm

Norlington Gate Farm

Howell's Bank

Upper Broyle Farm

Broyle Mill Farm

BROYLE LA

BROYLE CL
KILN
BALLARD
SPINNEY
NEW TREE CR
MANOR DR
FOXGLOVE
CL
BROYLE PADDOCK
BROYLESIDE COTT

Broyle Side

Turnpike Farm

THE BROYLE

B 2192

HALE MILE DRO

Norlington

Norlington Farm

NORLINGTON LA

Fingerpost Farm

13

HAM LA

NORLINGTON FIELDS

Lower Barn East

Green Man Hotel (PH)

B 2124

LAUGHTON RD

Lower Lodge Farm

Barnfield Farm

Longacre

CHRISTIE AVE
POTTERS FIELD
BISHOP'S LA
CROWHURST GREEN CL
CROSS KENDALE
DELVES
CHURCH HILL
NORTH RD
LEWES RD

Delves House

Broyle Gate Farm

Schs

Ringmer

Sch

Sewage Works

Barnfield Farm

ARCHES FARM

3

VICARAGE WAY
VICARAGE CL
THE ELMS
STEERS LA
HARRIS RD
SPRINGETT AVE
ANCHOR FIELD
SHELLEY RD
FAIRLIGHT
SHEPHERDS WAY
RUSHEY
HARRISONS LA
GREATER
WILL WATT

MILL MEAD

Chamberlaines Farmhouse

Arches Farm

NEAVES LA

Rushy Green

POTATO LA

Ashton Green

Moorland Farm

Middleham

MIDDLEHAM
GREENACRES DR
SADLERS WAY
MILL VIEW
MILL CL
MILL RD

GOTE LA

B 2192

Goat Farm

Moor House

MOOR LA

Little Heaven

Reservoir Cottages

New Barn

NEW RD

WEEK LA

The Holt

Oldhouse Farm

Old Hag

The Lawn

Wakelands

Saxon Cross

Tumuli

Glyndebourne

Lower Wood

Cows Wood

Saxon Down

Glyndebourne Farm

Glyndebourne Pit

10

44   A   45   B   46   C

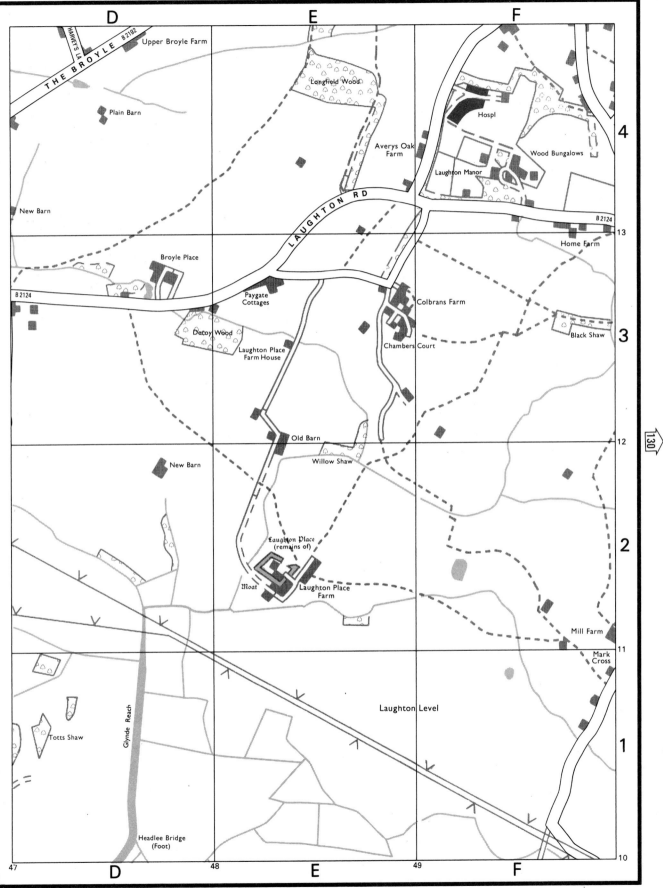

D E F

HARVEY'S LA
THE BROYLE B 2192
Upper Broyle Farm
Plain Barn
New Barn
Longfield Wood
Averys Oak Farm
LAUGHTON RD
Hospl
Laughton Manor
Wood Bungalows
B 2124
Home Farm
13
Broyle Place
Paygate Cottages
Decoy Wood
Laughton Place Farm House
Colbrans Farm
Chambers Court
Black Shaw
3
B 2124
New Barn
Old Barn
Willow Shaw
Mill Farm
12
Laughton Place (remains of)
Moat
Laughton Place Farm
Mark Cross
11
2
Totts Shaw
Glynde Reach
Laughton Level
1
Headlee Bridge (Foot)
10
47 48 49
D E F

130

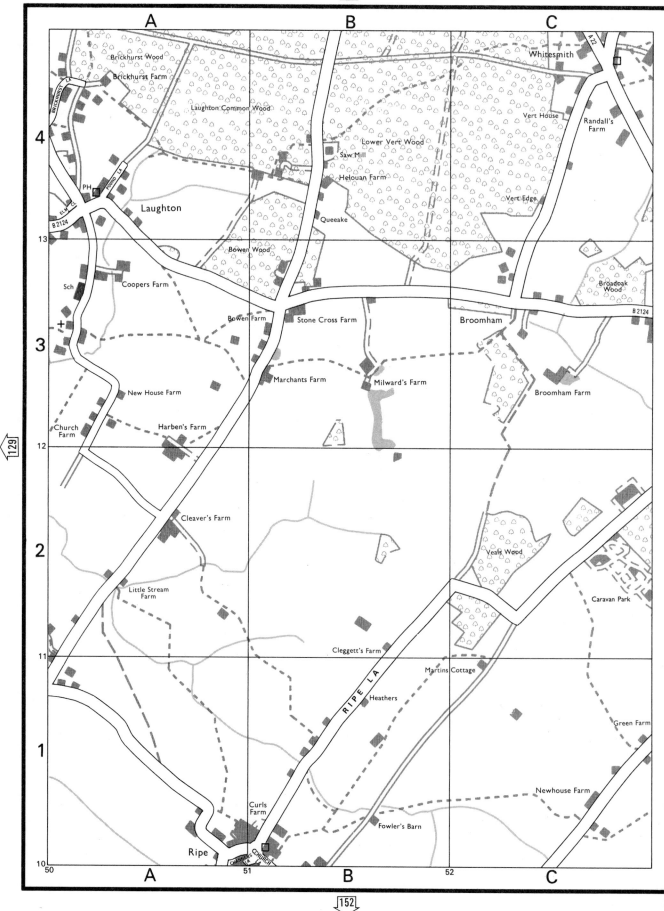

129

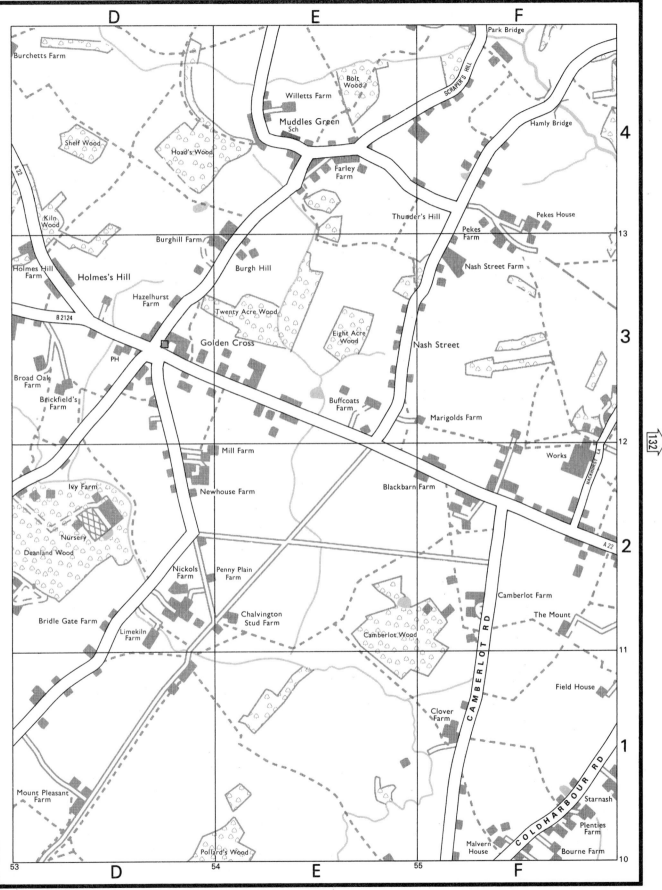

D E F

132

Burchetts Farm

Bolt Wood

Willetts Farm

SCRAPER'S HILL

Park Bridge

Hamly Bridge

Shelf Wood

Hoad's Wood

Muddles Green
Sch

4

Farley Farm

Thunder's Hill

Pekes House

A 22

Kiln Wood

Burghill Farm

Pekes Farm

13

Holmes Hill Farm

Holmes's Hill

Burgh Hill

Nash Street Farm

Hazelhurst Farm

Twenty Acre Wood

Eight Acre Wood

Nash Street

3

B 2124

Golden Cross

PH

Broad Oak Farm

Buffcoats Farm

Marigolds Farm

Brickfield's Farm

Works

12

Mill Farm

Ivy Farm

Newhouse Farm

Blackbarn Farm

HACKHURST LA.

A 22

2

Nursery

Deanland Wood

Nickols Farm

Penny Plain Farm

Camberlot Farm

The Mount

Bridle Gate Farm

Chalvington Stud Farm

Camberlot Wood

CAMBERLOT RD

11

Limekiln Farm

Field House

Clover Farm

1

Mount Pleasant Farm

Starnash

COLDHARBOUR RD

Plenties Farm

Pollard's Wood

Malvern House

Bourne Farm

10

53 D 54 E 55 F

109

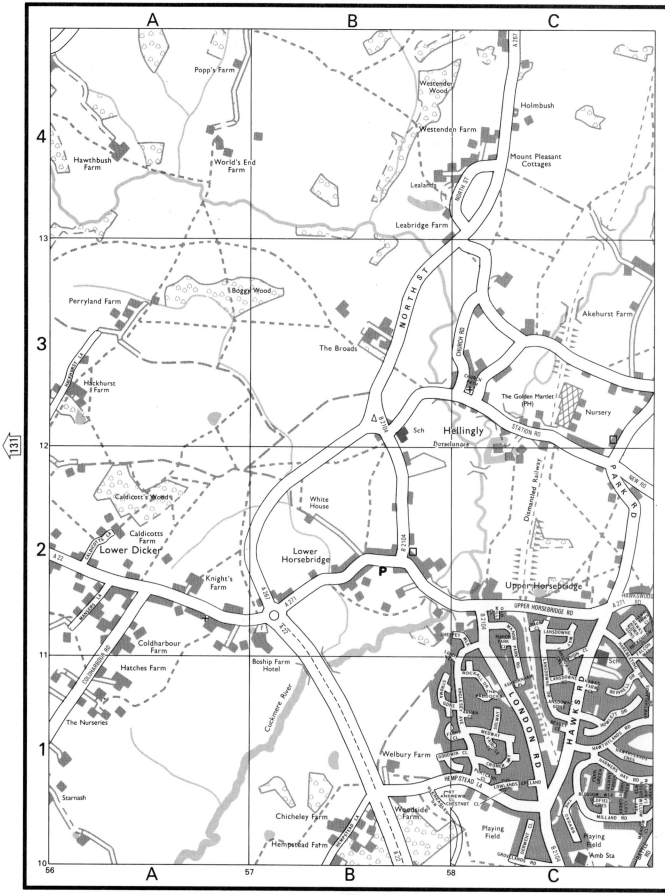

131

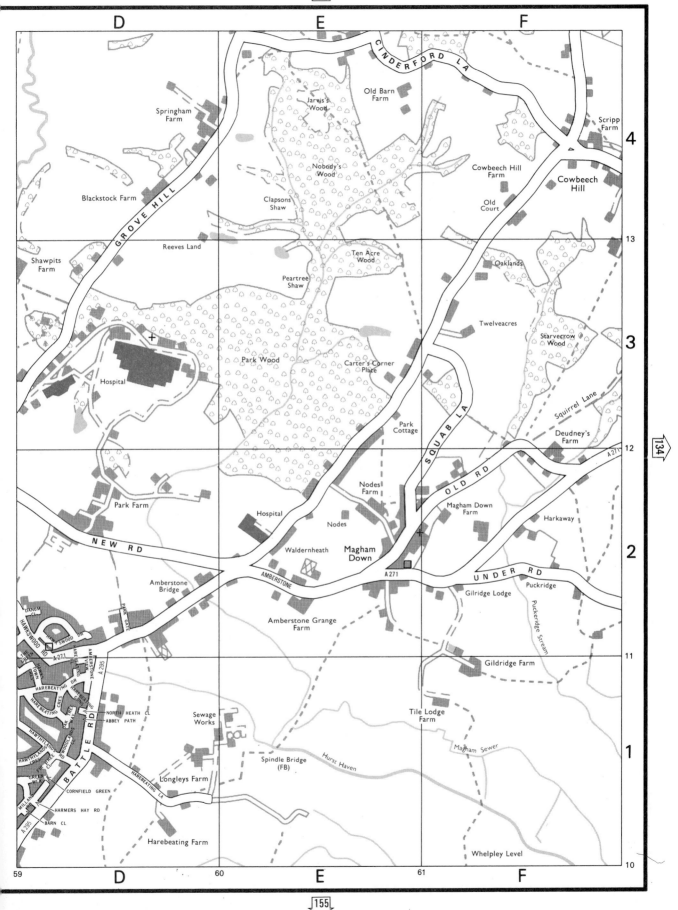

PAGE III STEPHEN/SUE

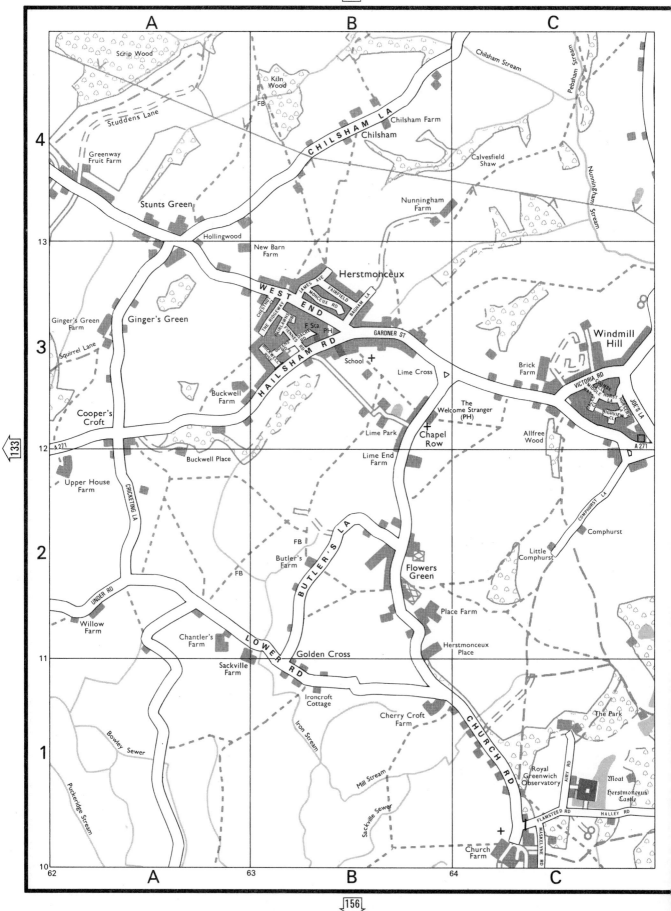

A   B   C

Scrip Wood

Kiln Wood

FB

CHILSHAM LA

Chilsham Stream

Chilsham Farm

Chilsham

4

Studdens Lane

Greenway Fruit Farm

Calvesfield Shaw

Pebsham Stream

Nunningham Stream

Stunts Green

Nunningham Farm

Hollingwood

13

New Barn Farm

Herstmonceux

WEST END

JAMES AVE FAIRFIELD

MONCEUX RD

CHESTNUT

THE RIDGEWAY

PIRLAINES

BAGHAM LA

F Sta PH

GARDNER ST

Windmill Hill

3

Ginger's Green Farm

Ginger's Green

Squirrel Lane

HAILSHAM RD

QUEENS RD

BRICKFIELD

DUCKELL

School

Lime Cross

Brick Farm

VICTORIA RD

COMBE

MIDDLE HURST LA

HIGHVIEW

JOE'S LA

Cooper's Croft

Buckwell Farm

Lime Park

The Welcome Stranger (PH)

Chapel Row

Allfree Wood

A 271

12

A 271

Buckwell Place

Lime End Farm

Upper House Farm

CRICKETING LA

COMPHURST LA

Comphurst

2

FB

FB

Butler's Farm

BUTLER'S LA

Flowers Green

Little Comphurst

UNDER RD

Willow Farm

Chantler's Farm

LOWER RD

Golden Cross

Place Farm

Herstmonceux Place

11

Sackville Farm

Ironcroft Cottage

Iron Stream

Cherry Croft Farm

CHURCH RD

The Park

1

Bowley Sewer

Puckeridge Stream

Mill Stream

Sackville Sewer

Royal Greenwich Observatory

AIRY RD

Moat

Herstmonceux Castle

FLAMSTEED RD

HALLEY RD

MASKELYNE RD

Church Farm

10

62   A   63   B   64   C

133

112

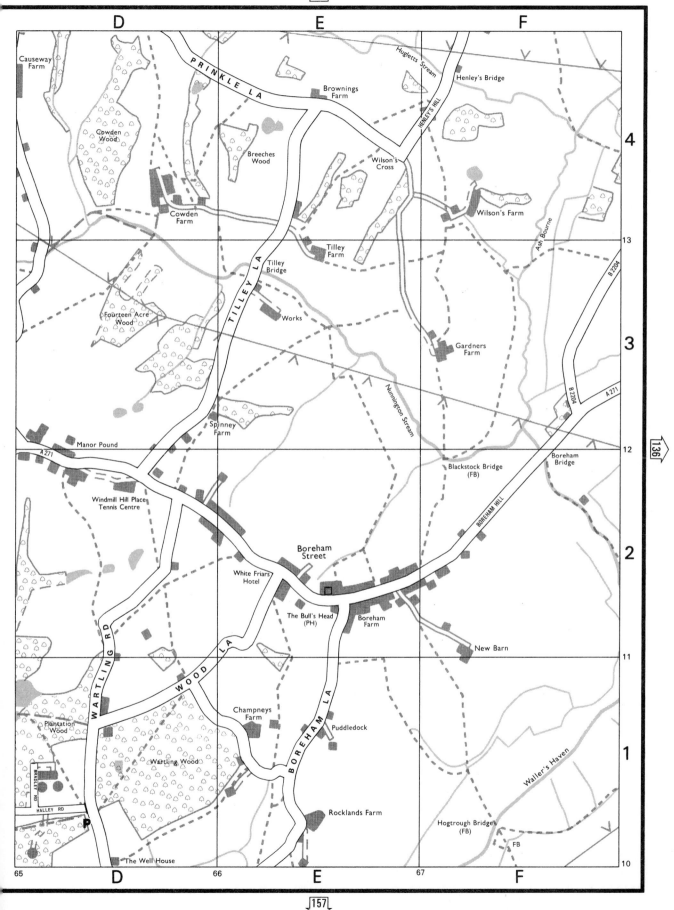

136

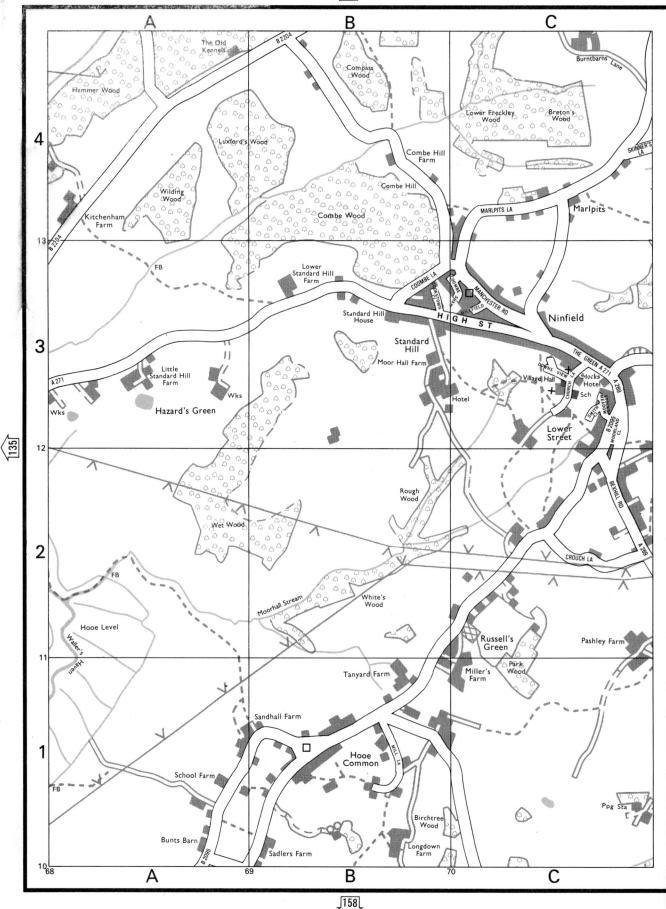

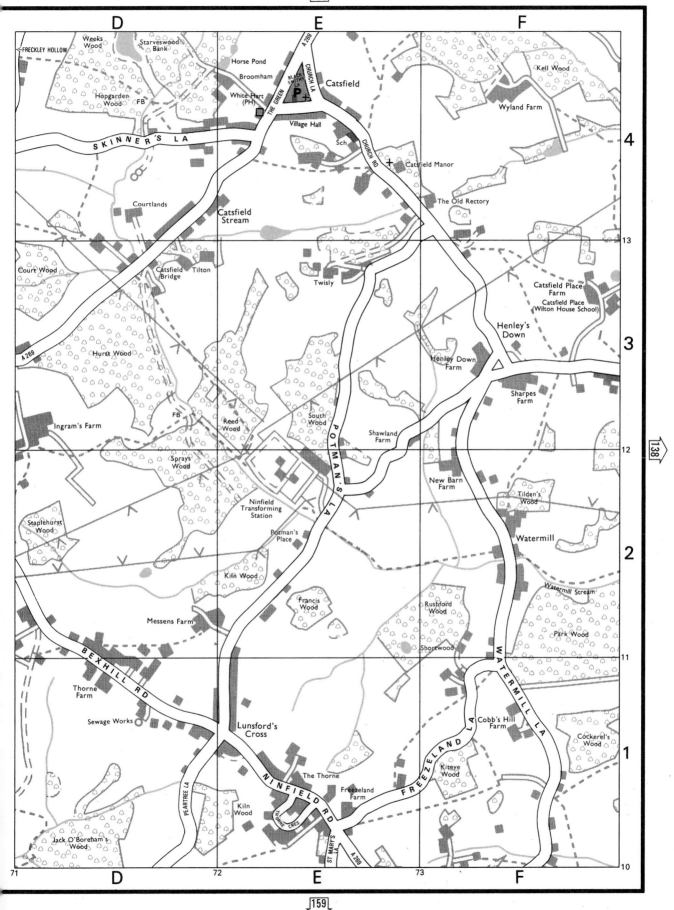

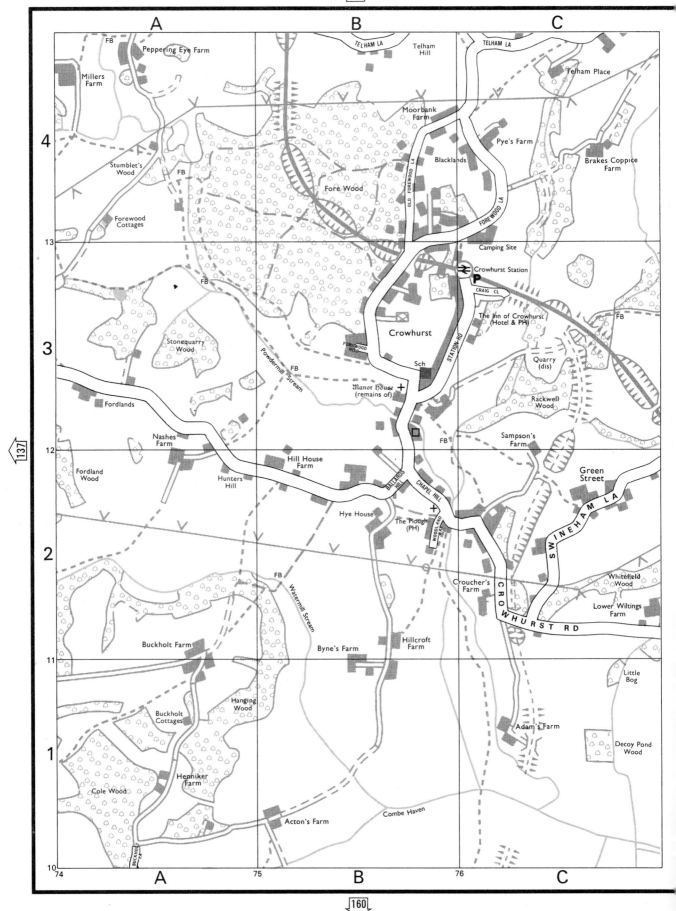

D   E   F

Water Tower
Circle Pond
Crowhurst Park
Crowhurst Park
Long Plantation
New Wood
Park Farm
Marline Wood
Stonebridge Farm
SWINEHAM LA
Park Wood
Chapel Wood
Mayfield Farm
Upper Wilting Farm
Monkham Wood
Redgeland Wood
Dogkennel Wood

A 2100
HASTINGS RD
Breadsell Farm
Wychnour
Maze Pond
BREADSELL LA
Birchen Wood
Hoad's Wood
High Beech
QUEENSWAY
NAPIER RD
HARVEY CL
CHATSFIELD CL
INGLESIDE
Tilekiln
ARM STRONG CL
CUBITT WAY
BRUNEL RD
PAXHILL CL
SILVAN RD
Sch
Church Wood Dr
HIGHFIELD DR
PINEWOOD
JUNIPER WAY
PLOVER HAVEN
Church Wood
WESTMORELAND CL
PH
Hollington
CHURCH IN THE WOOD LA
THE SLIDES
WISHING TREE RD
Robsack Wood
BLUESTONE CL
SWALLOW BANK
BEDGEBURY CL
SALCEY CL
ROBSACK AVE
THE SUTTONS
Rocky Shaw
BECKLEY CL
MAYFIELD LA
BODIAM DR
ICKLESHAM DR
LINTON RD
CROWHURST RD
P
IRONLATCH AVE
WISHING TREE RD
School
DARWELL CL
SPALDING WAY THE
GILLSMAN'S PARK
SPRINGSIDE
B 2092 HARLEY SHUTE RD
FERN RD

Beauport Wood
Red River Wood
Baldslow Wood
Beauport Park Hotel
STONEBRIDGE DR
B 2159
THE RIDGE WEST
Caravan Site
Mon
EBDEN'S HILL
A 21(T)
WESTFIELD LA
MAPLE HURST RD
B 2093
Baldslow
JUNCTION
A 2100 THE RIDGE
WHITWORTH RD
Beauharrow Road
REGENT
BLIDE
FLETCHER CRES
CEDAR AVE
STONELINK CL
TRAFALGAR
HOOVER DR
FAIRLAWN DR
EISENHOWER DR
WARGREAVON AVE
MOORHURST INDUSTRIAL ESTATE
AUGUSTUS WAY
Castleham
CASTLEHAM RD
GRESLEY RD
STANIER RD
THE KESTRELS
FINCHDEAN
SWYNFORD
LANCASTER RD
KENT RD
TAYLOR RD
ADAM RD
CARPENTER DR
HUGHES RD
TRENHAM RD
FREWYN CL
PARSONS CL
HOWLETT CL
Schs
OLD CHURCH RD
MEADOW RD
LINCOLN
BUCHAN RD
ORMEROD
WISHING TREE RD
LOWER GLEN
UPPER CHURCH RD
BELLINGHAM CL
Marline Rd
Schs
HOLLINGTON OLD LA
BLACKMAN AVE
JAMESON RD
BURDEN PL
DYMOND RD
BRISTOL RD
GIBERD RD
OXFORD RD
LEWES RD
COVENTRY RD
WESTERN RD
ADELA RD
CHAMBERS RD
WING
CHARD RD
WISHING TREE RD
REDGELAND RISE
CHURCHWOOD DR
GILLSMAN'S HILL
HOLLINGTON PARK RD
MARLBOROUGH RD
HOLLINGTON PARK CL
AVONDALE RD
THE GREEN
CLINTON CRES

Red River Wood
SEDLESCOMBE RD N
BATTLE RD
A 21(T)
THE HIDE
HOLLINGTON
Offices
Greenfields CL
HARLEQUIN GDNS
SEVEN ACRE RD
BRASSEY CL
KINGSLEY CL
THOMAS RD
WELLINGTON RD
WELLINGTON MEWS
UPPER GLEN RD
Ledsham Ave
HOLLINGHURST RD
MARLOW CL
APPLEWOOD
MENDOW
A 21(T)
SHIRLEY RD
ASHBROOK RD
OLD HARROW RD
BATTLE CRES
RYMILL RD
PERTH RD
PAYNTON RD
WINDSOR RD
STEVENSON RD
MEWS
CHICHESTER RD
DUKE TERR
SILVERLANDS RD
B 2159
A 21(T)
ROCHESTER RD
THEAKLEN DR
DRURY LA
ELLENSLEA RD
STONEHOUSE DR
Hollington Stream
PONSWOOD RD
HORSESHOE CL
WINDMILL CL
DRAPERS WAY
DOUCEGROVE
DELL
SEDLESCOMBE RD S
ARBOURVALE
ANDINE DR
School
HILL BANK
St Matthew's
Sch
SPRINGFIELD RD
SPRINGFIELD VALLEY RD
Hospl

77   D   78   E   79   F

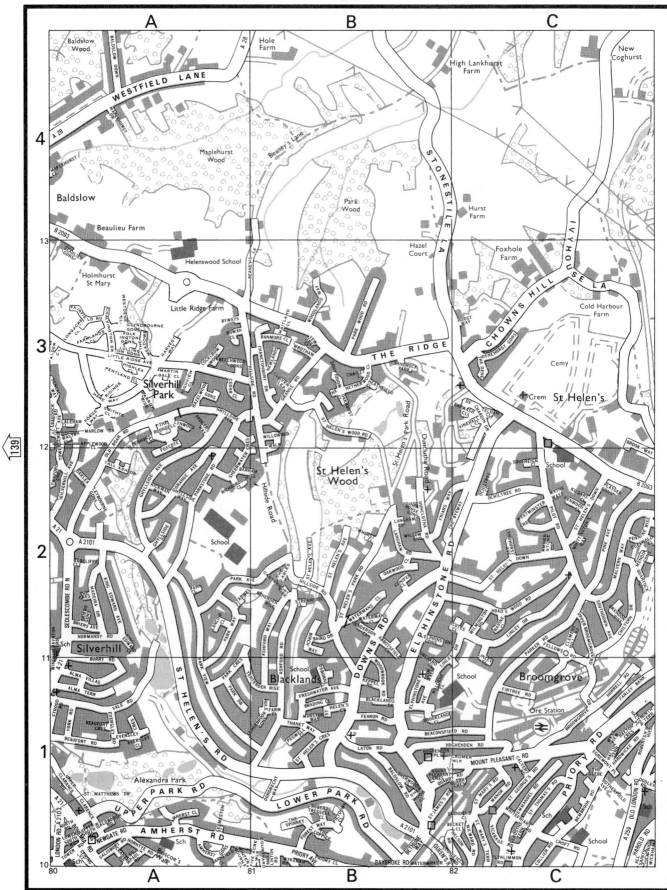

139

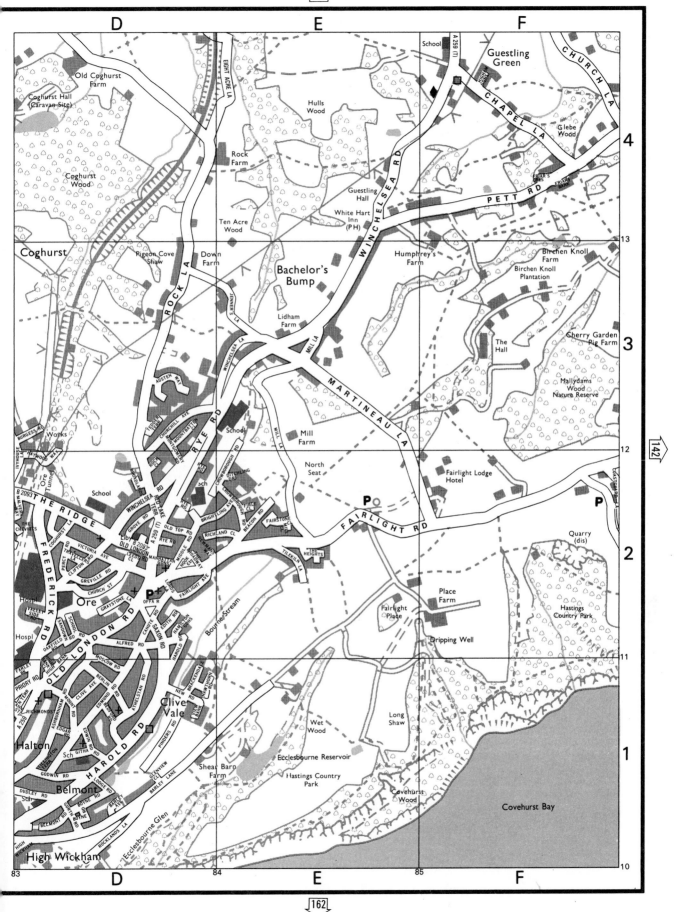

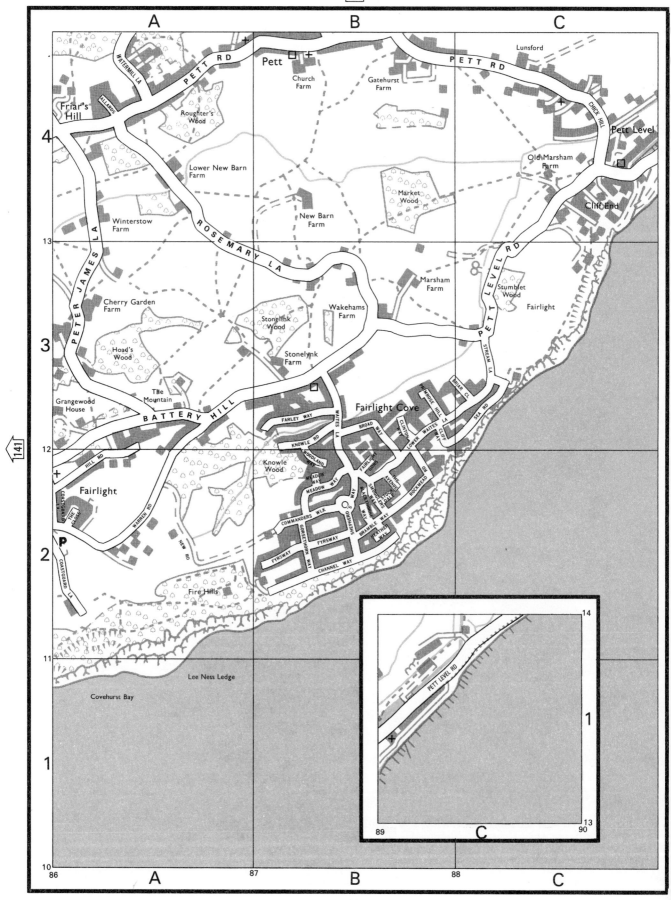

119

141

A   B   C

Pett

Friar's
Hill

PETT RD

WATERMILL LA

Lunsford

PETT RD

Church
Farm

Gatehurst
Farm

Roughter's
Wood

CHICK HILL

Pett Level

Old Marsham
Farm

Lower New Barn
Farm

4

Market
Wood

Cliff End

PETER JAMES LA

ROSEMARY LA

Winterstow
Farm

New Barn
Farm

13

PETT LEVEL RD

Marsham
Farm

Cherry Garden
Farm

Wakehams
Farm

Stumblet
Wood

Fairlight

Stonelink
Wood

Hoad's
Wood

3

STREAM LA

Stonelynk
Farm

The
Mountain

BATTERY HILL

Grangewood
House

BRIAR CL.

Fairlight Cove

PRIMROSE HILL LA

SEA RD

FARLEY WAY

WAITES LA

BROAD WAY

CLINTON

LOWER WAITES

CLIFF

KNOWLE RD

12

HILL RD

Knowle
Wood

WOODLAND WAY

FAIRLIGHT GDNS

AVENUE

ROCKMEAD RD

Fairlight

MEADOW WAY

MEADOW WAY

THE DALE

WARREN RD

COASTGUARD LA

THE CHASE

BLACKWAY

SHEPHERDS WAY

BRAMBLE WAY

HEATHER WAY

NEW RD

COMMANDERS WLK

GORSETHORN WAY

SHEPHERDS

P

GORSETHORN WAY

FYRSWAY

CHANNEL WAY

2

COASTGUARD LA

FYRSWAY

FYRSWAY

Fire Hills

11

Lee Ness Ledge

14

Covehurst Bay

PETT LEVEL RD

1

89   90

13

C

1

86   A   87   B   88   C

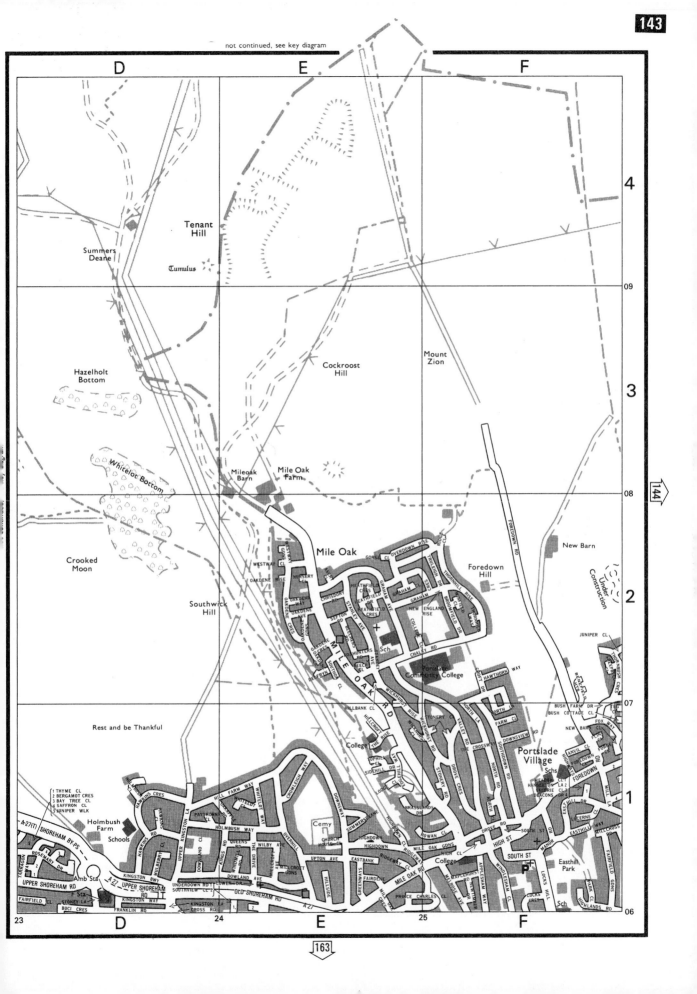

not continued, see key diagram

D E F

4

09

3

Tenant Hill

Summers Deane

Tumulus

Hazelholt Bottom

Cockroost Hill

Mount Zion

Whitelot Bottom

08

144

Mileoak Barn

Mile Oak Farm

Crooked Moon

Mile Oak

Foredown Hill

New Barn

Under Construction

2

Southwick Hill

WESTWAY GDNS
WESTWAY
NURSERY CL
OAKDENE RISE
OAKDENE WAY
CHRISDORY RD
OAKDENE AVE
OAKDENE CRES
GORSE CL
OVERDOWN RISE
HEATHFIELD CRES
HEATHFIELD DR
HEATHFIELD CRES
STANLEY AVE
SEFTON RD
GRAHAM AVE
GRAHAM CL
GRAHAM
THORNHILL RISE
TRULEIGH DR
RIDGE
BROMFIELD DR
UNITED DR
NEW ENGLAND RISE
COLLEGE
JUNIPER CL
THORNBUSH CRES
BENFIELD WAY

HUNTERS CL
BEECH CL
SCH
CHALKY RD
Portslade Community College
HAWTHORN WAY
FORT DR

BELFRYN
OXON CL
WICKHURST RISE
WICKHURST
WICKHURST RD
NORTH LA
NORTH
FARM RD
BUSH FARM DR
BUSH COTTAGE CL
NEW BARN CL
FOX WAY
FOXDOWN RD

07

Rest and be Thankful

HILLBANK CL
HILCROFT CL
THE RISE
College CL
TOPHILL CL
SIDEHILL DR
AVON CL
THREE
LODGE CL
STONERY CL
VALLEY RD
THE CROSSWAY
SOUTHVIEW RD
DOWNSVIEW RD
ANVIL CL
HIGHBANK
FOREDOWN RD
FOREDOWN DR

Portslade Village
Schs
MEADOW CL
HANGLETON
JASMINE CL
DEACONS DR

1 THYME CL
2 BERGAMOT CRES
3 BAY TREE CL
4 SAFFRON CL
5 JUNIPER WLK

Holmbush Farm
Schools

A-27(T) SHOREHAM BY-PS

ROSEMARY DR
TARRAGON
UPPER SHOREHAM RD
FAIRFIELD CL
STONEY LA
BUCI CRES
Amb Sta
F Sta
A 27
UPPER SHOREHAM RD
KINGSTON BWY
FRANKLIN RD

HAWKINS CRES
HAWKINS RD
MULBERRY CL
UPPER KINGSTON LA
DOWN
KINGSTON LA
KINGSTON CROSS RD

HILL FARM WAY
PAYTHORNE CL
HOLMBUSH WAY
HOLMBUSH WAY
QUEENS RD
THE DRIVE
KINGS RD
DOWLAND AVE
UNDERDOWN RD
SOUTHVIEW CL
OLD SHOREHAM RD

WHITELOT WAY
CROMLEIGH WAY
OVERHILL
WILBY AVE
WILLCROFT GDNS
UPTON AVE
HILLSIDE
EASTBANK
GREENWAYS
FAIRDENE

Cemy
CHURCH HOUSE CL
DOWNSWAY
SUMMERSDEANE
HIGHDOWN
HIGHDOWN
HIGHDOWN
RIDGEWAY
HOWAN CL
MILE OAK GDNS
EASTDOWN
MILE OAK CRES
PRINCE CHARLES CL

BRASSLANDS DR
DROVE CRES
STONERY RD
DROVE RD
NORTH RD
HIGH ST
SOUTH ST
MANOR
LOCKS HILL
WINDLESHAM WAY
MAPLEHURST RD
APPLESHAM WAY
MELROSE AVE
HEATH HILL AVE

College
South St
P
Easthill Park

CERNE RD
EASTHILL DR
EASTHILL WAY
HILLCROSS AVE
PARK RD
FAIRFIELD GDNS
HIGHLANDS RD
Sch

23 24 25

D E F

06

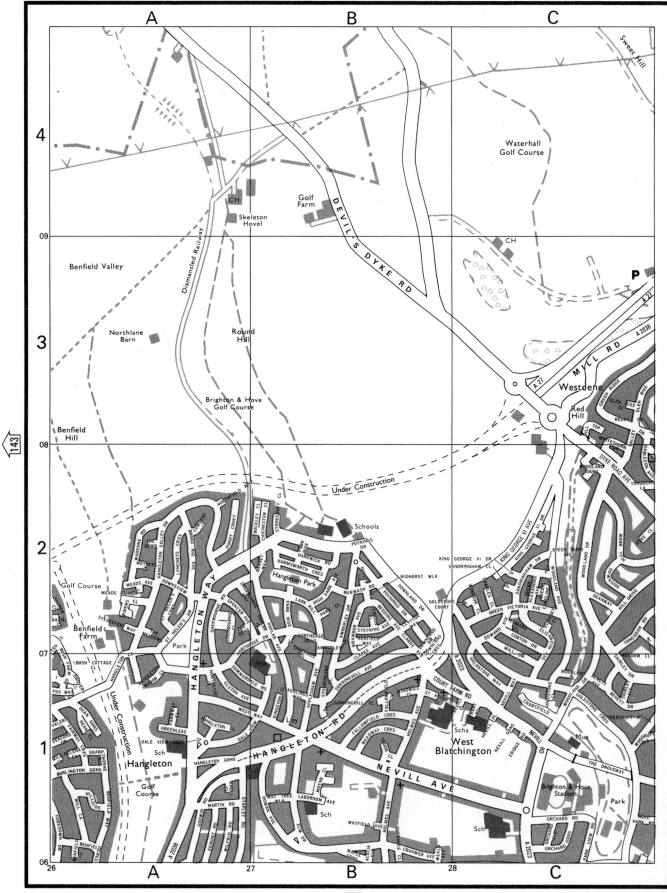

A   B   C

Sweet Hill

4

Waterhall
Golf Course

CH

Skeleton
Hovel

Golf
Farm

DEVIL'S DYKE RD

09

Benfield Valley

CH

P

A 27

Northlane
Barn

Round
Hill

Westdene

3

Brighton & Hove
Golf Course

Red
Hill

MILL RD   A 2038

A 27

Benfield
Hill

08

Under Construction

Schools

King George VI Ave

Golf Course

Hangleton Park

2

Benfield
Farm

Park

Under Construction

07

West
Blatchington

Hangleton

1

Golf
Course

NEVILL AVE

Brighton & Hove
Stadium

Park

THE DROVEWAY

06

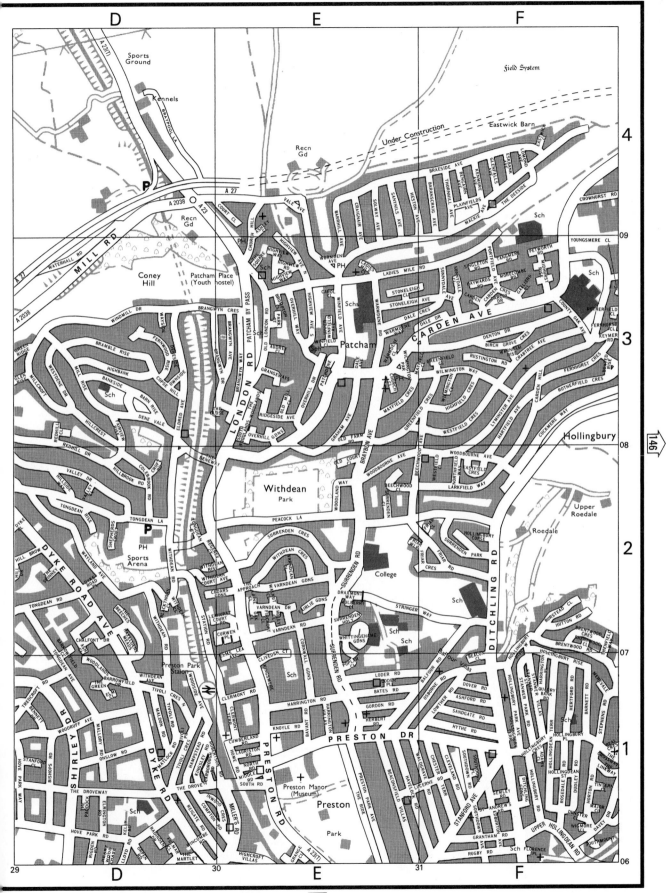

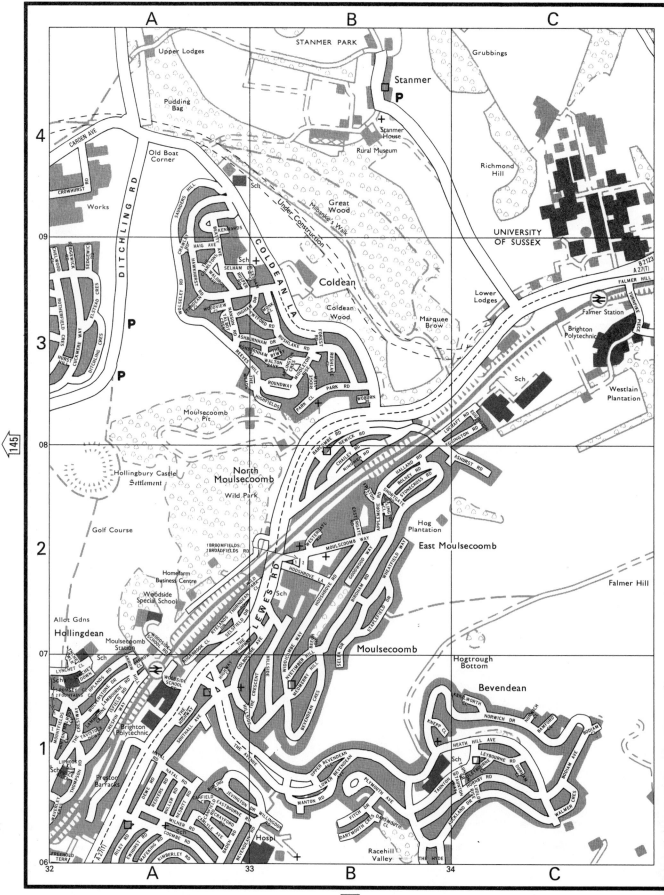

A   B   C

4

09

3

08

2

07

1

06

32   A   33   B   34   C

Upper Lodges

STANMER PARK

Grubbings

Pudding Bag

Stanmer

P

Stanmer House

Rural Museum

Richmond Hill

CARDEN AVE

Old Boat Corner

CROWHURST RD

Works

DITCHLING RD

Great Wood

Milbanke's Walk

Under Construction

COLDEAN LA

Coldean

Coldean Wood

Marquee Brow

UNIVERSITY OF SUSSEX

Lower Lodges

FALMER HILL

Falmer Station

Brighton Polytechnic

Westlain Plantation

Sch

RIDGEWICK
CHELWOOD
SEDGEWICK
ROTHERFIELD CRES
HURST HILL
CUCKMERE WAY
ELSTED CRES
DITCHLING CRES

P

P

SAUNDERS HILL
CRAWLEY RD
HAWKHURST RD
HAIG AVE
BEATTY AVE
WOLSELEY RD
HODIAN RD
WALDRON
WOODVIEW
HANSON RD
INGRAM
BEKENWARDS
SELHAM DR
HUSSET
TWYFORD RD
ASHBURNHAM DR
RUSHLAKE RD
REEVES HILL
CLAYTON CRES
MIDDLETON
WALTON BANK
THE BYWAY
FOREST RD
RUSHLAKE
HIGHFIELDS
ROUNDWAY
PARK CL RIDGE
PARK RD
WOBURN PL

Sch

Moulsecoomb Pit

North Moulsecoomb

Hollingbury Castle Settlement

Wild Park

Golf Course

Homefarm Business Centre

Woodside Special School

Allot Gdns

Hollingdean

Moulsecoomb Station

Sch

BARCOMBE RD
NEWICK RD
CHAILEY RD
RINGMER RD
APPLEMORE
PRESTON
SHORTGATE
FRISTON
RALLAND RD
BOLNEY RD
STONECROSS
ASHURST RD

LUGRAFT RD
EGGINGTON RD
EGGINGTON

Hog Plantation

East Moulsecoomb

Falmer Hill

LEWES RD

WILD PARK
RYELANDS
THORNDEAN
SELSFIELD AVE
HIGHBROOK CL
WOODSIDE SCHOOL RD

1 BROOMFIELDS CL
2 BROADFIELDS RD

HODSHROVE LA
WESTERGATE
MOULSECOOMB WAY
GOODWOOD WAY
WHEATFIELD WAY
HODSHROVE RD
BIRDHAM RD
STAPLEFIELD DR
BEECH

Moulsecoomb

Hogtrough Bottom

Bevendean

KENILWORTH CL
NORWICH DR
NORWICH
BAMFORD
BODIAM AVE

LYNCHET CL
CHET DOWN
ROMSEY CL
2 FOUNTAINS CL
WOLSTONEBURY DR
UPLANDS DR
LAMBOURNE DR
CRESTWAY
TAVISTOCK DOWN
LANGDALE
CRESPIN WAY

Brighton Polytechnic

WOODSIDE SCHOOL

Sch

THE HIGHWAY
SOUTHALL AVE
THE CRESCENT
HILLSIDE
REDMERRY HILL
BEVENDEAN CRES
WIDDICOMBE WAY
NYETIMBER HILL
REDMERRY HILL
SELBA DR

HEATH HILL AVE
Sch
KNEPP CL
LEYBOURNE RD
LEYBOURNE RD
TAUNTON RD
BODIAM AVE
WALMER CRES
DUDLEY RD
HORNBY RD

UPPER BEVENDEAN
LOWER BEVENDEAN

MOUNTFIELDS
LIPHOOK CL
THOMPSON RD
Sch
WAVERLEY CRES
FREEHOLD TERR

Preston Barracks

NATAL RD
DEENE RD
BULLER RD
NESBITT RD
HARTFIELD
BURTON
MILNER RD
COOMBE RD
KIMBERLEY RD
EWHURST RD
MAFEKING RD
BEVENDEAN RD
RILEY RD

A 27(T)

Sch

JEVINGTON DR
EASTBOURNE RD
WILLINGDON
CRAYFORD RD
CARLTIE AVE
BADEN

Hospl

MANTON RD
PLYMOUTH AVE
FITCH DR
DARTMOUTH CRES
DARTMOUTH CL
AUCKLAND DR

Racehill Valley

THE HYDE

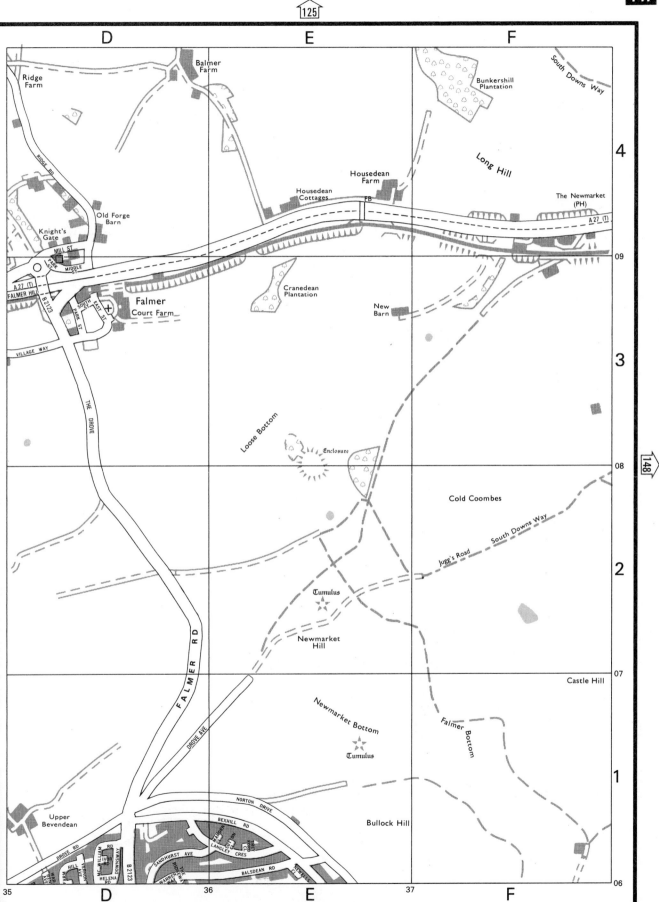

D   E   F

Ridge Farm

Balmer Farm

South Downs Way

Bunkershill Plantation

Long Hill

4

Housedean Farm

Housedean Cottages

FB

The Newmarket (PH)

Knight's Gate

Old Forge Barn

A 27 (T)

MILL ST

PARK ST

MIDDLE ST

A 27 (T)

FALMER HILL

B 2123

09

Falmer Court Farm

SOUTH PARK ST

EAST ST

Cranedean Plantation

New Barn

VILLAGE WAY

3

THE DROVE

Loose Bottom

Enclosure

Cold Coombes

08

Jugg's Road   South Downs Way

2

FALMER RD

Tumulus

Newmarket Hill

07

Castle Hill

DROVE AVE

Newmarket Bottom

Tumulus

Falmer Bottom

1

Upper Bevendean

NORTON DRIVE

Bullock Hill

DROVE RD

BEXHILL RD

WILLIAM RD

IVOR RD

AYLESMORE

LANGLEY CRES

HYAMMERTON RD

SANDHURST AVE

THE HIGHWAY

WARREN WAY

ROWELLS CL

BALSDEAN RD

HELENA RD

VERNON AVE

HILL

B 2123

06

35   D   36   E   37   F

148

126

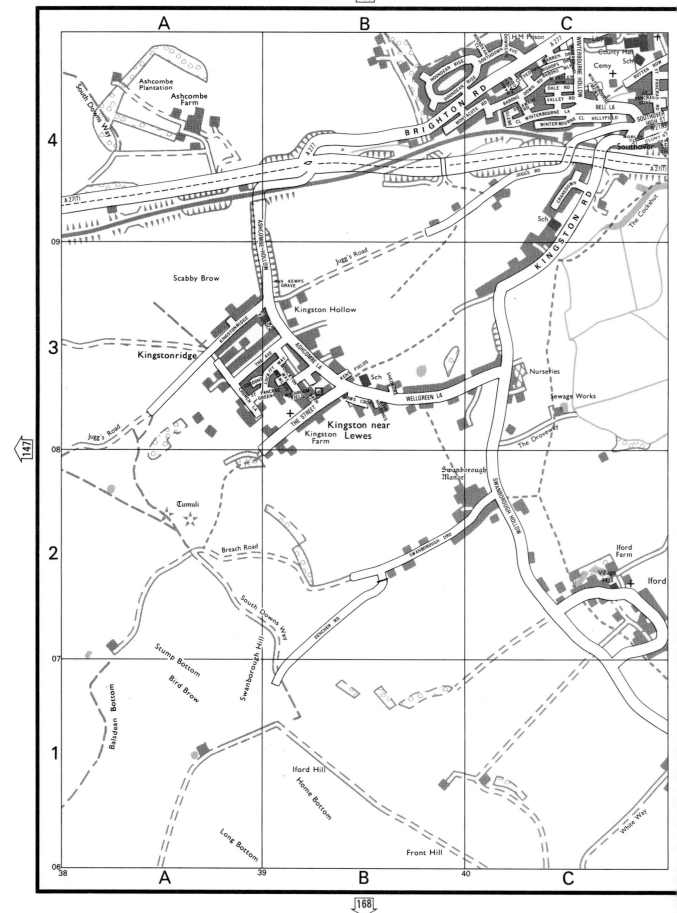

147

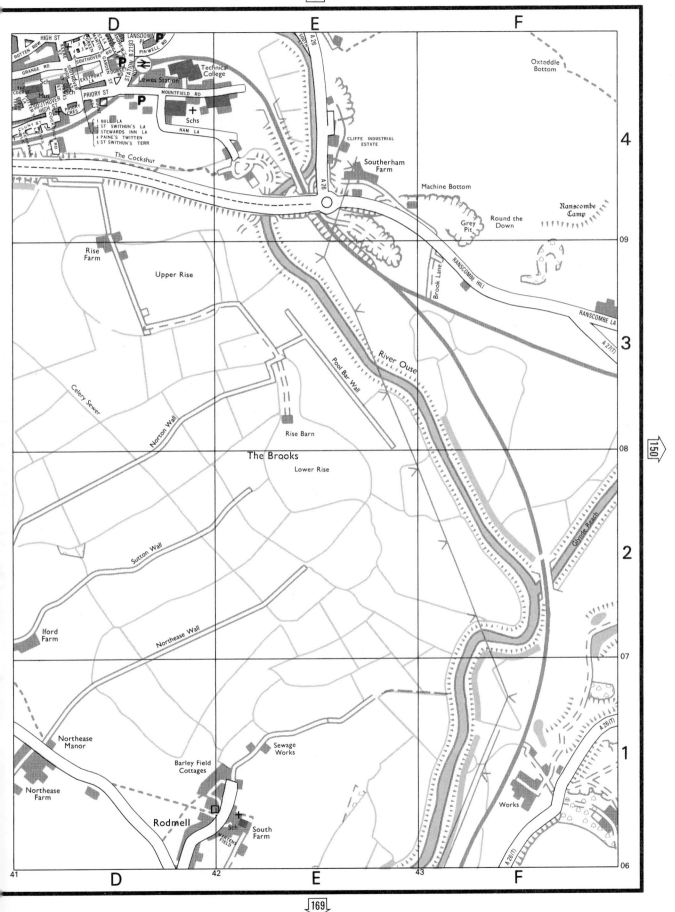

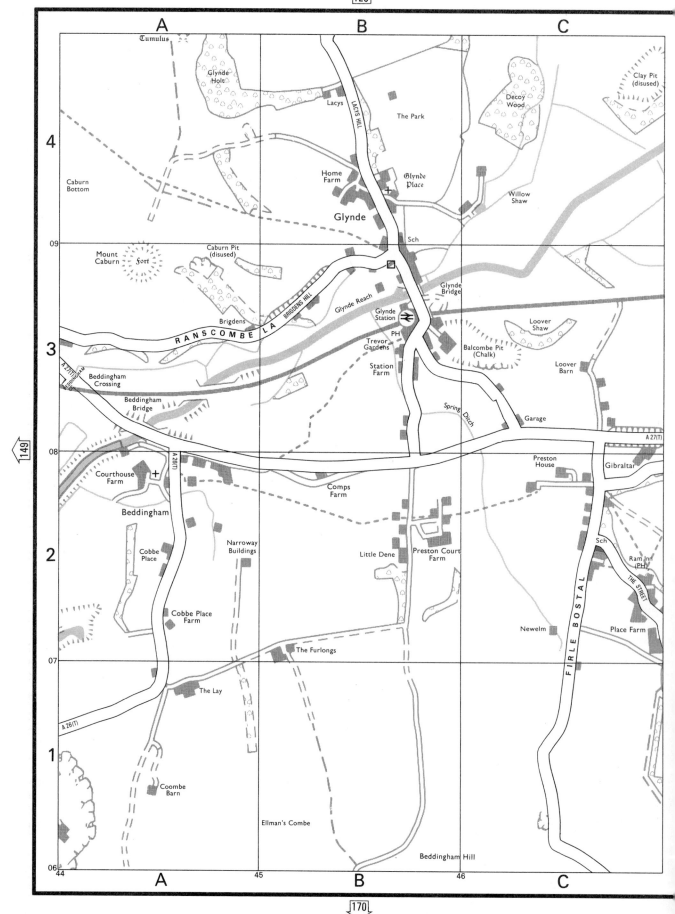

A   B   C

Tumulus

Glynde Holt

Lacys

LACYS HILL

The Park

Decoy Wood

Clay Pit (disused)

Caburn Bottom

Home Farm

Glynde Place

Willow Shaw

Glynde

Sch

Mount Caburn Fort

Caburn Pit (disused)

Glynde Bridge

Brigdens

BRIGDENS HILL

Glynde Reach

Glynde Station

Loover Shaw

RANSCOMBE LA

PH

Balcombe Pit (Chalk)

Loover Barn

Trevor Gardens

Beddingham Crossing

Station Farm

A 27(T)

BEDDINGHAM

Beddingham Bridge

Spring Ditch

Garage

A 27(T)

Courthouse Farm

A 26(T)

Comps Farm

Preston House

Gibraltar

Beddingham

Cobbe Place

Narroway Buildings

Little Dene

Preston Court Farm

Sch

Ram Inn (PH)

THE STREET

Cobbe Place Farm

Newelm

Place Farm

FIRLE BOSTAL

The Furlongs

The Lay

A 26(T)

Coombe Barn

Ellman's Combe

Beddingham Hill

A   B   C

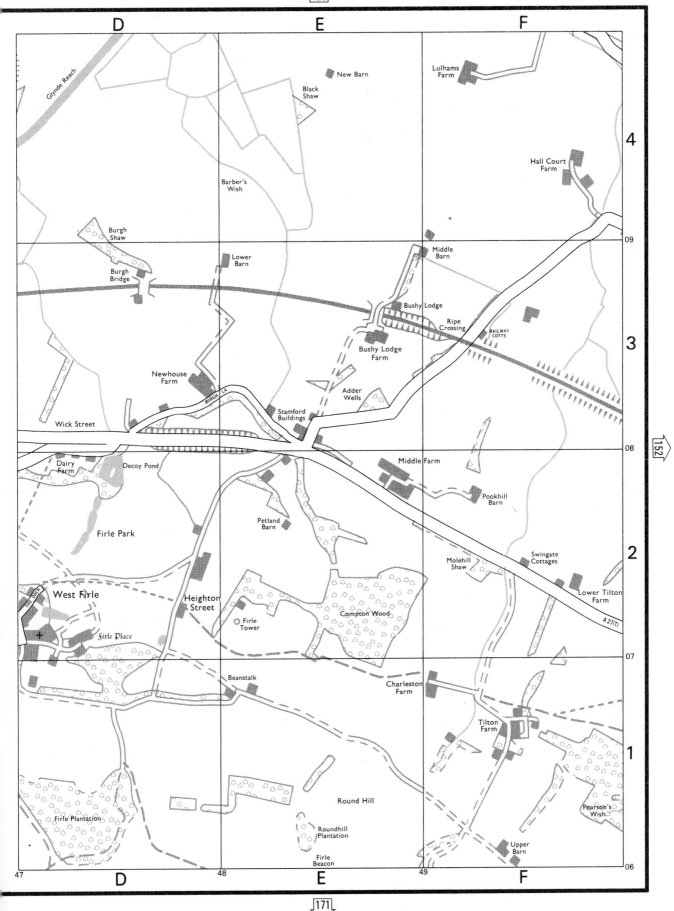

D E F

Glynde Reach

New Barn

Black Shaw

Lulhams Farm

4

Barber's Wish

Hall Court Farm

Burgh Shaw

09

Burgh Bridge

Lower Barn

Middle Barn

Bushy Lodge

Ripe Crossing

RAILWAY COTTS

3

Newhouse Farm

BURGH LA

Bushy Lodge Farm

Adder Wells

Wick Street

Stamford Buildings

08

Dairy Farm

Decoy Pond

Middle Farm

Pookhill Barn

Firle Park

Petland Barn

Molehill Shaw

Swingate Cottages

2

Lower Tilton Farm

A 27(T)

THE DOCK

West Firle

Heighton Street

Firle Tower

Compton Wood

Charleston Farm

07

Firle Place

Beanstalk

Tilton Farm

1

Firle Plantation

Round Hill

Pearson's Wish

Roundhill Plantation

Upper Barn

Firle Beacon

06

47 D 48 E 49 F

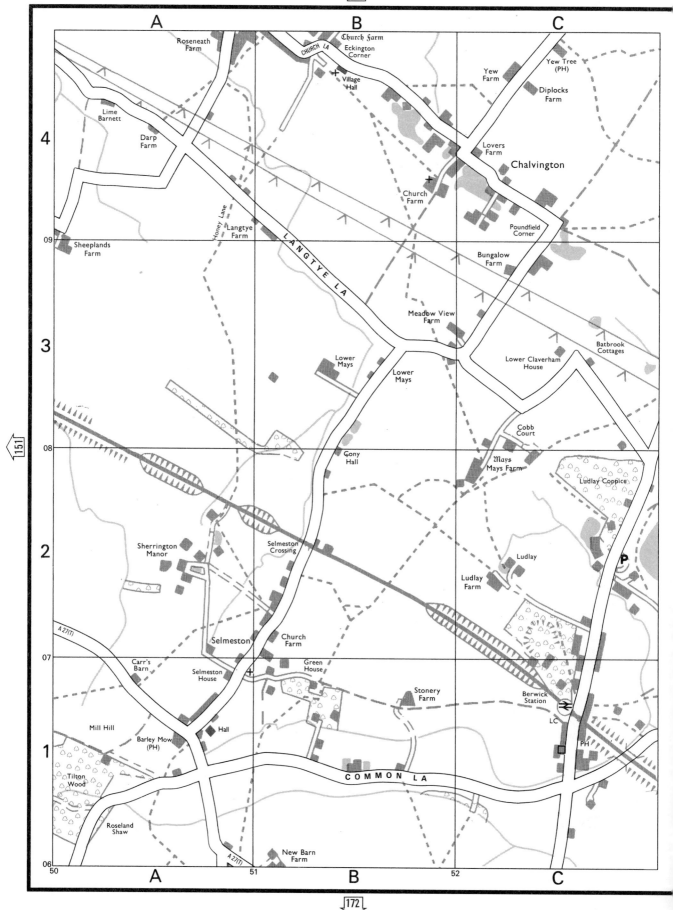

151

Roseneath Farm
Church Farm
CHURCH LA
Eckington Corner
Yew Farm
Yew Tree (PH)
Diplocks Farm
Village Hall
Lime Barnett
Darp Farm
Lovers Farm
Chalvington
Church Farm
Honey Lane
Langtye Farm
Poundfield Corner
4
Sheeplands Farm
09
LANGTYE LA
Bungalow Farm
Meadow View Farm
3
Lower Mays
Lower Mays
Lower Claverham House
Batbrook Cottages
Cobb Court
08
Gony Hall
Mays Mays Farm
Ludlay Coppice
A 27(T)
Sherrington Manor
Selmeston Crossing
2
Ludlay
P
Ludlay Farm
Selmeston
Church Farm
07
Carr's Barn
Selmeston House
Green House
Stonery Farm
Berwick Station
LC
Mill Hill
Barley Mow (PH)
Hall
1
PH
Tilton Wood
COMMON LA
Roseland Shaw
A 27(T)
New Barn Farm
06
50
51
52

A   B   C

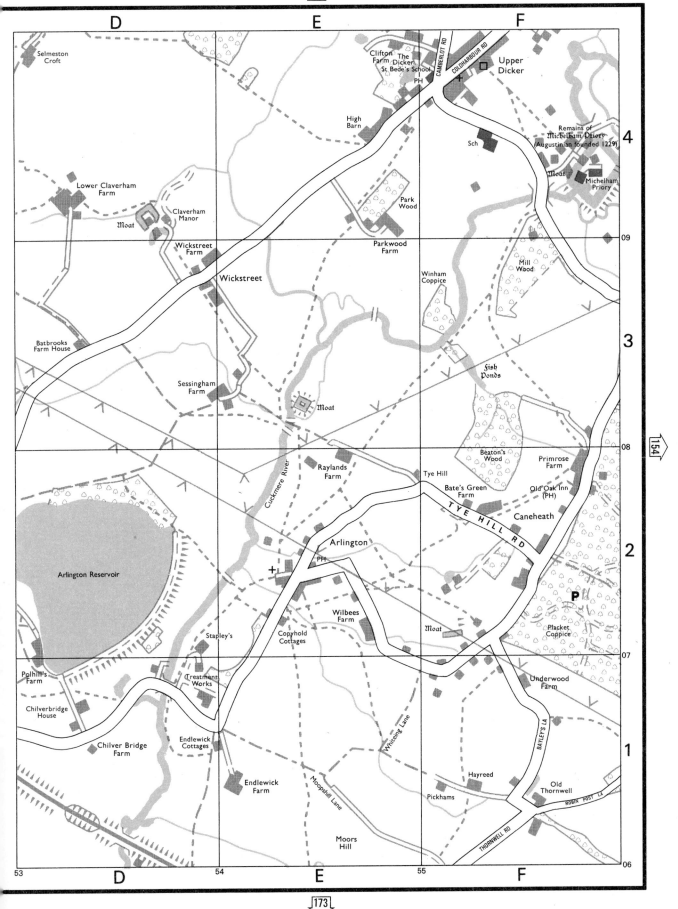

D   E   F

Selmeston
Croft

Clifton
Farm
The
Dicker
St Bede's School
PH

Upper
Dicker

High
Barn

Sch

Remains of
Michelham Priory
(Augustinian founded 1229)

Lower Claverham
Farm

Park
Wood

Moat

Moat
Michelham
Priory

Claverham
Manor

4

Moat

Wickstreet
Farm

Parkwood
Farm

09

Wickstreet

Winham
Coppice

Mill
Wood

Batbrooks
Farm House

3

Fish
Ponds

Sessingham
Farm

Moat

154

Beaton's
Wood

Primrose
Farm

08

Raylands
Farm

Tye Hill

Cuckmere River

Bate's Green
Farm

Old Oak Inn
(PH)

Arlington Reservoir

TYE HILL RD

Caneheath

Arlington

PH

2

Mill
Wood

P

Stapley's

Wilbees
Farm

Moat

Placket
Coppice

Copyhold
Cottages

Polhill's
Farm

Treatment
Works

Underwood
Farm

Chilverbridge
House

Bayley's La

Whiteing Lane

Chilver Bridge
Farm

Endlewick
Cottages

1

Hayreed

Old
Thornwell

Moopshill Lane

Endlewick
Farm

Pickhams

ROBIN POST LA

Moors
Hill

THORNWELL RD

06

53   D   E   54   55   F

07

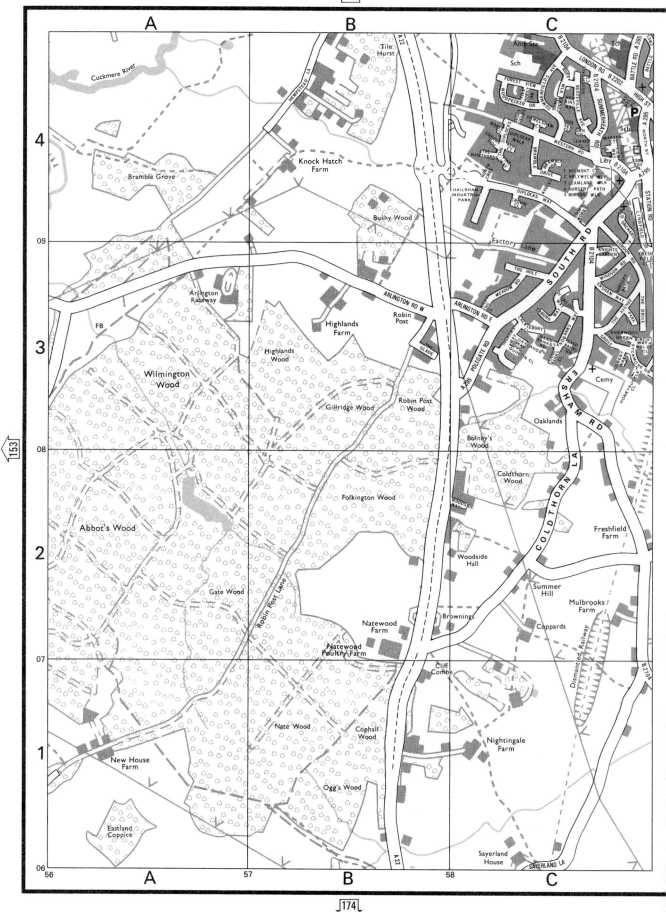

A   B   C

Cuckmere River

4

Bramble Grove

Knock Hatch Farm

Tile Hurst

HEMPSTEAD LA

A 22

Amb Sta

Sch

Sch

LONDON RD

B 2104

B 2202

B 2104

FOREST VIEW

WOODPECKER DR

SUMMERHEATH RD

BATTLE RD A 295

Battle

High St

A 295

Sch

P

HAILSHAM INDUSTRIAL PARK

Bushy Wood

Factory Lane

09

STATION RD

Liby

1 BELMONT CT
2 HOLYWELL WLK
3 LEAMLAND WLK
4 NURSERY PATH
5 BURTON WLK

OLD ORCHARD

B 2104

Arlington Raceway

FB

Highlands Farm

ARLINGTON RD W

Robin Post

THE GLADE

ARLINGTON RD E

POLEGATE RD

A 295

SOUTH RD

B 2104

Factory Lane

THE HOLT

MEADOW RD

Knights Garden

GORDON RD

WINDSOR RD

ERESH FIELD

3

Wilmington Wood

Highlands Wood

Gilridge Wood

Robin Post Wood

Oaklands

Cemy

ERSHAM RD

THE DRIVE

SHERWOOD GREEN

08

Abbot's Wood

Folkington Wood

Bolney's Wood

Coldthorn Wood

COLDTHORN LA

Freshfield Farm

2

Gate Wood

Robin Post Lane

Natewood Farm

Woodside Hall

Summer Hill

Mulbrooks Farm

Brownings

Coppards

Dismantled Railway

07

Natewood Poultry Farm

Cliff Combe

Nightingale Farm

1

New House Farm

Nate Wood

Cophall Wood

Ogg's Wood

Eastland Coppice

Sayerland House

SAYERLAND LA

B 2104

A 22

06

56   A   57   B   58   C

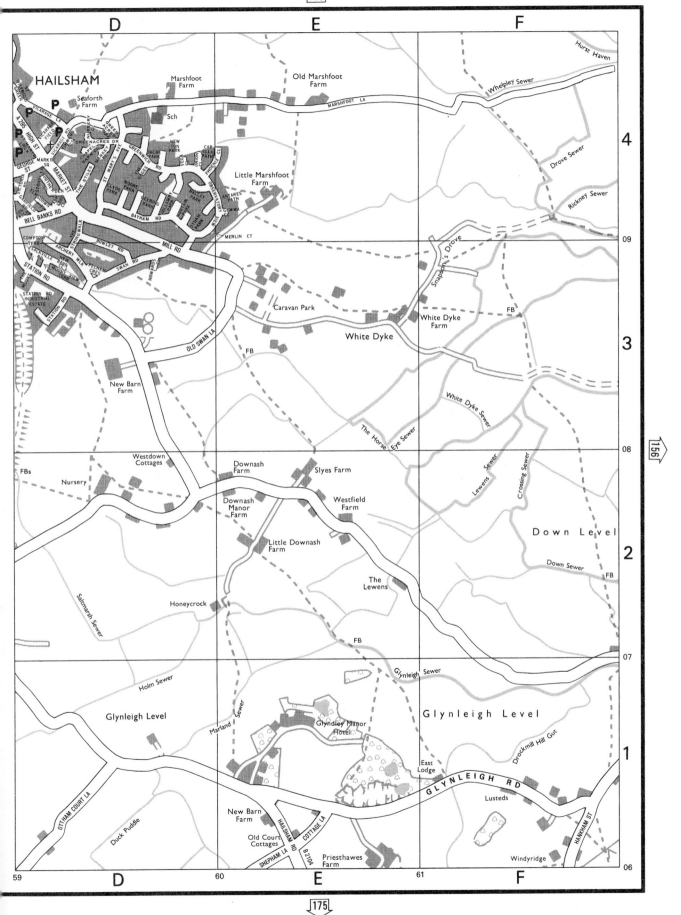

D E F

HAILSHAM

P P
P P
P

Seaforth Farm

Marshfoot Farm

Old Marshfoot Farm

Hurst Haven

Whelpley Sewer

MARSHFOOT LA

Sch

Drove Sewer

Rickney Sewer

Little Marshfoot Farm

09

MERLIN CT

Snapson's Drove

FB

Caravan Park

White Dyke Farm

White Dyke

3

Old Swan La

FB

New Barn Farm

White Dyke Sewer

The Horse Eye Sewer

Lewens Sewer

Crossing Sewer

08

Westdown Cottages

Downash Farm

Slyes Farm

FBs

Nursery

Downash Manor Farm

Westfield Farm

Down Level

Little Downash Farm

Down Sewer

FB

2

Saltmarsh Sewer

Honeycrock

The Lewens

FB

07

Holm Sewer

Glynleigh Sewer

Glynleigh Level

Marland Sewer

Glyndley Manor Hotel

Glynleigh Level

Drockmill Hill Gut

East Lodge

1

OTTHAM COURT LA

Duck Puddle

New Barn Farm

GLYNLEIGH RD

Lusteds

Old Court Cottages

HAILSHAM RD B2104

COTTAGE LA

SHEPHAM LA

Priesthawes Farm

Windyridge

HANKHAM ST

06

59 D 60 E 61 F

4

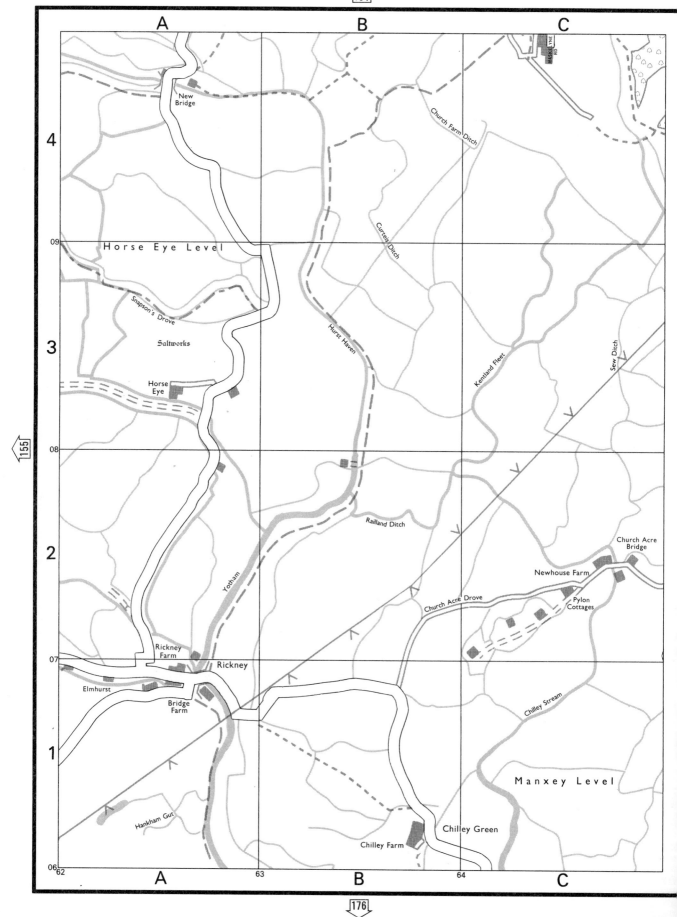

A   B   C

New Bridge

MASKELYNE RD

Church Farm Ditch

4

Curteis Ditch

09

Horse Eye Level

Snapson's Drove

Hurst Haven

Saltworks

Kentland Fleet

Sew Ditch

3

Horse Eye

08

Railland Ditch

Yotham

2

Church Acre Bridge

Newhouse Farm

Church Acre Drove

Pylon Cottages

Rickney Farm

07

Rickney

Elmhurst

Chilley Stream

Bridge Farm

1

Manxey Level

Hankham Gut

Chilley Green

Chilley Farm

06   62   A   63   B   64   C

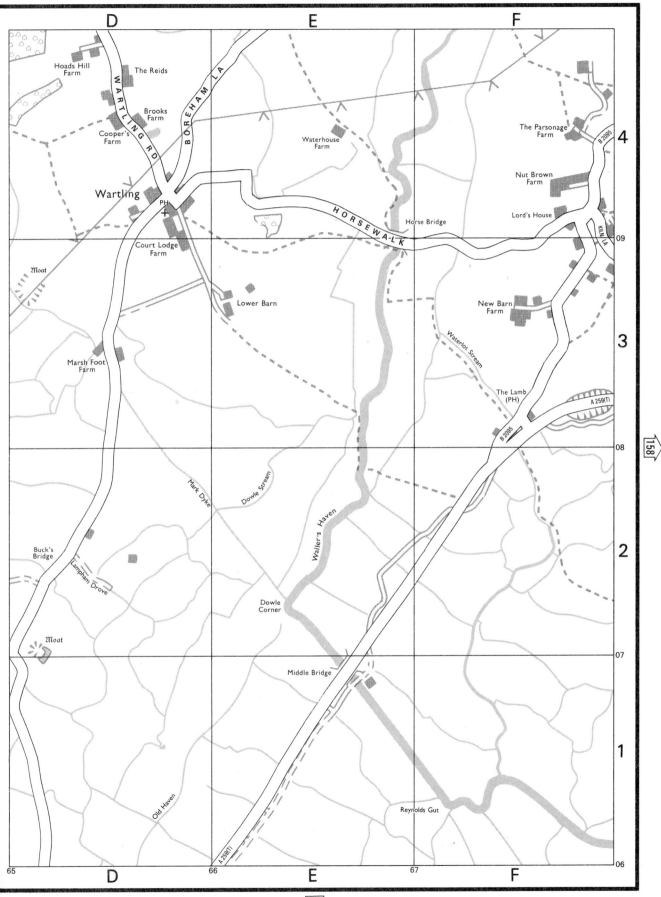

D E F

4

3

2

1

Hoads Hill Farm

The Reids

Brooks Farm

Cooper's Farm

WARTLING RD

BOREHAM LA

Wartling

PH

Court Lodge Farm

Moat

Lower Barn

Marsh Foot Farm

Waterhouse Farm

HORSE-WALK

Horse Bridge

The Parsonage Farm

Nut Brown Farm

Lord's House

KILN LA

B 2095

New Barn Farm

Waterlot Stream

The Lamb (PH)

A 259(T)

B 2095

Buck's Bridge

Lampham Drove

Moat

Mark Dyke

Dowle Stream

Waller's Haven

Dowle Corner

Middle Bridge

Old Haven

A 2591(T)

Reynolds Gut

09

08

07

06

65 D 66 E 67 F

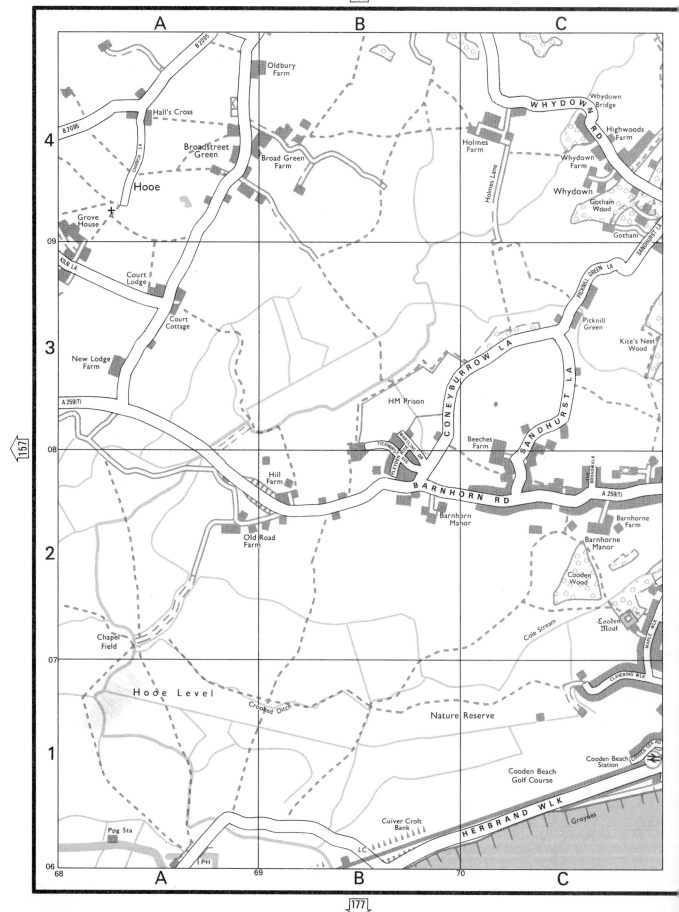

A   B   C

4

3

2

1

B 2095

Oldbury Farm

Hall's Cross

CHURCH LA

Broadstreet Green

Broad Green Farm

B 2095

Hooe

Grove House

KILN LA

Court Lodge

Court Cottage

New Lodge Farm

A 259(T)

Hill Farm

Old Road Farm

Chapel Field

Hooe Level

Crooked Ditch

Ppg Sta

PH

LC

Cuiver Croft Bank

HERBRAND WLK

Groynes

WHYDOWN RD

Whydown Bridge

Highwoods Farm

Holmes Farm

Holmes Lane

Whydown Farm

Whydown

SANDHURST LA

Gotham Wood

Gotham

PICKNILL GREEN LA

Picknill Green

Kite's Nest Wood

CONEYBURROW LA

HM Prison

WARTLING DR

TICEHURST AVE

PLEYDEN AVE

Beeches Farm

SANDHURST LA

THE BROADWALK

A 259(T)

BARNHORN RD

Barnhorn Manor

Barnhorne Farm

Barnhorne Manor

Cooden Wood

Cooden Moat

Cole Stream

MAPLE WLK

Nature Reserve

CLANERING WLK

COODEN SEA RD

Cooden Beach Station

Cooden Beach Golf Course

09   08   07   06

68   69   70

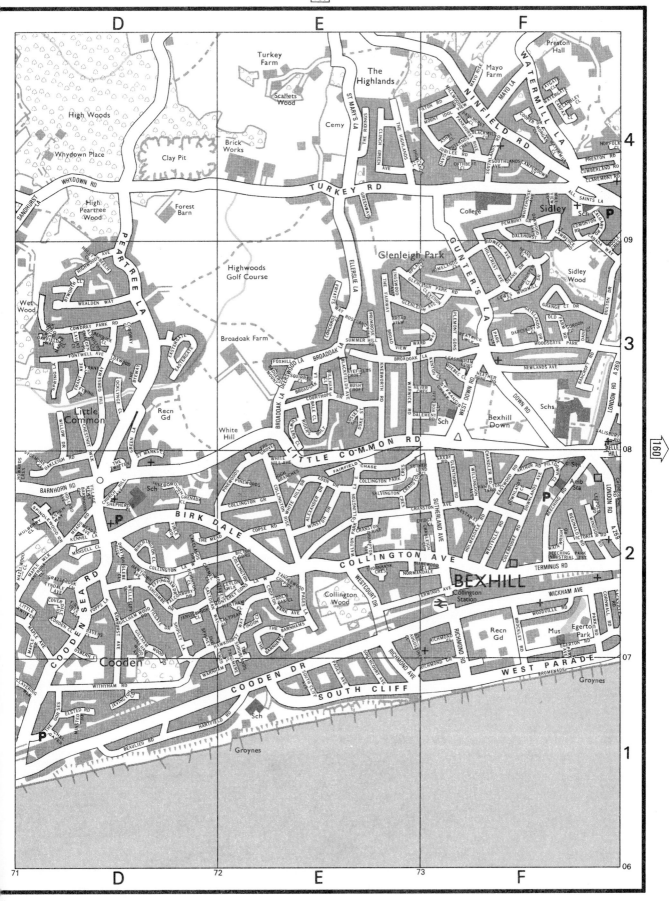

160

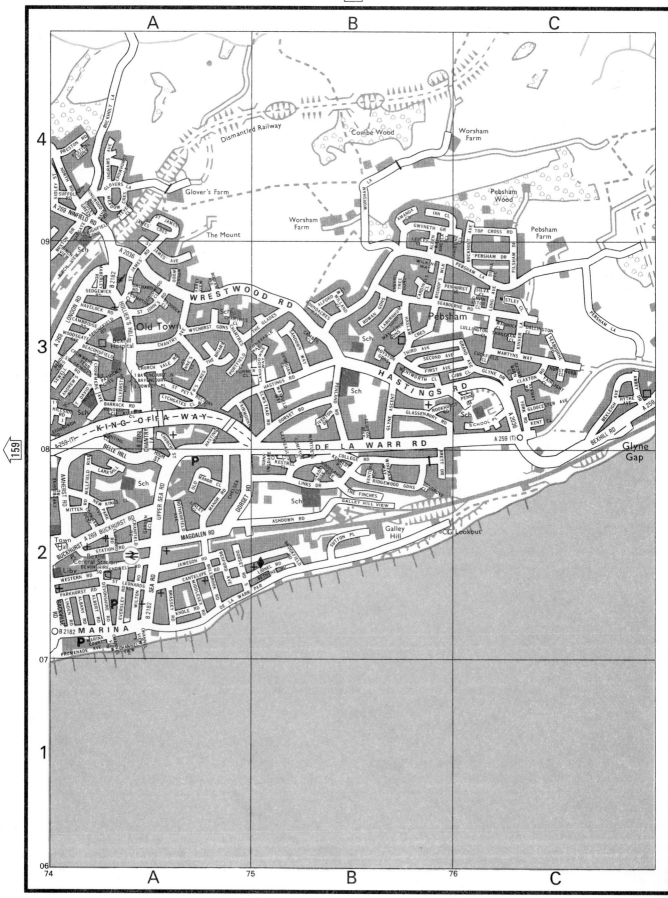

138

159

139
162

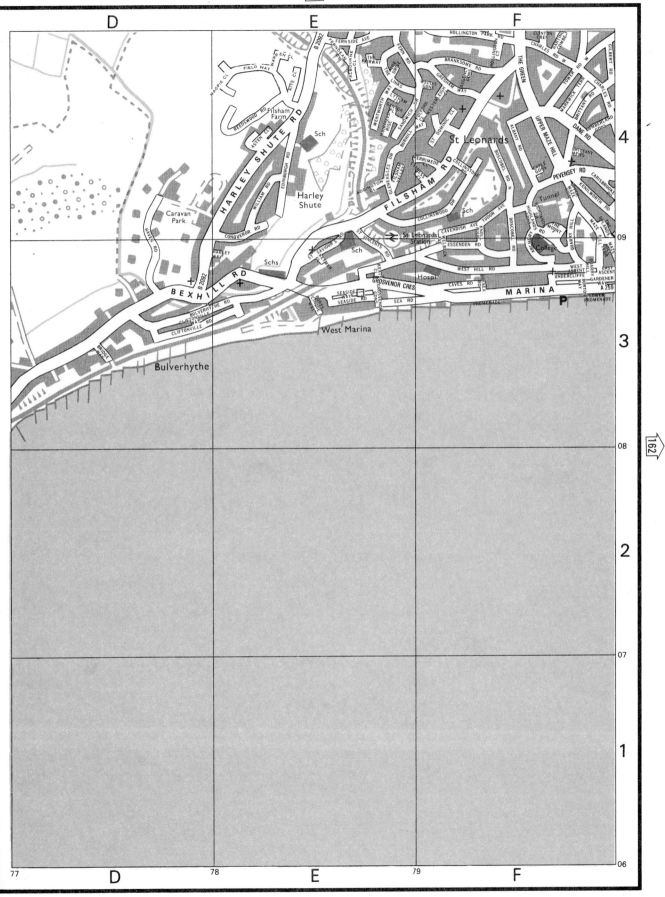

D E F

4

HOLLINGTON PARK RD
CLINTON CRES
CHARLES RD W
CHARLES RD W
GILBERT RD
THE GREEN
BRANKSOME RD
TOWER RD W
TOWER RD
WARWICK TERR
BRITTANY RD
CHARLES RD
CUMBERLAND GDNS
FERNSIDE AVE
THE FAIRWAY
FERN RD
GRESHAM RD
WELLS GDNS
WILTON RD
CLEMENTINE AVE
SANDWICH WAY
ST DOMINIC CL
DANE RD
MARYLAND
BRITTANY MEWS
FIELD WAY
MAGPIE CL
EASTERN CL
REEDSWOOD RD
Filsham Farm
Sch
WENTWORTH RISE
WESTWOOD RISE
GLYNE DR
LYTHAM CL
BURHILL WAY
UPPER MAZE HILL
ALBANY RD
PEVENSEY RD
CARISBROOKE RD
KENILWORTH RD
St Leonards
HARLEY SHUTE RD
WILLIAM RD
EDINBURGH RD
CONQUEROR RD
Harley Shute
EDDINGTON DR
GLENEAGLES DR
FILSHAM RD
MERRIMEDE CL
COLLINSTONE RD
CHICHESTER RISE
BOSCOBEL RD
CASTLE GDNS
THE MOUNT
HIGHLANDS RD
KNOLL
Caravan Park
HAVEN RD
Tunnel
KENILWORTH RD
BULVERHYTHE RD
CLIFTONVILLE RD
CLIFTONVILLE RD
COLLINSWOOD RD
Sch
CAVENDISH AVE
TUDOR AVE
BOSCOBEL RD
College
MAZE HILL
MARINA
BEXHILL RD
HARLEY WAY
B 2092
ST SAVIOUR'S RD
ST KILDA
Schs
St VINCENTS RD
Sch
St Leonards Station
WELBECK
ESSENDEN RD
WEST HILL RD
CAVES RD
HOSPl
WEST ASCENT
EAST ASCENT
GARDENER
WAY
UNDERCLIFFE
BRIDGE WAY
CLIFTONVILLE WAY
SEASIDE
CLIFTONVILLE
SEASIDE
GROSVENOR CRES
SEA RD
PROMENADE
BULWER RD
Hospl
A 259
West Marina
Bulverhythe
PROMENADE
P
9

09

08

3

07

2

1

06

77 D 78 E 79 F

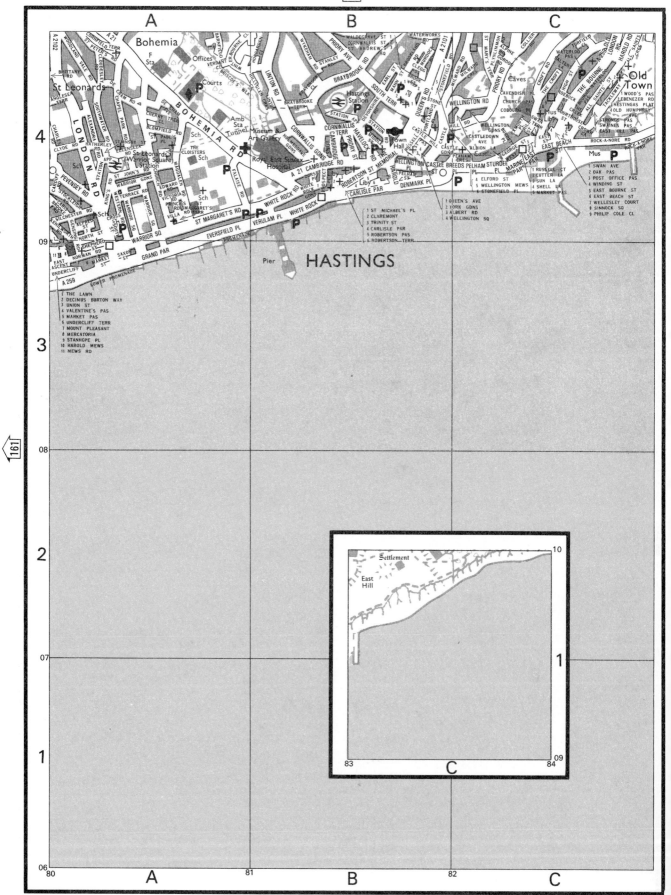

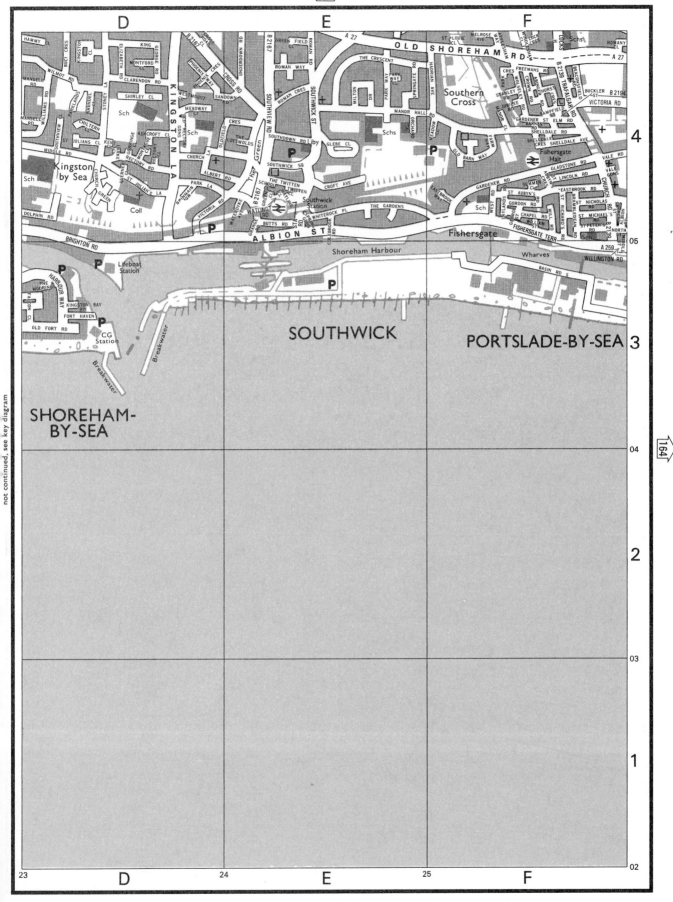

164

D E F

OLD SHOREHAM RD A 27

Southern Cross

Kingston by Sea

KINGSTON LA

Southwick Station

ALBION ST

Shoreham Harbour

Fishersgate

Wharves

SOUTHWICK

PORTSLADE-BY-SEA

SHOREHAM-BY-SEA

not continued, see key diagram

Breakwater

23 D 24 E 25 F

05

04

03

02

4

3

2

1

144

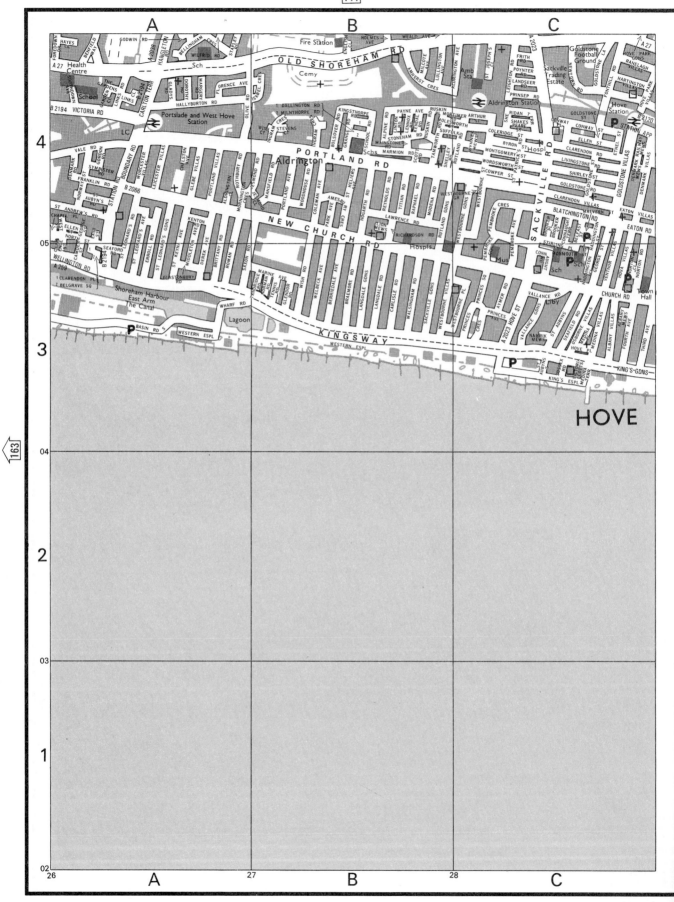

HOVE

163

BRIGHTON

Palace Pier

West Pier

Information Centre

Aquarium

1 NORFOLK ST
2 NORFOLK MEWS
3 NORFOLK BLDGS
4 NORFOLK PL
5 LITTLE WESTERN ST

1 SHIP ST CT
2 BRIGHTON SQ
3 BRIGHTON PL
4 BLACK LION ST
5 BARTHOLOMEWS
6 LITTLE EAST ST
7 BRILLS LA

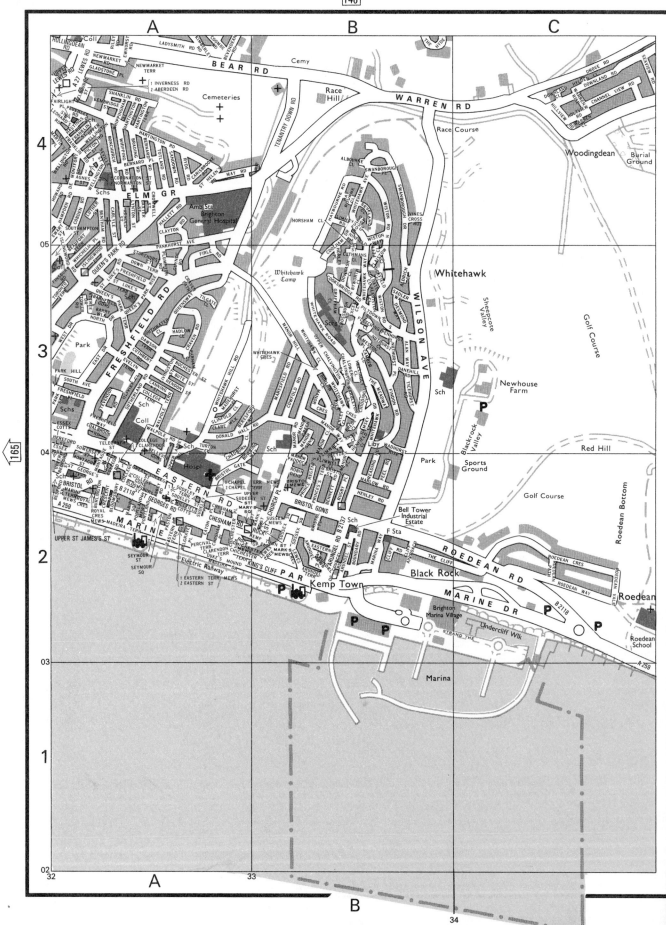

146
165

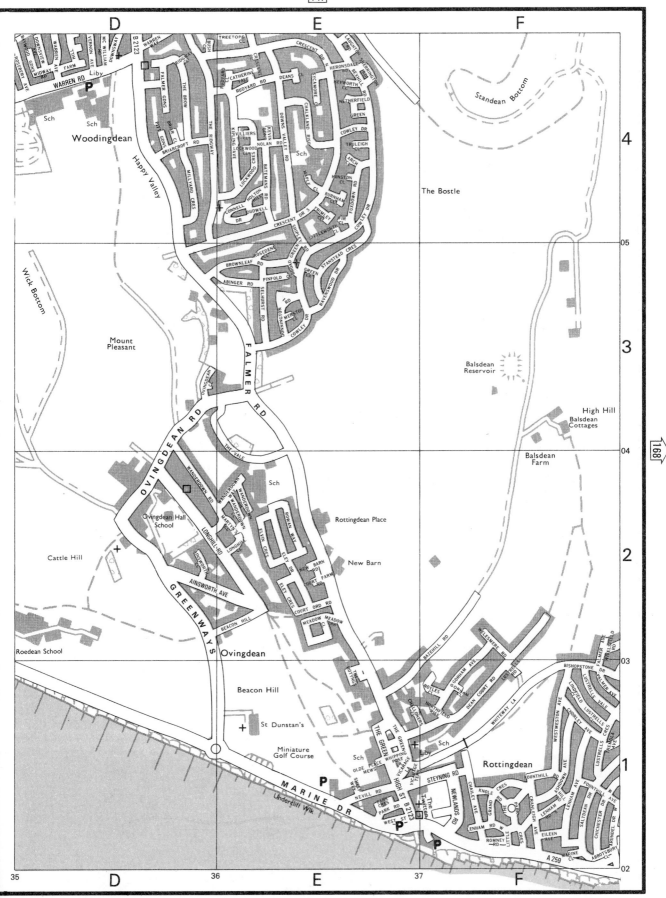

D

E

F

4

05

3

04

2

03

1

02

35

D

36

E

37

F

Standean Bottom

The Bostle

Balsdean
Reservoir

High Hill
Balsdean
Cottages

Balsdean
Farm

WARREN RD

Woodingdean

Happy Valley

Wick Bottom

Mount
Pleasant

Cattle Hill

OVINGDEAN RD

FALMER RD

The Vale

GREENWAYS

AINSWORTH AVE

Ovingdean Hall
School

LONGHILL RD

BEACON HILL

Roedean School

Ovingdean

Beacon Hill

St Dunstan's

Miniature
Golf Course

MARINE DR

Undercliff Wlk

Rottingdean Place

New Barn

New Barn

Rottingdean

A 259

FALMER GDNS

THE BROW

THE RIDGWAY

MILLYARD CRES

BRIARCROFT RD

PIT GDNS

BRIAR GDNS

KIPLING AVE

LOCKWOOD CRES

LOCKWOOD RD

BATEMANS RD

NOLAN RD

KEVIN GDN

NANDOWN RD

WANDERDOWN RD

MARTYN'S

ELVIN CRES

ELEY DR

ELEY CRES

ROMAN WAY

CATHERINE VALE

RUDYARD RD

DOWNS VALLEY RD

MAPLE RD

SYCAMORE CL

DEANS

CRESCENT DR N

HERONSDALE RD

HEYWORTH RD

NETHERFIELD

GREEN

COWLEY DR

THULEIGH CL

LARCH

HUNSTON RD

FOXDOWN RD

BURNHAM CL

PRIMLEY CL

FIR CL

CONNELL DR

HOLTON CL

DUDWELL RD

CRESCENT DR S

SHIPLEY RD

LITTLEWORTH CL

COWLEY DR

BROWNLEAF RD

ABINGER RD

SELHURST RD

PINFOLD

ROSEDENE

OVINGDEAN RD

GREEN

PAVILION RD

ROTTINGDEAN DR

STANSTEAD CRES

MERSTON RD

COWLEY DR

Sch

Sch

Sch

Sch

Sch

Sch

Sch

P

P

P

P

P

Liby

Liby

WANDERDOWN RD

NEW BARN
COURT FARM

LONGHILL

ORD RD

MEADOW

MEADOW

THE
ROTYNS

BAZEHILL RD

WELLESMERE RD

GORHAM AVE

DEAN COURT RD

LUSTRELLS

WHITEWAY LA

NORTHFIELD

ROYLES

CHALLONERS

BISHOPSTONE

FALMER AVE

WHITELOT

WESTMESTON AVE

CHORLEY AVE

LUSTRELLS VALE

LINDFIELD AVE

LUSTRELLS CRES

FALMER AVE

FOUNTHILL RD

CAMBELL RD

LENHAM AVE

LENHAM AVE

FOUNTHILL RD

GRAND AVE

CRANLEIGH AVE

SALTDEAN DR

CHICHESTER DR

ARUNDEL DR

EILEEN AVE

MARINE CL

ABBOTSBURY

KNOLE CRES

CHAILEY AVE

NEWLANDS RD

STEYNING RD

Steyning Rd

VICARAGE TERR

VICARAGE

THE GREEN

WHIPPING
POST LA

OLDE PLACE

HIGH ST B 2123

THE GREEN

NEVILL RD

PARK RD

PARK CRES

WEST ST

LITTLE
ROMNEY RD

ENHAM RD W

The
Twitten

St Dunstan's

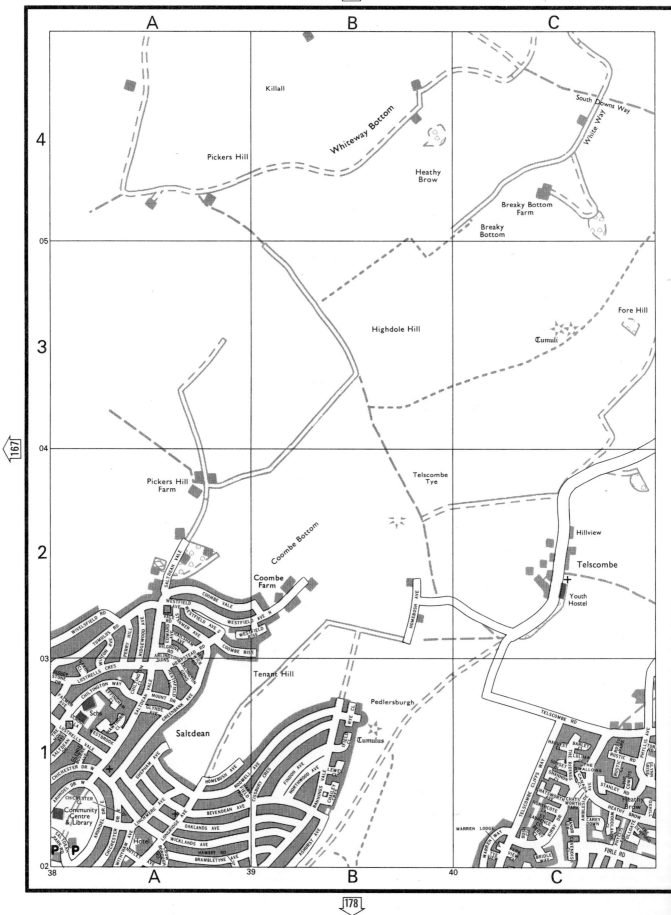

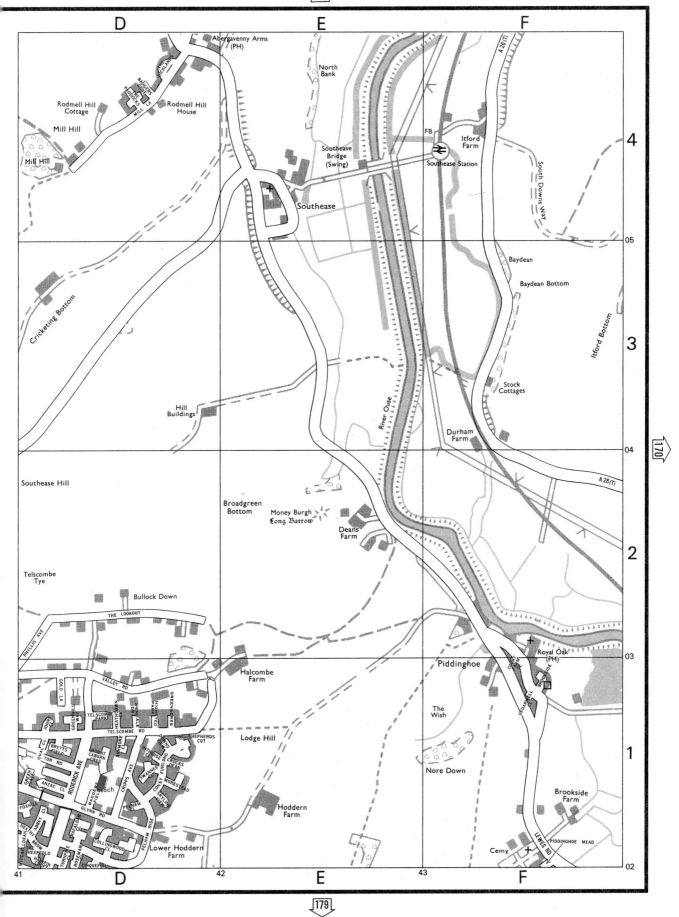

149

D   E   F

Abergavenny Arms
(PH)

ACKLANDS

North
Bank

BADGERS
CLOSE
PADDOCK'S LA
RODMELL MILL

Rodmell Hill
Cottage

Rodmell Hill
House

Mill Hill

Southease
Bridge
(Swing)

FB

Itford
Farm

A 26 (T)

4

Southease Station

Mill Hill

Southease

South Downs Way

05

Baydean

Cricketing Bottom

Baydean Bottom

3

River Ouse

Itford Bottom

Hill
Buildings

Stock
Cottages

Durham
Farm

04

Southease Hill

A 26 (T)

Broadgreen
Bottom

Money Burgh
Long Barrow

Deans
Farm

2

Telscombe
Tye

Bullock Down

Royal Oak
(PH)

THE LOOKOUT

Piddinghoe

03

PHYLLIS AVE

VALLEY RD

GREENACRES

Halcombe
Farm

The
Wish

CEDARWELL
BROOKSIDE

OLD LA

GOLD LA

JOHN

GREENHILL CL
HEATHDOWN

Telscombe
Park

HIGHFIELD
PARK

WENDYLN

Lodge Hill

Nore Down

1

TELSCOMBE RD

SHEPHERDS
COT

JOHN
SOUTH CL
STANMER

BRETTS
FIELD
MOUNT
CABURN

WHITMORE
SWANBE

DENE
COVE FURLONG

CRICKS
DEAN

Brookside
Farm

GREEN
LEAF CL
ANZAC CL

Sch

MORESTEAD

LEWES RD

Cemx

PIDDINGHOE MEAD

FOXHILL
HEATH

PELHAM
RISE

PELHAM

BADGERS
FIELD

RODERICK AVE
GLYNN RD

CRIPPS AVE

Hoddern
Farm

TRAFALGAR
ROSEMARY
COLLINGWOOD
THIRLMERE

Lower Hoddern
Farm

CINQUEFOIL

D   E   F

02

41   42   43

170

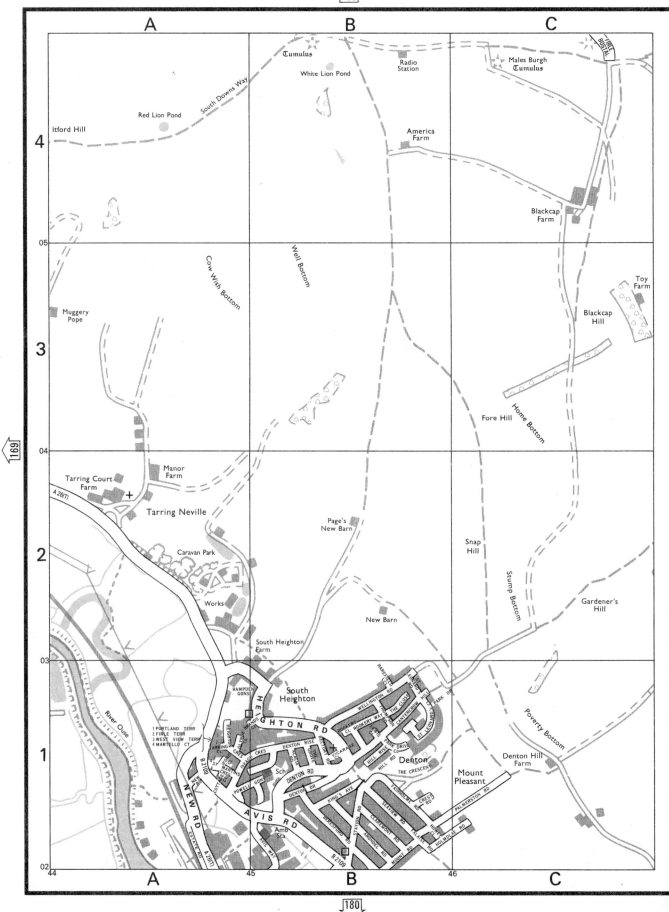

A   **B**   **C**

Itford Hill

Red Lion Pond

South Downs Way

Tumulus

White Lion Pond

Radio Station

Males Burgh

Tumulus

America Farm

Blackcap Farm

4

05

Cow Wish Bottom

Well Bottom

Toy Farm

Blackcap Hill

Muggery Pope

Fore Hill

Home Bottom

3

04

Manor Farm

Tarring Court Farm

A 26(T)

Tarring Neville

Page's New Barn

Snap Hill

Stump Bottom

Gardener's Hill

2

Caravan Park

Works

New Barn

South Heighton Farm

03

HAMPDEN GDNS

HEIGHTON RD

South Heighton

Poverty Bottom

Denton Hill Farm

1

1 PORTLAND TERR
2 FIRLE TERR
3 WEST VIEW TERR
4 MARTELLO CT

River Ouse

WELLINGTON RD

THE CLOSE

Denton

Mount Pleasant

NEW RD

B 2109

Sch

DENTON RD

AVIS RD

Amb Sta

B 2109

AVIS WAY

02

44   **A**   **45**   **B**   **46**   **C**

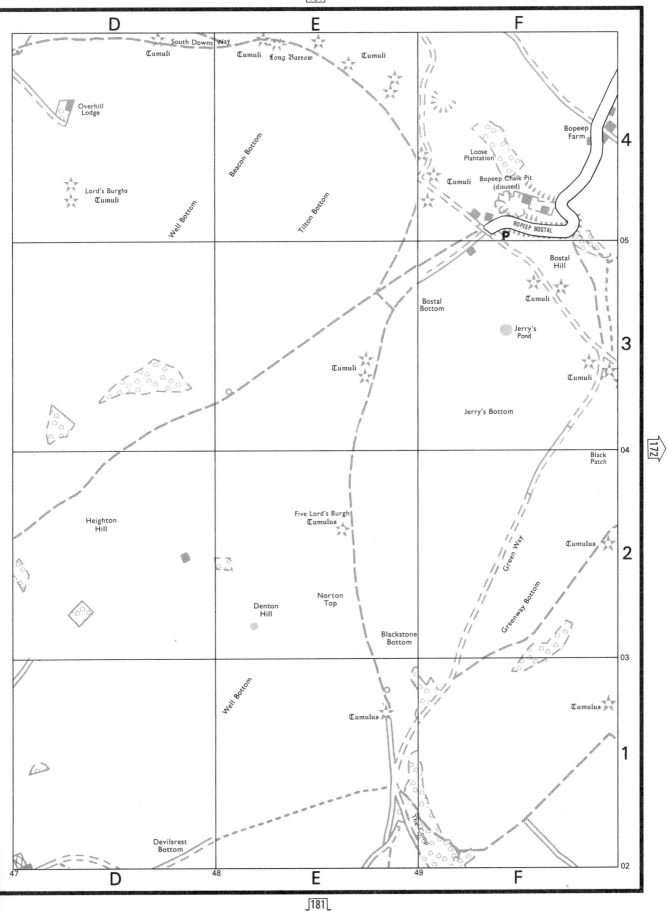

D   E   F

South Downs Way

Tumuli

Tumuli

Long Barrow

Tumuli

Overhill
Lodge

Bopeep
Farm

4

Loose
Plantation

Lord's Burghs
Tumuli

Tumuli

Bopeep Chalk Pit
(disused)

Well Bottom

Beacon Bottom

Tilton Bottom

BOPEEP BOSTAL

P

05

Bostal
Hill

Bostal
Bottom

Tumuli

Jerry's
Pond

3

Tumuli

Tumuli

Jerry's Bottom

04

Black
Patch

Heighton
Hill

Five Lord's Burgh
Tumulus

Green Way

Tumulus

2

Denton
Hill

Norton
Top

Greenway Bottom

Blackstone
Bottom

03

Well Bottom

Tumulus

Tumulus

1

The Comp

Devilsrest
Bottom

02

47   D   48   E   49   F

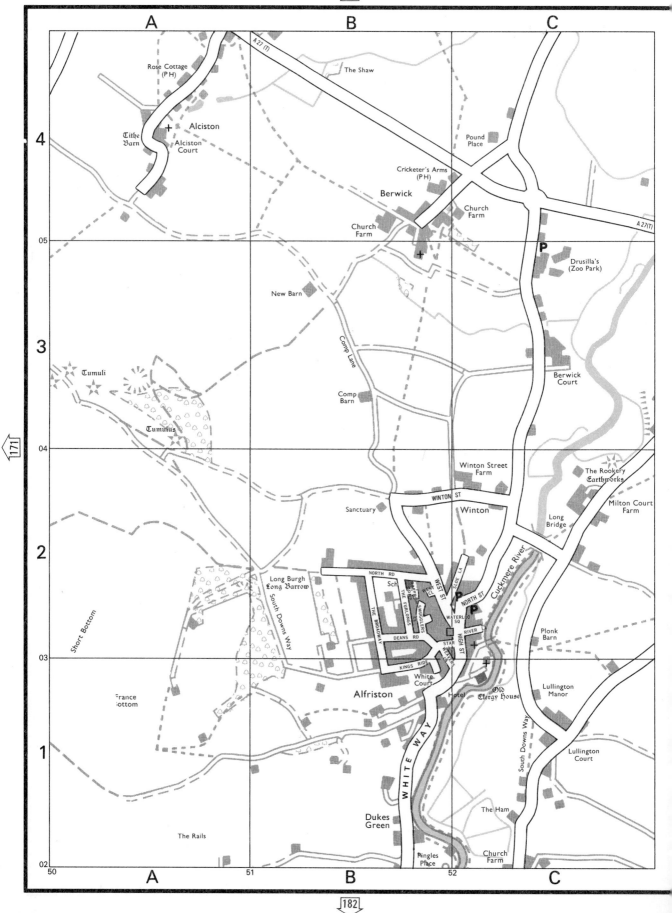

A   B   C

A 27 (T)

The Shaw

Rose Cottage
(P H)

Alciston

Tithe
Barn

Alciston
Court

Pound
Place

Cricketer's Arms
(P H)

Berwick

Church
Farm

Church
Farm

Drusilla's
(Zoo Park)

New Barn

Comp Lane

Tumuli

Comp
Barn

Berwick
Court

Tumulus

The Rookery
Earthworks

Winton Street
Farm

Milton Court
Farm

Sanctuary

Winton

Long
Bridge

Long Burgh
Long Barrow

South Downs Way

WINTON ST

Cuckmere River

NORTH RD

Sch

THE FURLONGS

WEST
CL

WEST ST

SLOE LA

NORTH ST

WATERLOO
SQ

Short Bottom

THE BROADWAY

SMUGGLERS

Plonk
Barn

DEANS RD

HIGH ST

RIVER

STAR

KINGS RIDE

WEAVERS

White
Court

Alfriston

Hotel

Old
Clergy House

Lullington
Manor

France
Bottom

WHITE WAY

South Downs Way

Lullington
Court

The Ham

The Rails

Dukes
Green

Pingles
Place

Church
Farm

A 27 (T)

50   A   51   B   52   C

D   E   F

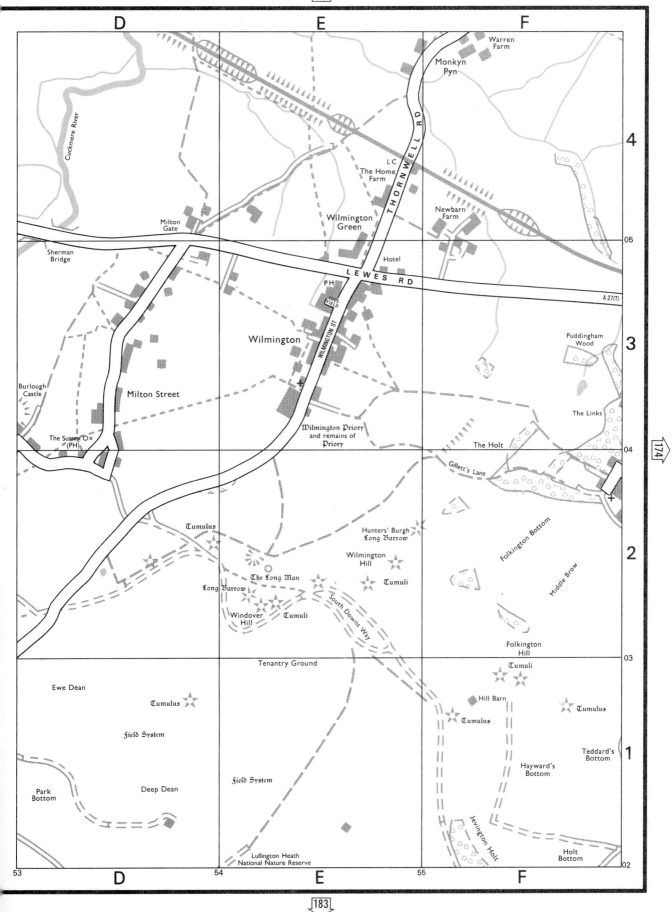

Cuckmere River

Warren Farm

Monkyn Pyn

LC
The Home Farm

Milton Gate

Wilmington Green

THORNWELL RD

Newbarn Farm

05

Sherman Bridge

Hotel

LEWES RD

A 27(T)

PH

Puddingham Wood

Wilmington

WILMINGTON ST

3

Burlough Castle

Milton Street

The Links

Wilmington Priory
and remains of
Priory

The Holt

04

174

The Sussex Ox
(PH)

Gillett's Lane

Tumulus

Hunters' Burgh
Long Barrow

Folkington Bottom

2

Wilmington Hill

Long Barrow

The Long Man

Tumuli

Middle Brow

Windover Hill

Tumuli

South Downs Way

Folkington Hill

Tenantry Ground

03

Ewe Dean

Tumuli

Tumulus

Field System

Hill Barn

Tumulus

Tumulus

Teddard's Bottom

1

Field System

Park Bottom

Deep Dean

Hayward's Bottom

Jevington Holt

Holt Bottom

Lullington Heath
National Nature Reserve

02

53   D   54   E   55   F

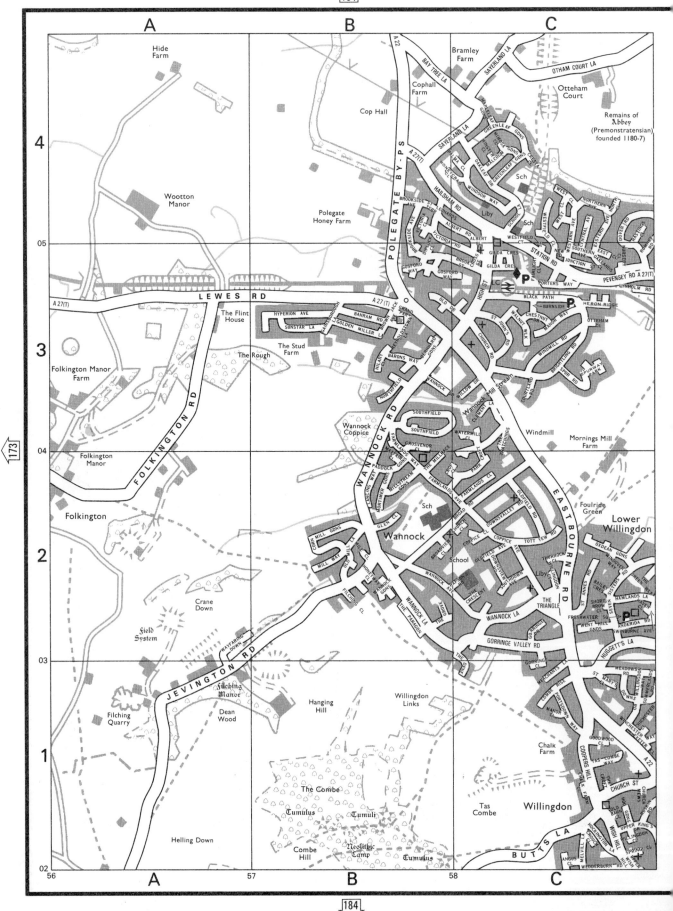

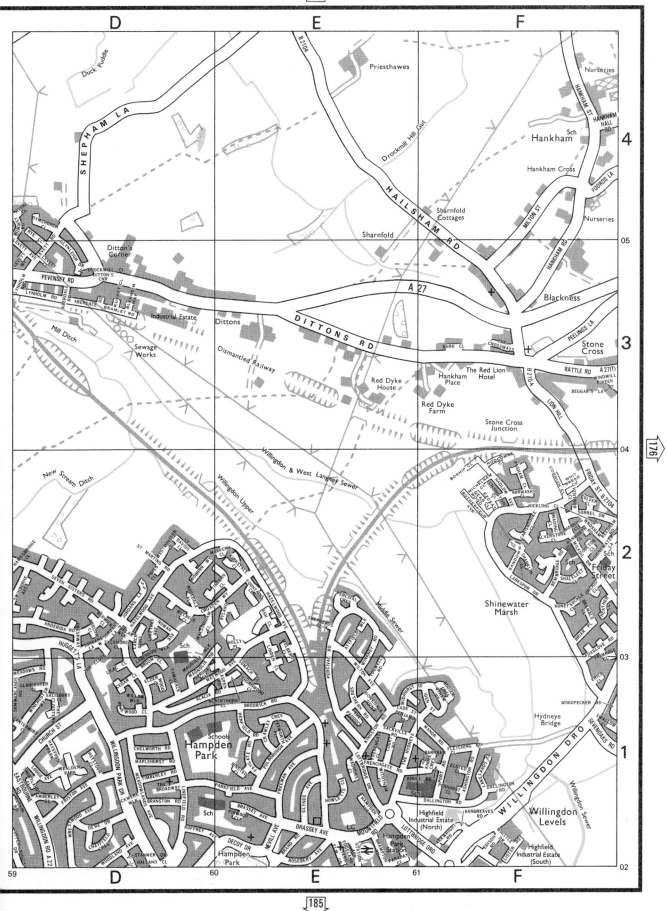

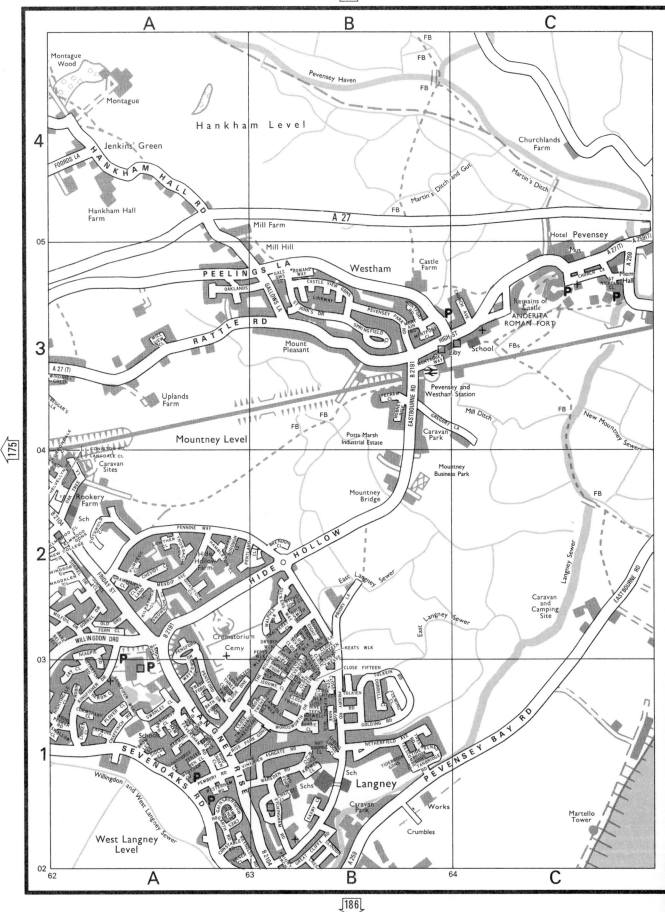

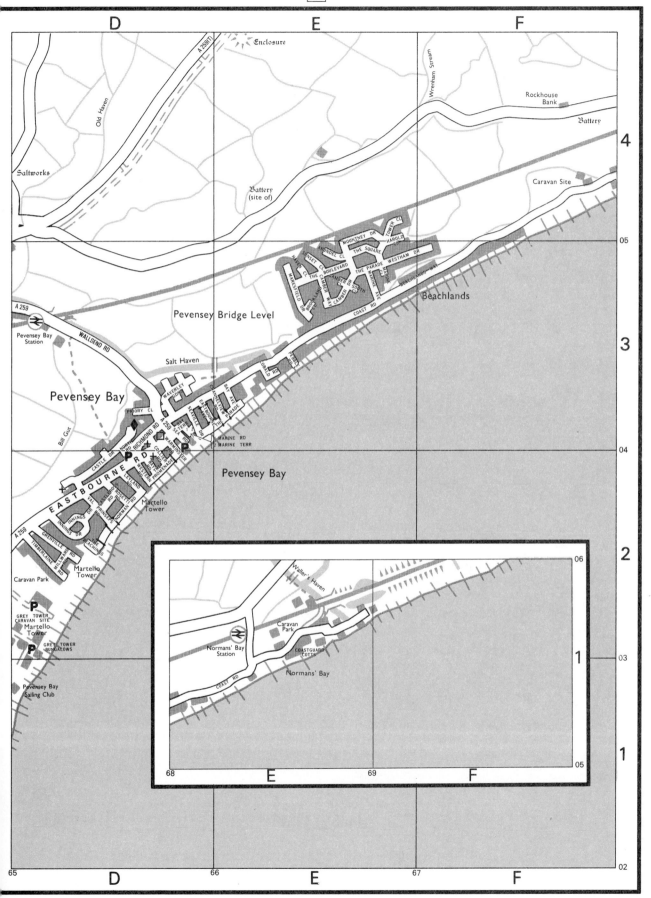

D   E   F

Enclosure

Old Haven

Saltworks

Battery
(site of)

Wrenham Stream

Rockhouse
Bank

Battery

Caravan Site

4

MOUNTNEY DR

TOWER CL

THE SQUARE

HAROLD
CL

ARUNDEL CL

SUNSET CL

THE BOULEVARD

CAMBER DR

WESTHAM DR

PAYNE CL

CAMBER WAY

THE PARADE

MARINE AVE

MARESFIELD DR

CAMBER CL SOUTH

BROOKLANDS

BEACHLANDS WAY

Beachlands

05

Pevensey Bridge Level

COAST RD

A 259

Pevensey Bay
Station

WALLSEND RD

3

Salt Haven

PETER'S RD

JOHN RD

Pevensey Bay

WAVERLEY

BAY AVE

THE PARADE

CARAVELLE RD

EASTBOURN

Bill Gut

PRIORY CL

RICHMOND RD

A 259

SEVILLE RD

SEAVILLE DR

SEA RD

WARMINSTER

MARINE RD

MARINE TERR

Eastbourne

CASTLE DR NORTH

RD

COTT

P R D

Pevensey Bay

04

EASTBOURNE

VAL PRINSEP'S RD

CASSOBURY RD

ROSE

NORMAN RD

WESTON

LELAND RD

SOUTH PROMENADE

Martello
Tower

A 259

INNINGS DR

GRENVILLE

INNINGS DR

MILLWARD RD

BEACHINGS

Caravan Park

TIMBERLAINE RD

Martello
Tower

2

P

GREY TOWER
CARAVAN SITE
Martello
Tower

P

GREY TOWER
BUNGALOWS

Pevensey Bay
Sailing Club

Waller's Haven

06

Caravan
Park

Normans' Bay
Station

COASTGUARD
COTTS

COAST RD

Normans' Bay

03

1

68   E   69   F

05

02

65   D   66   E   67   F

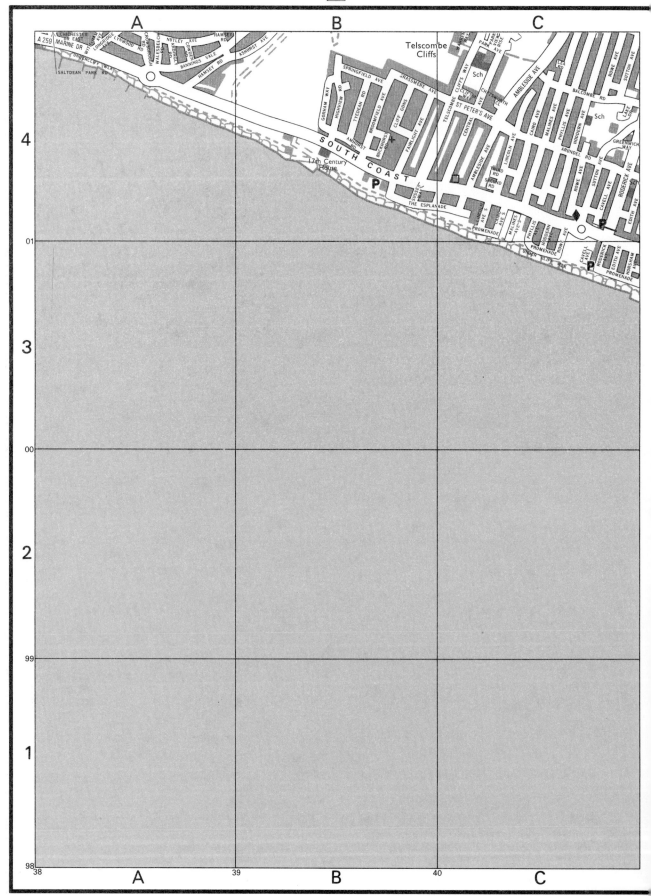

Telscombe Cliffs

SOUTH COAST

17th Century House

THE ESPLANADE

PROMENADE

UNDER CLIFF WAY

PROMENADE

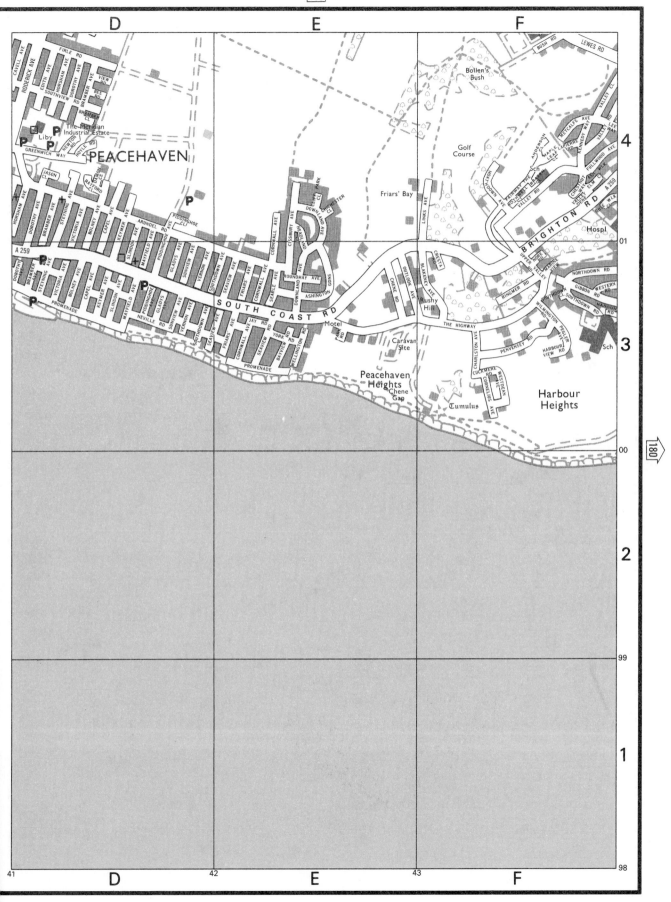

D E F

CAVELL AVE
RODERICK AVE
FIRLE RD
EDITH AVE
HORSHAM RD
SOUTHVIEW RD
DOROTHY RD
BRAMBER AVE
VIEW RD
BEE RD
BRAMBER CL

The Meridian
Industrial Estate
Liby
P P P
NEWTON RD
HOYLE RD
GREENWICH WAY

PEACEHAVEN

JASON CL
DARWIN CL
RAYFORD CL

HORSHAM AVE
DOROTHY AVE
BRAMBER AVE
STEYNING AVE
VICTORIA AVE
BOLNEY AVE
CAPEL AVE
KEYMER AVE
SLINDON AVE
MAYFIELD
PIDDINGHOE AVE
ARUNDEL AVE

P

PIDDINGHOE CL
DOWNLAND AVE
CHAPEL PARK
CHICHESTER
CISSBURY AVE
CORNWALL AVE
SEAVIEW AVE
SEARLE AVE
FRIARS
ROUNDHAY AVE
ASHINGTON GDNS
MIDLAND AVE
DOWNLAND AVE
CHICHESTER CL
CHAPEL PARK

Friars' Bay

Bollen's Bush

Golf
Course

LEWES RD
BUSH RD
VALLEY CL
LEE WAY
METCALFE AVE
LAPIERRE
KENNEDY WAY
VALLEY RD
ANDERSON
MAPLE LEAF CL
CHESTNUT
FULLWOOD AVE
ELM CL
WYVERN
TREE WLK
A 259

Sch

BRIGHTON RD

Hospl

01

A 259
DOROTHY AVE
BRAMBER AVE
STEYNING AVE
VICTORIA AVE
BOLNEY AVE
CAPEL AVE
KEYMER AVE
SLINDON AVE
MAYFIELD
PIDDINGHOE AVE
P P
P

PROMENADE
NEVILLE RD
CLADYS
SUNVIEW AVE
VERNON AVE
SOUTHDOWN AVE
SEAVIEW AVE

SOUTH COAST RD

CRESTA RD
BLAKENEY AVE
OUTLOOK AVE
CHENE RD
Rushy Hill
THE HIGHWAY
UPPER HOLT
UPPER VALLEY
RINGMER RD
WILMINGTON
FEGLER RD
NORTHDOWN
SOUTHDOWN RD
GIBBON RD
WESTERN
NORTHDOWN RD

Sch

LINKS AVE

CORNWALL
JAY RD
SEAVIEW AVE
BAYVIEW RD
YORK RD
WELLINGTON RD
PROMENADE
Motel
PARK RD

Caravan
Site

CHARLISTON AVE
CUCKMERE RD
PEVENSEY RD
WESTDEAN AVE
CORNELIUS AVE
HARBOUR VIEW RD

Sch

Peacehaven
Heights
Chene
Gap

Tumulus

Harbour
Heights

00

180

4

3

2

99

1

98

41 D 42 E 43 F

A ↓ 259
170

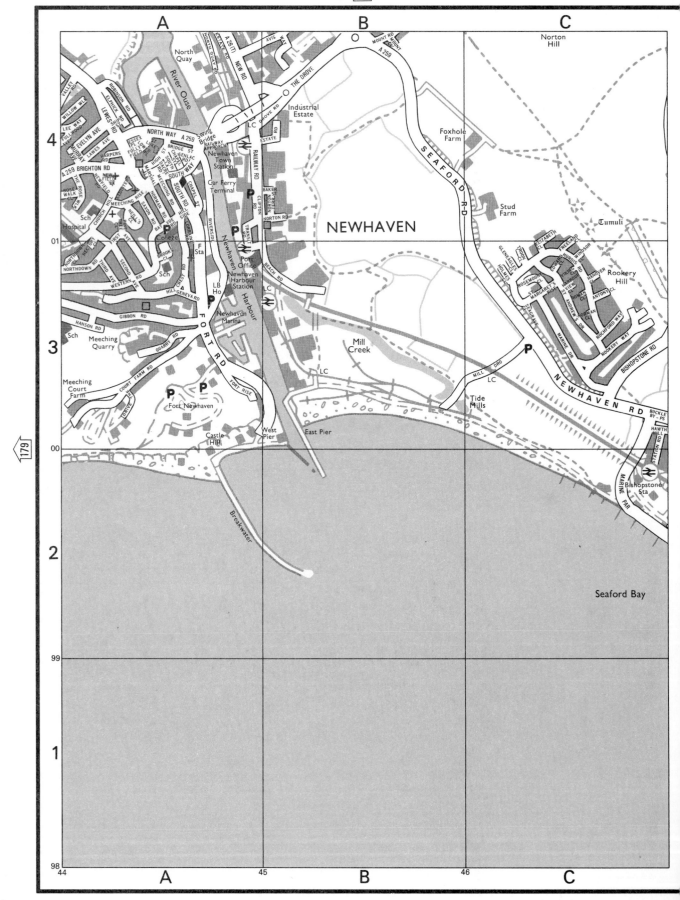

NEWHAVEN

Seaford Bay

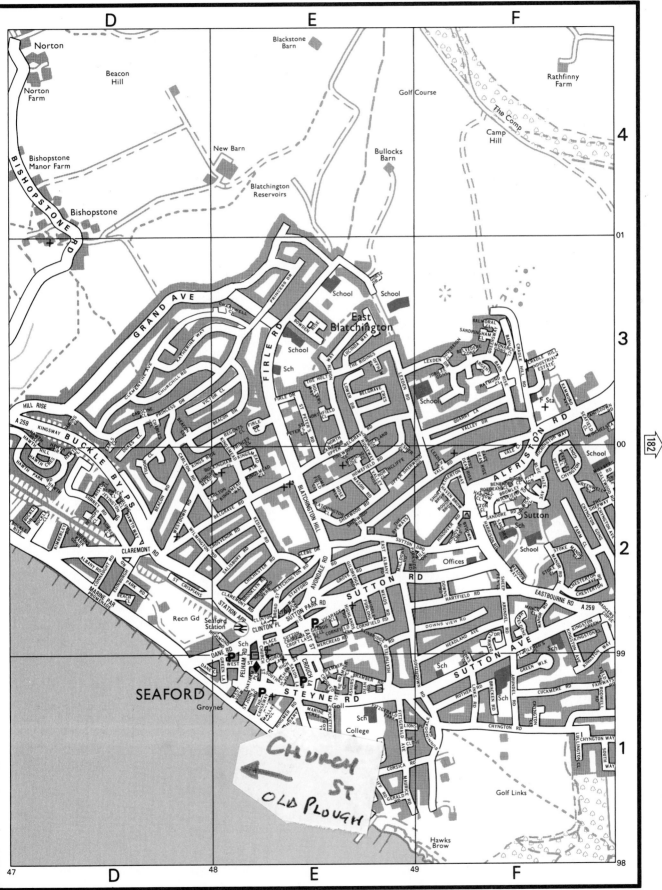

182

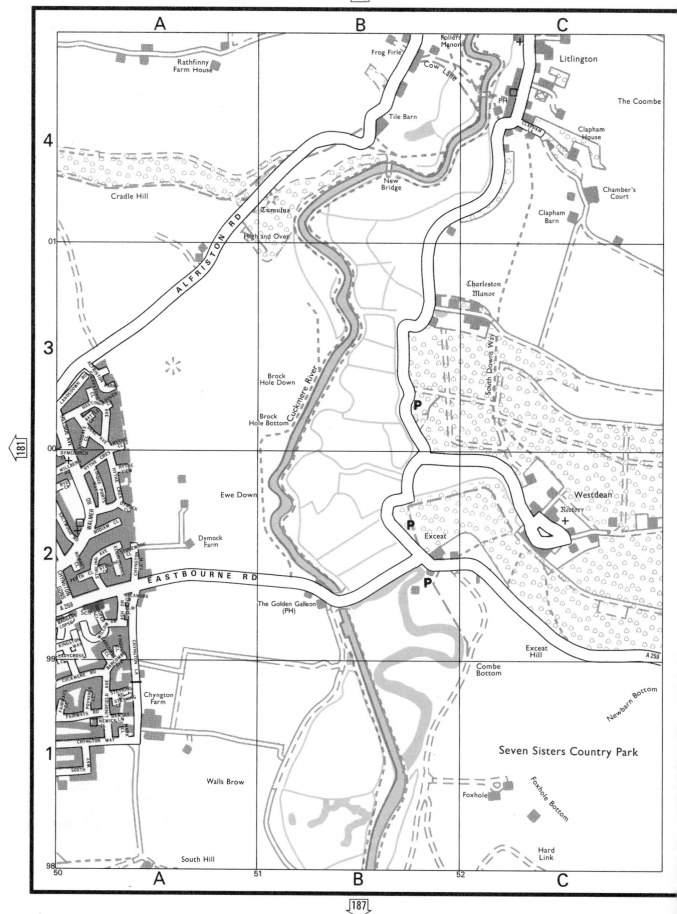

181

A   B   C

4

01

3

00

2

99

1

98

50   51   52

A   B   C

Rathfinny Farm House
Frog Firle
Follers Manor
Litlington
The Coombe
Cow Lane
Tile Barn
PH
CLAPHAM
Clapham House
Cradle Hill
New Bridge
Chamber's Court
Tumulus
Clapham Barn
High and Over
ALFRISTON RD
Charleston Manor
Brock Hole Down
Cuckmere River
South Downs Way
Brock Hole Bottom
P
Westdean
DYMCHURCH
Ewe Down
Rectory
P
Exceat
Dymock Farm
P
EASTBOURNE RD
The Golden Galleon (PH)
Exceat Hill
A 259
Combe Bottom
Chyngton Farm
Newbarn Bottom
Chyngton Way
Seven Sisters Country Park
South Way
Walls Brow
Foxhole
Foxhole Bottom
South Hill
Hard Link

173

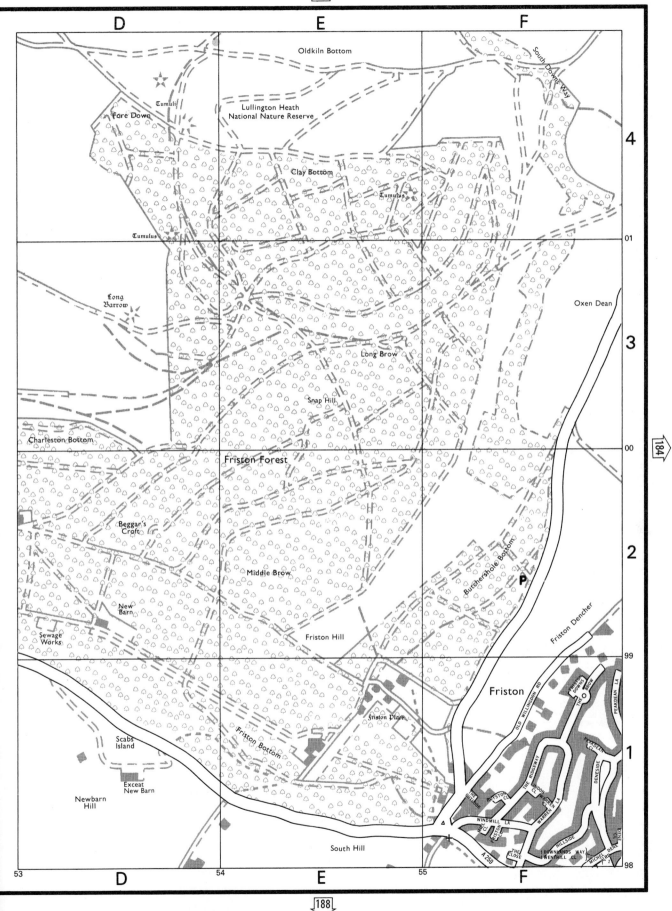

D   E   F

Oldkiln Bottom

South Downs Way

Tumuli

Fore Down

Lullington Heath
National Nature Reserve

4

Clay Bottom

Tumulus

01

Oxen Dean

Long
Barrow

3

Long Brow

Snap Hill

Charleston Bottom

00

Friston Forest

Beggar's
Croft

Burchershole Bottom

2

Middle Brow

P

New
Barn

Friston Dencher

Sewage
Works

Friston Hill

99

Friston

Scabs
Island

OLD WILLINGDON RD

THE BROW

FRISTON DOWNS

PEAKDEAN LA

Friston Bottom

Friston Place

THE RIDGEWAY

LINDON CL

PEAKDEAN CL

DENESIDE

1

Exceat
New Barn

THE
BULLOCK

RUTSTON CL

WARREN LA

Newbarn
Hill

WINDMILL LA

HILLSIDE

South Hill

THE
CLOSE

1 DOWNLANDS WAY

DENE RISE

MICHEL DENE RD

A 259

1 TWENTHILL CL

53   D   54   E   55   F   98

184

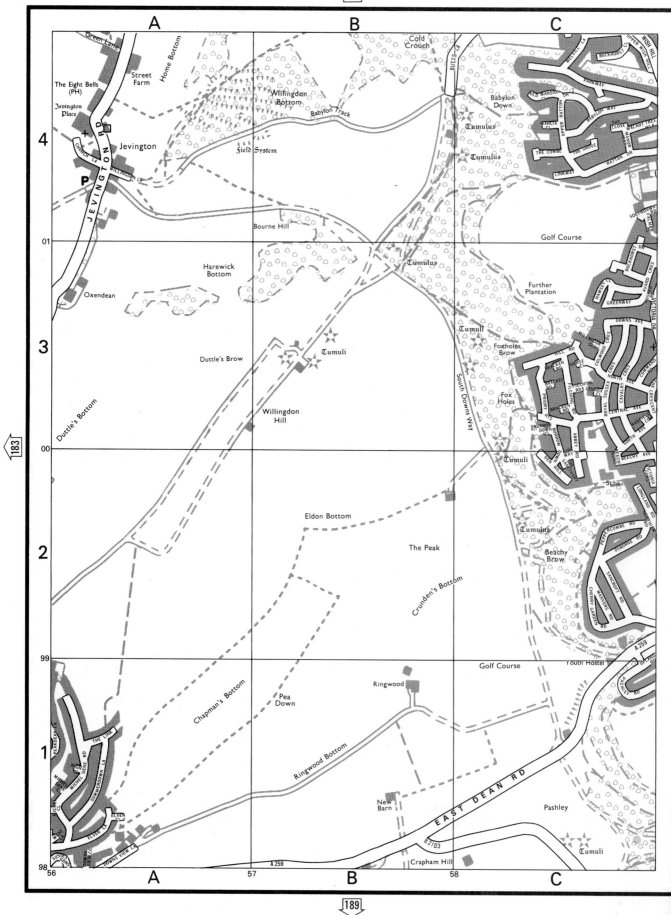

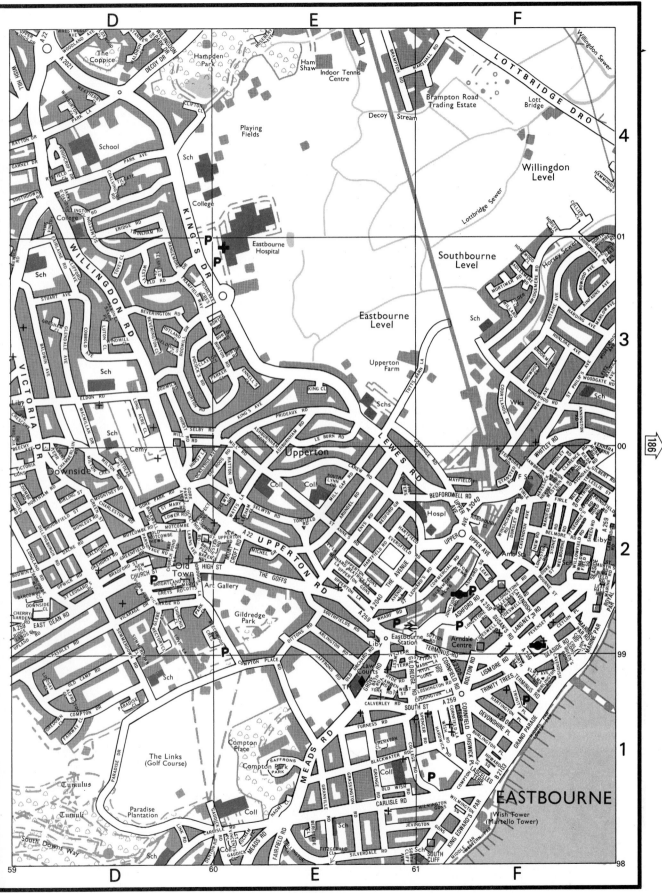

EASTBOURNE

Wish Tower
(Martello Tower)

176

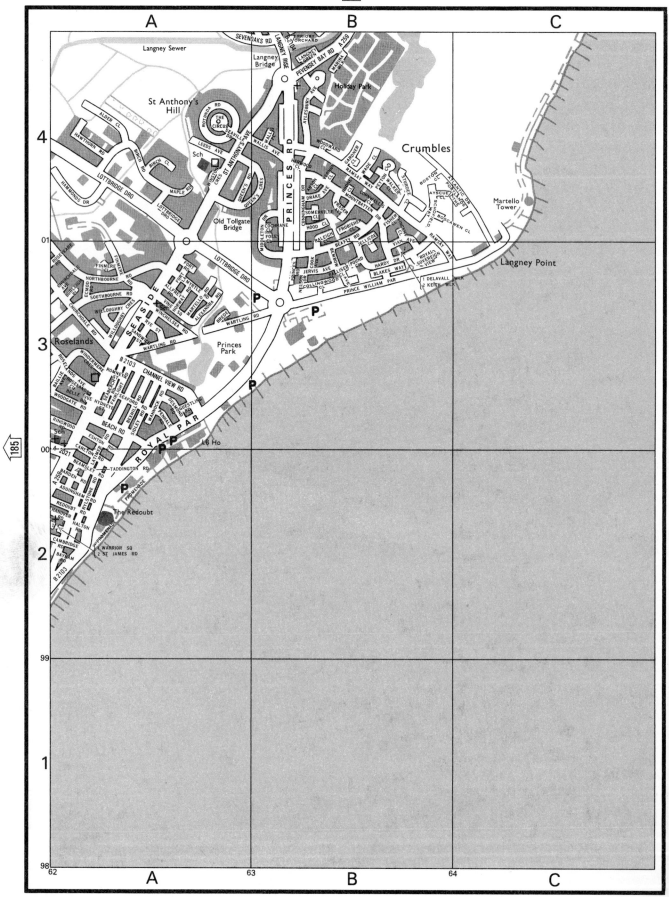

185

A   B   C

Langney Sewer

St Anthony's Hill

SEVENOAKS RD

PRIORY ORCHARD

Langney Bridge

PEVENSEY BAY RD

A 259

Holiday Park

Crumbles

THE CIRCUS

ROTUNDA RD

LEEDS AVE

Sch

ST ANTHONY'S AVE

SEAVILLE DR

WALLIS AVE

PRINCES RD

Martello Tower

Old Tollgate Bridge

Lottbridge Dro

LOTTBRIDGE DRO

QUEEN'S RD

QUEEN'S CRES

Langney Point

Roselands

FINMERE RD

NORTHBOURNE RD

SOUTHBOURNE RD

WILLOUGHBY CRES

SEASIDE

LOTTBRIDGE DRO

WARTLING RD

Princes Park

WARTLING RD

CHANNEL VIEW RD

B 2103

WINDERMERE

ROYAL PAR

BEACH RD

Sch

A 2021

LB Ho

The Redoubt

PROMENADE

TADDINGTON RD

REDOUBT

B 2103

CAMBRIDGE RD

A 259

BATHAM RD

1 WARRIOR SQ
2 ST JAMES RD

98 62   A   63   B   64   C

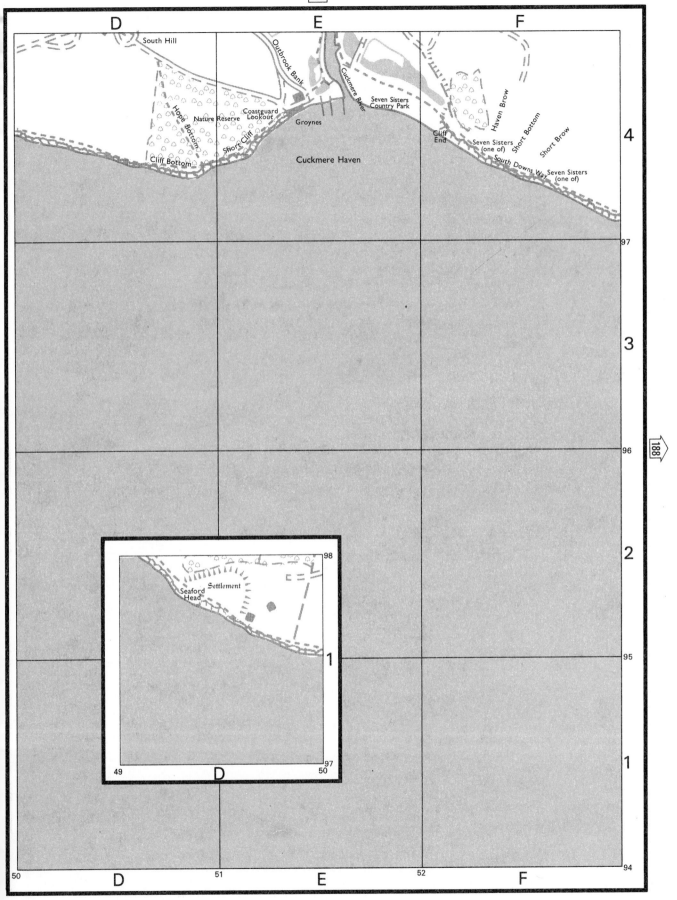

D   E   F

South Hill

Outbrook Bank

Cuckmere River

Seven Sisters
Country Park

Hope Bottom

Nature Reserve   Coastguard
Lookout   Groynes

Short Cliff

Cliff Bottom

Cuckmere Haven

Cliff
End

Haven Brow

Seven Sisters
(one of)   Short Bottom
                         Short Brow

South Downs Way   Seven Sisters
                                (one of)

4

97

3

96

2

98

Seaford
Head   Settlement

1

97
49   D   50

95

1

50   D   51   E   52   F   94

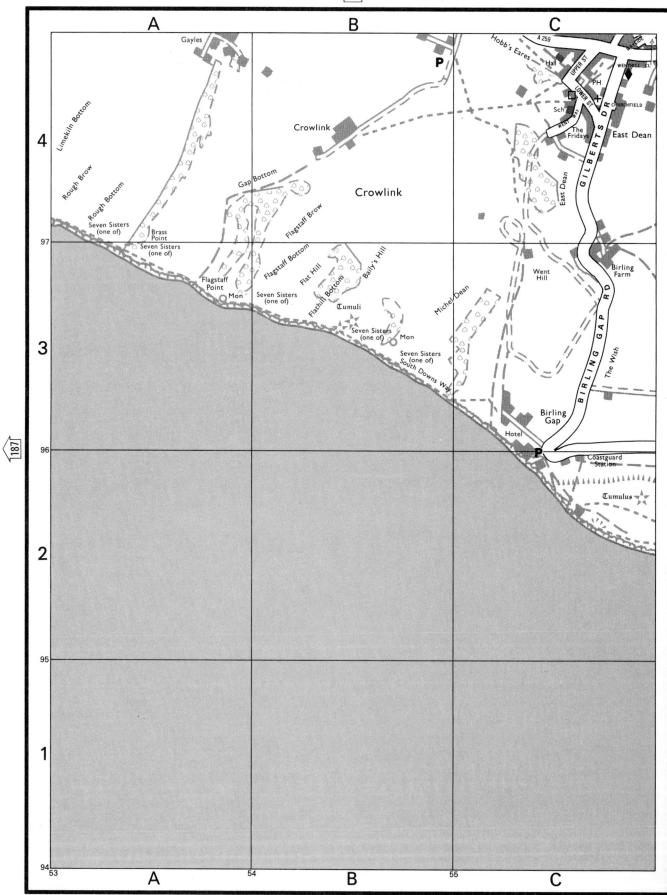

◁187

A   B   C

4

Gayles

Limekiln Bottom

Rough Brow

Rough Bottom

Seven Sisters (one of)

Brass Point

Seven Sisters (one of)

Gap Bottom

Crowlink

Crowlink

Flagstaff Brow

Hobb's Eares

Hall

A 259

WESTSIDE

UPPER ST

PH

WENTHILL EL

LOWER ST

Sch

WENT WAY

GILBERTS DR

CHURCHFIELD

The Fridays

East Dean

East Dean

97

Flagstaff Point

Mon

Flagstaff Bottom

Flat Hill

Flathill Bottom

Bally's Hill

Tumuli

Seven Sisters (one of)

Seven Sisters (one of)

Mon

Michel Dean

Went Hill

Birling Farm

3

Seven Sisters (one of)

South Downs Way

The Wish

BIRLING GAP RD

Birling Gap

Hotel

96

P

Coastguard Station

Tumulus

2

95

1

94

53   54   55

A   B   C

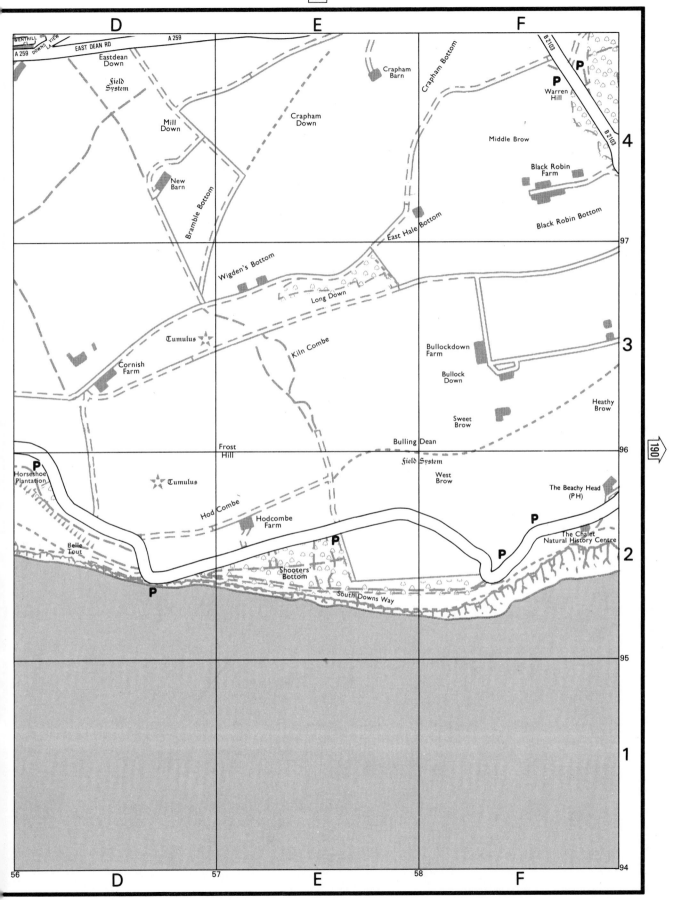

D E F

WENTHILL
DOWNS LA VIEW
A 259 EAST DEAN RD A 259

Eastdean
Down

Field
System

Mill
Down

New
Barn

Bramble Bottom

Crapham
Down

Crapham
Barn

Crapham Bottom

B 2103

Warren
Hill

P
P

Middle Brow

Black Robin
Farm

Black Robin Bottom

East Hale Bottom

97

Wigden's Bottom

Long Down

Kiln Combe

Tumulus

Cornish
Farm

Bullockdown
Farm

Bullock
Down

Heathy
Brow

Sweet
Brow

3

Bulling Dean

Frost
Hill

Field System

West
Brow

The Beachy Head
(PH)

96

P
Horseshoe
Plantation

Tumulus

Hod Combe

Hodcombe
Farm

Shooters'
Bottom

P

P
The Chalet
Natural History Centre

P

Belle
Tout

P

South Downs Way

2

95

1

56 D 57 E 58 F 94

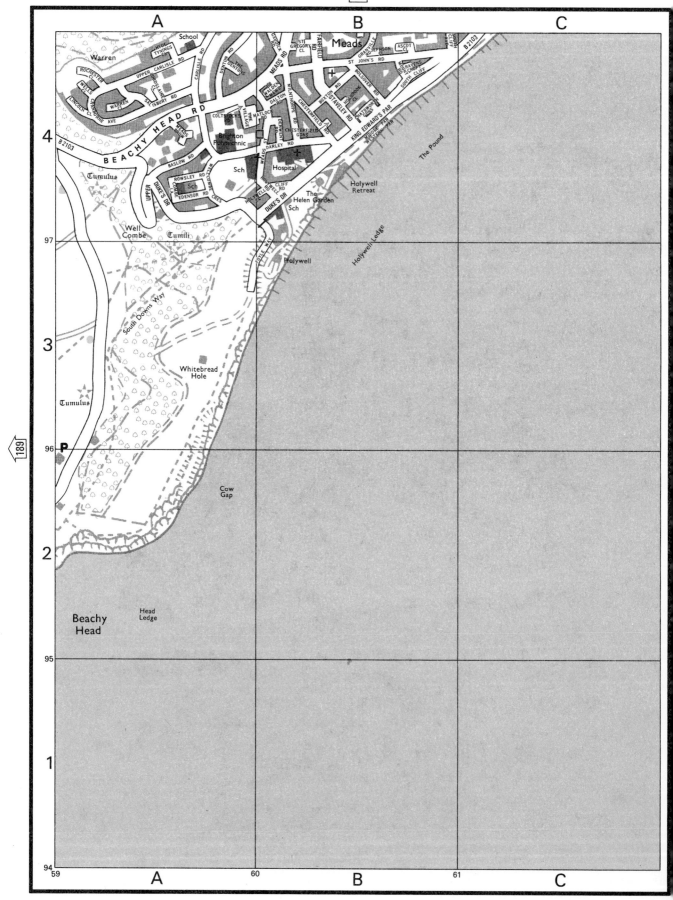

	A	B	C

Warren
School
ROCHESTER CL
UPPER CARLISLE RD
WELL'S
CLABORNE AVE
WARREN
LINCOLN CL
CRANBORNE AVE
ST ISBURY RD
TYNINGS
BRIDGE
THE JENTONS
DENTON RD
CARLISLE RD
B E A C H Y   H E A D   R D
COLTSTOCKS RD
THE VILLAGE
ATTAGS BROW
UPPER DUKE'S DR
BASLOW RD
LOWER DUKE'S DR
ROWSLEY RD
EDENSOR RD
Sch
WYE COMBE CRES
Sch
Brighton Polytechnic
MEADS ST
MATLOCK RD
DARLEY RD
Hospital
HOLYWELL RD
CLIFF RD
Sch
DUKE'S DR
FOYLE WAY

Meads
ST GREGORY CL
FAIRFIELD RD
ST JOHN'S RD
GRANVILLE RD
JEPHSON
ASCOT
ROWSLEY RD
BOLSOVER RD
MEADS RD
MILNTHORPE RD
DALTON RD
CHESTERFIELD RD
BUXTON RD
STAVELEY RD
ROBERTSON RD
BLATCHMORE GDNS
SOUTH CLIFF
RAVENS CHOPS
KING EDWARD'S PAR
MOORE PAR
WESTERN PAR
SOUTH CLIFF
B 2103

CHESTERFIELD GDNS
The Helen Garden
Sch
Holywell Retreat
The Pound
Holywell Ledge
Holywell

B 2103

Tumulus
Well Combe
Tumuli

South Downs Way

Whitebread Hole

Tumulus

P

Cow Gap

Beachy Head

Head Ledge

USER'S NOTES

EXPLANATION OF THE STREET INDEX REFERENCE SYSTEM

Street names are listed alphabetically and show the locality, the page number and a reference to the square in which the name falls on the map page.

Example: West St.   Dit..101 D2

West St   This is the full street name, which may have been abbreviated on the map.

Dit   This is the abbreviation for the town, village or locality in which the street falls.

101   This is the page number of the map on which the street name appears.

D2   The letter and figure indicate the square on the map in which the centre of the street falls. The square can be found at the junction of the vertical column carrying the appropriate letter and the horizontal row carrying the appropriate figure.

ABBREVIATIONS USED IN THE INDEX
Road Names

Approach	App	Lane	La
Avenue	Ave	North	N
Boulevard	Bvd	Orchard	Orch
Broadway	Bwy	Parade	Par
By-Pass	By-Ps	Passage	Pas
Causeway	Cswy	Place	Pl
Common	Comm	Pleasant	Plea
Corner	Cnr	Precinct	Prec
Cottages	Cotts	Promenade	Prom
Court	Ct	Road	Rd
Crescent	Cres	South	S
Drive	Dr	Square	Sq
Drove	Dro	Street,Saint	St
East	E	Terrace	Terr
Gardens	Gdns	Walk	Wlk
Grove	Gr	West	W
Heights	Hts	Yard	Yd

Place	Abbr.	Page	Grid
Albourne	Alb	99	D3
Alciston	Alc	172	A4
Alfriston	Alfn	172	B1
Arlington	Arl	153	E2
Ashurst (Langton Green)	Asht	6	A1
Ashurst Wood	Ash W	13	E3
Barcombe	Bar	104	B1
Barcombe Cross	Bar C	104	B2
Battle	Bat	115	D3
Beckley	Bec	69	F2
Beddingham	Bed	150	A2
Bells Yew Green	Bel G	19	E3
Berwick	Ber	172	B4
Bexhill	Bex	159	F2
Bishopstone	Bis	181	D4
Blackboys	Blas	81	F3
Blackham	Blam	5	F2
Boarshead	Boa	28	A3
Bodiam	Bod	67	E4
Bodle Street Green	Bod G	112	A1
Boreham Street	Bor S	135	E2
Brede	Bre	91	F1
Brightling	Bril	87	D3
Brighton	Bri	165	F2
Broad Oak (Heathfield)	Bro O	61	E1
Broad Oak (Westfield)	Bro O W	91	F2
Buckland Hill	Buc	20	C1
Burgess Hill	Bur H	74	C3
Burwash	Bur	63	F3
Burwash Common	Bur C	62	C2
Buss's Green	Bus G	20	C1
Buxted	Bux	57	F2
Cackle Street	Cac S	37	E1
Cade Street	Cad S	84	B3
Camber	Cam	96	B2
Catsfield	Cat	137	E4
Chailey	Chay	77	E2
Chalvington	Chal	152	C4
Chelwood Common	Che Co	36	A3
Chelwood Gate	Che G	36	A4
Chiddingly	Chi	108	B1
Chiddingstone Hoath	Chi H	6	A4
Churches Green	Chur	111	F4
Clayton	Clay	123	E4
Cliff End	C End	142	C4
Coghurst	Cog	141	D3
Coleman's Hatch	Col H	25	E4
Cooksbridge	Coo	126	C4
Cousley Wood	Cou W	32	A4
Cowbeech	Cowb	110	C1
Cowden	Cowd	4	C3
Crawley Down	Cra D	11	D4
Cripp's Corner	Cri C	90	A4
Cross in Hand	Cro H	82	C4
Crow borough	Cro	27	F1
Crowhurst	Crow	138	B3
Dallington	Dal	86	A2
Danehill	Dan	35	F2
Ditchling	Dit	101	E2
Domewood	Dom	1	A3
Dormans Park	Dor P	2	B3
Dormansland	Dor	2	C4
Earl's Down	Ear D	85	F2
Easbourne	East	185	F1
East Chiltington	E Chi	102	C1
East Dean	E Dean	188	C4
East Grinstead	E Gri	2	B1
East Guldeford	E Gul	95	E4
East Hoathly	E Hoa	107	F3
Eridge Green	Eri G	17	F2
Etchingham	Etc	46	A1
Etchingwood	Etcd	58	A1
Ewhurst Green	Ewh G	67	F3
Fairlight	Fai	142	B3
Fairwarp	Fair	37	F1
Falmer	Fal	147	D3
Felbridge	Fel	1	C2
Five Ashes	Five A	59	F3
Fletching	Fle	55	F2
Flimwell	Fli	34	A2
Folkington	Fol	174	A2
Fordcombe	Ford	6	C3
Forest Row	For R	13	F1
Four Oaks	Four O	70	A3
Four Throws	Four T	48	A4
Framfield	Fra	80	C3
Frant	Frant	19	D2
Friar's Gate	Fri G	26	C4
Friston	Fri	183	F1
Glynde	Gly	150	B4
Golden Cross	Gol C	131	E3
Groombridge	Gro	16	C4
Guestling Green	Gue G	141	F4
Hadlow Down	Had D	59	D3
Hailsham	Hai	155	D4
Halland	Hall	107	D3
Hammerwood	Hamm	3	F2
Hamsey	Ham	127	D3
Hankham	Hank	175	F4
Hartfield	Hart	15	D2
Hassocks	Hass	100	B2
Hastings	Hast	162	B3
Haywards Heath	Hay H	52	B3
Heathfield	Hea	83	F4
Hellingly	Hel	132	C3
Herstmonceux	Hers	134	B3
High Hurstwood	H Hur	38	C1
Highbrook	Higk	22	B1
Hooe	Hooe	158	A4
Horam	Hor	109	E4
Horsted Keynes	Hor K	35	D2
Hove	Hove	164	C3
Hurst Green	Hur G	46	C2
Hurstpierpoint	Hur	99	E3
Icklesham	Ick	119	E3
Iden	Iden	71	F2
Iford	Iford	148	C2
Isfield	Isf	105	E4
Jevington	Jev	184	A4
Keymer	Key	100	C2
Kingstone near Lewes	Kin L	148	B3
Kipping's Cross	Kip	10	C2
Lamberhurst	Lam	21	F3
Langton Green	Lan G	7	E2
Laughton	Lau	130	A4
Lewes	Lew	127	D1
Litlington	Litl	182	C4
Little Bayham	Lit B	20	B2
Little Horsted	Lit H	80	A1
Lower Dicker	Low D	132	A2
Lower Horsebridge	Low H	132	B2
Lower Willingdon	Low W	174	C2
Lunsford's Cross	Lun C	137	E1
Lydd	Lydd	98	C3
Magham Down	Mag D	133	E2
Maresfield	Mar	56	C3
Mark Cross	Mar C	29	F2
Mayfield	May	41	F1
Mill Corner	Mill C	68	C2
Milton Street	Milt S	173	D3
Mountfield	Mou	88	C3
Netherfield	Net	88	A1
New Cut	New Cut	117	E3
Newenden	Newd	50	A2
Newhaven	Newh	180	B4
Newick	Newk	78	A4
Ninfield	Nin	136	C3
Normans' Bay	Nor B	177	E1
North Chailey	N Cha	77	E4
Northbridge Street	N St	65	F3
Northiam	Norm	68	C3
Norton	Nort	181	D4
Nutley	Nut	37	D2
Offham	Off	126	B3
Ovingdean	Oving	167	E2
Oxley's Green	Oxl G	87	E4
Peacehaven	Pea	179	D4
Peasmarsh	Peas	70	C1
Pell Green	Pel G	31	F4
Pembury	Pem	10	A3
Penhurst	Pen	113	E3
Pett	Pett	142	B4
Pevensey	Pev	176	C4
Pevensey Bay	Pev B	177	D3
Piddinghoe	Pid	169	F1
Piltdown	Pil	56	A1
Plumpton	Plu	125	E4
Plumpton Green	Plu G	102	B3
Polegate	Pole	174	C3
Ponts Green	Pon G	112	C2
Portslade Village	Por V	143	C1
Portslade-by-Sea	Por S	163	F3
Poynings	Poy	122	A3
Punnett's Town	Pun T	85	D3
Pyecombe	Pye	122	C3
Ridgewood	Rid	80	A2
Ringmer	Rin	128	B3
Ripe	Ripe	130	A1
Robertsbridge	Rob	65	F2
Rodmell	Rod	149	D1
Rotherfield	Rot	40	C4
Rottingdean	Rottn	167	F1
Rushlake Green	Rus	85	D1
Rye	Rye	95	D3
Rye Harbour	Rye H	95	E1
Salehurst	Sale	66	A3
Saltdean	Salt	168	A1
Sandhurst	San	48	C3
Scayne's Hill	Sca H	53	E2
Seaford	Sea	181	D1
Sedlescombe	Sed	90	B1
Selmeston	Selm	152	A2
Selsfield Common	Sel C	11	D1
Sharpthorne	Sha	22	C3
Shoreham-by-Sea	S Sea	163	D3
Shortgate	Sho	106	C2
South Chailey	S Cha	103	E4
South Heighton	S Hei	170	B1
South Malling	S Mal	127	D2
South Street	S Str	77	E1
Southborough	Sgh	3	C4
Southease	S	169	E4
Southwick	Sock	163	E3
Speldhurst	Spe	7	F4
Spithurst	Spi	104	B4
Staplecross	Stas	67	E1
Stone Bridge	St B	31	E4
Stone Cross	St Cro	175	F3
Stonegate	Ston	44	B3
Streat	Strt	102	A2
Tarring Neville	Tar N	170	A2
Telscombe	Tel	168	C2
The Moor	The M	47	E4
The Moor	The Moor	117	E2
Three Cups Corner	Thr C C	95	E3
Three Leg Cross	Thr C	33	D2
Three Oaks	Thr O	113	A1
Ticehurst	Tic	33	E1
Tidebrook	Tid	42	C4
Town Row	Tow R	29	D1
Tunbridge Wells, Royal	T W	3	B2
Turner's Green	Tur G	85	E2
Uckfield	Uck	30	A4
Udimore	Udi	93	D1
Upper Dicker	Upp D	153	F4
Upper Hartfield	Upp H	14	C1
Vines Cross	Vin C	110	A4
Wadhurst	Wad	31	F2
Waldron	Wald	82	B2
Wallcrouch	Wal	32	B1
Warbleton	War	34	C1
Wartling	Wart	157	D4
West Firle	W Firle	151	D2
West Hoathly	W Hoath	22	B3
Westdean	Wes	182	C2
Westfield	Wfd	117	E2
Westham	Whm	176	B3
Westmeston	Wmes	124	C4
Whatlington	Wha	39	F1
Whitesmith	Whi	130	C4
Willingdon	Willn	174	C1
Wilmington	Wil	173	E3
Winchelsea	Winc	120	B4
Winchelsea Beach	Winc B	120	C3
Windmill Hill	Wln H	134	C3
Witherenden Hill	Wit H	43	F1
Withyham	Wit	15	F2
Wivelsfield	Wiv	75	F3
Wivelsfield Green	Wiv G	76	A2
Wood's Green	Woo G	31	E4
Woodingdean	Wood	167	D4
Wych Cross	Wych C	24	B2

Abberton Field. Hur 99 F3
Abbey Cl. Pea 169 D1
Abbey Dr. Bex 160 C3
Abbey Rd. Bri 166 A2
Abbey Rd. East 184 C3
Abbey View. Bex 160 A3
Abbey Way. Bat 115 D3
Abbots Cl. Bat 115 E2
Abbots Cl. Hass 100 B2
Abbotsbury Cl. Salt 167 F1
Abbotsfield Rd. Hast 140 B2
Aberdale Rd. Pole 175 D3
Aberdeen Rd. Bri 166 A4
Abergavenny Rd. Lew 126 C1
Abinger Pl. Lew 127 D1
Abinger Rd. Por S 163 F4
Abinger Rd. Wood 167 E3
Acacia Rd. Hove 144 B1
Acacia Rd. East 175 D1
Acacia Rd. Newh 170 B1
Acer Ave. Bel G 19 D4
Acorn Cl. E Gri 12 B4
Acorn Green. Hai 132 C1
Acorn Way. Hur G 46 C2
Acorns The. Ston 44 B3
Acre Cl. Hay H 52 A1
Acres Rise. Tic 33 E1
Adam Cl. Hast 139 E2
Adams Cl. Bri 145 F1
Adams La. Ewh G 68 A1
Adams La. Mill C 68 A2
Adastra Ave. Key 100 C2
Addingham Rd. East 186 A2
Addington Cl. Hast 161 E4
Addison Rd. Hove 165 E4
Adelaide Cres. Hove 165 D3
Adelaide Rd. Hast 139 F2
Ades Field. Wil 173 E3
Admiral's Bridge La. E Gri 12 A1
Adur Rd. Bur H 75 D2
Agincourt Cl. Hast 139 E4
Ailsworth La. Rye 95 D3
Ainsworth Ave. Oving 167 E2
Ainsworth Cl. Oving 167 D2
Air St. Bri 165 E3
Airy Rd. Hers 134 C1
Alan Way. Bri 166 B3
Albany Hill. T W 9 D3
Albany Mews. Hove 164 C3
Albany Rd. Bex 160 A2
Albany Rd. Hast 161 F4
Albany Rd. Sea 181 D2
Albany Villas. Hove 164 C3
Albert Cl. Hay H 52 C2
Albert Dr. Bur H 74 B1
Albert Mews. Hove 165 D3
Albert Pl. Pole 174 C4
Albert Rd. Bex 160 A2
Albert Rd. Bri 165 E3
Albert Rd. Hast 162 B4
Albert Rd. Pole 174 C4
Albert Rd. Rid 80 A3
Albert Rd. Sock 163 D4
Albert St. T W 8 C2
Albert Terr. East 185 D2
Albion Ct. Bur H 74 B1
Albion Hill. Bri 165 F3
Albion La. Hast 162 C4
Albion Pl. Bri 165 F3
Albion Rd. East 185 F2
Albion Rd. T W 9 D3
Albion St. Bri 165 F3
Albion St. Lew 127 D1
Albion St. Sock 163 E4
Albourne Cl. Bri 166 B4
Albourne Cl. Hast 161 E4
Aldborough Rd. Hast 140 A1
Alder Cl. East 186 A4
Alder Cl. Hast 140 A3
Alder Cl. Hea 83 F3
Alderbrook Cl. Cro 39 F3
Alderbrook Path. Cro 39 F3
Alderbrook Way. Cro 39 F3
Alders Ave. E Gri 2 B2
Alders View Dr. E Gri 2 B2
Aldervale Cotts. Cro 39 F4
Aldrich Cl. Bri 166 B3
Aldrington Ave. Hove 164 C4
Aldrington Cl. Hove 164 A4
Alexander Dr. Bex 159 E2
Alexandra Rd. East 186 A3
Alexandra Rd. Hast 162 A4
Alexandra Rd. Hea 83 F3
Alexandra Rd. May 42 A2
Alexandra Rd. Rid 80 A3
Alexandra Villas. Bri 165 E3
Alford Way. Bex 160 B3
Alfray Rd. Bex 160 C3
Alfred Rd. Bri 165 E3
Alfred Rd. Hast 141 D2
Alfred St. Hast 162 A4
Alfriston Cl. Bex 159 D3
Alfriston Cl. Bri 166 B3
Alfriston Cl. East 185 D1
Alfriston Park. Sea 182 A3
Alfriston Rd. Sea 182 A3
Alice Bright La. Cro 39 E4

Alice St. Hove 165 D3
All Saints Cres. Hast 140 C1
All Saints La. Bex 159 F4
All Saints Rd. T W 8 C3
All Saints Rise. T W 8 C3
All Saints' St. Hast 162 C4
Allan Cl. T W 8 A2
Allandale Rd. T W 9 D4
Allards. Gue G 142 A4
Allen Rd. Hay H 52 C3
Allen Way. Bex 160 B4
Allen's Cl. Ash W 13 D3
Allfrey Rd. East 186 A3
Allington Cres. Newk 78 A4
Allington La. Coo 126 A4
Allington La. Off 126 A4
Allington Rd. Newk 78 A3
Allwood Cres. Wiv G 76 A2
Alma Rd. Hay H 52 C4
Alma Terr. Hast 140 A1
Alma Villas. Hast 140 A1
Alpine Rd. Hast 162 C4
Alpine Rd. Hove 164 B4
Alverstone Cl. East 175 F2
Amanda Cl. Bex 160 B4
Amberleaze Dr. Pem 10 A3
Amberley Cl. Bur H 74 C2
Amberley Cl. Hay H 52 A2
Amberley Cl. Hove 144 B2
Amberley Dr. Hove 144 B2
Amberley Rd. East 175 D1
Amberstone. Mag D 133 E2
Amberstone Cl. Hast 140 C2
Amberstone View. Hai 133 D1
Amberstone View. Hai 133 D2
Ambleside Ave. Pea 178 C4
America La. Hay H 52 C3
Amesbury Cres. Hove 164 B4
Amherst Cl. Hast 140 A1
Amherst Cres. Hove 164 B4
Amherst Gdns. Hast 140 A1
Amherst Rd. Bex 160 A2
Amherst Rd. Hast 140 A1
Amherst Rd. T W 8 C3
Amhurst Rd. Pea 178 B4
Anchor Field. Rin 128 B3
Anchor Hill. Sca H 53 F1
Anchor La. Spi 104 C3
Anderida Rd. Willn 175 D2
Anderson Cl. Newh 179 F4
Andrew Rd. Sgh 9 D4
Andrews Cl. Sale 66 A3
Andrews Cl. T W 9 D3
Angela Cl. Bex 160 B4
Anglesea Terr. Hast 162 A4
Anglesey Ave. Hai 132 C1
Angus Cl. East 174 C1
Ann Cl. Key 100 C3
Ann St. Bri 165 F4
Ann St. Hast 141 D1
Anne's Path. Lew 148 C4
Annington Rd. East 185 F3
Anson Cl. East 186 B4
Ansty Cl. Bri 166 B3
Antares Path. Hai 155 E4
Antony Cl. Sea 180 C3
Antrona Cl. Bex 159 D2
Anvil Cl. Por S 143 F1
Anzac Cl. Pea 169 D1
Apple Tree La. T W 9 D4
Appledene Cnr. S Cha 103 E4
Appledore Cl. East 176 A1
Appledore Gdns. Hay H 52 C3
Appledore Rd. Bri 146 B2
Applesham Ave. Hove 144 B1
Applesham Way. Por S 143 F1
Applewood Cl. Hast 140 A3
Approach The. Bri 145 E2
Approach The. Dor P 2 B3
Apsley St. T W 8 A2
Arbor Cl. Hay H 52 B3
Arbourvale. Hast 139 F1
Archery Rd. Hast 161 F4
Archery Wlk. Hai 155 D3
Ardingly Rd. Salt 178 A4
Ardingly St. Bri 165 F3
Argent Cl. Sea 181 F3
Argos Hill Rd. May 41 D2
Argyle Rd. Bri 165 E4
Arkwright Rd. East 175 F1
Arlington Cres. Bri 146 B3
Arlington Gdns. Salt 168 A1
Arlington Rd. East 185 E2
Arlington Rd E. Hai 154 C3
Arlington Rd W. Hai 154 B3
Armstrong Cl. Hast 139 E2
Arnold St. Bri 166 A4
Arnside Rd. Hast 161 E3
Arran Cl. Hai 132 C1
Arthur Rd. Bex 159 F2
Arthur St. Hove 164 C4
Arun Path. Uck 57 E1
Arundel Cl. Pev B 177 E3
Arundel Cl. S Sea 163 D4
Arundel Dr E. Salt 168 A1
Arundel Dr W. Salt 168 A1
Arundel Green. Lew 126 C1
Arundel Mews. Bri 166 B2
Arundel Pl. Bri 166 B2

Arundel Rd. Bri 166 B2
Arundel Rd. East 185 E2
Arundel Rd. Newh 170 B1
Arundel Rd. Pea 179 D4
Arundel Rd. Sea 181 F1
Arundel Rd. T W 8 C1
Arundel St. Bri 166 B2
Arundel Terr. Bri 166 B2
Ascham Pl. East 185 E1
Ascot Cl. East 190 B4
Ash Cl. Cra D 11 D4
Ash Cl. East 175 E2
Ash Cl. Hove 145 D2
Ash Ct. Hai 154 C4
Ash Ct. Whm 176 A3
Ash Dr. Sea 182 A2
Ash Gr. Hay H 52 A1
Ashbrook Rd. Hast 139 F2
Ashburnham Cl. Bri 146 A3
Ashburnham Dr. Bri 146 A3
Ashburnham Gdns. East 185 E3
Ashburnham Pl. Hai 132 C1
Ashburnham Rd. East 185 E3
Ashburnham Rd. Hast 141 D1
Ashby Cl. Bex 159 F4
Ashcombe Dr. Bex 159 D2
Ashcombe Hollow. Lew 148 B3
Ashcombe La. Kin L 148 B3
Ashcroft Cl. Rin 128 A3
Ashcroft Cl. S Sea 163 D4
Ashdown Ave. Salt 167 F1
Ashdown Cl. For R 13 F1
Ashdown Cl. Hay H 52 C2
Ashdown Cl. T W 8 B2
Ashdown Rd. Bex 160 B2
Ashdown Rd. Bri 165 F4
Ashdown Rd. For R 13 E1
Ashdown View. E Gri 12 B4
Ashdown View. Nut 37 D3
Ashenden Ave. Rye 94 C3
Ashenden Wlk. T W 9 E4
Ashenground Cl. Hay H 52 B2
Ashenground Rd. Hay H 52 B2
Asher Reeds. Lan G 7 F2
Ashford Cl. Hai 155 D4
Ashford Rd. Bri 145 F1
Ashford Rd. East 185 F2
Ashford Rd. Hast 140 B1
Ashford Sq. East 185 F2
Ashford Way. Hast 140 B2
Ashgate Rd. East 176 B1
Ashington Gdns. Pea 179 E3
Ashley Cl. Bri 145 E4
Ashley Gdns. May 41 F1
Ashley Gdns. T W 8 A3
Ashley Park. T W 8 A3
Ashley Park Cl. T W 8 A3
Ashlings Way. Hove 144 B1
Ashmore Cl. Pea 169 D1
Ashton Rise. Bri 165 F3
Ashtonville Cl. Rin 128 B3
Ashurst Ave. Salt 168 B1
Ashurst Rd. Asht 6 B2
Ashurst Rd. Bri 146 C2
Ashurst Rd. Lan G 7 D1
Ashurst Rd. Sea 181 E1
Ashway. Bur H 74 C1
Aslington Rd. East 175 F1
Aspen Cl. Hay H 52 C2
Aspen Rd. East 175 E1
Aspen Way. Bex 159 D2
Astaire Ave. East 185 F3
Asten Cl. Hast 161 E4
Asten Fields. Bat 115 D3
Athelstan Rd. Hast 141 D1
Atlantic Dr. East 186 C4
Atlingworth St. Bri 165 F2
Attree Dr. Bri 166 A3
Auckland Dr. Bri 146 C1
Auckland Rd. T W 9 D3
Audrey Cl. Bri 145 E3
Augustines Way. Hay H 52 B2
Augustus Way. Hast 139 E3
Austen Cl. E Gri 1 C1
Austen Way. Hast 141 D3
Austen Wlk. East 176 A1
Avard Cres. East 184 C3
Avenue. Bri 165 F3
Avenue La. East 185 E2
Avenue The. Bri 146 A1
Avenue The. Dor 2 C3
Avenue The. East 185 E2
Avenue The. Fai 142 B2
Avenue The. Hai 154 C3
Avenue The. Hor 109 E4
Avenue The. Kin L 148 A3
Avenue The. Lew 126 C1
Avenue The. May 41 F1
Avery Cl. Por S 143 E2
Aviary Way. Cra D 1 A1
Aviemore Rd. Cro 27 D1
Avis Rd. S Hei 170 A1
Avis Way. Newh 180 B4
Avocet. Hai 154 C4
Avon St. T W 9 D3
Avondale Rd. East 185 F2
Avondale Rd. Hast 139 F1
Avondale Rd. Hove 165 D4

Avondale Rd. Sea 181 E2
Avonhurst. Bur H 74 C2
Awbrook Cl. Sca H 53 E2
Aylesbury Ave. East 186 B4
Aymer Rd. Hove 164 C3
Ayscue Cl. East 186 B4
Babylon Way. East 184 C4
Back La. Cro H 83 D4
Back La. Rus 85 D1
Back La. Winc 120 B4
Back Rd. San 48 C3
Backwoods Cl. Hay H 52 C3
Backwoods La. Hay H 52 C3
Baden Rd. Bri 146 A1
Badger Dr. Hay H 52 A3
Badgers Cl. Cro 27 E2
Badgers Copse. Sea 182 A2
Badgers Dene. Rod 169 D4
Badgers Field. Pea 169 D1
Badgers Mount. Bex 159 E3
Badgers Way. Hast 140 A3
Badgers Wlk. Bur H 75 D1
Badlesmere Rd. East 185 F3
Bagham La. Hers 134 B3
Bahram Rd. Pole 174 B3
Bailey Cres. Willn 174 C2
Baillie Ave. East 186 A3
Bainbridge Cl. Sea 181 E2
Baird Dr. Hast 140 B2
Baker St. Bri 165 F4
Baker St. Newh 180 B4
Baker St. Rid 80 A3
Baker's Rd. East 185 D2
Bakewell Rd. East 185 D2
Balaclava La. Wad 31 F3
Balcombe La. Hor K 23 E1
Balcombe La. Sha 23 D2
Balcombe Rd. Hay H 52 A4
Balcombe Rd. Pea 178 C4
Baldock Rd. Wad 31 E3
Baldslow Down. Wfd 140 A4
Baldslow Rd. Hast 140 B1
Baldwin Ave. East 185 D3
Bale Cl. Bex 159 E3
Balfour Gdns. For R 13 E1
Balfour Rd. Bri 145 F1
Ball's Green. Wit 15 F3
Ballard Dr. Rin 128 B4
Ballards Hill. Crow 138 B2
Ballsocks La. Vin C 110 A4
Balmoral. E Gri 12 C4
Balmoral Cl. Sea 181 F3
Balsdean Rd. Wood 147 E1
Bamford Cl. Bri 146 C1
Bampfield St. Por S 163 F4
Bancroft Rd. East 159 F3
Bank Rd. Bex 160 A4
Banks Rd. N Cha 54 B1
Bankside. Bri 145 D3
Bankside. Hass 100 B3
Bankside. Wad 31 E3
Banner Farm Rd. T W 8 C1
Bannings Vale. Salt 168 B1
Bannisters Field. Newk 78 A4
Baranscraig Ave. Bri 145 F4
Barcombe Ave. Sea 182 A1
Barcombe Cl. East 185 D2
Barcombe Cl. Sea 182 A2
Barcombe Mills Rd. Bar C 104 B2
Barcombe Rd. Bri 146 B3
Barcombe Rd. Wick. East 185 D2
Barden Rd. East 186 A2
Barden Rd. Spe 7 F4
Bargate Cl. Bex 160 A4
Barham Cl. Hast 140 A2
Barkdale. Bur H 75 D3
Barley Ave. East 141 D1
Barley Cl. Pea 168 C1
Barley La. Hast 141 D1
Barleycroft. Alb 99 D3
Barming Cl. East 176 A1
Barn Cl. Alb 99 D3
Barn Cl. Kin L 148 B3
Barn Cl. St Cro 175 F3
Barn Cottage La. Hay H 52 C3
Barn Hatch Cl. Lew 148 C4
Barn La. Fra 81 D4
Barn Rd. S Mal 127 D2
Barn Rise. Bri 145 D3
Barn Rise. Sea 181 F3
Barnes Rd. Por S 163 F4
Barnet Way. Hove 144 B2
Barnett Rd. Bri 145 F1
Barnett Way. Uck 80 A4
Barnetts Way. Sgh 9 D4
Barnfield. Cro 27 E2
Barnfield. Plu 102 B3
Barnfield. T W 18 B4
Barnfield Cl. Hast 162 A4
Barnfield Gdns. Bri 166 A3
Barnfield Gdns. Dit 101 E2
Barnhams The. Bex 159 E2
Barnhorn Cl. Bex 159 D2

Barnhorn Rd. Bex 158 B2
Barnmead. Hay H 52 A4
Barnside Ave. Bur H 75 D1
Barons Cl. Sea 181 D3
Barons Ct. Bur H 74 C1
Barons Down Rd. Lew 148 C4
Barons Way. Pole 174 B3
Barons Wlk. Lew 148 C4
Barrack Rd. Bex 160 A4
Barrack Sq. Winc 120 B4
Barrhill Ave. Bri 145 E4
Barrie Cl. East 176 B3
Barrington Cl. Hay H 52 B4
Barrington Rd. Hay H 52 B4
Barrow Cl. Bri 146 A1
Barrow Hill. Bri 146 A1
Barrow Rise. Hast 140 A3
Barrowfield Cl. Hove 145 D2
Barrowfield Dr. Hove 145 D2
Barry Wlk. Bri 166 A3
Bartholomews. Bri 165 F3
Barton Cres. E Gri 12 C4
Basin St S. Hove 164 A3
Basin Rd S. Por S 164 A3
Basin Rd S. Sock 163 F3
Basinghall St. T W 8 C2
Baslow Rd. East 190 A4
Batchelor Way. Uck 79 F4
Batchelors. Pem 10 B4
Bateman's La. Bur 63 F2
Batemans Rd. Wood 167 E4
Bates Rd. Bri 145 E1
Bath Rd. East 185 E1
Bath St. Bri 165 E4
Bathford Cl. East 176 A1
Battery Hill. Fai 142 A3
Battle Cl. East 182 A3
Battle Cres. Hai 154 C4
Battle Cres. Hast 139 F2
Battle Gates. Bat 114 C3
Battle Hill. Bat ....
Battle Rd. Hai 133 D1
Battle Rd. Hast 139 F2
Batts Bridge Rd. Mar 56 C2
Bavant Rd. Bri 145 E1
Baxter Rd. Lew 126 C1
Baxter St. Bri 166 A4
Baxters La. Che Co 36 A3
Bay Ave. Pev B 177 D3
Bay Pond Rd. East 185 D2
Bay Rd. Pev B 177 D3
Bay Terr. Pev B 177 D3
Bay Tree Cl. Hea 83 F3
Bay Tree Cl. S Sea 143 D3
Bay Tree La. Pole 174 B4
Bay Vue Rd. Newh 180 A4
Baywood Gdns. Wood 167 E4
Bazehill Rd. Rottn 167 F2
Beach Cl. Sea 181 D3
Beach Rd. East 186 A3
Beach Rd. Newh 180 B4
Beachings The. Pev B 177 D3
Beachlands Way. Pev B 177 F3
Beachy Head Rd. East 190 A4
Beacon Cl. Bri 145 F1
Beacon Cl. Cro 27 E1
Beacon Cl. Sea 181 D3
Beacon Dr. Sea 181 D3
Beacon Gdns. Cro 27 E2
Beacon Hill. Dor 2 C4
Beacon Hill. Oving 167 E2
Beacon Hurst. Key 100 C2
Beacon Rd. Cro 27 E2
Beacon Rd. Dit 101 D1
Beacon Rd. Hast 141 D2
Beacon Rd. Sea 181 D2
Beacon Rd. Wmes 124 A4
Beacon Rd W. Cro 27 D1
Beacon The. W Hoa 22 B4
Beaconsfield Rd. Bex 160 A4
Beaconsfield Rd. East 165 E4
Beaconsfield Rd. Che G 78 B4
Beaconsfield Rd. Hast 140 B1
Beaconsfield Rd. Por S 163 F4
Beaconsfield Villas. Bri 145 E1
Beagles Wood Rd. Pem 10 B4
Beal Cres. Bri 145 F1
Beales La. Norm 68 C3
Beamsley Rd. East 186 A4
Beaney's La. Hast 140 B3
Beaney's La. Wfd 140 B3
Bear Rd. Bri 166 A4
Bear Yd. Lew 127 D1
Beatrice La. East 185 E2
Beatrice Wlk. Bex 159 F3
Beatty Ave. Bri 146 A3
Beatty Rd. East 186 B4
Beauchamp Rd. Hast 139 E3
Beauford Rd. Hor 109 E4
Beaufort Cres. Hast 140 A1

Beaufort Rd. Hast 140 A1
Beaufort Terr. Bri 166 A3
Beauharrow Rd. Hast 139 F3
Beaulieu Gdns. Hast 140 A3
Beaulieu Rd. Bex 159 D1
Beauport Gdns. Hast 139 F4
Beauport Hone Fm Cl. Hast . 139 F3
Beaver Cl. Cro 27 F1
Beckenham Cl. Hai 132 C2
Becket Cl. Hast 140 C1
Beckets Way. Fra 80 C3
Beckett Way. E Gri 12 B4
Beckett Way. S Mal 127 D2
Beckley Cl. Bri 166 B3
Beckley Cl. Hast 139 D1
Beckworth Cl. Hay H 52 C3
Beckworth La. Hay H 52 C3
Bedales Hill. Hay H 53 D2
Beddingham Cl. Gly 150 A3
Bedelands Cl. Bur H 74 C3
Bedford Ave. Bex 160 A2
Bedford Ct. Uck 80 A4
Bedford Gr. East 185 E2
Bedford Pl. Bri 165 E3
Bedford Rd. Hast 141 D1
Bedford Sq. Bri 165 E3
Bedford St. Bri 166 A2
Bedford Terr. T W 8 C1
Bedfordwell Rd. East 185 F2
Bedgebury Cl. Hast 139 E1
Bee Rd. Pea 179 D4
Beech Cl. Bat 115 D4
Beech Cl. Bex 159 D3
Beech Cl. Por S 143 E2
Beech Farm Rd. Sed 90 A2
Beech Fields. E Gri 2 B2
Beech Gr. Bri 146 B2
Beech Hill. Hay H 52 C2
Beech House La. Sale 66 A3
Beech Hurst. Pem 10 A4
Beech Hurst Cl. Hay H 52 A2
Beech St. T W 8 C3
Beechers Rd. Por S 143 E2
Beeches Cl. Uck 80 A4
Beeches Farm Rd. Cro 27 F1
Beeches La. Ash W 13 D3
Beeches Rd. Cro 27 F1
Beeches The. Bri 145 D2
Beeches The. Cro 27 F1
Beeching Park Ind Est. Bex . 159 F2
Beeching Rd. Bex 159 F2
Beeching Way. E Gri 2 B1
Beechwood Ave. Bri 145 E2
Beechwood Cl. Bri 145 E2
Beechwood Cl. Bur 63 F4
Beechwood Cres. East 185 D2
Beechwood Gdns. Hast 140 A3
Beechwood La. Coo 126 B4
Beechwood Mews. T W 9 E2
Beechwoods. Bur H 74 C1
Beechy Ave. East 184 C2
Beechy Gdns. East 184 C2
Beechy Rd. Blas 81 F1
Beeding Ave. Hove 144 B2
Beggar's La. Poy 122 A3
Beggar's La. St Cro 176 A3
Beggar's Wood Rd. N Cha 77 D3
Belfast St. Hove 164 C4
Belfry Orch. Rid 80 A3
Belgrave Cres. Sea 181 E3
Belgrave Pl. Bri 166 A2
Belgrave Rd. Sea 181 E2
Belgrave Rd. T W 8 C2
Belgrave Sq. Por S 164 A3
Belgrave St. Bri 165 F3
Belgrove. T W 8 C1
Bell Alley Rd. Bur 63 F3
Bell Banks Rd. Hai 155 D4
Bell La. Lew 148 C4
Bell La. Nut 36 C2
Bell La. Uck 79 F3
Belle Hill. Bex 160 A3
Belle Vue Rd. East 186 A3
Bellevue Gdns. Bri 166 A2
Bellfield Rd. Pem 10 A3
Bellhurst Rd. Rob 65 F2
Bellingham Cl. Hast 139 F2
Bellingham Cres. Hove 164 A4
Belmont. Bri 165 E4
Belmont Cl. Hass 100 B3
Belmont Ct. Hai 154 C4
Belmont La. Hur 100 A3
Belmont Rd. Hast 141 D1
Belmont Rd. Uck 80 A4
Belmont St. Bri 165 F4
Belmore Rd. East 185 F4
Belton Rd. Bri 165 F4
Beltring Rd. East 185 F4
Beltring Rd. T W 8 C3
Beltring Terr. East 185 F4
Belvedere Gdns. Cro 27 F1
Belvedere Gdns. Sea 181 F3
Bembridge Rd. East 175 F2
Bembridge St. Bri 166 A4
Bembrook Rd. Hast 140 C1
Benbow Ave. East 186 B3
Benchfield Cl. E Gri 2 C1
Bending Cres. Bex 160 A3
Benefield Hts. Pors 143 F2

Benenden Cl. Sea 181 F2
Benenden Rise. Hast 140 B2
Benett Ave. Hove 144 C1
Benett Dr. Hove 144 C1
Benfield Cl. Por S 144 A1
Benfield Cres. Por S 144 A1
Benfield Way. Por S 144 A1
Bengairn Ave. Bri 145 F4
Benhall Mill Rd. Bel G 19 D4
Benhall Mill Rd. T W 19 D4
Benjamin Cl. East 175 E1
Bennett Rd. Bri 166 B2
Bentham Hill. Sgh 8 A4
Bentham Rd. Bri 166 A4
Bentswood Cres. Hay H 52 C3
Bentswood Rd. Hay H 52 B3
Berbow Ave. East 186 B3
Beresford Rd. Bri 166 A3
Beresford Rd. Newh 170 B1
Bergamot Cres. S Sea 143 D1
Beristede Cl. East 185 E1
Berkeley Rd. T W 8 C1
Berkeley Row. Lew 148 C4
Berkeley Wlk. East 176 B2
Berkley Rd. May 41 E1
Berlin Rd. Hast 141 D1
Bernard La. East 185 E2
Bernard Pl. Bri 166 A4
Bernard Rd. Bri 166 A4
Bernhard Gdns. Pole 174 B3
Berriedale Ave. Hove 164 B3
Berry Cl. Bur H 74 C3
Berry Cl. Pea 168 C1
Berwick Cl. Bex 159 D3
Berwick Cl. East 175 D2
Berwick Cl. Sea 181 D2
Berwick Rd. Salt 168 A2
Betchley Cl. E Gri 2 B2
Bethune Rd. Bex 160 B2
Bethune Way. Hast 140 B1
Beulah Rd. T W 9 D2
Beuzeville Ave. Hai 154 C4
Bevendean Ave. Salt 168 A1
Bevendean Cres. Bri 146 B1
Bevendean Rd. Bri 146 A1
Beverington Cl. East 185 D3
Beverington Rd. East 185 D3
Bewl Bridge Cl. Fli 33 F2
Bewlbridge La. Cou W 32 B4
Bexhill Rd. East 186 A3
Bexhill Rd. Hast 161 D3
Bexhill Rd. Lun C 137 D1
Bexhill Rd. Nin 137 D1
Bexhill Rd. Wood 147 E1
Bexleigh Ave. Bex 160 C3
Bexley Cl. Hai 132 C1
Bicton Gdns. Bex 159 E2
Biddenden Cl. East 176 A1
Bidwell Ave. Bex 159 F3
Bigwood Ave. Hove 165 D4
Billingham La. Udi 93 D2
Binsted Cl. East 175 E1
Birch Ave. Hay H 52 C2
Birch Cl. Cra D 11 D4
Birch Cl. East 186 A4
Birch Cl. Hay H 52 C2
Birch Cl. T W 9 D4
Birch Cl. Uck 80 B4
Birch Grove Cres. Bri 145 F3
Birch Rd. East 186 A4
Birch View. Bex 160 A3
Birch Way. Hai 154 C3
Birch Way. Hast 140 B2
Birch Way. Hay H 52 C1
Birch Way. Hea 83 F3
Birch Way. T W 9 D4
Birchen La. Hay H 52 B4
Birches Close. Cro 27 E2
Birches Ind Est. E Gri 1 C2
Birchetts Ave. Lan G 7 E2
Birchetts Green La. Tic 32 C2
Birchgrove La. Hor K 23 E1
Birchgrove Rd. Hor K 35 E4
Birchington Cl. Bex 159 D2
Birchwood Grove Rd. Bur H . 75 D1
Bird In Eye Hill. Fra 80 B3
Bird In Hand St. Asht 16 C4
Bird La. Wad 30 C3
Birdham Rd. Bri 146 B2
Birk Dale. Bex 159 D2
Birken Rd. T W 9 D3
Birling Cl. Bri 146 A1
Birling Cl. Sea 181 D2
Birling Dr. T W 18 C4
Birling Gap Rd. E Dean 188 C3
Birling Park Ave. T W 18 C4
Birling Rd. T W 18 C4
Birling St. East 185 D2
Birling Way. Uck 80 B4
Bishop's Cl. Hur 99 F4
Bishop's Cl. Rin 128 B3
Bishop's Down. T W 8 B2
Bishop's Down Park Rd. T W . 8 A2
Bishop's Down Rd. T W 8 B2
Bishop's La. Rin 128 B3
Bishop's La. Rob 65 F2
Bishop's Wlk. Bex 160 B3
Bishops Cl. Sea 181 D2
Bishops Dr. Lew 148 C4

Bishops Rd. Hove 145 D1
Bishopstone Rd. Bis 181 D4
Bisky Bar. Peas 70 C1
Bixley La. Bec 69 F1
Black Hill. Hay H 52 C4
Black Lion St. Bri 165 F3
Black Path. Pole 174 C3
Blackberry La. Dor P 2 B4
Blackberry Rd. Dor P 2 A4
Blackbrook La. N Cha 54 B2
Blackbrook La. Sca H 54 B2
Blackdon Hill. Tow R 28 C3
Blackfields Ave. Bex 159 E3
Blackhouse La. Bur H 74 C2
Blackhurst La. T W 9 E3
Blacklands Cres. For R 13 E1
Blacklands Dr. Hast 140 B1
Blackman Ave. Hast 139 F2
Blackman St. Bri 165 F3
Blackmill Cl. Bex 159 F4
Blackness Rd. Cro 39 F4
Blacksmiths La. Cat 137 E4
Blackstone Way. Bur H 74 C3
Blackthorn Cl. Bri 145 D2
Blackthorn Cl. East 175 E1
Blackthorn Way. Fai 142 B2
Blackthorns. Hay H 52 C4
Blackthorns Cl. Hay H 52 C3
Blackthorns The. Bur H 74 C3
Blackwater Rd. East 185 E1
Blackwell Farm Rd. E Gri 2 B2
Blakeney Ave. Pea 179 F3
Blaker St. Bri 165 F3
Blakes Way. East 186 B3
Blatchington Cl. Sea 181 E2
Blatchington Hill. Sea 181 E2
Blatchington Rd. Hove 164 C4
Blatchington Rd. Sea 181 E2
Blatchington Rd. T W 8 C1
Blenheim Cl. E Gri 2 C2
Blenheim Ct. Rob 65 F2
Blenheim Pl. Bri 165 F3
Blenheim Way. Fli 34 A2
Blenheim Way. Pole 175 D3
Bletchinglye La. Tow R 29 E1
Blind La. Newk 78 B3
Blois Rd. Lew 126 C1
Blomfield Rd. Hast 162 A4
Bloomsbury Pl. Bri 166 A2
Bloomsbury St. Bri 166 A2
Blossom Wlk. Hai 132 C1
Blount Ave. E Gri 2 A1
Blowers Hill. Cowd 5 D4
Blue Haze Ave. Sea 181 F2
Bluebell Cl. E Gri 1 C1
Bluebell Cl. Hay H 52 B2
Bluemans La. Wfd 116 C2
Bluestone Cl. Hast 139 E1
Blytons The. E Gri 1 C1
Boarders La. Tic 33 D2
Boast La. Spi 104 B3
Bocking Cl. Wad 31 E2
Boddingtons La. Dit 101 D2
Bodiam Ave. Bex 160 A3
Bodiam Ave. Bex 146 C1
Bodiam Cl. Bri 146 C1
Bodiam Cl. Sea 182 A2
Bodiam Cres. East 175 F1
Bodiam Dr. Hast 139 D1
Bodiam Rd. San 48 B2
Bodle Cres. Bex 159 F3
Bodmin Cl. East 185 D2
Bohemia Rd. Hast 162 A4
Bolding Way. Hay H 52 B3
Bolebrook Rd. Bex 160 A2
Bolney Ave. Pea 179 D4
Bolney Rd. Bri 146 B2
Bolnore Rd. Hay H 52 A2
Bolsover Rd. East 190 B4
Bolsover Rd. Hove 164 B4
Bolton Cl. Uck 79 F3
Bolton Rd. East 185 F1
Boltro Rd. Hay H 52 A3
Bonchurch Rd. Bri 166 A4
Bond St. Bri 165 F3
Bond Street Row. Bri 165 F3
Bonfire La. Hor K 35 D3
Bonny Wood Rd. Hass 100 B2
Booker Cl. Cro 27 F1
Bopeep Bostal. Alc 171 F4
Bordehill La. Hay H 52 A4
Boreham Hill. Bor S 135 F2
Boreham La. Bor S 135 E1
Borough La. East 185 D2
Borough St. Bri 165 E3
Borrowdale Cl. East 176 A2
Boscawen Cl. East 186 B4
Boscobel Cl. Hast 161 F4
Boscobel Rd N. Hast 161 F4
Boship Cl. East 175 F2
Boston Cl. East 186 B4
Boston Rd. Hay H 52 C3
Boston St. Bri 165 F3
Bough Beeches. Bur H 75 D1

Boulevard The. Pev B 177 E3
Boundary Rd. Bri 166 B2
Boundary Rd. Hove 164 A4
Boundary Rd. T W 9 D1
Boundary The. Lan G 7 F2
Boundary The. Sea 181 E1
Bourg-de-peage Ave. E Gri .. 2 C1
Bourne La. Sale 66 B4
Bourne Pas. Hast 162 C4
Bourne St. East 185 F2
Bourne The. Hass 100 B3
Bourne The. Hast 162 C4
Bowden Rise. Sea 181 E3
Bowen Rd. T W 7 F2
Bower Cl. Hast 139 F2
Bower The. Hay H 52 A3
Bowley Rd. Hai 155 D4
Bowmans Dr. Bat 115 D4
Bowood Ave. East 185 F3
Bowrey Pl. Bex 160 A3
Bowring Way. Bri 166 A3
Box La. Ash W 13 E3
Box's La. Che Co 36 A3
Boxes La. Hor K 35 D3
Boxgrove Cl. Bex 160 B2
Boyce's St. Bri 165 E3
Boyne Park. T W 8 B2
Boyne Rd. Hast 141 D1
Bracken Cl. Cro 28 A1
Bracken Cl. T W 9 E3
Bracken Rd. East 184 C3
Bracken Rd. Sea 181 F1
Bracken Rd. T W 9 E3
Brackendale. Hast 141 D1
Bradford Cl. Lew 126 C1
Bradford St. East 185 D2
Brading Cl. East 175 F2
Brading Cl. Hast 140 B1
Brading Rd. Bri 166 A4
Bradley Rd. Chid H 6 A3
Braemore Rd. Hove 164 B3
Braeside Ave. Bri 145 F4
Bramber Ave. Hove 144 B2
Bramber Ave. Pea 179 D4
Bramber Cl. Hay H 52 A2
Bramber Cl. Pea 179 D4
Bramber Cl. Sea 181 E1
Bramber La. Sea 181 E1
Bramber Rd. Sea 181 E1
Bramber Way. Bur H 74 C2
Bramble Cl. East 175 F2
Bramble Croft. Cro 27 F1
Bramble Dr. Hai 154 C4
Bramble Reed La. Kip 10 C4
Bramble Rise. Bri 145 D3
Bramble Twitten. E Gri 2 C1
Brambledean Rd. Por S 163 F4
Brambles. Hass 100 B3
Brambleside. Uck 79 F3
Brambletyne Ave. Salt 168 A1
Bramley Rd. Pole 175 D3
Bramleys. Kin L 148 B3
Brampton Ave. Bex 159 E2
Brampton Rd. East 185 E4
Brampton Rd Tdg Est. East .. 185 F4
Brand Rd. East 175 E1
Brands Cl. S Hei 170 B1
Brangwyn Ave. Bri 145 E3
Brangwyn Cres. Bri 145 E3
Brangwyn Dr. Bri 145 D3
Brangwyn Way. Bri 145 E3
Branksome Rd. Hast 161 F4
Branston Rd. East 175 E1
Brassey Ave. East 175 E1
Brassey Rd. Bex 160 A2
Brasslands Dr. Por S 143 E1
Braybon Ave. Bri 145 E2
Braybrooke Cl. Hast 162 B4
Braybrooke Rd. Hast 162 B4
Braybrooke Terr. Hast 162 B4
Braypool La. Hove 145 D4
Brazen Cl. Newh 179 F4
Bread St. Bri 165 F3
Breadsell La. Crow 139 D3
Breckley Rd. Bex 159 F2
Brede Cl. Bri 166 B3
Brede Cl. East 186 A3
Brede Cl. Hast 139 E4
Brede Hill. Bre 91 F1
Brede La. Bre 91 D1
Brede La. Sed 90 C1
Brede Valley View. Ick 119 E3
Breeds Pl. Hast 162 B4
Brendon Cl. East 176 B2
Brendon Cl. T W 9 D3
Brendon Rise. Hast 140 C2
Brentwood Cl. Bri 145 E2
Brentwood Cres. Bri 145 E2
Brentwood Rd. Bri 145 F2
Bretland Rd. T W 8 A2
Brett Dr. Bex 160 B2
Bretton. Bur H 74 B3
Bretts Field. Pea 169 D1
Brewer St. Bri 165 F4
Brewer St. Lam 21 F3
Brian Cres. Sgh 8 A4
Briar Cl. Fai 142 C3
Briar Cl. Wood 167 D4

Briar Pl. East 175 F2
Briarcroft Rd. Wood 167 D4
Briary The. Bex 160 A3
Brickfield Estate. Peas 70 C1
Brickyard La. Mar C 29 E3
Brickyard La. Tow R 29 E3
Bridge Cl. Bur H 74 B2
Bridge Cl. Hor 109 F4
Bridge Pl. Rye 95 D3
Bridge Rd. Hay H 52 B3
Bridge St. Newh 180 A4
Bridge Way. Hast 161 F4
Bridgemere Rd. East 185 F3
Bridger Way. Cro 27 F1
Bridgersmill. Hay H 52 A3
Bridgewick Cl. S Mal 127 D2
Bridle Way. Pea 168 C1
Briers Ave. Hast 140 A2
Briers Gdns. Hast 140 A2
Brigden St. Bri 165 E4
Bright Ridge. Sgh 8 A4
Brightland Rd. East 185 D2
Brightling Ave. Hast 141 D2
Brightling Rd. Oxl G 64 C1
Brightling Rd. Pole 174 C3
Brightling Cl. Rob 65 E2
Brighton Pl. Bri 165 F3
Brighton Rd. Alb 99 E2
Brighton Rd. Hass 100 A1
Brighton Rd. Hur 99 E2
Brighton Rd. Lew 148 C4
Brighton Rd. Newh 179 F4
Brighton Rd. S Sea 163 D3
Brighton Sq. Bri 165 F3
Brills La. Bri 165 F2
Brinker's La. Wad 31 F1
Briscoe's Wlk. Hast 162 A4
Bristol Gate. Bri 166 A2
Bristol Gdns. Bri 166 B2
Bristol Mews. Bri 166 B2
Bristol Pl. Bri 166 B2
Bristol Rd. Bri 166 A2
Bristol Rd. Hast 139 F2
Bristol St. Bri 166 B2
Bristol Way. Hast 139 F2
Brittany Mews. Hast 161 F4
Brittany Rd. Hast 161 F4
Brittany Rd. Hove 164 A3
Brittenden La. Cro H 82 B3
Brittenden La. Wald 82 B3
Britts Farm Rd. Bux 58 A2
Broad Gr. T W 8 C1
Broad Green. Wood 167 E3
Broad Green Ave. Bur H 75 D1
Broad La. Ford 6 C2
Broad Oak. Gro 17 D3
Broad Oak. T W 8 B1
Broad Rd. Willn 174 C2
Broad Rig Ave. Hove 144 A2
Broad St. Bri 165 F2
Broad St. Ick 119 D3
Broad St. Sea 181 D2
Broad View. Bro O 159 E3
Broad View. Bro O 61 E1
Broad Way. Fai 142 B3
Broadcroft. T W 18 B4
Broadfield. W Hoa 22 B4
Broadfields. Bri 146 B2
Broadfields Rd. Bri 146 B2
Broadhill Orch. Bro O 61 E1
Broadlands. Bur H 100 C4
Broadlands. Hast 141 D2
Broadlands Rd. Bur H 100 C4
Broadmead. T W 18 B4
Broadmead Ave. T W 18 B4
Broadoak La. Bex 159 E3
Broadview The. Willn 174 B2
Broadwalk The. Bex 158 C2
Broadwater Down. T W 18 B4
Broadwater La. T W 8 B1
Broadwater La. T W 18 B4
Broadwater Rise. T W 8 B1
Broadway The. Alfn 172 B2
Broadway The. Cro 27 E2
Broadway The. East 175 D1
Broadway The. Hast 141 D1
Broadway The. Hay H 52 A3
Broadway The. Lam 21 F3
Brodie Pl. East 185 D2
Brodrick Rd. East 175 E1
Brokes Way. Sgh 8 C4
Bromley Cl. East 176 A1
Bromley Cl. Key 100 C2
Bromley Rd. Bri 165 F4
Bromley Rd. Sea 181 F2
Brompton Cl. Bri 145 E3
Brontes The. E Gri 2 A1
Brook Ave. Key 100 B2
Brook Cl. Cro 28 A1
Brook Cl. E Gri 2 C1
Brook La. Hay H 52 B4
Brook Rd. T W 9 D4
Brook St. Hast 162 B4
Brook St. Lew 127 D1
Brook St. Pole 174 C3
Brook Way. Hast 140 C3
Brooker Pl. Hove 164 C4
Brooker St. Hove 164 C4

Brookfield Rd. Bex 160 B2
Brookhouse Bottom. Che Co .. 36 A2
Brookland Cl. Hast 140 B1
Brookland Cl. Pev B 177 E3
Brookland Rd. Hast 162 B4
Brooklands. T W 9 D4
Brooklands Ave. Cro 39 E4
Brooklands Farm Cl. Ford 6 C3
Brooklyn Rd. Sea 181 E2
Brookmead Cl. East 185 F3
Brooks Cl. Newh 180 A3
Brooks Gdns. Newk 78 A3
Brooks Rd. Lew 127 E1
Brooks The. Bur H 74 B3
Brookside. Pid 169 F1
Brookside. Uck 79 F3
Brookside Ave. Pole 174 B4
Brookway. Bur H 75 D2
Brookway. Hay H 52 C4
Broom Cl. East 175 D1
Broom La. Lan G 7 E1
Broom Park. Lan G 7 E2
Brooman's La. Lew 127 D1
Broomfield Ave. Pea 178 B4
Broomfield Dr. Por S 143 F2
Broomfield St. East 185 D2
Broomgrove Rd. Hast 140 C1
Broomhill Park Rd. Sgh 8 A4
Broomhill Rd. T W 8 A4
Brow The. Bur H 74 C2
Brow The. Fri 183 F1
Brow The. Wood 167 D4
Brown Jack Ave. Pole 174 B3
Brown's Cl. Uck 80 A4
Brown's La. Uck 57 D1
Brown's Path. Uck 80 B4
Browning Rd. Hea 83 F4
Browning Wlk. East 176 B1
Brownings The. E Gri 2 A1
Brownleaf Rd. Wood 167 E3
Browns Wood. E Gri 2 B2
Broyle Cl. Rin 128 B4
Broyle La. Rin 128 B4
Broyle Paddock. Rin 128 B4
Broyle The. Rin 129 D4
Broyleside. Rin 128 C4
Bruce Cl. Hay H 52 B2
Brunel Rd. Hast 139 E2
Brunswick Mews. Hove 165 D3
Brunswick Pl. Hove 165 D3
Brunswick Rd. Hove 165 D3
Brunswick Row. Bri 165 F4
Brunswick Sq. Hove 165 D3
Brunswick St. Hove 165 D3
Brunswick St W. Hove 165 D3
Brunswick Terr. Hove 165 D3
Brushes La. Hay H 52 C4
Bryants Field. Cro 27 E2
Buckholt Ave. Bex 160 C4
Buckholt La. Bex 160 A4
Buckhurst Cl. E Gri 2 A2
Buckhurst Cl. East 184 C4
Buckhurst Cl. S Mal 127 D2
Buckhurst La. Wad 30 C3
Buckhurst Mead. E Gri 2 A2
Buckhurst Pl. Bex 160 A2
Buckhurst Rd. Bex 160 A2
Buckhurst Rd. Pea 178 B4
Buckhurst Way. E Gri 2 A2
Buckingham Cl. Sea 181 D2
Buckingham Dr. E Gri 12 C4
Buckingham Pl. Bri 165 E4
Buckingham Rd. Bri 165 E3
Buckingham Rd. Hast 139 F2
Buckingham Rd. T W 8 C1
Buckingham St. Bri 165 E3
Buckland Rd. Sea 181 E3
Buckle By-ps. Sea 181 D2
Buckle Cl. Sea 181 D2
Buckle Dr. Sea 181 D2
Buckle Rise. Sea 181 D2
Buckler St. Por S 163 F4
Bucklers Cl. T W 9 D2
Buckley Cl. Hove 144 B2
Buckwell Ct. Lew 126 C2
Buckwell Rise. Hers 134 B3
Bull La. Lew 149 D4
Bulldogs Bank. W Hoa 22 B3
Buller Cl. Cro 27 F1
Buller Rd. Bri 146 A1
Bullingstone La. Ford 7 E4
Bullingstone La. Spe 7 E4
Bulls Pl. Pem 10 A3
Bulverhythe Rd. Hast 161 D3
Burchetts Cl. Hay H 52 A1
Burden Rd. Hast 139 F2
Burdett Pl. Hast 162 C4
Burdett Rd. T W 7 F2
Burdocks Dr. Bur H 75 D1
Burfield Rd. East 185 F2
Burgess Rd. Hast 141 D3
Burgh Hill. Etc 46 B1
Burgh La. H Fir 151 D2
Burhill Way. Hast 161 E4
Burleigh Pl. East 186 A3
Burlington Gdns. Por S 144 A1
Burlington Pl. East 185 F1
Burlington Rd. East 185 F1

Burlington St. Bri 166 A2
Burlow Cl. Bri 166 B3
Burlow Cl. Willn 175 D2
Burma Cl. Hay H 53 D2
Burnham Cl. Wood 167 E4
Burns Way. E Gri 2 A1
Burnside. Pole 174 C3
Burnt House La. Lan G 7 F3
Burnt Lodge La. Wal 32 C1
Burrel Rd. Hay H 52 A3
Burrell Rd. Hay H 52 A3
Burrow Down. East 184 C3
Burrow Down Cl. East 184 C3
Burry Rd. Hast 140 A1
Burslem Rd. T W 9 E4
Burstead Cl. Bri 145 F2
Burton Rd. East 185 E3
Burton Villas. Hove 165 D4
Burton Way. Hast 161 F3
Burton Wlk. Hai 154 C4
Burwash Cl. East 175 F2
Burwash Cl. Hast 140 C3
Burwash Rd. Bro O 61 E1
Burwash Rd. Hea 83 F4
Burwash Rd. Hove 144 B2
Bush Cl. Pea 168 C1
Bush Cl. Wood 167 D4
Bush Cottage Cl. Por S 144 A1
Bush Farm Dr. Por S 144 A2
Bush Rd. Newh 179 F4
Bushbury La. Blas 81 F2
Busheyfields. Hai 154 C4
Bushy Croft. Bex 159 E3
Bushy Gill. Lan G 7 F2
Butcher's La. Cog 118 A1
Butcher's La. Thr O 118 B1
Butcherfield La. Hart 14 C4
Bute St. Bri 166 A3
Butler's Green Rd. Hay H 52 A2
Butler's La. Hers 134 B2
Butlers Way. Rin 128 A3
Butterbox La. Sca H 54 A2
Butterfield. E Gri 1 C2
Butts La. East 174 C1
Buttsfield La. E Hoa 107 F3
Buxted Rise. Bri 145 F3
Buxted Wood La. Bux 58 B3
Buxton Dr. Bex 159 F3
Buxton Rd. Bri 165 E4
Buxton Rd. East 190 B4
By Sunte. Hay H 52 B4
Bydown. Sea 181 F2
Byefields Croft. Bex 159 E3
Byeway The. Bex 159 D3
Byeway The. Hast 140 C2
Byeways The. Sea 181 E2
Byland Cl. East 175 E2
Byng Rd. T W 8 B3
Byron Gr. E Gri 2 A1
Byron St. Hove 164 C4
Byron Wlk. East 176 B2
Byway The. Bri 146 B3
Byways. Hast 140 A3
Byworth Cl. Bri 159 D3
Byworth Cl. Bri 166 B3

Cabbage Stalk La. T W 8 B1
Caburn Cres. Lew 126 C1
Caburn Rd. Hove 165 E4
Caburn Way. Hai 154 C3
Cackle St. Bri 91 F1
Cackle St. Nut 37 E1
Cacklebury Cl. Hai 154 C3
Cadborough Cliff. Rye 94 B2
Cade St. East 175 E1
Cadogan Gdns. T W 8 C2
Cairo Ave. Pea 178 C4
Cairo Ave S. Pea 178 C4
Caister's Cl. Hove 165 D4
Calbourne. Hay H 52 A3
Caldbec Hill. Bat 115 D3
Caldecot La. Lydd 98 C4
Caldicotts La. Low D 132 A2
Caledonian Rd. Bri 165 F4
Caley Rd. T W 9 D1
Calgary Rd. Bex 159 F4
Calverley Park. T W 8 C2
Calverley Park Cres. T W 8 C2
Calverley Park Gdns. T W 9 D2
Calverley Rd. East 185 E1
Calverley Rd. T W 8 C2
Calverley St. T W 8 C2
Calvert Cl. Uck 79 F4
Calvert Rd. Hast 140 C1
Calvert Rd. Uck 79 F4
Camber Cl. Bex 160 B3
Camber Cl. Bri 166 B3
Camber Cl. Pev B 177 E3
Camber Dr. Pev B 177 E3
Camber Rd. Cam 95 E3
Camber Rd. E Gul 95 E3
Camber Way. Pev B 177 E3
Camberlot Rd. Gol C 131 F1
Camberlot Rd. Upp D 131 F1
Cambrian St. Bri 9 D4
Cambridge Gdns. Hast 162 B4
Cambridge Gdns. T W 8 C1

Cambridge Gr. Hove 165 D4
Cambridge Rd. Bex 160 A3
Cambridge Rd. East 186 A4
Cambridge Rd. Hast 162 B4
Cambridge Rd. Hove 165 D3
Cambridge St. T W 9 D2
Cambridge Way. Uck 57 D1
Camden Ave. Pem 10 A3
Camden Hill. T W 9 D1
Camden Park. T W 9 D2
Camden Rd. East 185 E1
Camden Rd. T W 8 C2
Camden St. Por S 164 A3
Camelford St. Bri 165 F2
Campbell Cl. Uck 57 D1
Campbell Cres. E Gri 1 C1
Campbell Rd. Bri 165 E4
Campbell Rd. T W 8 C3
Camperdown St. Bex 159 F4
Canada Cl. Pea 168 C1
Canada Way. Bex 159 F4
Canadia Rd. Bat 115 D4
Canfield Cl. Bri 146 A1
Canfield Rd. Bri 146 A1
Canning St. Bri 166 A3
Cannon Pl. Bri 165 E3
Cansiron La. Ash W 13 E3
Cansiron La. For R 13 F3
Cansiron La. Hart 4 B1
Cantelupe Rd. Bex 160 A2
Cantelupe Rd. E Gri 2 B1
Canterbury Cl. Willn 175 D1
Canterbury Dr. Bri 165 F4
Canterbury Rd. Pem 10 B3
Canterbury Rise. Hast 140 B2
Cantercrow Hill. Newh 170 B1
Cants Cl. Bur H 75 D2
Cants La. Bur H 75 D2
Canute Rd. Hast 141 D2
Capel Ave. Pea 179 D4
Capella Path. Hai 155 D4
Caple Gdns. Hast 161 F4
Carden Ave. Bri 145 F3
Carden Cl. Bri 145 F3
Carden Cres. Bri 145 F3
Carden Hill. Bri 145 F3
Cardiff Rd. Hast 162 A4
Cardinals Cl. Bex 160 B3
Carew Rd. East 185 E2
Carey Down. Pea 168 C1
Carfax Cl. Bex 159 F4
Carinus Gdns. Hast 139 F3
Carisbrooke Cl. East 175 F2
Carisbrooke Rd. Bri 166 A4
Carisbrooke Rd. Hast 162 A4
Carlisle Par. Hast 162 B4
Carlisle Rd. East 185 E1
Carlisle Rd. Hove 164 B3
Carlton Cl. Sea 181 D2
Carlton Cres. T W 9 D2
Carlton Hill. Bri 165 F3
Carlton Pl. Bri 165 F3
Carlton Rd. East 186 A2
Carlton Rd. Sea 181 D2
Carlton Rd. T W 9 D2
Carlton Terr. Por S 164 A4
Carlyle Ave. East 146 A1
Carlyle St. Bri 166 A4
Carmel Cl. Bex 159 D2
Carol Cl. Bri 145 E3
Caroline Cl. Sea 181 D3
Carpenter Dr. Hast 139 E2
Carpenters Croft. E Hoa 107 F3
Carriers Path. Hai 154 C4
Carriers Pl. Cowd 5 F2
Carroll Wlk. East 176 B1
Castle Banks. Lew 127 D1
Castle Ditch La. Lew 127 D1
Castle Dr. Pev B 177 D2
Castle Gate. Lew 127 D1
Castle Gdns. Hast 162 B4
Castle Hill Pas. Hast 162 B4
Castle Hill Rd. Hast 162 C4
Castle Hurst. Sale 66 C4
Castle La. Lew 127 D1
Castle Prec. Lew 127 D1
Castle Rd. T W 8 C2
Castle Rise. Lew 127 D1
Castle Rise. Rid 80 A2
Castle Sq. Bri 165 F3
Castle St. Bri 165 E3
Castle St. Hast 162 B4
Castle St. T W 8 C1
Castle St. Winc 120 B4
Castle View
    Caravan Site. Pev Bay 176 C2
Castle View Gdns. Whm 176 B3
Castle View Rd. Rid 80 A2
Castle Wlk. Wad 31 E2
Castledown Ave. Hast 162 C4
Castlefields. Hart 15 E2
Castleham Rd. Hast 139 E3
Castleross Rd. Pev B 177 D2
Cat St. Upp H 14 B1
Catherine Pl. T W 8 C1
Catherine Vale. Wood 167 E4
Catkin Rd. Hay H 52 C2
Catsfield Cl. Hast 139 D1
Catt's Hill. Tow R 29 E1

Causeway The. Sea 181 E1
Cavalier Way. E Gri 12 B4
Cavalry Cres. East 184 C3
Cavell Ave. Pea 178 C4
Cavendish Ave. East 185 F2
Cavendish Ave. Hast 161 F4
Cavendish Cl. Pea 168 C1
Cavendish Dr. T W 8 C1
Cavendish Pl. Bri 165 E3
Cavendish Pl. East 185 F2
Cavendish Pl. Hast 162 C4
Cavendish St. Bri 165 F3
Caveridge La. S Cha 103 E4
Caves Rd. Hast 161 F3
Caxton Way. Hay H 52 B2
Cedar Cl. Bur H 74 C3
Cedar Cl. East 175 D1
Cedar Cl. Hast 140 A3
Cedar Ct. T W 8 C3
Cedar Ridge. T W 9 D3
Cedar Way. Hay H 52 C2
Cedars Cl. Uck 80 A4
Cedars Gdns. Bri 145 E2
Cedars The. Hai 132 C1
Cedars The. Hay H 52 A4
Cedarwell Cl. Pid 169 F1
Celandine Dr. Hast 139 F1
Central Ave. East 184 C3
Central Ave. Pea 178 C4
Central Ave. Pole 174 C4
Centurion Rd. Bri 165 E3
Ceylon Pl. East 185 F2
Ceylon Wlk. Bex 159 E2
Chadborn Cl. Bri 166 A3
Chaffinch Rd. East 176 A1
Chafford Cl. Ford 6 B3
Chailey Ave. Rottn 167 F1
Chailey Cl. East 176 B1
Chailey Cl. Hast 140 B3
Chailey Cres. Salt 168 B1
Chailey La. Chay 77 F3
Chailey Rd. Bri 146 B2
Chain La. Bat 115 D3
Chalden Pl. Bex 159 D3
Chalfont Dr. Hove 145 D2
Chalk Farm Cl. East 174 C1
Chalkers La. Hur 99 F4
Chalket La. Pem 10 A3
Chalkland Rise. Wood 167 E4
Chalky Rd. Por S 143 E2
Challoners Cl. Hor K 35 D2
Challoners Cl. Rottn 167 F1
Challow Cl. Hass 100 B2
Chaloner Cl. Hay H 52 C4
Chaloner Rd. Hay H 52 C4
Chalvington Dr. Hast 140 A3
Chalvington Rd. East 185 D4
Chamberlain Rd. East 185 D2
Chambers Cres. Hast 139 E2
Chambers Rd. Hast 139 E2
Chancellors Park. Hass 100 B2
Chanctonbury Dr. Hast 140 B3
Chanctonbury Rd. Bur H 74 C1
Chanctonbury Rd. Hove 165 E4
Chandler Rd. Bex 159 F2
Chandler's Mead. Coo 126 C4
Chandos Rd. T W 9 D3
Channel View. Bex 160 A2
Channel View E. Bex 160 A2
Channel View Rd. East 186 A3
Channel View Rd. Wood 166 C4
Channel View W. Bex 160 A2
Channel Way. Fai 142 B2
Channelview Rd. Pev B 177 E3
Channers La. Ripe 130 A1
Chant La. Tow R 29 D1
Chantlers Cl. E Gri 2 A1
Chantlers Mead. Cowd 4 C3
Chantry Ave. Bex 160 A3
Chantry La. Bex 160 A3
Chapel Barn Cl. Hai 155 D4
Chapel Burn Cl. Hai 155 D4
Chapel Cl. Bur H 74 B2
Chapel Field. Norm 68 C4
Chapel Green. Cro 27 E1
Chapel Hill. Crow 138 B2
Chapel Hill. Lew 127 E1
Chapel Hill. Sed 188 B4
Chapel La. Ash W 13 D3
Chapel La. E Chi 102 C2
Chapel La. For R 13 E1
Chapel La. Gue G 141 F4
Chapel Mews. Hove 165 D3
Chapel Park Rd. Hast 162 A4
Chapel Pl. Por S 164 A4
Chapel Pl. T W 8 C1
Chapel Rd. Plu G 102 B4
Chapel Rd. Por S 144 A4
Chapel Row. W Hoa 22 B4
Chapel St. Bri 165 F3
Chapel St. Newh 180 A4
Chapel Terr. Bri 166 A2
Chapel Terr Mews. Bri 166 A2
Chapman Way. Sgh 9 D4
Chapman's La. E Gri 2 A1
Charity Farm Way. Cro 27 F2
Charles Ave. Bur H 74 A1
Charles Ave. Bur H 74 B1
Charles Cl. Hove 144 C2

Charles Cl. Sea 181 D3
Charles Rd. Hast 161 F4
Charles Rd W. Hast 161 F4
Charles St. Bri 165 F2
Charles St. Sgh 8 C4
Charleston Rd. East 8 C4
Charlesworth Park. Hay H 53 D2
Charlewood Gdns. Bur H 75 D1
Charlotte St. Bri 165 F2
Charlston Ave. Newh 179 F3
Charlton's Way. T W 8 B1
Charltons The. Bri 146 A3
Charlwood Rd. Bur H 75 D3
Charlwoods Busn Cen. E Gri .. 2 A1
Charlwoods Pl. E Gri 2 B2
Charlwoods Rd. E Gri 2 B2
Chartfield. Hove 144 C1
Chartres. Bex 160 A3
Chartres Cl. Bex 160 A3
Chartwell Cl. Sea 181 E3
Chase The. T W 9 D1
Chatfield Cres. East 175 D1
Chatham Pl. Bri 165 E4
Chatham Pl. Sea 181 E1
Chatham Rd. Hast 139 F1
Chatsworth Ave. Pea 168 C1
Chatsworth Cl. Pea 178 C4
Chatsworth Gdns. East 190 B4
Chatsworth Park. Pea 168 C1
Chatsworth Rd. Bri 165 E4
Chaucer Ave. E Gri 2 A1
Chaucer Wlk. East 176 B2
Chawbrook Rd. East 185 F2
Cheapside. Bri 165 F3
Cheeleys. Hor K 35 D3
Chelgates. Bex 159 D1
Chelsea Cl. Bex 160 A2
Chelston Ave. Hove 164 A4
Cheltenham Pl. Bri 165 F3
Chelwood Cl. Bri 146 A3
Chelworth Rd. East 175 D1
Chene Rd. Pea 179 E3
Chenies Cl. T W 18 C4
Chepbourne Rd. Bex 160 A2
Chequer Cl. For R 13 E1
Chequer Rd. E Gri 2 B1
Chequers Cl. Cro 27 F1
Chequers Way. Cro 27 F1
Cherington Cl. Hur 99 F3
Cherry Cl. Bur H 74 B2
Cherry Garden Rd. East 184 C2
Cherry Gdns. H Hur 57 F4
Cherry Gdns. Hea 83 F3
Cherry Side. Hai 154 C4
Cherry Tree Cl. Hast 162 A4
Cherry Tree Cotts. Fle 55 E2
Cherry Tree Gdns. Bex 160 B3
Cherry Tree Rd. T W 8 B1
Cherwell Rd. Hea 83 F4
Chesham Pl. Bri 166 A2
Chesham Rd. Bri 166 A2
Chesham St. Bri 166 A2
Chester Ave. T W 9 D2
Chester Terr. Bri 145 F1
Chesterfield Cl. Cra D 1 A2
Chesterfield Gdns. East 190 B4
Chesterfield Rd. East 190 B4
Chesterton Ave. Sea 181 E2
Chesterton Cl. E Gri 12 B4
Chesterton Dr. Sea 181 F2
Chestnut Ave. Sgh 8 C4
Chestnut Cl. Bro O W 91 F3
Chestnut Cl. Bur H 74 C3
Chestnut Cl. E Gri 2 C1
Chestnut Cl. Hai 132 C1
Chestnut Cl. Hers 134 B3
Chestnut Cl. Sgh 8 C4
Chestnut Dr. Pole 174 C3
Chestnut Gr. Hur 99 D4
Chestnut Way. Newh 179 F4
Chestnut Wlk. Bex 159 D3
Chestnut Wlk. Dor P 2 A4
Chestnuts Cl. Hay H 52 C4
Chestnuts The. Hay H 52 B4
Chestnuts The. The M 47 E4
Chetnole. E Gri 2 A1
Cheviot Cl. East 176 A2
Cheviots The. Hast 141 D2
Chichester Cl. Bex 159 F3
Chichester Cl. Hove 144 B2
Chichester Cl. Pea 179 E4
Chichester Cl. Salt 168 A1
Chichester Cl. Willn 174 C1
Chichester Dr E. Salt 168 A1
Chichester Dr W. Salt 167 F1
Chichester Mews. Bri 166 A2
Chichester Pl. Bri 166 A2
Chichester Rd. Hast 139 F1
Chichester Rd. Sea 181 E2
Chichester Terr. Bri 166 A2
Chichester Way. Bur H 75 D3
Chick Hill. Pett 142 C4
Chiddingly Cl. Bri 166 B3
Chieveley Dr. T W 9 D1
Chilcomb. Bur H 75 D1
Chilham Cl. East 176 A1
Chillies La. H Hur 38 C2
Chilling St. Hor K 23 D1

Chilling St. Sha 23 D2
Chillis Wood Rd. Hay H 52 A3
Chilsham La. Bod G 111 F1
Chilsham La. Hers 111 F1
Chilston Cl. T W 8 C3
Chilston Rd. T W 8 C3
Chiltern Cl. S Sea 163 D4
Chiltern Dr. Hast 140 C2
Chiltern Wlk. T W 9 D2
Chiltington Cl. Bur H 74 B3
Chiltington Cl. Salt 168 A1
Chiltington La. Bar 103 D1
Chiltington La. E Chi 103 D2
Chiltington Way. Salt 168 A1
Chiswick Pl. East 185 F1
Chitcombe Rd. Bro Ow 91 E3
Chorley Ave. Hast 167 F1
Chowns Hill. Cog 140 C3
Chrisdory Rd. Por S 143 E2
Christ Church Ave. T W 8 C1
Christie Ave. Rin 128 A3
Christie Rd. Lew 126 C1
Christies. E Gri 12 A4
Christine Cl. Bex 160 C4
Christopher Rd. E Gri 2 B1
Church App. Fra 80 C3
Church Ave. Hay H 52 B3
Church Ave. Whm 176 C3
Church Cl. Bri 145 E3
Church Cl. Bur H 74 C2
Church Cl. Willn 174 C2
Church Fields. Hur 99 E3
Church Green. S Sea 163 D4
Church Hill. Bri 145 E4
Church Hill. Etc 45 F1
Church Hill. Newh 180 A4
Church Hill. Rin 128 A3
Church Hill. Wex. Bex 159 D2
Church House Cl. Sock 143 E1
Church in the Wood La. Hast 139 E2
Church La. Alb 99 D3
Church La. Bec 69 E2
Church La. Bux 58 A3
Church La. Cat 137 E4
Church La. Dan 35 F2
Church La. Dit 101 D2
Church La. E Gri 2 B1
Church La. East 185 D2
Church La. Etc 46 A1
Church La. Frant 18 C2
Church La. Gue G 141 F4
Church La. Hooe 158 A4
Church La. Hor K 35 D3
Church La. Jev 184 A4
Church La. Kin L 148 A3
Church La. Nin 136 C3
Church La. Norm 69 D3
Church La. Peas 71 D1
Church La. Pev 176 C3
Church La. Poy 122 A4
Church La. Ripe 152 B4
Church La. S Mal 127 D2
Church La. Sea 181 E1
Church La. Sock 163 D4
Church La. Wfd 117 E2
Church La. Wiv 75 E3
Church Marks La. E Hoa 107 E3
Church Mead. Key 100 C2
Church Mews. Willn 174 C1
Church Pas. Hast 162 C4
Church Path. Hel 132 C3
Church Path. Nin 136 C3
Church Pl. Bri 166 B2
Church Rd. Bar 104 B2
Church Rd. Bar C 104 B2
Church Rd. Bux 57 F2
Church Rd. Cat 137 E4
Church Rd. Cro 27 E1
Church Rd. Hast 162 A4
Church Rd. Hay H 52 B2
Church Rd. Hel 132 C3
Church Rd. Hers 134 C1
Church Rd. Hove 165 D3
Church Rd. Lam 21 F3
Church Rd. Mou 88 C3
Church Rd. Newk 78 B4
Church Rd. Pem 10 A4
Church Rd. Pole 174 C3
Church Rd. Por S 163 F4
Church Rd. Sale 66 A3
Church Rd. San 48 B2
Church Rd. Sca H 53 E2
Church Rd. T W 8 C2
Church Rd. W Hoa 22 B3
Church Row. Lew 127 D1
Church Sq. Rye 95 D3
Church St. Bex 160 A3
Church St. Bri 165 F3
Church St. Cad S 84 A3
Church St. Cowd 4 C3
Church St. East 185 D2
Church St. Hart 15 D2
Church St. Hast 141 D2
Church St. Por S 163 F4
Church St. Rot 40 C4
Church St. Sea 181 E2
Church St. Uck 80 A4
Church St. Willn 175 D1
Church Twitten. Lew 127 D1

Church Vale Rd. Bex 160 A3
Church Wood Dr. Hast 139 E2
Church Wood Way. Hast 139 E1
Churchdale Ave. East 186 A3
Churchdale Pl. East 185 F3
Churchdale Rd. East 186 A3
Churchfield. E Dean 188 C4
Churchfield. Wfd 117 D2
Churchfields. Nut 37 D2
Churchill Ave. Hast 141 D3
Churchill Cl. East 185 D2
Churchill Rd. Hea 83 F3
Churchill Rd. Lew 126 C2
Churchill Rd. Sea 181 D3
Churchill Way. Bur H 75 D1
Churchland La. Sed 90 B2
Churchsettle La. Tic 32 A1
Chyngton Ave. Sea 181 F2
Chyngton Cl. East 175 F2
Chyngton Cl. Sea 181 F1
Chyngton Gdns. Sea 181 F2
Chyngton La. Sea 182 A2
Chyngton La N. Sea 182 A2
Chyngton Rd. Sea 181 F1
Chyngton Way. Sea 182 A1
Cider House Wlk. E Hoa 107 F3
Cinder Hill. Chay 77 F2
Cinderford La. Cowb 133 F4
Cinque Ports St. Rye 94 C3
Cinque Ports Way. Hast 161 E3
Cinque Ports Way. Sea 182 A2
Cinquefoil. Pea 169 D1
Circus St. Bri 165 F3
Cissbury Ave. Pea 179 E4
Cissbury Cres. Salt 168 B1
Cissbury Rd. Bur H 74 B2
Cissbury Rd. Hove 165 E4
Civic Way. Bur H 74 C1
Clackhams La. Rot 40 A4
Clair Ct. Hay H 52 B3
Clair Rd. Hay H 52 B3
Clanricarde Gdns. T W 8 C2
Clanricarde Rd. T W 8 C2
Clapham La. Litl 182 C4
Clapatch La. Tic 32 C3
Clappers The. Rob 65 F2
Clappers The. Sale 65 F2
Clare Rd. Lew 126 C1
Clare Wlk. Bri 166 A3
Claremont. Hast 162 B4
Claremont Gdns. T W 8 C1
Claremont Rd. Bex 159 F4
Claremont Rd. Newh 170 B1
Claremont Rd. Sea 181 D2
Claremont Rd. T W 8 C1
Claremont Rise. Uck 57 D1
Clarence Dr. Gri 12 B4
Clarence Rd. East 185 F2
Clarence Rd. Hast 140 A1
Clarence Rd. T W 8 C2
Clarence Row. T W 8 C2
Clarence Sq. Bri 165 E3
Clarence St. Por S 164 A3
Clarendon Cl. Hast 139 F2
Clarendon Gdns. T W 8 C1
Clarendon Pl. Bri 166 A2
Clarendon Pl. Por S 164 A3
Clarendon Rd. Hove 164 C4
Clarendon Rd. S Sea 163 D4
Clarendon Terr. Bri 166 A2
Clarendon Villas. Hove 164 C4
Clarendon Way. T W 8 C1
Clarke Ave. Hove 144 B2
Claverham Cl. Bat 114 C2
Claverham Way. Bat 114 C2
Clavering Wlk. Bex 158 C1
Claxton Cl. East 185 D3
Claxton Rd. Bex 160 C3
Clay Hill Rd. Lam 21 D3
Clays Cl. E Gri 12 B4
Clayton Ave. Hass 100 B2
Clayton Dr. Bur H 74 B1
Clayton Hill. Pye 123 D4
Clayton Rd. Bri 166 A4
Clayton Rd. Dit 101 D2
Clayton Way. Hove 144 B2
Clayton's La. Asht 6 B1
Clearwater La. Sca H 53 F2
Clearwaters La. Bur H 75 D4
Cleeve Ave. T W 9 D1
Clegg St. Hast 162 B4
Clement Hill Rd. Hast 140 C1
Clement La. Pole 174 C3
Clementine Ave. Sea 181 D3
Clerks Acre. Key 100 C2
Clermont Rd. Bri 145 E1
Clermont Terr. Bri 145 E1
Cleve Cl. Fra 80 C3
Cleve Terr. Lew 149 D4
Clevedon Rd. Bex 159 F3
Clevedown. Lew 148 C4
Cleveland. T W 9 D1
Cleveland Cl. East 176 A2
Cleveland Gdns. Bur H 74 C1
Cleveland Rd. Bri 145 F1
Cliff Approach. Bri 166 B2
Cliff Cl. Sea 181 E1
Cliff Gdns. Pea 178 B4

Cliff Gdns. Sea 181 E1
Cliff Park Cl. Pea 179 E4
Cliff Rd. Bri 166 B2
Cliff Rd. East 190 B4
Cliff Rd. Sea 181 E1
Cliff Way. Fai 142 B3
Cliffe High St. Lew 127 E1
Cliffe Ind Est. Lew 149 E4
Clifford Ave. East 185 D3
Clifford Rd. Bex 160 A2
Clifton Cl. East 185 D4
Clifton Hill. Bri 165 E3
Clifton Pl. Bri 165 E3
Clifton Pl. T W 8 C1
Clifton Rd. Bri 165 E3
Clifton Rd. Hast 141 D2
Clifton Rd. Newh 180 A4
Clifton Rd. T W 9 D4
Clifton Rise. Bex 160 B3
Clifton St. Bri 165 E3
Clifton Terr. Bri 165 E3
Clifton Way. Pea 178 C4
Climbing Cl. Hay H 52 A2
Clinch Green Ave. Bex 159 E4
Clinton Cres. Hast 139 F1
Clinton Hill. Dor 2 C4
Clinton La. Sea 181 E2
Clinton Pl. Sea 181 E2
Clinton Way. Fai 142 B3
Clive Ave. Hast 141 D1
Cliveden Ct. Bri 145 E2
Clockhouse. T W 9 E3
Clockhouse La. Nut 37 D2
Cloisters. Newh 180 A4
Cloisters The. East 175 D1
Cloisters The. Hast 162 A4
Close Eight. East 176 B2
Close Eighteen. East 176 B1
Close Eleven. East 176 B2
Close Fifteen. East 176 B1
Close Five. East 176 B2
Close Four. East 176 B1
Close Fourteen. East 176 B1
Close Nine. East 176 B1
Close Nineteen. East 176 B1
Close One. East 176 A1
Close Seven. East 176 B2
Close Seventeen. East 176 B1
Close Six. East 176 B2
Close Sixteen. East 176 B1
Close Ten. East 176 B1
Close The. Bri 145 D3
Close The. Bur H 75 D2
Close The. Cro 27 E2
Close The. E Gri 12 A4
Close The. East 184 C4
Close The. Fai 142 A2
Close The. Fri 183 F1
Close The. Key 100 B2
Close The. Newh 170 B1
Close The. Rye 94 C3
Close The. Sea 181 E1
Close The. Willn 175 D2
Close Three. East 176 A1
Close Twelve. East 176 B1
Close Twenty. East 176 B1
Close Twentyfive. East 176 A1
Close Twentyfour. East 176 A1
Close Two. East 176 A1
Cloudesley Rd. Hast 162 A4
Cloverlea. Hast 140 B3
Cluny St. Lew 149 D4
Clyde Park. Hai 155 D4
Clyde Rd. Bri 165 F4
Clyde Rd. Hast 162 A4
Coach and Horses La.
  Che Co 36 A3
Coach and Horses Pas.
  T W 8 C1
Coach La. Che Co 36 A3
Coalbrook Rd. Bri 166 A3
Coast Rd. Nor B 177 E1
Coast Rd. Pev B 177 E3
Coastguard Cotts. Nor B ... 177 E2
Coastguard La. Fai 142 A2
Coastguard La. Hast 142 A2
Cob Cl. Cra D 11 D4
Cob La. Ard 22 A1
Cobald Rd. Pev B 177 E3
Cobbett's Ride. T W 8 B1
Cobbetts Mead. Hay H 52 C2
Cobbold Ave. East 185 D3
Cobden Rd. Bri 166 A4
Cobhams. Spe 7 F4
Cobourg Pl. Hast 162 C4
Cobton Dr. Hove 144 C2
Cochrane Cl. East 186 B4
Cockcrow Wood. Hast 140 A3
Cockmount La. Wad 31 E3
Cockshut Rd. Lew 149 D4
Cogger's La. Hel 109 E2
Coggins Mill Rd. May 42 A2
Coghurst La. Hast 141 D2
Colbourne Ave. Bri 146 A1
Colbourne Rd. Hove 165 E4
Colchester Vale. For R 13 E1
Coldean La. Bri 146 B3

Coldharbour Cl. Cro 27 F1
Coldharbour La. N Cha 77 F4
Coldharbour Rd. Ford 6 B4
Coldharbour Rd. Low D 132 A2
Coldharbour Rd. Upp D 131 F1
Coldthorn La. Hai 154 C2
Coldwaltham La. Bur H 75 D1
Colebrook Rd. Bri 145 D2
Colebrook Rd. Sgh 9 D4
Colebrook Rd. Sock 163 E4
Colebrooke Rd. Bex 159 F2
Coleman Ave. Hove 164 B4
Coleman St. Bri 165 F4
Coleridge St. Hove 164 C4
Coleridge Wlk. East 176 B1
Colgate Cl. Bri 166 B3
College Cl. E Gri 2 B1
College Cl. Por S 143 E2
College Dr. T W 9 D2
College Gdns. Bri 166 A2
College La. E Gri 2 B1
College La. Hur 100 A3
College Pl. Bri 166 A2
College Pl. Hur 100 A3
College Rd. Bex 160 B2
College Rd. Bri 166 A2
College Rd. East 185 E1
College Rd. Hay H 52 B4
College Rd. Sea 181 E1
College St. Bri 166 A2
College Terr. Bri 166 A3
Collett Cl. Hast 139 E3
Collier Cl. East 185 F4
Collier Rd. Pev B 177 D2
Collingford La. Dan 35 F2
Collington Ave. Bex 159 E2
Collington Cl. East 185 E1
Collington Gr. Bex 159 E2
Collington La E. Bex 159 E2
Collington La W. Bex 159 D2
Collington Park Cres. Bex .. 159 E2
Collington Rise. Bex 159 E2
Collingwood Ave. Hea 83 F4
Collingwood Cl. E Gri 12 B4
Collingwood Cl. East 186 B3
Collingwood Cl. Pea 169 D1
Collingwood Rise. Hea 83 F4
Collinstone Rd. Hast 161 F4
Collinswood Dr. Hast 161 F4
Colmer Ct. Bur H 74 B2
Colmer Pl. Bur H 74 B2
Colonnade Gdns. East 185 F2
Colonnade Rd. East 185 F2
Coltstocks Rd. East 190 A4
Colwell Cl. Hay H 52 A2
Colwell Gdns. Hay H 52 B2
Colwell La. Hay H 52 C1
Colwell Rd. Hay H 52 B1
Colwood Cres. East 184 C3
Combe End. Cro 39 E4
Combe La. East 190 A4
Combe Rise. Willn 174 C1
Combe The. East 184 C4
Combermere Rd. Hast 139 F1
Command Rd. East 184 C3
Commanders Wlk. Fai 142 B2
Commercial Rd. Bur H 74 B2
Commercial Rd. East 185 F2
Commercial Rd. T W 8 C3
Commercial Sq. Lew 127 D1
Common La. Ber 152 B1
Common La. Dit 101 D3
Common La. Selm 152 B1
Common View. T W 8 A2
Common Wood Rise. Cro 27 E2
Compasses La. Sed 90 A3
Comphurst La. Win H 134 C2
Compton Ave. Bri 165 E4
Compton Cl. Bex 160 B2
Compton Dr. East 185 D1
Compton Place Rd. East 185 E1
Compton Rd. Bri 145 D1
Compton Rd. Hay H 52 C4
Compton St. East 185 F1
Compton Terr. Hai 155 D3
Compts The. Pea 168 C1
Concord Cl. T W 9 D2
Concorde Cl. Bex 159 E3
Condor Way. Bur H 74 B2
Conduit Hill. Rye 95 D3
Coney Furlong. Pea 169 D1
Coneyburrow La. Bex 158 B3
Coneyburrow Rd. T W 9 E3
Conghurst La. Upp T 48 A4
Conghurst La. The M 47 F3
Conifer Cl. Hast 140 B2
Conifers The. East 185 E2
Coniston Ave. T W 8 B3
Coniston Rd. East 176 A2
Connaught Rd. East 185 F1
Connaught Rd. Hove 164 C3
Connaught Rd. Sea 181 D2
Connaught Terr. Hove 164 C4
Connaught Way. T W 8 B3
Connell Dr. Wood 167 E4
Conqueror Ind Est. Hast ... 139 E3
Conqueror Rd. Hast 161 E4
Consort Way. Bur H 74 B1
Constable Rd. East 176 A1

Constable Way. Bex 160 B3
Conway Pl. Hove 164 C4
Conway St. Hove 164 C4
Cooden Cl. Bex 159 D2
Cooden Dr. Bex 159 E1
Cooden Sea Rd. Bex 158 C1
Cook Ave. East 186 B3
Cookham Dene. Bex 160 A2
Cooksbridge Rd. Bri 166 B3
Cookstown Cl. Nin 136 B3
Coolham Dr. Bri 166 B4
Coombe Cl. Win H 134 C3
Coombe Hill Rd. E Gri 12 A3
Coombe La. Nin 136 B3
Coombe Rd. Bri 146 A3
Coombe Rd. East 185 D2
Coombe Rd. S Mal 127 D1
Coombe Rise. Salt 168 A2
Coombe Shaw. Nin 136 C3
Coombe Vale. Salt 168 A2
Coombers La. Hay H 52 C3
Coombs Cl. Four O 70 A3
Coombs Cotts. Four O 70 A3
Cooper Dr. Bex 159 F4
Cooper Rd. Rye 94 C3
Coopers Cl. Bur H 74 C3
Coopers Hill. Willn 174 C1
Coopers La. Cro 27 D2
Coopers La. Ford 7 D4
Coopers Wood. Cro 27 D2
Copestake Dr. Bur H 75 D2
Coplands Rise. Norm 68 C4
Coppards Cl. Wiv G 76 A2
Coppards La. Norm 69 D4
Copper's Hill. Bar 63 E3
Copperfields. Lydd 98 C3
Coppice Ave. Willn 174 C2
Coppice Cl. Willn 174 C2
Coppice The. Bat 115 F2
Coppice The. Hast 140 B1
Coppice The. Pem 10 A3
Coppice Way. Hay H 52 A2
Copse Cl. E Gri 2 C2
Copse Hill. Bri 145 D3
Copse Rd. Bex 159 E2
Copse The. Hay H 52 B3
Copthorne Rd. Fel 1 B2
Copwood Ave. Uck 79 F4
Copyhold Rd. E Gri 12 A4
Cordons. Kin L 148 A3
Cormorant Cl. East 176 A1
Cornelius Ave. Newh 179 F3
Cornfield Cl. Sea 181 E2
Cornfield Green. Hai 133 D1
Cornfield La. East 185 F1
Cornfield Rd. East 185 F1
Cornfield Rd. Sea 181 D2
Cornfield Terr. East 185 F1
Cornfield Terr. Hast 162 A4
Cornford Cl. Bur H 74 B3
Cornford Cl. Cro 27 F1
Cornford Cl. Pem 10 A3
Cornford La. T W 9 F2
Cornford Pk. Pem 10 A3
Cornish Cl. East 175 F2
Cornmill Gdns. Willn 174 C2
Cornwall Ave. Pea 179 E3
Cornwall Gdns. Bri 145 E1
Cornwall Rd. Bex 159 F2
Cornwallis Cl. East 186 B4
Cornwallis Gdns. Hast 162 B4
Cornwallis St. Hast 162 B4
Cornwallis Terr. Hast 162 B4
Coronation Cotts. Sale 66 A3
Coronation Gdns. Bat 115 E3
Coronation Gdns. Hur G 46 B2
Coronation Rd. E Gri 12 B4
Coronation St. Bri 166 A4
Corseley Rd. Gro 17 D3
Corsica Cl. Sea 181 E1
Corsica Rd. Sea 181 F1
Costells Edge. Sca H 53 E2
Cotswold Cl. East 176 A2
Cotswold Cl. Hast 140 C2
Cotswolds The. Sock 163 E4
Cottage Cl. S Hei 170 A1
Cottage La. Hank 155 E1
Cottage La. Sed 116 C2
Cottage La. Wfd 117 E3
County Oak Ave. Bri 145 F3
Course The. Lew 149 D4
Court Cl. Bri 145 D3
Court Cl. E Gri 2 B1
Court Cres. E Gri 2 B1
Court Farm Cl. Pid 169 F1
Court Farm Rd. Hove 144 C1
Court Farm Rd. Newh 180 A3
Court Farm Rd. Rottn 167 E2
Court Meadow. Rot 40 C4
Court Meadow Cl. Rot 40 C4
Court Ord Rd. Rottn 167 E2
Court Rd. East 175 E1
Court Rd. T W 8 A2
Courtenwell. Lan G 7 E2
Courthope Ave. Wad 31 E2
Courthope Dr. Bex 159 E3
Courthouse St. Hast 162 C4
Courtland Rd. Pole 174 C3
Courtlands. Hay H 52 B2

Courtlands. Nut 37 D1
Courtlands Rd. East 185 F3
Courtyard The. E Gri 2 C1
Courtyard The. Hast 140 B1
Cousley Wood Rd. Cou W 32 A4
Cousley Wood Rd. Wad 31 F3
Coventry Rd. Hast 139 F2
Coventry St. Bri 165 E4
Coverdale Ave. Bex 159 D2
Covers The. Sea 181 E1
Cowden Cl. The M 47 E4
Cowden Rd. Salt 178 A4
Cowden Wlk. Hast 139 F1
Cowdens Cl. Hove 144 A2
Cowdray Cl. Bex 159 D3
Cowdray Park Rd. Bex 159 D3
Cowfold Rd. Bri 166 B3
Cowley Dr. Wood 167 E4
Cowper St. Hove 164 C4
Cox Gr. Bur H 74 B2
Crabtree Ave. Bri 145 F3
Cradle Hill Ind Est. Sea 181 F3
Cradle Hill Rd. Sea 181 F3
Craig Cl. Crow 138 C3
Craignair Ave. Bri 145 E4
Cranborne Ave. East 190 A4
Cranbourne St. Bri 165 E3
Cranbrook Rd. Hast 140 A1
Cranedown. Lew 148 C4
Cranfield Rd. Bex 160 A2
Cranleigh Ave. Salt 167 F1
Cranleigh Cl. Bex 159 F2
Cranmer Ave. Hove 144 B1
Cranmer Cl. S Mal 127 C1
Cranston Ave. Bex 159 E2
Cranston Cl. Bex 159 E2
Cranston Rd. E Gri 2 B1
Cranston Rise. Bex 159 E2
Cranwell Rd. T W 8 A2
Craven Rd. Bri 166 A3
Crawford Way. E Gri 2 B2
Crawley Cres. East 175 E1
Crawley Down Rd. Fel 1 B2
Crawley Rd. Bri 146 A3
Crayford Rd. Bri 146 A1
Crazy La. Sed 116 B4
Creek The. Hast 162 C4
Crendon Park. Sgh 8 C4
Crescent Cl. Bur H 74 C2
Crescent Cl. Wood 167 E4
Crescent Dr N. Wood 167 E4
Crescent Dr S. Wood 167 E4
Crescent Pl. Bri 166 A2
Crescent Rd. Bri 165 F4
Crescent Rd. Bur H 74 C2
Crescent Rd. E Gri 2 A1
Crescent Rd. T W 8 C2
Crescent The. Bri 146 B1
Crescent The. Dor P 2 A4
Crescent The. East 184 C3
Crescent The. Hast 140 A2
Crescent The. Key 100 C2
Crescent The. Newh 170 B1
Crescent The. Sock 163 E4
Crescent The. Willn 174 C2
Crescent Way. Bur H 74 C2
Crespin Way. Bri 146 A1
Crest Rd. Newh 170 B1
Cresta Cl. Pole 174 C4
Cresta Rd. Newh 179 F3
Crestway The. Bri 146 A1
Cricketers Field. Stas 67 E1
Cricketfield. Newk 78 A4
Cricketfield Rd. Sea 181 E1
Cricketing La. Hers 134 A2
Criers La. Five A 59 F4
Crink Hill. Bar C 104 B2
Cripland Cl. Hay H 52 C3
Cripps Ave. Pea 169 D1
Crisp Rd. Lew 126 C2
Crittle's Ct. Wad 134 B2
Crockendale Field. Rin 128 B3
Crockers Hatch Cnr. Lan G 7 D1
Crocks Dean. Pea 169 D1
Croft Ave. Sock 163 E4
Croft Cl. Pole 174 B2
Croft Dr. Por S 143 F2
Croft La. Sea 181 E2
Croft Rd. Bri 145 D2
Croft Rd. Cro 27 E1
Croft Rd. Hast 162 C4
Croft The. Hass 100 B3
Croft The. Hast 162 C4
Croft The. Willn 174 C1
Croft Works. Hai 154 C4
Crofton Park Ave. Bex 159 E2
Croham Rd. Cro 27 E2
Cromer Way. Hai 132 C1
Cromer Wlk. Hast 140 B1
Cromleigh Way. Sock 143 E1
Cromwell Pl. E Gri 12 B4
Cromwell Rd. Bur H 74 B2
Cromwell Rd. Hove 165 D4
Cromwell Rd. T W 9 D2
Cromwell St. Bri 166 A4
Crooked La. Sea 181 E1
Cross La. Tic 33 D1
Cross Rd. Sock 163 D4

Cross Road Cl. Sock 163 D4
Cross St. Bri 165 F4
Cross St. Hast 162 A4
Cross St. Hove 165 D3
Cross St. Pole 174 C3
Cross Way. Lew 126 C1
Crossbush Rd. Bri 166 B3
Crossway The. Bri 145 F1
Crossway The. Por S 143 F1
Crossway The. T W 8 A1
Crossways Ave. E Gri 2 A1
Crossways The. St Cro 175 F3
Crouch Cl. East 174 C1
Crouch La. Nin 136 C2
Crouch La. San 49 E4
Crouch La. Sea 181 E1
Crowborough Hill. Cro 40 A4
Crowborough Rd. Hast 141 E2
Crowborough Rd. Salt 168 A1
Crowhurst La. Bex 160 A4
Crowhurst Rd. Bri 146 A4
Crowhurst Rd. Crow 138 C2
Crowhurst Rd. Hast 139 D1
Crowmere Ave. Bex 160 A3
Crowmere Terr. Bex 160 A3
Crown Cl. Hai 154 C4
Crown Cl. Uck 80 A4
Crown Gdns. Bri 165 E3
Crown La. Hast 162 C4
Crown Rd. Por S 163 F4
Crown St. Bri 165 E3
Crown St. East 185 D2
Croxden Wy. East 175 E2
Croxton La. Hay H 52 C3
Crunden Rd. East 185 D2
Cubitt Way. Hast .... 139 E2‘
Cuckfield Cl. Bex 160 C3
Cuckfield Rd. Hur 99 F4
Cuckmere Path. Uck 57 E1
Cuckmere Rd. Newh 179 F3
Cuckmere Rd. Sea 181 F1
Cuckmere Rise. Hea 83 F4
Cuckmere Way. Bri 145 F3
Cuckmere Wlk. East 175 D1
Cuckoo Dr. Hea 83 F3
Cuilfail Tunnel. Lew 127 E1
Culpepper. Bur H 74 B2
Culross Ave. Hay H 52 A3
Culver Cl. East 175 F2
Culverden Ave. T W 8 C3
Culverden Down. T W 8 B3
Culverden Park. T W 8 B3
Culverden Park Rd. T W 8 B3
Culverden Sq. T W 8 C3
Culverden St. T W 8 C2
Cumberland Gdns. Hast 161 F4
Cumberland Gdns. T W 8 C1
Cumberland Rd. Bex 159 F4
Cumberland Rd. Bri 145 E1
Cumberland Wlk. T W 8 C1
Cumberland Yd. T W 8 C1
Cumbrian Cl. East 176 A2
Cunningham Dr. East 186 B4
Cunningham Rd. T W 8 C3
Curlew Ct. Hast 139 E2
Curren Pl. Bri 145 E2
Curwen Pl. Bri 145 E2
Cuthbert Cl. Bex 159 F4
Cuthbert Rd. Bri 166 A3
Cutter La. Hast 162 C4
Cuttinglye Rd. Cra D 1 A1
Cypress Cl. Hast 161 F4
Cypress Gr. Bel G 19 D4
Cyprus Pl. Rye 94 C4
Cyprus Rd. Bur H 74 C2

Dacre Park. Hai 155 D4
Dacre Rd. East 185 D2
Dacre Rd. Hers 134 B3
Dacre Rd. Newh 180 A4
Dagg La. Ewh G 67 D3
Dale Ave. Bri 145 E3
Dale Ave. Key 100 C2
Dale Cres. Bri 145 E3
Dale Dr. Bri 145 F3
Dale Hill. Pye 122 C3
Dale Rd. For R 13 E1
Dale Rd. Lew 148 C4
Dale St. T W 8 C2
Dale View. Hove 144 B1
Dale View Gdns. Hove 144 A1
Dalehurst Rd. Bex 159 F4
Dalemeny Rd. Bex 159 F3
Dales Cl. Win H 134 C3
Dalewood Gdns. Bur H 75 F1
Dallas La. Spi 104 B3
Dallaway Gdns. E Gri 2 B1
Dallington Cl. Bex 160 C3
Dallington Rd. East 175 F1
Dallington Rd. Hove 164 B4
Dalton Rd. East 190 B4
Damian Way. Key 100 C2
Damon Cl. Pea 179 D4
Dane Cl. Sea 181 D1
Dane Ct Cl. Bex 159 F3
Dane Rd. Hast 161 F4
Dane Rd. Sea 181 E2
Danehill La. Hor K 35 E3
Danehill Rd. Bri 166 B3

Danum Cl. Hai 133 D2
Darby's La. Wad 31 F1
Darcey Dr. Bri 145 F3
Daresbury Cl. Bex 159 F3
Darley Rd. East 190 B4
Dartmouth Cl. Bri 146 B1
Dartmouth Cres. Bri 146 B1
Darvel Down. Net 88 A1
Darwall Dr. Sea 181 F2
Darwell Cl. Hast 139 E1
D'aubigny Rd. Bri 165 F4
Davey Dr. Bri 145 F1
Davey's La. Lew 127 E1
Davidgor Rd. Hove 165 E4
Davis Cl. Bex 159 F4
Dawson Terr. Bri 166 A3
De Cham Ave. Hast 162 A4
De Cham Rd. Hast 162 A4
De Chardin Dr. Hast 140 C3
De Courcel Rd. Bri 166 B2
De La Warr Green. Lew 126 C2
De La Warr Par. Bex 160 B2
De La Warr Rd. Bex 160 B3
De La Warr Rd. E Gri 2 B1
De Monkfort Rd. Bri 166 A4
De Montfort Rd. Lew 126 C1
De Roos Rd. East 185 E2
De Walden Mews. East 190 B4
De Warrenne Rd. Lew 126 C1
Deacons Dr. Por S 144 A1
Deadmantree Hill. Bar 103 F2
Deadmantree Hill. Bar C 103 F2
Deal Ave. Sea 182 A3
Deals The. Rye 94 C3
Dean Cl. Por S 144 A1
Dean Ct Rd. Rottn 167 F1
Dean Gdns. Por S 144 A1
Dean Rd. Sea 181 E1
Dean St. Bri 165 E3
Dean Wood. East 175 F2
Deanery Cl. S Mal 127 D2
Deans Cl. Bex 159 F3
Deans Cl. Wood 167 E4
Deans Dr. Bex 159 F3
Deans Meadow. Bar C 104 B3
Deanway. Hove 144 C2
Deanway. Alfn 172 B2
Deanway. Hove 144 C2
Decimus Burton Way. Hast 162 A4
Decoy Dr. East 175 E1
Deepdene. Wad 31 E3
Deersswood La. Bex 159 E3
Deeside The. Bri 145 F4
Delaware Rd. Lew 148 C4
Delfryn. Por S 143 E2
Dell Cl. Hast 139 F1
Dell Dr. T W 9 D2
Dell The. E Gri 2 C1
Dellney Ave. Hay H 52 B2
Delmonden Rd. Fli 34 C1
Delves Ave. T W 9 D1
Delves Cl. Rin 128 A3
Delves Way. Rin 128 A3
Den Hill. East 184 C2
Denbigh Rd. T W 9 D4
Dencher Rd. Iford 148 B2
Dene Cl. Fri 183 F1
Dene Dr. East 175 D1
Dene Path. Uck 57 D1
Dene The. Hast 140 C3
Dene The. Hove 144 A2
Dene The. Uck 57 D1
Dene The. Willn 174 C2
Dene Vale. Bri 145 D3
Denehurst Gdns. Hast 140 C3
Deneside. Bri 145 D3
Deneside. Fri 183 F1
Deneway. Spe 7 F4
Deneway The. Bri 145 D2
Denge La. Lydd 98 C4
Denham Cl. Hast 139 E2
Denham Rd. Bur H 74 A2
Denham Way. Cam 96 B1
Denman's Cl. Hay H 52 C3
Denman's La. Hay H 52 C3
Denmark Mews. Hove 164 C4
Denmark Pl. Hast 162 B4
Denmark Rd. Por S 164 A4
Denmark Terr. Bri 165 E3
Denmark Villas. Hove 164 C4
Denne's La. Lydd 98 C4
Denton Cl. Rye 94 C3
Denton Dr. Bri 145 F3
Denton Rd. East 190 A4
Denton Rd. Newh 170 B1
Denton Rise. Newh 170 B1
Dentons The. East 190 A4
Derek Ave. Hove 164 A3
Derings The. Lydd 98 C4
Derwent Cl. Hai 132 C1
Derwent Dr. T W 8 B3
Derwent Rd. East 190 B4
Desmond Rd. East 186 A3
Desmond Way. Bri 166 B3
Devil's Dyke Rd. Hove 144 B3
Devil's Dyke Rd. Poy 122 A1
Devonshire Cl. T W 18 B4
Devonshire Pl. Bri 165 F3

Devonshire Pl. East 185 F1
Devonshire Rd. Bex 160 A2
Devonshire Rd. Hast 162 B4
Devonshire Sq. Bex 160 A2
Dew La. Peas 70 C1
Dewe Rd. Bri 146 A1
Dewpond The. Pea 168 C1
Diana Cl. Bex 160 C3
Dickens Cl. E Gri 2 A1
Dickens Way. East 176 B2
Dicklands The. Rod 169 D4
Dillingburgh Rd. East 185 D2
Dillon Way. T W 9 D3
Diplock Cl. Pole 174 B3
Diplocks The. Hai 154 C4
Diplocks Way. Hai 154 C4
Diplocks Wlk. Hai 154 C4
Dirty La. Ash W 13 E3
Dirty La. Hamm 13 D3
Ditchling Bostal. Wmes 124 A4
Ditchling Cres. Bri 146 A3
Ditchling Dr. Hast 141 E2
Ditchling Gdns. Bri 145 F1
Ditchling Rd. Bri 145 F2
Ditchling Rd. Wmes 124 A2
Ditchling Rise. Bri 165 F4
Ditchling Way. Hai 154 C3
Ditton's Cnr. Pole 175 D3
Dittons Mews. Hast 139 E1
Dittons Rd. East 185 E2
Dittons Rd. St Cro 175 E3
Dixter La. Norm 68 C4
Dixter Rd. Norm 68 C3
Dock The. W Fir 151 D2
Dodshill. Cro 27 F1
Dog Kennel La. Five A 59 F3
Dogs Hill Rd. Winc B 120 C3
Doleham Hill. Thr O 118 A3
Doleham Hill. Wfd 118 A3
Doleham La. Wfd 117 F3
Dolphin Rd. Hay H 52 A2
Donald Hall Rd. Bri 166 A3
Donald Way. Winc B 120 C3
Donkey Mews. Hove 165 D3
Donnington Rd. Wood 167 E3
Dordrecht Way. Hast 140 B1
Dorking Rd. T W 9 D3
Dormans Cl. Dor 2 C1
Dormans Gdns. Dor P 2 B3
Dormans High St. Dor 2 C4
Dormans Park Rd. Dor P 2 B3
Dormans Park Rd. E Gri 2 A2
Dormans Station Rd. Dor 2 B4
Dornden Dr. Lan G 7 F2
Dornden Park. T W 7 F2
Dorothy Ave. Pea 179 D4
Dorothy Rd. Hove 164 A4
Dorset Ave. E Gri 2 A2
Dorset Gdns. Bri 165 F3
Dorset Gdns. E Gri 2 A2
Dorset Pl. Bri 165 F3
Dorset Pl. Hast 162 B4
Dorset Rd. Bex 160 B3
Dorset Rd. Lew 149 D4
Dorset Rd. T W 9 D1
Dorset Rd S. Bex 160 A2
Dorset St. Bri 165 F3
Doubledays. Bur H 74 C1
Doucegrove. Hast 139 F1
Douglas Rd. Tow R 29 D1
Dovedale Gdns. East 175 E1
Dover Cl. Sea 182 A3
Dover Rd. Bri 145 F1
Dover Rd. Pole 174 C4
Dowland Ave. Sock 143 E1
Downland Ave. Pea 179 E3
Downland Cl. Sock 143 D1
Downland Cl. Wood 166 C4
Downland Copse. Uck 80 A4
Downland Cres. Hove 144 B2
Downland Dr. Hove 144 B2
Downland Rd. Wood 166 C4
Downlands Ave. Bex 159 F2
Downlands Cl. Bex 159 F2
Downlands Way. Fri 183 F1
Downline Cl. Hor 109 E4
Downs Ave. East 184 C3
Downs Cl. Lew 126 C1
Downs Rd. Bur H 74 B2
Downs Rd. Hast 140 B2
Downs Rd. Sea 181 F2
Downs Rd. Willn 174 C1
Downs Valley Rd. Wood 167 E4
Downs View. N Cha 77 E4
Downs View. Nin 136 C3
Downs View. Pea 169 D1
Downs View Cl. Fri 184 A1
Downs View Cl. N Cha 77 E4
Downs View La. Fri 184 A1
Downs View Rd. Hass 100 B2

Downs View Rd. Sea 181 F2
Downs Way. Sock 143 E1
Downscroft. Bur H 75 D3
Downside. Hove 144 C2
Downside. Lew 148 C4
Downside Cl. East 185 D2
Downsvalley Rd. Willn 174 C2
Downsview. Hea 83 F4
Downsview. Hove 144 A2
Downsview Ave. Wood 167 D4
Downsview Cres. Uck 80 A4
Downsview Dr. Wiv G 76 A2
Downsview Rd. Por S 143 F1
Downsview Rd. Willn 174 C2
Downsview Way. Hai 154 C4
Downsway. Wood 147 D1
Draffin La. Cam 96 A2
Drake Ave. East 186 B4
Drapers Way. Hast 139 F1
Draxmont Way. Bri 145 E2
Drayton Rise. Bex 159 D2
Drive The. Bur H 74 C2
Drive The. Cro 27 D1
Drive The. Hai 154 C3
Drive The. Hast 161 E4
Drive The. Hove 165 D4
Drive The. Mar 56 C3
Drive The. Newh 180 A3
Drive The. Sock 143 E1
Drive The. T W 8 C1
Drive The. Uck 80 A4
Drockmill Cl. Pole 175 D3
Drove Ave. Kin L 147 D1
Drove Ave. Wood 147 D1
Drove Cres. Por S 143 F1
Drove Rd. Newh 180 B4
Drove Rd. Por S 143 F1
Drove Rd. Wood 166 C4
Drove The. Bri 145 E1
Drove The. Fal 147 D3
Drove The. Newh 180 B4
Drove The. Off 126 C3
Drovers Cl. Por S 144 A1
Drovers Way. Bur H 75 D3
Droveway The. Hay H 52 A3
Droveway The. Hove 145 D1
Drummond Cl. Hay H 52 A2
Drury La. Hast 139 F1
Dryden Wlk. East 176 B2
Dudley Rd. Bri 145 F1
Dudley Rd. East 185 F2
Dudley Rd. Hast 141 D1
Dudley Rd. T W 8 C2
Dudwell Rd. Wood 167 E4
Duke Rd. Hast 139 F1
Duke St. Bex 159 E3
Duke St. Bri 165 E3
Duke St. East 185 F2
Duke St. Hast 139 F1
Duke Terr. Hast 139 F1
Duke's Dr. East 190 B4
Duke's Mound. Bri 166 A2
Duke's Pas. Bri 165 E3
Dukes Cl. Sea 181 D2
Dukes Hill. Bat 115 D3
Dukes La. Bri 165 E3
Dukes Rd. Hay H 52 C4
Dukes Rd. T W 9 D3
Dulwich Cl. Sea 181 F2
Dumb Woman's La. Udi 94 A3
Dumbrells Cl. Dit 101 D2
Dumbrills Cl. Bur H 74 C3
Dunclutha Rd. Hast 140 B2
Duncton Cl. Hay H 52 A2
Dundale Rd. Bel G 10 C1
Dundale Rd. Kip 10 B1
Dunes Ave. Cam 96 B1
Dunning's Rd. E Gri 12 B4
Dunstall Ave. Bur H 74 B2
Dunstall Farm Rd. Bur H 74 B2
Dunstan Gr. T W 8 C3
Dunstan Rd. T W 8 C3
Dunstans Croft. May 42 A2
Dunster Cl. Bri 145 F1
Dunvan Cl. S Mal 127 C2
Durham Cl. Bri 146 C1
Durkins Rd. E Gri 2 A1
Durrell Cl. East 176 B1
Dursley Rd. East 185 F2
Dyall Cl. Bur H 74 B2
Dyke Cl. Hove 144 C2
Dyke Cl. Poy 122 A2
Dyke La. Poy 122 A2
Dyke Rd. Bri 165 E4
Dyke Road Ave. Hove 145 D2
Dyke Road Dr. Bri 165 E4
Dyke Road Mews. Bri 165 E4
Dyke Road Pl. Bri 145 D2
Dymchurch Cl. Pole 175 D4
Dymchurch Cl. Sea 182 A2
Dymock Cl. Sea 182 A2
Dymock's The. Dit 101 D2
Dymond Rd. Hast 139 F2
Dynevor Rd. T W 9 D4

Eagle Rd. Rye 95 D3
Earl St. Hast 162 B4
Earl's Rd. T W 8 A2
Earls Cl. Sea 181 D3

Earls Gdn. Lew

Earls Gdn. Lew 127 D1
East Albany Rd. Sea 181 E2
East Ascent. Hast 162 A3
East Beach St. Hast 162 C4
East Beeches Rd. Cro 27 F1
East Bourne St. Hast 162 C4
East Cl. Pole 174 C3
East Cliff. Rye 95 D3
East Cliff Rd. T W 8 C3
East Dean Rd. East 184 C1
East Dean Rise. Sea 181 F2
East Dr. Bri 166 A3
East End La. Dit 101 D2
East Gdns. Dit 101 D2
East Hill. Dor P 2 B3
East Hill Pas. Hast 162 C4
East Mascalls Rd. Hay H ... 53 E3
East Par. Hast 162 C4
East Park La. Dom 1 A4
East St. Bri 165 F2
East St. Fal 147 D3
East St. Hast 162 C4
East St. Lew 127 D1
East St. May 42 A4
East St. Por S 164 A4
East St. Rye 95 D3
East St. Sea 181 E2
East St. Tur H 11 D2
East View Fields. Plu 102 B3
East View Terr. Sed 90 B1
East Way. Lew 126 B1
East Wick. Hay H 53 D4
Eastbank. Sock 143 E1
Eastbourne Ave. Pev B ... 177 D3
Eastbourne Rd. Bri 146 A1
Eastbourne Rd. Fel 1
Eastbourne Rd. Pev B 177 D2
Eastbourne Rd. Pole 174 C3
Eastbourne Rd. Rid 80 A2
Eastbourne Rd. Sea 182 A2
Eastbourne Rd. Whm 176 B3
Eastbourne Rd. Willn 174 C2
Eastbrook Rd. Bur H 75 D2
Eastbrook Way. Por S 163 F4
Eastdale. Bex 159 D3
Eastergate. Bex 159 D3
Eastergate Rd. Bri 146 B2
Eastern Ave. Pole 174 C4
Eastern Pl. Bri 166 B2
Eastern Rd. Bri 166 A2
Eastern Rd. Hay H 52 B2
Eastern Rd. Hay H 53 D4
Eastern Rd. Wiv 75 F2
Eastern St. Bri 166 A2
Eastern Terr. Bri 166 A2
Eastern Terr Mews. Bri ... 166 A2
Eastfield Cres. Bri 145 F2
Eastgate St. Lew 127 D1
Eastgate Wharf. Lew 127 D1
Easthill Dr. Por S 143 F1
Easthill Way. Por S 143 F1
Eastlands Cl. T W 18 B4
Eastlands Rd. T W 8 B1
Eastport La. Lew 149 D4
Eastwell Pl. Hai 154 C4
Eastwick Cl. Bri 145 F4
Eastwood Rd. Bex 159 F2
Eatenden La. Mou 88 C1
Eatenden La. Net 88 C1
Eaton Gdns. Hove 165 D4
Eaton Gr. Hove 165 D4
Eaton Pl. Bri 166 A2
Eaton Rd. Hove 165 D3
Eaton Villas. Hove 164 C4
Ebden's Hill. Hast 139 F4
Ebden's Hill. Wfd 139 F4
Ebenezer Rd. Hast 162 C4
Ecmod Rd. East 186 A3
Edburton Ave. Bri 145 F1
Edgar Rd. Hast 141 D1
Edgehill Way. Por S 143 E1
Edgeland Terr. East 175 E1
Edinburgh Rd. Bex 160 A3
Edinburgh Rd. Bri 165 F4
Edinburgh Rd. Hast 161 E4
Edinburgh Rd. Sea 181 D2
Edinburgh Way. E Gri 12 B4
Edison Rd. East 175 F1
Edith Ave. Pea 178 C4
Edith Rd. Hast 141 D2
Edmonton Rd. Bex 159 F4
Edmund Rd. Hast 141 D1
Edward Ave. Hove 144 C2
Edward Cl. Salt 168 A2
Edward Cl. Hove 144 C2
Edward Cl. Sea 180 C3
Edward Rd. Hast 162 A4
Edward Rd. Hay H 52 B1
Edward St. Bri 165 F3
Edward St. Lew 127 D1
Edward St. Sgh 8 B4
Edward St. T W 8 A2
Edward Terr. Hast 139 F2
Edward Way. Bur H 74 A1

Edwin Rd. Hast 141 D1
Effingham Cl. Salt 168 A1
Effingham Dr. Bex 159 D2
Egerton Rd. Bex 159 F2
Eggington Cl. Bri 146 C3
Eggington Rd. Bri 146 C3
Egles Gr. Uck 79 F4
Egmont Rd. Hove 144 A1
Egremont Pl. Bri 165 F3
Egremont Pl. Hast 140 C1
Eight Acre La. Thr O 118 A1
Eight Bells Cl. Bux 58 A2
Eileen Ave. Salt 167 F1
Eisenhower Dr. Hast 139 E3
Elder Pl. Bri 165 F4
Elderwood Cl. East 175 D1
Eldon Rd. East 185 D3
Eldred Ave. Bri 145 D3
Eleanor Cl. Lew 126 C1
Eley Cres. Rottn 167 E2
Eley Dr. Rottn 167 E2
Elford St. Hast 162 B4
Elgin Gdns. Sea 182 A2
Elim Ct Gdns. Cro 27 E2
Elim Wlk. Hast 140 B1
Elizabeth Ave. Hove 144 C2
Elizabeth Cl. Hove 144 C2
Elizabeth Cl. Sea 180 C3
Elizabeth Cres. E Gri 2 B2
Elizabeth Rd. Hast 139 F1
Elizabeth Rd. S Sea 163 D4
Ellen St. Hove 164 C4
Ellen St. Por S 164 A4
Ellenslea Rd. Hast 162 A4
Ellenwhorne La. Cri C 90 C4
Ellenwhorne La. Ewh G ... 90 C4
Ellerslie La. Bex 159 E3
Elliots Way. Hea 83 F4
Ellis Way. Uck 79 F4
Elm Cl. Hove 145 D1
Elm Cl. Lau 130 A4
Elm Cl. Sea 182 A2
Elm Ct. Newh 179 F4
Elm Dr. E Gri 2 C1
Elm Dr. Hove 144 B1
Elm Gr. Bri 166 A4
Elm Gr. East 175 E1
Elm Green. Hai 132 C1
Elm Rd. Por S 163 F4
Elm Way. Hea 83 F3
Elmhurst Ave. Pem 10 A4
Elmore Rd. Bri 165 F3
Elms Ave. East 185 F1
Elms La. Pett 119 E1
Elms Lea Ave. Bri 145 E2
Elms Rd. East 185 F1
Elms The. Rin 128 A3
Elmsdown Pl. Hai 155 D4
Elmsmead. Iden 71 F2
Elmstead Rd. Bex 160 B3
Elmwood Cl. East 176 A2
Elmwood Gdns. East 176 A2
Elphick Rd. Newh 180 A4
Elphick's Pl. T W 18 C4
Elphinstone Ave. Hast 140 B1
Elphinstone Gdns. Hast ... 140 B2
Elphinstone Rd. Hast 140 B2
Elrington Rd. Hove 145 D1
Elstead Cres. Bri 146 A3
Elsted Cl. East 175 F1
Elsted Rd. Bex 159 D1
Elven Cl. Fri 184 A1
Elven La. Fri 184 A1
Elvin Cres. Rottn 167 E2
Ely La. T W 8 C2
Emmanuel Rd. Hast 140 C1
Endwell Rd. Bex 160 A2
Engalee. E Gri 2 A1
English Cl. Hove 164 B4
English's Pas. Lew 127 D1
Enys Rd. East 185 E2
Epeland. Hai 132 C1
Erica Cl. East 175 F1
Eridge Cl. Bex 159 F2
Eridge Dr. Cro 27 F2
Eridge Gdns. Cro 27 F2
Eridge Green. Lew 126 C1
Eridge Rd. Boa 28 A3
Eridge Rd. Cro 27 F2
Eridge Rd. East 185 D4
Eridge Rd. Hove 144 C1
Eridge Rd. T W 18 B4
Erin Way. Bur H 74 B2
Erroll Rd. Hove 164 A3
Ersham Rd. Hai 154 C3
Ersham Way. Hai 154 C3
Esher Cl. Sea 181 E2
Eshton Rd. East 186 A3
Eskbank Ave. Bri 145 F4
Eskdale Cl. East 176 A2
Eskine Park Rd. T W 8 A2
Esplanade. Sea 181 E1
Esplanade The. Pea 178 B4
Essenden Rd. Hast 161 F3
Essex Cl. T W 18 B4
Essex Cotts. Bri 166 A2
Essex Pl. Newh 180 A4
Essex Rd. Hast 139 F2
Essex St. Bri 166 A2

Estate Rd. Newh 180 A4
Estate Rd. Newh 180 B4
Estate Rd. S Hei 170 A1
Estcots Dr. E Gri 2 C1
Etchingham Rd. East 176 B1
Ethel St. Hove 164 C4
Etherington Hill. Spe 8 A4
Etherton Way. Sea 181 F2
Ethnan La. San 49 E2
Eton Cl. Sea 181 F2
Eton Mews. East 185 F2
Evelyn Ave. Newh 180 A4
Evelyn Rd. Lew 126 C1
Evelyn Terr. Bri 166 A3
Eversfield Pl. Hast 162 A4
Eversfield Rd. East 185 E2
Eversley Cl. Hast 140 A1
Eversley Cres. Hast 140 A1
Eversley Rd. Bex 160 A2
Eversley Rd. Hast 140 A1
Ewart St. Bri 165 F3
Ewehurst Cl. Hast 140 B2
Ewehurst La. Spe 7 B3
Ewhurst Cl. Hast 140 B2
Ewhurst La. Mill C 68 B3
Ewhurst La. Norm 68 B3
Ewhurst Rd. Bri 146 A1
Exceat Cl. Bri 166 B3
Exceat Cl. East 175 F2
Exeter Cl. Willn 174 C1
Exeter St. Bri 165 E4
Exmouth Pl. Hast 162 C4

Factory La. Hai 154 C3
Fair La. Rob 65 F2
Fair Meadow. Rye 95 D4
Fair Oak Cl. Hea 83 F4
Fairbanks. Hay H 52 B3
Faircrouch La. Wad 31 D3
Fairdene. Sock 143 E1
Fairfax Ave. Hast 139 E3
Fairfield. Hers 134 B3
Fairfield Ave. T W 9 D3
Fairfield Chase. Bex 159 E2
Fairfield Cl. Bur H 74 B2
Fairfield Cl. S Sea 143 D1
Fairfield Cres. Hur 99 F3
Fairfield Gdns. Por S 143 F1
Fairfield Rd. Bur H 74 B2
Fairfield Rd. E Gri 12 B4
Fairfield Rd. East 185 E1
Fairfield Rd. Hast 140 A3
Fairfield Way. Hay H 52 A4
Fairford Cl. Hay H 52 B3
Fairglen Rd. Wad 30 C2
Fairholme Rd. Newh 170 B1
Fairisle Cl. Hai 132 C1
Fairlaine Rd. East 185 D3
Fairlawn Cres. E Gri 1 C1
Fairlawn Dr. E Gri 1 C1
Fairlawns. Dr. Hers 134 B3
Fairlea Cl. Bur H 74 B2
Fairley Bank. Hast 141 D1
Fairlie Gdns. Bri 145 E2
Fairlight. Uck 57 E1
Fairlight Ave. Hast 141 D2
Fairlight Ave. Pea 178 B4
Fairlight Cl. Bex 160 C3
Fairlight Cl. Pole 174 C3
Fairlight Field. Rin 128 A3
Fairlight Gdns. Fai 142 B2
Fairlight Pl. Bri 166 A4
Fairlight Rd. East 186 A3
Fairlight Rd. Hast 141 D2
Fairmile Rd. T W 9 E3
Fairmount Rd. Bex 160 A3
Fairstone Cl. Hast 141 E2
Fairview Cotts. Cro 27 E2
Fairview La. Cro 27 E2
Fairview Rise. Bri 145 D3
Fairway Cl. East 185 D1
Fairway Cres. Por S 144 A1
Fairway The. Bex 159 E3
Fairway The. East 161 E4
Fairway The. Newh 179 F4
Fairways Cl. Sea 182 A1
Fairways Rd. Sea 182 A1
Fairways The. Sgh 8 C4
Falaise Rd. Hast 162 A4
Falaise Rd. Newh 170 A1
Falcon Cl. S Sea 163 D3
Falcon Way. Hai 132 C2
Falconbury Dr. Bex 159 D2
Falconers Dr. Bat 115 E2
Fallowfield Cl. Hove 144 B1
Fallowfield Cres. Hove 144 B1
Falmer Ave. Salt 168 A1
Falmer Cl. East 184 C4
Falmer Gdns. Wood 167 D4
Falmer Hill. Bri 146 C3
Falmer Hill. Fal 147 D3
Falmer Rd. Rottn 167 E2
Falmer Rd. Wood 167 D4
Faraday Ave. E Gri 12 B3
Faraday Cl. East 175 E1
Farley Bank. Hast 140 C1
Farley Way. Fai 142 B3
Farlington Ave. Hay H 52 B3
Farlington Cl. Hay H 52 B3
Farm Cl. E Gri 12 C4

Farm Cl. Hass 100 B2
Farm Cl. Por S 143 F1
Farm Cl. Sea 181 E2
Farm Hill. Wood 167 D4
Farm Rd. Hove 165 D3
Farm Way. Bur H 75 D1
Farm Way. Por S 163 F4
Farm Yd. Bri 165 E3
Farman St. Hove 165 D3
Farmcombe Cl. T W 8 C1
Farmcombe La. T W 8 C1
Farmcombe Rd. T W 9 D1
Farmland Way. Hai 133 D1
Farmlands Ave. Willn 174 B2
Farmlands Cl. Hast 140 A3
Farmlands Cl. Willn 174 C2
Farmlands Way. Pole 174 B3
Farmway Cl. Hove 144 A1
Farncombe Cl. Wiv G 76 A2
Farncombe Rd. Lew 127 E1
Farne Cl. Hai 132 B1
Farnham Ave. Key 100 C3
Farnham Cl. Lan G 7 F2
Farnham La. Lan G 7 F2
Farningham Rd. Cro 40 A4
Farnlea Rd. Bur H 75 D3
Farriers Way. Rid 80 A3
Farthing Hill. Tic 33 E1
Farthing La. Pon G 112 B3
Farthings The. Cro 27 F2
Faulkners Way. Bur H 74 C3
Faversham Rd. East 176 A1
Faygate Cl. Bex 159 F4
Faygate Rd. East 175 E1
Fayre Meadow. Rob 65 F2
Fearon Rd. Hast 140 B1
Felbridge Cl. E Gri 2 A2
Felbridge Ct. E Gri 1 C2
Felbridge Rd. Cra D 1 A2
Felcot Rd. Cra D 1 A2
Felcourt La. Dor P 2 A4
Felcourt Rd. Dor P 2 A4
Fellows Rd. Hast 140 C2
Fennell's Cl. East 185 E3
Ferbies. Spe 7 F4
Ferguson Rd. Lydd 98 B1
Fermor Rd. Cro 39 E4
Fermor Row. Cro 39 E4
Fermor Way. Cro 39 F4
Fern Cl. East 176 A2
Fern Green. Hai 132 C1
Fern Rd. Hast 161 E4
Ferndale. T W 9 D3
Ferndale Cl. T W 9 D2
Ferndale Rd. Bur H 75 D1
Ferndale Rd. Hove 165 D4
Ferndean Cl. Hast 161 E4
Fernhurst Cl. Bri 145 F3
Fernhurst Cres. Bri 145 F3
Fernlea Cl. Wfd 117 E2
Ferns The. T W 8 C2
Fernside Ave. Hast 161 E4
Fernwood Rise. Bri 145 D3
Ferrers Rd. Lew 126 C1
Ferring Cl. Rye 94 C3
Ferry Hill. Winc 120 B4
Ferry Rd. Rye 94 C3
Festival Gdns. Bex 160 A4
Field Cl. Bur H 74 B2
Field Cl. Sea 181 E1
Field Way. Hast 161 E4
Fielden La. Cro 27 D1
Fielden Rd. Cro 27 D1
Fieldway. Bro Ow 91 F3
Fieldway. Dit 101 D2
Fieldway. Hay H 52 B4
Fiennes Rd. Hers 134 B3
Figg La. Cro 39 E4
Filching Cl. Willn 174 B2
Filching Rd. East 184 C4
Filder Cl. East 185 F3
Filsham Dr. Bex 160 C3
Filsham Rd. Hast 161 E4
Filsham Valley. Hast 161 E4
Finches Gdns. Hay H 52 C4
Finches Park Rd. Hay H ... 52 C4
Finches The. Bex 160 B2
Finches The. Hast 139 F3
Findon Ave. Salt 168 B1
Findon Cl. Bex 159 E2
Findon Cl. Hove 144 B2
Findon Cl. Sea 182 A2
Findon Rd. Bri 166 B3
Finmere Cl. East 186 A3
Finmere Rd. East 186 A3
Fir Cl. Wood 167 E4
Fir Grove Rd. Cro H 82 C4
Fir Toll Rd. May 41 E1
Fir Tree Cl. Bex 159 D2
Fir Tree Cl. Hai 133 D1
Fir Tree Rd. T W 8 B2
Fir Tree Way. Key 100 C2
Fircroft Cl. Bri 145 E2
Firlands. Hay H 52 B2
Firle Bostal. W Fir 150 C2
Firle Cl. Hast 141 D2
Firle Cl. Sea 181 E3

Firle Cres. Lew 126 B2
Firle Dr. Sea 181 E3
Firle Green. Uck 57 E1
Firle Rd. Bex 159 D2
Firle Rd. Bri 166 A3
Firle Rd. East 185 F2
Firle Rd. Pea 179 D4
Firle Rd. Sea 181 E3
Firle Terr. S Hei 170 A1
First Ave. Bex 160 B3
First Ave. Cam 96 B1
First Ave. Hove 165 D3
First Ave. Newh 180 A3
First St. Lan G 7 E2
Firtoft Cl. Bur H 74 C2
Firtree Rd. Hast 140 C1
Firwood Cl. East 175 E1
Firwood Rd. Hea 83 F4
Firwood Rise. Hea 83 F4
Fisher Cl. East 186 B4
Fisher St. Lew 127 D1
Fishmarket Rd. Rye 95 D3
Fishponds La. Wfd 117 E2
Fitch Dr. Bri 146 B1
Fitzgerald Ave. Sea 181 E1
Fitzgerald Cl. East 185 E1
Fitzgerald Park. Sea 181 E1
Fitzgerald Rd. S Mal 127 D2
Fitzjohns Rd. Lew 126 C1
Fitzmaurice Ave. East 185 F3
Fitzroy Rd. Lew 126 C1
Five Acre Wlk. Hast 161 B1
Five Ways. T W 8 C2
Flamsteed Rd. Hers 134 C1
Fleming Cl. East 176 B1
Fletcher Ave. Hast 139 E4
Fletching Cl. Bri 166 B3
Fletching Rd. East 175 F1
Fletching St. May 42 A2
Flimwell Cl. Bri 166 B2
Flimwell Cl. Fli 34 A2
Flint Cl. Por S 143 F1
Flitterbrook La. Pun T 85 D2
Flitterbrook La. Rus 85 D2
Florence Ave. Hove 164 A4
Florence Pl. Bri 145 F1
Florence Rd. Bri 165 F4
Folders Cl. Bri 75 D1
Folders La. Bur H 75 D1
Foley Cl. East 186 B4
Folkestone Cl. Sea 182 A3
Folkestone Rd. E Gul 95 E4
Folkestone Rd. Rye 72 C1
Folkington Gdns. Hast ... 140 A3
Folkington Rd. Fol 174 A3
Folly Field. Newh 180 A4
Fonthill Rd. Hove 164 C4
Fontridge La. Bur 64 C3
Fontridge La. Etc 64 C3
Fontwell Ave. Bex 159 D3
Foords La. St Cro 176 A4
Foot's La. Bur C 62 C2
Ford Rd. Hast 139 E1
Fordcombe La. Ford 7 D3
Fordcombe Rd. Ford 6 C3
Fordcombe Rd. Lan G 7 D2
Foredown Cl. East 185 D1
Foredown Cl. Por S 143 F1
Foredown Dr. Por S 164 A4
Foredown Rd. Por S 143 F1
Forest Dene. Cro 28 A1
Forest Park. Cro 27 D1
Forest Pl. Cro H 82 B3
Forest Rd. Bri 146 B3
Forest Rd. For R 13 F1
Forest Rd. T W 9 D1
Forest Ridge. Sha 22 C3
Forest Rise. Cro 28 A1
Forest View. Hai 154 C4
Forest View. Nut 37 D2
Forest View Rd. E Gri 12 B3
Forest Way. Hast 140 B1
Forest Way. Pem 10 A4
Forest Way. T W 9 D1
Forewood La. Crow 138 C4
Forewood Rise. Crow 138 B3
Forge Cl. Por S 143 F1
Forge Cl. Stas 67 E1
Forge Cl. Uck 80 A3
Forge Field. Ston 44 B3
Forge La. Stas 67 E1
Forge Lane Cotts. Mar ... 56 C4
Forge Rise. Uck 80 A3
Forge Way. Bur H 74 C2
Forge Way. Hast 140 A3
Forstal The. Eri G 17 E2
Forstal The. Pem 10 B4
Forstall. Lan G 7 F2
Fort Haven. S Sea 163 D3
Fort La. East 186 A3
Fort Rd. East 186 A3
Fort Rd. Newh 180 A3
Fort Rise. Newh 180 A3
Foundry La. Lew 127 E1
Foundry St. Bri 165 F3
Fountains Cl. Bri 146 A1
Fountains Cl. East 175 E2
Founthill Ave. Salt 167 F1
Founthill Rd. Salt 167 F1

Founthill Rd. Salt

Fourteen Acre La. Thr O 118 B2
Fourth Ave. Hove 164 C3
Fowlers Cl. Bex 159 E3
Fowly La. H Hur 57 F3
Fox Hill. Hay H 52 B1
Fox Hill Cl. Hay H 52 B1
Fox Hill Village. Hay H 52 B1
Fox Way. Por S 143 F1
Foxcote. Hast 140 A3
Foxdown Rd. Wood 167 E4
Foxglove Cl. Rin 128 C4
Foxglove Rd. East 175 F2
Foxhill. Bex 159 E3
Foxhill. Pea 168 C1
Foxhole La. Four T 48 A4
Foxhole La. Wad 31 F2
Foxhunters Rd. Por S 143 E2
Foxwarren. Hay H 52 A3
Foyle Way. East 190 B3
Framelle Mount. Fra 80 C3
Framfield Bux 57 F2
Framfield Rd. Rid 80 A3
Framfield Way. East 185 D3
Francis Rd. Hay H 52 C4
Francis St. Bri 165 F4
Frankfield Rise. T W 8 C1
Franklands Cl. Bur H 74 C1
Franklands Gdns. Bur H 100 C4
Franklands Way. Bur H 100 C4
Franklin Rd. Bri 166 A4
Franklin Rd. Por S 164 A4
Franklin Rd. S Sea 143 D1
Franklin St. Bri 166 A4
Franklynn Rd. Hay H 52 B2
Frankton Ave. Hay H 52 C2
Frant Ave. Bex 159 D3
Frant Cl. Bex 159 D3
Frant Rd. Hove 144 C1
Frant Rd. T W 8 C1
Frary Wlk. Hea 83 F2
Fraser Ave. East 186 B4
Freckley Hollow. Cat 113 F1
Frederick Gdns. Bri 165 F3
Frederick Pl. Bri 165 F3
Frederick Rd. Hast 141 D2
Frederick St. Bri 165 F3
Free Heath Rd. Lam 21 D2
Freehold Terr. Hast 146 A1
Freeks La. Bur H 74 C3
Freeland Cl. Sea 180 C3
Freeman Ave. East 175 E1
Freezeland La. Bex 137 F1
Fremlin Cl. T W 7 F2
French Gdns. Hay H 52 C3
Frenches Farm Dr. Hea 83 F3
Frenchgate Cl. East 175 E1
Frenchgate Rd. East 175 E1
Freshfield. Bri 166 A3
Freshfield. Hai 154 C3
Freshfield Bank. For R 13 E1
Freshfield La. Dan 35 E1
Freshfield La. Hor K 35 E1
Freshfield Rd. Bri 166 A3
Freshfield St. Bri 166 A3
Freshfield Way. Bri 166 A3
Freshford Cl. East 176 A1
Freshwater Ave. Hast 140 B1
Freshwater Sq. Willn 174 C2
Freshway. Willn 175 D2
Frewen Cl. Norm 68 C4
Frewyn Cl. Hast 139 E2
Friar Cl. Bri 145 F2
Friar Cres. Bri 145 F2
Friar Rd. Bri 145 F2
Friar Wlk. Bri 145 E2
Friar's Cres. Gue G 141 F4
Friars Bank. Gue G 141 F4
Friars Cl. Hass 100 B2
Friars Oak Rd. Hass 100 B3
Friars Rd. Winc 120 B4
Friars Way. Hast 140 B2
Friars Way. T W 9 D3
Friars' Ave. Pea 179 E3
Friars' Wlk. Lew 127 D1
Friday St. East 176 A2
Fridays The. E Dean 188 C4
Friezland Rd. T W 8 A1
Frimley Cl. Wood 167 E4
Friston Ave. East 175 D1
Friston Cl. Bri 146 B2
Friston Cl. Fri 183 F1
Friston Cl. Sea 181 D2
Friston Downs. Fri 183 F1
Frith Rd. E Gri 2 B2
Frith Rd. Hove 164 C4
Frobisher Cl. East 186 B4
Frog La. T W 8 C1
Fry Cres. Bur H 74 B3
Fryatts Way. Bex 159 E3
Fryman's La. Bre 91 D1
Fulford Cl. Hast 161 F4
Fuller Cl. Wad 31 E3
Fuller Rd. Lew 126 C2
Fuller's Pas. Lew 127 D1
Fullwood Ave. Newh 179 F4
Fulmer Way. Pea 145 D1
Fulmar Dr. E Gri 2 C2
Furlongs The. Alfn 172 B2

Furnace Ave. Lam 21 F2
Furnace Farm Rd. Cra D 1 A2
Furnace La. Bec 92 B4
Furnace La. Bro Ow 92 A3
Furnace La. Cad S 84 B1
Furnace La. Hor 109 D4
Furnace La. Lam 21 D4
Furnace La. War 84 B1
Furnace Rd. Cra D 1 A2
Furness Rd. East 185 E1
Furze Hill. Hove 165 D3
Furze La. E Gri 1 C2
Furzefield Ave. Spe 7 F4
Furzefield Chase. Dor P 2 B3
Furzefield Rd. E Gri 2 A2
Furzeland Way. Say C 99 D4
Fyning Pl. Bex 159 D3
Fyrsway. Fai 142 B2
Fysie La. Etc 46 A2

Gables The. Hast 140 B2
Gableson Ave. Bri 144 C2
Gage Cl. Cra D 1 A1
Gage Ridge. For R 13 E1
Gages The. Hai 155 D4
Gainsborough Cres. East 176 A1
Gainsborough La. Pole 174 B3
Galley Hill View. Bex 160 B2
Galliers Cl. Bri 145 F3
Gallops The. Lew 126 C1
Gallows Cl. Whm 176 B3
Gallows La. Whm 176 B3
Gammons Way. Sed 90 B1
Gander Cl. Bur H 74 C3
Gander Green. Hay H 52 B4
Gander Hill. Hay H 52 B4
Ganton Pl. Hast 161 E4
Garden Cl. Bex 160 A2
Garden Cl. E Gri 12 A3
Garden Cl. Por S 164 A4
Garden House La. Gri 12 A4
Garden Mead. W Hoa 22 B3
Garden Pl. T W 8 C2
Garden St. Lew 149 D4
Garden St. T W 8 C2
Garden Wood Rd. E Gri 12 A4
Gardener Rd. Por S 163 F4
Gardener St. Por S 163 F4
Gardens The. Por S 164 A4
Gardens The. Sock 163 E4
Gardner Cl. East 186 B4
Gardner St. Bri 165 F3
Gardner St. Hers 134 B3
Gardner Way. Hast 161 F3
Gardner's Hill. Iden 71 F3
Garfield Rd. Hai 155 D4
Garland Rd. E Gri 2 A1
Garnet Dr. East 185 D4
Garston Park. Bur 63 F3
Gatehouse La. Bur H 74 C3
Gatehouse La. Fra 81 D4
Gatelands Dr. Bex 159 E3
Gatesmead. Hay H 52 B4
Gattons The. Bur H 74 B2
Gaudick Cl. East 185 E1
Gaudick Rd. East 185 E1
Gavin Astor Cl. Bex 160 C3
Geary Pl. Wfd 117 E2
Geering Park. Hai 155 D4
Geers Wood. Hea 83 E3
Gemma Cl. Hai 155 E4
Geneva Rd. Newh 180 A3
Gensing Rd. Hast 162 A4
George Hill. Rob 65 F2
George St. Bri 165 F3
George St. Hai 155 D4
George St. Hast 162 C4
George St. Hove 164 C3
George St. Por S 163 F4
George St. Sock 164 A4
George St. T W 9 D2
George St. Wad 31 E3
Georgian Cl. Bex 160 B3
Gerald Cl. Bur H 75 D2
Gerald Rd. Sea 181 E1
Gerard St. Bri 165 F4
German St. Winc 120 B4
Ghyll Rd. Cro 27 E2
Ghyll Rd. Hea 83 E3
Ghyll Side Rd. Norm 68 C4
Ghyllside Ave. Hast 140 A2
Ghyllside Dr. Hast 140 A2
Ghyllside Way. Hast 140 A2
Gibb Cl. Bex 160 C3
Gibbetts. Lan G 7 E2
Gibbon Rd. Newh 180 A3
Gibraltar Rise. Hea 83 F4
Giffards Cl. E Gri 2 B1
Gilbert Rd. East 185 F2
Gilbert Rd. Hast 161 F4
Gilbert Way. Hai 154 C3
Gilberts Dr. E Dean 188 C4
Gilda Cres. Pole 174 C3
Gildredge Rd. East 185 E1
Gildredge Rd. Sea 181 E2
Gilham La. For R 13 E1
Gill The. Pem 10 B3
Gillham Wood Ave. Bex 159 D2

Gillham Wood Rd. Bex 159 D2
Gilligans The. Bur H 74 B3
Gillridge Green. Cro 27 E2
Gillsman's Dr. Hast 139 E1
Gillsman's Hill. Hast 139 F1
Gillsman's Park. Hast 139 E1
Gimble Way. Pem 10 A4
Gingerbread La. Fli 34 B1
Gipps Cross La. Lan G 7 E2
Githa Rd. Hast 141 D1
Glade The. Hai 154 B3
Glade The. May 41 F2
Glades The. Bex 160 B3
Glades The. E Gri 2 C1
Gladstone Pl. Bri 166 A4
Gladstone Rd. Bur H 75 D2
Gladstone Rd. Cro 27 E1
Gladstone Rd. Por S 163 F4
Gladstone Rd. T W 7 F2
Gladstone Terr. Hast 140 C1
Gladys Ave. Pea 179 D3
Gladys Rd. Hove 164 A4
Glassenbury Rd. Bex 160 B3
Glastonbury Rd. Hove 164 A3
Gleave Cl. E Gri 2 C1
Glebe Cl. Bex 159 D2
Glebe Cl. East 185 D2
Glebe Cl. Lew 148 C4
Glebe Cl. Sock 163 E4
Glebe Dr. Sea 181 E2
Glebe The. Fel 1 C2
Glebe The. Hast 140 C1
Glebe The. Hay H 52 C4
Glebe The. Pem 10 A4
Glebe The. Pett 119 E1
Glebe Villas. Hove 164 A4
Glen Cl. Willn 174 B2
Glen Rise. Bri 144 C3
Glen Rise Cl. Bri 144 C3
Glen The. Uck 57 D1
Glen Vue. E Gri 2 B1
Glendale Ave. East 185 D3
Glendale Rd. Bur H 74 C1
Glendale Rd. Hove 165 D4
Glendor Rd. Hove 164 B3
Glendyne Cl. E Gri 12 C4
Glendyne Way. E Gri 12 C4
Gleneagles Cl. Bex 160 B2
Gleneagles Cl. Sea 180 C3
Gleneagles Dr. Hai 132 B1
Gleneagles Dr. Hast 161 E4
Glenfalls Ave. Bri 145 F4
Glenleigh Ave. Bex 159 E3
Glenleigh Park Rd. Bex 159 E3
Glenmore Mews. East 185 F2
Glenmore Park. T W 18 B4
Glenmore Rd. Cro 27 D2
Glenmore Rd E. Cro 27 D2
Glenthorn Rd. Bex 159 F2
Glenview Cl. Hast 141 D1
Gleton Ave. Hove 144 A1
Gloucester Ave. Bex 160 C3
Gloucester Cl. Willn 175 D1
Gloucester Pas. Bri 165 F3
Gloucester Pl. Bri 165 F3
Gloucester Rd. Bri 165 F3
Gloucester Rd. Bur H 74 B2
Gloucester Rd. Wad 31 E3
Gloucester St. Bri 165 F3
Glovers La. Bex 160 A4
Glyndbourne Gdns. Hast 140 A3
Glynde Ave. East 175 E1
Glynde Ave. Salt 168 A1
Glynde Cl. S Hei 170 A1
Glynde Rd. Bri 166 A3
Glyndebourne Ave. Salt 168 A1
Glyndleigh Dr. Pole 175 D3
Glynleigh Rd. Hank 155 F1
Glynn Rd. Pea 169 D1
Glynn Rise. Pea 168 C1
Goatham La. Bro Ow 91 E3
Godden Rd. Newh 78 A4
Goddens Cl. Norm 68 C4
Goddens Gill. Norm 68 C4
Godfrey Cl. S Mal 127 D2
Godwin Rd. Hast 141 D1
Godwin Rd. Hove 144 A1
Goffs The. East 185 E2
Gold La. Pea 169 D1
Goldbridge Rd. Newk 78 B4
Goldcrest Dr. Rid 80 A3
Golden Hill. Bur H 75 D2
Golden La. Bri 165 D3
Golden Miller La. Pole 174 B3
Goldhurst Green. Ick 119 E3
Golding St. T W 8 C2
Goldring Rd. East 176 B1
Goldsmid Rd. Hove 165 E4
Goldsmith Cl. East 176 B2
Goldsmiths Ave. Cro 27 D2
Goldstone Cl. Hove 144 C1
Goldstone Cres. Hove 144 C1
Goldstone La. Hove 144 C2
Goldstone La. Hove 164 C4
Goldstone Rd. Hove 164 C4

Goldstone St. Hove 164 C4
Goldstone Villas. Hove 164 C4
Goldstone Way. Hove 144 C1
Goods Station Rd. T W 8 C2
Goodtrees La. Hart 4 C1
Goodwin Cl. Hai 132 B1
Goodwins Cl. E Gri 2 A2
Goodwins The. T W 8 B1
Goodwood Cl. Bex 160 A3
Goodwood Cl. Willn 174 C1
Goodwood Way. Bri 146 B2
Gordon Cl. Hay H 52 B3
Gordon Pl. Bex 159 F3
Gordon Rd. Bri 145 E1
Gordon Rd. Bur H 75 D2
Gordon Rd. Bux 57 F2
Gordon Rd. Hai 154 C4
Gordon Rd. Hast 162 C4
Gordon Rd. Hay H 52 B3
Gordon Rd. Por S 163 F4
Gordon Rd. Sgh 9 D4
Gordon Rd. Sock 164 A4
Gore Park Ave. East 185 D2
Gore Park Rd. East 185 D2
Gorham Ave. Rottn 167 F1
Gorham Cl. Rott 167 F1
Gorham Way. Pea 178 B4
Gorringe Cl. S Sea 163 D4
Gorringe Dr. Willn 174 C2
Gorringe Rd. East 185 F2
Gorringe Valley Rd. Willn 174 C2
Gorse Cl. East 184 C3
Gorse Cl. Por S 143 E2
Gorse Dr. Sea 181 E3
Gorse Hill. Bro O 61 E1
Gorse Rd. T W 9 E3
Gorselands. Sed 90 B1
Gorses The. Bex 159 D1
Gorsethorn Way. Fai 142 B2
Gorseway The. Bex 159 D3
Gosford Way. Pole 174 B3
Gote La. Rin 128 A2
Goudhurst Cl. East 176 A1
Gower Rd. Hay H 52 B2
Gows Croft. Kin L 148 B3
Graffham Cl. Bri 166 B3
Grafton St. Bri 165 F2
Graham Ave. Bri 145 E3
Graham Cl. Por S 143 E2
Graham Cres. Por S 143 E2
Grampian Cl. East 176 A2
Grampian Cl. T W 9 D3
Grand Ave. Bex 160 C3
Grand Ave. Hove 165 D3
Grand Ave. Key 100 C3
Grand Ave. Sea 181 D3
Grand Cres. Rottn 167 F1
Grand Junction Rd. Bri 165 F2
Grand Par. Bri 165 F3
Grand Par. East 185 F1
Grand Par. Hast 162 A3
Grand Par. Pole 174 B3
Grange Ave. Hast 140 A2
Grange Cl. Bri 145 E1
Grange Cl. Bur H 75 D3
Grange Cl. Cro 27 D1
Grange Cl. Hor 109 E3
Grange Ct Dr. Bex 159 F3
Grange Gdns. T W 8 A2
Grange Rd. Bar C 104 A2
Grange Rd. East 185 E1
Grange Rd. Hast 140 B3
Grange Rd. Hove 164 B4
Grange Rd. Lew 149 D4
Grange Rd. Sock 163 E4
Grange Rd. T W 8 A2
Grange Rd. Uck 80 A4
Grange The. Bar C 104 A2
Grangeways. Bri 145 E3
Granston Way. Cra D 11 A4
Grant St. Bri 165 F4
Grantham Bank. Bar C 104 B2
Grantham Cl. S Cha 103 E4
Grantham Rd. Bri 145 F1
Granville Rd. East 185 E1
Granville Rd. Hove 165 E4
Granville Rd. T W 9 D3
Grassington Rd. East 185 E1
Grassmere Ave. Pea 178 B4
Gravelye La. Hay H 52 C3
Gravett Ct. Bur H 74 B1
Graycoats Dr. Cro 27 E1
Graystone La. Hast 141 D2
Grazebrook Cl. Bex 159 D2
Great Brooms Rd. Sgh 9 D4
Great Cliffe Rd. East 176 B1
Great College St. Bri 166 A2
Great Courtlands. Lan G 7 F2
Great Footway. Lan G 7 E2
Great Hall Arc. T W 8 C2
Great Heathmead. Hay H 52 A3
Great Oak. Hur G 46 C2
Great Rough. Chay 77 F3
Greater Paddock. Rin 128 B3
Grecian Rd. T W 8 C1
Green Cl. Rin 128 B3

Green Cl. Sock 163 E4
Green Field Cl. Sock 163 D4
Green Gate. Pea 169 D1
Green Gr. Hai 154 C4
Green Hedges Ave. E Gri 2 A1
Green Hedges Cl. E Gri 2 A1
Green La. Bex 159 D3
Green La. Cro 27 F1
Green La. Hea 83 F3
Green La. Jev 184 A4
Green La. Lew 149 D4
Green La. Rin 105 F1
Green La. S Cha 103 E4
Green La. S Str 77 E1
Green La. Sea 181 E1
Green La. Wood 167 D3
Green Meadows. Hay H 52 C4
Green Park Cnr. Wiv 75 F2
Green Ridge. Bri 144 C3
Green Sq. Wad 31 E3
Green St. East 185 D2
Green The. Blas 81 F3
Green The. Cat 137 E4
Green The. Hai 133 D1
Green The. Hast 139 F1
Green The. Hove 145 D1
Green The. Lan G 7 E2
Green The. Newk 78 A4
Green The. Nin 136 C3
Green The. Rottn 167 E1
Green The. Stas 67 F3
Green Wall. Lew 127 D1
Green Way. Lydd 98 C3
Green Way. T W 9 E4
Green Wlk. Hai 133 D1
Green Wlk. Sea 181 F1
Green Wlk The. Willn 174 C2
Greenacres. Pea 169 D1
Greenacres. Wfd 117 E2
Greenacres Dr. Hai 155 D4
Greenacres Dr. Hai 155 D4
Greenacres Dr. Rin 128 A3
Greenacres Way. Hai 155 D4
Greenbank Ave. Salt 168 A1
Greenfield Cl. Bri 145 F3
Greenfield Cl. T W 8 A3
Greenfield Cres. Bri 145 F3
Greenfield Dr. Rid 80 A2
Greenfield Rd. Bur 64 A4
Greenfield Rd. East 185 D2
Greenfields Cl. Hast 139 F3
Greenhill Park. Hay H 52 C1
Greenhill Way. Hay H 52 C1
Greenhill Way. Pea 169 D1
Greenlands Cl. Bur H 100 C4
Greenlands Dr. Bur H 100 C4
Greenleaf Gdns. Pole 174 C4
Greenleas. Hove 144 A1
Greenleas. Pem 10 A3
Greenstede Ave. E Gri 2 B1
Greenway. East 184 C3
Greenways. Bex 159 E4
Greenways. Hay H 52 B3
Greenways. Oving 167 D2
Greenways. Sock 143 E1
Greenwell Cl. Sea 181 F2
Greenwich Rd. Hai 155 D4
Greenwich Way. Pea 179 D4
Greenwoods La. Pun T 85 D4
Greggs Wood Rd. T W 9 E4
Gregory La. Whm 176 B3
Gregory Wlk. Sed 116 B4
Grenada Cl. Bex 159 D2
Grenville Rd. Pev B 177 D2
Grenville St. Bri 165 E3
Gresham Cl. East 185 D3
Gresham Way. Hast 161 F4
Gresley Rd. Hast 139 E3
Greville Rd. Hast 141 D2
Grey Alders. Hay H 52 C3
Grey Tower Bungalows.
    Pev B 177 D2
Grey Tower Caravan Site.
    Pev B 177 D2
Greyfriars Pl. Winc B 120 C3
Greys Rd. East 185 D2
Grinstead La. Sha 23 D4
Gromenfield. Gro 17 D4
Groombridge Hill. Lan G 7 D1
Groombridge Rd. Asht 6 C1
Grosvenor Bridge. T W 8 C3
Grosvenor Cl. Pole 174 B3
Grosvenor Cres. Hast 161 E3
Grosvenor Gdns. Hast 161 E3
Grosvenor Park. T W 8 C3
Grosvenor Rd. E Gri 2 A1
Grosvenor Rd. Sea 181 E2
Grosvenor Rd. T W 8 C2
Grosvenor St. Bri 165 F3
Grosvenor Wlk. T W 8 C2
Grove Ave. T W 8 C1
Grove Hill. Bri 165 F3
Grove Hill. Hel 110 B1
Grove Hill Gdns. Tw 8 C1
Grove Hill Rd. T W 8 C2
Grove La. Rye 72 A2
Grove Rd. Bur H 74 C2
Grove Rd. Chid H 6 A4
Grove Rd. East 185 E1

Grove Rd. Hast 141 D2
Grove Rd. Sea 181 E2
Grove St. Bri 165 F3
Grove The. Bex 159 E3
Grove The. Cro 27 E1
Grove The. East 184 C4
Grove The. Hai 154 C3
Grove The. Hay H 52 C2
Grove The. May 41 F1
Grove The. Newh 170 B1
Grove The. Pem 10 A4
Grove The. Rye 95 D3
Grove The. Willn 174 B2
Grovelands Cl. Bur H 74 B1
Grovelands Rd. Hai 132 C1
Grovely La. Chur 85 F1
Grover St. T W 8 C2
Growers End. Newk 78 A4
Guardswell Pl. Sea 181 E2
Guestling Rd. East 186 A3
Guildford Rd. Bri 165 E3
Guildford Rd. T W 8 C2
Guildford St. Bri 165 E3
Guldeford La. Brok 73 E2
Guldeford Rd. E Gul 95 E3
Gun Rd. Blas 81 F3
Gundreda Rd. Lew 126 C1
Gunters La. Bex 159 F3
Gurth Rd. Hast 141 D1
Gwyneth Gr. Bex 160 B4
Gwynne Gdns. E Gri 2 A1

Hackenden Cl. E Gri 2 B2
Hackenden La. E Gri 2 B2
Hackhurst La. Low D 132 A3
Hackwood. Rob 65 E2
Haddington Cl. Hove 164 C3
Haddington St. Hove 164 C4
Hadley Ct. T W 8 B3
Hadlow Ave. East 175 F2
Hadlow Cl. Bri 166 A3
Hadrian Ave. Sock 163 F4
Hadrian Gdns. Hast 139 F3
Haig Ave. Bri 146 A3
Hailsham Ave. Salt 168 A2
Hailsham Ind Park. Hai 154 C4
Hailsham Rd. Hank 175 E4
Hailsham Rd. Hea 83 F3
Hailsham Rd. Hers 134 B3
Hailsham Rd. Pole 174 B4
Hairpin Croft. Pea 169 D1
Half Mile Dro. Her 128 C4
Hall's Hole Rd. T W 9 E2
Halland Cl. East 175 D1
Halland Rd. Bri 146 B2
Hallett Rd. Bri 166 A4
Halley Park. Hai 155 D4
Halley Rd. Bro O 84 B4
Halley Rd. Cad S 84 A4
Halley Rd. Hers 134 C1
Hallsland. Cra D 11 D4
Hallyburton Rd. Hove 164 A4
Halsford Green. E Gri 1 C2
Halsford La. E Gri 1 C1
Halsford Park Rd. E Gri 2 A1
Halton Cres. Hast 140 C1
Halton Pl. Hast 140 C1
Halton Rd. East 186 A2
Halton Shaws. Hur 99 F3
Halton Terr. Hast 140 C1
Ham La. Bur 63 F4
Ham La. Lew 149 D4
Ham La. Rin 128 A3
Ham La. Sca H 53 E2
Hambleton Cl. East 176 A2
Hambrook. Bur H 75 D1
Hamelsham Ct. Hai 154 C4
Hamilton Gdns. Hast 141 D2
Hamilton Rd. Bri 165 E4
Hamilton Terr. Bex 159 F2
Hamlands La. Willn 174 C2
Hammer La. Cowb 110 B2
Hammer La. War 110 B2
Hammerwood Rd. Ash W 13 D3
Hammington La. W Hoa 22 B2
Hammonds Dr. East 185 F4
Hammy Cl. S Sea 163 D4
Hampden Ave. East 175 E1
Hampden Cl. Bat 114 C2
Hampden Gdns. S Hei 170 A1
Hampden Rd. Bri 166 A4
Hampshire Ct. Bri 166 A2
Hampstead Rd. Hove 145 D1
Hampton Pl. Bri 165 E3
Hampton St. Bri 165 E3
Hampton Way. E Gri 12 B4
Hamsey Cl. Bri 166 B3
Hamsey Cl. East 184 C3
Hamsey Cres. Lew 126 B1
Hamsey La. Coo 126 C4
Hamsey La. Ham 126 C4
Hamsey La. Sea 182 A1
Hamsey Rd. Salt 178 A4
Hamsey Rd. Sha 22 C3
Hamsland. Hor K 35 D2
Hanbury La. Hay H 52 C3
Hanging Birch La. Hor 83 D1
Hangleton Cl. Hove 144 A1
Hangleton Gdns. Hove 144 A1

Hangleton La. Hove 144 A1
Hangleton Manor Cl. Hove 144 A1
Hangleton Rd. Hove 144 B1
Hangleton Valley Dr. Hove 144 A2
Hangleton Way. Hove 144 A2
Hankham Hall Rd. St Cro 176 A4
Hankham Hall Rd. Whm 176 B3
Hankham St. Cro 175 F3
Hankham St. Hank 175 F4
Hanlye La. Hay H 52 A4
Hannington Pl. Hur 99 F4
Hanover Cl. Bex 160 A3
Hanover Cl. Sea 180 C3
Hanover Cres. Bri 165 F4
Hanover Rd. East 186 A2
Hanover St. Bri 165 F4
Hanover Terr. Bri 165 F4
Hanson Rd. Newh 179 F3
Hanson Rd. Newh 180 A3
Harbour Farm. Winc B 120 C3
Harbour Rd. Rye 95 E2
Harbour Rd. Rye H 95 E2
Harbour View Cl. Sea 180 C3
Harbour View Rd. Newh 179 F3
Harcourt Cl. Rid 80 A3
Harcourt Rd. Rid 80 A3
Harding Ave. East 185 F3
Hardwick Rd. East 185 F1
Hardwick Rd. Hove 144 B2
Hardwicke Rd. Hast 140 C1
Hardy Dr. East 186 B3
Hare Way. Hast 140 A3
Harebeating Cl. Hai 133 D1
Harebeating Cres. Hai 133 D1
Harebeating Dr. Hai 133 D1
Harebeating Gdns. Hai 133 D1
Harebeating La. Hai 133 D1
Harebell Cl. East 176 A2
Harecombe Rd. Cro 39 E4
Harecombe Rise. Cro 39 E4
Harefield Cl. Newh 170 B1
Haremere Hill. Etc 46 A1
Harescroft. T W 18 B4
Harewood Cl. Bex 159 F2
Hargate Cl. T W 18 B4
Hargreaves Rd. East 175 F1
Harlands Cl. Hay H 52 A3
Harlands Rd. Hay H 52 A3
Harlequin Gdns. Hast 139 F3
Harlequin La. Cro 39 E4
Harlequin Pl. Cro 39 E4
Harley La. Hea 83 F3
Harley Shute Rd. Hast 161 E4
Harley Way. Hast 161 E3
Harmans Dr. E Gri 2 C1
Harmans Mead. E Gri 2 C1
Harmers Hay Rd. Hai 132 C1
Harmers Hill. Newk 78 A4
Harmony St. T W 8 A2
Harmsworth Cres. Hove 144 B2
Harold Cl. Pev B 177 E4
Harold Mews. Hast 162 A3
Harold Pl. Hast 162 B4
Harold Rd. Hast 141 D1
Harold Terr. Bat 115 E2
Harpers Rd. Newh 180 A4
Harrier La. Bat 115 E2
Harries Rd. T W 9 D4
Harrington Pl. Bri 145 F1
Harrington Rd. Bri 145 E1
Harrington Villas. Bri 145 E1
Harrison Rd. Sea 181 F2
Harrisons La. Rin 128 B3
Harrow Cl. Sea 181 F2
Harrow La. Hast 139 F3
Hart Cl. Uck 79 F4
Hartfield Ave. Bri 145 F3
Hartfield Rd. East 185 E2
Hartfield Rd. Bex 159 D1
Hartfield Rd. Cowd 5 D3
Hartfield Rd. East 185 E2
Hartfield Rd. For R 14 A1
Hartfield Rd. Salt 168 A1
Hartfield Rd. Sea 181 F2
Harting Combe. Hast 161 F4
Hartington Pl. Bri 166 A4
Hartington Pl. East 185 F1
Hartington Rd. Bri 166 A4
Hartington Terr. Bri 166 A4
Hartington Villas. Hove 164 C4
Harvard Cl. S Mal 127 D2
Harvard Rd. Rin 128 A3
Harvest Cl. Hay H 52 C4
Harvest Cl. Pea 168 C1
Harvest Hill. E Gri 12 B4
Harvest Way. Hast 140 A3
Harvey Cl. Hast 139 E2
Harvey's La. Fra 106 A2
Harvey's La. Rin 106 A2
Harwarden Cl. Cra D 11 D4
Harwood Cl. East 186 B4
Harwood's La. E Gri 12 B3
Harwoods Cl. Gri 12 B4
Haslam Cres. Bex 160 B3
Hasletts Cl. T W 8 C3
Hassocks Rd. Hur 99 F3
Hastings Ave. Sea 182 A3
Hastings Cl. Pole 174 C4

Hastings Rd. Bat 115 F2
Hastings Rd. Bex 160 B3
Hastings Rd. Bri 166 A4
Hastings Rd. Kip 10 C3
Hastings Rd. Newd 49 F2
Hastings Rd. Pem 10 B3
Hastings Rd. Rol L 50 A4
Hastings Rd. The M 47 E3
Hatch End. For R 13 E1
Hatherley Rd. Hast 162 A4
Havelock Rd. Bex 160 A3
Havelock Rd. Bri 145 E1
Havelock Rd. East 185 F2
Havelock Rd. Hast 162 B4
Haven Brow. Sea 181 F2
Haven Cl. Pev B 177 E3
Haven Cl. Willn 174 C2
Haven Rd. Hast 161 D4
Hawkenbury Cl. T W 9 D1
Hawkenbury Rd. T W 9 E1
Hawkenbury Way. Lew 126 C1
Hawkhurst Cl. East 176 A1
Hawkhurst Rd. Bri 146 A3
Hawkhurst Rd. Fli 34 B1
Hawkhurst Way. Bex 159 E2
Hawkins Cl. S Sea 143 D1
Hawkins Cres. S Sea 143 D1
Hawkins Rd. S Sea 143 D1
Hawkins Way. Hai 154 C4
Hawks Farm Cl. Hai 132 C2
Hawks Rd. Hai 132 C1
Hawks Town Cl. Hai 132 C2
Hawks Town Cres. Hai 133 D1
Hawks Town Gdns. Hai 132 C2
Hawksbridge Cl. Willn 175 D2
Hawkswood Dr. Hai 133 D2
Hawkswood Rd. Hai 132 C2
Hawmead. Cra D 11 D4
Hawth Cl. Sea 181 D2
Hawth Cres. Sea 181 D2
Hawth Gr. Sea 181 D3
Hawth Hill. Sea 181 D3
Hawth Park Rd. Sea 181 D2
Hawth Pl. Sea 181 D2
Hawth Rise. Sea 181 D3
Hawth Way. Sea 181 D2
Hawthorn Ave. Bex 159 D2
Hawthorn Cl. Bur H 75 D3
Hawthorn Cl. Hea 83 F3
Hawthorn Cl. Salt 168 A1
Hawthorn Rd. East 186 A4
Hawthorn Rd. Hast 141 D1
Hawthorn Way. Por S 143 D2
Hawthorn Wlk. T W 9 E4
Hawthornes The. Bro Ow 91 F2
Hawthorns The. Bur H 74 C3
Hawthorns The. Hai 154 C4
Hawthylands Cres. Hai 132 C1
Hawthylands Dr. Hai 132 C1
Hawthylands Rd. Hai 132 C1
Haybourne Cl. Bri 166 B4
Haybourne Rd. Bri 166 B4
Hayes Cl. Por S 164 A4
Hayes Cl. Rin 128 A3
Hayes La. Bec 92 C3
Hayes La. Peas 93 D3
Hayland Green. Hai 133 D1
Haylind Rd. Hay H 52 C3
Haystoun Cl. East 175 D1
Haystoun Park. East 175 D1
Hayward Rd. Lew 126 C2
Haywards Rd. Bri 145 F3
Haywards Rd. Hay H 52 B2
Haywood Way. Hast 141 D2
Hazel Cl. Cra D 11 D4
Hazel Cl. Por S 144 A2
Hazel Dr. Bur H 74 C1
Hazel Gr. Willn 174 C2
Hazel Way. Cra D 11 D4
Hazelbank. Lan G 7 E2
Hazeldene. Sea 181 F2
Hazeldene Meads. Bri 145 D2
Hazeledene La. N Cha 77 E4
Hazelgrove Rd. Hay H 52 B2
Hazelwood Ave. East 175 D2
Hazelwood Cl. Bex 159 D2
Hazelwood Gdns. Hast 140 A3
Headland Ave. Sea 181 F2
Headland Cl. Pea 179 E3
Heartwood Chase. Hove 145 D1
Heartwood Chase. Hove 165 D4
Heath Cl. Hay H 52 B2
Heath Rd. Hay H 52 B3
Heathcote Dr. E Gri 2 A1
Heathdown Cl. Pea 169 D1
Heather Bank. Hay H 52 A3
Heather Cl. East 175 F2
Heather Way. Fai 142 B2
Heather Wlk. Cro 28 A1
Heatherdune Rd. Bex 159 F3
Heatherway. Fel 1 B4
Heathfield Ave. Salt 168 A1
Heathfield Cl. Hast 140 B3
Heathfield Cres. Por S 143 E2
Heathfield Dr. Por S 143 E2
Heathfield Gdns. Rob 65 F2
Heathfield Rd. Sea 181 E2

Heathlands. Wfd 117 E2
Heathy Brow. Pea 168 C1
Heavegate Rd. Cro 39 D4
Heighton Cl. Bex 159 D2
Heighton Cres. S Hei 170 A1
Heighton Rd. S Hei 170 B1
Heights The. Hast 141 D4
Helena Cl. Por S 144 A1
Helena Rd. Wood 147 D1
Hellingly Cl. Bri 166 B3
Helvellyn Dr. East 176 A2
Hempstead Gdns. Uck 80 A4
Hempstead La. Hai 132 B1
Hempstead La. Uck 80 A4
Hempstead Rd. Salt 168 A2
Hempstead Rd. Uck 80 A4
Hempstead Rise. Uck 80 A4
Henderson Cl. Hast 140 B2
Hendon St. Bri 166 A3
Henfield Cl. Bri 166 B3
Henfield Rd. East 175 E1
Henfield Way. Hove 144 B2
Henley Cl. Rye 94 C3
Henley Cl. T W 9 D3
Henley Rd. Bri 166 B2
Henley's Hill. Pon G 135 F4
Henshill La. The M 47 E4
Henwood Cres. Pem 10 A3
Henwood Green Rd. Pem 10 A3
Henwoods Mount. Pem 10 B3
Herbert Rd. Bri 145 E1
Herbrand Wlk. Bex 158 C1
Hereford St. Bri 166 A3
Hereward Way. S Mal 127 D2
Hermitage La. E Gri 12 B4
Hermitage Rd. E Gri 2 A2
Herne Down. Cro 39 F4
Herne Rd. Cro 39 E4
Heron Cl. East 176 A1
Heron Pl. E Gri 12 B4
Heron Ridge. Pole 174 C3
Herons Way. Pem 10 B4
Heronsdale Rd. Wood 167 E4
Herontye Dr. E Gri 12 B4
Herring's Rd. Dal 86 B1
Herring's Rd. Pon G 112 B4
Hertford Cl. Hast 139 F2
Hertford Rd. Bri 145 F1
Heskett Park. Pem 10 A3
Hestingas Plat. Hast 162 C4
Heston Ave. Bri 145 E4
Hever Cl. East 176 A1
Hever Cres. Bex 159 F3
Heyworth Cl. Wood 167 E4
Hickling Cl. East 175 F2
Hickman Way. Hast 140 A2
Hickman's Cl. Hay H 52 C4
Hickman's La. Hay H 52 C4
Hide Hollow. East 176 B2
High Bank. Hast 141 D1
High Bank Cl. Hast 141 D1
High Beech Cl. Hast 139 E3
High Beeches. T W 9 D3
High Branches. Bex 159 E2
High Broom La. Cro 39 E4
High Broom Rd. Cro 39 E4
High Brooms Rd. Sgh 9 D4
High Cl. Por S 143 F1
High Cl. Fri. Fri 184 A1
High Cross Fields. Cro 27 E2
High Fords. Ick 119 E3
High Fords Cl. Ick 119 E3
High Hurst Cl. Newk 78 A4
High Park. Norm 68 C4
High Park Ave. Hove 144 B2
High Point. Hay H 52 C2
High Rocks La. T W 8 A1
High St. Alfn 172 C2
High St. Bar C 104 A2
High St. Bat 115 D3
High St. Bex 160 A3
High St. Bri 165 F3
High St. Bur 63 F3
High St. Bux 57 F2
High St. Cowd 4 C3
High St. Cro 27 E2
High St. Dit 101 D2
High St. E Gri 12 B4
High St. E Hoa 107 F3
High St. East 185 D2
High St. Etc 64 C4
High St. Fli 34 A2
High St. Frant 19 D2
High St. Hai 155 D4
High St. Hart 15 D2
High St. Hast 162 C4
High St. Hay H 52 C4
High St. Hea 83 F4
High St. Hur 99 F3
High St. Lam 21 F3
High St. Lew 149 D4
High St. Lydd 98 C3
High St. Mar 56 C2
High St. May 41 F1
High St. Newh 180 A4
High St. Newk 78 A4
High St. Nin 136 C3
High St. Nut 37 D2
High St. Pem 10 A3

High St. Pole 174 C3
High St. Rid 80 A3
High St. Rob 65 F2
High St. Rot 40 C4
High St. Rottn 167 E1
High St. Rye 95 D3
High St. Sea 181 E1
High St. T W 8 C1
High St. Uck 80 A3
High St. Wad 31 E2
High St. Wal 32 C1
High St. Whm 176 B3
High St. Winc 120 B4
High Trees. Hay H 52 B3
High Wickham. Hast 140 C1
High Woods La. T W 9 E1
Higham Gdns. Gue G 141 F4
Highbank. Bri 145 D3
Highbridge La. E Chi 102 C2
Highbrook Cl. Bri 146 A2
Highcroft Cres. Hea 83 F4
Highcroft Rd. Sha 22 C3
Highdown. Sock 143 E1
Highdown Cl. Sock 143 E1
Highdown Rd. Hove 165 E4
Highdown Rd. Lew 126 C1
Highfield Cl. Pem 10 A3
Highfield Cres. Bri 145 F3
Highfield Dr. Hast 139 D2
Highfield Dr. Hur 99 F3
Highfield Gdns. Bex 160 A4
Highfield Rd. Bro O 61 E1
Highfield Rd. E Gri 2 A2
Highfield Rd. Hor 109 E4
Highfield Rd. Sgh 9 D4
Highfields. Bri 146 B3
Highfields. Bur 63 F4
Highfields. For R 13 E1
Highgate Rd. For R 13 E1
Highgrove. T W 18 C4
Highland Ct. Hay H 52 B2
Highland Rd. Hay H 52 B2
Highlands Ave. Rid 80 A2
Highlands Cl. Bex 159 E4
Highlands Cl. Cro 27 E2
Highlands Cl. Key 100 C2
Highlands Dr. Bur H 74 C2
Highlands Dr. Hast 161 F4
Highlands Gdns. Hast 161 F4
Highlands Rd. Por S 143 F1
Highlands Rd. Sea 181 D2
Highlands The. Bex 159 E4
Highlea Cl. Hast 140 A3
Highsted Park. Pea 169 D1
Highview Ave N. Bri 145 E3
Highview Ave S. Bri 145 E3
Highview Cl. Hast 140 A3
Highview Cl. Win H 134 C3
Highview La. Rid 80 A2
Highview Rd. Bri 145 E3
Highview Rd. Pea 178 B4
Highview Way. Bri 145 E3
Highway Cl. Bri 146 A1
Highway The. Bri 146 B2
Highway The. Newh 179 F3
Highway The. Pea 179 F3
Highways. Por S 143 F1
Highwoods Ave. Bex 159 D4
Hiham Green. Winc 120 B4
Hilary Cl. Pole 174 B3
Hilbert Cl. T W 9 D3
Hilbert Rd. T W 9 D3
Hilders Farm Cl. Cro 27 F1
Hilgrove Rd. Salt 168 A2
Hill Brow. Hove 144 C2
Hill Cl. Cro 27 E1
Hill Cl. Poy 122 A3
Hill Crest. Dor P 2 B3
Hill Crest. Sgh 8 C4
Hill Crest Rd. Newh 180 A3
Hill Dr. Hove 144 C2
Hill Farm Way. Sock 143 E1
Hill Mead. Nut 37 D2
Hill Rd. East 184 C4
Hill Rd. Fai 142 A2
Hill Rd. Lew 126 C2
Hill Rd. Salt 167 F1
Hill Rise. Newh 170 B1
Hill Rise. Sea 181 D3
Hill Side. Newh 180 A4
Hill St. Hast 162 C4
Hill St. T W 8 C3
Hill Top. Bri 144 C3
Hill View Rd. T W 8 A2
Hillary Cl. E Gri 2 C2
Hillbank Cl. Por S 143 E2
Hillborough Cl. Bex 159 D2
Hillbrow Rd. Bri 145 D2
Hillbury Gdns. Tic 33 D1
Hillcrest. Bri 145 D3
Hillcrest Ave. Bex 159 F3
Hillcrest Cl. Sca H 53 E2
Hillcrest Dr. T W 9 D4
Hillcrest La. Sca H 53 E2
Hillcroft. Por S 143 E1
Hillgarth. Sgh 8 C4
Hillrise. Cro 27 F1
Hillside. Bri 146 B1
Hillside. For R 13 E2

Hillside. Fri 183 F1
Hillside. Por S 144 A1
Hillside. Sock 143 E1
Hill'side Ave. Sea 182 A3
Hillside Cl. E Gri 2 B2
Hillside Rd. Bex 160 A3
Hillside Rd. Hast 140 B3
Hillside Way. H 145 D2
Hillside Wlk. Hay H 52 A3
Hilltop Rd. W Hoa 22 B3
Hillview Rd. Wood 166 C4
Hillyfield. Lew 148 C4
Hillyglen Cl. Hast 162 B4
Hindover Cres. Sea 181 F2
Hindover Rd. Sea 181 F2
Hinton Cl. Bri 146 A1
Hither Chantlers. Lan G 7 F1
Hoad Rd. East 185 F2
Hoad's Wood Rd. Hast 140 C2
Hoadleys La. Cro 27 D3
Hoath Hill. Mou 89 D3
Hoathdown Ave. Newh 179 F4
Hobbs Ind Est. Fel 1 A4
Hobbs La. Four O 70 A3
Hoblands. Hay H 52 C2
Hobney Rise. Whm 176 B3
Hockington La. East 174 C1
Hodcombe Cl. East 175 F2
Hoddern Ave. Pea 178 C4
Hodshrove La. Bri 146 B2
Hodshrove Rd. Bri 146 B2
Hoe The. Hast 139 F3
Hogarth Rd. East 176 A1
Hogarth Rd. Hove 164 B4
Hoghole La. Lam 21 E1
Hogtrough La. Winc 120 B4
Holbrook Cl. East 190 B4
Holden Park Rd. Sgh 8 B4
Holdings The. Kin L 148 B3
Hole Farm Cl. Hast 140 B1
Hollamby Park. Hai 155 D4
Holland Ave. Bex 159 D2
Holland Mews. Hove 165 D3
Holland Rd. Hove 165 D3
Holland St. Bri 165 F3
Hollands Way. E Gri 2 C2
Holliers Hill. Bex 160 A3
Hollin Cl. T W 8 A2
Hollingbury Copse. Bri ... 145 F2
Hollingbury Cres. Bri 145 F1
Hollingbury Park Ave. Bri 145 F1
Hollingbury Pl. Bri 145 F1
Hollingbury Rd. Bri 145 F1
Hollingbury Rise. Bri 145 F1
Hollingbury Rise W. Bri .. 145 F1
Hollingbury Terr. Bri 145 F1
Hollingdean Rd. Bri 166 A4
Hollingdean St. Bri 145 F1
Hollingdean Terr. Bri 145 F1
Hollinghurst Cl. Hast 139 F2
Hollinghurst Rd. Hast 139 F2
Hollington Ct. Hast 161 F4
Hollington Old La. Hast .. 139 F2
Hollington Park Cl. Hast . 139 F1
Hollington Park Rd. Hast 139 F1
Hollow La. Blas 81 F2
Hollow La. Dor 3 D3
Hollow The. Hay H 52 C3
Hollow The. W Hoa 22 B3
Holly Cl. Bex 159 D3
Holly Cl. Bri 145 E2
Holly Cl. Hai 154 C3
Holly Cl. Hea 83 F3
Holly Dr. Hea 83 F3
Holly Pl. East 175 E2
Holly Rd. Hay H 52 C2
Hollybank Gdns. Hast 139 F1
Hollydene Rd. Wad 31 E3
Hollyshaw Cl. T W 9 D1
Holm Oak Cl. Bex 159 E2
Holmbush Cl. Hay H 52 B1
Holmbush Cl. S Sea 143 D1
Holmbush Way. Sock 143 E1
Holmdale Rd. Newh 170 B1
Holmes Ave. Hove 164 B4
Holmes Cl. Sea 180 C3
Holmesdale Cl. Wad 31 E3
Holmesdale Gdns. Hast .. 162 B4
Holmesdale Rd. Bex 159 F2
Holmesdale Rd. Bur H 74 C1
Holmewood Rd. T W 9 D4
Holmhurst La. Hast 139 F3
Holt The. Bur H 75 D1
Holt The. Hai 154 C3
Holt The. Sea 181 E3
Holters Way. Sea 181 E3
Holton Hill. Wood 167 E4
Holtview Rd. Wood 166 C4
Holtye Ave. E Gri 2 C2
Holtye Rd. E Gri 2 C2
Holyrood. E Gri 12 C4
Holywell Rd. East 190 B4
Holywell Wlk. Hai 154 C4
Home Farm Ct. Frant 19 D2
Home Farm La. T W 9 E4
Home Platt. Sha 22 C3
Home Rd. Bri 145 E1

Homebush Ave. Salt 168 A1
Homebush Ave. Salt 168 B2
Homefield Cl. Sea 181 E2
Homefield Rd. Sea 181 E2
Homewood Cl. East 185 F3
Homewood Ridge. Lan G .. 7 E2
Honey Croft. Hove 144 A2
Honeycrag Cl. Pole 174 C4
Honeypot La. E Chi 102 C4
Honeysuckle Cl. East 175 F2
Honeysuckle Cl. Hai 154 C3
Honeyway Cl. Willn 174 B2
Hoo Gdns. East 174 C1
Hood Cl. East 186 B4
Hook Hill. Tic 32 C3
Hook La. Brok 73 F4
Hook La. W Hoa 22 A2
Hookswood Cl. Cro 27 F2
Hoopers Cl. S Mal 127 D2
Hoover Cl. Hast 139 E3
Hop Gdn. Fair 38 A1
Hopfield Gdns. Uck 80 A4
Hopgarden Cl. Hast 162 B4
Hophurst Hill. Cra D 1 A1
Hophurst La. Cra D 1 A1
Hopwood Gdns. T W 8 C3
Horam Park Cl. Hor 109 F4
Horebeech La. Hor 109 F3
Horley Pl. Bri 166 B3
Hornbeam. Bur 63 F4
Hornbuckles Cl. S Cha ... 103 E4
Hornby Rd. Bri 146 C1
Horning Cl. East 175 F2
Horns Rd. The M 47 D4
Hornshurst Rd. Rot 40 C4
Horntye Rd. Hast 140 A1
Horsegrove Ave. Tic 33 E1
Horsegrove La. Rot 40 C4
Horseshoe Cl. Hast 139 F1
Horseshoe La. Bec 92 C4
Horsewalk. Hooe 157 E4
Horsewalk. Wart 157 E4
Horsfield Rd. Lew 126 C2
Horsham Ave. Pea 179 D4
Horsham Cl. Bri 166 B3
Horsted La. Dan 35 F2
Horsted La. Isf 105 E4
Horsted La. Lit H 105 E4
Horsted La. Sha 22 C2
Horsye Rd. East 185 F4
Horton Rd. Bri 145 F1
Hoskins Pl. E Gri 2 C2
Hosmers Field. Tow R 41 D4
Houghton La. Rye 72 A1
Houndean Cl. Lew 148 C4
Houndean Rise. Lew 148 B4
Hova Villas. Hove 164 C3
Hove Park Gdns. Hove ... 164 C4
Hove Park Rd. Hove 145 D1
Hove Park Villas. Hove .. 164 C4
Hove Park Way. Hove 145 D1
Hove Pl. Hove 164 C3
Hove Sea Wall. Hove 165 D3
Hove St. Hove 164 C3
How's Cl. Bro O W 91 F3
Howard Ave. Bur H 74 B2
Howard Gdns. T W 8 C1
Howard Pl. Bri 165 E4
Howard Rd. Bri 166 A4
Howard Sq. East 185 F1
Howard Terr. Bri 165 E4
Howards Cl. Hai 155 D3
Howards Cres. Bex 159 D2
Howbourne La. Bux 58 B3
Howey Cl. Newh 170 B1
Howlett Cl. Hast 139 E2
Howlett Dr. Hai 132 C1
Howletts Cl. East 175 E1
Hoyle Rd. Pea 179 D4
Hudson Cl. East 186 C4
Hudson Rd. Hay H 52 B3
Huggett's La. Willn 174 C2
Hughenden Pl. Hast 140 B1
Hughendon Rd. Hast 140 C1
Huglets La. Cad S 84 C3
Humboldt Ct. T W 9 D3
Hundred Acre La. Dit 75 F1
Hundred Acre La. Wiv G .. 75 F2
Hundredhouse La. Bec 92 B3
Hundredhouse La. Bro O W 92 B2
Hungershall Park. T W 8 B1
Hunloke Ave. East 185 F3
Hunston Cl. Wood 167 E4
Hunter's Mead. Alb 99 D3
Hunters Way. T W 8 B1
Hunters Way. Uck 79 F4
Hunting Cl. Bex 160 A3
Huntingdon Rd. Cro 39 E4
Huntingdon Way. Bur H ... 75 D3
Huntley Mill Rd. Tic 33 E2
Hurdis Rd. Sea 180 C3
Hurrell Rd. Hast 140 C1
Hurst Cres. Por S 163 F4
Hurst Farm Rd. E Gri 12 A4
Hurst Gdns. Hur 99 E4
Hurst Hill. Bri 146 A3
Hurst La. East 185 D4
Hurst La. Sed 90 B2

Hurst La. Win H 134 C3
Hurst Rd. East 185 D3
Hurst Rd. Hass 100 A2
Hurst The. T W 9 E4
Hurst Way. Wfd 140 C3
Hurst Wickham Cl. Hur ... 100 A3
Hurstfield Cl. Hay H 52 C1
Hurstwood Cl. Bex 160 C3
Hurstwood La. Hay H 52 C1
Hurstwood La. Hor K 23 D1
Hurstwood La. T W 8 B2
Hurstwood Rd. H Hur 57 E2
Hurstwood Rd. Uck 57 E2
Hurtis Hill. Cro 39 E4
Hutton Rd. Bri 145 F2
Hyde Gdns. East 185 F1
Hyde Rd. East 185 E1
Hyde The. Bri 166 B4
Hyde Tynings Cl. East 190 A4
Hydehurst Cl. Cro 27 E1
Hydneye St. East 186 A3
Hydneye The. East 175 E1
Hylden Cl. Wood 166 C4
Hyperion Ave. Pole 174 B3
Hythe Ave. Bex 160 C3
Hythe Cl. Pole 175 D4
Hythe Cl. Sea 182 A3
Hythe Cres. Sea 182 A2
Hythe Rd. Bri 145 F1
Hythe View. Sea 182 A2

Ian Cl. Bex 160 B4
Icklesham Dr. Hast 139 D2
Iden Cl. Bri 166 B3
Iden Hurst. Hur 99 F4
Iden Rd. Rye 71 F1
Iden St. East 175 F1
Iden's La. Bro O 84 A4
Ifield Cl. Salt 168 B1
Iford Cl. S Hei 170 A1
Ilex Green. Hai 132 C1
Imberholme La. E Gri 1 C1
Imberhorne La. E Gri 11 F4
Imberhorne Way. E Gri 1 C2
Impala Gdns. T W 8 C3
Imperial Arc. Bri 165 E3
Ingham Dr. Bri 146 A3
Ingleside. Hast 139 E2
Ingleside Dr. Cro 27 E1
Inglewood Gdns. Hast 139 E2
Ingram Cres. Hove 164 B4
Ingrams Ave. Bex 160 A4
Ingrams Way. Hai 154 C3
Inholmes Cl. Bur H 75 D2
Inholmes Park Rd. Bur H .. 74 C2
Ink Pen La. For R 13 E1
Innham's Wood. Cro 27 E2
Innings Dr. Pev B 177 D2
Institute Wlk. E Gri 2 B1
Invicta Rd. Lydd 98 C1
Inwood Cres. Bri 145 E1
Iona Way. Hay H 52 B2
Irelands La. Lew 126 C1
Ironlatch Ave. Hast 139 E1
Ironlatch Cl. Hast 139 E1
Ironstone Way. Uck 80 A4
Ironstones. Lan G 7 F2
Isaac's La. East 74 B4
Isaac's La. Hay H 52 A2
Isabel Cres. Hove 164 B4
Isfield Rd. Bri 146 A1
Islingwood Pl. Bri 166 A3
Islingword Rd. Bri 165 F4
Islingword St. Bri 165 F3
Iveagh Cres. S Hei 170 B1
Ivor Rd. Wood 147 D1
Ivory Pl. Bri 165 F3
Ivy Dene La. Ash W 13 D3
Ivy La. East 185 E2
Ivy Pl. Hove 165 D3
Ivy Terr. East 185 E1
Ivyhouse La. Cog 140 C4
Ivyhouse La. Hast 140 C3

Jaarlen Rd. Lydd 98 C3
Jack O'dandy Cl. East 185 D4
Jackies La. Chay 77 F4
Jackson St. Bri 165 F4
James Ave. Hers 134 B3
Jameson Cres. Hast 139 F2
Jameson Rd. Bex 160 A2
Janes Cl. Bur H 75 D3
Janes La. Bur H 75 D3
Janes La. Wiv 75 E2
Jarvisbrook Cl. Bex 159 D2
Jasmine Green. Hai 132 C1
Jason Cl. Pea 179 D4
Jay Cl. East 176 A1
Jay Rd. Pea 179 E3
Jays The. Bur H 74 B2
Jefferies Way. Cro 27 E2
Jeffreys Way. Uck 57 D1
Jellicoe Cl. East 186 B4
Jenner's La. Hast 141 E3
Jephson Cl. East 190 B4
Jerome Cl. East 176 B1
Jersey St. Bri 165 F3
Jervis Ave. East 186 B3

Jesmond Cl. Hove 164 B4
Jesmond Rd. Hove 164 B4
Jesters. Bur H 75 D4
Jevington Cl. Bex 159 D1
Jevington Dr. Bri 146 A1
Jevington Dr. Sea 181 D2
Jevington Gdns. East 185 E1
Jevington Rd. Jev 184 A4
Jevington Rd. Willn 174 B2
Jew St. Bri 165 F3
Jireh Ct. Hay H 52 B3
Joe's La. Win H 134 C3
John St. Bri 165 F3
John St. T W 8 C3
John's Cross Rd. Mou 89 D4
John's Cross Rd. Rob 65 F1
Johns Cl. Pea 169 D1
Johnson Dr. Bur H 75 D2
Jonas Dr. Wad 31 E3
Jonas La. Wad 31 E3
Jordans La. East 175 D2
Jordans La E. East 175 D2
Jordans La W. East 175 D2
Jordans La W. Willn 175 D2
Jordans The. E Gri 12 B4
Jubilee Gdns. Sea 181 F3
Jubilee Rd. Bex 159 F4
Jubilee Rd. Bur H 74 B1
Jubilee Rd. Por S 163 F4
Jubilee St. Bri 165 F3
Jubille Cl. Hay H 52 C2
Juggs Rd. Lew 148 C4
Julian Rd. Hove 165 E4
Julian Rd. Hove 165 E4
Junction Cl. Bur H 75 D2
Junction Rd. Bri 165 E3
Junction Rd. Bur H 74 C2
Junction Rd. Cri C 90 A4
Junction Rd. East 185 F2
Junction Rd. Hast 139 F4
Junction Rd. Sale 66 C4
Junction Rd. Stas 67 D2
Junction St. Pole 174 C3
Juniper Cl. Hast 139 E2
Juniper Cl. Por S 143 F2
Juniper Cl. Sea 182 A2
Juniper Wlk. S Sea 143 D1
Jury's Gap Rd. Lydd 98 B3

Kammond Ave. Sea 181 F3
Katherine Way. Sea 181 E3
Keats Cl. Hast 161 E3
Keats Pl. E Gri 2 A1
Keats Wlk. East 176 B2
Kebworth Cl. Bex 159 E3
Kedale Rd. Sea 181 E2
Keel Gdns. Sgh 8 B4
Keere St. Lew 149 D4
Keith Wlk. East 186 B3
Keld Ave. Rid 80 A3
Keld Cl. Rid 80 A3
Keld Dr. Rid 80 A3
Kelly Rd. Hove 145 D1
Kemble Cl. T W 9 E4
Kemp St. Bri 165 F3
Kemp Town Pl. Bri 166 A2
Kemps. Hur 99 E4
Kemps Farm Rd. Cro 27 F1
Kemps Way. Sale 66 A3
Kendal Park. T W 8 B3
Kendal Rd. Hove 164 B4
Kenilworth Cl. Bri 146 C1
Kenilworth Rd. Hast 161 F4
Kenmure Ave. Bri 145 F4
Kennedy Ave. E Gri 2 A2
Kennedy Cl. Hea 83 F3
Kennedy Rd. Bex 160 B2
Kennedy Way. Newh 179 F4
Kennel La. Bex 159 D2
Kensington Gdns. Bri 165 F3
Kensington Pl. Bri 165 F3
Kensington St. Bri 165 F3
Kensington St. T W 8 C2
Kent Cl. Bex 160 C3
Kent Cl. S Sea 163 D4
Kent Cl. Winc 120 B4
Kent Fields. Kin L 148 B3
Kent La. Bril 87 E4
Kent Rd. Hast 139 E2
Kent Rd. T W 8 C3
Kent St. Sed 116 B3
Kent St. Wfd 116 C2
Kentish Gdns. Hay H 18 B4
Kenton Cl. Bex 159 F3
Kenton Rd. Hove 164 A4
Kents Bank. Hay H 52 B2
Kenwards. Bri 146 A4
Kenwood Cl. Hast 140 C2
Keppel Rd. Hast 140 B1
Kerrara Terr. East 185 F2
Kestrel Cl. Bex 160 B2
Kestrel Cl. Hove 165 D4
Kestrels The. Hast 139 E3
Ketche's La. Hor K 54 B4
Ketches La. Fle 54 B3
Kevin Gdns. Wood 167 E4
Kew St. Bri 165 E3
Kewhurst Ave. Bex 159 D2
Keymer Ave. Pea 179 D4
Keymer Cl. East 176 B1

Keymer Cl. Hast 161 E2
Keymer Ct. Bur H 74 C1
Keymer Gdns. Bur H 74 C1
Keymer Park. Key 100 C3
Keymer Rd. Bri 145 F3
Keymer Rd. Bur H 74 C1
Keymer Rd. Dit 101 D2
Keymer Rd. Hass 100 B2
Keymer Rd. Key 100 C2
Kibbles La. Sgh 8 B4
Kidbrook. Hay H 52 C3
Kidbrooke Rise. For R 13 E1
Kidd's Hill. Col H 25 F2
Kilda St. East 185 F2
Kildare Cl. Hast 140 C2
Kiln Cl. Rid 80 A2
Kiln La. Hay H 52 C3
Kiln La. Hooe 157 F4
Kiln The. Bur H 75 D2
Kilnwood La. S Cha 103 E4
Kilpatrick Cl. East 175 E1
Kimberley Cl. East 146 A1
Kimberley Rd. Sea 181 D2
Kindersley Cl. E Gri 2 C2
Kinfauns Ave. East 185 F3
King Cl. East 185 E3
King Edward Ave. Hast ... 140 A2
King Edward Cl. Hast 140 A2
King Edward's Par. East .. 190 B4
King George Ave. E Gri 2 A2
King George Rd. S Sea ... 163 D4
King George V Hill. T W 9 D3
King George Vi Ave. Hove 144 C2
King George Vi Dr. Hove .. 144 C2
King Henry's Rd. Lew 126 C1
King Offa Way. Bex 160 A3
King Pl. Bri 165 F3
King St. Bri 165 F3
King St. Brok 73 F4
King St. E Gri 2 B1
King Wood Hill. Bro O W .. 91 F2
King's Ave. East 185 E3
King's Ave. Newh 170 A3
King's Ave. Rye 95 D3
King's Bank La. Bec 69 F2
King's Cliff. Bri 166 A2
King's Espl. Hove 164 C3
King's Gdns. Hove 164 C3
King's Hill Rd. Bur 63 F2
King's Mead La. Sea 181 D2
King's Mews. Hove 165 D3
King's Rd. Bri 165 E3
King's Rd. Hast 162 A4
Kingfisher Dr. East 176 A1
Kingfisher Rise. E Gri 12 B4
Kings Chase. Cro 27 D2
Kings Cl. Bex 160 A2
Kings Copse. E Gri 12 B4
Kings Ct. Cro 27 E1
Kings Dr. Key 100 B2
Kings Holiday Park and
  Country Club. East 186 B4
Kings Rd. Hay H 52 B2
Kings Rd. Sock 143 E1
Kings Ride. Alfn 172 B1
Kings Ride. Bur H 75 D1
Kings Ride. Sea 181 D2
Kings Toll Rd. Pem 10 C3
Kings Way. Bur H 75 D1
Kingsbury Rd. Bri 165 F4
Kingsbury St. Bri 165 F3
Kingsdale Cl. Bat 115 E2
Kingsley Cl. Hast 139 F3
Kingsley Ct. Wad 31 F2
Kingsley Rd. Lew 126 C1
Kingsmead. Sea 181 E3
Kingsmead Cl. Sea 181 E2
Kingsmead Way. Sea 181 E2
Kingsmead Wlk. Sea 181 E2
Kingsmere. Bri 145 E1
Kingsthorpe Rd. Hove 164 B4
Kingston Ave. Sea 181 F2
Kingston Bay Rd. S Sea .. 163 D3
Kingston Bwy. S Sea 143 E1
Kingston Cl. Hove 144 B1
Kingston Cl. S Sea 163 D4
Kingston Cl. Sea 181 E2
Kingston Green. Sea 181 F2
Kingston La. S Sea 163 D4
Kingston Rd. East 175 E1
Kingston Rd. Lew 148 C4
Kingston Way. S Sea 143 D1
Kingston Way. Sea 182 A2
Kingstonridge. Kin L 148 A3
Kingsway. Hove 164 B3
Kingsway. Sea 181 D2
Kingswood Ave. Bex 159 E3
Kingswood Cl. T W 9 D2
Kingswood Rd. T W 9 D2
Kingswood St. Bri 165 F3
Kinver La. Bex 160 C3
Kipling Ave. Wood 167 E4
Kipling Way. E Gri 2 A1
Kipling Wlk. East 176 B1
Kirby Dr. Pea 168 C1
Kirdford Cl. Bur H 75 D1
Kirk Way. East 184 C2

Kirkdale Rd. T W 8 C2
Kirkstall Cl. East 175 E2
Kitchenour La. Four O 70 B3
Kitchenour La. Peas 70 B3
Kite Cl. Hast 161 E4
Knebworth Rd. Bex 159 E3
Knelle Rd. Rob 65 F2
Knepp Cl. Bri 146 B1
Knight's Ridge. Pem 10 A4
Knights Cl. Pem 10 A4
Knights Garden. Hai 154 C3
Knights Meadow. Uck 80 B4
Knightsbridge Cl. T W 8 B3
Knole Gr. E Gri 2 A2
Knole Rd. Bex 160 A2
Knole Rd. Rottn 167 F1
Knoll Cl. Hove 144 A1
Knoll Cres. East 175 F1
Knoll Rd. East 175 F1
Knoll Rise. Hast 161 F4
Knowle Cl. Cro 40 A4
Knowle Cl. Lan G 7 E2
Knowle Hill. May 41 F1
Knowle Park Rd. May 41 F1
Knowle Rd. Fai 142 B3
Knoyle Rd. Bri 145 E1
Kymer Gdns. Key 100 C2

Laburnum Ave. Hove 144 B1
Laburnum Gdns. Bex 160 B3
Laburnum Green. Hai 132 C1
Laburnum Way. Hay H 52 C2
Laburnum Wlk. East 175 D2
Lacys Hill. Gly 150 B4
Ladies Mile Cl. Bri 145 E3
Ladies Mile Rd. Bri 145 E3
Lady Oak La. Fli 34 A4
Lady's Gift Rd. Sgh 8 B4
Ladycross Cl. Sea 182 A2
Ladymead. Bur H 75 D3
Ladysmith Rd. Bri 166 A4
Lagwood Cl. Hass 100 B2
Laine Cl. Bri 145 E2
Lake Dr. Pea 178 C4
Lake Rd. T W 8 A2
Lake St. May 42 A4
Lake St. Wad 29 F1
Lake View Rd. Cra D 1 A2
Lake View Rd. Dor P 2 B3
Lakehurst La. Pon G 112 C4
Lakelands Cl. East 175 F1
Lakelands Dr. Bex 159 D2
Laleham Cl. East 185 E2
Laleham Cl. Hast 140 A3
Lambert Pl. S Mal 127 D2
Lamberts Rd. T W 9 D4
Lambourn. E Gri 2 B2
Lambourn Way. T W 9 D1
Lambourne Cl. Bri 146 A1
Lambourne Rd. Bri 146 A1
Lampington Row. Lan G 7 E2
Lancaster Dr. E Gri 2 C2
Lancaster Dr. Bri 165 E4
Lancaster Rd. Hast 139 E3
Lancaster St. Lew 127 D1
Lancing Cl. Hast 140 A2
Lancing Way. Willn 174 B2
Landgate. Rye 95 D3
Landport Rd. Lew 126 C2
Landsdown Rd. Sea 181 F3
Landsdowne Way. Bex 160 B3
Landseer Rd. Hove 164 C4
Langdale Cl. East 176 A2
Langdale Gdns. Hove 164 B3
Langdale Rd. Hove 164 B3
Langham Cl. Hast 140 B2
Langham Cl. Rin 128 A3
Langham Rd. Hast 140 B2
Langham Rd. Rob 65 E3
Langholm Rd. Lan G 7 E2
Langley Cl. Bex 159 F4
Langley Cres. Wood 147 E1
Langney Green. East 186 B4
Langney Rd. East 185 F2
Langney Rise. East 176 A1
Langridge La. Hay H 52 C3
Langridge Way. Bur H 74 B3
Langton La. Hur 99 E4
Langton Rd. Lan G 7 F2
Langton Rd. T W 8 A2
Langton Ridge. Lan G 7 F2
Langtye La. Chal 152 B3
Langtye La. Ripe 152 B3
Lansdown Pl. Lew 149 D4
Lansdowne Cres. Hai 132 C1
Lansdowne Dr. Hai 132 C1
Lansdowne Gdns. Hai 132 C1
Lansdowne Pl. Hove 165 D3
Lansdowne Rd. Hai 132 C1
Lansdowne Rd. Hove 165 D3
Lansdowne Rd. T W 8 C2
Lansdowne Sq. Hove 165 D3
Lansdowne Sq. T W 8 C2
Lansdowne St. Hove 165 D3
Lansdowne Way. Hai 132 C1
Lapierre Rd. Newh 179 F4
Lapwing Cl. East 176 A1
Larch Cl. Hast 139 F1
Larch Cl. Wood 167 E4

Larch Gdns. East 175 D2
Larches Way. Cra D 11 D4
Lark Hill. Hove 144 B2
Larke Cl. S Sea 163 D4
Larkfield Cl. Hast 139 F2
Larkfield Way. Bri 145 F2
Larkhill. Bex 160 A2
Larkspur Dr. East 175 F2
Lascelles Terr. East 185 F1
Lashbrooks Rd. Uck 79 F4
Latimer Rd. East 186 A2
Latnach Cl. Uck 80 A4
Laton Rd. Hast 140 B1
Laughton Rd. Lau 129 E4
Laughton Rd. Rin 129 E4
Laughton Rd. Wood 167 E4
Laundry La. Che G 24 A1
Laurel Bank. Sgh 8 C4
Laurel Cl. Bur H 75 D3
Laurel Dene. E Gri 2 B1
Laurel La. Ick 119 E3
Laurel Rd. T W 9 D4
Laurel Way. T W 9 D4
Laurel Wlk. Hast 139 E2
Laurels The. Uck 80 B4
Lauriston Rd. Bri 145 E1
Lavant Cl. Bex 159 D3
Lavender St. Bri 165 F3
Lawes Ave. Newh 180 A4
Lawn The. Hast 162 A4
Lawns Ave. East 185 D2
Lawrence Cl. East 176 A1
Lawrence Rd. Hove 164 B4
Lawrie La. Hay H 52 C2
Laylands Rd. Por S 163 F4
Le Brun Rd. East 185 E3
Lea Ave. Rye 94 C3
Lea Rd. Pea 178 C4
Leaf Hall Rd. East 185 F2
Leaf Rd. East 185 F2
Leahurst Court Rd. Bri 145 E2
Lealands Cl. Gro 17 D3
Lealands Dr. Uck 57 D1
Leamland Wlk. Hai 154 C4
Leas The. Wad 31 F3
Leasam La. Rye 94 C4
Leasingham Gdns. Bex 159 F3
Ledsham Ave. Hast 139 F3
Ledsham Cl. Hast 139 F3
Ledsham Park. Hast 139 F3
Ledsham Way. Hast 139 F3
Lee Rd. Lew 126 C1
Lee Way. Newh 179 F4
Leeds Ave. East 186 A4
Leeds Cl. Hast 141 D2
Leeves Cl. Hea 83 F3
Leeves Way. Hea 83 F3
Leggs La. Lan G 7 E3
Legsheath La. Gri 12 A1
Legsheath La. For R 23 E4
Leicester Dr. T W 18 B4
Leicester Rd. Lew 126 C1
Leicester St. Bri 165 F3
Leicester Villas. Hove 164 A4
Leighton Cl. T W 8 C4
Leighton Rd. Hor K 35 D3
Leighton Rd. Hove 164 C4
Leneda Dr. T W 18 B4
Lenham Ave. Salt 167 F1
Lenham Rd. E. Salt 167 F1
Lenham Rd E. Rottn 167 F1
Lenham Rd W. Rottn 167 F1
Lennox Cl. East 184 C3
Lennox Rd. Hove 164 B4
Lennox St. Bri 165 F3
Leopold Rd. Bex 159 F2
Leopold Rd. Bri 165 E3
Lesley Cl. Bex 160 B4
Leslie St. East 185 F2
Leveller End. Newk 78 A4
Leveller Rd. Newk 78 A4
Levett Ave. Pole 175 D3
Levett Cl. Pole 175 D3
Levett Cl. Pole 175 D3
Levett Way. Pole 175 D3
Levetts La. Bod 48 B1
Lewes Cl. Bex 159 F3
Lewes Cl. Salt 168 B1
Lewes Cres. Bri 166 B2
Lewes Rd. Ash W 13 D3
Lewes Rd. Bri 165 F4
Lewes Rd. Dan 35 F2
Lewes Rd. Dit 101 D1
Lewes Rd. E Gri 12 C4
Lewes Rd. East 185 E2
Lewes Rd. Fol 174 A3
Lewes Rd. For R 24 B4
Lewes Rd. Hay H 52 C2
Lewes Rd. Hay H 52 C4
Lewes Rd. Hor K 35 D3
Lewes Rd. Lit H 80 A2
Lewes Rd. Newh 180 A4
Lewes Rd. Pole 174 B3
Lewes Rd. Rid 80 A2
Lewes Rd. Rin 128 A3
Lewes Rd. Sca H 53 E2
Lewes Rd. Wil 173 F3
Lewes Rd. Wmes 124 B4
Lewes St. Bri 165 F3

Lewis Cl. Newh 170 B1
Lewis Rd. Hast 139 F2
Lewis's Bldgs. Bri 165 E3
Lexden Cl. Sea 181 F2
Lexden Dr. Sea 181 F3
Lexden Rd. Sea 181 E3
Leybourne Cl. Bri 146 C1
Leybourne Gdns. Hast 140 A2
Leybourne Rd. Bri 146 C1
Leyfield. Alb 99 D3
Leyland Rd. Pev B 177 D2
Leylands Park. Bur H 74 C3
Leylands Rd. Bur H 74 C2
Lilac Cl. East 175 D1
Limden Cl. Ston 44 B3
Lime Cl. East 175 D1
Lime Cl. Uck 80 A4
Lime Hill Rd. T W 8 C2
Lime Tree Ave. Uck 80 A4
Lime Way. Hea 83 F3
Limekiln Ct. Cro 28 A2
Limes La. Bux 58 A2
Limes The. Fel 1 C3
Limetree Ave. East 175 D2
Limeway. Hea 83 F3
Limney Rd. Bri 166 B4
Linchmere Ave. Salt 168 A1
Lincoln Ave. Pea 178 C4
Lincoln Ave S. Pea 178 C4
Lincoln Cl. East 190 A4
Lincoln Cl. Hast 139 F2
Lincoln Cotts. Bri 165 F3
Lincoln Rd. Por S 163 F4
Lincoln St. Bri 165 F4
Lincoln Wood. Hay H 52 A3
Linden Ave. E Gri 2 A1
Linden Chase. Uck 80 A4
Linden Cl. East 175 E1
Linden Ct. Uck 80 A4
Linden Gdns. T W 8 B1
Linden Gr. Hay H 52 C4
Linden Park Rd. T W 8 C1
Linden Rd. Bex 160 A2
Lindfield Ave. Sea 182 A1
Lindfield Cl. Rottn 167 F1
Lindfield Dr. Hai 154 C4
Lindfield Rd. East 175 D1
Lindon Cl. Fri 183 F1
Lindsay Cl. East 185 D1
Lingfield Rd. E Gri 2 A2
Link Rd. East 185 D1
Link The. Fri 184 A1
Link The. Rye 94 C3
Link Way. T W 9 E4
Links Cl. Cro 27 D1
Links Cl. Por S 164 A4
Links Cl. Sea 181 F2
Links Dr. Bex 160 B2
Links Rd. Por S 164 A4
Links Rd. Sea 181 F1
Links The. Hast 161 E4
Links Way. Cam 96 B1
Linkway. East 184 C4
Linkway. Whm 176 B3
Linkway The. Bri 145 F1
Linley Cl. Bex 160 A2
Linley Dr. Hast 140 B1
Linley Dr. Hast 140 C2
Linnet Cl. East 176 A1
Linthouse Cl. Pea 169 D1
Linton Ave. Bri 166 B3
Linton Cres. Hast 162 B4
Linton Rd. Hast 162 B4
Linton Rd. Hove 164 B4
Lion Hill. St Cro 175 F3
Lion La. East 185 F2
Lion Mews. Hove 164 B4
Lion St. Rye 95 D3
Lionel Rd. Bex 160 B2
Lions Pl. Sea 181 E1
Liphook Cl. Bri 146 A1
Lipscombe Rd. T W 9 D3
Liptraps La. T W 9 D4
Lismore Rd. East 185 F1
Lister Ave. E Gri 12 B3
Lister Rd. East 175 F1
Little Bentswood. Hay H 52 B3
Little Bentswood Cl. Hay H ... 52 B3
Little Common Rd. Bex 159 E3
Little Copse Rd. Hass 100 B2
Little Cres. Rottn 167 F1
Little East St. Bri 165 F3
Little East St. Lew 127 D1
Little Footway. Lan G 7 E2
Little George St. Bri 165 F3
Little King St. E Gri 2 B1
Little London Rd. Hor 109 E4
Little Mallett. Lan G 7 E2
Little Mead. Coo 126 C4
Little Mount Sion. T W 8 C1
Little Paddock. Rin 128 B3
Little Preston St. Bri 165 E3
Little Ridge Ave. Hast 139 F3
Little Ridge Ave. Hast 140 A3
Little Sunnyside. Cro 27 E1
Little Trodgers La. May 42 A3

Little Twitten. Bex 159 D2
Little Western St. Hove 165 E3
Littleworth Cl. Wood 167 E4
Liverpool St. Bri 165 F3
Livingstone Rd. Bur H 74 B2
Livingstone Rd. Hove 164 C4
Livingstone St. Bri 166 A3
Lloyd Rd. Hove 165 D4
Lockitt Way. Kin L 148 B3
Locks Cres. Por S 143 F1
Locks Hill. Por S 143 F1
Lockwood Cl. Wood 167 E4
Lockwood Cres. Wood 167 E4
Loder Pl. Bri 145 E1
Loder Rd. Bri 145 E1
Lodge Ave. Willn 175 D1
Lodge Cl. E Gri 2 A1
Lodge Cl. Por S 143 E1
Lodge Hill La. Dit 101 D2
Lodge La. Key 100 C1
Lodge Rd. Hast 141 D1
Lomas La. San 49 E3
Lomond Ave. Bri 145 F4
London Rd. Alb 122 B4
London Rd. Bat 115 D4
London Rd. Bex 159 F3
London Rd. Bri 145 E3
London Rd. Bri 165 F4
London Rd. Bur H 100 B4
London Rd. Cro 27 E2
London Rd. Dan 35 F2
London Rd. E Gri 2 A1
London Rd. E Hoa 107 F3
London Rd. Fli 34 A2
London Rd. For R 13 E2
London Rd. Hai 132 C1
London Rd. Hass 100 B3
London Rd. Hast 162 A4
London Rd. Hur G 46 C1
London Rd. Mou 89 D2
London Rd. Sgh 8 C4
London Rd. T W 8 C2
London Rd. Uck 57 D1
London Terr. Bri 165 F4
Long Acre Cl. East 185 D3
Long Ave. Bex 160 C3
Long La. Sed 90 B1
Long Meads. Lan G 7 F2
Long Meads. T W 7 F2
Long Park Cnr. Dit 101 D1
Long Slip. Lan G 7 F2
Longacre Cl. Hast 140 A3
Longfield. T W 9 D4
Longfield Cl. Oving 167 E2
Longhill Rd. Oving 167 E2
Longhurst. Bur H 75 D1
Longland Rd. East 185 D2
Longridge Ave. Salt 168 A1
Longstone Rd. East 185 F2
Longview. Hea 83 F3
Longview Way. T W 9 D4
Lonsdale Dr. T W 8 C2
Lookout The. Pea 169 D2
Lordine La. Ewh G 67 F2
Lords La. Hast 141 D2
Lordslaine Cl. East 190 A4
Lordswell La. Cro 39 E4
Lorna Rd. Hove 165 D4
Lorne Rd. Bri 165 F4
Lorraine Rd. Newh 180 A4
Lossenham La. New 50 A2
Lottbridge Dr. East 175 E1
Lottbridge Dro. East 185 F4
Love La. East 185 D2
Love La. May 41 E1
Love La. Rye 94 C3
Lover's Wlk. Bri 165 E4
Lowdell's La. E Gri 2 A2
Lowdells Cl. E Gri 2 A2
Lowdells Dr. E Gri 2 A2
Lower Bevendean Ave. Bri ... 146 B1
Lower Chalvington Pl. Bri ... 166 B3
Lower Church Rd. Bur H 74 B2
Lower Dene. E Gri 2 C1
Lower Dr. Sea 181 E3
Lower Dr. Sock 143 E1
Lower Glen Rd. Hast 139 F2
Lower Green Rd. Pem 10 A4
Lower Green Rd. Spe 8 A4
Lower Green Rd. T W 8 A2
Lower Hazelhurst. Tic 32 C2
Lower High St. Wad 31 F2
Lower Lake. Bat 115 E2
Lower Market St. Hove 165 D3
Lower Mere. E Gri 12 B4
Lower Par. East 185 F1
Lower Park Rd. Hast 140 B1
Lower Pl. Newh 180 A4
Lower Platts. Tic 33 E1
Lower Prom. Hast 161 F3
Lower Rd. East 185 D2
Lower Rd. For R 13 E2
Lower Rd. Hers 134 B2
Lower Rock Gdns. Bri 165 F2
Lower South Rd. Hast 140 A1
Lower Sq. For R 13 E2
Lower St. E Dean 188 C4
Lower St. Rye 95 D3

Lower Station Rd. Chay 77 B2
Lower Waites La. Fai 142 B3
Lowfield Rd. Hay H 52 B2
Lowlands Rd. Bur H 74 C3
Lowlands The. Hai 132 C1
Lowther Cl. East 176 A2
Lowther Rd. Bri 145 F1
Loxfield Cl. May 41 F1
Loxfield Gdns. Cro 27 F1
Loxwood Cl. Bex 159 D3
Loxwood Cl. East 175 D1
Lucas. Hor K 35 D3
Lucas Cl. E Gri 2 C1
Lucas Grange. Hay H 52 A3
Lucas Way. Hay H 52 A3
Lucastes Ave. Hay H 52 A3
Lucastes La. Hay H 52 A3
Lucastes Rd. Hay H 52 A3
Lucerne Cl. Por S 143 F1
Lucerne Rd. Bri 145 F1
Lucinda Way. Sea 181 E3
Lucroft Rd. Bri 146 C3
Ludley Hill. Bec 92 C3
Ludlow Rise. Bri 146 C1
Ludpit La. Bur 65 D3
Ludpit La. Etc 65 D3
Lulham Ct. Pea 168 C1
Lullington Ave. Hove 164 B4
Lullington Cl. Bex 160 C3
Lullington Cl. East 185 D4
Lullington Cl. Sea 181 F1
Lullington Gdns. Hast 140 A3
Lumberpit La. E Chi 102 C4
Lunces Hill. Wiv 75 E4
Lundy Wlk. Hai 132 B1
Lurgashall Rd. Bri 75 D1
Lushington La. East 185 F1
Lushington Rd. East 185 F1
Lustrells Cl. Salt 167 F1
Lustrells Cres. Salt 168 A1
Lustrells Rd. Rottn 167 F1
Lustrells Vale. Salt 168 A1
Luther St. Bri 166 A4
Luton Cl. East 185 D3
Luxford Dr. Cro 39 F4
Luxford La. Cro 39 F4
Luxford Rd. Cro 39 F4
Luxford Rd. Hay H 52 C4
Luxford's La. E Gri 12 C3
Lychgates Cl. Bex 160 A3
Lydd Cl. East 176 A1
Lydd Rd. Cam 96 C1
Lymden La. Ston 44 C4
Lymden La. Wal 32 C1
Lyminster Ave. Bri 145 F3
Lynchet Down. Bri 146 A1
Lynchet Wlk. Bri 146 A1
Lynchets Cres. Hove 144 A2
Lynchets The. S Mal 127 E2
Lyndhurst Ave. Hast 140 C2
Lyndhurst Rd. Hove 165 D4
Lynholm Rd. Pole 175 D3
Lynton Cl. E Gri 2 C1
Lynton Cl. Hur 99 F3
Lynton Park Ave. E Gri 2 C1
Lynton St. Bri 166 A4
Lynwood Cl. Hast 140 A3
Lynwood Rd. Salt 178 A4
Lyoth La. Hay H 53 D2
Lytham Cl. Hast 161 E4

Mabb's Hill. Ston 44 B4
Maberley Rd. Bex 160 A3
Mackerel Hill. Peas 70 B2
Mackie Ave. Bri 145 F4
Mackie Ave. Key 100 C3
Macmillan Dr. East 185 D3
Madehurst Cl. Bri 166 A3
Madeira Dr. Hast 140 A2
Madeira Park. T W 8 C1
Madeira Pl. Bri 165 F2
Madeira Terr. Bri 166 A2
Mafeking Rd. Bri 146 A1
Magdalen Cl. East 176 A2
Magdalen Rd. Bex 160 A2
Magdalen Rd. Hast 162 A4
Magnolia Dr. East 175 D1
Magnolia Wlk. East 175 D2
Magpie Cl. Bex 159 D3
Magpie Cl. Hast 161 E4
Magpie Rd. East 176 A2
Maidstone Rd. Pem 10 B4
Main Rd. Ick 119 D3
Main Rd. Wfd 117 E2
Main St. Iden 71 F2
Main St. Norm 68 C3
Main St. Peas 70 C1
Mainstone Rd. Hove 164 B4
Maitland Cl. Hast 140 B3
Major Cl. Bri 145 F1
Major York's Rd. T W 8 B1
Malcolm Gdns. Pole 174 C4
Maldon Rd. Bri 145 D1
Malines Ave. Pea 178 C4
Malines Ave S. Pea 178 C4
Mallard Dr. Rid 80 A3
Mallard Pl. E Gri 12 B4
Mallet Cl. Sea 181 E1

Malling Cl. S Mal 127 D2
Malling Down. S Mal 127 E2
Malling Hill. S Mal 127 E1
Malling Ind Est. Lew 127 E1
Malling St. Lew 127 E1
Mallory Rd. Hove 145 D1
Malthouse La. Bur H 74 A1
Malthouse La. Hur 100 A4
Maltings The. Peas 70 C1
Malton Way. T W 9 E3
Malvern Cl. East 175 E2
Malvern St. Hove 164 C4
Malvern Way. Hast 140 C2
Manaton Cl. Hay H 52 B2
Manchester Rd. Nin 136 C3
Manchester St. Bri 165 F2
Manhattan Gdns. Hast 141 D2
Manifold Rd. East 185 F2
Mann St. Hast 162 B4
Manning Cl. E Gri 2 A1
Manor Ave. Key 100 C3
Manor Cl. Bri 166 B3
Manor Cl. Bur H 75 D2
Manor Cl. Hor 109 E4
Manor Cl. Ick 119 E3
Manor Cl. Rin 128 B4
Manor Cl. Sea 181 F2
Manor Cl. Sock 163 F4
Manor Cl. T W 8 B2
Manor Cl. Uck 80 A4
Manor Cl. Willn 174 C1
Manor Cres. Bri 166 B3
Manor Dr. Pea 168 C1
Manor End. Uck 80 A4
Manor Gdns. Bri 166 B3
Manor Gdns. Hur 99 E3
Manor Green. Bri 166 B3
Manor Hall Rd. Sock 163 E4
Manor Hill. Bri 166 B3
Manor Paddock. Bri 166 B2
Manor Park. T W 8 B2
Manor Park Cl. Hai 132 C2
Manor Park Rd. Hai 132 C2
Manor Pl. Bri 166 B2
Manor Rd. Bex 160 A2
Manor Rd. Bri 166 B3
Manor Rd. Bur H 75 D2
Manor Rd. E Gri 2 A1
Manor Rd. East 175 F1
Manor Rd. Hast 140 C1
Manor Rd. Hor 109 E4
Manor Rd. Hur 99 E3
Manor Rd. Por S 143 F1
Manor Rd. Sea 181 F2
Manor Rd. T W 8 A2
Manor Rd N. Sea 181 F2
Manor Way. Bri 166 B3
Manor Way. Cro 39 E4
Manor Way. East 184 C4
Manor Way. Pole 174 C3
Manor Way. Uck 80 A4
Mansell Cl. Bex 159 D2
Mansers La. Low D 132 A2
Mansfield Rd. Hove 164 B4
Mansion Cl. Bur H 75 D2
Manston Way. Hast 140 B1
Mantell Cl. S Mal 127 D2
Manton Rd. Bri 146 B1
Manvers Rd. East 184 C2
Maple Ave. Bex 159 D2
Maple Cl. Bex 159 D2
Maple Cl. Bur H 75 D3
Maple Cl. Hay H 52 C2
Maple Cl. T W 8 C1
Maple Cl. Wood 167 E4
Maple Cl. Hai 154 C4
Maple Dr. Bur H 74 C3
Maple Dr. E Gri 2 C1
Maple Gdns. Hove 144 B1
Maple Hts. Hast 139 F4
Maple Leaf Cl. Newh 179 F4
Maple Rd. East 186 A4
Maple Wlk. Bex 159 D2
Maplehurst Cl. Hast 140 A4
Maplehurst Dr. Wfd 140 A4
Maplehurst Rd. East 175 D1
Maplehurst Rd. Hast 139 F4
Maplehurst Rd. Por S 143 F1
Maplehurst Rise. Hast 139 F4
Mapleleaf Gdns. Pole 174 C4
Marbles Rd. Newk 78 A4
Marchants Dr. Cam 96 B1
Marchants Rd. Hur 99 F3
Marchants Way. Bur H 74 B3
Marcia Cl. East 184 C4
Marcus Gdns. Hast 139 F3
Marden Cl. Wood 147 E1
Marden's Hill. Cro 27 D3
Marden's Hill. Fri G 26 C3
Maresfield Dr. Pev B 177 E3
Maresfield Rd. Bri 166 B3
Margaret St. Bri 165 F2
Margery Rd. Hove 164 A4
Marina. Bex 160 A2
Marina. Hast 161 F3
Marina Ct Ave. Bex 160 A2
Marina Way. Bri 166 B2
Marina Wlk. East 186 B4
Marine Ave. Hove 164 B3

Marine Ave. Pev B 177 E3
Marine Cl. Pev B 177 E3
Marine Cl. Salt 167 F1
Marine Cres. Sea 181 E1
Marine Dr. Bri 166 C2
Marine Dr. Oving 167 D1
Marine Dr. Rottn 167 E1
Marine Dr. Salt 167 E1
Marine Dr. Sea 180 C3
Marine Gdns. Bri 165 F2
Marine Par. Bri 166 A2
Marine Par. East 185 F2
Marine Par. Hast 162 C4
Marine Par. Sea 181 D2
Marine Par Rd. East 185 F2
Marine Rd. East 185 F2
Marine Rd. Pev B 177 D3
Marine Sq. Bri 166 A2
Marine Terr. Pev B 177 D3
Marine Terr Mews. Bri 166 A2
Marine View. Bri 165 F3
Marine View. Newh 179 F3
Mark Cl. Sea 182 A1
Mark La. Lew 127 D1
Market Pas. Hast 162 A3
Market Pas. Hast 162 C4
Market Pl. Hai 155 D4
Market Pl. Hai 155 D4
Market Pl. T W 8 C1
Market Rd. Bat 115 D3
Market Rd. Rye 95 D3
Market Rd. T W 8 C2
Market Sq. Bat 115 D3
Market Sq. Hai 155 D4
Market St. Bri 165 F3
Market St. Hast 162 A3
Market St. Lew 127 D1
Market St. Rye 95 D3
Market St. T W 8 C1
Markland Way. Uck 79 F4
Marklye La. Hea 83 F4
Markstakes Cnr. S Str 77 E1
Markstakes La. S Str 77 F1
Markwick Terr. Hast 161 F4
Marlborough Cl. East 176 A2
Marlborough Cl. Hast 139 F1
Marlborough Cl. T W 8 A2
Marlborough Dr. Bur H 75 D1
Marlborough Pl. Bri 165 F3
Marlborough St. Bri 165 E3
Marle Ave. Bur H 74 C2
Marley Cl. Bat 115 E2
Marley Gdns. Bat 115 E2
Marley La. Bat 115 F3
Marley La. Sed 116 A4
Marley Rd. Rye 94 C3
Marley Rise. Bat 115 E2
Marline Ave. Hast 139 F2
Marline Rd. Hast 139 F2
Marlow Ave. East 185 F3
Marlow Dr. Hast 139 F3
Marlow Dr. Hay H 53 D2
Marlow Rd. Bri 166 B2
Marlpit Cl. E Gri 2 B2
Marlpit Cl. Sha 22 C3
Marlpit The. Wad 31 E3
Marlpits La. Nin 136 C4
Marmion Rd. Hove 164 B4
Marsden Rd. East 176 B1
Marsh Quarter La. San 49 D2
Marshall La. Newh 180 A4
Marshall Rd. East 185 F4
Marshalls Row. Bri 165 F4
Marshfoot La. Hai 155 D4
Marshlands La. Hea 83 F4
Martello Ct. S Hei 170 A1
Martello Rd. East 186 A4
Martello Rd. Sea 181 E1
Martens Field. Rod 149 E1
Martin Rd. Hove 144 A1
Martineau La. Hast 141 E3
Martingale Cl. Hast 140 A3
Martins The. Cra D 11 D4
Martlet Ct. Cro 27 E1
Martlets The. Bro Ow 92 A2
Martlets The. Cro 27 E1
Martlets The. S Mal 127 D2
Martletts. Bex 160 B3
Martletts The. Rin 128 B3
Martyn's Cl. Oving 167 E2
Martyns Pl. E Gri 12 B4
Martyns Way. Bex 160 C3
Mary Stamford Green.
Rye H 95 F2
Maryan Ct. Hai 154 C4
Maryland Rd. T W 9 D1
Maskelyne Rd. Hers 134 C1
Mason Cl. E Gri 2 B1
Mason Rd. Rye 94 C3
Mason Rd. Sea 181 E2
Matlock Rd. East 190 B4
Matlock Rd. Hove 145 D1
Maunsell Rd. Hast 139 E3
Maurice Rd. Sea 181 E1
Maxfield Cl. East 184 C3
Maxfield La. Thr O 118 A1
May Rd. Bri 166 A4

May Tree Gdns. Bex 160 B3
May Tree Wlk. Hove 144 B1
Mayfair Cl. Pole 174 B2
Mayfield Ave. Pea 179 D3
Mayfield Cl. Bri 145 F3
Mayfield Cl. May 41 E1
Mayfield Cres. Bri 145 E3
Mayfield Flat. Blas 82 C4
Mayfield Flat. Five A 59 F1
Mayfield La. Hast 139 D1
Mayfield La. Wad 31 D2
Mayfield Park. Wad 31 D3
Mayfield Pl. East 185 F2
Mayfield Rd. T W 8 B2
Mayfield Way. Bex 160 B3
Mayflower Ct. Hay H 52 B2
Mayflower Rd. Hay H 52 B2
Mayflower Sq. Bri 165 F4
Maynards Mead. Cro 40 A4
Mayne Waye. Hast 140 C2
Mayo La. Bex 159 F4
Mayo Rd. Bri 165 F4
Mayo Rise. Bex 159 F4
Maypole Cotts. H Hur 57 F4
Maypole Rd. Ash W 13 E3
Maypole Rd. E Gri 2 A1
Maytham Rd. Rol L 51 D4
Mayview Cl. Bro O 61 F1
Maywood Ave. East 175 D1
Maze Hill. Hast 161 F4
Maze Hill Terr. Hast 161 F4
Mc Indoe Rd. E Gri 2 A2
Mc William Rd. Wood 147 D1
Meachants La. Willn 174 C1
Mead The. Bex 159 D2
Meadow Cl. Hast 139 E2
Meadow Cl. Hove 144 C2
Meadow Cl. Por S 143 F1
Meadow Cl. Rottn 167 E2
Meadow Cl. Sock 163 F4
Meadow Cres. Bex 160 A4
Meadow Dr. Hay H 52 C3
Meadow Hill Rd. T W 8 C2
Meadow La. Bur H 74 B1
Meadow La. Hay H 52 C3
Meadow Par. Rottn 167 E2
Meadow Pl. Rid 80 A3
Meadow Rd. Gro 17 D4
Meadow Rd. Hai 154 C3
Meadow Rd. T W 8 C2
Meadow The. Pem 10 B4
Meadow Way. Fai 142 B2
Meadow Way. Hea 83 F3
Meadow Way. Sea 181 F2
Meadow Wlk. Rob 65 F2
Meadowcroft Cl. E Gri 2 A1
Meadowlands Ave. East 175 D1
Meadows. Hass 100 B3
Meadows Rd. Willn 174 C1
Meadows The. Cro 27 E1
Meadows The. Hast 140 A3
Meadows The. Hove 144 A2
Meadows The. S Mal 127 E2
Meads Ave. Bex 159 D2
Meads Ave. Hove 144 A2
Meads Brow. East 190 A4
Meads Cl. Hove 144 A2
Meads Rd. Bex 159 D2
Meads Rd. East 185 E1
Meads Rd. Sea 181 E2
Meads St. East 190 B4
Meads The. Bri 146 A3
Meads The. E Gri 12 B4
Meads The. T W 9 D1
Meadway Cres. Hove 144 B1
Meadway Ct. Sock 163 D4
Meadway The. Bri 166 B3
Mealla Cl. S Mal 127 D2
Medina Pl. Hove 164 C3
Medina Terr. Hove 164 C3
Medina Villas. Hove 164 C3
Medmerry Hill. Bri 146 B1
Medway. Cro 28 A1
Medway. Hai 132 C1
Medway Dr. E Gri 12 A3
Medway Dr. For R 13 F1
Medway Rd. T W 8 C3
Meeching Rd. Newh 180 A4
Meeching Rise. Newh 180 A4
Meeds Rd. Bur H 74 C1
Meeting House La. Bri 165 F3
Megrims Hill. San 48 C3
Melbourne Rd. East 185 F2
Melbourne St. Bri 166 A4
Melfort Rd. Cro 27 D1
Melrose Ave. Por S 143 F1
Melrose Cl. Bri 146 A1
Melvill La. East 174 C1
Melville Rd. Hove 165 E4
Memorial The. Hast 162 B4
Mendip Ave. East 176 A3
Mendip Gdns. Hast 140 C2
Mendip Wlk. T W 9 D3
Mendow Rd. T W 8 A2
Menzies Rd. Hast 139 F1
Mercatoria. Hast 162 A3
Mercer St. T W 8 C3

Mercers. Lan G 7 D2
Mercread Rd. Sea 181 E2
Merevale. Bri 145 F1
Mereworth Rd. T W 8 C3
Meridian Way. E Gri 2 B2
Meridian Way. E Gri 2 B2
Merlin Cl. Hove 165 D4
Merlin Ct. Hai 155 E4
Merlin Way. E Gri 2 C2
Mermaid St. Rye 94 C3
Merrimede Cl. Hast 161 F4
Merrion Cl. T W 8 C4
Merrion Way. T W 8 C4
Merston Cl. Wood 167 E3
Metcalfe Ave. Newh 179 F4
Mews Rd. Hast 162 A3
Mews The. E Hoa 107 F3
Meyners Cl. Hove 144 A2
Michael Fields. For R 13 E1
Michel Cl. Fri 184 A1
Michel Dene Cl. Fri 184 A1
Michel Dene Rd. Fri 183 F1
Michel Gr. East 185 E2
Michele Cl. Hast 139 F1
Michelham Cl. East 175 F2
Michelham Rd. Uck 57 E1
Michelson Cl. Hast 139 E2
Middle Dr. Mar 56 C3
Middle Field. Pem 10 B4
Middle Furlong. Sea 181 E2
Middle Par. East 185 F1
Middle Rd. Bel G 19 F3
Middle Rd. Bri 145 E1
Middle Rd. Hast 141 D2
Middle St. Bri 165 E3
Middle St. Fal 147 D3
Middle St. Hast 162 B4
Middle St. Por S 163 F3
Middle Way. Bur H 74 C2
Middle Way. Lew 126 C1
Middle Wlk. T W 9 E4
Middleham Cl. Rin 128 A2
Middlesex Rd. Bex 160 A2
Middleton Ave. Hove 164 A3
Middleton Dr. East 186 B4
Middleton Rise. Bri 146 B3
Middleway. Win H 134 C3
Midfield Cl. Bur H 74 C2
Midfield Dr. Bur H 74 C2
Midfields Wlk. Bur H 74 C2
Midhurst Rd. East 175 E1
Midhurst Rise. Bri 145 F3
Midhurst Wlk. Hove 144 B2
Midway Rd. Wood 167 D4
Midway The. T W 8 A1
Mighell St. Bri 165 F3
Milcote Ave. Hove 164 B4
Mildenhall Dr. Hast 139 F2
Mildmay Cl. Rin 128 A3
Mildmay Rd. Lew 126 C1
Mile Oak Cres. Sock 143 E1
Mile Oak Gdns. Por S 143 F1
Mile Oak Rd. Por S 143 E2
Mile Oak Rd. Sock 143 E1
Milfoil Dr. East 175 F2
Military Rd. Iden 72 B3
Military Rd. Rye 95 D4
Mill Brooks. S Cha 103 D4
Mill Cl. E Gri 12 B4
Mill Cl. Fri 183 F1
Mill Cl. Hast 141 E2
Mill Cl. Hea 83 E4
Mill Cl. Por S 144 A1
Mill Cl. Rin 128 B3
Mill Cl. S Cha 103 D4
Mill Cl. Wfd 117 E3
Mill Cl. Willn 174 B2
Mill Cres. Cro 27 E2
Mill Dr. Cro 27 E2
Mill Dr. Hove 144 C1
Mill Dr. Sea 181 F2
Mill Dro. Rid 80 A3
Mill Dro. Sea 180 C3
Mill Gap Rd. East 185 E2
Mill Gdns. Hea 83 F3
Mill Gdns. Rin 128 A3
Mill Green Rd. Hay H 52 B3
Mill Hill Cl. Hay H 52 B4
Mill La. Bar 104 A1
Mill La. Clay 123 E4
Mill La. Cro 27 E1
Mill La. Dor 2 B4
Mill La. E Hoa 107 F3
Mill La. Fel 1 B3
Mill La. Hast 141 E3
Mill La. Hooe 136 B1
Mill La. Peas 70 B2
Mill La. Por S 144 A1
Mill La. Pye 123 D4
Mill La. Rid 80 A3
Mill La. Rod 169 D4
Mill La. S Cha 103 D4
Mill La. Wfd 117 E3
Mill Mead. Rin 128 B3
Mill Path. Rin 128 B3
Mill Rd. Bri 145 D3
Mill Rd. Bur H 74 C2
Mill Rd. East 185 D3

Mill Rd. Hai 155 D3
Mill Rd. Hea 83 E4
Mill Rd. Rin 128 A3
Mill Rd. Rye 95 D4
Mill Rd. S Mal 127 E2
Mill Rd. Sock 163 F4
Mill Rd. Winc 120 B4
Mill Rise. Bri 145 D3
Mill Rise. Rob 65 F2
Mill St. Fal 147 D4
Mill Stream Meadow.
Hay H 52 A4
Mill View. Rin 128 A2
Mill View Cl. Whm 176 A3
Mill View Rd. Bex 159 F4
Mill Way. E Gri 12 B4
Mill Way. Willn 174 B2
Mill Wood. Bur H 74 C2
Milland Cl. Bex 160 B3
Milland Rd. Hai 132 C1
Millbank. Bur H 74 C2
Millberg Rd. Sea 182 A2
Millbrook Cl. Hor 109 F4
Millbrook Gdns. East 184 C3
Millbrook Rd. Cro 27 F2
Millcroft. Bri 145 D3
Millcroft Ave. Sock 143 E1
Millcroft Gdns. Sock 143 E1
Millcross Rd. Por S 143 F1
Milldown Rd. Sea 181 E2
Miller's Hill. Wfd 117 E3
Miller's Rd. Bri 145 E1
Millers Way. Bur H 74 C2
Millfield. Nin 136 C3
Millfield Cl. Sea 181 F2
Millfield Cotts. Bri 166 A2
Millfield Rise. Bex 160 A2
Millham Cl. Bex 159 E3
Millrace The. Pole 174 B2
Millstream Cl. Asht 6 A1
Millstream Ct. Asht 6 A1
Millstream Gdns. Willn 174 B2
Millward Rd. Pev B 177 D2
Millwood Cl. Uck 57 D2
Millwood La. Mar 57 D2
Millwood La. Uck 57 D2
Millwood Rd. Bex 159 F4
Millyard Cres. Wood 167 D4
Milner Rd. Bri 146 A1
Milnthorpe Rd. East 190 B4
Milnthorpe Rd. Hove 164 B4
Milton Cres. E Gri 12 A3
Milton Cres. East 185 D2
Milton Dr. Sock 163 E4
Milton Dr. T W 9 D4
Milton Rd. Bri 165 F4
Milton Rd. East 185 D2
Milton Rd. Hay H 52 A3
Milton St. Hank 175 F4
Milward Cres. Hast 162 C4
Milward Rd. Hast 162 C4
Mimosa Cl. Pole 174 C4
Minnels The. Key 100 C2
Minsted Sq. Bex 159 D1
Minster Cl. Pole 174 C4
Mint The. Rye 94 C3
Mistley Cl. Bex 160 C3
Mitchelldean. Pea 169 D1
Mitten Rd. Bex 160 A2
Moat Croft Rd. East 185 E2
Moat Farm. T W 18 C4
Moat La. Wald 82 A1
Moat Cl. Wfd 116 C2
Moat Rd. E Gri 2 B1
Modena Rd. Hove 164 B4
Molesworth St. Hove 164 B4
Molyneux Almshouses. T W 7 F2
Molyneux Park Rd. T W 8 B2
Mona Rd. East 185 F2
Monarch Gdns. Sea 181 F3
Monastery Gdns. Rot 40 C4
Monceux Rd. East 185 D2
Monceux Rd. Hers 134 B3
Monckton Way. Kin L 148 B3
Monger's Mead. Bar C 104 B2
Monk Cl. Bri 146 A3
Monks La. Lew 149 D4
Monks La. Wad 31 F4
Monks Walk. Winc 120 B4
Monks Way. Norm 68 C4
Monks Way. S Mal 127 D2
Monmouth St. Hove 164 C4
Monson Rd. T W 8 C2
Montacute Gdns. T W 8 B1
Montacute Rd. Lew 148 C4
Montacute Rd. T W 8 B1
Montacute Way. Uck 80 A4
Montague Cl. S Sea 163 D4
Montague Pl. Bri 166 A2
Montague St. Bri 166 A2
Montague Way. Whm 176 B3
Montargis Way. Cro 27 F1
Montefiore Rd. Hove 165 E4
Monteith Cl. Lan G 7 F2
Monterey Gdns. Bex 159 E2
Montes Hill. Hay H 53 E4
Monteswood La. Hay H 53 F4
Monteswood La. Hor K 53 F4

Montford Cl. S Sea 163 D4
Montfort Cl. Whm 176 B3
Montford Rd. Whm 176 B3
Montgomery Rd. Hast 141 D3
Montgomery Rd. T W 8 C4
Montgomery St. Hove 164 C4
Montpelier Cres. Bri 165 E3
Montpelier Pl. Bri 165 E3
Montpelier Rd. Bri 165 E3
Montpelier St. Bri 165 E3
Montpelier Terr. Bri 165 E3
Montpelier Villas. Bri 165 E3
Montreal St. Bri 165 F3
Moon's La. Dor 3 D4
Moor La. Gly 128 C2
Moor La. Rin 128 C2
Moor La. Wfd 117 E2
Moor Pl. E Gri 2 A1
Moor Rd. Wfd 117 E2
Moor The. The M 47 E4
Moore Park. Hai 155 D4
Moore's La. Bec 92 B4
Moorhurst Rd. Hast 139 E3
Moorings The. S Sea 163 D3
Moorland Cl. Nin 136 C3
Moorsite. Wfd 117 E2
Morecambe Rd. Bri 145 F3
Morestead. Pea 169 D1
Morgan Cl. Bex 159 F4
Morlais Pl. Winc B 120 C3
Morlais Ridge. Winc B 120 C3
Morland Dr. Lam 21 F3
Morley Cl. Lew 148 C4
Morley St. Bri 165 F3
Morningside Cl. Sea 181 E4
Mornington Cres. Hove 164 C4
Morris Rd. Lew 127 E1
Mortain Park. Hai 175 D4
Mortain Rd. Whm 176 B3
Mortimer Gdns. Willn 174 B2
Mortimer Rd. East 185 F3
Mortimer Rd. Hove 164 B4
Morton Rd. E Gri 12 B4
Moscow Rd. Hast 141 D1
Motcombe La. East 185 D2
Motcombe Rd. East 185 D2
Motte Field. Hart 15 E2
Mottins Hill. Cro 40 A4
Moulsecoomb Way. Bri 146 B2
Mount Caburn Cres. Pea 169 D1
Mount Dr. Salt 168 A1
Mount Edgcumbe Rd. T W 8 C2
Mount Ephraim. T W 8 C2
Mount Ephraim Rd. T W 8 C2
Mount Harry Rd. Lew 126 C1
Mount Idol View. Bex 159 F4
Mount Joy. Bat 115 D3
Mount Pl. Lew 127 D1
Mount Pleasant. Blas 81 F3
Mount Pleasant. Bri 165 F3
Mount Pleasant. Cro 40 A4
Mount Pleasant. Hast 162 A3
Mount Pleasant. Lam 21 E3
Mount Pleasant. Lew 127 D1
Mount Pleasant. Rid 80 A3
Mount Pleasant. Spi 104 B3
Mount Pleasant. Wad 31 E3
Mount Pleasant Ave. T W 8 C2
Mount Pleasant Cres. Hast ... 140 B1
Mount Pleasant La. Lam 21 F3
Mount Pleasant Rd. Hast 140 C1
Mount Pleasant Rd. T W 8 C2
Mount Rd. East 190 B4
Mount Rd. Hast 141 D1
Mount Rd. Newh 170 B1
Mount Sion. T W 8 C1
Mount St. Bat 115 D3
Mount St. Lew 149 D4
Mount The. Hai 155 D3
Mount The. Hast 161 F4
Mount The. Uck 80 A4
Mount View Terr. Hai 155 D3
Mount Zion Pl. Bri 165 E3
Mountbatten Cl. Hast 141 D3
Mountbatten Dr. East 186 B4
Mountfield Gdns. T W 8 C2
Mountfield La. Mou 88 A4
Mountfield Rd. East 175 E1
Mountfield Rd. Lew 149 D4
Mountfield Rd. T W 8 C2
Mountfields. Bri 146 A1
Mountney Dr. Pev B 177 E4
Mountney Rd. East 185 D2
Mountreed. Five A 59 F4
Moy Ave. East 185 F3
Moyne Cl. Hove 144 B1
Muirfield Rise. Hast 161 E4
Mulberry Cl. Bex 159 D2
Mulberry Cl. Bri 145 E2
Mulberry Cl. East 175 E2
Mulberry Cl. S Sea 143 D1
Mulberry La. Dit 101 D2
Mulberry Way. Hea 83 F3
Munns Dr. Bur H 74 C2
Munster Green. Bar C 104 B2
Murdock Rd. Hast 162 B4
Murray Ave. Newh 180 A4
Musgrave Ave. E Gri 12 B4

Mushroom Field. Kin L 148 B3
Muster Green. Hay H 52 A2
Muster Green N. Hay H 52 A2
Muster Green S. Hay H 52 A2
Mutton Hall Hill. Hea 83 F4
Mutton Hall La. Hea 83 F4
Mutton Hill. Dor 2 C4
Myrtle Rd. Cro 27 E1
Myrtle Rd. East 186 A3

Namrik Mews. Hove 164 C3
Nan Kemps Grave. Kin L 148 B3
Nan Tucks La. Bux 58 A1
Nanson Rd. Bri 146 A3
Naomi Cl. East 185 E1
Napier Rd. Hast 139 E2
Napier Rd. T W 9 D1
Nash La. Sca H 53 F2
Natal Rd. Bri 146 A1
Neale Cl. E Gri 1 C2
Neath Rd. Cam 97 F1
Neaves La. Rin 128 C2
Neill's Cl. Newh 180 A4
Neills Rd. Lam 21 D1
Nellington Rd. T W 7 F2
Nelson Dr. East 186 B3
Nelson Rd. Hast 140 C1
Nelson Rd. T W 9 D1
Nesbitt Rd. Bri 146 A1
Nether La. Nut 37 D2
Netherfield. East 176 B1
Netherfield Green. Wood 167 E4
Netherfield Hill. Bat 114 C4
Netherfield Rd. Net 88 B1
Netherfield Way. Net 88 A1
Netherwood Cl. Hast 140 B3
Nevill Ave. East 175 E1
Nevill Ave. Hove 144 B1
Nevill Cl. Hove 144 C1
Nevill Cotts. Dit 101 D1
Nevill Cres. Lew 126 C1
Nevill Gate. T W 8 C1
Nevill Gdns. Hove 144 C1
Nevill Green. Uck 57 D1
Nevill Park. T W 8 A2
Nevill Pl. Hove 144 C1
Nevill Rd. Cro 27 E2
Nevill Rd. Hove 144 C1
Nevill Rd. Lew 126 C1
Nevill Rd. Rottn 167 E1
Nevill Rd. Uck 57 D1
Nevill Ridge. T W 8 A2
Nevill St. T W 8 C1
Nevill Way. Hove 144 C1
Neville Rd. East 185 F2
Neville Rd. Pea 179 D4
New Barn Cl. Hast 155 D3
New Barn Cl. Por S 143 F1
New Barn La. Rid 80 A3
New Barn Rd. Rottn 167 E2
New Church Rd. Hove 164 B4
New College Cl. East 176 A2
New Cut. Mou 89 D3
New Dorset St. Bri 165 E3
New England La. Sed 116 B3
New England Rd. Bri 165 E4
New England Rd. Hay H 52 B3
New England Rd. T W 8 C4
New England Rise. Por S 143 F2
New England St. Bri 165 F4
New Farthingdale. Dor 2 C4
New Lydd Rd. Cam 96 B1
New Park Ave. Bex 160 A2
New Pl. East 185 D2
New Pl. Rid 80 A3
New Pond Hill. Hea 83 D3
New Rd. Bec 69 D2
New Rd. Bri 165 F3
New Rd. Cro 27 E2
New Rd. Dit 100 C1
New Rd. East 185 F2
New Rd. Ford 6 C4
New Rd. Gly 128 A2
New Rd. Hast 141 D1
New Rd. Hel 133 D2
New Rd. Key 100 B1
New Rd. Lew 127 D1
New Rd. Mag D 133 D2
New Rd. Mill C 68 C2
New Rd. Newh 180 A4
New Rd. Pole 174 C3
New Rd. Rid 80 A2
New Rd. Rin 128 A2
New Rd. Rot 40 C4
New Rd. Rye 95 D3
New Rd. Tow R 41 D4
New Steine. Bri 165 F2
New Steine Mews. Bri 165 F2
New Upperton Rd. East 185 E2
New Way La. Hur 99 F2
New Winchelsea Rd. Rye 94 C2
Newark Pl. Bri 165 F3
Newbury Rd. Cou W 32 A4
Newcomen Rd. T W 8 C3
Newells Cl. Wood 147 E1
Newfield La. Newh 180 A4
Newfield Rd. Newh 180 A4
Newgate Rd. Hast 140 A1
Newham Rd. Hea 83 F4

Newhaven Rd. Sea 180 C3
Newhaven St. Bri 165 F3
Newhaven Wlk. Hast 139 F2
Newick Cl. Sea 182 A1
Newick Dr. Newk 78 A4
Newick Hill. Newk 78 A4
Newick La. Hea 61 D1
Newick La. May 60 C4
Newick Rd. Bri 146 B3
Newick Rd. East 185 D3
Newlands. Lan G 7 F2
Newlands Ave. Bex 159 F3
Newlands Cl. Hast 140 B3
Newlands Cl. Key 100 C2
Newlands Cres. E Gri 2 A1
Newlands Rd. Rottn 167 F1
Newlands Rd. T W 8 C4
Newlands Rise. T W 8 C4
Newlands Way. T W 8 C4
Newmans Way. Hast 141 D2
Newmarket Rd. Bri 166 A4
Newmarket Terr. Bri 166 A4
Newport Rd. Bur H 74 B2
Newport St. Bri 165 F4
Newtimber Dr. Por S 143 F1
Newton Ave. E Gri 12 B3
Newton Park. Hai 155 D4
Newton Rd. Hay H 53 D4
Newton Rd. Lew 126 C1
Newton Rd. Pea 179 D4
Newton Rd. T W 8 C2
Newtown Cl. Hay H 52 C4
Newtown Crt. Hay H 52 B3
Newtown Rd. Hove 164 C4
Nightingale Cl. E Gri 12 A4
Nightingale Cl. Hast 176 A1
Nightingale La. Bur H 100 C4
Nightingale Rise. Rid 80 A2
Nile St. Bri 165 F3
Ninfield Pl. Bri 166 B4
Ninfield Rd. Bex 159 F4
Ninfield Rd. Lun C 137 E1
Nizells Ave. Hove 165 E4
Noahs Ark La. Hay H 53 D4
Noel Green. Bur H 74 C2
Noel Rise. Bur H 74 C2
Nolan Rd. Wood 167 E4
Norbury Cl. Cro 27 F1
Nore Rd. Newh 179 F3
Norfolk Bldgs. Bri 165 E3
Norfolk Cl. Bex 159 F4
Norfolk Dr. Hast 139 E2
Norfolk Mews. Bri 165 E3
Norfolk Pl. Bri 165 E3
Norfolk Rd. Bri 165 E3
Norfolk Rd. T W 8 C1
Norfolk Sq. Bri 165 E3
Norfolk St. Bri 165 E3
Norfolk Terr. Bri 165 E3
Norfolk Way. Uck 80 A4
Norlington Fields. Rin 128 A3
Norlington La. Rin 128 A4
Norman Cl. Bat 115 E2
Norman Cl. Sea 180 C3
Norman Rd. Bur H 74 C2
Norman Rd. Hast 162 A4
Norman Rd. Hove 164 B3
Norman Rd. Newh 180 A4
Norman Rd. Pev B 177 D2
Norman Rd. T W 8 C3
Normandale. Bex 159 F2
Normandy Rd. Hast 140 A2
Normansland. Fair 37 F1
Normanton St. Bri 166 A4
Norstead Gdns. Sgh 8 C4
North Ave. East 184 C3
North Bank. Hass 100 B2
North Beeches Rd. Cro 27 F1
North Camp La. Sea 181 E3
North Cl. Pole 174 C4
North Cl. Por S 143 F1
North Common Rd. N Cha 76 B3
North Common Rd. Plu G 76 B3
North Common Rd. Wiv G 76 B3
North Cres. Hai 154 C4
North Ct. Hass 100 B2
North Ct. Lew 127 E1
North Dr. Bri 166 A3
North End. Dit 101 D2
North Farm La. T W 9 D4
North Farm Rd. Sgh 9 D4
North Gdns. Bri 165 E3
North Heath Cl. Hai 133 D1
North La. Por S 143 F2
North La. Thr O 118 B3
North La. W Hoa 22 B3
North Pl. Bri 165 F3
North Quay Rd. Newh 180 A4
North Rd. Alfn 172 B2
North Rd. Bex 160 A4
North Rd. Bod G 112 A1
North Rd. Bri 165 E1
North Rd. Bri 165 F3
North Rd. Hast 140 A1
North Rd. Hay H 52 C4
North Rd. Pev B 177 D3
North Rd. Por S 143 F1
North Rd. Rin 128 A3

North Row. Uck 80 A4
North Salts. Rye 95 D3
North St. Alfn 172 C2
North St. Bri 165 F3
North St. Cowd 4 C3
North St. Cro H 82 B3
North St. East 185 F1
North St. Hai 154 C4
North St. Hast 162 A4
North St. Hel 132 C4
North St. Lew 127 D1
North St. Low H 132 C3
North St. May 41 F2
North St. Por S 164 A4
North St. Pun T 85 D3
North St. Rot 40 C4
North St. T W 9 D2
North St. Wald 82 B2
North St. Winc 120 B4
North St Quadrant. Bri 165 E3
North Trade Rd. Bat 114 C2
North Way. Lew 126 C1
North Way. Newh 180 A4
North Way. Sea 181 E3
Northampton Way. Hast 139 F2
Northbridge. Sale 65 F3
Northcliffe Cl. Sea 181 E2
Northcote La. Pea 168 C1
Northdown Cl. Newh 180 A3
Northdown Rd. Newh 180 A3
Northease Cl. Hove 144 A1
Northease Dr. Hove 144 B2
Northease Gdns. Hove 144 B2
Northern Ave. Pole 174 C4
Northfield. Pole 174 B3
Northfield Cl. Sea 181 E3
Northfield Cotts. Isf 105 D4
Northfield Rise. Hove 144 A2
Northfield Rise. Rottn 167 F1
Northfield Way. Bri 145 F2
Northfields. Spe 7 F3
Northiam Rd. Bro O W 91 F3
Northiam Rd. East 185 D2
Northiam Rd. Mill C 91 F3
Northlands Ave. Hay H 52 C2
Northridge. Norm 68 C4
Northway. Bur H 75 D2
Northwood Ave. Salt 168 B1
Norton Cl. Hove 164 C3
Norton Dr. Wood 147 E1
Norton Rd. Hove 164 C3
Norton Terr. Newh 180 B4
Norway Rd. East 186 A3
Norway St. Por S 164 A4
Norwich Cl. Bri 146 C1
Norwich Dr. Bri 146 C1
Nottidge Rd. T W 8 A1
Novington La. E Chi 102 C2
Nunnery La. Ford 6 B4
Nursery Cl. Hai 155 D4
Nursery Cl. Hay H 52 A3
Nursery Cl. Hur 99 E4
Nursery Cl. Pole 174 C3
Nursery Cl. Por S 143 F2
Nursery Field. Bux 58 A2
Nursery La. Blas 82 B4
Nursery La. Fair 37 F1
Nursery La. Had D 59 E1
Nursery La. Mar 56 C3
Nursery La. Nut 37 D2
Nursery La. Rid 80 A2
Nursery La. Win H 134 C3
Nursery Path. Hai 154 C4
Nursery Rd. Sgh 8 C4
Nursery The. Bur H 75 D2
Nursery Way. Hea 83 E4
Nutbourne Cl. East 176 B1
Nuthatch Rd. East 176 A1
Nuthurst Cl. Bri 166 B3
Nuthurst Pl. Bri 166 B3
Nutley Ave. Salt 178 A4
Nutley Cl. Hove 144 B2
Nutley Cl. Rye 94 C3
Nye Cl. Cro 27 E1
Nye La. Dit 101 E1
Nye La. Wmes 124 A4
Nye Rd. Bur H 75 D2
Nyetimber Hill. Bri 146 B1

Oak Bank. Hay H 52 B4
Oak Cl. Bri 145 E2
Oak Croft. E Gri 12 C4
Oak Hall Park. Bur H 74 C1
Oak La. Lydd 98 C3
Oak Pas. Hast 162 C4
Oak Rd. T W 9 D4
Oak Tree Cl. T W 8 C1
Oak Tree Cotts. Dan 35 F2
Oak Tree Ct. Uck 80 A4
Oak Tree La. East 176 A2
Oak Tree Way. Hai 133 D1
Oakapple Rd. Sock 143 E1
Oakdale Rd. Hay H 52 B2
Oakdale Rd. T W 8 B2
Oakdene Ave. Por S 143 E2
Oakdene Cl. Por S 143 E2
Oakdene Cres. Por S 143 E2
Oakdene Gdns. Por S 143 E2

Oakdene Rise. Por S 143 E2
Oakdene Way. Por S 143 E2
Oakenfield. Bur H 74 B3
Oakfield. Hay H 52 C4
Oakfield Ct Rd. T W 9 D2
Oakfield Rd. Hast 141 D2
Oakfield The. Rye 94 C4
Oakfield Way. Bex 159 D3
Oakfield Way. E Gri 2 B2
Oakhill Cotts. Four O 70 A2
Oakhill Dr. Bro O W 91 F3
Oakhurst. Hay H 52 A4
Oakhurst Cl. Hast 140 B3
Oakhurst Dr. Cro 27 F2
Oakhurst Gdns. E Gri 2 A1
Oakhurst Rd. Bat 115 D4
Oakland Dr. Rob 65 D2
Oaklands. Whm 176 B3
Oaklands Ave. Salt 168 A1
Oaklands Cl. Pole 174 C3
Oaklands Rd. Gro 16 C3
Oaklands Rd. Hay H 52 A3
Oaklands Way. Hai 154 C3
Oaklea Cl. Hast 140 A2
Oaklea Way. Uck 79 F4
Oakleaf Dr. Pole 174 C4
Oakleigh Rd. Bex 159 D2
Oakley Cl. E Gri 12 C4
Oakmead Rd. Bur H 74 B1
Oakmede Way. Rin 128 A3
Oakroyd Cl. Bur H 75 D3
Oaks Forstal. San 49 D3
Oaks The. E Gri 12 C4
Oaks The. Hea 83 F3
Oaktree. Bar C 104 B2
Oakwood Ave. Bex 159 F4
Oakwood Cl. Bur H 74 C1
Oakwood Cl. Hast 140 B2
Oakwood Dr. Bur H 74 C1
Oakwood Dr. Uck 80 B4
Oakwood Park. Nut 37 D3
Oakwood Rise. Bur H 75 D1
Oakwood Rise. T W 9 D4
Oast Cl. T W 9 D4
Oast House Field. Ick 119 E3
Oast House Rd. Ick 119 E3
Oathall Ave. Hay H 52 B3
Oathall Rd. Hay H 52 B3
Oban Rd. Hast 139 F2
Observatory View. Hai 155 E4
Ochiltree Cl. Hast 140 C2
Ochiltree Rd. Hast 140 C2
Ockenden Way. Hass 100 B2
Ockley Hill. Key 100 C3
Ockley La. Bur H 100 C4
Ockley La. Key 100 C3
Ockley Way. Key 100 C3
Ocklynge Ave. East 185 D2
Ocklynge Cl. Bex 159 D3
Ocklynge Rd. East 185 D2
Offa Rd. Hast 141 D2
Offham Cl. Sea 181 E3
Offham Rd. Lew 126 C1
Okehurst Rd. East 185 D2
Old Barn Cl. East 174 C1
Old Barn Way. Por S 163 F4
Old Camp Rd. East 185 D1
Old Church Rd. Hast 139 F2
Old Court Cl. Bri 145 E2
Old Dr. Pole 174 B3
Old Dro. East 176 A2
Old Farm Rd. Bex 159 F3
Old Farm Rd. Bri 145 E3
Old Foord Cl S Cha 103 D4
Old Forest La. Rot 40 B4
Old Forewood La. Crow 138 B4
Old Forge La. Fair 37 F1
Old Forge La. Mar 56 B4
Old Gardens Cl. T W 18 C4
Old Harrow Rd. Hast 139 F2
Old House Gdns. Hast 140 B2
Old House La. Ford 7 D3
Old House La. Lan G 7 D2
Old Humphrey Ave. Hast 162 C4
Old La. Cro 27 D2
Old La. Cro 27 F1
Old London Rd. Bri 145 E3
Old London Rd. Hast 141 D2
Old Lydd Rd. Cam 96 B1
Old Malling Way. S Mal 127 D2
Old Manor Cl. Bex 160 A2
Old Mansion Cl. East 184 C4
Old Mill Cl. Bri 145 E3
Old Mill Cl. Hai 132 C2
Old Mill La. Willn 174 B2
Old Motcombe Mews. East ... 185 D2
Old Orchard Pl. Hai 154 C4
Old Orchard Rd. East 185 E1
Old Rd. E Gri 2 B1
Old Rd. Hers 133 F2
Old Rd. Mag D 133 F2
Old Rectory Gdns. Sock 163 D4
Old River Way. Winc B 120 C4
Old Roar Rd. Hast 140 A2
Old Shoreham Rd. Hove 164 B4
Old Shoreham Rd. Por S 163 F4
Old Shoreham Rd. Soc 143 E1
Old Shoreham Rd. Sock 163 E4
Old Station Rd. Wad 31 E3

Old Steine. Bri

Prince Albert St. Bri

Old Steine. Bri 165 F3
Old Swan La. Hai 155 D3
Old Timbers La. Rid 80 A3
Old Top Rd. Hast 141 D2
Old Wickham La. Hay H 52 B4
Old Willingdon Rd. Fri 183 F1
Old Wish Rd. East 185 E1
Oldaker Rd. Newk 78 A4
Olde Place Mews. Rottn 167 E1
Oldfield Ave. Willn 174 C2
Oldfield Cres. Hai 132 C1
Oldfield Cres. Sock 163 D4
Oldfield Rd. Willn 174 C2
Oldlands Ave. Key 100 C2
Oldlands Hill. Fair 38 A1
Oldlands Hill. Uck 38 A1
Olive Rd. Hove 164 A4
Oliver Cl. Cro 27 F1
Olives Meadow. Uck 80 A4
Olives Yd. Uck 80 A4
Olivier Cl. Bri 166 A3
Onslow Rd. Hove 145 D1
Orange Row. Bri 165 F3
Orchard Ave. Hove 144 C1
Orchard Cl. Hast 140 B1
Orchard Cl. Hay H 52 A4
Orchard Cl. Sca H 53 E2
Orchard Cl. Sock 163 E4
Orchard Cl. T W 9 D3
Orchard Gdns. Hove 144 C1
Orchard La. Dit 101 D2
Orchard La. Key 100 B2
Orchard Rd. Bex 160 A3
Orchard Rd. Bur H 74 B2
Orchard Rd. Hove 144 C1
Orchard Rd. S Mal 127 C4
Orchard Rise. Gro 16 C4
Orchard The. Bro O W 91 F2
Orchard The. Hass 100 B2
Orchard Way. Bur H 74 B2
Orchard Way. E 2 B1
Orchard Way. Hay H 52 A4
Orchard Way. Hur 99 E3
Orchid Cl. East 175 F2
Orchid Park. Hay H 53 D2
Oriental Pl. Bri 165 E3
Orion Cl. Hai 155 D4
Ormerod Ave. Hast 139 F2
Ormerod Cl. Hay H 52 B3
Orpen Rd. Hove 145 D1
Osbern Cl. Bex 159 D2
Osborne Cl. Hast 140 B1
Osborne Hill. Cro 40 A4
Osborne Rd. Bri 145 F1
Osborne Rd. Cro 40 A4
Osborne Rd. East 184 C2
Osborne Villas. Hove 164 C3
Osmers Hill. Wad 31 F4
Osmond Rd. Hove 165 E4
Osmunda Bank. Dor P 2 B3
Otham Ct La. Pole 174 C4
Otham Park. Hai 155 D4
Otham Rd. East 175 F1
Otteham Cl. Pole 174 C3
Oulton Cl. East 175 F2
Ousedale Cl. Lew 126 C1
Outlook Ave. Pea 179 E3
Outlook The. Fri 183 F1
Oval Cl. Pea 169 D1
Over St. Bri 165 F3
Overdown Rise. Por S 143 E2
Overhill. Sock 143 E1
Overhill Dr. Bri 145 E3
Overhill Gdns. Bri 145 E3
Overhill Way. Bri 145 E3
Overton Shaw. E Gri 2 B2
Ovingdean Cl. Oving 167 D3
Ovingdean Rd. Oving 167 D3
Ownside. Bri 145 D3
Ox Lea. Lan G 7 F2
Oxbottom Cl. Chay 77 F3
Oxdean Gdns. Willn 174 C2
Oxenbridge La. Etc 65 D4
Oxford Ct. Bri 165 F4
Oxford Pl. Bri 165 F4
Oxford Rd. East 185 F2
Oxford Rd. Hast 139 F2
Oxford St. Bri 165 F4

Packham Way. Bur H 74 B2
Paddock Cl. Bex 160 A3
Paddock Cl. Ford 6 C3
Paddock Gdns. E Gri 12 B4
Paddock Gdns. Willn 174 B2
Paddock La. Lew 127 D1
Paddock Rd. Hast 140 A3
Paddock Rd. Lew 127 D1
Paddock The. East 175 E1
Paddock The. Hove 145 D1
Paddock The. Mar 56 C2
Paddock The. Norm 68 C4
Paddock The. Pem 10 A4
Paddockhall Rd. Hay H 52 B4
Paddocks The. Cowd 4 C4
Paddocks The. Hai 132 C1
Paddocks The. Plu 102 B3
Paddocks The. Rod 169 D4
Padgham La. Chur 112 A4
Pages Ave. Bex 159 E1

Pages Cl. Hea 83 E4
Pages Hill. Hea 83 E4
Pages La. Bex 159 E2
Pagets The. Newk 78 A4
Pagham Cl. East 175 F2
Paine's Twitten. Lew 149 D4
Pains Flat. Bur H 74 A4
Palace Pl. Bri 165 F3
Palesgate Rd. Cro 28 A1
Palliser Cl. East 186 B3
Palma Cl. Pole 174 C4
Palmeira Ave. Hove 165 D3
Palmeira Pl. Hove 165 D4
Palmeira Sq. Hove 165 D3
Palmerston Rd. Newh 170 C1
Pankhurst Ave. Bri 166 A3
Pankhurst Cl. Bex 159 F4
Pankhurst Rise. Bex 159 F4
Pannel La. Pett 119 E1
Pannell Cl. E Gri 2 A1
Pantiles The. T W 8 C1
Parade The. E Gri 1 C2
Parade The. Pev B 177 E3
Paradise Cl. East 185 D1
Paradise Dr. East 185 D1
Parham Cl. Bri 166 A3
Park Ave. Bex 159 F2
Park Ave. East 185 D4
Park Ave. Hast 140 A4
Park Ave. Hove 164 B4
Park Ave. Key 100 C1
Park Ave. Pea 178 C4
Park Cl. Bri 146 B3
Park Cl. Bur H 74 B2
Park Cl. East 185 D2
Park Cl. Hai 154 C3
Park Cl. Hast 140 A2
Park Cl. Hove 144 B2
Park Cl. Hur 99 F3
Park Cl. Por S 143 F1
Park Cres. Cro 27 E2
Park Cres. For R 13 F1
Park Cres. Hast 140 A1
Park Cres. Por S 163 F4
Park Cres. Rottn 167 E1
Park Cres Pl. Bri 165 F4
Park Cres Rd. Bri 165 F4
Park Cres Terr. Bri 165 F4
Park Croft. Pole 174 C4
Park Croft. Willn 174 B2
Park Ct. Bri 145 E3
Park Dr. Hast 140 A1
Park Dr Cl. Newh 170 B1
Park Farm Cl. Etc 64 C4
Park Gate. Hai 133 D2
Park Hill. Bri 166 A3
Park La. Ash W 13 D3
Park La. Bat 115 D2
Park La. Bex 159 F3
Park La. Cro 27 E2
Park La. East 185 D4
Park La. Sock 163 D4
Park La. Wha 89 F3
Park Par. Hay H 52 B2
Park Rd. Bex 159 F2
Park Rd. Bri 146 B3
Park Rd. Bur H 74 C2
Park Rd. Cro 27 E2
Park Rd. Dor P 2 B3
Park Rd. E Gri 2 A1
Park Rd. For R 13 F1
Park Rd. Hai 132 C2
Park Rd. Hay H 52 B2
Park Rd. Hea 84 A3
Park Rd. Hel 132 C2
Park Rd. Lew 127 D1
Park Rd. Pea 179 E3
Park Rd. Rottn 167 E1
Park Rd. Sea 181 D2
Park Rd. T W 8 C2
Park Rise. Hove 144 B2
Park Road Terr. Bri 165 F3
Park Shaw. Sed 90 B1
Park St. Bri 166 A3
Park St. Fal 147 D3
Park St. Lydd 98 C3
Park St. T W 9 D2
Park The. Cro 27 E1
Park The. Rottn 167 E1
Park View. Bux 58 A2
Park View. Hast 140 A1
Park View. Hay H 52 B3
Park View. Norm 68 C3
Park View. Peas 70 C1
Park View Cl. Pea 168 C1
Park View Rd. Hove 144 C1
Park View Rise. Pea 178 C4
Park Way. Hast 140 A2
Park Way Cl. Sock 163 E4
Park Wood Rd. Hast 140 B3
Parker Cl. East 185 E3
Parker Rd. Hast 140 C2
Parkfield Ave. East 175 E1
Parkhurst Rd. Bex 160 A2
Parklands. Mar 56 C3
Parklands. S Sea 163 D4
Parklands Rd. Key 100 B2
Parkmore Terr. Bri 165 E4

Parkrise. Hove 144 B2
Parkside. E Gri 2 A1
Parkside. Hea 83 F3
Parkside. Key 100 C2
Parkside Rd. Sea 181 E2
Parkstone Rd. Hast 140 A2
Parkview Rd. Uck 57 D1
Parkway. East 184 C4
Parkwood. Iden 71 F2
Parkwood Cl. T W 9 D3
Parrock La. Col H 14 B1
Parrock La. Upp H 14 B1
Parsonage Cl. T W 7 F3
Parsonage La. Ick 119 E3
Parsonage La. Lam 21 F3
Parsonage La. Wfd 117 D2
Parsonage Rd. East 185 D2
Parsonage Rd. T W 7 F3
Parsons Cl. Hast 139 E2
Partridges La. Wad 30 B3
Pashley Rd. East 185 D1
Paston Pl. Bri 166 A2
Pasture Hill Road. Hay H 52 A3
Patcham By-ps. Bri 145 E3
Patchdene. Bri 145 E3
Paton Rd. Bex 159 F4
Paul Cl. Hai 132 C2
Pavilion Bldgs. Bri 165 F3
Pavilion Par. Bri 165 F3
Pavilion St. Bri 165 F3
Paxhill Cl. Hast 139 E2
Paygate Rd. Sed 116 B4
Payne Ave. Hove 164 B4
Paynsbridge Way. Hor 109 F4
Paynters Way. Newk 78 A4
Paynton Rd. Hast 139 F2
Paythorne Cl. Sock 143 D1
Peace Cl. Bri 146 A1
Peacock La. Bri 145 E2
Peakdean Cl. Fri 183 F1
Peakdean La. Fri 183 F1
Pearse Pl. Lam 21 F3
Peartree Cl. Bur H 74 B2
Peartree Hill. Ston 44 B2
Peartree La. Bex 137 D1
Peartree La. Lun C 137 D1
Pebble Rd. Pev B 177 E3
Pebsham Dr. Bex 160 C3
Pebsham La. Bex 160 C3
Pebsham La. Hast 160 C3
Peckham Cl. S Mal 127 D2
Peel Rd. Bri 166 B2
Peelings La. St Cro 175 F3
Peelings La. Whm 176 A3
Pegasus Way. E Gri 2 C2
Pegler Ave. Newh 179 F3
Pegwell Cl. Hast 140 B1
Pelham Cl. Pea 169 D1
Pelham Cl. Whm 176 B3
Pelham Cres. Hai 155 D3
Pelham Cres. Hast 162 C4
Pelham Pl. Hast 162 C4
Pelham Rd. Hay H 52 C3
Pelham Rd. Sea 181 E1
Pelham Rise. Pea 169 D1
Pelham Sq. Bri 165 F3
Pelham St. Bri 165 F3
Pelham St. Hast 162 B4
Pelham Terr. Lew 127 D1
Pelham Yd. Sea 181 E1
Pell Cl. Wad 31 F3
Pellbrook Rd. Lew 126 C2
Pelwood Rd. Cam 96 C1
Pembroke Ave. Hove 164 C4
Pembroke Cres. Hove 164 C4
Pembroke Gdns. Hove 164 C3
Pembury Cl. Hay H 52 C2
Pembury Cl. Pem 10 A4
Pembury Gr. Bex 159 F4
Pembury Grange. T W 9 F3
Pembury Rd. Hast 176 A1
Pembury Rd. T W 9 E3
Pendean. Bur H 75 D1
Penhale Rd. East 186 A3
Penhurst Cl. East 175 F1
Penhurst Cl. Hast 140 A3
Penhurst Dr. Bex 160 C3
Penhurst La. Brill 87 E1
Penhurst La. Pen 113 E3
Penhurst Pl. Bri 166 B3
Penhurst Rd. Ford 7 E4
Penland Cl. Hay H 52 A4
Penland Rd. Bex 160 B3
Penland Rd. Hay H 52 A4
Penn Cres. Hay H 52 C3
Penn Cres. Rin 128 A3
Pennine Rise. Hast 140 C2
Pennine Way. East 176 A2
Pennine Wlk. T W 9 D3
Penny La. Bex 160 C3
Pennybridge La. May 42 A3
Pensford Dr. East 176 A1
Penshurst Rd. Spe 7 E4
Pentland Cl. East 176 B2
Pentland Cl. Hast 140 A3
Penvensey Rd. Newh 179 F3
Peppercombe Rd. East 184 C2
Pepys Wlk. East 176 B1
Percival Cres. East 175 E2

Percival Rd. East 175 E1
Percival Terr. Bri 166 A2
Percy Rd. Hast 141 D2
Perry Ave. E Gri 2 B2
Perry Hill. Salt 168 A2
Perryman's La. Che Co 36 A2
Perrymount Rd. Hay H 52 B3
Perth Cl. Sea 182 A2
Perth Rd. Hast 139 F2
Pet Level Rd. Pett 120 B2
Peter James Cl. Cam 96 B1
Peter James La. Fai 142 A3
Peter James La. Gue G 142 A4
Petersfield. Pem 10 B4
Petlands Gdns. Hay H 52 B2
Petlands Rd. Hay H 52 B2
Pett Cl. Bri 166 B3
Pett La. Ick 119 F2
Pett Level Rd. Fai 142 C4
Pett Level Rd. Pett 142 C4
Pett Level Rd. Winc B 120 C2
Pett Rd. Gue G 142 A4
Pett Rd. Pett 142 B4
Petworth Dr. Bur H 74 C2
Petworth Pl. East 175 E1
Petworth Rd. Bri 145 F3
Pevensey Bay Rd. Pev B 176 B1
Pevensey Cl. Sea 181 F2
Pevensey Park Rd. Whm 176 B3
Pevensey Rd. Bri 166 A4
Pevensey Rd. East 185 F2
Pevensey Rd. Hast 161 F4
Pevensey Rd. Pole 175 D3
Peyton Cl. East 186 B4
Philip Cole Cl. Hast 162 C4
Phoenix Cl. Hai 155 D4
Phoenix Cres. Sock 163 D4
Phoenix Cswy. Lew 127 D1
Phoenix La. Ash W 13 E3
Phoenix Pl. Bri 165 F3
Phoenix Pl. Lew 127 D1
Phoenix Way. Sock 163 D4
Phyllis Ave. Pea 168 C1
Picardy Cl. Bat 115 E2
Piccadilly La. May 42 A2
Pickers Green. Hay H 52 C4
Picketts La. Mar 56 B4
Pickforde La. Tic 33 D1
Picknill Green La. Bex 158 C3
Picton St. Bri 166 A4
Piddinghoe Ave. Pea 179 D3
Piddinghoe Mead. Newh ... 169 F1
Piddinghole Cl. Pea 179 D4
Pilgrim Ct. Hay H 52 C3
Pilmer Rd. Cro 27 E2
Pilot Rd. Hast 140 C2
Piltdown Cl. Bex 159 F2
Piltdown Cl. Hast 140 B1
Piltdown Rd. Bri 166 B3
Piltdown Rise. Uck 80 A4
Pimms Gdns. Bri 165 F3
Pinders Rd. Hast 141 D1
Pine Ave. Hast 140 C2
Pine Gr. Cro 27 E2
Pine Gr. E Gri 1 C2
Pine Tree Cl. Hur 99 F3
Pine Tree Cl. Newh 180 A4
Pine Tree Rd. Hea 83 F3
Pine Trees. Hast 100 A2
Pine Way. Hai 154 C4
Pine Way Cl. E Gri 12 B4
Pine Wlk. Uck 80 A4
Pineham Copse. Hay H 52 B2
Pinehurst. Bur H 74 C1
Pines The. Hay H 52 C2
Pinewood Cl. East 175 D1
Pinewood Cl. Sea 181 D1
Pinewood Rd. T W 9 D3
Pinewood Way. Hast 139 E2
Pinewoods. Bex 159 E2
Pinfold Cl. Wood 167 E3
Pink Alley. T W 8 C1
Pinton Hill. Tic 32 C2
Pinwell Rd. Lew 149 D4
Pipe Pas. Lew 127 D1
Piper's Gate. Rid 80 A2
Piper's La. Rob 65 F2
Pipers Cl. Bex 160 A3
Pipers Cl. Hove 144 A2
Pipers Cl. Wad 31 F2
Pipers Field. Rid 80 A3
Pit Rd. Hur 99 F3
Pitt Dr. Sea 181 F3
Pitt Gdns. Wood 167 D4
Place La. Sea 181 E2
Plainfields Ave. Bri 145 E4
Plaistow Cl. Bri 166 B3
Platt The. Dor 2 C4
Platt The. Hay H 52 C3
Plaw Hatch La. For R 23 E3
Plaw Hatch La. Sha 23 D3
Playden Gdns. Hast 140 C2
Playden Cl. Rye 72 C1
Pleasant View Rd. Cro 27 E2
Plemont Gdns. Bex 159 F3
Pleyden Cl. Bri 166 B2
Pleyden Rise. Bex 158 B2
Plough La. Hast 139 F1
Plover Cl. East 176 A1

Plover Ct. Hast 139 E2
Plumpton Bostall. Plu 125 D3
Plumpton Cl. Bex 160 A3
Plumpton La. Plu 102 B2
Plumpton Rd. Bri 166 A3
Plymouth Ave. Bri 146 B1
Pocock's Rd. East 185 D3
Polegate By-ps. Pole 174 B4
Polegate Rd. Hai 154 C3
Polesden Rd. T W 9 D1
Pond Cl. Bro Ow 91 F3
Pond Way. E Gri 2 C1
Pondcroft Rd. Hay H 52 C4
Ponswood Rd. Hast 139 F1
Pont Cl. Pun T 85 D3
Pook Reed Cl. Hea 83 E3
Pook Reed La. Hea 83 E3
Pool Valley. Bri 165 F2
Poona Rd. T W 8 C1
Poplar Ave. Hove 144 B2
Poplar Cl. Bri 145 E1
Poplar Cl. Hove 144 B2
Poplar Wlk. East 175 D2
Poppinghole La. Rob 66 A1
Poppinghole La. Sed 89 F4
Popps La. Bex 159 D2
Poppyfield. Rye 72 A1
Port Hall Ave. Bri 165 E4
Port Hall Pl. Bri 165 E4
Port Hall Rd. Bri 165 E4
Port Hall St. Bri 165 E4
Port Rd. East 175 F1
Porters Way. Pole 174 C3
Portfield Ave. Bri 145 F3
Portfield Cl. Bex 160 A3
Portland Ave. Hove 164 B4
Portland Ave. Hai 132 C1
Portland Mews. Bri 166 A2
Portland Pl. Bri 166 A2
Portland Pl. Hast 162 B4
Portland Rd. Bur H 74 B2
Portland Rd. E Gri 12 B4
Portland Rd. Hove 164 B4
Portland St. Bri 165 E3
Portland Stps. Hast 162 B4
Portland Terr. S Hei 170 A1
Portland Villas. Hove 164 A4
Portlands The. East 186 C4
Portsdown. Willn 174 C1
Portsmouth La. Hay H 52 B4
Portsmouth Wood. Hay H ... 52 B4
Portsmouth Wood Cl. Hay H ... 52 B4
Possingworth Cl. Cro H 82 B4
Post Horn Cl. For R 13 F1
Post Horn La. For R 13 F1
Post Office Pas. Hast 162 C4
Potato La. Rin 128 B3
Potman's La. Cat 137 E2
Potman's La. Lun C 137 E2
Pottens Mill La. Bro O 61 E3
Potter's La. Lew 149 D4
Potteries The. Rid 80 A2
Potters Field. Rin 128 A3
Potters La. Bur H 74 B1
Pottery Cl. Bre 91 F1
Pottery La. Bre 91 F1
Pottingfield Rd. Rye 94 C3
Pound Cl. East 186 B3
Pound La. Bux 58 B1
Pound La. Fra 81 E4
Pound La. Lau 130 A4
Pound The. Bur H 74 B2
Poundfield Rd. Cro 27 F1
Poundfield Rd. San 48 C3
Poundsbridge Hill. Ford 7 D4
Poveys Cl. Bur H 74 A2
Powder Mill La. Sgh 9 D4
Powder Mill La. T W 8 C4
Powdermill Cl. Sgh 9 D4
Powdermill La. Bat 115 D1
Powdermill La. Bre 91 D2
Powdermill La. Bro O W 91 D2
Powdermill La. Cat 114 C1
Powdermill La. Sed 90 C1
Powell Gdns. Newh .(....... 170 A1
Powell Rd. Newk 78 A4
Powis Gr. Bri 165 E3
Powis Rd. Bri 165 E3
Powis Sq. Bri 165 E3
Powis Villas. Bri 165 E3
Poynings Cl. Sea 182 A1
Poynings Dr. Hove 144 B2
Poynter Rd. Hove 164 C4
Pratt's Folly La. Cro 27 E1
Prescott Gdns. Bur H 74 C2
Preston Circ. Bri 165 F4
Preston Dro. Bri 145 E1
Preston Gr. Fra 80 C3
Preston Park Ave. Bri 145 E1
Preston Rd. Bex 159 F4
Preston Rd. Bri 145 E1
Preston St. Bri 165 E3
Prestonville Rd. Bri 165 E4
Prideaux Rd. East 185 E3
Primrose Cl. East 175 F2
Primrose Hill. Bex 159 E3
Primrose Hill. Fai 142 B3
Primrose La. For R 13 F1
Prince Albert St. Bri 165 F3

Prince Charles Cl. Sock 143 E1
Prince Charles Rd. S Mal 127 E2
Prince Edward's Rd. Lew 126 C1
Prince Regent's Cl. Bri 166 B2
Prince William Par. East 186 B3
Prince's Cres. Bri 165 F4
Prince's Rd. Bri 165 F4
Prince's Rd. Hast 162 A4
Prince's St. Bri 165 F3
Prince's St. T W 9 D2
Princes Ave. Hove 164 C3
Princes Cl. Sea 181 E3
Princes Cl. Uck 79 F4
Princes Cres. Hove 164 C3
Princes Pl. Bri 165 F3
Princes Rd. East 186 B4
Princes Sq. Hove 164 C3
Princes's Terr. Bri 166 B2
Princess Dr. Sea 181 D3
Princess Dr. Sea 181 E3
Prinkle La. Bod G 112 A1
Prinkle La. Bor S 112 A1
Prinsep Rd. Hove 164 C4
Prior's Way. Cowd 4 C3
Priory Ave. Hast 162 B4
Priory Cl. Hast 140 B1
Priory Cl. Pev B 177 D2
Priory Cres. Lew 149 D4
Priory Hts. East 184 C3
Priory La. East 176 B2
Priory Orch. East 176 B1
Priory Orchard. East 186 B4
Priory Rd. Bur H 74 C1
Priory Rd. East 176 B1
Priory Rd. For R 24 A4
Priory Rd. Hass 100 B3
Priory Rd. Hast 140 C1
Priory St. Hast 162 B4
Priory St. Lew 149 D4
Priory Way. Hay H 52 B2
Prom. Bex 160 A2
Prom. East 186 A2
Prom. Hast 162 A4
Prom. Pea 179 D3
Prom. Sea 181 D2
Prom The. Pev B 177 D2
Prospect Gdns. East 185 D2
Prospect Pl. Hast 162 B4
Prospect Rd. Hea 83 F3
Prospect Rd. Sgh 8 B4
Prospect Rd. T W 9 D2
Providence Pl. Bri 165 F4
Pudding Cake La. Uck 80 A4
Pulborough Ave. East 175 E1
Pulborough Cl. Bri 166 B4
Pump La. Fra 81 D2
Purbeck Cl. East 176 A2
Putlands Cres. Bex 159 F4
Pyecombe St. Pye 122 C3

Quadrant The. Key 100 C2
Quakers La. Hay H 52 C3
Quantock Cl. East 176 A2
Quantock Gdns. Hast 140 C2
Quarry Bank Rd. Bri 145 F1
Quarry Cl. Bur H 75 D2
Quarry Cres. Hast 140 C1
Quarry Hill. Hast 161 F4
Quarry Hill. Hay H 52 A3
Quarry La. Sea 181 F3
Quarry Rd. Hast 140 B1
Quarry Rd. Newh 180 A3
Quarry Rd. T W 8 C3
Quarry Rise. E Gri 2 C2
Quebec Cl. Bex 159 F3
Quebec Rd. Hast 139 F2
Quebec St. Bri 165 F3
Queen Alexandra Ave. Hove 144 C2
Queen Anne's Cl. Lew 127 D1
Queen Caroline Cl. Hove 144 C2
Queen Elizabeth Ave. Bur H .. 74 B1
Queen Mary Ave. Hove 144 C2
Queen Sq. Bri 165 E3
Queen St. San 48 C3
Queen Victoria Ave. Hove ... 144 C2
Queen's Ave. Hast 162 B4
Queen's Cres. Bur H 186 B4
Queen's Dr. Mar 56 B2
Queen's Gdns. Bri 165 F3
Queen's Gdns. East 185 F2
Queen's Gdns. Hove 165 D3
Queen's Gdns. T W 8 C3
Queen's Park Rd. Bri 166 A3
Queen's Park Rise. Bri 166 A3
Queen's Park Terr. Bri 166 A3
Queen's Pl. Bri 165 F4
Queen's Pl. Hove 165 D3
Queen's Rd. Bri 165 E3
Queen's Rd. E Gri 2 B1
Queen's Rd. East 186 A4
Queen's Rd. Hast 162 B4
Queen's Rd. S Mal 127 D2
Queen's Rd. T W 8 C3
Queen's Rd Quadrant. Bri ... 165 E3
Queen's Wlk. E Gri 2 B1
Queens App. Uck 57 D1
Queens Cotts. Wad 31 E3
Queens Cres. Bur H 74 C1
Queens Dr. Key 100 B2

Queens Park Gdns. Sea 181 D2
Queens Rd. Cro 27 E1
Queens Rd. Hay H 52 B3
Queens Rd. Hers 134 B3
Queens Rd. Sock 143 E1
Queensbury Mews. Bri 165 E3
Queensmount. Five A 59 F4
Queensway. Bri 166 A3
Queensway. E Gri 2 B1
Queensway. Hast 139 E3
Queensway. Sea 181 F3
Querneby Cl. S Sea 163 D4
Quickbourne La. Norm 69 D4
Quinnell Dr. Hai 132 C1
Quintin Cl. Hai 154 C3

Radcliffe Cl. Hast 140 A2
Radinden Dr. Hove 145 D1
Radinden Manor Rd. Hove ... 165 D4
Ragged Dog La. Hea 82 C2
Railway App. E Gri 2 B1
Railway App. Newh 180 A4
Railway Cotts. W Fir 151 E3
Railway La. Lew 127 D1
Railway Mews. Hove 164 C4
Railway Rd. Newh 180 A4
Railway St. Bri 165 E3
Raleigh Cl. East 186 B4
Ramsay Way. East 186 B4
Ramslye Rd. T W 18 B4
Randiddles Cl. Hur 99 F2
Randolph La. Rye 71 F2
Ranelagh Villas. Hove 164 C4
Rangemoor Dr. East 185 D3
Rankine Rd. T W 9 D4
Ranmore Cl. Hast 140 B3
Rannoch Rd. Cro 27 D1
Rannoch Rd W. Cro 27 D1
Ranscombe Hill. S Mal 149 F3
Ranscombe La. Gly 150 A3
Ranworth Cl. East 175 F2
Rapson's Rd. Willn 174 C2
Raphael Rd. Hove 164 B4
Ratton Dr. East 184 C4
Ratton Rd. East 185 E2
Raven Ct. Bat 115 E2
Raven Cl. Hast 139 E2
Ravens Cl. Bex 159 D2
Ravens Croft. East 190 B4
Ravenswood Ave. T W 9 D3
Ravenswood Dr. Wood 167 E3
Ravenswood Rd. Bur H 74 C2
Ravine Cl. Hast 140 C2
Rayford Cl. Pea 179 D4
Raymond Cl. Sea 181 F3
Rayners La. Iden 71 E3
Reading Rd. Bri 166 B2
Rectory Cl. Bur 63 F4
Rectory Cl. E Hoa 107 F3
Rectory Cl. East 185 D2
Rectory Cl. Hast 139 F1
Rectory Cl. Newh 180 A3
Rectory Cl. S Sea 163 D4
Rectory Field. Hart 15 E2
Rectory La. Bec 69 E2
Rectory La. Iden 71 E2
Rectory La. Winc 120 B4
Rectory Park. Pett 119 E1
Rectory Rd. Newh 170 B1
Rectory Rd. S Sea 163 D4
Rectory Way. Bex 160 A3
Red Lake Terr. Hast 141 D2
Red Oak. The M 47 E4
Redbridge La. Cro 39 D3
Redbrook La. Bux 58 A2
Redcross St. Bri 165 F3
Redford Cl. East 176 B1
Redgeland Rise. Hast 139 E1
Redgill La. N Cha 54 C1
Redhill Cl. Bri 145 D3
Redhill Dr. Bri 145 D2
Redleaf Cl. T W 9 D3
Redoubt Rd. East 186 A2
Redvers Rd. Bri 146 A1
Redwood Dr. Hay H 52 A2
Reed Pond Wlk. Hay H 52 C2
Reed's La. Alb 99 D4
Reedham Rd. East 175 F2
Reedswood Rd. Bro O W 91 F3
Reedswood Rd. Hast 161 E4
Reeves Hill. Bri 146 A3
Regal Dr. E Gri 12 B4
Regency Cl. Uck 80 A4
Regency Cl. Bri 145 E2
Regency Gdns. Hast 161 F4
Regency Mews. Bri 165 E3
Regency Sq. Bri 165 E3
Regent Arc. Bri 165 F3
Regent Hill. Bri 165 E3
Regent Pl. Hast 139 E4
Regent Row. Bri 165 E3
Regent Sq. Rye 95 D3
Regent St. Bri 165 F3
Regents Cl. Sea 181 E3
Reginald Rd. Bex 159 D2
Reigate Rd. Bri 145 D1

Resting Oak Hill. Bar C 103 E2
Reynolds La. Sgh 8 B4
Reynolds Rd. East 176 B1
Reynolds Rd. Hove 164 B4
Reynoldstown La. Pole 174 B3
Riccards La. Wha 89 F1
Rices Hill. E Gri 2 B1
Richardson Rd. Hove 164 B4
Richardson Rd. T W 8 C3
Richborough Cl. Hast 140 A2
Richington Way. Sea 181 F2
Richland Cl. Hast 141 E2
Richmead Gdns. May 41 F1
Richmond Ave. Bex 159 E2
Richmond Cl. Bex 159 F2
Richmond Gr. Bex 159 F1
Richmond Pl. Bri 165 F3
Richmond Rd. Bex 159 F1
Richmond Rd. Bri 165 F4
Richmond Rd. Pev B 177 D3
Richmond Rd. Sea 181 D2
Richmond Sq. E Gri 2 A2
Richmond St. Bri 165 F3
Richmond St. Hast 141 D1
Richmond Terr. Sea 181 E2
Richmond Way. E Gri 12 B4
Riddens Cl. Plu 102 B3
Riddens La. Plu 102 B3
Riddlesdale Ave. T W 8 C3
Ride The. Bri 145 E1
Riders Bolt. Bex 159 E3
Ridge Cl. Nut 37 D3
Ridge Rd. Fal 147 D4
Ridge The. Hast 139 F4
Ridge The. Winc B 121 D3
Ridge View. Bri 146 B3
Ridge Way. Hay H 52 C1
Ridge West The. Hast 139 F4
Ridgelands Cl. East 185 D2
Ridgeside Ave. Bri 145 E3
Ridgeway. E Gri 12 B4
Ridgeway. Pem 10 A4
Ridgeway. Sock 143 E1
Ridgeway Cl. Hea 83 F4
Ridgeway Cl. Sock 143 E1
Ridgeway Paddock. Kin L 148 B3
Ridgeway The. Bur H 74 C2
Ridgeway The. Fri 183 F1
Ridgeway The. Hers 134 B3
Ridgeway The. Sea 181 E2
Ridgewaye The. Sgh 8 C4
Ridgewick Rd. Bri 146 A3
Ridgewood Ave. Salt 168 A2
Ridgewood Cl. Rid 80 A2
Ridgewood Gdns. Bex 160 B2
Ridgway Cl. Wood 167 D4
Ridgway The. Wood 167 D4
Ridings The. Bex 159 E4
Ridings The. Bur H 75 D1
Ridings The. Hast 140 A3
Ridings The. Newk 78 A4
Ridings The. Pea 168 C1
Ridings The. Sea 181 E3
Ridings The. T W 9 E3
Ridleys. W Hoa 22 B3
Rigden Rd. Hove 145 D1
Riley Rd. Bri 146 A1
Rill Wlk. E Gri 2 C1
Ringmer Rd. Bri 146 B2
Ringmer Rd. Newh 179 F3
Ringmer Rd. Sea 181 E1
Ringwood Cl. East 185 F3
Ringwood Rd. Bex 160 A4
Ringwood Rd. East 185 F3
Ripe La. Ripe 130 B1
Ripsley Cl. East 176 B1
Risden La. Four T 48 A4
Rise Park Gdns. East 176 B1
Rise The. E Gri 12 B4
Rise The. Hay H 52 C3
Rise The. Por S 143 E1
Riseden Rd. Wad 31 D1
Rising The. East 176 B1
River La. Alfn 172 C2
River Way. Uck 80 A3
Riverdale. S Mal 127 D1
Riverside. For R 13 E2
Riverside. Newh 180 A4
Riverside Ind Est. Lew 127 D1
Rixons Cl. Hor K 35 D3
Rixons Orch. Hor K 35 D3
Robert Rd. Bri 165 F3
Robert Tressell Cl. Hast 140 B1
Robert's Hill. Winc 120 B2
Robertson Pas. Hast 162 B4
Robertson Rd. Bri 145 D1
Robertson St. Hast 162 B4
Robertson Terr. Hast 162 B4
Robertson's Hill. Hast 140 C1
Robian Cl. Mar 56 C2
Robin Cl. East 176 A1
Robin Dene. Bri 166 B2
Robin Post La. Will 153 F1
Robinson Rd. Newh 180 A4
Roborough Cl. East 185 F2
Robsack Ave. Hast 139 E1

Rochdale Rd. T W 9 D3
Rochester Cl. East 190 A4
Rochester Gdns. Hove 165 D3
Rochester Rd. Hast 139 F1
Rochester St. Bri 166 A3
Rochester Way. Cro 27 F1
Rochford Way. Sea 180 C3
Rock Cl. Hast 141 D2
Rock Gr. Bri 166 A2
Rock La. Cog 118 A3
Rock Pl. Bri 165 F2
Rock St. Bri 166 B2
Rock Villa Rd. T W 8 C2
Rock's Hill. Wfd 117 E4
Rock-a-nore Par. Hast 162 C4
Rock-a-nore Rd. Hast 162 C4
Rockall Dr. Hai 132 C1
Rockhurst Dr. East 184 C3
Rockington Way. Cro 39 F4
Rocklands La. Hast 141 D1
Rockmead Rd. Fai 142 B2
Rocks Hill. Sale 66 B3
Rocks La. H Hur 57 E4
Rocks Park Rd. Uck 79 F4
Rocky La. Hay H 52 A1
Roderick Ave. Pea 178 C4
Roderick Ave. Pea 179 D4
Rodmell Ave. Salt 168 A1
Rodmell Rd. Sea 181 F1
Rodmell Rd. T W 8 C1
Rodmill Dr. East 185 D3
Rodmill Rd. East 185 D3
Rodney Cl. East 186 B4
Roebuck St. Hast 162 C4
Roedale Rd. Bri 145 F1
Roedean Cl. Bex 159 F3
Roedean Cl. Sea 181 F2
Roedean Cres. Bri 166 C2
Roedean Path. Bri 166 C2
Roedean Rd. Bri 166 C2
Roedean Rd. T W 8 C1
Roedean Vale. Bri 166 C2
Roedean Way. Bri 166 C2
Roffrey Ave. East 175 D1
Rolfe Dr. Bur H 75 D2
Romaine Cl. Bur H 75 D3
Roman Cl. Sea 180 C3
Roman Cres. Sock 163 E4
Roman Rd. Hove 164 A3
Roman Rd. Sock 163 E4
Roman Way. Sock 163 E4
Roman Way. Uck 80 B4
Romans Way. Whm 176 B3
Romany Cl. Por S 163 F4
Romford Rd. Pem 10 B4
Romney Cl. Sea 182 A2
Romney Rd. Pole 174 C4
Romney Rd. Rottn 167 F1
Romney St. East 186 A3
Romsey Cl. Bri 146 A1
Rookery Cl. Newh 170 B1
Rookery La. Winc 120 B4
Rookery Way. Hay H 52 B1
Rookery Way. Newh 170 B1
Rookery Way. Sea 180 C3
Rookhurst Rd. Bex 160 B3
Rookley Cl. T W 9 D1
Rookwood Cl. Uck 80 B4
Roopers. Spe 7 F2
Rope Wlk. Hai 154 C4
Rope Wlk. Rye 95 D3
Rope Wlk The. San 48 C3
Roper's Gate. T W 8 B1
Rose Hill. Bri 165 F4
Rose Hill Cl. Bri 165 F4
Rose Hill Terr. Bri 165 F4
Rose Wlk. Sea 181 E2
Rose Wlk Cl. Newh 179 F4
Rose Wlk The. Newh 180 A4
Rosebarn Cl. Bur H 75 D1
Rosebery Ave. East 175 E1
Rosebery Ave. Wood 167 D4
Rosedale Pl. East 175 D2
Rosedene Cl. Wood 167 E3
Rosehill Wlk. T W 8 C2
Roselands. Bex 159 E3
Roselands Ave. May 41 E1
Roselands Cl. East 186 A3
Roseleigh Gdns. Sca H 53 E2
Rosemary Cl. Pea 169 D1
Rosemary Dr. S Sea 143 D1
Rosemary La. Fai 142 A4
Rosemary La. Tic 33 F2
Rosemount Cl. Sea 180 C3
Rosetti Rd. Pev B 177 D2
Rossdale. T W 9 D3
Roswell Wlk. East 176 B1
Rothbury Rd. Hove 164 A4
Rother Cl. Bur 63 F4
Rother Cl. Cro 39 F4
Rother Rd. Sea 181 F1
Rother View. Bur 63 F4
Rotherfield Ave. Bex 160 A2
Rotherfield Ave. East 175 F2
Rotherfield Ave. Hast 140 C1
Rotherfield Cl. Bri 145 F3
Rotherfield Cres. Bri 145 F3
Rotherfield La. May 41 E2
Rotherfield Rd. Cro 40 A4

Rotherfield Rd. Rot 40 B4
Rotherhill Rd. Cro 39 F4
Rothermead. May 41 E1
Rotherview. Sale 66 A3
Rothley Chase. Hay H 52 B2
Rothsay Rd. Hast 161 F4
Rothwell Ct. Newh 179 F4
Rotten Row. Lew 149 D4
Rotunda Rd. East 186 A4
Rotyngs The. Rottn 167 E1
Rough Brow. Sea 181 E1
Rough Field. E Gri 2 A2
Rough The. Newk 78 A4
Round Hill Cres. Bri 165 F4
Round Hill Rd. Bri 165 F4
Round Hill St. Bri 165 F4
Roundacres Way. Bex 160 B3
Roundell The. Hast 140 A3
Roundhay Ave. Pea 179 E3
Roundhill Rd. T W 9 D1
Roundway. Bri 146 B3
Roundwood La. Hay H 52 B4
Roundwood Rd. Hast 139 F3
Rowan Ave. East 175 D2
Rowan Ave. Hove 144 B1
Rowan Cl. Hast 140 A3
Rowan Cl. Hay H 52 C2
Rowan Cl. Hea 83 F3
Rowan Cl. Por S 143 F1
Rowan Gdns. Bex 160 B3
Rowan Tree Rd. T W 8 B1
Rowan Way. Rottn 167 E2
Rowan Wlk. Cra D 11 D4
Rowbarns. Bat 115 D3
Rowe Ave. Pea 178 C4
Rowplatt La. Fel 1 B2
Rowsley Rd. East 190 A4
Royal Chase. T W 8 A2
Royal Cres. Bri 166 A2
Royal Cres Mews. Bri 166 A2
Royal George Rd. Bur H 74 B2
Royal Par. East 186 A3
Royal Military Rd. Winc 94 C1
Royal Sovereign View. East . 186 B3
Royal Sussex Cres. East 184 C3
Royles Cl. Rottn 167 F1
Royston Cl. Fri 183 F1
Royston Gdns. Bex 160 B3
Rudyard Cl. Wood 167 E4
Rudyard Rd. Wood 167 E4
Rue De Bayeux. Bat 115 D3
Rufus Cl. Lew 127 D1
Rugby Cl. Sea 181 F2
Rugby Pl. Bri 166 B2
Rugby Rd. Bri 145 F1
Rumbolds La. Hay H 52 A1
Rushetts. Lan G 7 E2
Rushey Cl. Rin 128 B3
Rushlake Cl. Bri 146 B3
Rushlake Cres. East 185 D3
Rushlake Rd. Bri 146 B3
Rushlye Cl. Bel G 19 E3
Rushwood Cl. Hay H 52 C2
Ruskin Pl. Hove 164 B4
Ruskin Rd. East 174 C1
Ruskin Rd. Hove 164 B4
Rusper Rd. Bri 146 A3
Rusper Rd. East 184 C3
Ruspers. Bur H 75 D1
Russell Cres. Bri 165 E4
Russell Ct. Hast 162 C4
Russell Pl. Bri 165 E3
Russell Rd. Bri 165 E3
Russell Row. S Mal 127 D2
Russell Sq. Bri 165 E3
Russet Cl. Pole 175 D3
Russet Cl. Hast 162 B4
Russet Cl. Pole 175 D3
Rusthall Grange. T W 8 A2
Rusthall Rd St. T W 8 A2
Rusthall Park. T W 8 A2
Rusthall Rd. T W 8 A2
Rustic Cl. Pea 168 C1
Rustic Park. Pea 168 C1
Rustic Rd. Pea 168 C1
Rustington Rd. Bri 145 F3
Rustlings Cl. Hay H 52 C3
Rustwick. T W 8 A2
Rutland Cl. East 185 D3
Rutland Gdns. Hove 164 B4
Rutland Rd. Hove 164 C4
Rutley Cl. Sale 66 A3
Rydal Cl. T W 8 B3
Rydal Dr. T W 8 B3
Rydal Way. East 176 A2
Ryde Rd. Bri 166 A4
Ryders. Lan G 7 F2
Rye Cl. Pole 175 D4
Rye Cl. Salt 168 B1
Rye Cl. Sea 182 A2
Rye Rd. Four T 48 A4
Rye Rd. Hast 141 D3
Rye Rd. Rye 71 E1
Rye Rd. Witt 71 F4
Rye St. East 186 A3
Ryecroft. Hay H 52 B2
Ryefield Cl. East 185 D4
Ryelands Dr. Bri 146 A2
Rylstone Rd. East 186 A2
Rymers Cl. T W 9 D4

Rymill Rd. Hast ...139 F2
Ryst Wood Rd. For R ...14 A1

Sackville Cl. Lew ...127 D1
Sackville Gdns. E Gri ...2 A2
Sackville Gdns. Hove ...164 B3
Sackville La. E Gri ...1 C2
Sackville Rd. Bex ...160 A2
Sackville Rd. East ...175 E1
Sackville Rd. Hai ...155 D3
Sackville Rd. Hove ...164 C4
Saddler's Wall La. Brok ...73 F4
Saddlers Cl. Bur H ...75 D1
Saddlers Ct. Hast ...161 F3
Sadler Rd. Bri ...166 B3
Sadlers Way. Rin ...128 A2
Saffron Cl. S Sea ...143 D1
Saffron Gdns. Alfn ...172 B2
Saffrons Park. East ...185 E1
Saffrons The. Bur H ...74 B3
St Agnes Rd. E Gri ...2 B1
St Andrew's Dr. Sea ...180 C3
St Andrew's La. Lew ...149 D4
St Andrew's Rd. Bex ...160 A3
St Andrew's Rd. East ...145 F1
St Andrew's Rd. Por S ...164 A4
St Andrew's Sq. Hast ...162 B4
St Andrews Cl. Hai ...132 C1
St Andrews Rd. Bur H ...75 D2
St Anne's Cl. Bex ...160 A3
St Anne's Cres. Lew ...126 C1
St Anne's Rd. East ...185 E2
St Annes Rd. Willn ...174 C2
St Anthony's Ave. East ...186 A4
St Aubyn's Cres. Sock ...163 F4
St Aubyn's Mead. Rottn ...167 F1
St Aubyn's Rd. East ...185 F2
St Aubyn's Rd. Por S ...164 A4
St Aubyns. Hove ...164 C3
St Aubyns Rd. Sock ...163 F4
St Aubyns S. Hove ...164 C3
St Augustine's Cl. Bex ...159 E2
St Augustine's Cl. Sca H ...53 E2
St Christopher's Rd. Hur ...99 F3
St Crispians. Sea ...181 D2
St Cuthmans Cl. Bri ...166 B3
St David's Ave. Bex ...160 A3
St David's Rd. T W ...8 C3
St Davids Cl. East ...175 D2
St Dominic Cl. Hast ...161 F4
St Edmund's Rd. Hay H ...52 B2
St Edward's Cl. E Gri ...2 A1
St Francis Chase. Bex ...159 F3
St George's La. Hur ...99 F3
St George's Mews. Bri ...165 F3
St George's Pl. Bri ...165 F3
St George's Park. T W ...18 B4
St George's Pl. Hur ...99 F3
St George's Rd. Bex ...160 A3
St George's Rd. East ...185 F2
St George's Rd. Hast ...140 C1
St George's Terr. Bri ...166 A2
St Georges Rd. Bri ...166 A2
St Giles Cl. Winc ...120 B4
St Gregory Cl. East ...190 B4
St Helen's Ave. Hast ...140 B2
St Helen's Cres. Hast ...140 B1
St Helen's Cres. Hove ...144 A2
St Helen's Ct. Hast ...140 B1
St Helen's Down. Hast ...140 C2
St Helen's Dr. Hove ...144 A2
St Helen's Park Rd. Hast ...140 B2
St Helen's Rd. Bri ...166 A4
St Helen's Rd. Hast ...140 A1
St Helen's Wood Rd. Hast ...140 B3
St Heliers Ave. Hove ...164 B4
St Hill Rd. E Gri ...12 A3
St James La. Nut ...37 D2
St James Rd. E Gri ...2 B1
St James Rd. East ...186 A2
St James St. Lew ...149 D4
St James Wlk. S Str ...77 E1
St James' Ave. Bex ...160 A4
St James' Cl. Bex ...160 A4
St James' Cres. Bex ...160 A4
St James' Park. T W ...9 D3
St James' Rd. Bex ...160 A3
St James' Rd. T W ...9 D3
St James's Ave. Bri ...165 F3
St James's Pl. Bri ...165 F3
St James's Rd. Hast ...140 B1
St James's St. Bri ...165 F2
St James's St Mews. Bri ...165 F3
St John Cl. Lew ...127 D1
St John's Ave. Bur H ...74 B2
St John's Bank. S Cha ...103 D4
St John's Cl. E Gri ...2 B1
St John's Dr. Whm ...176 B3
St John's Hill. Lew ...127 D1
St John's Park. T W ...8 C4
St John's Pl. Bri ...165 F3
St John's Pl. Hove ...165 D3
St John's Rd. Bex ...160 A3
St John's Rd. Cro ...27 D2
St John's Rd. E Gri ...2 B1
St John's Rd. East ...190 B4
St John's Rd. Hast ...162 A4
St John's Rd. Hay H ...52 B1

St John's Rd. Pole ...174 C3
St John's Rd. Sea ...181 E1
St John's Rd. T W ...8 C3
St John's Terr. Lew ...127 D1
St Johns Rd. Bur H ...74 C2
St Johns Rd. Hove ...165 D3
St Joseph's Cl. Hove ...164 C4
St Josephs Way. Hay H ...52 B2
St Julian's La. S Sea ...163 D4
St Julians Cl. S Sea ...163 D4
St Keyna Ave. Hove ...164 A3
St Laurence Cl. Pea ...168 C1
St Lawrence Rd. Bex ...159 F4
St Lawrence Way. Hur ...99 F4
St Leonard's Ave. Hove ...164 A4
St Leonard's Cl. Newh ...170 B1
St Leonard's Gdns. Hove ...164 A3
St Leonard's Pl. East ...185 D2
St Leonard's Rd. Bri ...166 A4
St Leonard's Rd. East ...185 E2
St Leonard's Rd. Hove ...164 A4
St Leonard's Rd. Newh ...170 B1
St Leonards Park. E Gri ...2 B1
St Leonards Rd. Bex ...160 A2
St Leonards Terr. Pole ...174 B4
St Louie Cl. Sock ...163 F4
St Luke's La. Newh ...180 A4
St Luke's Rd. Bri ...166 A3
St Luke's Rd. T W ...8 C3
St Luke's Terr. Bri ...166 A3
St Mark's St. Bri ...166 B2
St Marks Cl. Bex ...159 D2
St Margaret's Ave. Dor P ...2 B3
St Margaret's Pl. Bri ...165 E3
St Margaret's Rd. E Gri ...2 B2
St Margaret's Rd. Hast ...162 A4
St Margaret's Rise. Sea ...180 C3
St Margaret's Terr. Hast ...162 A4
St Margarets Terr. Rye ...94 C3
St Mark's Mews. Bri ...166 B2
St Mark's Mews. Bri ...166 B2
St Mark's Rd. T W ...18 B4
St Martin's La. Lew ...149 D4
St Martin's Pl. Bri ...166 A4
St Martin's St. Bri ...165 F4
St Martins Cres. S Hei ...170 A1
St Martins Rd. East ...175 D2
St Mary Magdalene St. Bri ...165 F4
St Mary's Ave. Hai ...155 D4
St Mary's Cl. Bre ...91 F1
St Mary's Cl. Tic ...33 D1
St Mary's Cl. Willn ...174 C1
St Mary's Cotts. East ...185 D2
St Mary's La. Bex ...159 E4
St Mary's La. Spe ...7 F4
St Mary's La. Tic ...33 D1
St Mary's Pl. Bri ...165 F2
St Mary's Rd. Bur H ...74 B2
St Mary's Rd. East ...185 D2
St Mary's Rd. Hast ...140 C1
St Mary's Rd W. Bur H ...74 B2
St Mary's Sq. Bri ...166 A2
St Mary's Sq. Bri ...166 A2
St Mary's Terr. Bat ...115 E2
St Mary's Terr. Hast ...140 C1
St Mary-in-the-fields. May ...41 F1
St Marys Garth. Bux ...58 A2
St Marys Wlk. Hai ...155 D4
St Matthew's Cl. Hast ...140 A1
St Matthew's Gdns. Hast ...139 F1
St Matthew's Rd. Hast ...139 F1
St Michael's Cl. Cro ...39 F4
St Michael's Pl. Bri ...165 E3
St Michael's Pl. Hast ...162 B4
St Michael's Rd. Por S ...163 F4
St Michael's Rd. T W ...8 C4
St Michael's Terr. S Mal ...127 D2
St Michaels Rd. E Gri ...2 B1
St Nicholas La. Lew ...127 D1
St Nicholas Rd. Bri ...165 E3
St Nicholas Rd. Por S ...163 F4
St Nicolas Cl. Pev ...176 C3
St Olive's Cl. Cro H ...83 D4
St Pancras Gdns. Lew ...148 C3
St Pancras Green. Kin L ...148 B3
St Pancras Rd. Lew ...148 C4
St Patrick's Cres. Bex ...160 A3
St Patrick's Rd. Hove ...164 C4
St Paul's Cl. Hay H ...52 B3
St Paul's Pl. Hast ...162 A4
St Paul's Rd. Hast ...140 A1
St Paul's St. Bri ...165 F4
St Paul's St. T W ...8 A2
St Pauls Cl. East ...175 D2
St Peter's Ave. Pea ...178 C4
St Peter's Cl. Hove ...144 B1
St Peter's Cres. Bex ...160 A3
St Peter's Pl. Bri ...165 F3
St Peter's Pl. Lew ...127 D1
St Peter's Rd. Hast ...162 A4
St Peter's Rd. Por S ...163 F4
St Peter's Rd. Sea ...181 E3
St Peter's St. Bri ...165 F4
St Peter's St. T W ...9 D2
St Peters Rd. Bur H ...74 C2
St Peters Row. Ford ...6 C3
St Philip's Ave. East ...185 F1
St Richard's Rd. Por S ...163 F4

St Richard's Rd. Sock ...163 F4
St Richards Rd. Cro ...39 F4
St Saviour's Rd. Hast ...161 E3
St Swithun's Cl. E Gri ...2 B1
St Swithun's La. Lew ...149 D4
St Swithun's Terr. Lew ...149 D4
St Thomas's Rd. Hast ...140 C1
St Thomas's St. Winc ...120 B4
St Vincents Pl. East ...185 E1
St Vincents Rd. Hast ...161 E4
St Wilfred's Pl. Sea ...181 F2
St Wilfrid's Green. Hai ...155 D4
St Wilfrid's Way. Hay H ...52 B2
St Wilfrids Rd. Bur H ...74 C2
Saints Hill. Ford ...6 C4
Salcey Cl. Hast ...139 E1
Salehurst Rd. East ...185 D2
Salisbury Cl. East ...175 D1
Salisbury Rd. Bex ...159 F3
Salisbury Rd. East ...190 A4
Salisbury Rd. Hast ...140 A1
Salisbury Rd. Hove ...165 D3
Salisbury Rd. Lan G ...7 E2
Salisbury Rd. Sea ...181 E2
Salisbury Rd. Sgh ...9 D4
Salomons Rd. T W ...8 A2
Saltcote St. Rye ...95 D4
Saltdean Cl. Bex ...159 E2
Saltdean Dr. Salt ...168 A1
Saltdean Park Rd. Salt ...178 A4
Saltdean Vale. Salt ...168 A1
Saltdean Way. Bex ...159 D2
Salter's La. Brok ...73 F4
Salters La. Hast ...162 C4
Saltwood Rd. Sea ...182 A2
Salvington Cres. Bex ...159 E2
San Feliu Ct. E Gri ...2 C1
Sancroft Rd. East ...184 C2
Sanctuary The. East ...184 C2
Sand Hill La. Fra ...106 C4
Sand Rd. Lam ...21 F2
Sandbanks Cl. Hai ...154 C3
Sandbanks Gr. Hai ...154 C3
Sandbanks Rd. Hai ...154 C3
Sandbanks Way. Hai ...154 C3
Sandfield Rd. Ford ...6 C4
Sandgate Cl. Sea ...182 A3
Sandgate Rd. Bri ...145 F1
Sandhawes Hill. E Gri ...2 C2
Sandhill La. Boa ...27 F4
Sandhill La. Chur ...111 F3
Sandhurst Ave. Pem ...10 B3
Sandhurst Ave. Wood ...147 D1
Sandhurst Cl. San ...48 C2
Sandhurst Cl. T W ...9 D3
Sandhurst La. Bex ...158 C3
Sandhurst Park. T W ...9 D3
Sandhurst Rd. T W ...9 D3
Sandore Cl. Sea ...181 F2
Sandore Rd. Sea ...181 F2
Sandown Cl. East ...175 F2
Sandown Cl. T W ...9 E3
Sandown Gr. T W ...9 E3
Sandown Park. T W ...9 E3
Sandown Rd. Bri ...166 A4
Sandown Rd. Hast ...141 D2
Sandown Rd. Sock ...163 D4
Sandown Way. Bex ...160 B3
Sandpiper Wlk. East ...176 A1
Sandridge. Cro ...27 E1
Sandringham Cl. E Gri ...12 C4
Sandringham Cl. Hove ...144 C2
Sandringham Cl. Sea ...181 F3
Sandringham Dr. Hove ...144 C2
Sandrock Park. Hast ...140 B3
Sandrock Rd. T W ...9 D2
Sandrocks Way. Hay H ...52 B1
Sandwich Dr. Hast ...161 E4
Sandwich St. East ...186 A3
Sandy Cl. Hast ...139 F3
Sandy Cross Cotts. Hea ...83 F3
Sandy Cross La. Hea ...83 F3
Sandy La. Cro H ...25 D3
Sandy La. E Gri ...2 B1
Sandy La. Fra ...80 C4
Sandy La. Hor ...83 E1
Sandy La. W Hoa ...22 B3
Sandy Vale. Hay H ...52 B1
Sanyhils Ave. Bri ...145 E4
Saunders Cl. Hast ...140 C1
Saunders Hill. Bri ...146 A4
Saunders Rd. T W ...8 B1
Saunders Way. Cam ...96 C1
Savill Rd. Hay H ...52 C4
Sawyers Cl. Bur H ...75 D1
Saxby Cl. East ...176 B1
Saxby Rd. Bex ...159 F2
Saxon Cl. East ...185 D3
Saxon Cl. Salt ...168 A1
Saxon La. Sea ...181 E1
Saxon Rd. East ...185 D3
Saxon Rd. Hast ...141 D2
Saxon Rd. Hove ...164 A3
Saxon Rd. Newh ...180 A4
Saxon Rise. Bex ...160 B2
Saxon St. Hast ...162 A3
Saxonbury Cl. Cro ...27 E1
Saxonwood Rd. Bat ...115 D3
Sayerland La. Pole ...174 C4

Sayers The. E Gri ...2 A1
Scamps Hill. Hay H ...53 D3
Scarborough Rd. Bri ...145 D1
Scarletts Cl. Uck ...79 F4
Schofield Way. East ...186 B4
School Cl. Bur H ...74 B1
School Cl. Sock ...163 E4
School Field. Bar C ...104 A3
School Gdns. Bar C ...104 A2
School Hill. Lam ...21 F3
School Hill. Lew ...127 D1
School Hill. Mar ...56 C2
School Hill. Winc ...120 B4
School La. Ash W ...13 E3
School La. Bar C ...104 B3
School La. Che Co ...36 A3
School La. Cro ...27 E1
School La. Dan ...35 F3
School La. Had D ...58 C3
School La. Nut ...37 D3
School La. Peas ...70 C1
School La. Pole ...174 C4
School La. Pye ...123 D3
School La. Rye ...72 A1
School La. Salt ...168 A1
School Path. Bar C ...104 A2
School Pl. Bex ...160 C3
School Rd. Hast ...141 D2
School Rd. Hove ...164 B4
Scotland St. Bri ...165 F3
Scotsford Rd. Bro O ...61 E3
Scott Rd. Hove ...164 B4
Scotts Acre. Cam ...96 B1
Scotts Way. T W ...18 B4
Scraper's Hill. Chi ...131 F4
Scutes Cl. Hast ...140 C2
Scuthview Dr. Uck ...80 A4
Sea Rd. Bex ...160 A2
Sea Rd. Cam ...96 B1
Sea Rd. Fai ...142 C3
Sea Rd. Hast ...161 E3
Sea Rd. Pev B ...177 D3
Sea Rd. Winc ...120 C4
Sea Rd. Winc B ...120 C3
Seabeach Rd. East ...186 A3
Seabourne Rd. Bex ...160 C3
Seafield Cl. Sea ...181 F3
Seafield Rd. Hove ...164 C3
Seaford Rd. East ...186 A3
Seaford Rd. Hove ...164 A3
Seaford Rd. Newh ...180 B4
Seaford Rd. Sea ...180 B4
Seagrave Cl. Sea ...180 C3
Seaside. East ...186 A3
Seaside Rd. East ...185 F2
Seaside Rd. Hast ...161 E3
Seaside Way. Hast ...161 E3
Seaview Ave. Pea ...179 E3
Seaview Rd. Newh ...170 B1
Seaview Rd. Pea ...179 E3
Seaview Rd. Wood ...166 C4
Seaview Terr. Rye ...95 D3
Seaville Dr. East ...186 A4
Seaville Dr. Pev B ...177 D3
Second Ave. Bex ...160 B3
Second Ave. Cam ...96 B1
Second Ave. Hove ...165 D3
Second Ave. Newh ...180 A3
Second Rd. Pea ...178 C4
Sedgebrook Gdns. Hast ...140 B1
Sedgewick Rd. Bex ...160 A3
Sedgwick Rd. Bri ...146 A3
Sedlescombe Rd N. Hast ...140 A2
Sedlescombe Rd S. Hast ...139 F1
Sedlescombe Gdns. Hast ...139 F1
Sefton Chase. Cro ...27 F2
Sefton Rd. Por S ...143 E2
Sefton Way. Cro ...27 F2
Segrave Cl. Lew ...126 C1
Selba Dr. Bri ...146 B2
Selborne Pl. Hove ...165 D4
Selborne Rd. Hove ...165 D3
Selby Cl. Rid ...80 A3
Selby Ct. Hay H ...52 B2
Selby Gdns. Rid ...80 A3
Selby Rd. East ...185 D3
Selby Rd. Rid ...80 A3
Selby Rise. Rid ...80 A3
Selham Cl. Bri ...146 A3
Selham Dr. Bri ...146 A3
Selhurst Rd. Wood ...167 E3
Selmeston Cl. Hast ...140 A1
Selmeston Pl. Bri ...166 B3
Selmeston Rd. East ...185 D4
Selsfield Cl. East ...185 D3
Selsfield Dr. Bri ...146 A2
Selsfield Rd. W Hoa ...22 A4
Selwyn Dr. East ...185 E2
Selwyn Rd. East ...185 E2
Semley Rd. Bri ...145 F1
Semley Rd. Hass ...100 B2
Senlac Gdns. Bat ...115 E2
Senlac Green. Uck ...57 E1
Senlac Rd. Newh ...180 A4
Senlac Way. Hast ...140 A3
Sergison Cl. Hay H ...52 A3
Sergison Rd. Hay H ...52 A3
Setfords Field. S Str ...77 E1

Sevelands Cl. Bri ...166 B4
Seven Acre Cl. Hast ...139 F3
Seven Sisters Rd. Willn ...175 D2
Sevenoaks Rd. East ...176 A1
Seville St. Bri ...166 A4
Sewell Ave. Bex ...160 A3
Seymour Sq. Bri ...166 A2
Seymour St. Bri ...166 A2
Shaftesbury Pl. Bri ...165 F4
Shaftesbury Rd. Bri ...165 F4
Shaftesbury Rd. T W ...8 C3
Shakespeare St. Hove ...164 C4
Shakespeare Wlk. East ...176 B1
Shalesbrook La. For R ...13 F1
Shalfleet Cl. East ...175 F2
Shandon Cl. T W ...9 D2
Shanklin Cl. East ...175 F2
Shanklin Rd. Bri ...166 A4
Shannon Cl. Pea ...168 C1
Sharpthorne Cres. Por S ...144 A1
Sharrow Cl. Hay H ...52 B3
Shaw The. T W ...9 D1
Shawfield. Cro ...27 E1
Sheddingdean Cl. Bur H ...74 C2
Sheen Rd. East ...185 F2
Sheep Pen La. Sea ...181 F2
Sheep Plain. Cro ...39 D4
Sheep Wlk. Rottn ...167 E1
Sheepbell Cl. Por S ...143 F2
Sheepfair. Lew ...126 C3
Sheepfold The. Pea ...169 D1
Sheepsetting La. Hea ...83 E4
Sheepstreet La. Etc ...45 E2
Sheepstreet La. Ston ...45 E2
Sheerwater Cres. Hast ...140 A2
Sheffield Mill La. Che G ...55 D4
Sheffield Mill La. Dan ...54 C4
Sheiling Rd. Cro ...27 E2
Shell La. Hast ...162 C4
Shelldale Ave. Por S ...163 F4
Shelldale Cres. Por S ...163 F4
Shelldale Rd. Por S ...163 F4
Shelley Cl. Lew ...126 C1
Shelley Rd. E Gri ...2 A1
Shelley Rd. Hove ...164 B4
Shelley Rd. Rin ...128 A3
Shelley Wlk. East ...176 B1
Shenfield Way. Bri ...145 F2
Shenstone. Hay H ...52 C4
Shepham Ave. Salt ...168 A1
Shepham La. Pole ...175 D4
Shepherd St. Hast ...162 A3
Shepherd's Cl. Bex ...159 D2
Shepherd's Hill. Col H ...25 D4
Shepherd's Way. Fai ...142 B2
Shepherds Cl. East ...175 E2
Shepherds Cl. Rin ...128 B3
Shepherds Cot. Pea ...169 D1
Shepherds Croft. Bri ...145 D2
Shepherds Mead. Bur H ...74 B2
Shepherds Way. Rin ...128 B3
Shepherds Wlk. Cro ...28 A1
Shepherds Wlk. Hass ...100 B3
Shepherds Wlk. T W ...9 D2
Shepherdsgrove La. Hamm ...3 F2
Sheppey Wlk. Hai ...132 C2
Sheppeys. Hay H ...52 A1
Shepway The. Sea ...181 F2
Sheraton Cl. East ...185 E1
Sherborne Cl. T W ...9 D1
Sherborne Cl. Hove ...144 A2
Sherborne Rd. Hove ...144 A2
Sherbourne Way. Hove ...144 A2
Sheridan Cl. E Gri ...2 A1
Sheridan Terr. Hove ...164 C4
Sheriff's La. Tow R ...41 D4
Sheringham Cl. Stas ...67 E3
Sherrington Rd. Wood ...167 E4
Sherwood Cl. Hast ...140 B1
Sherwood Dr. Hay H ...52 A3
Sherwood Green. Hai ...154 C3
Sherwood Rd. Sea ...181 E2
Sherwood Rd. T W ...9 D3
Sherwood Rise. Sea ...181 E2
Sherwood Way. T W ...9 D3
Shinewater La. East ...175 F2
Ship St. Bri ...165 E3
Ship St. E Gri ...12 B3
Ship St. Newh ...180 A4
Ship St Ct. Bri ...165 F3
Ship St Gdns. Bri ...165 E3
Shipley La. Bex ...159 D2
Shipley Rd. Wood ...167 E3
Shirlea View. Bat ...115 E2
Shirley Ave. Hove ...144 C1
Shirley Cl. S Sea ...163 D4
Shirley Dr. Hast ...139 F2
Shirley Dr. Hove ...145 D1
Shirley Gdns. T W ...8 A3
Shirley Gr. T W ...8 A3
Shirley Rd. Hove ...165 D4
Shirley Rd. Hove ...164 C4
Shirleys. Dit ...101 E1
Shoreham By-ps. S Sea ...143 C4
Short Brow. Sea ...181 F2
Short Brow Cl. Willn ...174 C2
Shortdean Pl. East ...185 D2
Shortgate Rd. Bri ...146 B2

Shortlands Cl. Willn

Shortlands Cl. Willn 175 D1
Showfields Rd. T W 8 B1
Shrub La. Bur 64 A4
Shrub La. Ston 45 D1
Shrublands Ct. T W 9 D2
Shrublands The. Bex 159 E2
Sicklehatch La. Hor 83 F1
Sidcup Cl. East 176 A1
Sidehill Dr. Por S 143 E1
Sidley Green. Bex 160 A4
Sidley Rd. East 186 A3
Sidley St. Bex 160 A4
Sidney Cl. Hast 139 F2
Sidney Cl. T W 18 B4
Sidney Little Rd. Hast 139 D2
Silchester Rd. Hast 162 A4
Sillwood Pl. Bri 165 E3
Sillwood Rd. Bri 165 E3
Sillwood St. Bri 165 E3
Sillwood Terr. Bri 165 E3
Silva Cl. Bex 160 C3
Silvan Rd. Hast 139 E2
Silver Birches. Hay H 52 C2
Silverdale. Key 100 C2
Silverdale. Hove 165 D4
Silverdale Ct. Hai 154 C4
Silverdale La. T W 8 C3
Silverdale Rd. Bur H 75 D1
Silverdale Rd. East 185 E1
Silverdale Rd. Hove 165 D4
Silverdale Rd. T W 8 C3
Silverhill Ave. Hast 140 A2
Silverhill Ave. Hast 140 A3
Silverlands Rd. Hast 139 F1
Silverwick's La. Pon G 112 B4
Silvester Rd. Bex 160 A3
Silwood Cl. T W 9 E4
Simons Cl. Cro 27 F1
Singleton Rd. Bri 145 F3
Singleton Way. Bur H 75 D1
Sinnock Sq. Hast 162 C4
Sir David's Park. Sgh 8 B4
Skinner's La. Cat 137 D4
Skyline View. Pea 169 D1
Slade The. Lam 21 F2
Sleeches Cross. Frant 18 C1
Sleepers Stile Rd. Lam 20 C1
Slider's La. Dan 54 C4
Slider's La. Fle 54 C4
Slides The. Hast 139 E2
Slimbridge Rd. Bur H 74 B2
Slindon Ave. Pea 179 D3
Slindon Cres. East 176 B1
Slinfold Cl. Bri 166 A3
Sloe La. Alfn 172 C2
Slugwash La. Hay H 53 D1
Slugwash La. Wiv 76 A4
Smeatons La. Winc B 120 C3
Smith Cl. Nin 136 C3
Smithys Cl. Hast 140 A3
Smolletts. E Gri 12 A4
Smugglers Cl. Alfn 172 B2
Smugglers La. Cro 27 D3
Smugglers Way. Fai 142 B2
Snape View. Wad 31 E2
Snatt's Rd. Uck 79 F4
Snednore. Kin L 148 B3
Snipe Cl. Pem 10 B4
Snowdon Cl. East 176 A2
Snowdrop La. Hay H 53 D2
Solomon's La. Mou 89 D2
Solway. Hai 132 C1
Solway Ave. Bri 145 E4
Somerhill Ave. Hove 165 D4
Somerhill Rd. Hove 165 D3
Somerset Rd. T W 8 C3
Somerset St. Bri 166 A3
Somerville Cl. East 186 B4
Somerville Gdns. T W 8 B2
Sorrel Cl. East 176 A2
Sorrel Dr. East 176 A2
South Ave. Bri 166 A3
South Ave. East 184 C3
South Ave. Hur 99 F3
South Bank. Hass 100 B2
South Brooks Rd. Lydd 98 B1
South Cl. Bur H 74 B2
South Cl. Pev B 177 E3
South Cliff. Bex 159 E1
South Cliff. East 190 B4
South Cliff Ave. Bex 159 E1
South Cliff Ave. East 185 E1
South Coast Rd. Pea 179 E3
South Coast Rd. Salt 178 B4
South Ct. Lew 127 E1
South Downs. Plu 102 B3
South Dr. Bur H 74 B2
South Gr. T W 8 C1
South La. Dal 86 B1
South La. Newh 180 A4
South Lodge Cl. Bur H 74 B2
South Lynn Dr. East 185 E2
South Rd. Bri 145 E1
South Rd. Hai 154 C3
South Rd. Hay H 52 B2
South Rd. Newh 180 A4
South Rd. Plu G 76 A2
South Rd. Wiv G 76 A2
South Rough. Newk 78 A4

South St. Bri 165 E3
South St. Cro 27 E1
South St. Dit 101 D2
South St. E Hoa 107 E2
South St. East 185 E1
South St. Fal 147 D3
South St. Hast 162 A4
South St. Lew 149 E4
South St. May 41 F1
South St. Por S 143 F1
South St. Rot 40 C4
South St. Sea 181 E1
South Terr. Hast 162 B4
South Undercliff. Rye 95 D3
South View. Dit 101 E3
South View Rd. Cro 27 E1
South View Rd. Sgh 8 C4
South View Rd. Wad 31 E3
South Way. Lew 126 C1
South Way. Newh 180 A4
South Way. Sea 182 A1
South Woodlands. Bri 145 E3
Southall Ave. Bri 146 A1
Southampton St. Bri 166 A3
Southcourt Ave. Bex 159 E1
Southdown Ave. Bri 145 F1
Southdown Ave. Hast 140 C2
Southdown Ave. Lew 148 C4
Southdown Ave. Pea 179 E3
Southdown Ave. Por S 164 A4
Southdown Ave. Willn 174 C2
Southdown Cl. Hay H 52 A1
Southdown Cl. Newh 179 F3
Southdown Pl. Bri 145 F1
Southdown Pl. Lew 127 E1
Southdown Rd. Bri 145 F1
Southdown Rd. East 185 D4
Southdown Rd. Newh 179 F3
Southdown Rd. Por S 143 F1
Southdown Rd. Sea 181 E1
Southdown Rd. Sock 163 E4
Southerden Cl. Hai 155 D4
Southern Ave. Pole 174 C3
Southern Rd. East 175 E1
Southfield. Pole 174 B3
Southfield Rd. Spe 7 F4
Southfield Rd. T W 8 C3
Southfields. Wad 31 E3
Southfields Rd. East 185 E2
Southfields Way. Sgh 8 C4
Southlands. E Gri 12 B4
Southlands Ave. Bex 159 F4
Southlands Rd. Bex 159 F4
Southmead Cl. May 42 A2
Southmount. Bri 145 F1
Southon Cl. Por S 143 E2
Southover High St. Lew 149 D4
Southover Pl. Bri 165 F4
Southover Rd. Lew 149 D4
Southover St. Bri 165 F3
Southridge Rd. Cro 39 E4
Southridge Rise. Cro 39 E4
Southview Cl. Cro 27 E1
Southview Cl. S Sea 163 D4
Southview Cl. Sock 143 E1
Southview Rd. Pea 179 D4
Southview Rd. Sock 163 E4
Southwater Cl. Bri 166 A3
Southwater Rd. Hast 162 A4
Southway. Bur H 74 A2
Southwick Cl. E Gri 2 A1
Southwick Sq. Sock 163 E4
Southwick St. Sock 163 E4
Southwood Ave. T W 8 C3
Southwood Rd. T W 7 F2
Sovereign Cl. Hast 140 C2
Sovereign Cl. Sea 181 F3
Spa Ind Park. T W 9 E4
Spaldings The. Hast 139 E1
Sparrows Green Rd. Wad 31 E3
Spatham La. Dit 101 E3
Speldhurst Hill. Spe 7 F4
Speldhurst Rd. Lan G 7 E2
Speldhurst Rd. Sgh 8 B4
Speldhurst Rd. Spe 7 E3
Spencer Ave. Hove 144 A2
Spencer Rd. East 185 F1
Spencers Field. S Mal 127 E1
Spences La. S Mal 127 D1
Spicers Cl. Bur H 74 B3
Spindewood Dr. Bex 159 D2
Spinnais Gr. Sock 163 D4
Spinnais Gr. Sock 163 D4
Spinney Cl. Cra D 11 D4
Spinney Cl. Hur 99 F3
Spinney The. Bat 115 E2
Spinney The. Bex 159 D2
Spinney The. Hass 100 B3
Spinney The. Hast 140 B1
Spinney The. Hay H 52 A4
Spinney The. Hay H 52 B2
Spinney The. Hove 145 D2
Spinney The. Rob 65 E2
Spinneys The. Hea 83 F3
Spinneys The. Lew 127 E1
Spital Rd. Lew 126 C1
Spithurst Rd. Spi 104 C3
Spode La. Cowd 4 C4

Sponden La. Four T 48 C4
Sponden La. San 48 C4
Spotted Cow La. Bux 58 B3
Spray Hill. Lam 21 F2
Sprays La. Wfd 116 C2
Spring Cl. East 174 C1
Spring Gdns. Bri 165 F3
Spring Gdns. Lew 127 D1
Spring Gdns. Sock 163 E4
Spring Hill. Ford 6 C3
Spring La. Bex 159 D3
Spring La. Bur 63 E3
Spring La. Clay 123 E4
Spring Lodge Cl. East 176 B1
Spring Meadow. For R 13 E1
Spring St. Bri 165 E3
Spring St. Hast 140 A1
Spring Way. E Gri 2 C2
Springate Rd. Sock 163 E4
Springett Ave. Rin 128 A3
Springfield. E Gri 2 A2
Springfield Ave. Pea 178 B4
Springfield Cl. Cro 27 F1
Springfield Cl. Whm 176 B3
Springfield Rd. Bex 160 A3
Springfield Rd. Bri 165 F4
Springfield Rd. East 185 F2
Springfield Rd. Gro 17 D4
Springfield Rd. Hast 139 F1
Springfield Valley Rd. Hast 139 F1
Springfields. Tic 33 E1
Springhead. T W 9 D3
Springhead Way. Cro 39 E4
Springside Wlk. Hast 139 E1
Springwood Rd. Hea 83 F4
Spruce Cl. East 175 D1
Spur Rd. Pole 174 C3
Spurway Park. Pole 174 C3
Spurway The. T W 8 A1
Squab La. Mag D 133 F3
Square The. Bri 145 E3
Square The. Cowd 4 C3
Square The. Pev B 177 E3
Square The. Wad 31 F2
Squirrel Cl. Bex 159 E3
Squirrel Way. T W 9 E4
Stabledene Way. Pem 10 A3
Stablefield. Wfd 117 E2
Stafford Rd. Bri 165 E4
Stafford Rd. Sea 181 E2
Stafford Rd. T W 9 E2
Stafford Way. Key 100 C2
Stag Rd. T W 9 D4
Stainsby St. Hast 162 A4
Stanam Rd. Pem 10 B3
Standean Cl. Bri 146 A3
Standen Cl. E Gri 1 C2
Standen Sch. San 49 E4
Standen St. T W 8 C3
Stanford Ave. Bri 145 F1
Stanford Ave. Hass 100 B2
Stanford Cl. Hass 100 B2
Stanford Cl. Hove 145 E1
Stanford Rd. Bri 165 E4
Stanhope Pl. Hast 162 C4
Stanhope Rd. T W 9 D3
Stanier Rd. Hast 139 E3
Stanley Ave. Por S 143 E3
Stanley Ave S. Por S 143 E2
Stanley Rd. Bri 165 F4
Stanley Rd. East 185 F2
Stanley Rd. Hast 162 B4
Stanley Rd. Pea 168 C1
Stanley Rd. Por 163 F4
Stanley Rd. T W 8 C3
Stanley St. Bri 165 F3
Stanmer Ave. Salt 168 A2
Stanmer Dr. East 185 D4
Stanmer Park Rd. Bri 145 F1
Stanmer St. Bri 145 F1
Stanmer Villas. Bri 145 F1
Stansfield Rd. Lew 126 C1
Stanstead Cres. Wood 167 E3
Stansted Rd. East 185 F2
Staplefield Dr. Bri 146 B2
Stapley Rd. Hove 144 A1
Star La. Alfn 172 C2
Star La. Blas 81 F3
Star La. May 41 F1
Star Rd. East 185 E2
Starr's Green La. Bat 115 E2
Starrs Mead. Bat 115 E2
Starvecrow La. Bec 92 C3
Starvecrow La. Peas 93 E4
Starwell Cl. Hast 140 A2
Station App. Bat 115 E2
Station App. East 175 E1
Station App. Hass 100 B2
Station App. Hast 162 A4
Station App. Hea 83 F4
Station App. Hove 164 C4
Station App. Sea 181 E2
Station Cl. Plu 102 B3
Station Cotts. Hass 100 B2
Station Rd. Bex 160 A2
Station Rd. Bri 145 D2
Station Rd. Bur H 74 C1
Station Rd. Chay 77 E4
Station Rd. Crow 138 B3

Station Rd. E Gri 2 A1
Station Rd. For R 13 E2
Station Rd. Gro 17 D4
Station Rd. Hai 155 D3
Station Rd. Hast 162 B4
Station Rd. Hea 83 F4
Station Rd. Hel 132 C3
Station Rd. Hor K 35 D3
Station Rd. Hur G 46 C2
Station Rd. Lew 149 D4
Station Rd. May 41 F1
Station Rd. N Cha 77 E4
Station Rd. Newh 170 B1
Station Rd. Norm 68 C4
Station Rd. Plu 102 B3
Station Rd. Pole 174 C3
Station Rd. Por S 164 A4
Station Rd. Rob 65 F2
Station Rd. Rot 40 C4
Station Rd. Sea 180 C2
Station Rd. Sha 22 C3
Station Rd. Sock 163 E4
Station Rd. Tow R 29 D1
Station Rd. Wad 31 D3
Station Rd. Winc 94 B1
Station Rd. Wit 15 F3
Station Rd Ind Est. Hai 155 D3
Station St. Bri 165 F3
Station St. East 185 F1
Station St. Lew 127 D1
Staveley Rd. East 190 B4
Steep Hill. Bre 91 E1
Steine Gdns. Bri 165 F3
Steine La. Bri 165 F3
Steine St. Bri 165 F2
Stephen's Rd. T W 8 C3
Stephens Cl. Rin 128 A3
Stephens Rd. Bri 145 F1
Stephenson Dr. E Gri 12 B4
Stevens Cl. Bex 160 A4
Stevens Ct. Hove 164 B4
Stevenson Cl. East 176 B2
Stevenson Rd. Bri 166 A3
Stevenson Rd. Hast 139 F1
Stewards Inn La. Lew 149 D4
Stewart Rd. Sgh 9 D4
Steyne Cl. Sea 181 E1
Steyne Rd. Sea 181 E1
Steyning Ave. Hove 144 B2
Steyning Ave. Pea 179 D4
Steyning Cl. Sea 182 A1
Steyning Rd. Rottn 167 F1
Steyning Rd. Sea 182 A1
Stiles The. Hai 155 D4
Stirling Ave. Sea 182 A2
Stirling Cl. Bur H 75 D2
Stirling Cl. Sea 182 A2
Stirling Ct Rd. Bur H 75 D2
Stirling Pl. Hove 164 C3
Stirling Rd. Hast 139 E3
Stock Dale. Fai 142 B2
Stockland Green Rd. Spe 8 A4
Stockleigh Rd. Hast 162 A4
Stocks Meadow. Nin 136 C3
Stockwell Rd. E Gri 12 B3
Stoddards La. Bec 69 E3
Stoke Cl. Sea 181 F2
Stoke Manor Cl. Sea 181 F2
Stone Cross Rd. Cro 39 F3
Stone Cross Rd. Wad 31 F2
Stone Ct La. Pem 10 B4
Stone Hill. E Gri 12 A2
Stone Pit La. San 49 E3
Stone Quarry Rd. Che G 36 A4
Stone St. Bri 165 E3
Stone St. Hast 162 B4
Stone St. T W 9 D2
Stonecroft Cl. Hove 144 B2
Stonecross Rd. Bri 146 B2
Stonedene Cl. For R 13 F1
Stonefield Pl. Hast 162 B4
Stonefield Rd. Hast 162 C4
Stonefield Way. Bur H 74 B3
Stonegate Rd. Ston 44 A4
Stonegate Rd. Tic 32 A1
Stoneham Cl. S Mal 127 D2
Stoneham Rd. Hove 164 B4
Stonehouse Dr. Batt 116 B1
Stonehouse Dr. Hast 139 F1
Stonehouse Dr. Wfd 116 C1
Stonehurst Dr. Bri 166 A3
Stoneleigh Ave. Bri 145 E3
Stoneleigh Cl. Bri 145 E3
Stoneleigh Cl. E Gri 2 B1
Stonelink Cl. Hast 139 E4
Stonepark Dr. For R 13 F1
Stonepound Rd. Hass 100 B2
Stonery Cl. Por S 143 F1
Stonery Rd. Por S 143 F1
Stonestile La. Hast 140 B4
Stonewall Park Rd. Lan G 7 E2
Stonewood Cl. Sea 182 A2
Stoney La. S Sea 163 D4
Stony La. Hai 155 D4
Storrington Cl. Hove 144 B1
Straight Half Mile. Mar 56 C3
Strand. Rye 94 C3
Strand Hill. Winc 120 B4
Strand Meadow. Bur 63 F4

Sutherland Ave. Bex

Stratford St. T W 9 D3
Strathfield Cl. Hay H 52 B2
Strawberry Cl. T W 18 B4
Stream La. Fai 142 C3
Stream La. Sed 90 A1
Stream La. The M 47 F4
Stream La. Wha 89 F1
Stream Park. E Gri 1 C2
Stream Pit La. San 48 C3
Streamside Cl. Hast 140 B2
Streat La. Dit 102 A2
Streat La. N Cha 102 A2
Streat La. Strt 102 A2
Streatfield Rd. Hea 83 E4
Streatfield Rd. Uck 79 F4
Streele View. Uck 80 B4
Street End La. Bro O 61 E1
Street The. Fra 80 C3
Street The. Kin L 148 B3
Street The. Sed 116 B4
Street The. W Fir 150 C2
Street The. Wmes 124 B4
Streetlands. Sed 90 B1
Stringer Way. Bri 145 E2
Stringwalk The. Hai 155 D4
Stroma Gdns. Hai 132 B1
Strongs Pas. Hast 162 C4
Strood Rd. Hast 140 A1
Stuart Ave. East 185 D3
Stuart Cl. T W 18 B4
Stuart Way. E Gri 12 B4
Stubb La. Bre 92 A1
Stubb La. Bro Ow 92 B2
Stubpond La. Fel 1 A4
Studdens La. Cowb 111 D1
Studdens La. Hers 134 A4
Sturdee Cl. East 186 B4
Sturdee Pl. Hast 162 C4
Sturton Pl. Hai 154 C4
Subworth Cl. Hay H 52 A4
Sudeley Pl. Bri 166 A2
Sudeley St. Bri 166 A2
Sudeley Terr. Bri 166 A2
Suffolk Rd. Bex 160 A4
Suffolk St. Hove 164 B4
Sugar La. Hor K 35 D2
Sullington Cl. Bri 146 B2
Sumach Cl. East 175 E1
Summer Cl. Por S 163 F4
Summer Hill Rd. Bex 159 E3
Summercourt. Hai 154 C4
Summerdale Rd. Hove 144 A1
Summerdown Cl. East 185 D2
Summerdown La. Fri 184 A1
Summerdown Rd. East 185 D2
Summerfields Ave. Hai 154 C4
Summerheath Rd. Hai 154 C4
Summerhill Cl. Hay H 52 B4
Summerhill Dr. Hay H 52 C4
Summerhill Grange. Hay H 52 B4
Summerhill La. Hay H 52 B4
Summerlands Rd. Willn 175 D1
Summersdeane. Sock 143 E1
Summervale Rd. T W 8 B1
Sun La. Hast 162 C4
Sun Patch. Hai 155 D4
Sun St. Lew 127 D1
Sunningdale Cl. Bex 160 B2
Sunningdale Cl. Sea 181 F1
Sunninghill Ave. Hove 144 B1
Sunninghill Cl. Hove 144 B1
Sunnybank Cl. May 41 F1
Sunnydale Ave. Bri 145 F3
Sunnydale Cl. Bri 145 F3
Sunnyside Rd. T W 8 A2
Sunnywood Dr. Hay H 52 A2
Sunset Cl. Pea 168 C1
Sunset Cl. Pev B 177 E3
Sunstar La. Pole 174 B3
Sunte Ave. Hay H 52 B4
Sunte Cl. Hay H 52 B4
Sunview Ave. Pea 179 D3
Surrenden Cl. Bri 145 E2
Surrenden Cres. Bri 145 E2
Surrenden Holt. Bri 145 E2
Surrenden Park. Bri 145 E2
Surrenden Rd. Bri 145 E2
Surrey Cl. Sea 181 D2
Surrey Cl. T W 18 B4
Surrey Rd. Sea 181 D2
Surrey St. Bri 165 E3
Susan's Rd. East 185 F2
Susans Cl. E Hoa 107 F3
Sussex Ave. Hai 154 C4
Sussex Cl. Bex 159 E3
Sussex Cl. Hai 154 C4
Sussex Cl. T W 9 D1
Sussex Gdns. Fri 184 A1
Sussex Mews. Bri 166 B2
Sussex Mews. T W 8 C1
Sussex Pl. Bri 165 F3
Sussex Rd. Hast 161 F3
Sussex Rd. Hay H 52 B2
Sussex Rd. Hove 164 C3
Sussex Sq. Bri 166 B2
Sussex St. Bri 165 F3
Sussex Terr. Bri 165 F3
Sussex Way. Bur H 74 B3
Sussex Way. Pea 178 C4
Sutherland Ave. Bex 159 F2

Sutherland Cl. Bex

Sutherland Cl. Bex 159 E2
Sutherland Rd. Bri 166 A3
Sutherland Rd. T W 8 C2
Sutton Ave. Pea 178 C4
Sutton Ave. Sea 181 F1
Sutton Cl. Wood 147 E1
Sutton Croft La. Sea 181 E2
Sutton Dro. Sea 181 E2
Sutton Park Rd. Sea 181 E2
Sutton Pl. Bex 160 B2
Sutton Rd. East 185 F2
Sutton Rd. Sea 181 E2
Suttons The. Cam 96 C1
Suttons The. Hast 139 E1
Swaines Pas. Hast 162 C4
Swaines Way. Hea 83 F3
Swainsthorpe Cl. Hay H 52 B2
Swallow Bank. Hast 139 E1
Swallow Cl. East 176 A1
Swallow Ct. Rid 80 A3
Swallow Dr. Bat 115 E2
Swallow Dr. T W 9 E3
Swallows The. Pea 168 C1
Swan Ave. Hast 162 C4
Swan Cl. S Cha 103 E4
Swan Rd. Hai 155 D3
Swan Terr. Hast 162 C4
Swanborough Dr. Bri 166 B4
Swanborough Dro. Kin L 148 B2
Swanborough Hollow. Iford 148 C2
Swanborough Pl. Bri 166 B4
Swanley Cl. East 176 A1
Swann Cl. Bur H 75 D2
Swannee Cl. Pea 169 D1
Swaylands Ave. Cro 39 E4
Sweeps Hill Cl. Pem 10 A4
Sweethaws La. Cro 39 D3
Sweetings La. Cou W 21 D1
Sweetlands. Key 100 C3
Swife La. Bro O 62 A2
Swift Cl. Cro 27 D1
Swinburne Ave. Willn 175 D2
Swinehan La. Crow 138 C2
Swissland Hill. Dor P 2 B2
Swynford Dr. Hast 139 F3
Sybron Way. Cro 40 A4
Sycamore Cl. Bex 159 D2
Sycamore Cl. East 175 D2
Sycamore Cl. Hast 139 F1
Sycamore Cl. Hea 83 F3
Sycamore Cl. Sea 182 A2
Sycamore Cl. Wood 167 E4
Sycamore Cl. Uck 80 A4
Sycamore Dr. E Gri 2 C1
Sycamore Dr. Hai 154 C3
Sydney Rd. East 185 F2
Sydney Rd. Hay H 52 B3
Sydney St. Bri 165 F3
Sylvan Cl. Hay H 52 C2
Sylvester Way. Hove 144 A2
Symbister Rd. Por S 164 A4
Syresham Gdns. Hay H 52 B2

Tackleway. Hast 162 C4
Taddington Rd. East 186 A2
Tainters Brook. Uck 80 B4
Talbot Cres. Bri 146 A3
Talbot Park. T W 9 D3
Talbot Rd. The M 47 E4
Talbot Terr. Lew 127 D1
Tall Ash Dr. Hast 140 A2
Tamarack Cl. East 175 D1
Tamworth Rd. Hove 164 B4
Tanbridge Rd. East 176 A1
Tandridge Rd. Hove 164 B3
Tangier La. Frant 18 C3
Tangle Fel 1 B2
Tanglewood Coppice. Bex 159 E2
Tangmere Cl. Bex 159 E2
Tangmere Rd. Bri 145 F3
Tanhouse La. Peas 70 B1
Tanners Way. Cro 27 F1
Tanyard. San 48 C3
Tanyard Ave. E Gri 12 C4
Tanyard Cotts. Bux 58 A1
Tanyard La. Che Co 36 A3
Tanyard La. Dan 35 F1
Tanyard La. Winc 120 B4
Tapsell's La. Wad 31 D3
Tarner Rd. Bri 165 F3
Tarragon Way. S Sea 143 D1
Tarring Cl. S Hei 170 A1
Tas Combe Way. Willn 174 C1
Tate Cres. Bur H 74 B3
Taunton Gr. Bri 146 C1
Taunton Rd. Bri 146 B1
Taunton Way. Bri 146 C1
Tavistock Down. Bri 146 A1
Taylor Cl. Hast 139 E2
Taylor St. Sgh 8 C4
Tea Gdn La. T W 8 A1
Teal Ct. Hast 139 E2
Teasley Mead. Wit 6 A2
Tedder Rd. T W 8 C4
Tedder Terr. Hast 141 D3
Teg Cl. Por S 144 A1
Telegraph St. Bri 166 A2
Telford Rd. Hast 139 F3
Telham Cl. Hast 140 C3

Telham La. Bat 115 D1
Telscombe Cliffs Way. Pea 178 C4
Telscombe Park. Pea 169 D1
Telscombe Rd. East 176 B1
Telscombe Rd. Pea 169 D1
Temple Gdns. Bri 165 E3
Temple St. Bri 165 E3
Tenantry Down Rd. Bri 166 B4
Tennis Cl. Hai 154 C4
Tennis Rd. Hove 164 B3
Tennyson Rise. E Gri 2 A1
Tennyson Wlk. East 176 B2
Tenterden Cl. East 176 A1
Tenterden Rise. Hast 140 B1
Terminus Ave. Bex 159 F2
Terminus Pl. Bri 165 E4
Terminus Rd. Bex 159 F2
Terminus Rd. Bri 165 E4
Terminus Rd. East 185 F1
Terminus St. Bri 165 E3
Terrace Rd. Hast 162 A4
Thackeray Cl. East 176 B2
Thakeham Cl. Bex 160 C3
Thames Cl. Bri 165 F3
Thanet Way. Hast 140 B1
Thatchers Cl. Bur H 75 D1
Thatchings The. Pole 174 C3
Theaklen Dr. Hast 139 F1
Theobalds Green. Hea 83 F3
Theobalds Rd. Bur H 75 D3
Theobalds Rd. Wiv 75 E4
Theodore Cl. T W 9 E4
Third Ave. Bex 160 B3
Third Ave. Hove 164 C3
Third Ave. Newh 180 A3
Third Rd. Pea 178 C4
Third St. Lan G 7 E2
Thirlmere Rd. T W 8 B3
Thomas Brassey Cl. Hast 139 F3
Thomas St. Lew 127 E1
Thomas St. T W 8 C3
Thomas Turner Dr. E Hoa 107 F3
Thompson Rd. Bri 146 A1
Thompson Rd. Newh 170 B1
Thorden La. Rol L 50 C4
Thornbank Cres. Bex 159 E2
Thornbush Cres. Por S 143 F2
Thorndean Rd. Bri 146 A2
Thorne Cres. Bex 137 E1
Thornfield Gdns. T W 9 E3
Thornhill Ave. Bri 145 F4
Thornhill Cl. Hove 144 B1
Thornhill Rise. Por S 143 F2
Thornhill Way. Por S 143 F2
Thornwell Rd. Wil 173 E4
Thornwood Cl. East 175 E1
Thorny Cl. Hea 83 F4
Three Leg Cross Rd. Tic 33 D1
Three Oaks La. Wad 31 D4
Thurrock Cl. Willn 174 C2
Thyme Cl. S Sea 143 D1
Tibbs Mill La. Cro 39 E1
Ticehurst Ave. Hooe 158 B3
Ticehurst Rd. Bri 166 B3
Ticehurst Rd. Ston 44 B3
Tickerage La. Blas 81 E3
Tidebrook Gdns. East 176 B1
Tideswell Rd. East 185 F2
Tidy St. Bri 165 F3
Tilbury Pl. Bri 165 F3
Tilbury Way. Bri 165 F3
Tile Barn Rd. Hast 139 E2
Tilehurst Dr. Hai 154 C4
Tilekiln La. Hast 141 E2
Tilers Cl. Bur H 75 D2
Tilgate Cl. Bri 166 A3
Tilgate Cl. East 185 D4
Tilgate Dr. Bex 159 D2
Tilley La. Bor S 135 E3
Tillingham Ave. Rye 94 C3
Tillingham La. Peas 93 E3
Tillingham View. Bro O W 91 F3
Tillington Terr. Hast 141 D1
Tillstone St. Bri 165 F3
Tilsmore Rd. Hea 83 E4
Tiltwood Dr. Cra D 1 A1
Timber Yard Cotts. Lew 127 E1
Timberlaine Rd. Pev B 177 D2
Timberley Rd. East 175 D1
Timbers Ct. Hai 155 D4
Tindal Cl. Bri 75 D2
Tinker's La. Had D 59 E2
Tinkers La. Tic 33 E2
Tintern Cl. Bri 145 F1
Tintern Cl. East 175 E2
Tisbury Rd. Hove 165 D3
Titchborne St. Bri 165 F3
Titchfield Cl. Bur H 75 D1
Tithe Orch. Fel 1 B4
Titian Rd. Hove 164 B4
Tiverton Dr. Bex 160 B3
Tivoli Cres. Bri 145 D1
Tivoli Cres N. Bri 145 D1
Tivoli Pl. Hove 145 D1
Tivoli Rd. Bri 145 D1
Tolkien Rd. East 176 B1
Toll Wood Rd. Hor 109 E4
Tollgate. Pea 168 C1
Tollgates. Bat 114 C2

Tollwood Park. Cro 27 F1
Tollwood Rd. Cro 39 F4
Tompset's Bank. For R 13 E1
Tonbridge Rd. Pem 9 F4
Tonbridge Way. Cam 96 B1
Tongdean Ave. Hove 145 D1
Tongdean Ct. Bri 145 D2
Tongdean La. Bri 145 D2
Tongdean Rd. Hove 145 D2
Tongdean Rise. Bri 145 D2
Top Cross Rd. Bex 160 C4
Top Dr. Mar 56 C3
Top Rd. Sha 22 C3
Tophill Cl. Por S 143 E1
Tor Rd. Pea 169 D1
Torfield Cl. Hast 162 C4
Torfield Rd. East 185 E2
Toronto Terr. Bri 165 F3
Toronto Terr. Lew 127 D1
Torrance Cl. Hove 144 B1
Totland Rd. Bri 166 A4
Tott Yew Rd. Willn 174 C2
Tourney Rd. Lydd 98 C3
Tovey Cl. East 185 D3
Tower Cl. E Gri 2 B1
Tower Cl. Pev B 177 E4
Tower Rd. Bri 166 A3
Tower Rd. Hast 140 A1
Tower Rd W. Hast 161 F4
Tower Ride. Uck 57 D1
Tower St. Hea 83 F4
Tower View. Uck 80 A4
Towerscroft Ave. Hast 140 A3
Town Hill. Lam 21 F2
Townlands Rd. Wad 31 E2
Trading Estate. Rye H 95 D2
Trafalgar Cl. Hast 139 E4
Trafalgar Cl. Pea 169 D1
Trafalgar Ct. Bri 165 F3
Trafalgar La. Bri 165 F3
Trafalgar Rd. Por S 163 F4
Trafalgar St. Bri 165 F3
Trafalgar Terr. Bri 165 F3
Tram Rd. Rye H 95 F1
Transit Rd. Newh 180 A4
Travellers La. Hast 141 D2
Treblers Rd. Rot 40 B3
Tredcroft Rd. Hove 145 D1
Treemaines Rd. East 176 B1
Treemans Rd. Hor K 54 A4
Treetops Cl. Hast 167 E4
Tremola Ave. Salt 168 A1
Trenches Rd. Cro 27 E1
Treyford Cl. Wood 147 E1
Triangle Rd. Hay H 52 B2
Triangle The. Willn 174 C2
Trinity Cl. T W 9 D2
Trinity Pas. Hast 162 B4
Trinity Pl. East 185 F1
Trinity Rd. Hur 99 F3
Trinity St. Bri 165 F4
Trinity St. Hast 162 B4
Trinity Trees. East 185 F1
Tristan Gdns. T W 8 A2
Troon Cl. Sea 180 C3
Trossachs Cl. East 176 A2
Troy Cl. Cro 27 F1
Truleigh Cl. Wood 167 E4
Truleigh Dr. Por S 143 F2
Tubwell La. Cro 40 A4
Tubwell La. Hor 83 E1
Tudor Ave. Hast 161 F4
Tudor Cl. E Gri 12 B4
Tudor Cl. Hove 144 B1
Tudor Cl. Sea 181 D2
Tudor Ct. T W 8 B1
Tudor Gdns. Bur H 74 B2
Tudor Wlk. Fra 80 C3
Tugwell Rd. East 175 E1
Tumulus Rd. Salt 168 A2
Tunnel Rd. T W 8 C2
Turkey Rd. Bex 159 E4
Turner Cl. Bex 160 B3
Turner Cl. East 176 A1
Turner Ct. E Gri 2 C2
Turner's Hill Rd. E Gri 12 A4
Turners Green La. Wad 31 E3
Turners Mill Cl. Hay H 52 A3
Turners Mill Rd. Hay H 52 A3
Turners Way. Bur H 74 B2
Turnpike Cl. Pea 169 D1
Turnpike Cl. Rin 128 C4
Turnpike Piece. Bri 146 C3
Turton Cl. Bri 166 A3
Tutts Barn La. East 185 E3
Tuxford Rd. T W 7 F3
Twineham Rd. East 185 D4
Twitten Cl. Sock 163 E4
Twitten La. Fel 1 B2
Twitten The. Alb 99 D3
Twitten The. Bex 159 D2
Twitten The. Cro 27 E1
Twitten The. Dit 101 D2
Twitten The. Sock 163 D4
Twittens The. Bur H 74 C2
Twyford Cres. Hast 140 A2
Twyford Rd. Bri 146 A3
Twyfords. Cro 27 D1
Tye Hill Rd. Arl 153 F2

Tye View. Pea 168 C1
Tyedean Rd. Pea 178 B4
Tylers La. Nut 37 E1
Tyndale Ave. Bex 159 D2

Uckfield Cl. Bri 166 B3
Uckfield Rd. Cro 38 C4
Uckfield Rd. Rin 127 F4
Uckham La. Bat 115 E3
Udimore Rd. Bro O W 92 B2
Udimore Rd. Rye 94 B2
Udimore Rd. Udi 93 E1
Under Rd. Hers 134 A2
Under Rd. Mag D 133 F2
Undercliff Terr. Hast 162 A3
Undercliffe. Hast 161 F3
Underdown Rd. Sock 163 D4
Underhill. Mar 56 C3
Underhill La. Clay 123 E4
Underhill La. Wmes 124 A4
Union Cl. Hai 132 C2
Union Rd. Bri 165 F4
Union St. Bri 165 F3
Union St. Hast 162 A4
Upland Rd. East 185 D2
Uplands Cl. Bex 159 E3
Uplands Park. Bro O 61 E1
Uplands Rd. Bri 146 A1
Uplands The. Hast 161 F4
Upper Abbey Rd. Bri 166 A2
Upper Ave. East 185 F2
Upper Bedford St. Bri 166 A2
Upper Belgrave Rd. Sea 181 E2
Upper Bevendean Ave. Bri 146 B1
Upper Broomgrove Rd. Hast 140 C2
Upper Carlisle Rd. East 190 A4
Upper Chalvington Pl. Bri 166 B3
Upper Church Rd. Hast 139 F2
Upper Chyngton Gdns. Sea 181 F2
Upper Cl. For R 13 E1
Upper Clarance Rd. Hast 140 A1
Upper Cumberland Wlk. T W 8 C1
Upper Dr The. Hove 165 D4
Upper Duke's Dr. East 190 A4
Upper Dunstan Rd. T W 8 C3
Upper Gardner St. Bri 165 F3
Upper Glen Rd. Hast 139 F3
Upper Gloucester Rd. Bri 165 E3
Upper Greenwoods La. Pun T 85 D3
Upper Grosvenor Rd. T W 8 C3
Upper Hamilton Rd. Bri 165 E3
Upper Hollingdean Rd. Bri 145 F1
Upper Horsebridge Rd. Hai 132 C2
Upper King's Dr. East 175 D1
Upper Kingston La. S Sea 143 D1
Upper Lake. Bat 115 E2
Upper Lewes Rd. Bri 165 F4
Upper Market St. Hove 165 D3
Upper Maze Hill. Hast 161 F4
Upper Nellington. Lan G 7 F2
Upper North St. Bri 165 E3
Upper Park Pl. Bri 165 F3
Upper Park Rd. Hast 140 A1
Upper Profit. Lan G 7 F2
Upper Ratton Dr. East 184 C4
Upper Rock Gdns. Bri 165 F3
Upper Sea Rd. Bex 160 A2
Upper Sherwood Rd. Sea 181 E2
Upper Shoreham Rd. S Sea 143 D1
Upper South Rd. Hast 140 A1
Upper Sq. For R 13 E2
Upper St. E Dean 188 C4
Upper St. T W 8 A2
Upper St James's St. Bri 166 A2
Upper St Johns Rd. Bur H 74 C2
Upper Station Rd. Hea 83 F4
Upper Stephens. Lan G 7 F2
Upper Sudeley St. Bri 166 A2
Upper Valley Rd. Newh 179 F3
Upper Wellington Rd. Bri 166 A4
Upper Winfield Ave. Bri 145 E3
Upper Wish Hill. East 184 C4
Upperton Gdns. East 185 E2
Upperton La. East 185 E2
Upperton Rd. East 185 E2
Upton Ave. Sock 143 E1
Upton Quarry. Lan G 7 E2
Upwick Rd. East 185 D2

Val Prinseps Rd. Pev B 177 D2
Vale Ave. Bri 145 E4
Vale Ave. T W 8 C2
Vale Cl. Sea 181 F2
Vale Gdns. Por S 163 F4
Vale Rd. Bat 114 C3
Vale Rd. Hast 140 A1
Vale Rd. Hay H 52 B1
Vale Rd. May 41 F2
Vale Rd. Por S 164 A4
Vale Rd. Salt 168 A2
Vale Rd. Sea 181 F2
Vale Rd. T W 8 C2
Vale The. Oving 167 E2
Vale View Rd. Hea 83 F3
Valebridge Cl. Bur H 75 D3
Valebridge Dr. Bur H 75 D3
Valebridge Rd. Bur H 75 D3
Valence Rd. Lew 126 C1
Valentine's Pas. Hast 162 A3

Vinehall Rd. Mou 89 E3
Vineries The. Bur H 75 D2
Vineries The. East 176 A1
Vines Cross Rd. Bri 166 B4
Vines Cross Rd. Hor 109 F4
Vineyard La. Tic 33 D1
Vintry The. East 185 D4
Vintry The. Nut 37 D2
Virgin's Croft. Bat 115 D3
Virgins La. Bat 115 D3
Vowels La. Sel C 11 D1

Wade Cl. East 186 B4
Wadhurst Cl. East 175 E1
Wadhurst La. Bat 139 F3
Wadhurst La. Bat 114 B3
Wadhurst Par. Wad 31 E2
Wadhurst Rise. Bri 166 B3
Wadlands Brook Rd. Dor P 2 A3
Wagg Cl. E Gri 2 C1
Wainwright Cl. Hast 139 D2
Wainwright Cl. Bex 159 F2
Waite Cl. S Mal 127 D1
Waites La. Fai 142 B3
Wakefield Rd. Bri 165 F4
Waldegrave Rd. Bri 145 F1
Waldegrave St. Hast 162 B4
Waldene Cl. East 140 B1
Waldron Ave. Bri 146 A3
Waldron Cl. East 185 D4
Waldron Ct. Hea 83 F4
Waldron Rd. E Hoa 107 F3
Waldron Thorns. Hea 83 F4
Waldshut Rd. Lew 126 C2
Walesbeech Rd. Salt 178 A4
Walker Cl. East 186 B4
Wall Hill Rd. Ash W 13 E3
Wall Hill Rd. For R 13 E3
Wallace Cl. T W 18 C4
Wallands Cres. Lew 127 D1
Wallers. Spe 7 F4
Wallinger's Wlk. Hast 162 C4
Wallis Ave. East 186 B4
Wallis Cl. Cro 27 F1
Wallis Pl. East 186 B4
Wallsend Rd. Pev B 177 D3
Walmer Cres. Bri 146 C1
Walmer Rd. Sea 182 A2
Walnut Cl. Bri 145 E2
Walnut Cl. Hea 83 F3
Walnut Tree Wlk. East 184 C4
Walnut Wlk. Pole 174 C3
Walpole Rd. Bri 166 A3
Walpole Terr. Bri 166 A3
Walpole Wlk. Bex 176 B2
Walshes Rd. Cro 39 F4
Walsingham Cl. East 175 D2
Walsingham Rd. Hove 164 B3
Walters Green Rd. Ford 6 B4
Walton Bank. Bri 146 B3
Walton Cl. Hast 140 A3
Walwers La. East 127 D1
Wanderdown Cl. Oving 167 E2
Wanderdown Rd. Oving 167 D2
Wanderdown Way. Oving 167 E2
Wannock Ave. Willn 174 B2
Wannock Cl. Bex 160 C3
Wannock Dr. Pole 174 B3
Wannock Gdns. Willn 174 B2
Wannock La. Willn 174 B2
Wannock Rd. East 186 A3
Wannock Rd. Pole 174 B3
Warbleton Cl. Bri 166 B3
Warburton Cl. E Gri 12 C4
Warburton Cl. East 185 D4
Warburton Cl. Uck 80 A4
Ward Way. Bex 159 E3
Ward's La. Wal 32 B2
Wardsbook Rd. Tic 45 D4
Warenne Rd. Hove 144 A2
Wares Field. Rid 80 A2
Wares Rd. Rid 80 A2
Warliegh Rd. Bri 165 F4
Warmdene Ave. Bri 145 E3
Warmdene Cl. Bri 145 E3
Warmdene Rd. Bri 145 E3
Warmdene Way. Bri 145 E3
Warminster Rd. Pev B 177 D3
Warnham Gdns. Bex 159 D1
Warnham Rise. Bri 145 F3
Warren Ave. Wood 167 D4
Warren Cl. Cro H 82 B3
Warren Cl. East 190 A4
Warren Cl. Fel 1 B2
Warren Cl. Fri 183 F1
Warren Cl. Hast 161 E4
Warren Cl. Lew 148 C4
Warren Cl. Wood 166 C4
Warren Dr. Lew 148 C4
Warren Gdn. Cro 27 E1
Warren La. Cro H 82 C4
Warren La. Fri 183 F1
Warren La. N Cha 77 E4
Warren Lodge. Pea 168 C1
Warren Rd. Bri 166 B4
Warren Rd. Cro 27 D1
Warren Rd. Fai 142 A2
Warren Rd. Fri G 26 C1
Warren Rd. Wood 166 C4

Warren Ridge. Frant 19 D2
Warren Rise. Wood 166 C4
Warren The. Bur H 75 D1
Warren The. May 42 A1
Warren Way. N Cha 77 E4
Warren Way. Pea 168 C1
Warren Way. Wood 167 D4
Warrior Gdns. Hast 162 A4
Warrior Sq. East 186 A2
Warrior Sq. Hast 162 A4
Warrs Hill La. N Cha 77 E4
Wartling Cl. Hast 139 E1
Wartling Dr. Bex 158 B3
Wartling Rd. Bor S 135 D1
Wartling Rd. East 186 A3
Wartling Rd. Wart 157 D4
Warwick Park. T W 8 C1
Warwick Rd. Bex 159 E3
Warwick Rd. Sea 181 E2
Warwick Rd. T W 8 C1
Washington Ave. Hast 139 E3
Washington Rd. Hay H 52 C3
Washington St. Bri 165 F4
Washwell La. Wad 31 E2
Wassall La. Rol L 50 B4
Watchbell La. Rye 95 D3
Watchbell St. Rye 95 D3
Watemill La. Bex 137 F1
Waterdown Rd. T W 8 B1
Waterdyke Ave. Sock 163 E4
Waterfield. T W 18 C4
Watergate. Bex 159 F4
Waterhall Rd. Bri 145 D3
Waterloo Cl. Hast 139 E4
Waterloo Pas. Hast 162 C4
Waterloo Pl. Bri 165 F3
Waterloo Pl. Hast 162 C4
Waterloo Pl. Lew 127 D1
Waterloo Sq. Alfn 172 C2
Waterloo St. Hove 165 D3
Watermans Cl. Hast 140 B2
Watermill Cl. Bex 159 F4
Watermill Cl. Pole 174 C3
Watermill La. Bec 69 D1
Watermill La. Gue G 119 D1
Watermill La. Ick 119 D2
Waters Cotts. Wad 31 F2
Waterside. E Gri 2 C1
Waterworks Dr. For R 13 E4
Waterworks Rd. East 185 F2
Waterworks Rd. Hast 140 B1
Watling Cl. Sock 163 E4
Watling Rd. Sock 163 E4
Watton Park. Bex 159 E2
Watts Cl. Wad 31 E2
Watts La. East 185 E2
Watts' Palace La. Ewh G 91 D4
Waverley Cres. Bri 146 A1
Waverley Dr. T W 9 E3
Waverley Gdns. Pev B 177 D3
Wayfaring Down. Jev 174 A2
Wayfield Ave. Hove 144 B1
Wayford Cl. East 176 A1
Wayland Ave. Bri 145 D2
Wayside. Bri 145 D3
Wayside. Fri 188 C4
Weald Ave. Hove 164 B4
Weald Cl. Bar C 104 B2
Weald Cl. Hur 99 E3
Weald Rd. Bur H 74 B2
Weald Rise. Hay H 52 B1
Weald The. E Gri 2 B2
Weald View. Bar C 104 B2
Weald View. Stas 67 E1
Weald View. Wad 31 E3
Wealden Cl. Cro 27 E2
Wealden Park. East 175 D1
Wealden View. Bur 63 F4
Wealden Way. Bex 159 D3
Wealden Way. Hay H 52 A2
Wealdview Rd. Hea 83 E4
Weare Rd. Sgh 9 D4
Weatherby Cl. East 185 D4
Weavers Cl. Bur H 75 D1
Weavers La. Alfn 172 B2
Wedderburn Rd. East 174 C1
Week La. Gly 128 A1
Welbeck Ave. Hast 161 F4
Welbeck Ave. Hove 164 B3
Welbeck Ave. Sgh 9 D4
Welbeck Cl. Bur H 75 D2
Welbeck Cl. East 175 D2
Welbeck Dr. Bur H 75 D2
Welesmere Rd. Rottn 167 F2
Welkin The. Hay H 52 C4
Well Hollow Pl. Lew 127 D1
Wellcombe Cres. East 190 A4
Weller Rd. T W 8 A2
Wellesley Cl. Bex 159 D2
Wellesley Cl. Cro 27 D1
Wellesley St. Hast 162 C4
Wellesley Rd. East 185 F2
Wellfield. Ash W 13 D4
Wellgreen La. Kin L 148 B3
Wellhouse La. Bur H 100 C4
Wellingham La. Rin 127 D1
Wellingham La. S Mal 127 F4
Wellington Gdns. Bat 115 D3

Wellington Gdns. Hast 162 C4
Wellington Mews. Hast 162 B4
Wellington Pl. Hast 162 B4
Wellington Rd. Bri 166 A4
Wellington Rd. Hast 162 C4
Wellington Rd. Newh 170 B1
Wellington Rd. Pea 179 E3
Wellington Rd. Por S 164 A3
Wellington Sq. Hast 162 B4
Wellington St. Bri 166 A4
Wellington St. Lew 127 D1
Wellington Town Rd. E Gri 2 A1
Wellis Gdns. Hast 161 F4
Wells Cl. East 190 A4
Wells Cl. Plu G 102 B3
Wells Cl. T W 8 C2
Wells Meadow. E Gri 2 A2
Wendale Dr. Pea 169 D1
Went Hill Gdns. Willn 174 C2
Went La. Fri 184 A1
Went Way. E Dean 188 C4
Wenthill Cl. Fri 189 D4
Wentworth Cl. Bex 160 B3
Wentworth St. Bri 165 F2
Wentworth Way. Hast 161 E4
West Ascent. Hast 161 F3
West Beeches Rd. Cro 27 F1
West Cl. Alfn 172 B2
West Cl. Pole 174 C4
West Comm. Hay H 52 B4
West Comm Dr. Hay H 52 C4
West Dean Rise. Sea 181 F2
West Down Rd. Bex 159 F3
West Dr. Bri 166 A3
West End. Hers 134 B3
West Furlong La. Hur 99 F3
West Hill. Dor P 2 B3
West Hill. E Gri 12 A4
West Hill Pl. Bri 165 E3
West Hill Rd. Bri 165 E3
West Hill Rd. Hast 161 F3
West Hill St. Bri 165 E3
West Hoathly Rd. E Gri 12 A3
West La. E Gri 12 A4
West Leigh. E Gri 12 B4
West Mallion. Hay H 52 B2
West Par. Bex 159 F1
West Park Cres. Bur H 74 A2
West Park Rd. Dom 1 A4
West Rd. Por S 163 F4
West Rd. Poy 122 B4
West Rd. Pye 122 C3
West St. Alfn 172 B2
West St. Bri 165 E3
West St. Bur H 74 B2
West St. Dit 101 D2
West St. Dor 2 C4
West St. E Gri 12 B4
West St. East 185 E1
West St. Hast 162 C4
West St. Lew 127 D1
West St. May 41 F1
West St. Por S 164 A4
West St. Rottn 167 E1
West St. Rye 95 D3
West St. Sea 181 E1
West St La. Hor 83 E1
West Terr. East 185 E1
West Undercliff. Rye 94 C3
West View. Hast 140 C1
West View. Hay H 52 C3
West View. Sea 181 E1
West View. Uck 57 D1
West View Gdns. E Gri 12 B4
West View Terr. S Hei 170 A1
West Way. Hove 144 B1
Westaway Dr. Bex 159 F2
Westbourne Gdns. Hove 164 C4
Westbourne Gr. Hove 164 C4
Westbourne Pl. Hove 164 C3
Westbourne St. Hove 164 C4
Westbourne Villas. Hove 164 B3
Westbrook. Salt 168 A1
Westbrook La. Wfd 117 E3
Westbrook Terr. T W 9 D1
Westcourt Dr. Bex 159 E2
Westdean Ave. Newh 179 F3
Westdene Cl. Hast 140 A3
Westdene Dr. Bri 145 D3
Westdown La. Bur C 62 C2
Westdown Rd. Sea 181 D2
Westergate Rd. Bri 146 B2
Westerham Rd. East 176 A1
Westerleigh Cl. Hast 161 F4
Western Ave. Pole 174 C4
Western Espl. Hove 164 B3
Western Gdns. Cro 40 A4
Western Par. East 190 B4
Western Rd. Bex 160 A2
Western Rd. Bri 165 E3
Western Rd. Bur H 74 B2
Western Rd. Chay 77 F3
Western Rd. Cro 40 A4
Western Rd. East 185 F2
Western Rd. Hai 154 C4
Western Rd. Hast 162 A4
Western Rd. Hay H 52 B2
Western Rd. Hur 99 E3

Western Rd. Lew 126 C1
Western Rd. Newh 180 A3
Western Rd. Newk 78 A4
Western Rd. Pev B 177 D2
Western Rd. T W 9 D3
Western Rd. Wad 31 E3
Western St. Bri 165 D3
Western Terr. Bri 165 E3
Westfield Ave. Salt 168 A2
Westfield Ave N. Salt 168 B2
Westfield Ave S. Salt 168 A2
Westfield Cl. Bri 145 F2
Westfield Cl. Five A 59 F3
Westfield Cl. Pole 174 C4
Westfield Cres. Bri 145 F3
Westfield Ct. Pole 174 C3
Westfield La. Hast 139 F4
Westfield La. Wfd 117 D1
Westfield Rd. East 185 D3
Westfield Rise. Salt 168 B2
Westgate St. Lew 127 D1
Westham Cl. Bex 159 E2
Westham Dr. Pev B 177 E3
Westlands Rd. Hay H 52 C3
Westmeston Ave. Salt 167 F1
Westminster Cl. East 175 D2
Westminster Cres. Hast 140 C2
Westmoreland Cl. Hast 139 E2
Westmount Cl. Sock 163 D4
Westpoint. Newk 78 A4
Westville Rd. Bex 159 F2
Westway. Pem 10 A4
Westway Cl. Por S 143 E2
Westway Gdns. Por S 143 E2
Westwood Rd. T W 8 A3
Wharf Rd. East 185 E2
Wharf Rd. Hove 164 A3
Whatlington Rd. Bat 115 E4
Whatlington Rd. Wha 89 F1
Whatlington Way. Hast 139 D1
Wheatfield Way. Bri 146 B2
Wheatsheaf Gdns. Lew 127 E1
Wheel La. Wfd 117 D2
Wheelers La. Had D 59 D3
Wheelwright La. Bur H 75 D1
Whichelo Pl. Bri 166 A3
Whiffens Cl. Hast 154 C3
Whincroft Park. Cro 39 D4
Whipping Post La. Rottn 167 E1
Whipping Rd. Bri 166 A4
Whippingham St. Bri 166 A4
Whitbread Cl. East 175 F2
White Hill. Lew 127 D1
White Hill Ave. Bex 159 E2
White Hill Dr. Bex 159 E2
White Rock. Hast 162 B4
White Rock Gdns. Hast 162 B4
White Rock Rd. Hast 162 B4
White St. Bri 165 F3
White Way. Alfn 172 B1
White's Cl. Hur 99 F4
Whitebread La. Bec 69 E4
Whitebread La. Four O 70 A3
Whitebread La. Norm 69 E4
Whitecross St. Bri 165 F3
Whitefield Rd. T W 8 C3
Whitefriars Rd. Hast 140 C1
Whitegates Cl. S Cha 103 E4
Whitegates La. Wad 31 D4
Whitehawk Ave. Bri 166 B4
Whitehawk Cl. Bri 166 B3
Whitehawk Cres. Bri 166 B3
Whitehawk Hill Rd. Bri 166 A3
Whitehawk Rd. Bri 166 B3
Whitehawk Way. Bri 166 B3
Whitehill Cl. Cro 27 E1
Whitehill Rd. Cro 27 E1
Whitehouse Ave. Bex 159 F4
Whitehouse La. Hea 82 C2
Whitehouse La. Wald 82 C2
Whitelot Way. Sock 143 E1
Whitelot Way. Sock 143 E1
Whiterock Pl. Sock 163 E4
Whiteway La. Rottn 167 F1
Whitley Rd. East 185 F2
Whittingehame Gdns. Bri 145 E2
Whittington College. Fel 1 C2
Whittington's Way. Hast 140 C2
Whittle Dr. East 175 F1
Whitworth Rd. Hast 139 F4
Whybourne Crest. T W 9 D1
Whydown Hill. Sed 116 B3
Whydown Rd. Bex 159 D4
Wickham Ave. Bex 159 F2
Wickham Cl. Hay H 52 B4
Wickham Dr. Hur 99 F3
Wickham Dr. Hur 100 A3
Wickham Gdns. Tw 9 D1
Wickham Hill. Hur 100 A2
Wickham La. Bar 103 E1
Wickham La. Bar C 103 E1
Wickham Rock La. Ick 119 F2
Wickham Rock La. Winc 120 A3
Wickham Way. Hay H 52 B4
Wickhurst Cl. Por S 143 E1
Wickhurst Rd. Por S 143 F1
Wickhurst Rise. Por S 143 E2

Wicklands Ave. Salt 168 A1
Widbury Cl. Lan G 7 E2
Widdicombe Way. Bri 146 B1
Wigmore Cl. Bri 145 F1
Wilbury Ave. Hove 165 D4
Wilbury Cres. Hove 165 D4
Wilbury Gdns. Hove 165 D4
Wilbury Gr. Hove 165 D3
Wilbury Rd. Hove 165 D3
Wilbury Villas. Hove 165 D4
Wilby Ave. Sock 143 E1
Wild Park Cl. Bri 146 B2
Wilderness La. Had D 59 D2
Wilderness Park. Cro 27 E1
Wilderness Rd. Hur 99 F3
Wilderness Rise. Dor P 2 C3
Wilderness The. Hay H 52 C4
Wilderwick Rd. Dor 2 C3
Wilderwick Rd. E Gri 2 C2
Wilfred Rd. Hove 144 A1
Wilkins Way. Bex 160 B3
Willard Cl. East 185 F3
William Allen La. Hay H 52 C3
William Rd. Hast 161 E4
William St. Bri 165 F3
William St. Sock 163 F4
William St. T W 8 C3
Williams Rd. S Sea 163 D4
Willingdon Ave. Bex 159 F2
Willingdon Ave. Hast 139 F3
Willingdon Cl. East 174 C1
Willingdon Cl. Hast 139 F3
Willingdon Ct. Willn 174 C2
Willingdon Dro. East 175 F1
Willingdon La. Jev 184 A4
Willingdon Park Dr. East 175 D1
Willingdon Rd. Bri 146 B1
Willingdon Rd. East 185 D3
Willingdon Way. Hast 139 F3
Willingdon Way. Willn 174 C1
Willingford La. Bur 63 D1
Willoughby Cres. East 186 A3
Willow Ave. Hai 132 C1
Willow Bank. Rob 65 F2
Willow Cl. E Gri 2 A2
Willow Cl. Etc 64 C4
Willow Cl. Hea 83 F4
Willow Dr. Bex 159 D3
Willow Dr. Pole 174 C3
Willow Dr. Sea 182 A2
Willow End. Hast 140 B2
Willow Gdns. Hur 99 F4
Willow La. Winc B 120 C3
Willow Mead. E Gri 12 B4
Willow Park. Hay H 52 C2
Willow Tree Rd. T W 8 B1
Willow Way. Hur 99 E4
Willow Wlk. East 175 D1
Willow Wlk. Newh 180 A4
Willow Wlk. T W 9 E4
Willowbed Wlk. Hast 140 B3
Willowbrook Way. Key 100 C2
Willowfield Rd. East 185 F2
Willowfield Sq. East 185 F2
Willowmead. Cro 39 E4
Willows Rise. Fra 80 C3
Willows The. Bur H 75 D3
Willowstream Cl. Thr O 118 C2
Wilman Rd. T W 8 C4
Wilmington Cl. Bri 145 E3
Wilmington Cl. Key 100 B2
Wilmington Gdns. East 185 F1
Wilmington Par. Bri 145 E3
Wilmington Rd. Hast 140 C2
Wilmington Rd. Newh 179 F3
Wilmington Rd. Sea 181 D2
Wilmington Sq. East 185 F1
Wilmington St. Wil 173 E3
Wilmington Way. Bri 145 F3
Wilmington Way. Hay H 52 C3
Wilmot Rd. S Sea 163 D4
Wilson Ave. Bri 166 B3
Wilson Gr. Uck 79 F4
Wilton Ave. East 175 E1
Wilton Rd. Bex 160 A2
Wiltshire Way. T W 9 D4
Winchcombe Rd. East 185 F2
Winchelsea Cl. Sea 181 F3
Winchelsea La. Hast 141 F4
Winchelsea La. Udi 94 A1
Winchelsea Rd. East 186 A3
Winchelsea Rd. Hast 141 E4
Winchelsea Rd. Rye 94 C3
Winchester St. Bri 165 E4
Winchester Wy. Willn 175 D1
Wincombe Rd. Bri 145 D1
Windermere Cres. East 186 A3
Windermere Rd. Hay H 52 B2
Winding St. Hast 162 C4
Windlesham Ave. Bri 165 E3
Windlesham Cl. Por S 143 F1
Windlesham Gdns. Bri 165 E3
Windlesham Rd. Bri 165 E3
Windmill Ave. Key 100 B2
Windmill Cl. East 185 D3
Windmill Cl. Hea 83 F4
Windmill Dr. Bex 159 F3
Windmill Dr. Bri 145 D3

Windmill Dr. Bur H 74 C2
Windmill Green. St Cro 176 A3
Windmill La. Ash W 13 D4
Windmill La. Cou W 32 A4
Windmill La. E Gri 2 A2
Windmill La. Fri 183 F1
Windmill La. Wad 31 D2
Windmill Rd. Hast 139 F1
Windmill Rd. Pole 174 C3
Windmill Rd. Sock 143 E1
Windmill St. Bri 165 E3
Windmill St. T W 9 D2
Windmill Terr. Bri 165 F3
Windover Cres. Lew 126 C1
Windover Way. Willn 174 C2
Windsor Cl. East 176 A2
Windsor Cl. Hove 144 C2
Windsor Cl. Sea 180 C3
Windsor Ct. Cro 40 A4
Windsor Pl. Cro 40 A4
Windsor Pl. E Gri 12 C4
Windsor Rd. Bex 159 F2
Windsor Rd. Cro 40 A4
Windsor Rd. Hai 154 C3
Windsor Rd. Hast 139 F2
Windsor St. Bri 165 E3
Windsor Way. Pole 174 C4
Windsor Way. Winc B 120 C3
Wineham Way. Bex 160 B2
Winfield Ave. Bri 145 E3
Winfield Cl. Bri 145 E3
Winfield Cl. Por S 143 F2
Wingate Cl. Hast 139 F1
Wingle Tye Rd. Bur H 100 C4
Winkhurst Way. Bur H 75 D1
Winkney Rd. East 175 E2
Winston Cres. East 186 A4
Winston Dr. Bex 159 E2
Winstone Scott Ave. Lan G 7 E2
Winterbourne Cl. Hast 162 A4
Winterbourne Cl. Lew 148 C4
Winterbourne Hollow. Lew .. 148 C4
Winterbourne La. Lew 148 C4
Winterbourne Mews. Lew 148 C4

Winton Ave. Salt 168 A2
Winton St. Alfn 172 B2
Wire Mill La. Fel 1 B4
Wisden Ave. Bur H 74 B3
Wiseacre. Lam 21 F2
Wish Ct. Hove 164 B4
Wish Hill. East 184 C4
Wish Rd. East 185 F1
Wish Rd. Hove 164 B3
Wish St. Rye 94 C3
Wish Ward. Rye 94 C3
Wishing Tree Cl. Hast 139 E1
Wishing Tree La. Hast 139 E1
Wishing Tree Rd. Hast 139 E2
Wishing Tree Rd N. Hast 139 F2
Wiston Rd N. Bri 166 B4
Wiston Rd S. Bri 166 B3
Wiston Way. Bri 166 B4
Withdean Ave. Bri 145 D1
Withdean Cl. Bri 145 D2
Withdean Cres. Bri 145 E2
Withdean Ct Ave. Bri 145 D2
Withdean Rd. Bri 145 D2
Withdean Rise. Bri 145 D2
Withy Bush. Bur H 74 B3
Withyham Ave. Salt 168 A1
Withyham Cl. East 175 E1
Withyham Rd. Bex 159 D1
Withyham Rd. Gro 16 C3
Wittersham Rd. Iden 71 F4
Wittersham Rd. Rol L 51 D3
Wittersham Rd. Witt 51 F3
Wivelsfield Green Rd. Wiv 75 F3
Wivelsfield Green Rd. Wiv G .. 76 A3
Wivelsfield Rd. Hay H 52 B1
Wivelsfield Rd. Salt 168 A2
Woburn Pl. Bri 146 B3
Woburn Wy. East 175 D2
Wolfe Cl. Cro 39 F4
Wolseley Rd. Bri 146 A3
Wolseley Rd. Por S 163 F4
Wolseley Rd. Sgh 9 D4
Wolstonbury Cl. Hur 99 F2
Wolstonbury Rd. Hove 165 E4

Wolstonbury Way. Bur H 74 C1
Wolverstone Dr. Bri 146 A1
Wood La. Bor S 135 D1
Wood Ride. Hay H 52 A2
Wood St. Bri 165 F3
Wood St. E Gri 2 A1
Wood St. T W 8 C2
Wood's Pas. Hast 162 C4
Woodbine La. Newk 78 A4
Woodbourne Ave. Bri 145 F2
Woodbrook Rd. Hast 140 B1
Woodbury Ave. E Gri 2 C1
Woodbury Cl. E Gri 12 C4
Woodbury Park Gdns. T W 8 C3
Woodbury Park Rd. T W 8 C3
Woodcock Hill. Fel 1 B3
Woodcote Rd. For R 13 E1
Woodcrest Rd. Bur H 74 B1
Woodcroft. Bur H 74 B3
Woodcroft Dr. East 185 D4
Woodgate Meadow. Plu G ... 102 B4
Woodgate Rd. East 186 A3
Woodhams Cl. Bat 115 D3
Woodhill Park. Pem 10 A3
Woodhouse Rd. Hove 164 B4
Woodland Ave. Bur H 75 D2
Woodland Ave. East 175 D1
Woodland Ave. Hove 144 C1
Woodland Cl. Bur H 75 D2
Woodland Cl. Hove 144 C1
Woodland Cl. T W 8 C4
Woodland Ct. Hove 144 C2
Woodland Dr. Hove 144 C2
Woodland Rd. T W 9 D4
Woodland Rise. Bex 160 B2
Woodland Vale Rd. Hast 162 A4
Woodland Way. Bri 145 E2
Woodland Way. Cro 39 E4
Woodland Way. Crow 138 B2
Woodland Way. Fai 142 B2
Woodlands. Hove 145 D1
Woodlands. Pem 10 B4
Woodlands Cl. Hai 133 D1
Woodlands Cl. Hass 100 B2

Woodlands Cl. Hea 83 F3
Woodlands Cl. Pea 168 C1
Woodlands Cl. Uck 80 A4
Woodlands Rd. E Gri 2 C2
Woodlands Rd. Hass 100 B2
Woodlands Rd. Hay H 52 B2
Woodlands The. Bri 145 E3
Woodlands The. Hast 140 B3
Woodlands Way. Hea 83 F3
Woodleigh Rd. Bur H 75 D2
Woodpecker Dr. Hai 154 C4
Woodpecker Rd. East 175 F1
Woodridge Cl. Hay H 52 C2
Woodruff Ave. Hove 145 D1
Woods Hill Cl. Ash W 13 D3
Woods Hill La. Ash W 13 D3
Woodsgate Ave. Bex 160 A3
Woodsgate Park. Bex 159 F3
Woodsgate Way. Pem 9 F3
Woodside. Cro 27 E1
Woodside Ave. Hove 145 D1
Woodside Cl. Pem 10 B3
Woodside Rd. Pem 10 B3
Woodside Rd. T W 8 A2
Woodside School Rd. Bri 146 A1
Woodspring Cl. Hast 139 F3
Woodstock. E Gri 2 A1
Woodstock Rd. Bex 159 D3
Woodview Cl. Bri 146 A3
Woodville Rd. Bex 159 F2
Woodward Cl. East 186 B4
Woodwards Cl. Bur H 74 C1
Worcester Villas. Hove 164 A4
Wordsworth Dr. East 176 B1
Wordsworth Rise. E Gri 2 A1
Wordsworth St. Hove 164 C4
Workhouse La. Ick 119 E3
Worsham La. Bex 160 B4
Worsted La. E Gri 12 C4
Wray Cl. Ash W 13 D3
Wren Cl. Hea 83 F4
Wren Ct. Bat 115 E2
Wren Ct. Hast 139 E2

Wrestwood Ave. East 175 D1
Wrestwood Cl. Bex 160 A3
Wrestwood Rd. Bex 160 B3
Wrotham Cl. East 176 A1
Wrotham Cl. Hast 140 B3
Wroxham Rd. East 175 F2
Wyatts La. Hor K 35 D3
Wyberlye Rd. Bur H 74 C2
Wybourne Rise. T W 18 C4
Wychperry Rd. Hay H 52 A3
Wychurst Gdns. Bex 160 A3
Wykeham Rd. Hast 162 B4
Wykeham Way. Bur H 75 D1
Wyndham St. Bri 165 E3
Wynnes Mews. Hove 164 C4
Wyshe The. Pye 123 D3
Wythwood. Hay H 52 B1

Yardley St. Bri 165 F4
Yeomans. Rin 128 C4
Yew La. E Gri 1 C2
Yew Tree Cl. Hast 140 B3
Yew Tree Cl. Hea 83 F3
Yew Tree Cl. Rin 128 B4
Yew Tree Rd. Sgh 8 C4
Yewtree La. Tow R 41 E4
Yielding's Cl. East 185 D3
York Ave. E Gri 12 B4
York Ave. Hove 165 E3
York Gdns. Hast 162 B4
York Gr. Bri 165 F4
York Hill. Bri 165 F4
York Pl. Bri 165 F3
York Rd. Bex 160 C3
York Rd. Bur H 74 A4
York Rd. East 185 E1
York Rd. Hast 140 A1
York Rd. Hove 165 E3
York Rd. Pea 179 E3
York Rd. T W 8 C2
York Villas. Bri 165 E4
Youngsmere Cl. Bri 145 F3

Zion Gdns. Bri 165 E3